OPERATIONS RESEARCH SOCIETY OF AMERICA

Publications in Operations Research

Number 5

PUBLICATIONS IN OPERATIONS RESEARCH

No. 1. QUEUES, INVENTORIES AND MAINTENANCE
Philip M. Morse

No. 2. FINITE QUEUING TABLES
L. G. Peck and R. N. Hazelwood

No. 3. EFFICIENCY IN GOVERNMENT THROUGH SYSTEMS ANALYSIS
Roland N. McKean

No. 4. A COMPREHENSIVE BIBLIOGRAPHY ON OPERATIONS RESEARCH
Operations Research Group, Case Institute

No. 5. PROGRESS IN OPERATIONS RESEARCH, VOLUME I
Edited by Russell L. Ackoff

PROGRESS IN OPERATIONS RESEARCH

Volume I

edited by
RUSSELL L. ACKOFF
CASE INSTITUTE OF TECHNOLOGY

NEW YORK · LONDON, JOHN WILEY & SONS, INC.

Library of Congress Catalog Card Number: 61–10415

Printed in the United States of America

PREFACE

The overabundance of scientific literature has become a serious problem for the traditional scientific and engineering disciplines. As a consequence, considerable attention is being given to problems of indexing, abstracting, filtration, and so on in these fields. The Office of Scientific Information of the National Science Foundation and the Council of Library Resources, among others, have been sponsoring considerable research to alleviate the documentation problem.

In a new field like operations research we have a unique opportunity to take the necessary steps now to minimize the documentation problem of the future. Recognition of this fact led to the support by the Operations Research Society of America of the preparation of *A Comprehensive Bibliography on Operations Research* by the Operations Research Group at Case Institute of Technology. This bibliographic work is being continued under the support of the National Science Foundation with the cooperation of the Society. In addition, the Society will shortly publish a journal of abstracts.

The foundation of the series Publications in Operations Research, issued by John Wiley and Sons, with the collaboration of the Society, was another move to prevent a future documentation problem. Through this series technical works of restricted but significant interest can be made readily available to the operations research worker.

Over a year ago the Council of the Society (ORSA) approved a proposal of its Publication Committee to initiate a review series, also intended to ease future documentation problems. No commitment was made as to the frequency with which review volumes should appear. It was felt that this would best be determined by the rate of development of the field itself. When the next volume will appear will depend in part on the reception which this volume receives.

Having suggested this series to the Publication Committee, I was drafted to edit the first volume. I agreed to do so under two conditions: first, that the Publication Committee play an active role in the design of the volume's contents, and second, that the editing of future volumes be assigned to different men in rotation. Review volumes are bound to reflect the opinions and philosophy of the editor and, hence, it seems desirable to me that different points of view be reflected in subsequent volumes.

The emphasis of this volume lies in the area of technical progress: in the development of modeling techniques and ways of using these techniques to solve problems. This, I believe, reflects the major type of progress which has taken place in OR, but by no means the only type of progress. For this reason, the first and last chapters, my own and that by Ernst and Magee, consider other dimensions of progress and how much or how little we have moved along these dimensions. The technical content of the volume, then, is "sandwiched" between philosophical and professional considerations.

An attempt has been made to include discussions of the areas of greatest interest and use to practicing operations researchers; hence the inclusion of inventory theory, linear and dynamic programming, queuing theory, sequencing theory, replacement theory, simulation, and gaming. Other areas might also have been included, but restrictions on space necessitated some selection. It was hoped that the volume would contain a treatment of business gaming, but my efforts to obtain an article on this subject failed. The lack of a chapter on game theory is conspicuous, but it was not included because of the paucity of practical applications of the theory.

In addition to these technical chapters, a chapter is included on what I think of as the foundation of operations research, decision and value theory.

The individual authors were given complete freedom in their treatments. They were asked to portray the current state of the art and to survey applications which have been made. They were encouraged to be critical as well as expository. Different authors have emphasized different aspects of their subject matter, and this is as it should be because a review is necessarily a personal document. Cold, impartial inventories of such subject matter are not possible, and if they were, they would probably not be desirable.

Much could be said about the qualifications of the contributors, but these are better demonstrated by the contents of their reviews than by anything which I might say about them.

I would like to express my appreciation to each of them for their cooperativeness in the preparation of this volume and to apologize for having had to play the role of an unpleasant taskmaster at times. I am also greatly indebted to the members of the Publication Committee of ORSA: Martin L. Ernst, John F. Magee, Eliezer Naddor, and George Shortley, Chairman. Without the moral and financial support of the Council of ORSA this volume would not have been possible.

I am indebted to the following for permission to use material from their publications: American Institute of Industrial Engineers (*The Journal of Industrial Engineering*), American Mathematical Society (*Bulletin of the American Mathematical Society*), Chance Vought Aircraft Company, Constable and Company, *Data Processing,* Cornell University Computing Center, Department of the Army (Office of Military History), Henry Holt and Company, Hudson Kimberly Publishing Company, McGraw-Hill Book Company, New York University (A.E.C. Computing and Applied Mathematics Center), Office of Naval Research (*Naval Research Logistics Quarterly*), Operations Research Society of America (*Operations Research* and *Proceedings of the First International Conference on Operational Research*), Princeton University Press, *Scientific American,* Springfield Printing and Binding Company, System Development Corporation, The Institute of Management Sciences (*Management Science*), The Operational Research Society (*Operational Research Quarterly*), The Riverside Press, and John Wiley and Sons.

RUSSELL L. ACKOFF

Cleveland, Ohio
January, 1961

CONTENTS

Chapter 1

THE MEANING, SCOPE, AND METHODS OF OPERATIONS RESEARCH

RUSSELL L. ACKOFF
Case Institute of Technology, Cleveland, Ohio

Contents

"Now," said Rabbit, "this is a Search, and I've Organized it——"
"Done what to it?" said Pooh.
"Organized it. Which means—well, it's what you do to a Search when you don't all look in the same place at once."

—*From* THE HOUSE AT POOH CORNER *by A. A. Milne*

1. TOWARDS A STRATEGY OF OPERATIONS RESEARCH [1]

This volume is largely concerned with the technical progress of OR. It deals primarily with techniques of model construction and of deriving solutions from these models. There are, of course, many other aspects of OR's progress. Some of these are:

a. The creation and growth of OR societies in this and other countries,[2] and the formation of the International Federation of Operational Research Societies.

b. The increase in the number of OR groups in military, governmental, and industrial organizations and in consulting research agencies.[3]

c. The rapid growth of relevant literature in journals and books.

d. The introduction and expansion of courses and curricula in OR in academic institutions.[4]

In addition to these technical, professional, and educational aspects of OR's progress one can also point to what might be called its "strategy." The sense in which "strategy" is used here is reflected in a passage of an unsigned review which appeared in the *Operational Research Quarterly* in 1959:

[1] For their helpful suggestions and criticisms of an early draft of this chapter I am deeply indebted to Glen D. Camp, C. West Churchman, Merrill M. Flood, J. S. Minas, and Vernon C. Mickelson.

[2] See, for example, the *Proceedings of the First International Conference on Operations Research,* pp. 400–513; and the *Bulletin of the Operations Research Society of America,* **7,** Supplement 2, pp. B108–B114 (1959).

[3] See, for example, Churchman (1955), Goodeve and Ridley (1953), Johnson (1954), Hertz (1957), and Rivett (1959).

[4] See "Formal Educational Offerings in Operations Research," *Bull. Opns. Res. Soc. of Amer.,* **7,** Supplement 2, pp. E1–E29 (1959).

The strategy of science must be distinguished from its tactics. By strategy is meant largely the continued and open-minded revision of scientific values and standards, the allocation of priorities for research topics, and the development of measures of efficiency and a readiness by science to observe itself dispassionately and to submit its conclusions reached thereby to scientific verification (Vol. 10, No. 3, Sept. 1959, p. 180).

Discussions of OR's strategy in this sense tend to generate more heat than light. They are more philosophic than scientific. Because of this, perhaps, such discussions take place in dark corners of both meetings and the literature. Recorded observations of this type are likely to be found in editorials, letters to editors, reviews, discussion notes, and in an occasional publication of an address; but seldom in an article or book written for the purpose. Yet the emergence of what Churchman (1957, p. 519) called the "dignity" of a scientific activity must rest on the development of a sound strategy.

The purpose of this introductory chapter is to accumulate, consolidate, and synthesize what has been said and written about the strategy of OR. This is done in order to expose areas where further research and reflection are needed. I think it will become apparent that the expanding body of operations researchers does itself a disservice if it applies the standards of performance and concepts of methodology inherent in more traditional and less expanding areas of science. New concepts and methodologies must be developed if OR is to realize its ambitions even in part. Progress here, as in other aspects of science, can be accelerated by self-examination and self-evaluation, by as critical an appraisal by operations researchers of their own research operations as they give to the operations of others.

This discussion will be divided into three parts: (1) the meaning of OR, (2) its scope, and (3) its methodology.

2. THE MEANING OF OR

At the heart of any discussion of the strategy of a scientific discipline is the following question: What is the nature of the discipline? Efforts at answering this question are likely to appear "defensive" and characteristic of only a young and insecure discipline. For example, in 1956 W. N. Jessop wrote, "Operational Research is still young and self-conscious, it is therefore very much concerned with what it is, and what its standing is in comparison with other sciences—indeed whether it is a science at all" (p. 49).

Although Jessop's observation may still be valid, it does seem to me that operations researchers do not feel, as they did only a few years ago, that a completely satisfactory definition is essential to OR's progress or necessary for its survival. In the last decade there has been less and less defensiveness displayed by operations researchers and fewer efforts made at self-justification to others. This has been due in part to increasing acceptance by the scientific community.[5] Improved relations with other pure and applied scientific groups and the development of more effective means of collaborating with them have reduced the amount of discussion of how OR is similar to or different from a host of other disciplines. These disciplines are less preoccupied than they were a few years ago with showing that OR is nothing but what each of them (which claimed to be distinct from all the others) has been doing all along.

It should be possible, therefore, to reopen the question of definition for OR's sake and not for the sake of others. At least this is the intent here.

It seems to me that in the past those of us in OR have expected too much in one respect and too little in another from definitional efforts. Even the oldest scientific disciplines have failed to define themselves adequately, particularly where brevity was an objective. But even tentative definitions of a discipline can be useful to those in the discipline as well as to others. They can provide a basis for determining what research should be done and what standards should be maintained, that is, a basis for formulating a strategy of the discipline. This purpose is not well served by a so-called "operational" definition such as that of OR as "the activity carried on by members of the Society . . . as reported in our JOURNAL" (Page, 1954, p. 86).

This definition makes the editorial policy of this particular journal the definition of OR, and it requires those who want to know what OR is to read this journal (*Operations Research*), a burden the non-professional can hardly be expected to bear. It is true, of course, that we can find the characteristics of the field only by examining the activities of its practitioners; but such an examination is only the beginning, not the end of the defining process.

One might adopt the position of M. G. Kendall: "I shall not stay to try to find a sentence which might be inserted in a dictionary by way of definition. In my opinion subjects like ours are not to be defined by definitions" (1958, p. 266). If, however, one is inclined to drop the matter here he will not have caught Kendall's intent since

[5] For example, participation by ORSA in the National Research Council and the American Association for the Advancement of Science.

he also observed that "it would be convenient if we could be systematic and discuss . . . the scope and content of operational research" (p. 267). This is precisely the intention here.

Kendall goes on to say:

Operational research may be regarded as a branch of philosophy; as an attitude of mind towards the relation between man and environment; as a body of methods for the solution of problems which arise in that relationship (p. 267).

Others, like A. W. Swan (1957), have expressed similar beliefs in their references to OR as a "point of view." Although most practitioners would agree that OR has a point of view they would question its sufficiency for characterizing the field, even assuming that this point of view is made explicit.

Stafford Beer (1959) has attempted to analyze and expand Kendall's position and concludes that "operational research is not *a* science, for it is not *about* anything; it is science." He does not mean by this that OR has no subject matter, but that its subject—so to speak—is not matter:

I contend that operational research emerges as a subset of scientific methods appropriate to the analysis of *activity*. . . . And these sets of methods do not form a science—nor does operational research. And so I am saying let us do away with the idea of "*the* science of operational research"; and let us do away with the idea "but we do not know what it is." There is really a wonderful ambiguity about these two statements anyway, is there not? (p. 12).

Beer then suggests that:

(1) Operational research is the attack of modern science
(2) on problems of likelihood (accepting mischance)
(3) which arise in the management and control
(4) of men and machines, materials and money
(5) in their natural environment.
(6) Its special technique is to invent a strategy of control
(7) by measuring, comparing and predicting probable behavior
(8) through a scientific model of a situation (pp. 16–17).

Judging from the many definitions of OR which have appeared in the literature, I think most operations researchers are in substantial agreement with Beer's characterization. It does not go deep enough, however, to settle most of the issues involved in definitional discussions. The central issue in these discussions, it seems to me, involves the question of whether OR is a unique or unitary discipline. Beer's assertion that OR is not *a* science does not settle this question since unity and uniqueness might be found in other quarters.

Concern with this question is reflected in an observation by Morse:

"It should be demonstrable that we study a specific class of phenomena or that we have a unitary way of analyzing various phenomena, or both" (1957, p. 4). It will be noted that Morse makes no reference to a body of substantive knowledge about a class of phenomena. It is the lack of such a body of knowledge which is probably at the root of Beer's remark that OR is not *about* anything.

Do we lack such a body of knowledge because we have no subject to know about? Or do we have a subject about which knowledge cannot be obtained? Or, perhaps, have we only started to learn about our subject and the body of knowledge is yet to come? Each of these questions has been answered in the affirmative. Which answer is the most reasonable?

2.1. Operations

The ground apparently covered by OR has been claimed by a number of other disciplines. Does this preclude a claim by OR to a unique class of phenomena? Morse thinks not; the claims of others "need not be [unimpregnable] barriers to recognition. Other branches of science have taken recognized possession of intermediate ground; some have achieved independence even though most of the subject matter studied is common to other sciences" (1957, p. 3). Morse cites thermodynamics and biochemistry as examples. He further observes that:

> We're further along toward acceptance of the unitary nature of the phenomena we study than we are in having a coherent theory. While we can't yet give an inclusive definition of an *operation,* we have a pretty good idea what it is. . . . And we can make a pretty convincing argument that, while some operations are studied by economists, many are not appropriate subjects for economics; likewise many of them depend intimately on the physical properties of equipment, and so they cannot all be included in psychology or other social sciences; contrastingly, all of them involve people, so operations are not coincident with the subject matter of systems engineering. In short, I'm sure we can demonstrate that any one operation has many properties in common with other operations and that operations in general are phenomena which deserve study in a unitary way. . . .
>
> This ultimate definition of an operation should strip away the unessential aspects of an operation as well as make obvious that operations are similar. We, in operations research, study a pattern of activity, not a specific grouping of particular people. We are interested in those properties of an operation which would not change if we were to replace persons and/or equipment by others. The psychological aspects of interest to us are not those of individuals but those common to any group carrying out that operation. The physical properties of equipment which we need to know about are those pertaining to the mechanical aspects of a structured organization, with its links for transmitting orders and its feed-back loops. We look at an organization as a whole

with its human and its mechanical parts, engaged in doing its assigned task; we must utilize those portions of psychology, physics, systems engineering and economics which will aid us in understanding the workings of such operating organizations. I believe it will not be difficult for us to demonstrate that the structure of operating organizations does constitute a unitary field for study and that it is sufficiently distinct to merit separate classification as a subject for specialized scientific study (pp. 4–5).

Because of the name of our field there is considerable appeal to calling the special class of phenomena we study, if there is such, "operations." The word, unfortunately, has many different connotations, only some of which are relevant to OR. Therefore, the objective of this definitional excursion is to make precise what OR takes an operation to be, not necessarily what it is commonly taken to be.

Considering the military origin of the profession's name, we might expect to find the most satisfactory meaning of "operation" in the military context. *Webster's New Collegiate Dictionary* (1956) offers the following definition of an operation:

A military and/or naval action or mission including movement, supply, attack, defense, and *all requisite* maneuvers [italics mine].

I think this definition provides a clue to the essential characteristics of an operation. An operation is a *set* of acts *required* for the accomplishment of some desired outcome; that is, it is not a single act but a complex of interrelated acts performed simultaneously or in sequence, which lead to the accomplishment of some desired outcome (i.e., set of objectives). It seems clear to me that in OR we have been studying just such sets of interrelated acts. This concept of an operation, of course, is equally applicable to industrial, military, governmental, and other types of organizations.

Consider an example of a very simple operation: a clerk addressing and stamping envelopes. These acts are done in series in either of the two possible orders. If two clerks are involved they may be done simultaneously. Both acts are necessary for accomplishing the purpose of the acts: delivery of the envelopes to designated parties. Neither act alone is sufficient for the objective.

The acts are purposeful; that is, they involve choice either by the one who performs the acts or by someone who controls the performers. Two events such as sunshine and rain will produce growth of a plant but do not constitute an operation because choice is not involved. If, on the other hand, a horticulturist uses ultraviolet light and an indoor irrigation system we would say he performs an operation. The lighting and the watering, as the stamping and addressing, may be done by a machine but they would still constitute an operation because the control or programming of the machines would involve choice.

These observations concerning the nature of an operation can be synthesized and made more precise in a formal definition of the concept. The following symbols and concepts will be required:

O = outcome(s) desired by the decision maker(s)

a = an act

S = a set of acts

T = a set of subsets of acts $\{A_1, A_2, \cdots, A_i, \cdots, A_m\}$ such that

1. each subset (A_i) is included in S
2. there are at least two subsets: $m \geq 2$
3. the subsets are not identical: $A_i \neq A_j$ if $i \neq j$
4. each subset has at least two members

The following auxiliary definitions are required:

A *choice-set*, B, $= \{a_1, a_2 \cdots, a_i, \cdots, a_m\}$ such that a_i is included in A_i for each i.

A *sequence-set*, B_s, = the set of all (partially or completely) time-ordered sequences of elements of the choice-set B.

B is an *acceptable choice-set* if there is an environment in which at least one sequence in B_s has a probability greater than zero of producing the outcome O.

An operation can now be defined as *the set of sequences of acts contained in acceptable choice-sets* if the following three conditions hold:

1. Every act in the set S is relevant to the outcome O; that is, for every a included in S there is an acceptable choice-set, B, such that a is included in B.

2. One choice from each subset of acts $(A_1, A_2, \cdots, A_m)$ is necessary for the attainment of the outcome O; that is, the only sequences of acts included in S which have a probability greater than zero of producing O are included in acceptable choice-sets.

(Note that some choice-sets may have no chance of producing the outcome regardless of the order in which the acts are performed. There may be some choice-sets in which any order has some probability of producing the outcome.)

3. There is interaction among the acts in any sequence which has a probability greater than zero of producing the outcome O.

The meaning of "interaction" must be clarified. A set of acts can be said to interact relative to an outcome if the variables which characterize the actions chosen (choice-variables) and the outcome (outcome-variable) are related as follows: the amount of change in the outcome-variable which is affected by any choice-variable depends on the value of all other choice-variables in the sequence. If the choice-variables and outcome-variable are quantitative, and continuous, this condition can be restated: the partial derivative of the outcome-variable with respect to any choice-variable is a function of all other choice-variables in the sequence. In ordinary language, if an outcome is simply the sum of (or difference between) the properties of the necessary acts, these acts do not interact.

OR has *not* been concerned with *all* types of operations. For example, it has not been concerned with the operations of an individual who "operates" a machine. It has left such considerations to industrial engineers. In general, OR has not been concerned with the operations of individuals but rather with those of a certain type of *system*.

2.2. Systems and Organizations

Definitional discussions in OR repeatedly refer to the study of man-machine systems. An operator and his machine may constitute such a system. Man himself may be considered as a system, but he is not considered in this way in OR. In OR man is an element of a system and a system must have parts.

Now clearly not all systems are of interest to OR. The solar system is an example of such. The systems of concern to OR are purposeful, ones in which choices are made and objectives pursued. More precisely, a *purposeful system* can be defined as *an entity consisting of two or more parts whose acts constitute an operation* (as it was defined above).

OR has generally dealt with complex rather than simple systems. Some, like Solandt, apparently feel that complexity is essential to OR: "I feel that the essential feature of operations research is that it studies any complex organization in operation" (1955, p. 4).

The complexity of the systems studied by OR lies not only in the large number of parts which they usually have but also in the types of interaction between the parts. For example, most (if not all) the systems of interest involve communication between some of the parts, and many of these systems also involve feedback control. These are characteristics of that type of system called an "organization."

It will be recalled that in an earlier quotation from Morse he refers to OR's subject matter as the operation of an organization much as Solandt did in the preceding quote. Since most definitional efforts make similar references it is clear that "organization" is a central concept to OR.

An organization can be defined as a purposeful system with four essential characteristics:

1. Some of its components are human beings.

For example, wires, poles, switchboards, and telephones may make up a communication system but they do not constitute an organization. Men—or, more strictly speaking, animals—make up an organization. The employees of a telephone company make up the organization that runs the communication system. Men and equipment together constitute a more inclusive system than either does alone. It is this type of system with which OR is concerned.

2. Responsibility for choices from the set of acts $(A_1,A_2,\cdots,A_m)$ is divided among two or more individuals and/or groups of individuals.

Each subgroup (consisting of one or more individuals) is responsible[6] for one or more choices of action and the set of choices is divided between two or more subgroups. The classes of action and (hence) the subgroups may be individuated by a variety of types of characteristics; for example,

a. By function (e.g., an industrial organization may be divided into departments of production, marketing, research, finance, and personnel).

b. By geography (e.g., the division of the Army into areas of responsibility).

c. By time (e.g., "waves" of an invading force).

The classes of action may also be defined by combinations of these characteristics.

It should be noted that the individuals need not carry out the actions they select; the action may be performed by machines which are programmed or controlled by the individuals so as to act as desired. Thus the essential characteristic of human participation in organizations is decision making and need not involve overt action.

3. The functionally distinct subgroups are aware of each other's choices either through communication or observation.

In many laboratory experiments subjects are given tasks to perform and are rewarded on the basis of an outcome which is determined by

[6] A person, or group, is responsible for action if he can be rewarded or punished for the action.

their choices taken collectively. The subjects, however, are kept in complete ignorance of each other's actions. In such cases the subjects do not constitute an organization; they are *unorganized.* Allow them to communicate or observe each other and they may become an organization. Put another way, in an organization the human subgroups must be capable of reacting to each other.

4. A subgroup (or the total group) of individuals in the system has a control function: it compares achieved outcomes with desired outcomes and makes adjustments in the system intended to reduce the observed differences.

The control function is normally exercised by an executive body which operates on a feedback principle.

If any one of the last three conditions (2, 3, and 4) are not satisfied by a group it is *unorganized.* To the extent that any of these conditions, although satisfied, is not fulfilled efficiently, the group is *disorganized.*

It should be noted that none of these conditions require either the objectives or classes of action to remain fixed over time. They may be quite dynamic.[7]

We have now defined the class of phenomena which OR studies as the operations of organizations. Whether or not this class of phenomena is unique does not seem to be very important. Furthermore, I believe it will become less important as we develop more precise definitions of this class of phenomena than I have been able to provide here.

Now we want to examine some of the implications of the preceding definitions for the strategy of OR. Specifically, we will consider these implications with reference to the scope and methodology of OR.

3. THE SCOPE OF OR

Armed with detailed definitions of "operation" and "organization" it is possible to attack more effectively questions concerning the scope of OR. By "scope" I refer to the types of problems involving organizational operations which constitute the domain of OR.

Let us look at organizational operations from the point of view of

[7] The role of research in making organizational objectives dynamic was discussed by C. West Churchman in a paper delivered to the Second International Conference on OR: "Organizations and Goal Revisions" (1960, pp. 6–11).

the control function. It follows from the preceding definitions that changes in organized activity are of four types which correspond to the four requirements imposed on organizations above:

1. *Organizational Content:* changes of the people and/or equipment which make up the system, that is, addition, subtraction, or modification of these resources.
2. *Organizational Structure:* changes in the division of labor, that is, in the assignment of activity and the responsibility for it to the subgroups of men and/or equipment
3. *Communication:* changes in the generation, collection, treatment, and transmittal of information.
4. *Control:* changes in the way available resources are used.

3.1. Organizational Content

An organization may not function well because of the inefficiency of its personnel. This situation may be changed by selecting better personnel or improving personnel through training (personnel psychology), by improving human operations in ways revealed by work measurement (industrial engineering), by altering the work environment so as to motivate personnel to perform better (industrial social psychology), and by modifying the equipment used by people so as to increase their productivity, accuracy, and reliability (human engineering).

The equipment with which an organization operates may be inefficient. Here the various branches of engineering can come to the aid of management by designing or selecting new equipment or by improving the old. Design of systems of equipment and their control has increasingly become the domain of systems engineering (which we shall consider in some detail below).

OR has seldom been involved in such "content analyses."

3.2. Organizational Structure

Reorganization ("shaking up" the organization) is a common method of attacking organizational inefficiency. It consists of changing the composition of the subgroups and/or their responsibilities. Hence, the number, composition, and functions of organizational units may be modified. Reorganization (or organization) studies which are conducted by or for the executive group are largely qualitative in character. The body of knowledge and techniques on which they are based has come to be known as "organization theory," a theory which has not yet been effectively systematized or quantified. Beginnings in this direction have been made. (See, for example, Haire, 1959, and Rudner and Wolfson, 1958.)

Studies of this type have generally been made by management-consulting groups. Only a few such studies have been made by operations researchers. (See, for example, Glover and Ackoff, 1956.)

3.3. Communication

Research into information generation and processing in an organization has generally been performed by systems and procedures analysts and accountants, not by operations researchers. Such studies are also largely qualitative in character. Although there is a highly mathematized theory of communication based on the work of Hartley and Shannon, this theory does not include the psychological and social aspects of communication. Here too there have been recent efforts to extend the theory so as to make it more relevant to studies of organizational communication. (See, for example, Cherry, 1957, and Ackoff, 1958.)

3.4. Control

An organization with good personnel and equipment, and an efficient structure and communication system may still be inefficient because it does not make good use of its resources (men, machines, material, and money). That is, the operations of the organization (as contrasted with the activity of its components) may not be efficiently controlled. Control is a matter of directing the organization toward desired objectives and it is obtained by efficient decision making by those who manage the operations. Assisting managers to control organizations (i.e., improving their decision making) has been an important objective of OR. We will examine this research function in more detail in Section 4, but here we want to examine its relationship to the other types of technical assistance which management can obtain.

3.5. Integration at a Higher Level

In a number of OR studies it has been necessary to determine what changes in organizational content, structure, and communications are required in order to effect a proposed procedural change; but such concern has been secondary. Those concerned with studies of other aspects of organization have been similarly occupied with decision making. Is not an integration of these approaches desirable?

If the various professional groups dedicated to studies of organizational content, structure, communications, and control maintain their current division of labor, a residual problem will persist: Which approach to an organization's problems will yield the greatest improvement in its performance? In each case a decision must be based on either judgment or research. It seems apparent that research groups capable of working on all aspects of organizational performance would be likely to develop a sounder method for deciding which aspect(s) to work on than is currently available.

Many operations researchers are disinclined to extend their work into organizational content, structure, and communications because of the qualitative state of knowledge in all of these domains except those involving engineering. It is precisely because of their quantitative inclinations, however, that operations researchers can probably accelerate the development of theories applicable to personnel selection, training, and motivation; organizational structure; and human communication.

The spirit of disciplinary synthesis which pervades OR, it seems to me, dictates that it consider organizational content, structure, and communications more seriously and self-consciously in the future than it has in the past.

The implication of these remarks is not that OR should "absorb" all these other disciplines, but rather that a higher-order integration of management sciences and technologies is required. There is already evidence that at least some of these disciplines are approaching each other in the types of concepts and techniques which they employ.

In one instance a self-conscious effort at such a higher-order integration has been made. With funds provided by the Ford Foundation, Case Institute of Technology has established a Systems Research Center in which there is collaboration in teaching and research among autonomous groups from the following areas: operations research, systems engineering, communications engineering, computer technology, behavioral sciences (including human engineering), and industrial administration. The identities of the participating (inter)disciplines have not disappeared and will not as long as each has independent usefulness. Through this collaboration a broader spectrum of approaches to organizational problems is being taken than could be otherwise. It seems to me operations researchers can be most useful and can most rapidly develop their own particular abilities in such a context.

Of all the (inter)disciplines which have been mentioned systems engineering has, perhaps, a closer relationship to OR than any other. For this reason the relationship deserves closer examination.

3.6. OR and Systems Engineering

A decision consists of selecting one from a set of alternative courses of action, some of which have some chance of yielding a desired outcome. The types of decisions with which OR is concerned always involve alternative uses of resources. Usually the decision is restricted to available resources, but in some cases proposed or hypothetical resources may also be considered, for example, in weapon systems evaluation. OR itself has not been preoccupied with proposing new equipment systems but systems engineering has.

In a quotation cited above Morse asserted that the difference between these interdisciplines lies in the interest of OR in the human aspects of systems. This assertion is not one which most systems engineers would accept. Some of the essential similarities and differences between these two fields, as seen by systems engineers, are described by Goode and Machol as follows:

> In the first place, we are dealing with equipment systems . . . a primary function of the systems engineer is to make decisions involving choices of equipment. . . .
>
> The systems which are the subject of this book are automatic. The degree of automaticity varies, but it never reaches the state at one extreme where human beings perform all control functions and probably will never reach the state where no human beings are involved. Thus we shall always find computers in our systems, and the study of computers will be an important part of systems engineering. On the other hand the relationship between the machine and its human operator is also important, and so we must spend some time on human engineering (pp. 5–6).
>
> It will be evident at once that the competent operations analyst will make an excellent addition to the systems design team. . . . Each of the steps he normally uses in operations research is important in systems design. . . .
>
> . . . operations research is a very broad field. It is not like the other tools of systems design, because it is not well defined and because it includes many of these tools. In fact there has been a recent tendency to broaden the definition of operations research so that it is practically synonymous with systems design. However, there is a fundamental difference of approach: The operations analyst is primarily concerned in making procedural changes, while the systems engineer is primarily interested in making equipment changes (1957, p. 130).

It is clear from these selections that at least some systems engineers do not exclude consideration of the human element. Their concern with the human, however, is—so to speak—as an appendage to the machine. In OR, it seems to me, we are more likely to look at men and machines the other way around. The difference between their interdiscipline and ours, as they see it, lies in their preoccupation with equipment and ours with procedures. I think most operations researchers would accept the spirit of this distinction if it is realized that OR can no more ignore equipment than systems engineers can ignore human beings. Furthermore, experience seems to show clearly the necessity of integrating these approaches if we would create new systems or improve existing ones as efficiently as possible.

Problems involving the operation of an existing system are more likely to attract operations researchers than systems engineers; problems involving the design of new equipment systems are more likely to attract systems engineers. The design of an organized man-machine system, however, requires not only selecting equipment but also relating equipment to human agencies and determining the flow of information and control, and the procedures by which decisions ought to be made. Here, clearly, both systems engineering and operations research should be involved.

Flood observed that such an integration is particularly critical in automation studies:

> The automation of a system can normally be done efficiently only after a precise specification of the system's function is available, and a systematic evaluation of alternative designs and of alternative operating procedures has been completed so that an optimum solution may be selected (1958, p. 242).

3.7. Summary Remarks on the Scope of OR

I have tried to show that the aspect of organizations that OR has staked out for study is restricted to their operations and the decisions which control them. Improvement in organizational performance can be obtained in other ways which involve organizational content, structure, and communications. As the (inter)disciplines involved in the study of these other aspects of organizations increase their research power, the problem of selecting the most appropriate one(s) to improve an organization's performance will become increasingly difficult to solve. It can only be effectively solved by an integrated examination of the organization. Furthermore, each discipline and interdiscipline involved in such an integrated approach to organizational problems can be strengthened by its association with the others.

In my opinion OR and systems engineering will lead the way towards integration for two reasons: (*a*) they are the most advanced methodologically and technically, and (*b*) they already share much of their methodologies and techniques. I do not think the various disciplines and interdisciplines will lose their identity as a result of such integration any more than mathematics, physics, mechanical engineering, and the other disciplines involved in OR have lost or will lose their identity in OR; and for the same reason: they each have their independent uses.

4. THE METHODOLOGY OF OR

Whether or not OR has a unique area of study, the question remains as to whether or not it has a unique methodology or, put more constructively, what methodology it has.

In discussions of the general characteristics of OR's methodology three characteristics consistently appear: the use of mathematical models, the interdisciplinary team, and the "holistic" approach to problems. Although the latter two characteristics have seldom (if ever) been used by operations researchers as a basis for a claim to uniqueness, an understanding of their significance is essential for an understanding of OR's methodology. On the other hand, some have claimed that the way models are used in OR is unique, or at least that the essence of OR's methodology can be found here.

4.1. Know-How and Models

When Beer asserted that OR is not *a* science, the principal implication seemed to be that it does not have and cannot develop a unique body of knowledge about the phenomena which it studies. We want to examine this implication whether Beer intended it or not. Jessop is quite explicit in asserting this point of view:

> The dominant characteristic of operational research is that it is concerned with situations which apply in a vast number of human activities. . . . There cannot be an organized body of knowledge in the same sense as applies to physics: the subject matter of operational research is too diverse and variable in itself. Furthermore, in practice it is concerned with particular cases or situations, or in other words, its job is to solve problems that are specific or local. It is, therefore, a natural consequence that what constitutes operational research is not knowledge but know-how. Problem solving technique is the bond that links operational research workers in diverse fields.
>
> Operational research considered as a subject rather than as an activity is knowledge of particular situations and classes of situations and their associated methods. In natural science the unifying and synthesizing process takes the shape of the formulation of natural laws; in operational research it takes the form of recognizing analogous situations and developing techniques to meet them (1956, p. 50).

Whether or not one agrees completely with Jessop, it is certainly true that OR recognizes analogous mathematical structures in a large number of problems which arise in quite different contexts. The structure of the problem is revealed in the mathematical form of the model which represents the problem situation. In a very general sense all the models used in OR have one underlying structure. They all relate some measure of organizational performance to a set of controllable and uncontrollable variables.

In the application of OR one characteristic of organizational operations is of central interest: the exchange of values. Each operation consumes some valuable resource such as men, money, machines, time, or effort. In turn, the outcome also has some value. OR is concerned with decisions which affect the relationship between the value consumed (input) and the value created (output). The operations researcher may try to do any of the following:

a. Minimize input-value required to achieve a specified output.

b. Maximize output-value achieved from a specified input.

c. Maximize some function of these two values, for example, the difference between output- and input-values (profit, in a generalized sense), or their ratio (return on investment).

Operations may be studied, of course, without direct regard for the values of inputs and outputs, but only for the aspects of the operation which affect these values. For example, queues may be studied without reference to control and in so doing we need not account for the value of customer waiting time or equipment idle time. In such studies, however, we do consider those aspects of a queue which affect values.

An important characteristic of the scientific approach to problem solving is the act of abstraction which is performed: the analysis which conceptually separates what is never found separated in reality, form and content. Logic and mathematics are the language of structure and the scientist translates experience into these languages so that he can study structure. The operations researcher has done this repetitively for problems involving operations and has come to realize that most of these problems are composed of one or more of a small number of basic structures.

In Ackoff (1956) these forms are identified as the inventory structure, allocation, queuing, sequencing, routing, replacement, competition, and search. But even in a few years these distinctions have become less useful, for it is commonplace to find that a problem of one type can also be cast into the form of another type. Some inventory problems can be treated as either allocation or queuing problems. We are finding higher-order generalizations about structures of operating problems.

It seems to me quite likely that two things will happen in the near future. First, with increasing practical application of OR new forms will be discovered and identified. Secondly, these new forms together with the old ones will be synthesized into increasingly generalized formulations of structure. Though we may never attain it, we may continuously approach the definition of a single structure that will suit all of the problems with which we deal. Just as a variety of specific inventory models have been collected into generalized inventory models (see Arrow, Karlin, and Scarf, 1959) we may expect inventory and other types of models to become embedded in more generalized forms. When this has been done, even approximately, it may enable us—to quote Morse—"to demonstrate that the structure of operating organizations does constitute a unitary field for study and that it is sufficiently distinct to merit separate classification as a subject for specialized scientific study" (1957, p. 5).

If OR does have know-how it appears to consist essentially of the ability both to construct suitable mathematical models of operational problems and to derive "solutions" from them. These models fuse a representation of an operation and the decisions which are involved in the problem. They are decision models as well as operational models.

To be sure, the use of mathematical models is not unique to OR, but the use of these "fused" models to represent an operational problem is at least unique to that small complex of new interdisciplines which are devoted to the study of systems.

Knowledge and know-how. Jessop's view of OR as a body of know-how seems to be supported by the status of modeling in OR. Few problems solved by OR employ models which are already available. In almost every case it is necessary to develop a new model or adapt an old one. The fact that "ready-made" models are seldom used seems to support Jessop's contention that OR's subject matter is too diverse and variable. It could, however, also be explained by the youth of OR.

We have already noted a trend toward models of greater generality. As these are developed consequences deduced from them may form a generalized body of knowledge about operations. To preclude this possibility as Jessop does seems to ignore the fact that similar preclusions have been made about every area of inquiry in its early stages of development. Disciplinary progress has been characterized by finding unity in this diversity. As yet I can see no reason why OR should not eventually find a unifying body of knowledge. On the other hand, there is no doubt that at present we have more know-how than knowledge.

OR's preoccupation with applied problems tends to reveal and emphasize diversity and variability. The operations researcher, like the practicing physician, finds each patient different from all others. But doctors are effective in dealing with patients because generalized knowledge about sickness and health is available to them. The practicing physician is backed up by extensive medical research. Not so for the operations researcher. He conducts his research on patients and not on their diseases, ailments, anatomy, and physiology. OR has yet to develop extensive clinical and laboratory facilities which make large-scale basic research possible. The human being was no more accessible to medical experimenters a century ago than systems are to operations researchers today. Systems can and must be brought into clinics. In addition OR has its mice, rabbits, and monkeys in the form of simulated systems which it can produce on computers and paper.

A large portion of the model building being done in OR is concerned with more and more specialized situations. In queuing, for example, detailed variations of arrival-time and service-time distributions are being explored, as well as modifications in queue discipline and organization of facilities. Such exploration of the effect of changing conditions on outcomes is a necessary prelude to generalization, but the generalizations seem slow in coming. There appears to be too little effort to consolidate existing models into more general ones. This is undoubtedly due in part to the lack of experimentation on real and simulated systems.

A partial reorientation seems called for: we have created operational analysis; now we must begin to create operational synthesis.

Some methodological deficiencies. However much know-how OR has, it still has a great deal of know-not-how. Most research operations performed in OR have not yet been adequately modeled, let alone optimized. Before we can claim to do our job better than others do theirs we must at least turn our own methods of studying operations in on our own operations. Here, I think, we can perform a major service to science in general as well as to OR in particular.

It is not possible to consider all of OR's methodological shortcomings here, or even some of them in detail. Some of the more important ones, however, should at least be noted. First let us consider some of the methodological problems associated with obtaining an adequate measure of effectiveness of a system:

a. Necessary to obtaining an adequate measure of system effectiveness is a knowledge of the objectives of those who control the system. As yet we have no systematic and objective procedure for uncovering these objectives. We use informal methods of observation and interviewing. In his recent address to the Operations Research Society of America (November 11, 1959) Charles J. Hitch observed that these objectives are seldom, if ever, given to operations researchers. They must be "taken." "They must in general be developed as a *product* of the OR analysis . . ." (*Bulletin,* 1959, p. B-75). (See, for example, Leibowitz, 1958.)

b. Once objectives have been identified it is necessary to define the measures in terms of which their attainment is to be characterized. It is one thing to identify an objective in such terms as profit, growth, product leadership, market share, vulnerability, mobility, flexibility, readiness, and public service, but another to develop appropriate measures of these. Adequate measures of most of these objectives have yet to be developed.[8]

c. Once adequate measures for the relevant objectives have been obtained it is necessary to transform them so they can be put onto a single scale in order that the various aspects of the outcome can be made commensurate. In industrial problems, for example, delay time may have to be translated into a cost. Various objective and subjective methods of obtaining these transformations have been discussed in the literature but as yet no systematic methodology for this process has been developed. (See, for example, Feeney, 1955.)

d. After all the measures have been put on a single scale it is necessary to evaluate (measure the utility or value of) successive units on this scale. It is seldom, if ever, that these units have a linear transformation into a value scale, yet most of our current procedures make just such an assumption. (Problems of evaluation are discussed in the next chapter.)

e. Once outcomes can be characterized in terms of their values it still remains to decide what function of value should be maximized or minimized. That is, it is necessary to select a criterion for a "best" decision. At present we have no systematic way of selecting the most appropriate criterion. On this point Bevan observed:

> . . . our failure so far to build up a reasonable body of information or theory on criteria, standards, values, call them what you will. . . . The development

[8] The most detailed treatment of this yet available will appear in C. West Churchman's forthcoming book, *Prediction and Optimal Decisions.*

of a theory on criteria must inevitably be slow, but will even be slower unless we are prepared to devote more of our time to it, even if it means less time "getting on with the job" (1958, pp. 442–443).

After a suitable measure of effectiveness is developed it is usually converted into the dependent variable of a decision model. In most situations there are alternative modeling techniques available. As yet we have no effective way of selecting the best of the possible models. There are growing indications that relevant knowledge can be obtained by testing various modeling techniques against computer-simulated systems. Greater effort along these lines than has yet been expended is required before noticeable progress will be made.

The various problems associated with deriving solutions from models by analysis or simulation are discussed in detail in this volume. It will be apparent that many problems remain to be solved.

Solutions once obtained are normally evaluated retrospectively for obvious practical reasons. Too often, however, they are tested against the same data which was used to construct the model and hence we do not obtain an independent confirmation of the validity of the model. In order to make such evaluations meaningful not only are unused data required but also a way of measuring the value of the outcome which is independent of the model from which the solution is derived. If the derivation from the model has been executed correctly then the resulting solution must perform better than any other relative to the model, but not necessarily relative to the real situation. Adequacy of models and solutions can only be established by use of independent measures of the value of the outcome.

Since the systems with which we deal are dynamic, solutions must be periodically revised in order to take into account any significant changes which occur in the system; that is, it is necessary to exercise *control* over the solution. Not nearly enough work has been done on developing procedures for designing adequate controls of this type. (For an effort in this direction see Ackoff, 1957.)

Finally, it is necessary to see that a solution once obtained and made capable of control is properly implemented. The domain of implementation has been almost untouched by scientific hands. Our discussions of the subject are likely to be as unrevealing but as pompous and verbose as that type of management literature of which we are most critical. For example, the following list of "Principles of Presentation" were obtained by negating statements made at a panel discussion of "Effective Methods of Presenting OR Material" at the November 1959 meeting of the Operations Research Society of America:

Don't carry the customer along with you.
Don't be brief.
Don't use a brief summary.
Don't try to get a sympathetic project officer.
Don't try to communicate effectively.
Make complicated assumptions.
Change the assumptions frequently so as to accommodate the beliefs of the managers.
State the problem in a confusing way.
Be sure to see the problem differently from the way the manager does.

The fact that these principles are so ridiculous exposes the hollowness of the affirmative statements from which they were taken. Acknowledgment of such triviality is an essential first step if we are to make progress in the domain in which it abounds.

Problems in implementation are ones in which, in theory at least, behavioral scientists should be particularly useful. In a later section we will consider the role of these scientists in OR.

4.2. The Interdisciplinary Characteristic of OR

Contemporary scientists tend to overlook an important and interesting fact about the development of science. Until the middle of the eighteenth century all of what we refer to as science today was conducted under the name of "natural philosophy." The inventory of knowledge produced by these pursuits became too full for one man to store in his mind. Specialization was inevitable and it came about through the organization of scientific societies and the formation of departments of science in universities at about the middle of the nineteenth century.

We also have a tendency to think of the division of science into its various branches as corresponding to a natural classification of phenomena. The division of science into disciplines was accomplished by man, not by nature. The disciplines cannot be individuated by a unique set of objects or events which constitute their subject matter, but they are distinguished by the aspects of phenomena to which they direct their attention. Many phenomena may be studied fruitfully by each branch of science, but each will concern itself with different aspects of the phenomena. For example, a communicative act may have physical, chemical, biological, psychological, sociological, and economic aspects.

In the last hundred years it has been necessary to continue to divide our study of phenomena into more and more specialized domains so that progress in depth could be maintained. We began to reach a point, in the second quarter of this century, where the problems most pressing to mankind could no longer be fruitfully treated by specialists. A synthesis of scientific disciplines was inevitable. The effort to create scientific generalists, a much-discussed movement of the thirties, was directed along these lines; but it was doomed to failure because it acquired breadth at the cost of depth. Research by interdisciplinary teams was the only feasible alternative.

The second quarter of our century saw numerous interdisciplinary-team efforts. One such movement, philosophical in orientation, was the movement for a "Unified Science." It produced the *International Encyclopedia of Unified Science.* An Institute of Experimental Method was organized at the University of Pennsylvania in the early forties and conducted research on a wide variety of systems problem with interdisciplinary teams. (See, for example, Churchman et al., 1947.) These are but instances of a trend which Kenneth Boulding has described as follows:

> In recent years there has been a . . . development of great interest in the form of "multisexual" interdisciplines. . . . Cybernetics, for instance, comes out of electrical engineering, neurophysiology, physics, biology, with even a dash of economics. . . .
>
> On the more empirical and practical side the interdisciplinary movement is reflected in the development of interdepartmental institutes of many kinds. . . . Even more important than these visible developments, perhaps, though harder to perceive and identify, is a growing dissatisfaction in many [university] departments, especially at the level of graduate study, with the existing traditional theoretical backgrounds for the empirical studies which form the major part of the output of Ph.D. theses (1956, pp. 199–200).

The increasing use of interdisciplinary research teams results from the growing recognition of the fact that a large number of problems, particularly ones of practical interest, cannot be solved effectively within the boundaries of any one discipline. In the operation of a system, for example, the aspects of the system which can be manipulated so as to improve its performance are likely to come from many different disciplines. The determination of which of these variables can most effectively be manipulated from a control point of view requires the joint analysis of experts in the areas in which these variables are normally treated. Such joint analysis permits the construction of models in which variables from different disciplines interact.

The interdisciplinary approach to problems does *not* consist of a synthesis of research results obtained by independent *intra*disciplinary studies of the same phenomena. That is, it is not accomplished by first setting up disciplinary teams to study the same problem and then attempting to relate the results that are obtained in this way. Interdisciplinary research does not begin at the end of disciplinary inquiries but at the beginning of the research.

In practice, of course, it is seldom possible to have a wide variety of disciplines represented on a single research team. It is possible, however, to consult with representatives of a wide variety of disciplines and to use people on the team who are aware of the content and methods of other disciplines. It is no accident that so many operations researchers have multidisciplinary educational backgrounds.

The behavioral sciences. When one lists the types of variables which actually appear in OR models, the absence of psychological and social variables is conspicuous. Correspondingly, when one lists the disciplinary origin of operations researchers, few are found with backgrounds in the behavioral sciences. These facts seem inconsistent with the interdisciplinary principle and the avowed concern of OR with the human components of systems.

Although the systems with which operations researchers deal always involve human behavior, their models of these systems seldom reflect this fact. The characteristics of human beings which are of concern are usually no different from those of a machine which could perform the same task.

The operations researcher looks at human beings, separately or collectively, as a black box whose input and output characteristics alone are of interest. Therefore he has no direct concern with the psychological or social "mechanism" which converts input into output. This is the same way he looks at equipment. But this does not explain why inputs and outputs and the factors on which these depend are not more frequently characterized by psychological and social variables. The reason is that the types of measures of behavioral variables which are currently in use do not have the same mathematical properties as the types of measures primarily used in other disciplines; that is, they do not employ interval or ratio scales. (See Coombs, 1951, and Stevens, 1946.) As a consequence current psychological and social measures cannot be manipulated in a model in the same way as measures which are normally used in OR; that is, the same mathematical operations (e.g., addition and multiplication) cannot be performed on most of them.

Unfortunately there are relatively few behavioral scientists who are devoting their efforts to developing measures of psychological and social variables which permit the type of mathematical operations required in OR. What efforts there are along these lines have been primarily reported in the new journals *Behavioral Science* and *Conflict Resolution.* It is significant that a large portion of the contributors to these journals, though working in the behavioral sciences, were not formally educated in these areas.

It is difficult to determine what corrective measures should be taken. It does seem apparent, however, that to the extent that behavioral scientists are involved more directly in OR, they will be more strongly motivated to develop their own field in such a way that their results are of more use in OR. On the other side, students interested in operations research might well be encouraged to do some work in the behavioral sciences. By combining pressures from within and without, it may be possible to accelerate the type of conceptual and metrical development in the behavioral sciences which is required by OR.

Black boxes. OR's lack of concern with the contents of "black boxes" is not based on the conviction that they are uninteresting or unimportant. To the contrary, operations researchers recognize that they are both interesting and important but consider them to fall in the domain of other disciplines. Operations researchers are aware of the fact that research on what goes on inside the boxes can lead to system improvement and, as a matter of fact, has done so over a number of years. But this approach from within has limitations in what it can do about system performance. There are at least some major system problems that cannot be effectively researched from the particularized point of view. It is increasingly important that we become able to identify the characteristics of these problems.

The interdisciplinary-team approach to systems offers at least some safeguards against trying to solve a problem that is best solved by a look inside a box by a particular discipline. By having a psychologist present, for example, we may learn that operations of the system cannot be improved until the person in control is cured of his psychosis or is removed from control.

To a large extent operations researchers have failed to gain sympathetic understanding from those scientific disciplines which have engaged in particularized studies of systems because they have failed to make clear their belief in the potency of the traditional disciplines in handling some types of system problems.

Concentration on the input-output characteristics of the black boxes and the relationships between such characteristics of all the boxes that make up the system has come to be called by some the "holistic" approach to problems.

4.3. The Holistic Approach

In definitional discussion of OR there are repeated references to studying the system *as a whole.* For example, Solandt writes:

> But, the distinctive feature of operations research is that the researcher always looks at whatever element he is considering as a whole; not only does he study the whole of the problem, but he also tries to understand at least a little of how that specific problem fits into its larger background (1955, p. 4).

Most operations researchers seem to agree with this characterization of their activity. There is a question, however, as to what the "whole of a system" is.

It has been repeatedly observed that every system we study is part of a larger system. Ultimately, if one continues to generalize, he reaches (at least) the universe as a system. Now we do not mean that the largest all-inclusive system must be considered in solving every problem, for we cannot do so even if we wished to. There are both technological and practical obstacles to so doing. On the practical side we are usually constrained to study only that system under the control of the sponsor of the research. Since those in control can sometimes bring pressure on a larger system which contains theirs, we can and do try to point out significant linkages between these systems. But in general our work is limited by the span of control of those for whom we work. There is no real issue here.

Although in a theoretical or idealized sense one might argue that every decision that is acted on has some effect on every other decision that is ever subsequently made, no one would argue that all these effects are significant. It may be true that removing the speck of chalk from my finger displaces the sun but hardly by an amount that is significant relative to our present state of knowledge or purposes. On the other hand there is general agreement that we should consider all interactions which are significant. It seems to me that a real problem arises here, for if we are to keep this last assertion from being a hollow tautology the term "significant" must be operationally defined.

The field of mathematical statistics has provided one such definition of significance. Let us look at it in the context of a decision model. We never deal with systems so deterministic that the measure of performance is completely determined by the variables included in the model. Hence there is always an unexplained component of actual performance which arises at least in part from the influence of factors not included in the model. These are called "residual" or "chance" variables. If these variables account for more variation in outcome than those which are treated explicitly in our models, we have not taken a broad enough view of the system. The objective, of course, is to be able to reduce the unexplained variation as much as possible. We are limited in our efforts to do so by our ignorance of the structure of the system and by practical considerations. But it does seem as though we should examine at least as much of the system as is necessary in order to make sure that the unexplained variation is significantly less (statistically speaking) than that due to the variables under study.

Since Hitch's paper in 1953 the term "suboptimization" has come to be applied to the practice of dealing with anything less than what according to some criterion is the whole system. Merrill Flood commented on this practice in a recent private communication as follows:

> My own position regarding suboptimization is that it is a useless and unfortunate word, because optimization is normally taken to mean what Hitch refers to as "suboptimization"; specifically, optimization means the best within some clearly defined class of possibilities, where "best" is already defined and includes relevant measures pertaining to larger and higher worlds. In other words, optimum should mean simply the best according to some operationally clear measure within some precisely defined set of alternatives.

I agree with Flood but I do not think that removing the term will remove some of the problems which have been discussed in connection with it. These problems involve what can or must be left out of the statement of a problem.

A total system study would include consideration of all relevant objectives and all of the classes of action which make up the operation. That is, each choice would be considered as a controllable variable relative to all the organizational objectives.

One type of problem-reduction—I suggest this term in place of "suboptimization"—occurs if less than all the relevant objectives are taken into account. This is the type of problem-reduction with which Hitch was concerned in his 1953 paper. It is further discussed by Churchman in the next chapter.

In another type of problem-reduction not all the possible choices are considered as controllable; some may be "taken as given" and only a subset is considered to be subject to deliberate change. Finally, since the outcome is always dependent on environmental variables (which include competition if it is present), all of these may not be taken into account. Then the solution may have applicability over too restricted a range of possible situations.

Where these reductions are imposed on the researcher by external forces no problem arises other than the one of determining whether the problem should be tackled under the imposed constraints. Concern lies with reductions made by the researcher of his own free will, with his inclination to "cut the problem down to size." This means reducing the number of objectives, courses of action, or uncontrollable variables or modifying them in some way so that the resulting problem can be handled by familiar methods and techniques. This, in my opinion, is the heart of the problem that has come to be known as "sub-optimization."

OR has established its usefulness in dealing with problems of limited scope. It has also demonstrated its ability to refine the modeling techniques applicable to such problems. Witness the material in this volume. Continued development along these lines may lead to increased specialization in modeling techniques among operations researchers, a trend that is already in evidence. This will result, as it has in the past to some extent, in researchers looking for problems to fit their techniques. Worse yet, if they cannot find such problems they will be increasingly inclined to distort the problem so that their favorite technique can be applied. If OR is to survive it must maintain a strong problem orientation, not a technique orientation. It must expand its methods and techniques to fit the problems and not contract the problems to fit available methods and techniques.

For this reason it is important that operations researchers continually try to deal with problems of broader scope (e.g., long-range planning), that they try to deal with obstinate aspects of organizational operations (e.g., marketing and research in industry), and that they try to enlarge the category of types of systems that are studied so as to include even problems of national planning.

> . . . operational research should be applied essentially to broad problems, as for example to an industry as opposed to the bench, to a transport system as opposed to a railway truck. . . . Incidentally I can see no reason why operational research should not be applied in the future to studies concerned with national planning and national policy. (Bevan, 1958, p. 444.)

5. CONCLUSIONS

The principal purpose for this excursion into meaning, scope, and methods has been to identify the requirements for continued progress in OR. The conclusions reached may be summarized as follows:

1. OR should extend its approach to organizational operations to include consideration of changes in organizational structure and hence should support and contribute to the development of organization theory.
2. It should similarly extend itself to include consideration of information processing and hence should support and contribute to research efforts directed toward creating a theory of human communication.
3. A closer liaison (if not amalgamation) with systems engineering should be approached in order to obtain an integration of the methodologies and techniques of system development and system evaluation.
4. More active participation of behavioral scientists in OR is required to provide better coverage of relevant system variables and to assist in implementation problems. The behavioral sciences must develop their usefulness for such purposes. This can best be accomplished both by involving their representatives in OR and operations researchers in the behavioral sciences.
5. Research should be directed toward uncovering new problem structures, improving the current taxonomy of models, and developing more generalized specifications of these structures.
6. Theories should be developed which are sufficiently general to permit deductions which have potentially wide application, which can be experimentally confirmed or disconfirmed, and which generate hypotheses that when studied may lead to further generalizations.
7. Methodological (know-how) research should be intensified in order to obtain more satisfactory ways than are currently available for identifying objectives, defining suitable measures for them, transforming them into standard scales, evaluating units on these scales, and selecting a criterion of "best" choice. In addition, better methods of testing models and solutions, controlling them, and implementing results are required.
8. OR should attempt to deal with larger and larger segments of larger and larger systems so that deficiencies in procedures can be made more apparent and so that expansion of its methods and techniques is continually stimulated.

Who is to do all the research that is called for? It is clear that not all of it can or even should be done by operations researchers. But certainly some of it should. It cannot be expected to come from operations researchers in industrial or military units (unless they happen to be modeled after the RAND Corporation). In the main we will have to depend on academic institutions for such work. Although an increasing number of such institutions are developing OR activities there are still too few with a capacity for either basic or applied research in this area. There are many reasons for this, including indifference or hostility of university administrators; but, in my opinion, the principal reason is the unwillingness of academic operations researchers or systems engineers to separate themselves completely from their original disciplines and throw in their lot with the appropriate interdiscipline called by any name you will. People who straddle fences do not breed confidence in their activity by either students or administrators.

In some universities operations research is being taught in as many as four different departments, but research is being done in none. Energies are being consumed in interdepartmental rivalries. The organizational requirements for a successful activity differ from institution to institution but it does seem to me that the failure of OR and other interdisciplines to thrive in any institutions except those where they have some degree of autonomy is strong evidence of the need for academic operations researchers to strike out on their own under whatever name best suits the circumstances. Because the profession and practice of operations research has, it seems to me, grown more rapidly than any of the related interdisciplines its name is likely to be more useful than that of any of the related interdisciplines, at least for the near future.

A great deal has been accomplished by operations research in its short history. Much, however, remains to be done and it will be harder to do than what has already been done. Are we content with past accomplishments and willing to stop here? A great contemporary philosopher, E. A. Singer, Jr., has offered an answer:

> It might be, and commonly is, imagined that the labor of acquiring science may stop the moment one has all the power one needs to secure some limited prize, as it might be one's daily bread and all one would have of butter. But no; contentment lies not in having; it lies in the hope of having, and its measure is nicely proportioned to hope's measure of assurance (1923, pp. 109–110).

BIBLIOGRAPHY

Ackoff, R. L., "The Development of OR as a Science," *Opns. Res.,* **4,** 265–295 (1956).

———, "The Concept and Exercise of Control in Operations Research," *Proc. of the First Inter. Conf. on OR,* Opns. Res. Soc. of Amer., Baltimore (1957), 26–43.

———, "Towards a Behavioral Theory of Communication," *Mgmt. Sci.,* **4,** 218–234 (1958).

Arrow, K. J., "Decision Theory and Operations Research," *Opns. Res.,* **5,** 765–774 (1957).

———, Karlin, S., and Scarf, H., *Studies in the Mathematical Theory of Inventory and Production,* Stanford University Press, Stanford, California, 1958.

Beer, Stafford, "Cybernetics and Operational Research," *Opnal. Res. Quart.,* **10,** 1–21 (1959).

Bevan, R. W., "Trends in Operational Research," *Opns. Res.,* **6,** 441–447 (1958).

Boulding, Kenneth, "General Systems Theory," *Mgmt. Sci.,* **2,** 197–208 (1956).

Bulletin of the Operations Research Society of America, **7,** Supplement 2 (1959).

Camp, G. D., "Operations Research: The Science of Generalized Strategies and Tactics," *Textile Res. Jour.,* **25,** 629–634 (1955).

Cherry, Colin, *On Human Communication,* John Wiley and Sons, New York, 1957.

Churchman, C. W., "A Survey of Operations Research Accomplishments in Industry," *Proc. of the Conference on "What is Operations Research Accomplishing in Industry?,"* Case Inst. of Tech., Cleveland, 1955.

———, "A Summing-Up," *Proc. of the First Inter. Conf. on OR,* Opns. Res. Soc. of Amer., Baltimore (1957), 514–520.

———, "Organizations and Goal Revisions," *Proc. of the Second Inter. Conf. on OR* (uncorrected proof), English Universities Press, London (1960), 6–11.

———, Ackoff, R. L., and Arnoff, E. L., *Introduction to Operations Research,* John Wiley and Sons, New York, 1957.

———, Ackoff, R. L., and Wax, M. (ed.), *Measurement of Consumer Interest,* University of Pennsylvania Press, Philadelphia, 1947.

Coombs, C. H., "Mathematical Models in Psychological Scaling," *J. Amer. Stat. Assoc.,* **46,** 480–489 (1951).

Feeney, G. J., "A Basis for Strategic Decisions on Inventory Control Operations," *Mgmt. Sci.,* **2,** 69–82 (1955).

Flood, M. M., "Operations Research and Automation Science," *J. of Ind. Eng.,* **9,** 239–242 (1958).

Glover, W. S., and Ackoff, R. L., "Five-Year Planning for an Integrated Operation," *Case Studies in Operations Research,* Case Institute of Technology, Cleveland, 1956.

Goode, H. H., and Machol, R. E., *Systems Engineering,* McGraw-Hill Book Co., New York, 1957.

Goodeve, C. F., "Operational Research as a Science," *Opns. Res.,* **1,** 166–180 (1953).

———, "The Scientific Method," *Proc. of the First Inter. Conf. on OR,* Opns. Res. Soc. of Amer., Baltimore (1957), 9–19.

———, and Ridley, G. R., "A Survey of O.R. in Great Britain," *Opnal. Res. Quart.,* **4,** 21–24 (1953).

Haire, Mason (ed.), *Modern Organization Theory,* John Wiley and Sons, New York, 1959.

Hertz, D. B., "Progress in Industrial Operations Research in the United States," *Proc. of the First Inter. Conf. on OR,* Opns. Res. Soc. of Amer., Baltimore (1957), 455–467.

Hitch, Charles, "Sub-optimization in Operations Research," *Opns. Res.,* **1,** 87–99 (1953).

Jessop, W. N., "Operational Research Methods; What Are They?," *Opnal. Res. Quart.,* **7,** 49–58 (1956).

Johnson, Ellis, "A Survey of Operations Research in the U.S.A.," *Opnal. Res. Quart.,* **5,** 43–48 (1954).

Kendall, M. G., "The Teaching of Operational Research," *Opnal. Res. Quart.,* **9,** 265–278 (1958).

Koopman, B. O., "Fallacies in Operations Research," *Opns. Res.,* **4,** 422–426 (1956).

Leibowitz, M. J., "Metaphysical Considerations Involved in Choosing a Measure of Effectiveness," *Opns. Res.,* **6,** 127–130 (1958).

Morse, P. M., "Operations Research Is Also Research," *Proc. of the First Inter. Conf. on OR,* Opns. Res. Soc. of Amer., Baltimore (1957), 1–8.

———, and Kimball, G. E., *Methods of Operations Research,* Massachusetts Institute of Technology, The Technology Press, and John Wiley and Sons, New York, 1951.

Page, Thornton, "Operations Research as Defined in This Journal," *Opns. Res.,* **2,** 86–88 (1954).

Rivett, B. H. P., "A Survey of Operational Research in British Industry," *Opnal. Res. Quart.,* **10,** 189–205 (1959).

Rudner, R. S., and Wolfson, R. J., *Notes on a Constructional Framework for a Theory of Organizational Decision Making* (mimeographed), Michigan State University, East Lansing, 1958.

Singer, E. A., Jr., *On the Contented Life,* Henry Holt and Co., New York, 1923.

Solandt, Omand, "Observation, Experiment, and Measurement in Operations Research," *Opns. Res.,* **3,** 1–14 (1955).

Stevens, S. S., "Mathematics, Measurement, and Psychophysics," in *Handbook of Experimental Psychology,* ed. by S. S. Stevens, John Wiley and Sons, New York, 1951.

Swan, A. W., "The Name and Nature of OR," *Opnal. Res. Quart.,* **8,** 1–5 (1957).

"The Progress of Science: The Future Strategy of Science," *Opnal. Res. Quart.,* **10,** 179–180 (1959).

Williams, E. C., "Reflections on Operational Research," *Opnal. Res. Quart.,* **5,** 39–42 (1954).

Chapter **2**

DECISION AND VALUE THEORY

C. West Churchman
University of California, Berkeley

Contents

1. CONTRIBUTIONS TO DECISION AND VALUE THEORY

The subject of this chapter is given many different interpretations even in the same scientific discipline and radically different meanings between disciplines. Indeed, the phrase "decision making" has become almost as popular in the social sciences as "model." Virtually every social discipline has a deep concern about the way in which human beings do make and ought to make decisions. A brief account of these interests may help operations researchers to understand the enormous potentiality of intellectual resources at their disposal, as well as the bewildering complexity of concepts and results which a conscientious field of inquiry must try to scrutinize and evaluate.

For example, experimental psychology is interested in individual and group decision making in controlled and explicitly designed situations.[1] The situations are usually simple, as are the problems which the subject has to solve. There is usually some specific hypothesis which is to be tested by statistical techniques. The clinical psychologist, psychiatrist, and analyst study personal decision making in terms of "normal" and "abnormal" personality characteristics.[2] They stress both the hidden and the conscious motivations which underlie individual decision making.[3] The social psychologist and sociologist examine decision making of organizations and institutions.[4] They emphasize attitudes, cultural lags, traditions, status, and so on. Anthropologists do much the same thing for nations and cultures. Political scientists examine the structure and impact of decision making in political agencies.[5] They emphasize the role of power, conflict, and tradition in de-

[1] For a sample, see Edwards (1954, 1955, 1956), Lachman and Brown (1957), and McGlothin (1956), as well as others to be discussed below.

[2] The literature is obviously much too large to cite; some recent decision-making studies which are concerned with clinical data are to be found in Holzman (1958), Kaduskin (1958), and Scodel et al. (1959).

[3] Of considerable potential interest to operations research are the studies of preferences, and especially the pitfalls of questionnaire techniques; see, for example, Ferris (1957), Ishler, Lane, and Janish (1954), Lawler (1955), Mitchell (1957), Pangborn, Simone, and Leonard (1958), Pettit (1958), and Symposium (1957).

[4] See, for example, Calvin, Hoffman, and Harden (1957), Diesing (1958), Lazarsfeld (1954), Sutcliffe and Haberman (1956), and Torrance (1957).

[5] As examples, see Livingston (1958), Robinson (1958), Rose (1958), Snyder and

cision making. Lawyers try to discern the interplay of personal goals, tradition and ethics in the decisions of courts and other legal bodies. Students of education want to determine their community's educational goals and to evaluate educational policy in terms of these goals and certain implicit or explicit human ideals. Economists and business administrators attempt much the same thing for industrial policy makers; they have tended to subdivide policy making into fields: marketing, production, finance, and industrial relations, with quite distinct approaches in each case. Philosophers have often tried to construe man's aesthetic, cognitive, and moral enterprises as the outcome of decision making of individuals and groups.[6]

1.1. The Operations Researcher's Dilemma

What attitude shall the operations researcher take with respect to all this intellectual endeavor? On the one hand, the World War II tradition of operations research tells us that operations research should be "open minded" and receptive to all approaches. Presumably the workers within the disciplines have not been wasting their time and really have understood in depth some of the critical aspects of decision making which they have studied. Presumably, too, any real understanding of a class of phenomena can be generalized, so that the right way to understand how laws get adopted or labor disputes get settled should be useful in understanding how a firm's policies are made or a military agency's decisions are actualized.

But on the other hand the effort to appreciate another's mode of thinking and his discoveries is costly of time and status. Many operations researchers regard the analysis of decision making in other fields to be confusing in its terminology, lacking in precision, and indeterminate in its conclusions.

It is almost impossible at the present time to attempt to discern the rights and wrongs of these two points of view. For the purposes of this review, we shall recognize that although operations researchers have relied heavily on "traditional" or "classical" decision theory borrowed from economics, nevertheless operations research is not an applied branch of economics, and should certainly devote part of its basic

Glenn (1958), and Torrance (1957). Gore and Silander (1959) contains a number of other citations in sociology and political science.

[6] No attempt will be made here to cite the very broad literature in jurisprudence, education, economics, and philosophy, except for the specific items mentioned below.

research to the examination of the advantages and defects of other approaches to a theory of decision making.

2. MEANING OF DECISION AND VALUE THEORY

To set the stage for the survey, we follow Ackoff's formulation of decision making (Churchman et al., 1957, Chapter 7), because it seems to characterize very well what operations researchers normally do, and because it will enable us to distinguish between decision theory and value theory. The formulation will be modified somewhat to suit the purposes of this survey.

In operations research, then, we try to define a set of available alternative policies of a decision maker, and to measure the "effectiveness" of each policy in such a way that the policy with the highest effectiveness is the one which should be chosen. In this endeavor, we usually proceed by expressing the policies in terms of physically measurable attributes: the *quantity* ordered, the *number* of persons available, the *time* when a process starts, and so on. Hopefully, but not necessarily, each policy can be completely identified by a number along one physical scale. Thus, starting with a rather vague idea of a set of actions the decision maker can adopt, we end with a set of quantities, x_1, x_2, x_3, etc., such that each x_i denotes one and only one of the set of actions. More generally, we may arrive at a set of quantities (a vector) such that each set denotes one and only one of the members of the action set. For purposes of exposition, we shall consider the special case where each action is denoted by one quantity. Further, we shall say that the set of quantities is defined in terms of a continuous interval of some scale.

The quantities which denote the alternative actions are physical quantities. By this we mean that they reveal no information about their value to a decision maker. In other words, the quantities are the same no matter what may be the interests and other attributes of the decision maker. In operations research we try to take each of these quantities and translate it into an effectiveness measure. Usually this is done by developing two other kinds of quantities. One of these kinds depends on the decision maker's interests, needs, and wants. We shall call these the "value" quantities. More specifically, the value quantities assign weights to certain aspects (goals) of states of nature which may occur as a result of adopting one of the members of the action set. These weights are taken to represent the relative importance of the goals for the decision maker. The other kind of quantity depends on whatever other aspects of the situation are relevant in predicting which state will occur if a member of the action set is chosen. These are "non-value" quantities. The non-value quantities may or may not be independent of the decision maker. If they are independent, we call them "environmental," and if they are dependent, we call them (non-value) "personality" quantities.

By these steps we can describe operations research's final aim. Let x be used to symbolize the physical action quantities, y the value quantities, z the environmental quantities, and w the decision maker's personality quantities. We wish to express an effectiveness measure for each given y,z,w:

$$E(x) = f(x,y,z,w)$$

The function $E(x)$ has the following property: the quantity x which maximizes $f(x,y,z,w)$ for any fixed y,z,w is the best action for the decision maker to adopt in any situation describable by the given y,z,w. Further, if any set of the x-quantities is removed (i.e., if some of the actions are no longer available), and y,z,w do not change, then the quantity x in the reduced set which maximizes $f(x,y,z,w)$ is the best action.

The above description can be generalized in various ways: for example, y, z, and w need not be fixed as constants; they can be characterized instead by fixed random distributions, or by random distributions which change in a predetermined way over a time interval. In this case, the definition of the maximum of $f(x,y,z,w)$ has to be modified, and this is usually done by defining the expected value of f, and by asserting that if x is the best action, then the expected value of $f(x,y,z,w)$ or the discounted expected value is maximized.

Further, the set of action quantities may be restricted to an interval (e.g., x must be greater than zero). The terminal points of the interval we call "constraints." The constraints may be definitional (i.e., they may depend on the definition of the physical scale), environmental (they may depend on the physical or psychological aspects of the environment which the decision maker cannot change), or personal (they may depend on the non-value characteristics of the decision maker's personality).

In terms of this description we can define one meaning of "decision theory" and "value theory." The aim of decision theory is to derive, for a given set of decision makers, a given set of actions and a specified range of y,z,w, at least one function $f(x,y,z,w)$ which is the correct function for measuring effectiveness. The aim of value theory is to provide an empirically operational method of generating the value quantities (y).

The above account can be briefly illustrated by the well-known "newsboy" (one-shot) inventory problem. The newsboy's set of alternatives can be characterized completely by the number x of newspapers he orders. (In this case, the action quantities are not defined in terms of a continuous interval, of course.) The action quantities are definitionally constrained from below by zero, may be environmentally constrained by the newspaper company's refusal to let him have more than sixty copies, may be personality constrained by his predilection for ordering in even-numbered quantities. It is assumed that he wishes to maximize his long-run net return. Hence, the y-quantities can be expressed as the cost of overages (c_1) and the cost of lost customers (c_2). The influence of environmental variables (weather, locale, etc.) and the personality variables (method of sales approach, friendliness, etc.) are assumed to be expressible by means of a fixed random function of demand. Decision theory attempts to prove that the correct function is a *sum* of the average number of papers left over on days when he sells too few, linearly weighted by the cost of overage, *plus* the average number of papers short on days when he has too many customers, linearly weighted by the cost of shortage, for each quantity he orders. Value theory attempts to prove that a specified way of obtaining the cost of overage and the cost of shortage is correct.

This description of decision and value theory seems to make value theory a special case of decision theory, but a moment's reflection shows that the two are clearly interdependent: the correct function clearly depends on how the value quantities are obtained.

Finally, we shall recognize that the imputed aim of decision theory and of value theory may not be correct; that is, a researcher may legitimately investigate these aims. We shall include such investigations within "decision theory" and "value theory," by recognizing that the workers of any scientific discipline may always investigate their own methods and purposes.

2.1. *A Statistical Survey of Operations Research Contributions to Decision and Value Theory*

This chapter is concerned with the present state of decision and value theory in operations research. The "present state" can be described in terms of the amount of interest in the subject as is evidenced by articles which contribute to its development. This way of describing, however, is quite discouraging.

Suppose we say that an article contributes to decision and value theory if it either attempts to justify the form of the function f discussed above or tries to justify some method of obtaining the value quantities.

In the period January 1958 to July 1959, 249 articles appeared in the following journals, which are presumably devoted entirely to operations research and/or management science: *Operations Research, Journal of the Operational Research Society, Management Science, Naval Research Logistics Quarterly, Recherche Opérationelle, Unternehmungsforschung.* Of these 249 articles, only 5 can properly be described as contributing to decision or value theory.

Consequently, the present state of decision and value theory must be described primarily in terms of the articles appearing in journals of other fields, or in terms of monographs and books. The relevance of these contributions to operations research is therefore not easy to ascertain, simply because the contributors are not essentially interested in the types of problems and problem setting which concern the operations researcher. There is, of course, an obvious moral to be drawn about operations research, to the effect that a discipline which purports to study optimal decisions neglects the theory of decision making in its publications. One defense of this criticism of operations research is to assert that many of the successful operations research studies make use of a "traditional" form of the function f and to argue further that the value data are given to the operations research team, in the form which they require, by other research groups of the company or agency, notably the accounting departments or else the staffs of the top executives. This defense in effect is based on both a methodological axiom and an organizational principle. The methodological axiom asserts that the function f is expressible in terms of a set of variables which forecast the outcomes, linearly weighted by costs or profits. The forecasts may be determinate or probabilistic. The organizational principle states that the operations research team ought not to be responsible for developing the cost or profit data, but rather should make their requirements clear to other groups in the organization who will be assigned this responsibility. Of course the degree of involvement of the operations research team in the determination of costs is not clear even if the organizational principle be granted, because defining the cost-data requirements may in some cases virtually entail full responsibility on the part of the operations research team. But at least in the reported part of the work, the methodology of satisfying the cost data requirement is not discussed.

These comments suggest that the most useful kind of survey of decision and value theory will be one which describes research results and conceptual arguments that cast doubt on the adequacy of the "traditional" approach outlined above, that is, cast doubt on the methodological axiom and the organizational principle. Before examining these criticisms, it will be advantageous to mention several recent surveys and bibliographies of decision theory which will enable those interested to understand the current status of the field.

3. SURVEYS OF DECISION THEORY

Arrow's survey (1958) is a discussion of two important books which appeared in 1954: *Decision Processes* (Thrall et al., 1954) and *Mathematical Thinking in the Social Sciences* (Lazarsfeld, 1954). Both of these books are concerned with models of decision making and emphasize the concept of a preference relation over a set of alternative actions. Their significance for operations research is hard to assess, since they are primarily accounts of basic research, the payoff of which is still some distance off. *Decision Processes* contains several articles on the theory of rational decision making under uncertainty which demonstrate that the "obvious" intuitions about rational behavior are either inconsistent or else at variance with observed behavior. None of this necessarily implies a fundamental weakness in the use of traditional decision theory in operations research because the special circumstances which concern the operations researcher may be such that the subtle inadequacies do not occur in practice. *Mathematical Thinking* consists of a series of papers on attitude measurement, group interaction, and the like. Some of these may have the same kind of relevance to operations research as does the March and Simon book on organization theory (1958). Arrow appends a bibliography of papers which he takes to be relevant to the studies in these books. To this list should be added the book by Chernoff and Moses which deals with elementary decision theory (1959).

The *Administrative Science Quarterly* (1958) devoted an entire issue to decision theory and operations research. The papers seem primarily to be addressed to a lay audience. A similar set of papers, addressed to economists, appears in the *Review of Economics and Statistics* (1958), entitled "Economics and Operations Research." Some of this material will be discussed below. Perhaps the most surprising aspect of this symposium is the apparent assumption on the part of some of the writers that there exists in operations research the same kind of tradition and acceptance of methodology which occurs in economics. It seems oddly premature to speak of what "operations researchers do" or "try to do," when the recent beginnings of operations research explicitly refused to accept the historical precedent of any field and the last decade has introduced so many different methods, all claiming to be "cases" of operations research.

Recent bibliographies of decision theory are also to be found in two Cornell publications: Wasserman (1958) and Gore and Silander (1959). The latter is a survey article which contains a number of items not mentioned in the present chapter; the authors attempt to give a very broad picture of decision making; they contrast what they call the "organismic approach" of the sociologist and political scientist with the "management science orientation." Other extended bibliographies appear in Edwards (1955), Arrow (1951), Savage (1954), Case Institute (1957), and Batchelor (1959). Some recent models not mentioned in these surveys are contained in Adams and Fagot (1959) and Royden et al. (1959).

4. CRITICISMS OF TRADITIONAL DECISION THEORY

Suppose we turn now to the criticisms of the traditional approach to decision theory which are appearing in the current literature, and attempt to assess the importance of these relative to the future of operations research.

4.1. Learning Theory and Decision Theory

In the study of decision processes it is often unrealistic and economically bad research policy to consider the decision maker as one who is trying to select the optimal alternative from an action set; instead he should be conceived as a *learner* who attempts to improve his choices. For example, Simon (1957) and others have stressed the importance of learning and search in decision-making activity. The traditional theory requires that the decision maker be "faced with" a set of alternatives; but to get into a position in which one is "faced with" a set of thousands of alternatives may be very costly, or not even feasible. The real-life decision maker is, according to the heuristic viewpoint, a searcher. Models of decision making should emphasize this search activity, and not the simple maximization principle.

Simon has suggested that the word "satisficing" may more aptly describe the decision maker than the word "optimizing."[7] Perhaps the decision maker does not need to view all alternatives in the light of all future goals, but rather in specific circumstances he can use a much simpler model which will direct him to a choice that "satisfices"—for example, a single-goal model (Simon, 1957, Chapter 14).

These criticisms of traditional decision theory have tended to ally decision theory and learning theory, the latter being best illustrated by the Bush-Mosteller book (1955). Decision making is thus representable by models of tendencies to behave. In learning theory, these models are often expressed in terms of sets of differential (or difference) equations. The wary reader may wonder whether this alliance is altogether satisfactory. Learning theory does not depend fundamentally on conscious or unconscious decisions. The subject may show tendencies to behave in certain ways, without ever "deciding" anything. This tendency can be expressed by a rate of change in his behavior. But a differential equation would not necessarily describe the pattern of his *choices*. One might reply that all we have are the observed aspects of behavior, and a search for any more deeply rooted meaning of decision making is like a search for a man's soul. But it does seem that a necessary condition for the validity of "A decides" is that A in some sense produced his choice, and the concept of production does not seem to be observationally elusive, as Singer (1959) shows.

4.2. Suboptimization

The development of an optimal plan for a larger organization is essentially the study of a set of "suboptimal" problems which can realistically be solved, rather than the direct solution of the optimal over-all strategy. Hitch has argued most strenuously for this viewpoint (Hitch, 1953, 1958; and Symposium, 1958). His audience sometimes misconstrues his purpose to be one of damning all who ignore the goals of the whole organization, whereas he actually professes the great value of suboptimizing. His point is that optimal decision making is a planned series of suboptimizations. One must study the goals of a subgroup because to study the over-all problem is too costly. In this respect, Hitch and Simon are not too far apart, because a planned series of suboptima is one type of learning. Of course Hitch's viewpoint is itself subject to attack for its vagueness. He clearly implies that there is a decision to be made about how far to generalize a problem, but he is not clear how this decision ought to be made. The well-

[7] In this connection, see also Cyert, Dill, and March (1958).

known Hitch-Ackoff controversy on operations research and national planning (Ackoff, 1957, 1958; Hitch, 1957) is a case in point, because this showed that what appears to be obviously good suboptimization to a conservative mind is altogether too slow and costly to a non-conservative one. There is also the question of what the "whole" organization means; in one sense, the only optimal decisions are those that concern all mankind. In any event, it is clear that operations research lacks any general theory of research strategy based on suboptimization. Researchers may feel that this problem of strategy is to be solved by each person or team, and the solution is primarily an aspect of the art of research as opposed to the science of research. But few have tried to defend this feeling in any depth. Indeed, operations research itself is constantly breaking down the distinction between the art and science of decision making.

4.3. *Organization Theory*

Closely allied to both of the points raised above is the current interest in a behavioral theory of organizations, best illustrated by March and Simon (1958) and Haire (1959).[8] These books emphasize the difficulties in getting a whole organization to move along some preconceived pathway, and trying to determine what psychological and sociological behavior patterns influence the way in which an organization acts. Of course even within the so-called traditional viewpoint it has long been recognized that some models of decision making must include decentralization of responsibility and authority. For a recent contribution, see Dantzig (1959). More recently Marschak and Radner have investigated decentralization of information-receiving centers; for an early statement of their approach, see Marschak (1955). But March and Simon turn to non-economic properties of organization, and especially to psychological conflict and cooperation, as a basis for predicting organizational choices.

4.4. *Failure to Maximize Expected Return*

It is not at all clear that decision makers attempt to maximize the expected profit, or minimize the expected costs, in risk-taking situations. Experimental work as early as 1948 by Preston and Berrata (1948) indicated that subjects do not follow so-called rational rules in making choices when the outcomes are predictable within probability limits. This idea was investigated further, first by the experiments of

[8] For a bibliography of this area, see Ghiselli and Haire (1959) and also Wasserman (1959).

Mosteller and Nogee (1951), and later by Edwards (1954, 1955, 1956), Davidson, Suppes, and Siegel (1957), and Scodel, Ratoosh, and Minas (1959). The Mosteller-Nogee experiment seemed to show that the social class of a subject could bring about departures of his choice patterns from the traditional pattern; the Edwards results apparently indicate that some subjects "favor" certain probabilities independently of the expected value, and Scodel et al. believe they can show a dependence of choice patterns on personality characteristics. In a similar vein, Simon (1959) points out to economists that so-called "event matching" experiments cast doubt on traditional decision theory. These experiments show that a mature subject, when presented with simple binary choices (predictions about what will happen on the next try) and associated payoffs, will often tend to "event match"—that is, try to get as close as possible to the actual frequency of correct responses. But if the tries are selected by a random process with probabilities, say, of 0.70 or 0.30, then the optimal choice according to traditional theory is to predict the more frequent event each time. See, for example, Anderson, Grant, and David (1957).

There are naturally a number of questions to be asked about the significance of these results. The subjects may be ignorant of the true probabilities (no matter how well they are instructed), they may prefer gambling (or not gambling), they may have any one of several other objectives: to be different from the rest, to win more than anyone else, and so on. Davidson, Suppes, and Siegel (1957) and others have tried to sift out some of the confounding that occurs in decision-making experiments.

The relevance of these results to operations research is difficult to assess. They may mean that executives have their own personal styles of decision making which are valuable in and of themselves, and therefore a decision may be adopted because it accords with a man's style, even though it is "irrational." Of course, there is the defense of the traditional theory to the effect that a firm which fails to maximize its expected profits will "eventually" fail. This sentence, in fact, is a tautology under a suitable definition of the terms. But it seems reasonable enough to say that few if any firms maximize opportunity profit, perhaps because each firm is run in part to accord with its management's style.

At least the experiments on decision making should be taken by the operations researcher as evidence for the need to be cautious in accusing a reluctant management of being naive. At most, these experiments may be a prelude to a drastically revised theory of the firm.

4.5. Game Theory

Evidence of irrationality in decision making is also observed in competitive experimental games. Before turning to these results, however, we can note that traditional theory actually does not provide any clear-cut axioms of choice for competitive situations. For example, suppose the game consists of two choices for each player. If player 1 assumes that player 2 will play according to some fixed strategy, and tries to maximize his return accordingly, then player 2 may be able to ruin him. These reflections have resulted in a series of attempts to adapt the traditional theory so that it does provide rational rules of choice for each player, the minimax rule being the best-known example. But competitive situations seem peculiarly difficult to analyze in such a way that general rules of rationality are forthcoming; the best current treatment of the problem is to be found in Luce and Raiffa (1957). See also Shubik (1954) and the review of this work and much of current game theory by Wagner (1959).

One example will suffice to illustrate the difficulties. This is the well-known "prisoner's dilemma"—a non-zero-sum game. The situation is as follows: the players have two choices, A and B. If they both choose A they both are rewarded alike and rather well. If one chooses A and the other B, the A-chooser does badly and the B-chooser does very well. If both choose B they are rewarded rather poorly. How does the traditional theory decide this issue? Evidently, if the two players were "one" person, then A-A is the optimal choice. This self-evident assertion has apparently not been tested, but experiments have been run in which the subjects are given opportunities to communicate and cooperate, and in which the A-A choice is extraordinarily better than the B-B. Even so, subjects show a strong reluctance to converge on A-A. See Scodel et al. (1959). Hoggatt (1959) has investigated a similar situation in a competitive business game, with much the same result.

How concerned the operations researcher should be with these results is again difficult to say. Most reported operations research studies forecast demand independently of the consideration that the competitor may know that an operations research team is at work and therefore may try to thwart the recommended strategy. Further, there are legal restraints against cooperation. The results at least indicate that some decision makers are more interested in not being outsmarted than they are in making a profit. At most, the results are a prelude to a radically different theory of decision making in which competitive rules form the basis.

4.6. Probability of Choice

The traditional theory seems to restrict choice to one alternative. Of course, the extension to game theory often results in a recommendation for a mixed strategy, in which the plays are chosen by a random device. But quite apart from these considerations, it is important to ascertain whether utilities can be empirically measured in terms of probabilities of choice on the part of the subject, because subjects even under fairly rigidly defined situations do not always display the same preferences. Luce and Raiffa (1957) have given us a formalized version of such a theory, and Davidson and Marschak (1959) have reported some experimental results.

4.7. Group Decision Making

Most models of decision making assume that the decision maker is a single individual. But in many practical cases the alternatives have to be evaluated in terms of several individuals with conflicting interests. Operations researchers are familiar with this problem in several different contexts. They may find that the goals of one department of a company conflict with the goals of another, as the previous discussion of suboptimization suggests. Evidently, the conflict is eventually to be resolved by considering the "over-all" goals of the group to which the two departments belong. But on occasion the operations researcher finds himself faced with two groups which cannot conveniently be subsumed into one organization: for example, management and labor, or—in government research—the community and the enterprise. He may, of course, still look for the larger group to which both do belong. Or he may try to find some "fair" means of compromising between the conflicting aims of the groups. But what does "fair" mean in this context? Evidently, the single-decision-maker model is of no aid here. An earlier work of Arrow (1951) indicates that a set of intuitively obvious rules of fairness may turn out to be inconsistent, and later investigations have tried to overcome the difficulties by suitably weakening the rules. Pepper (1958) approaches the problem in a different way. He tries to form a hypothesis about the dynamics of group conflict and to suggest the ultimate end of a well-adjusted resolution of the conflict. An interesting example of the problem of group conflict occurs in a current operations research study conducted by the National Academy of Sciences designed to investigate maritime cargo handling. Whose interests should be used to develop effectiveness measures? The ship owners', the unions', the casual workers', or the community's? There are few guides for the operations researcher in this kind of a situation. In the maritime study the answer has been to try to determine a method of dividing the gains of the research which all parties will accept because they believe it to be fair. Evidently operations research in this context becomes involved in the intricacies of bargaining, and as yet has no model to guide the research process.

5. VERIFICATION

The criticisms of traditional decision theory so far discussed are mainly concerned with the model itself rather than the method of verifying the model. Yet it must be admitted on a little reflection that the major problem we face is the verification of the theory, and not the construction of alternative theories, no matter how elegant these may be. Perhaps the point can be made most strongly by arguing for the following two assertions:

a. Intuition by itself is a very poor guide in the process of verifying a decision theory.

b. There are no direct observations of behavior which by themselves constitute evidence for a decision theory.

Both of these assertions, if valid, imply that the methodology of verifying a theory of decision making is a very subtle one. Yet experience seems to favor both assertions quite strongly. In connection with assertion *a* it seems established that there is no obvious way of intuiting what a decision maker is trying to do, as is shown in the experiments mentioned above and in the experience of most operations researchers. He may be trying to maximize net profit, or gross profit, or cash, or total personnel, or probability of winning, or a number of other things. There is no purely rational argument which can satisfactorily establish which of these objectives accurately describes the decision maker's intent.

Even so, one might feel that assertion *a* is too strong because although it is true that the decision maker's objectives are never obvious, nonetheless some aspects of his patterns of choice are. These patterns, indeed, are the basis for inferring which objective the decision maker wants, or for measuring the utilities of the various objectives. Thus, one might argue that although we may not know whether the decision maker prefers A to B or B to C, nevertheless if we can verify that A is preferred to B and B to C by some method, then intuition alone verifies that A is preferred to C.

Now subjects do not in fact always behave even in accordance with this simple rule. One can explain their failure to do so in a number of ways. Perhaps they don't prefer A to B on a "pure" basis, so that probability of choice could account for their behavior (Davidson and Marschak, 1959). Perhaps the time between the choices explains the phenomenon. But whatever reason the researcher gives, the methodologist recognizes that the simple rule is verified because the researcher wants it to be, and is willing to modify his model so that it will be. The methodologist may agree with this research aim, but he cannot fail to point out that the verification is therefore not based on intuitive criteria, but on expediency.

In sum, whatever economists or statisticians may feel about the obviousness of their proposed rules of rational decision making, the operations researcher must assert that in the development of optimal strategies there are no obvious principles at all, no matter how simple the proposals may be.

Assertion *b* on the other hand is much more subtle, because it is concerned with the manner in which the researcher verifies a theory of decision making by observation. Indeed, it would seem almost obvious—if we hadn't already abandoned obviousness as a criterion—that the research verifies a theory either intuitively or by observation. Yet *b* asserts that direct observation alone supplies no evidence for or against a decision theory. The saving words of this assertion are, of course, "direct" and "alone." In order to understand assertion *b* more adequately, we examine it in several ways.

5.1. Measurement

We begin by noting that even though a researcher feels satisfied with a general form of the model of decision making, he still has to find the data which can be used to estimate the parameters: for example, costs and demands.

The moral that emerges from a study of data-collection problems of operations research is that the split between the task of formalizing the model and collection of the data which underlies the organizational principle mentioned earlier is ill-conceived.

Specifically, it is incorrect to assume that a set of cost or profit quantities are *measures* simply because they are quantitative. Measures have known formal properties which have to be tested empirically and which justify their use in models (e.g., which justify the multiplication of two quantities). Thus, by implication, it is generally unsafe for the operations research team to turn over to another less technically qualified team the responsibility of generating measures for models.

Hitch (1959), for example, is dismayed at the operations researcher's facile acceptance of indices as the basis of optimal decision making. He rightly points out that indices like "tons hauled per labor hour" or "items produced per direct cost" may be very dangerous bases for identifying optimal decisions or judging past performances. He might also have noted that such strange indices as setup cost per cost of unit inventory may be very fruitful bases. In any case, his cautions are certainly important to the operations researcher who lives in an environment of performance reports based on seemingly meaningful indices. They also indicate the inadvisability of trusting to other agencies the major task of measurement for operations research.

Hitch's concern about adequate measures is given detailed analytic study in present-day analyses of the concept of measurement, for example, in the collected papers of a recent symposium (Churchman and Ratoosh, 1959). The relevance of this effort to operations research can be illustrated by reference to some recent work in value theory of Karr (1958). Karr is interested in the problem of what spare parts to take along on a trip, a problem that bothers most of us householders and campers, but is particularly vexing for military aircraft. A previous study (Karr and Geisler, 1956) had suggested using the *probability* of requiring the part and the *weight* of the part. Both of these are measurements with known structures. Now the earlier suggestion was to divide the probability by the weight to obtain a criterion "measurement." The question is whether this ratio measures anything, and if so, what formal properties it has. At first sight it seems to measure in some sense the "urgency" of the part. We know that if the probability of requirement is zero, the part has no urgency, and this "checks" with one formal property of the ratio, provided the weight is positive. Unfortunately, the other extreme is not so obliging. If the probability is one, we will surely need the part, but if it is a very heavy item the criterion may tell us to leave it at home.

Karr attempts to overcome this difficulty by developing a psychological test of "essentiality." Experts are asked to judge each part in terms of a set of questions which (roughly) elicit responses about what would happen if the part failed (ranging from "virtually nothing" to "complete disability"). The resulting responses are "scaled." The paper does not tell us much about the property of this scale, since it is primarily a "briefing" of airforce personnel, and not an analysis. Each part receives a number depicting its "essentiality" in the eyes of the judges. This number is multiplied by the ratio. Now if a part is heavy, but will probably fail, it may come along nonetheless because its essentiality is high.

Students of measurement, however, may question a number of things about this procedure. Suppose, for example, that essentiality is no more than an ordering of the parts; in other words, the axioms of essentiality measurement do not infer any propositions like "A is x units more essential than B" or "The difference between A and B in essentiality is greater than the difference between C and D." Then it is highly questionable whether the multiplication of the rank orders by the ratio of probability to weight enables one to predict anything useful about the part in terms of its value on the trip. In particular, part A may be "greater than" part B, even though A's loss is only inconvenient and B's is disastrous, simply because A is much lighter than B. The student of measurement would want to axiomatize the measurement of the utility of parts and then study whether a given operational scheme ranks the parts in the manner prescribed by the axioms.

These comments and criticisms of value measurements are certainly important to operations researchers. For example, we often obtain the cost of shortages by questionnaires, or informal discussions with executives. We then divide these "costs" by, say, a holding cost which we also obtain by a series of questions. We then use this ratio to select an order quantity. But suppose our method does no more than rank items in terms of the seriousness of shortage and the inconvenience of holding. Does the ratio of rank orders mean anything? Furthermore, we often add these two costs, although the adding of rank orders is usually quite senseless. Of course, we defend ourselves by asserting that our methods do more than rank the items; they also (we say) provide estimates of the dollars that will be subtracted from liquid capital if a certain policy is carried out. But again, to be formally sound we ought to prove this, especially since the dollar amounts are personal expectations, and not outlays of cash. Many students of measurement feel that because we have not become formally sound in this regard, we do not have an adequate decision theory in operations research.

Returning now to assertion b on p. 50, we can easily see how this discussion supports its position. There are no observations, or records of past events, which by themselves constitute evidence of the validity of a decision theory. At the very least we need a framework that will translate observation into measurement. If the observations do not agree with an axiom of measurement, the axiom is not therefore discarded; instead some other rule may be modified in order to preserve the simplicity of the system. But the reader may feel that observations may lead us to reject a part of a theory, even though by themselves they never confirm the theory. In order to examine this viewpoint, we turn to other issues of verification.

5.2. *Stability of the System*

Littauer (1960) has adopted a different viewpoint on the problem of theory verification, by arguing that a model of a situation is applicable only if the measurement system which supplies the data is in a state of statistical control or "stability." Thus, unless one can show that the measurement of demand or of carrying costs in an inventory model satisfies the requirements of statistical stability, the model is probably meaningless, no matter how elegant. For one thing, all analyses of the sensitivity of models are fruitless if the system is not stable, because the standard errors are not predictors of the actual deviations that may occur. This point is no doubt important for operations researchers who like models and may feel they've done their best when they've studied their model's sensitivity. A strong form of Littauer's viewpoint is that the effort to construct a statistically stable system will reveal the optimal; in other words, optimal decision theory is a subbranch of the theory of technological stability.

The implication of Littauer's argument is that no test of a theory can take place unless the system is stable; a similar idea had been expressed earlier by Shewhart (1939) and Singer (1959). As applied to the study of decisions and values, this means that observations by themselves are not sufficient to test a theory; in addition one requires a set of rules for adjusting observations and a set of rules for determining the stability of the system. One illustration from preference testing will suffice. When a subject is given the same choices to make over and over, or when an executive is asked again to rank a set of objectives, one often finds a high degree of consistency in the responses. At first sight, one would be led to conclude that the "system" is quite stable. But a moment's reflection leads to the opposite conclusion, for the man's memory may be the dominating influence on his responses. The system is therefore contaminated by a nuisance variable which makes all the data turn out to be identical. Such a system is highly "unstable" relative to the aims of the researcher. We'd like to be able to remove the memory aspect which translates all responses into those made at one time, and adjust the observations to other times. Direct observation of choice in this circumstance is therefore of very little value in theory testing.

One inference from Littauer's methodological principle is that an observation becomes valid as evidence for or against a theory only if it can be shown to be a part of a stable system of operations; this, again, supports assertion *b*.

5.3. The Individual

Cowan (1959) has a quite different criticism of traditional theory. He feels that the decision process is essentially an expression of the uniqueness of the individual, a comment that is related to the criticism of the use of differential equations given above. What is decided by someone is what he himself has put into the situation. Put otherwise, decision theorists must themselves decide whether the individual decision maker is a dispensable component of their models. In the traditional theory, we conceptualize an environment in which there is a decision maker faced with choices. He selects that choice which best serves his interests. But couldn't we just as well say that given a state (which includes physical and psychological properties), a new series of states arises with predictable properties? Do we have to include the concept of a decision at all? If we do, what is meant by this requirement? Cowan seems to feel that what we ultimately mean is that some individual is essential in our description. He argues that traditional logic is incapable of capturing the meaning of this individuality. Operations researchers, though they may be a bit shaken by the possibility that their models do not necessarily include any decision makers, will probably view this criticism as irrelevant until a richer alternative to traditional modes of thinking becomes available. But no doubt the viewpoint lies in back of the scepticism about mathematical models and the emphasis on mathematics which was expressed by some of the U.K. members of the First International Conference on Operational Research (1957). The doubts they feel are doubts about the suitability of using certain kinds of mathematics to capture the essence of a decision-making problem, doubts which have been echoed on this side of the water, especially by Drucker (1959).[9]

[9] It is interesting to contrast these doubts with a recent article (Ledley and Lusted, 1959) which attempts to convince medical diagnosticians of the value of "decision theory" for their practice. No doubt individualism is the basic philosophy of the doctor who may, therefore, feel a strong intellectual antagonism toward the suggestions Ledley and Lusted make.

5.4. Presuppositions

A somewhat different criticism of some decision-theory models has been expressed by Churchman (1955) and Ackoff (1960). Their point is that the so-called problems of rational decision making under uncertainty are often problems of the researcher's own making and are not necessarily relevant in making recommendations to decision makers. Specifically, in experimental games the subjects are "given" the payoffs but are not given the method by which the payoffs arose; thus, the game-theoretic conceptualization includes informational cutoffs which do not occur in real situations. In other words, a model which depicts choices of strategies, "given" certain plays and payoffs, must not only be tested in terms of the behavior of experimental subjects; it must also be tested by determining whether the givens of the model are ever given in this form in reality. And all the evidence seems to be that they are not. Returning to the epistemological assertion made earlier, we can say that another reason that observation alone does not provide evidence for a decision theory is that before one trusts the observations of behavior one must also know the process by which the subject reached his present environment; in the case in point, it is doubtful if persons ever really reach a decision situation without knowing anything about the reasons why certain payoffs occur as a result of specified actions. The process of acquiring knowledge of the mechanism of payoffs is itself a decision process; it is methodologically wrong to separate this decision process from the decisions about the correct strategy. In other words, we could say that the player's strategic principle (minimax, max-max, minimax regret) is already contained in the process by which he comes to know the payoffs. Thus, he either knows nothing, or else he knows something. If he knows something, then a decision strategy is presupposed.

6. IDEALISM AND REALISM

The most important conclusion to be drawn from the present state of decision and value theory is that a certain philosophical issue is tremendously important for operations research. This is the issue classically referred to as ontology, the problem of *what* is and *how* we know what is. Two contrasting ontologies are evident at the present stage of our development, a form of idealism and a form of realism. The idealist believes that reality exists fundamentally in ideas, thought processes, and the like. If we borrow a term more familiar to operations research, the idealist holds that reality resides in the model. The realist believes that reality is independent of thought; he holds that reality resides in what is modeled.

To show that these opposing philosophies are of fundamental importance to operations research, we need to translate them into a framework more familiar to the attitudes of the scientific mind at work. The idealist believes in certain criteria which must be satisfied if the research effort is to be valuable: precision, simplicity, and non-triviality of conception. Precision stands for the ability to check our ideas and conclusions in a manner satisfactory to our intellectual peers, simplicity for the ability to express our ideas economically and forcefully, and non-triviality for our ability to create new and significant ideas and conceptions. Now few operations researchers would go so far as to claim that there is no reality beyond what is contained in models. Instead, the modern idealist would claim that the only adequate way to understand reality is to start with ideas and axioms which can be expressed precisely, simply, and non-trivially. The progress of research is an extension of models so that they gradually include more and more of what is contained in reality. The idea is a "first approximation," followed by "breakthroughs." Hence the idealist can respond to many of the criticisms of model building by pointing out that eventually the facets of the real situations which elude modeling at present will be encompassed in more elegant and subtle models.

Experimentation for the idealist has to be given a very precise meaning. The inputs of an experimental design must be sentences (hypotheses) of some model; observations must be simple, identifiable reports which can be interpreted in terms of certain of the symbols of the models. Thus, decision-theory experiments emphasize behavioral "choice" or "verbal response" because presumably these are readily identifiable types of behavior, and the reports of a subject's choices or responses can be interpreted simply in terms of certain elements of a model.

If we examine this form of idealism more closely, we cannot help but be struck by the role which "reality" plays; reality is in fact no more than the set of solved and unsolved problems which the scientist studies. To the idealist, the claim that a model fails to depict reality means nothing unless the claim can be phrased in the form of a problem which is conceivably solvable within some model. Otherwise the claim is vague or even meaningless. Thus, the idealist can appreciate the criticism of game theory that it fails to provide a solution for an n-person non-zero-sum game, because he can see that eventually a model can be built which will provide the solution, or else it will be possible to demonstrate in some model that no "solution" is possible. But if reality is the set of unsolved but solvable or undecidable problems, then the modern idealist is not so different from his ancient counterpart after all; to be real is to be what potentially can be part of a model.

The realist, on the other hand, tries to grasp all that exists by any means at his disposal, regardless of whether man can model it. Reality for him is all the things which we sense, intuit, and feel, in addition to the things we think. He is therefore most alert for the nuances of the situation which have not been included in the model. He emphasizes the complexity of most decisions made in organizations: for example, that the "decision maker" is not a single or easily recognizable entity, that his alternatives are not "laid out" like the apples and pears of traditional consumer economics, that his goals have to be created, and so on. He points out our inability to forecast, or to interpret, or to understand the essence of decision making. He is not concerned primarily with the problem of modeling reality; indeed if the model builders want to call their activity "science," the realist is quite willing to have them do so, and to then point out the "limits of science."

No doubt idealist and realist spend a great deal of time portraying the defects in the other's position. The realists have a predilection for detailed description—for example, for "cases" in which data are endlessly accumulated and tabulated. They ignore precision even when the effort to acquire it is minimal. The post World War II era seems to have witnessed a swing away from extreme realism, because to many researchers it became apparent that adding endlessly to the details of reality made reality as elusive as ever. But on the same score, to construct good models endlessly may also be to avoid the real.

The current status of decision and value theory is in effect an attempt to find a suitable ground between extreme realism and extreme idealism. For some, the proper ground is to restrict research to those problems which can be solved by traditional theory; this means searching reality for those segments where the traditional model is applicable. This proposal certainly narrows the domain of operations research, for example, to problems of production scheduling and control, sampling inspection, and the like. Others propose only to extend research to additional problems when suitable "breakthroughs" occur. Others insist that reality be grasped by any means we can find, and that precision is only one value dimension of good research.

Let us say first of all that any serious student of operations research must understand the idealist contributions of the last decade: that is, the development of "decision theory" and its applications. Having admitted this, then we can say that now the most significant problem of operations research is the problem of realism. We have come some distance by adherence to a form of idealism, but we ought to be aware of the serious impediments this philosophy has imposed upon us.

One aspect of idealism needs careful scrutiny. That one is the tendency to adopt meanings of "theory" and "solution" which are tied into the concept of a model: a theory, according to this viewpoint, is a model or set of models and a solution is a theorem developed in a model. But to the realist, a "theory" of inventory, for example, is an account of how inventories actually are created and maintained. The contrast is perhaps best illustrated by references to the theory of inventory contained in Arrow and Karlin (1958) as compared to the theory contained in Magee (1956). The realist's general requirement is a decision theory which classifies industries and agencies in terms of the kinds of decisions which each makes, the realistic restraints on the decisions, the kind of education and personality which the decision makers have, the nature of the consumer of the decision, and so on. Such a realist decision theory would enable the researcher to start his study with a realistic picture of the problem, something that no existing models of "decision theory" supply. Instead of saying, "Given the objectives, given the constraints, given the demand, this is the model that will work," the realist wants to say "If this is an organization of such-and-such a type, these are the objectives, these are the constraints, these are the demands, and so on." In more general terms still, the realist would like to know whether legal, legislative, medical, educational decisions are really different from the decisions of those businessmen and military strategists who have thus far been the almost exclusive examples used in the application of "decision theory." He would also like to understand how the realities of social morality and ethics can be incorporated into a theory of decision making.

One final point: the issue between idealism and realism in operations research is not a clear one. Clarity-first is after all the desideratum of the idealist. It's the idealist's personal problem—not the realist's—to try to understand how there can really be a problem without there being a precise way to state it.

BIBLIOGRAPHY

Ackoff, R. L., "Operations Research and National Planning," *Opns. Res.,* **5,** 457–468 (1957).

———, "On Hitch's Dissent on 'Operations Research' and National Planning," *Opns. Res.,* **6,** 121–124 (1958).

Adams, E., and Fagot, R., "A Model of Riskless Choice," *Behavioral Science,* **4,** 1–10 (1959).

Anderson, N. H., and Grant, D. A., "A Test of a Statistical Learning Theory Model for Two-Choice Behavior with Double Stimulus Events," *Journal of Experimental Psychology,* **54,** 305–317 (1957).

Arrow, K. J., "Alternative Approaches to the Theory of Choice in the Risk-Taking Situations," *Econometrica,* **19,** 404–437 (1951).

———, "Rational Choice Functions and Orderings," *Economica,* **24,** 121–127 (1959).

———, "Social Choices and Individual Values," Cowles Commission for Research in Economics, Monograph No. 12, John Wiley and Sons, New York, 1951.

———, "Utilities, Attitudes and Choices: A Review Note," *Econometrica,* **20,** 1–23 (1958).

———, and Karlin, S., *Studies in the Mathematical Theory of Inventory and Production,* Stanford University Press, Stanford, California, 1958.

Aumann, R. T., and Kruskal, T. B., "The Coefficients in an Allocation Problem," *Nav. Res. Log. Quart.* (Office of Naval Research), **5,** 111–123 (1958).

———, and ———, "Assigning Quantitative Values to Qualitative Factors in the Naval Electronics Problem," *Nav. Res. Log. Quart.* (Office of Naval Research), **6,** 1–15 (1959).

Batchelor, J., *An Annotated Bibliography of Operations Research,* University of St. Louis Press, St. Louis, 1959.

Bush, Robert C., and Mosteller, Frederick, *Stochastic Models for Learning,* John Wiley and Sons, New York, 1955.

Calvin, A. D., Hoffman, F. K., and Harden, E. L., "The Effect of Intelligence and Social Atmosphere on Group Problem Solving Behavior," *Journal of Social Psychology,* **45,** 61–74 (1957).

Case Institute of Technology, Operations Research Group, *A Comprehensive Bibliography on Operations Research,* John Wiley and Sons, New York, 1957.

———, *Proc. of the Conf. on OR,* Cleveland, Ohio, 1951.

Chernoff, H., and Moses, L. E., *Elementary Decision Theory,* John Wiley and Sons, New York, 1959.

Churchman, C. W., "Problems of Value Measurement for a Theory of Induction and Decisions," *Proceedings of the Third Berkeley Symposium on Mathematical Statistics and Probability,* University of California Press, Berkeley, 1955.

———, and Ackoff, R. L., "An Approximate Measure of Value," *J. of Opns. Res.,* **2,** 172–187 (1954).

———, ———, and Arnoff, L. E., *Introduction to Operations Research,* John Wiley and Sons, New York, 1957, Ch. 5, 105–135.

———, and Ratoosh, P. (eds.), *Measurement: Definitions and Theories,* John Wiley and Sons, New York, 1959.

Cowan, T. A., "Experience and Experiment," *Philosophy of Science,* **26,** 77–83 (1959).

Cyert, R. M., Dill, W. R., and March, J. G., "The Role of Expectations in Business Decision Making," *Administrative Sci. Quart.*, **3,** 307–340 (1958).

Dantzig, G. B., "On the Status of Multistage Linear Programming Problems," *Mgmt. Sci.,* **6,** 53–72 (1959).

Davidson, D., and Marschak, J., "Experimental Tests of Stochastic Decision Theory," in Churchman and Ratoosh, *Measurement: Definitions and Theories* (see Churchman and Ratoosh above).

———, Suppes, P., and Siegel, S., *Decision Making, An Experimental Approach,* Stanford University Press, Stanford, California, 1957.

Dean, B. V., "Operations Research and Managerial Decision Making," *Administrative Sci. Quart.,* **3,** 412–428 (1958).

Delmer, C. N., "Prediction of Sequential Two Choice Decisions from Event Runs," *J. of Experimental Psychology,* **57,** 105–114 (1959).

Diesing, P., "Socio-economic Decisions," *J. of Ethics,* **69,** 1–18 (1958).

Drucker, P., "Long Range Planning," *Mgmt. Sci.,* **5,** 238–249 (1959).

Edwards, W., "Probability Preferences among Bets with Differing Expected Values," *Amer. J. of Psychology,* **67,** 56–57, 68–95 (1954).

———, "An Attempt to Predict Gambling Decisions," in Dunlap, T. W. (ed.), *Mathematical Models of Human Behavior,* Dunlap & Associates, Inc., Stamford, Connecticut, 1955, 83–96.

———, "Reward Probability, Amount and Information as Determiners of Sequential Two-Alternative Decisions," *J. of Experimental Psychology,* **52,** 177–188 (1956).

———, "The Theory of Decision Making," *Psychological Bull.,* **51,** 380–417 (1954).

Estes, William K., "Individual Behavior in Uncertain Situations: An Interpretation in Terms of Statistical Association Theory," in Chapter 9 of Thrall, R. W., Coombs, C. H., and Davis, R. L. (eds.), *Decision Processes,* John Wiley and Sons, New York, 1954.

Ferris, G. E., "A Modified Latin Square Design for Taste-Testing," *Food Research,* **22,** 251–258 (1957).

First Inter. Conf. on OR (Proceedings), Operations Research Society of America, Baltimore, Maryland, 1957.

Friedman, M., and Savage, L. J., "The Expected Utility Hypothesis and the Measurability of Utility," *J. of Political Economy,* **50,** 463–474 (1952).

Gardner, A. R., "Probability Learning with Two and Three Choices," *The Amer. J. of Psychology,* **70,** 174–185 (1957).

Ghiselli, E. E., and Haire, M., *Annotated Bibliography of Organizational Theory* (mimeographed), Psychology Department, University of California, Berkeley, 1959.

Gore, W. J., and Silander, F. S., "A Bibliographic Essay on Decision Making," *Administrative Sci. Quart.,* **4,** 97–121 (1959).

Haire, M. (ed.), *Modern Organization Theory,* John Wiley and Sons, New York, 1959.

Hitch, C., "Operations Research and National Planning—A Dissent," *J. of the OR Soc. of Amer.,* **5,** 718–723 (1957).

———, "Sub-Optimization in Operations Problems," *J. of the OR Soc. of Amer.,* **1,** 87–99 (1953).

Hoffman, Fred S., "The Economic Analysis of Defense: Choice Without Markets," *American Economic Review,* **49,** 368–376 (1959).

Hoggatt, A., "An Experimental Business Game," *Behavioral Science,* **4,** 192–203 (1959).

Holzman, M., "Theories of Choice and Conflict in Psychology and Economics," *J. of Conflict Resolution,* **2,** 310–320 (1958).

Ishler, N., Lane, A., and Janisch, A., "Reliability of Taste-Testing and Consumer Testing Methods," *Food Technology,* **8,** 389 (1954).

Kaduskin, Charles, "Individual Decisions to Undertake Psychotherapy," *Administrative Sci. Quart.,* **3,** 379–411 (1958).

Karr, H. W., "A Method of Estimating Spare-Part Essentiality," *Nav. Res. Log. Quart.* (Office of Naval Research), **5,** 29–42 (1958).

———, and Geisler, M. A., "A Fruitful Application of Static Marginal Analysis," *Mgmt. Sci.,* **2,** 313–326 (1956).

———, and ———, "The Design of Military Supply Tables for Spare Parts," *Opns. Res.,* **4,** 431–442 (1956).

Lachman, J. S., and Brown, C. H., "Behavior in a Free Choice Multiple Path Elimination Problem," *J. of Psychology,* **43,** 27–40 (1957).

Lawler, M., "Cultural Influences on Preferences for Designs," *J. of Abnormal Social Psychology,* **51,** 690–692 (1955).

Lazarsfeld, P. F. (ed.), *Mathematical Thinking in the Social Sciences,* The Free Press, Glencoe, Illinois, 1954.

Ledley, R. S., and Lusted, L. B., "Reasoning Foundations of Medical Diagnosis," *Science,* **130,** 9–22 (1959).

Littauer, S. B., "On Some Aspects of Technological Measurement," *Management Technology,* Monograph of The Institute of Management Sciences, Waverly Press, Baltimore, Maryland, 1960.

Livingston, S. J., "Decision Making in Weapons Development," *Harvard Business Review,* **36,** 127–136 (1958).

Luce, D. R., and Raiffa, H., *Games and Decisions: Introduction and Critical Survey,* John Wiley and Sons, New York, 1957.

McGlothin, William H., "Stability of Choices among Uncertain Alternatives," *Amer. J. of Psychology,* **69,** 604–615 (1956).

Magee, J. F., *Production Planning and Inventory Control,* McGraw-Hill Book Co., New York, 1958.

March, J. G., and Simon, H. A., *Organizations,* John Wiley and Sons, New York, 1958.

Marschak, J., "Elements for a Theory of Teams," *Mgmt. Sci.,* **1,** 127–137 (1955).

Mitchell, John W., "Problems in Taste Difference Testing," *Food Technology,* **11,** 476–478 (1957).

Mosteller, Frederick, and Nogee, Philip, "An Experimental Measurement of Utility," *J. of Political Economy,* **59,** 371–404 (1951).

Nelson, Arthur W., "Present Accomplishments and Future Trends in Problem-Solving and Learning Theory," *Amer. Psychology,* **11,** 278–281 (1950).

Pangborn, R. M., Simone, M. J., and Leonard, S. T., "Comparison of Mass Panel and Household Consumer Responses to Canned Cling Peaches," *Food Technology,* **12,** 693–698 (1958).

Pepper, C. S., *The Sources of Value,* University of California Press, Berkeley, 1958.

Pettit, L. A., "Informational Bias in Flavor Preference Testing," *Food Technology,* **12,** 12–14 (1958).

Preston, M. C., and Barrata, P., "An Experimental Study of the Auction Value of an Uncertain Outcome," *Amer. J. of Psychology,* **61,** 183–193 (1948).

Robinson, James A., "Decision Making in the House Rules Committee," *Administrative Sci. Quart.,* **3,** 73–84 (1958).

Rose, Arnold M., "'Official' vs. 'Administrative' Criteria for Classifications of Combat Breakdown Cases," *Administrative Sci. Quart.,* **3,** 185–194 (1958).

Royden, L. Halsey, Suppes, Patrick, and Walsh, Karol, "A Model of the Experimental Measurement of the Utility of Gambling," *Behavioral Sci.,* **4,** 11–18 (1959).

Salveson, M. E., "An Analysis of Decisions," *Mgmt. Sci.,* **4,** 203–217 (1958).

Savage, L. J., *The Foundations of Statistics,* John Wiley and Sons, New York, 1954.

Scodel, A., Ratoosh, P., and Minas, J. S., "Some Personality Correlates of Decision Making under Conditions of Risk," *Behavioral Sci.,* **4,** 19–28 (1959).

———, ———, ———, and Lipetz, M., "Some Descriptive Aspects of Two-Person, Non Zero-Sum Games," *Conflict Resolution,* **3,** 114–119 (1959).

Seaton, R., and Gardner, B. W., "Acceptance Measurement of Unusual Foods," *Food Research,* **24,** 271–277 (1959).

Shewhart, W. A., *Statistical Method from the Viewpoint of Quality Control,* Graduate School, U.S. Dept. of Agriculture, Washington, D. C., 1939.

Shubik, M., "Studies and Theories of Decision Making," *Administrative Sci. Quart.,* **3,** 289–306 (1958).

——— (ed.), *Readings in Game Theory and Political Behavior,* Doubleday and Co., Garden City, New York, 1954.

———, *Strategy and Market Structure,* John Wiley and Sons, New York, 1959.

Siegel, S., and Goldstein, A. D., "Decision Making Behavior in a Free Choice Uncertain Outcome Situation," *J. of Experimental Psychology,* **57,** 37–42 (1959).

Simon, H. A., *Models of Man,* John Wiley and Sons, New York, 1957.

———, "Theories of Decision Making in Economics and Behavioral Science," *American Economic Review,* **49,** 253–283 (1959).

Singer, E. A., *Experience and Reflection,* University of Pennsylvania Press, Philadelphia, 1959.

Smith, J. W., "A Plan to Allocate and Procure Electronic Sets by the Use of Linear Programming Techniques and Analytical Methods of Assigning Values to Qualitative Factors," *Nav. Log. Res. Quart.,* **3,** 151–162 (1956).

Snyder, C. R., and Glenn, D. P., "The U.S. Decision to Resist Aggression in Korea: The Application of an Analytical Scheme," *Administrative Sci. Quart.,* **3,** 341–378 (1958).

Suppes, P., and Walsh, K., "A Non-linear Model for the Experimental Measurement of Utility," *Behavioral Science,* **4,** 204–211 (1959).

Sutcliffe, J. P., and Haberman, M., "Factors Influencing Choice in Role Conflict Situations," *American Sociological Review,* **21,** 695–703 (1956).

Symposium on "Economics and Operations Research," *Review of Economics and Statistics,* **40,** No. 3, whole issue (1958).

Symposium of the 7th Annual Meeting of the Institute of Food Technology, Pittsburgh, Pennsylvania, 1957, Proceedings inserted in Food Technology, **11,** No. 9 (1957).

Thrall, R. W., Coombs, C. H., and Davis, R. L. (eds.), *Decision Processes,* John Wiley and Sons, New York, 1954.

Torrance, E. P., "Group Decision Making and Disagreement," *Social Forces,* **35,** 314–318 (1957).

Wagner, H., "Advances in Game Theory: A Review Article," *American Economic Review,* **48,** 368–387 (1958).

Wasserman, P., and Silander, F. S., *Decision Making: An Annotated Bibliography,* Graduate School of Business and Public Administration, Cornell University, Ithaca, N. Y., 1958.

———, *Measurement and Evaluation of Organizational Performance: An Annotated Bibliography,* Graduate School of Business and Public Administration, Cornell University, Ithaca, N. Y., 1959.

Chapter **3**

A SURVEY OF INVENTORY THEORY FROM THE OPERATIONS RESEARCH VIEWPOINT

FRED HANSSMANN

Case Institute of Technology, Cleveland, Ohio

Contents

1. INTRODUCTION

Inventory theory, although originally suggested and motivated by applied problems, has developed into a mathematical discipline in its own right. It can be carried on with little or no reference to the so-called "real world" with which operations research is concerned. A useful analogy is found in, say, the theory of differential equations, which can be developed without any reference to the subjects of physics and engineering. The mathematician as such is not interested in the fact that some of his differential equations are useful models of certain processes in the physical world. On the other hand, the physicist is interested in differential equations only to the extent that they are useful to him. Existence proofs are of little concern to him. He knows that his problems have solutions. He considers lengthy and complex algorithms and methods for solution to be of no value. In the real world which interests him, simplicity and time are essential considerations to the extent that accuracy of the solution is sacrificed for them. Quite often, he restricts his search for solutions to certain types of functions, so that he is not always interested in generality to the same extent as the mathematician.

These remarks are equally valid for the operations researcher who looks at the mathematical theory of inventory. The author has thought along these lines in the selection of the material in this chapter, and in the distribution of emphasis. A certain element of subjectivity in judging the potential usefulness to operations research of a piece of theory is, however, unavoidable.

An attempt has been made to arrange the material in a systematic way in which the organization is based on certain features of the real-world phenomenon of inventory rather than mathematical aspects. Of course, these principles overlap. But preference is given here to the problem-oriented viewpoint over the technique-oriented viewpoint. The remainder of this introductory section is devoted to the discussion of the inventory notion and the classification of inventory problems.

1.1. The Inventory Problem

An inventory can be defined as an *idle resource* of any kind, provided that such resource has economic value. This implies that there is a *demand* for the resource. Demand may be satisfied by *outputs* from the inventory. On the other hand, the inventory is replenished by *inputs*. Input and output can be described by their respective rates $a(t)$ and $b(t)$ as functions of time. If the inventory level at time zero is I_0, the inventory level at time t will be

$$I(t) = I_0 + \int_0^t \{a(\tau) - b(\tau)\} \, d\tau \tag{3.1}$$

The rates $a(t)$ and $b(t)$ are not necessarily finite but their time integrals are. The inventory problem to which inventory theory has addressed itself is equivalent to finding input and output functions which maximize (or minimize) a given measure of effectiveness (or ineffectiveness) subject to certain restrictions. These restrictions may include the specification of classes of functions from which $a(t)$ and $b(t)$ must be chosen. Naturally, the availability of *some* information concerning the demand is always assumed.

1.2. Input and Output Patterns

The pattern according to which the demand for a resource materializes in time is a governing factor in every inventory problem. The existing inventory models usually employ one of these assumptions:

a. Demand arrives continuously in time.

b. Demand arrives (or can be treated as arriving) at discrete, equidistant points in time.

c. Demand arrives at discrete, irregular points in time.

As far as customer demand is concerned, assumption *c* appears to be the only one which rigorously holds. Nevertheless, the much more convenient assumptions *a* and *b* yield sufficient approximations in most cases. Only when the individual demands reach the order of magnitude of certain critical parameters of the problem—such as maximum possible inventory—may it be necessary to resort to assumption *c* and observe the precise arrival pattern of demands.

The same three patterns are possible for input and output. Most of the elementary theory of inventory is based on the combination of continuous demand (and output) and discrete inputs. These assumptions are obviously suggested by the nature of many production processes.

1.3. Inventory Networks

A complex system may contain several interacting "inventory stations." If the output from one inventory becomes the input to another we speak of a "series of stations." A series has various "levels." If there are several inventories on the same level, these are called "parallel stations." A given inventory station may have alternative input or output channels or both. Finally, it is possible that the outputs from several stations are combined into an input for another station. Then we shall speak of "fusion of channels."

These relationships can be conveniently illustrated by a network in which the links represent input and output channels and the nodes represent inventory stations or fusion points. The topology of this network is an important criterion in the classification of inventory problems. We shall classify as follows (see Fig. 3.1):

With respect to inventory stations:

The single station
Parallel stations
Series of stations

With respect to channels:

Single channels
Alternative channels
Fusion of channels

1.4. Deterministic and Probabilistic Problems

A second criterion for the classification of inventory problems is the quality of information about the pertinent "parameters" of the problem. The parameter of greatest interest usually is the demand rate. We speak of a deterministic problem when the parameters are known with certainty. If they are known subject to probability distributions the problem is referred to as probabilistic. Very few other alternatives—such as partially known probability distributions—have been explored.

1.5. Static and Dynamic Problems

If the parameters of a problem (or, alternatively, their probability distributions) do not change in time the problem is termed "static." Otherwise, we have a "dynamic" problem.

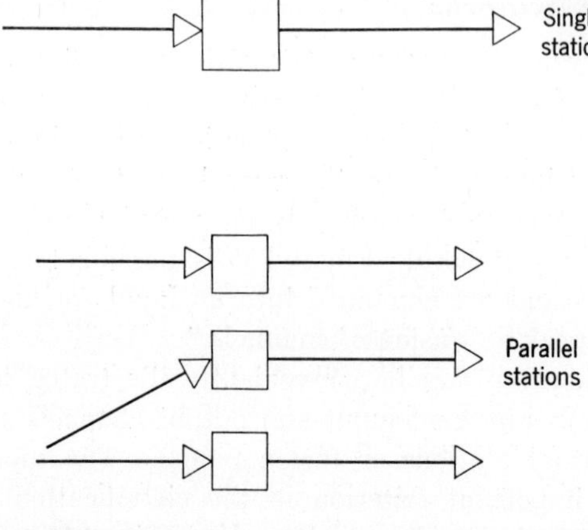

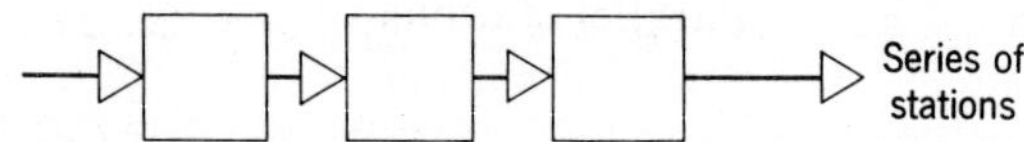

Fig. 3.1. Classification of inventory problems.

2. MATHEMATICAL MODELS

2.1. The Single Station

Static deterministic models. Most of the static deterministic models considered in the literature fall within the framework of the following typical assumptions.

1. Assumptions concerning the input-output-mechanism:

   a. Demand is continuous at a constant rate r. As long as the inventory level is positive, the output rate is held equal to the demand rate.

   b. Inputs occur at discrete points or during discrete intervals in time and must be "ordered" L time units ahead of time. L is the "lead time."

   c. Ordering time is to be signaled by a critical inventory level, the "reorder point."

   d. Input occurs at a constant rate p for a time span determined by the ordered quantity q. The possibility $p = \infty$ (instantaneous input) is admitted.

   e. Reorder point, input quantity, and time intervals between inputs are held constant in time.
   f. The process continues infinitely.
2. Assumptions concerning the measure of effectiveness (cost):
   a. There is a fixed charge for each input (setup cost).
   b. There is a charge per unit of input which may depend on the total input quantity q (e.g., quantity discounts).
   c. There is an inventory charge proportional to the time integral of the positive inventory level; less frequently, the inventory charge may be a more complex function of the inventory level and may depend on other parameters of the problem, such as the total input quantity q.
   d. There is a shortage charge proportional to the time integral of the negative inventory level. Here, too, more complex relationships have been considered. No demand is lost because of shortages (unfilled demand can be backlogged).

In the light of such simple models, the inventory control problem appears as one of determining optimal values for the reorder quantity and reorder point.

We shall discuss reorder points first. Without loss of generality let us assume that we plan for a zero inventory level immediately before delivery. Then, we shall not reorder if the actual inventory A "on the ground" satisfies the relationship

$$A > R_L + R_t - Q_L \tag{3.2}$$

where R_L = total demand during lead time L
Q_L = total input quantity during lead time L resulting from earlier orders
R_t = total demand during the "checking interval" t

The significance of the checking interval t is that orders can be placed only at equidistant points in time which are t time units apart. Equation 3.2 read at time zero says the following: if no additional order is placed now, the inventory level at time $L+t$ will still be positive. Hence, no order should be placed. In summary, the reorder point is the expression on the right-hand side of Eq. 3.1.

Reorder quantities q are determined optimally by writing down the total cost per unit time as a mathematical function of q, and by minimizing this function with respect to q.

As a prototype example consider the economic lot-size equation which is based on the simplest possible cost structure and the exclusion of shortages. The optimal input quantity is

$$\hat{q} = \sqrt{\frac{2rs}{h(1-r/p)}} \tag{3.3}$$

where s and h are cost parameters. Some authors have considered the demand rate as a function of selling price or average delivery time to the customer. In these and similar cases, profit is the appropriate measure of effectiveness, and additional decision variables—such as selling price—are introduced. No essential complications arise.

Finally, consider the case of discrete arrivals of demand in time. This assumption may be necessary for "slow-moving items." If there is a discrete demand for constant quantities at constant, given time intervals, it is not reasonable to allow values for q which are not multiples n of the quantity demanded at a time. In such cases, minimization is over a discrete set of ordering quantities. If $n=1$ turns out to be the optimal solution, the item should be produced to order.

In the case of sporadic demand, another complication may be introduced by the obsolescence behavior of the *individual* item in stock so that the order of withdrawal becomes a decision problem. Derman and Klein (1957–1958) have investigated this problem assuming that the utility derived from an item which is withdrawn at age S is a known function $U(S)$. They have shown that for convex $U(S)$ the optimal depletion policy is "LIFO" (last in, first out); for concave $U(S)$ it is "FIFO" (first in, first out). In the general case, the problem can be solved by the "assignment technique" of linear programming.

Static probabilistic models. The elementary inventory models of the type just discussed can be generalized without difficulty to include the case where one or more parameters of the model are subject to known probability distributions. Usually, the demand rate is the parameter of greatest interest, and it is assumed that the demanded quantities in each time unit come from identical, independent probability distributions. Particularly when the distributions are normal, this assumption permits easy handling of the demand during periods of arbitrary length.

It is common to replace the deterministic measures of effectiveness by their statistical expectations although this is by no means the only alternative in defining objective functions for probabilistic models. Strict restrictions are replaced by restrictions with a specified confidence.

As in the deterministic case, reorder point and reorder level assume the roles of two independent decision variables which are determined optimally by, say, minimizing expected cost per unit time.

A first step in constructing an objective function of these two variables is to study the effect of the reorder point on shortages during the lead time. This has merit in itself, particularly in practical applications of the reorder-point concept. We, therefore, give a brief generalization of the notion of reorder points.

By analogy with Eq. 3.2, let

$$G(R_L+R_t)$$

be the cumulative probability distribution of R_L+R_t. The probability that no shortage will occur between times L and $L+t$ is

$$G(A+Q_L)=\alpha \tag{3.4}$$

It is customary to specify a critical value α_0 below which α must not fall. If

$$G(H)=\alpha_0$$

then we shall not order if

$$A+Q_L>H$$

or

$$A>H-Q_L$$

Hence, $H-Q_L$ is the reorder point if shortages are to be avoided with a confidence of α_0.

In the case of given shortage cost and inventory cost it is usually not possible to give simple explicit solutions for the optimal reorder point P and reorder quantity q. This will become obvious by the following specific example where a cost of d dollars is placed on each shortage delay and the demand per unit time is normally distributed with parameters r and σ. All other symbols have the usual meaning. The expected cost per unit time of setups, inventory, and shortages is approximately equal to

$$E(C)=s\frac{r}{q}+h\left(\frac{q}{2}+P-rL\right)+d\frac{r}{q}\int_P^\infty \frac{(x-P)}{\sqrt{2\pi L}\,\sigma}\exp\left\{-\frac{(x-rL)^2}{2L\sigma^2}\right\}dx \tag{3.5}$$

In such cases, more extended numerical calculations are unavoidable.

An important characteristic of the elementary models considered so far is the fact that they have the notions of reorder point and reorder quantity built into them. In other words, optimization is over the restricted class of so-called (S,s)-policies where s designates the reorder point and $S-s$ designates the reorder quantity. Furthermore, the cost functions are usually very specific functions.

The more general and more theoretical model by Arrow, Harris, and

Marschak (1951) relaxes both of these assumptions. Orders can be placed at equidistant checking points and are filled immediately. The demands between checking points come from given, identical, independent probability distributions. An ordering policy is defined as a function

$$y = y(x) \tag{3.6}$$

where x is the stock on hand and $y-x$ is the quantity to be ordered. It is possible to define the notion of (long-run) expected cost associated with a given policy $y(x)$. This expected cost becomes the criterion for optimality. The optimal policy $y(x)$ can be obtained theoretically as the solution of an integral equation. General conditions for the cost functions and probability distributions are given under which the optimal policy is of the (S,s)-type. Furthermore, general methods are developed for finding the optimal values of S and s if optimization over the restricted class of (S,s)-policies is intended. This whole theory rests on the assumption that shortages can be carried over to the next period.

If delivery is not instantaneous (lead time $L>0$), then the optimal ordering policy can be shown to be of the form

$$y = y(x+Q_L) \tag{3.7}$$

where Q_L is the quantity "due in" during the lead time. Most results obtained in the case of instantaneous delivery hold up in terms of the "generalized stock level" $x+Q_L$. This is not the case, however, when shortages are lost rather than carried over.

The models considered up to this point have assumed infinite processes. A somewhat different type of problem arises when the inventory process is of finite duration. The "newsboy problem" is typical: the optimal supply for meeting a probabilistic one-time demand is sought. Elementary models of this situation are easily constructed.

The more sophisticated model developed by Arrow, Harris, and Marschak can handle finite processes of several periods. If the process lasts for n checking periods, then the optimal ordering policy $y_n(x)$ can be theoretically obtained by means of a set of recurrence relationships. This approach can be generalized for the dynamic case where the probability distributions of demand vary from period to period.

A significantly different input mechanism is introduced by the so-called "base-stock system." Under this system, each unit withdrawn from inventory is immediately reordered. Thus, the sum of inventory on the ground and inventory on order is constant in time. This constant is referred to as base stock. The amount of base stock is the essential decision variable. It can be determined by elementary methods so as to balance the cost of inventory on the ground and the cost of shortage.

All models considered so far have assumed continuous arrivals of demand and continuous decision variables. This model approximation may have to be dropped for "slow-moving items," which are demanded rather sporadically in time so that only a few—if any—items are kept in inventory. In such cases it may be necessary to use "discrete models," which take into account the discrete arrivals of demands in time and restrict the decisions to a few discrete alternatives.

If reordering decisions can be made after each transaction, queuing theory lends itself to the treatment of such problems (Karush, 1957). The base-stock system seems particularly appropriate for items with sporadic demand and hence will be used to illustrate the use of queuing concepts. The number of items in the base stock, M, corresponds to the number of channels of a queuing facility. An item on the ground is an idle channel and an item on order is a busy channel. It is assumed that demands "arrive" one at a time in Poisson fashion. The lead time for a reordered item corresponds to the "service time." Its probability is assumed to have an Erlang distribution. Customer demand which cannot be satisfied immediately is lost. The inventory problem of finding the optimal base stock has thus been brought into the form of the well-known queuing problem of optimizing the number of channels. This approach has been generalized for bulk ordering.

If reordering decisions can be made only at predetermined checking points, the theory of Markov processes lends itself to the construction of similar discrete models. It seems unlikely, however, that an item requiring discrete treatment of demand would not be checked after each transaction.

Dynamic models. We have called a problem dynamic when its parameters change in time. (The parameter of greatest interest in this context is the demand rate.) We assume that such parameters are known or at least probabilistically known as functions of time for a certain span of time extending into the future.

The definition of a long-run optimal policy encounters great conceptual difficulty because of the fact that each decision must be based on a continuously changing knowledge of the future. All solutions offered for this problem employ the concept of a "planning horizon" which is either shifting or fixed.

The method of the "shifting planning horizon" proposes to make decisions in the following way. A time interval of constant length T which immediately follows time t_0 is defined as the "planning horizon at time t_0." For this planning horizon, define an expected measure of effectiveness—say, expected cost—relative to the probability distributions as known at time t_0. This measure is a function of the planned policy during the horizon and of history up to time t_0. At time t_0, determine the optimal plan by minimizing expected cost for the horizon. Begin implementation of the optimal plan. At a later time t_1, make a new optimal plan based on the horizon at time t_1 and on the knowledge of history up to time t_1. Adjust implementation according to the new plan.

Which planning horizon yields the best long-run results is a difficult question and is not discussed here. In practice, it can be answered by simulating the system under different planning horizons. In most cases, the quality of obtainable forecasts suggests a planning horizon in a natural way.

The method of the "fixed planning horizon" proceeds as follows. The time interval T following time t_0 is fixed as the planning horizon once for all. Let t be an arbitrary point of time within this horizon. It seems reasonable that the decision at time t should be a function of t and the history up to time t. (The history up to time t may include information which is equivalent to an improved forecast.) For simplicity's sake, assume that the history can be summarized by a single state variable, say the inventory level I. Then, the decision rule for, say, the quantity to be produced in the next time segment should be of the form

$$q(t) = g(t,I) \tag{3.8}$$

where I depends on earlier decisions and on the values of random variables which have materialized up to time t. The optimal decision rule is given by the particular function $g(t,I)$ which minimizes the expected cost for the horizon. It should be noted, however, that "expected cost" is now defined relative to a preconceived *type* of decision rule. Once the optimal function $g(t,I)$ has been determined, decisions are made without further calculations by simply inserting the historical information and the time into the function.

Combinations of both methods are conceivable. Mathematically, both methods have to address themselves to the minimization of expected cost for a given planning horizon, the distinguishing feature of fixed horizon-planning being that it inserts a preconceived type of decision rule into the expression for expected cost. The following discussion will be centered on this general minimization (or maximization) problem.

The basic problem of minimizing setup and inventory costs over a deterministic horizon—the generalization of the economic lot-size formula—can be solved iteratively by employing certain tools of the differential calculus. The solution furnishes the optimal number of runs up to the horizon, their timing, and their quantities. The same problem can be solved by dynamic programming, using the finite Arrow-Harris-Marschak model discussed earlier.

Dvoretzky, Kiefer, and Wolfowitz (1952) have conceptualized the ordering problem for most general conditions, including dynamic cost functions. For example, in the case of the probabilistic single-station model they admit the possibility that the expected cost in period i is a (known) function

$$C_i = C_i(y_i \mid H_i) \tag{3.9}$$

of the ordering decision y_i at time i and the history H_i as known at time i where H_i is a vector with an arbitrary number of components one of which is the stock level at time i. These authors give:

1. A definition of an ordering *policy* by a set of functions

$$y_i = g_i(H_i) \qquad (i = 1, \cdots, \infty) \tag{3.10}$$

which represent at the same time decision rules applicable at time i.

2. A definition of long-run expected cost (or loss) relative to a *given* policy, from which follows the definition of an optimal policy.

3. Existence proofs for the optimal policy, and the mathematical operations by which the optimal policy may be constructed. Generally speaking, however, these operations are far from practicable, and the "construction" is one in the sense of pure mathematics.

Of any single problem, the so-called production-smoothing problem has received the most attention. The dynamic parameter is the demand rate. The problem is concerned with the conflict between the cost of imperfect synchronization of production and demand on one hand and the cost of changing the production rate plus the effect of nonconstant marginal production costs on the other hand. The problem has been treated for discrete and continuous production decisions.

In the discrete deterministic case, linear-programming formulations have been given (both of the general kind and the transportation type). In the discrete probabilistic case quadratic programming has proven a useful tool. The quadratic objective functions lead to linear decision rules. A very attractive feature is that the probability distributions of demand do not have to be known; knowledge of expected values is sufficient. In the case of stochastic production cost but deterministic demand, dynamic programming has been used to balance inventory costs and production costs. Charnes, Cooper, and Symonds (1958) have constructed a stochastic-demand, fixed-horizon model for the same problem and have solved it by linear-programming methods.

In the continuous case, work has been confined to deterministic horizons. Arrow, Karlin, and Scarf (1958) have given calculus-of-variations formulations. However, the solutions cannot be obtained with conventional tools of the calculus of variations but require a novel approach. The algorithms are rather tedious from the viewpoint of applications.

Another important class of problems is of the "warehousing" type. Inputs to and outputs from an inventory are to be controlled in the most profitable way when purchasing costs, sales prices, and demands change during the horizon. In this area, linear programming has been used extensively. A dynamic programming formulation of the warehousing problem has been given by Bellman (1956).

The "hydroelectric problem" deals with the output control for storage water in reservoirs. Input is probabilistic. Here, too, dynamic programming has proven a useful tool.

The "caterer problem" is somewhat of a dynamic generalization of the newsboy problem. The caterer knows his requirements of fresh napkins for each day of a planning horizon. Two kinds of laundry service are available which differ in speed and in cost. What initial stock of napkins should the caterer purchase, and how should he launder in order to meet all requirements at minimum cost? Several of the popular programming techniques can be employed to obtain a solution.

Occasionally, the decision rules derived from dynamic models pose the critical problem of stability. Holt and Simon (1954) have given concrete examples in which the decision rules derived by the calculus of variations or differential calculus represent unstable feedback rules. The methods and techniques discussed in this section should, therefore, always be supplemented by a check on stability, for which servo theory furnishes certain tools. Holt and Simon (1954) have employed servo theory to construct decision rules of a given type which minimize expected cost subject to the restriction that they be stable.

It appears that by these and similar approaches "good" decision rules can be obtained where goodness is judged by actual costs resulting from the application of the rule in comparison with, say, judgmental decisions. The theory seems to be largely in the dark, however, with regard to the "best" rule. The feedback behavior of dynamic decision rules calls for more theory of a general nature.

2.2. *Parallel Stations*

Problems involving parallel stations represent little more than a set of independent single-station problems unless there are interactions between the various inputs, outputs, and inventories.

One of the simplest inventory problems, the well-known newsboy problem, is significantly complicated if the newsboy can stock several kinds of newspapers with given demand distributions but has limited funds for purchasing. Let

c_i = unit cost of a paper of the ith kind
c = total available funds
x_i = amount spent for newspapers of the ith kind

$$(i=1,\cdots,n)$$

Clearly, the expected cost of shortage and overage for the ith paper is of the form $f_i(x_i/c_i)$ where $f_i(u)$ is a known function. The problem is mathematically equivalent to the minimization of

$$F(x_1,\cdots,x_n)=\sum_1^n f_i\left(\frac{x_i}{c_i}\right) \tag{3.11}$$

subject to

$$\sum_1^n x_i=c \tag{3.12}$$

Several algorithms, such as "convex programming," are available. Convex programming relies on equating marginal costs. Similar approaches have been proposed for dealing with limitations on space, weight, and the like.

If a given annual sales volume can be supplied from several factories with non-linear cost functions, then the question arises: How much—if anything—should a given factory contribute to this volume in order to minimize total costs? This problem of optimal factory location and size (in terms of output rate) is easily seen to be mathematically equivalent to the newsboy problem just discussed. Other interpretations of the newsboy problem will be discussed in the section on applications.

The problem is further complicated when there are several kinds of limited resources which are restricted in their use for the various kinds of "newspapers." This circumstance arises in the problem of allocating aircraft to routes with probabilistic passenger demand, which has been given a linear programming formulation by Dantzig (1955).

Very critical difficulties can arise when the elementary single-station models are applied to a set of parallel stations. For example, when economic production lots are established independently for a number of products, it is a common phenomenon that unfeasible production schedules—particularly because of overloading of facilities—result. One is thus faced with the "economic-lot scheduling problem." Vazsonyi (1957) has given a method for obtaining schedules which stay within available labor and machine restrictions but which are not necessarily optimal. An optimal solution would require the handling of a complicated large-scale non-linear-programming problem which is beyond the capacity of presently available computers.

Rogers (1958) has given an iterative scheduling method which uses the classical lot sizes as a point of departure and then modifies them to make a feasible schedule. The incremental cost which is due to deviations from the classical lot size is computed at each step and serves as a guide in making the modifications. Salveson (1956) has suggested minimizing total cost for all products involved by choosing a specific permutation (production sequence) of the products and introducing cycle length as the only control variable. By repeating this procedure for several permutations, low-cost, feasible schedules may be obtained.

In cases involving very few products and restrictions an exact solution may be obtained by the use of Lagrangian multipliers.

If items are not produced but purchased, the cost per order may have a fixed component and a variable component which is proportional to the number of items on the order. This interaction between items may influence the optimal reorder points. A solution for this case has been given by Naddor and Saltzman (1958).

Typical problems of parallel stations may arise in distribution systems. The routing of merchandise from factories i through rented warehouses j to retail outlets k poses the problem of warehouse selection. The following model by Baumol and Wolfe (1958) is based on the assumption that no significant fixed cost is associated with the use of rented warehouse space, and that an optimal ordering policy will be used for the total annual volume x_{ijk} on route ijk. Then, the total volume through warehouse j is

$$z_j = \sum_{i,k} x_{ijk} \tag{3.13}$$

and the annual transportation and inventory cost is of the form (the square root reflects the inventory policy):

$$C = \sum_{ijk} (c_{ij} + d_{jk}) x_{ijk} + \sum_j w_j \sqrt{z_j} \tag{3.14}$$

Restrictions are given by the supply at factory i:

$$\sum_{jk} x_{ijk} = q_i \tag{3.15}$$

and the demand at outlet k:

$$\sum_{ij} x_{ijk} = r_k \tag{3.16}$$

A simple algorithm can be employed to find a local minimum of this non-linear cost function by successive improvements. In the area of dynamic problems, the multiproduct case of the quadratic production-smoothing problem has been treated by Bonini (1958).

2.3. *Series of Stations*

In a series of inventory stations, all stations work together to produce a common result, which is the delivery of the end product of the process to the customer. Performance at the last level of the series is, therefore, of central interest. Inventories at earlier stages perform only auxiliary functions. Thus, the inventory problem presents itself in the form of two questions:

1. Should there be an inventory at a given stage?
2. If so, what should be the inventory policy at that stage?

We thus have the problem of inventory location and control. The few mathematical models which have been developed in this area handle these two aspects simultaneously.

Bryan, Wadsworth, and Whitin (1955) consider the problem of stocking for a one-time demand when stocks can be kept at four different production stages. The demand is probabilistic, and the respective fractions of demand which can be referred to the earlier production stages without loss are given. Under these assumptions, the optimal stock levels at the four respective stages are determined analytically.

Simpson (1958) has constructed a probabilistic model which employs the base-stock system of reordering. This means that any order against any stage i $(i=1,\cdots,n)$ is either filled immediately or placed into a backorder file, and in either case a replacement order is immediately placed with the preceding stage. Thus, when one unit is withdrawn from the finished stage ($i=n$), a process of "explosion" throughout the system is released. Performance at each inventory i can be characterized by a "service time" S_i. This is the (minimally chosen) time within which an order placed against inventory i is *always* filled (the maximum possible demand per unit time is finite). It is required that delivery to the customer as well as the fulfillment of raw-material requisitions be immediate:

$$S_n = S_1 = 0 \tag{3.17}$$

All other S_i are decision variables and at the same time the equivalent of inventory policies. If T_i is the production lead time between stages $i-1$ and i (see Fig. 3.2), it is clear that S_i obeys the inequality

$$0 \le S_i \le T_i + S_{i-1} \tag{3.18}$$

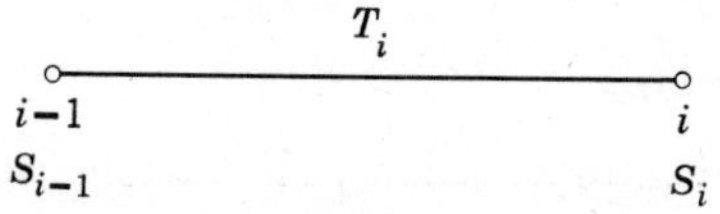

Fig. 3.2.

The right endpoint of this interval corresponds to an "empty inventory" at stage i (no orders are filled immediately), the left endpoint to a "full inventory" (all orders are filled immediately). The inventory cost at a given stage is assumed equal to a fixed cost plus an amount proportional to the average inventory level. Under these assumptions, it can be shown that the total relevant cost is of the form

$$C = \sum_i r_i \sqrt{S_{i-1} - S_i + T_i} \tag{3.19}$$

where the r_i are constants. The minimum of this function occurs at a cornerpoint of the space defined by Eq. 3.18 and, for a small number of stages, can be found readily by checking all cornerpoints.

In the model just discussed the level of performance to the customer had been fixed. In other instances, however, the value of delivery time to the customer may be the major consideration in the location of inventories. Hanssmann (1959) has proposed a model assuming that reordering can be done at constant checking intervals and that no setup cost is involved, whereas the expected number of units sold per unit time is a given function $s(t)$ of average delivery time t. This approach permits one to balance sales revenue against inventory carrying costs and to find the profit-maximizing set of inventory points in the system by a dynamic programming formulation of the interaction of stages.

Both the Simpson and Hanssmann models permit an arbitrary number of inventories generated by "branching," so that two important factors in inventory cost are recognized: (1) the rising intrinsic value of the products at more advanced stages, (2) the rising fluctuation (coefficient of variation) of inventories at more advanced stages.

2.4. Pipeline Inventory

So far, we have been entirely concerned with inventories at "stations" which we can represent as nodes of a network. (The channels of the network represent "operations.") A pipeline inventory can be defined as a resource on which an operation is being performed. In our network language, it is the amount of a resource which is in a channel at a given time. This resource is not idle in the strict sense since an operation is being performed on it but it is idle with respect to its end use or with respect to alternative uses of the capital tied up in it. For this reason, the pipeline inventory can be of great interest.

If the "traveling time" through a channel is t, and the average throughput rate of the channel is a, then the widely used expression

$$I(t) = at \tag{3.20}$$

is for the most part a satisfactory expression for the pipeline inventory. It follows that all techniques and methods aimed at changes of the traveling time have a pertinence to inventory theory via the pipeline inventory. Equipment policy, scheduling theory, and queuing theory can only be mentioned in this context. On the other hand, as long as the traveling time t is not under control but is fixed, pipeline inventory is of no consequence.

3. APPLICATIONS

3.1. Single-Station Problems

Static problems. A host of case studies on the installation of control systems for physical inventories testifies to the fact that the elementary notions of "scientific inventory control"—such as reorder points and economic ordering quantities—have found widespread application and acceptance in business and industry. The elementary static models for single inventory stations have helped to clarify the nature of the inventory problem and the conflicts inherent in it. From a practical viewpoint, it appears that the greatest contribution made by these inventory models has been to point out the need for specific information, without which these conflicts cannot be reconciled in a rational manner. Typically, the major portion of most case studies is devoted to a discussion of how setup costs, inventory carrying costs, shortage costs, demand patterns, and the like were established or could not be established, and what alternative steps were taken in the latter case. If all these data were given to begin with, it might not be difficult to arrive at a very nearly optimal solution even without the use of mathematical models. The role of the model becomes minor at the solution stage but it is major in the conceptualization of the problem.

It is not surprising, therefore, that inventory studies have often given rise to the first systematic forecasting activity in an organization or have led to considerable improvement in information processing and paper work, occasionally to the point of a major reorganization. Here lie major payoffs which, indirectly, are to the credit of inventory theory. An example of this kind is a study done for the Cummins Engine Company which involved installation of reorder points and reorder quantities for parts with price breaks but ultimately produced an integrated process-control system with substantially reduced production lead time because of improved parts availability and acceleration of paper work, in addition to significant out-of-pocket savings (Arnoff, Kania, and Small Day, 1958). Some companies have been able to reduce their inventories by as much as 50 per cent and simultaneously give improved delivery to the customer. It is clear that such results rest essentially on better information about customer demand.

A constantly recurring problem in all applications is that of reliability of information. Great difficulty, both conceptual and practical, is usually encountered in finding the cost parameters of inventory models. If a numerical estimate can be attained at all, one can ask the question: How much error would be required to make the "optimal" policy derived from the model worse than the present performance? If this error is quite large, one will be less reluctant to implement the "optimal" policy.

These difficulties have led some researchers to offer the opinion that ordering costs, inventory costs, and shortage costs are not "real" costs at all, but only a reflection of management policy in the allocation of resources (here the relevant resources are inventory investment and the capacity of the ordering mechanism). Feeney (1955) in an interesting case study parametrizes these "unreal" costs, derives optimal decision rules for each set of parameter values, and studies their consequences on resource allocation. Management is then presented with a tabulation of alternative allocations from which to choose. All these alternative allocations are the most "efficient" ones possible because of the use of optimal decision rules. Feeney's case study seems of sufficient interest to be considered in somewhat more detail.

A major railroad keeps inventories of spare parts and other items for internal consumption. Inventory control involves more than 20,000 end items. Optimal ordering rules were to be designed. It is almost impossible to establish demand characteristics, let alone cost parameters, for this many items. Hence the following assumptions of sweeping generality were made:

1. For all items, there is the same
   a. Ordering cost, s.
   b. Cost per shortage delay, d.
   c. Annual cost per dollar of inventory investment, h.
2. For each item, the demand per unit time (one year) is normally distributed with a mean r and a standard deviation σ characteristic for the item.

The problem of establishing optimal inventory control for an item is equivalent to finding the reorder point P and reorder quantity q which minimize expected annual cost of ordering, shortage delays, and inventory investment. If c is the value per piece (at cost) for the item under consideration, this annual cost is approximately given by

$$C=\frac{r}{q}s+hc\left(\frac{q}{2}+P-rL\right)$$

$$+\frac{dr}{q}\int_P^{\infty}(x-P)\frac{1}{\sqrt{I}\,\sigma\sqrt{2\pi}}\exp\left\{-\frac{(x-rL)^2}{2L\sigma^2}\right\}dx \tag{3.21}$$

The optimal decision rules can be derived from this equation and will take the form

$$\begin{aligned}\hat{P}&=\hat{P}(r,\sigma,c\,|\,s,h,d)\\ \hat{q}&=\hat{q}(r,\sigma,c\,|\,s,h,d)\end{aligned} \tag{3.22}$$

Given these decision rules, it is then possible to compute the following quantities for the item under consideration:

N = number of orders per year
I = average inventory investment
M = number of shortage delays per year

Of course, these quantities are reliable only as long as the model assumptions—in particular the normality of demand—are valid. These assumptions were, however, introduced mainly for convenience in deriving simple decision rules. It was felt that they could not be relied upon for analytical derivation of N, I, and M. For this reason, it was decided to derive these quantities by applying the decision rules (Eqs. 3.22) on paper, using actual demand data in retrospect. The demand parameters r and σ which represent an input to the decision rules were forecast by assuming that the next six months would be like the last six months. This simulation was carried out on a computer for a sample of 400 items and a period of two years. The computer was also used to evaluate the critical numbers (summing over all items):

$$\begin{aligned} n &= \Sigma N && \text{(total number of orders per year)} \\ J &= \Sigma I && \text{(average inventory investment in the system)} \\ R &= \frac{\Sigma M}{\Sigma r} && \text{(percentage of shortage delays or "system reliability")} \end{aligned} \tag{3.23}$$

This whole procedure was repeated for alternative sets of values for (s,h,d). Since the decision rules depend only on the values of the two ratios

$$\frac{h}{s}, \quad \frac{d}{s} \tag{3.24}$$

it is sufficient to consider pairs of ratios. In this way, the "cost-ratio plane" was mapped into the (n,J,R)-surface (see Fig. 3.3). The graph of this "efficient surface" was then presented to management and after a short discussion led to the selection of a point (n,J,R) which represented the desired compromise between the conflicting objectives inherent in the situation. The corresponding decision rules were implemented and, after a transition period with peak inventories, led to a steady state with a 20 per cent inventory reduction and no significant change in either reliability or number of orders processed.

The period of transition from an existing to a new control system poses a considerable problem in most applications. For example, if

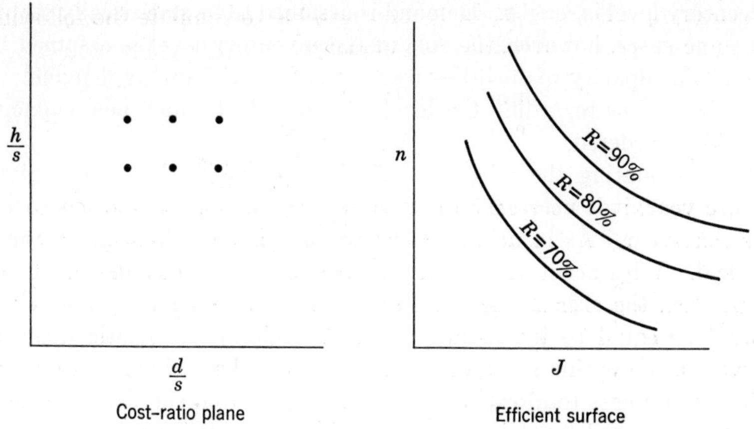

Fig. 3.3.

greater lot sizes are recommended, new storage facilities may be required, and care must be taken that the occurrence of shortages is not drastically increased in the transition period. In one case, the installation of economic lot sizes in the production of parts had to be gradually planned over a period of two years. Even when an inventory reduction is ultimately expected under a new system, the transition period may lead to peak inventories since all items with too low inventory levels under the new system are immediately ordered but no compensating effect is present for those items with too high levels under the new system. Sometimes it is necessary to change the system only for a few items at a time.

Probabilistic models with empirically established probability distributions of demand have been used almost exclusively in static situations, for example, for stocking spare parts with stable usage patterns. Because of their simplicity, static models have also been applied to situations with slowly changing demand patterns requiring forecasts. In such cases, the convenient assumption of a normal distribution of forecasting error seems inevitable although it is rarely established empirically and is often far from the truth. Nevertheless, decision rules based on such assumptions often yield good results.

The elementary concepts of inventory control have also been applied to a number of problems whose interpretation as inventory problems is not immediately apparent. This is true of the reorder-point concept in particular. Normally, a reorder point for a decreasing inventory level is sought. Demand is assumed to be statistically stable. In some cases, however, the role of the inventory level is assumed by the slack capacity of facilities used to satisfy a changing demand. A question arises regarding the level of demand at which new capacity should be ordered.

In evaluating the adequacy of airport parking lots for a given future year, it is necessary to forecast the demand for parking spaces for that year. As in all inventory problems, the forecasting error is critical. With accurate knowledge of demand, the optimal inventory level (i.e., the size of the parking lot) would be trivially known: it would be equal to the known demand. With probabilistic demand, however, the optimal size of the lot can only be defined as that size which minimizes total expected cost of overage and shortage of spaces for the year under consideration. If this optimal size falls below the actual size, the lot is still adequate.

The cost of shortage in this application was taken to consist of lost parking-lot revenues, airport revenues, and administrative cost of responding to bad will created among displaced parking-lot patrons. The cost of overage is the cost of building and operating an excess space. These costs could be determined. The forecast of demand for parking spaces was based on forecasts of air traffic and related traffic magnitudes and patterns (Hurst, 1955).

A similar study was conducted for an electric utility company. Here the question was: When should additional generating capacity be added to the existing system? In this case, no cost of shortage associated with inability to satisfy customer demand for power could be established. Rather, it was determined at what point of time the *probability* of shortage would rise above a certain specified level. This could be done by using historical data on generator outages and a forecast of demand for power. In order to give management all the pertinent information, the forecasting error of demand as well as several other variables of interest were parametrized (Arnoff and Chambers, 1956).

This approach has also been used for timing the acquisition of new electronic computing capacity (Operations Research Group, 1957).

Dynamic problems. The classical dynamic problem is the "production-smoothing problem" as it arises when demand is seasonal. The likewise classical quadratic programming approach to this problem by Holt, Simon, and Modigliani (1955) was applied to an actual case dealing with a paint factory whose product was demanded in a highly seasonal pattern. As a consequence, the company had a major problem of backorders on one hand, high inventories on the other hand, and at the same time considerable overtime and hiring and layoff costs were incurred. The extremely simple linear decision rule of quadratic programming requires as input—once all cost parameters are determined—the unbiased forecasts of demands for the next twelve months. It then quickly yields the optimal production quantity and work-force level for the next month. When tested in retrospect, this decision rule yielded an 8 per cent reduction of total annual costs of regular payroll, overtime, hiring, layoffs, inventory, and shortages. At the same time, the amount of backorders was considerably reduced. The test was made for various forecasting methods and yielded the interesting result that even with a relatively crude forecast substantial cost reduction could be achieved, and that the additional gain from a perfect forecast was not too great. Thus, the decision rule itself was of more importance than the quality of the forecast.

Similar studies of the smoothing problem have been made in various industries, some of them employing linear-programming methods. Charnes, Cooper, and Symonds (1958) have applied linear-programming methods to smoothing the production of heating oil in refineries where the relevant costs are production, transportation, and inventory costs and can be written as a convex function of production rates. Demand was weather-dependent and, therefore, stochastic. A fixed-horizon approach with a linear decision rule was employed.

Fluctuating raw material prices pose the problem of balancing purchasing costs and inventory costs. This problem arises in the purchasing of raw materials and was studied in that context by Fabian et al. (1959). It turned out that prices and requirements could be forecast reasonably well three to four months ahead of time. (The essential factors in the price-forecasting formulas were current and recent operating rates and the amount of prebooked capacity.) Using this period as a planning horizon, a purchasing decision rule was designed to minimize projected purchasing and inventory costs for the horizon. When tested in retrospect, the decision rule yielded a cost reduction of several million dollars.

A hydroelectric operation is faced with a seasonal supply of water. In the case of a shortage of water, electricity can be supplied by more costly means, say, from a steam generating plant. The outflow of water from the "water inventory" should be controlled so that the annual cost of satisfying the demand for electric energy is minimized. Several researchers have applied dynamic-programming techniques to this problem. John D. C. Little (1955) has found a potential annual cost reduction of 75,000 dollars for the Grand Coulee Dam.

In military logistics, the following problem arises. A fleet of airplanes is required to fulfill a specified flight program. The desired operational levels of the fleet are given as a function of time for a certain planning horizon. There is a slow and a fast repair service for engines. The two services differ in cost. What initial supply of spare engines and what repair policy will minimize the cost of the flight program? This problem gave rise to the mathematical formulation of the "caterer problem" by Jacobs (mentioned in Prager, 1956).

3.2. Problems of Parallel Stations

Problems of parallel stations often arise when several alternative inventory locations with differing characteristics are present on the same level of a distribution system. As a first example, consider a set of warehouses with differing storage-cost characteristics. A study pertaining to this situation was conducted by Eagle (1957) for the Hawaiian Pineapple Company, which is faced with the problem of allocating its highly seasonal production of canned pineapple to a number of warehouses scattered over the continental United States. Company policy precludes transshipments from warehouse to warehouse and carry-over of inventories from one season to the next. Warehouses differ in storage costs per case of goods per month as well as in the specific dates on which inventories at warehouses are taxed. If on a given date a certain quantity of canned goods is ready for shipment to the continent, allocation to warehouses is to be made such that total storage costs and taxes attributable to this quantity are minimized. Since the total future storage costs attributable to a certain quantity in a warehouse are proportional to the square of the quantity, it follows that the marginal storage cost at the warehouse is a linear function of the stock level. Figure 3.4 shows this relationship. Since the stock level is measured in months' supply, the jumps of marginal cost due to taxation on given dates can be incorporated into the figure as long as it is kept in mind that the figure refers to a given date. With curves of this kind available for all warehouses, one can find the optimal allocation of the total available quantity by making marginal costs equal at all warehouses. Simulated application in retrospect of this method demonstrated a potential for substantial savings. The company adopted the method and put a company officer in charge of its implementation.

The "newsboy problem" with limited resources has found numerous applications. In a competitive bidding situation where a specified amount of money is available for submitting closed bids on n objects,

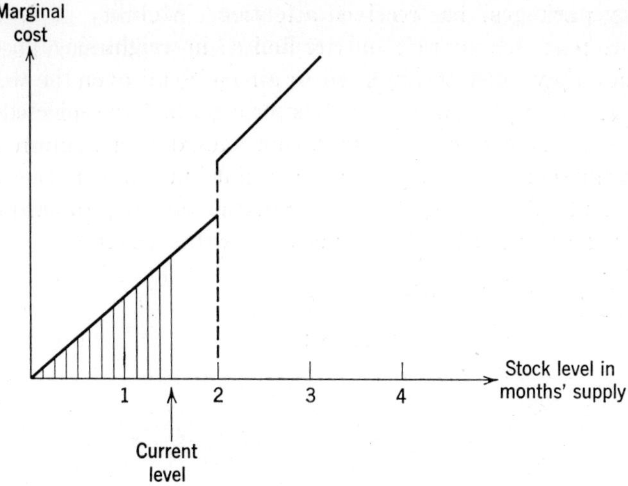

Fig. 3.4. Marginal costs at given warehouse on given date (next taxation in two months).

the submitted bids assume the role of stock levels, whereas demand is represented by the highest bid of the competition. Obviously, this demand is probabilistic and depends on the value of the object. If "demand" is higher than the "stock level" a rather serious cost of shortage is incurred: the object is lost. If the bid is successful, a cost of overage is incurred which is a function of the excess of the winning bid over the second highest bid. Competitive-bidding models in industrial applications have usually been set up in terms of total profit maximization. They then pose the problem of maximizing a function

$$F(x_1,\cdots,x_n)=\sum_1^n f_i(x_i) \tag{3.25}$$

subject to

$$\sum_1^n x_i=c \tag{3.26}$$

where x_i is the bid on object i and c is the total available amount of money. For convex return functions, simple numerical methods for solution have been developed, based on equalization of marginal gains. The "objects" could be contracts, property rights, etc. (Friedman, 1956; Hanssmann and Rivett, 1959).

In the area of military aircraft maintenance the problem of optimal "mobility packages" has received attention. Mobility packages contain spare parts for aircraft and are limited in weight since in cases of emergency they must be air-lifted to air bases all over the world. It is obviously important that the parts for a package be selected so that the expected total number of part shortages during a given maintenance period is minimized within the weight limitation of the package.

The solution of this problem presupposes knowledge of the probability distributions of demand for all eligible parts. Given these, it is then possible to tabulate the "usage probabilities" as in Table 3.1.

TABLE 3.1

USAGE PROBABILITIES FOR PART i

Number of Parts in Package (j)	Probability That All j Parts Are Used (p_{ij})
0	1
1	p_{i1}
2	p_{i2}
.	.
.	.
.	.

If w_i is the weight of the ith type of part, then the quantity

$$u_{ij}=\frac{p_{ij}}{w_i} \tag{3.27}$$

plays the role of a "marginal utility" due to the addition of the jth part of the ith type. These marginal utilities can be listed in decreasing order. In order to find the best parts selection for a given package weight, one need only to keep a running total of parts weights corresponding to the decreasing sequence of the u_{ij}. At the prescribed weight, the sequence is cut off, and all parts corresponding to the u_{ij} above the cutoff point are included in the package. Packages constructed in this way did better than the existing packages when tested in a simulation of emergency situations (Karr and Geisler, 1956).

Dantzig and Ferguson (1956) have applied linear-programming techniques to the problem of allocating aircraft to flying routes. The various types of aircraft in the available fleet are restricted in their usability on routes and differ in cost characteristics. The cost of shortage of airplanes on a route is the loss of potential revenue; the cost of overage is the cost of idle capacity. In this application, the demand for the airline's services is established in the form of discrete probability distributions which are incorporated into the linear-programming model.

3.3. Problems of Series of Stations

An interesting two-level inventory allocation problem poses itself in the scheduling of a trucking fleet which operates mostly between a central terminal and a number of outlying terminals (see Fig. 3.5). At the beginning of each scheduling period trucks at the central terminal must be dispatched to the outlying terminals, and at the same time empty trucks not presently needed at the outlying terminals may be ordered back to the central terminal. These decisions affect the match between demand for service and supply of service

a. At the central terminal now.
b. At the outlying terminals one period hence.
c. At the central terminal one period hence.

Imperfect match of supply and demand on a route means either a cost of delay of shipments (cost of shortage) or a cost of running empty vehicles (cost of overage)—a typical inventory situation. The problem has dynamic features in that demand changes significantly over time and in that each decision sets initial conditions for future decisions. In this study, a planning horizon of two periods was employed since no meaningful forecast could be obtained for periods farther in the future (Minas and Mitten, 1958).

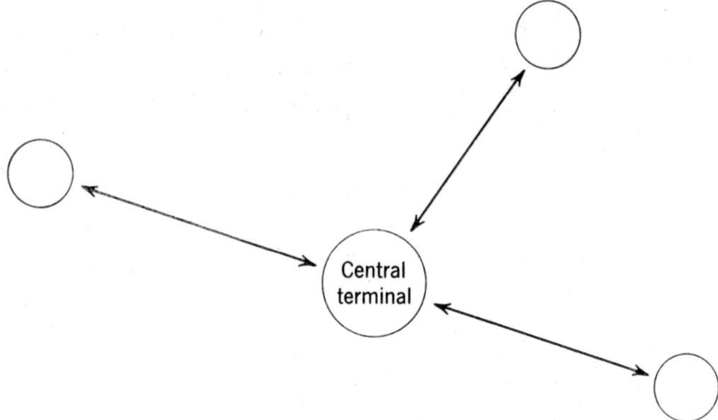

Fig. 3.5.

In this particular application, the role of the inventory level was assumed by the transportation *facilities*. In other applications, *demand* for transport services turns out to play a typical inventory role: so in railroading. Since there is a fixed cost associated with running a train, it is clear that demand must be accumulated for some time in order to warrant an economical train. On the other hand, high inventories of unfilled orders are costly since they "obsolete" in an obvious way. Thus, the problem of finding optimal train lengths in a complicated railway network can be viewed as a multistage economic-lot-size problem. Naturally, the intangible "inventory holding cost" must be parametrized in terms of the delay characteristics of shipments.

Simpson (1958) has conducted a multilevel inventory study for a manufacturing company which considered moving some of its inventories from an advanced stage in the production process to an earlier stage. The idea was to save by a reduction in inventory value and a gain in flexibility. At the same time, delivery performance to the customer was to be kept at the same level. The company used a base-stock system under which each unit withdrawn from any inventory was immediately reordered from the next-earlier inventory in the production process. In order to examine all possible inventory locations (say n), a model was set up which gave the total inventory cost as a function

$$f(I_1,\cdots,I_n) \tag{3.28}$$

of the inventory levels maintained at the n locations. The restriction on delivery performance was built into the model. $I_i=0$ means that no inventory is maintained at location i. The minimum-cost solution of this model yielded the best set of "inventory points" in the process, and the inventory levels to be maintained at these points. The study proved that the decision which had originally been made by management would not have yielded a cost reduction but, to the contrary, would have increased cost.

3.4. Pipeline-Inventory Problems

An airline intends to carry a monthly passenger volume V in each direction between two geographical locations which are d miles apart. One airplane of a given type will on the average carry l passengers. Obviously, the throughput rate of airplanes at either endpoint is V/l, and the traveling time of an airplane between the two endpoints is d/c, where d is the distance and c is its velocity. By Eq. 3.20, the required pipeline inventory of airplanes for both directions is

$$I=2\frac{V}{l}\cdot\frac{d}{c} \tag{3.29}$$

This formula may be used to determine the total investment required for different types of airplanes, which is an important factor in deciding on a given type. The formula shows the importance of speed for the pipeline inventory. In railroad systems, the speed with which freight cars travel between given points depends among other things on the number and location of classification yards. Mansfield and Wein (1958) considered the problem of locating an additional yard in a given system. By analogy with Eq. 3.29, the number of freight cars required to run the system is sensitive to the location of the new yard. Thus, the daily pipeline-inventory cost is an important component of the cost equation. Of course, there are many other considerations; for full detail of the cost equation we refer the interested reader to the article mentioned.

In principle, all queuing problems may be looked at as pipeline-inventory problems: if we consolidate service and waiting into one "operation," the total queue (number of units in the system) represents a pipeline inventory. It is certainly beyond the scope of this chapter to discuss applications of queuing theory. However, we wish to mention a few in which the role of the queue as an inventory is more obvious. In a job-shop operation, the material which has entered the production process forms a typical pipeline inventory. The fluctuations of this inventory can be kept under control by using overtime as soon as the inventory level reaches a certain control limit. The use of overtime reduces the average traveling time through the shop without affecting its average throughput. Thus, pipeline inventory is reduced. The corresponding savings in capital must be weighed against the cost of overtime. Of course, the traveling time itself is also an important consideration. Similarly, the dollar value of pipeline inventory may be reduced by using priority schemes which give preference to the high-value orders.

4. CONCLUSION

Inventory theory has developed its own body of mathematics. From the operations research viewpoint, the theory has been carried to a degree of mathematical sophistication in some areas which is not fruitful in light of the crudeness of data, and, perhaps more important, in light of the fact that the inventory problem is only *one* aspect of a complex system. From a realistic point of view, it seems more desirable for the theory to move in the direction of including other aspects of systems rather than to become oversophisticated in one area and to ignore others.

One of the most ignored aspects of inventory studies is the cost of using a theoretically derived procedure. This implementation cost may be more significant than all the inventory-connected costs which appear in a sophisticated model. The practitioner has solved this difficulty in his own way by restricting himself to models which give a reasonable fit to a real situation of interest and, at the same time, yield simple, operational decision rules and evaluations of alternative policies. It is these parts of the theory which have found their way to applications.

The theory has not yet thoroughly explored the effect of deviations from optimal policies. This area may hold some surprises. It is quite conceivable that in many cases it is not worth searching for an optimum.

As long as operations research remains true to itself by seeking results of practical, operational value, it will be mainly interested in the goodness of fit of models to real situations, simplicity and ease of solution, sensitivity of solutions to data, and an organic rather than isolated treatment of the inventory problem within the whole system. It follows that operations research will continue to be very selective in its use of what has been termed "inventory theory."

BIBLIOGRAPHY

Most titles in this bibliography were selected from *Operations Research, Management Science,* and *Naval Logistics Quarterly* up to and including the month of *April, 1959*. Some other articles and books published before that date are also included.

To assist in the use of the bibliography a classification of references corresponding to the organization of this chapter is appended. In this classification the articles are grouped by major subject areas, and are in alphabetical order within each area.

Ackoff, R. L., "Production and Inventory Control in a Chemical Process," *Opns. Res.,* **3,** 319–338 (1955).

Allen, S. G., "Redistribution of Total Stock Over Several User Locations," *Nav. Res. Log. Quart.,* **5,** 337–346 (1958).

Antosiewiez, H., and Hoffman, A. J., "A Remark on the Smoothing Problem," *Mgmt. Sci.,* **1,** 92–95 (1954).

Arnoff, E. L., and Chambers, J. C., "On the Determination of Optimum Reserve

Generating Capacity in an Electric Utility System," *Opns. Res.*, **4**, 468–479 (1956).

Arnoff, E. L., Kania, E. B., and Small Day, E., "An Integrated Process Control System at the Cummins Engine Company," *Opns. Res.*, **6**, 467–497 (1958).

Arrow, K. J., Harris, T., and Marschak, J., "Optimal Inventory Policy," *Econometrica*, **19**, 250–272 (1951).

Arrow, K. J., Karlin, S., and Scarf, H., *Studies in the Mathematical Theory of Inventory and Production*, Stanford University Press, Stanford, California, 1958.

Baumol, W. J., and Wolfe, P., "A Warehouse Location Problem," *Opns. Res.*, **6**, 252–263 (1958).

Beckman, M. J., "An Inventory Model for Repair Parts—Approximation in the Case of Variable Delivery Time," *Opns. Res.*, **7**, 256–258 (1959).

———, and Bobkoski, F., "Airline Demand: An Analysis of Some Frequency Distributions," *Nav. Res. Log. Quart.*, **5**, 43–52 (1958).

Beckman, M. J., and Muth, R., "An Inventory Policy for a Case of Lagged Delivery," *Mgmt. Sci.*, **2**, 145 (1956).

Bellman, R., "On the Theory of Dynamic Programming—A Warehousing Problem," *Mgmt. Sci.*, **2**, 272–275 (1956).

———, "Dynamic Programming and the Smoothing Problem," *Mgmt. Sci.*, **3**, 111–113 (1956).

———, "On a Dynamic Programming Approach to the Caterer Problem—I," *Mgmt. Sci.*, **3**, 270–278 (1957).

———, *Dynamic Programming*, Princeton University Press, Princeton, N. J., 1957.

———, Glicksberg, I., and Gross, O., "On the Optimal Inventory Equation," *Mgmt. Sci.*, **2**, 83–104 (1955).

Bishop, G. T., "On a Problem of Production Scheduling," *Opns. Res.*, **5**, 97–102 (1957).

Bonini, C. P., "Decision Rules for Buffer Inventories," *Mgmt. Sci.*, **4**, 457–471 (1958).

Bowman, E. H., "Production Scheduling by the Transportation Method of Linear Programming," *Opns. Res.*, **4**, 100–103 (1956).

———, "Scale of Operations—An Empirical Study," *Opns. Res.*, **6**, 320–328 (1958).

———, and Fetter, R. B., *Analysis for Production Management*, Richard D. Irwin, Inc., Homewood, Illinois, 1957.

Bryan, J. G., Wadsworth, G. P., and Whitin, T. M., "A Multi-Stage Inventory Model," *Nav. Res. Log. Quart.*, **2**, 25–38 (1955).

Case Institute of Technology, *Proceedings of the Conference on Operations Research in Production and Inventory Control* (Jan. 1954).

Chambers, J. C., Bond, A. F., and Leake, J. H., "Optimum Lot Sizes for Parts Used in Aircraft Production," *Opns. Res.*, **6**, 385–398 (1958).

Charnes, A., Cooper, W. W., and Mellon, B., "A Model for Optimizing Production by Reference to Cost Surrogates," *Econometrica*, **23**, 307–323 (1955).

Charnes, A., Cooper, W. W., and Symonds, G. H., "Cost Horizons and Certainty Equivalents: An Approach to Stochastic Programming of Heating Oil," *Mgmt. Sci.*, **4**, 235–263 (1958).

Churchman, C. W., Ackoff, R. L., and Arnoff, E. L., *Introduction to Operations Research*, John Wiley and Sons, New York, 1957.

Clark, C. E., "Mathematical Analysis of an Inventory Case," *Opns. Res.*, **5**, 627–643 (1957).

Dannerstedt, G., "Production Scheduling for an Arbitrary Number of Periods Given the Sales Forecast in the Form of a Probability Distribution," *Opns. Res.,* **3,** 300–318 (1955).

Danskin, J. M., "Mathematical Treatment of a Stockpiling Problem," *Nav. Res. Log. Quart.,* **2,** 99–110 (1955).

Dantzig, G. B., "Linear Programming under Uncertainty," *Mgmt. Sci.,* **1,** 197–206 (1955).

———, and Ferguson, A. R., "The Allocation of Aircraft Routes—An Example of Linear Programming under Uncertain Demand," *Mgmt. Sci.,* **3,** 45–73 (1956).

Derman, C., and Klein, M., "Inventory Depletion Management," *Mgmt. Sci.,* **4,** 450–456 (1958).

———, "A Note on the Optimal Depletion of Inventory," *Mgmt. Sci.,* **5,** 210–213 (1959).

Dillon, J. D., "Geographical Distribution of Production in Multiple Plant Operations," *Mgmt. Sci.,* **2,** 353–365 (1956).

Dreyfus, S. E., "An Analytic Solution of the Warehouse Problem," *Mgmt. Sci.,* **4,** 353–365 (1956).

Dvoretzky, A., Kiefer, J., and Wolfowitz, J., "The Inventory Problem," *Econometrica,* **20,** 187–222 (1952) and **20,** 450–466 (1952).

———, "On the Optimal Character of the (s_1S)-Policy in Inventory Theory," *Econometrica,* **21,** 586–596 (1953).

Eagle, A. R., "Distribution of Seasonal Inventory of the Hawaiian Pineapple Company," *Opns. Res.,* **5,** 382–396 (1957).

Eastman, W. L., "A Note on the Multi-Commodity Warehouse Problem," *Mgmt. Sci.,* **5,** 327–331 (1959).

Fabian, T., Fisher, J. L., Sasieni, M. W., and Yardeni, A., "Purchasing Raw Material on a Fluctuating Market," *Opns. Res.,* **7,** 107–122 (1959).

Feeney, G. J., "A Basis for Strategic Decisions on Inventory Control Operations," *Mgmt. Sci.,* **2,** 69–82 (1955).

Freeman, R. J., "*Ss* Inventory Policy with Variable Delivery Time," *Mgmt. Sci.,* **3,** 431–434 (1957).

Friedman, L., "A Competitive Bidding Strategy," *Opns. Res.,* **4,** 104–112 (1956).

Gaddum, J. W., Hoffman, A. J., and Sokolowsky, D., "On the Solution of the Caterer Problem," *Nav. Res. Log. Quart.,* **1,** 223–229 (1954).

Geisler, M. A., and Karr, H. W., "The Design of Military Supply Tables for Spare Parts," *Opns. Res.,* **4,** 431–442 (1956).

Gessford, J., "Scheduling the Use of Water Power," *Mgmt. Sci.,* **5,** 179–191 (1959).

Gourary, M. H., "A Simple Rule for the Consolidation of Allowance Lists," *Nav. Res. Log. Quart.,* **5,** 1–16 (1958).

———, Lewis, R., and Neeland, F., "An Inventory Control Bibliography," *Nav. Res. Log. Quart.,* **3,** 295–304 (1956).

Hanssmann, F., "Optimal Inventory Location and Control in Production and Distribution Networks," *Opns. Res.,* **7,** 483–498 (1959).

———, "Determination of Optimal Capacities of Service for Facilities with a Linear Measure of Inefficiency," *Opns. Res.,* **5,** 713–717 (1957).

———, and Rivett, B. H. P., "Competitive Bidding," *Opns. Res. Quart.,* **10,** 49–55 (1959).

Heyvaert, A. C., and Hurt, A., "Inventory Management of Slow Moving Parts," *Opns. Res.,* **4,** 572–580 (1956).

Hoffman, A. J., and Jacobs, W., "Smooth Patterns of Production," *Mgmt. Sci.,* **1,** 86–91 (1954).

Holt, C. C., Modigliani, F., and Muth, J. F., "Derivation of a Linear Decision Rule for Production and Employment Scheduling," *Mgmt. Sci.,* **2,** 159–177 (1956).

Holt, C. C., Modigliani, F., and Simon, H. A., "Linear Decision Rule for Production and Employment Scheduling," *Mgmt. Sci.,* **2,** 1–30 (1955).

Holt, C. C., and Simon, H. A., "Optimal Decision Rules for Production and Inventory Control," *Proceedings of the Conference on Operations Research in Production and Inventory Control,* Case Institute of Technology, Cleveland, Ohio, Jan. 20–22, 1954, p. 73.

Hu, T. C., Prager, W., "Network Analysis of Production Smoothing," *Nav. Res. Log. Quart.,* **6,** 17–24 (1959).

Hurst, F. V., Jr., "Evaluating the Adequacy of Airport Parking Lots," *Opns. Res.,* **3,** 522–535 (1955).

Isaac, E. J., "Note on Selection of Capital Equipment with Uncertain Delivery Date," *Opns. Res.,* **4,** 354–356 (1956).

Johnson, S. M., "Sequential Production Planning over Time at Minimum Cost," *Mgmt. Sci.,* **3,** 435–437 (1957).

Karr, H. W., "A Method of Estimating Spare Parts Essentiality," *Nav. Res. Log. Quart.,* **5,** 29–42 (1958).

———, and Geisler, M. A., "A Fruitful Application of Static Marginal Analysis," *Mgmt. Sci.,* **2,** 313–326 (1956).

Karush, W., "On a Class of Minimum Cost Problems," *Mgmt. Sci.,* **4,** 136–153 (1958).

———, "A Queuing Model for an Inventory Problem," *Opns. Res.,* **5,** 693–703 (1957).

———, and Vazsonyi, A., "Mathematical Programming and Service Scheduling," *Mgmt. Sci.,* **3,** 140–148 (1957).

———, "Mathematical Programming and Employment Scheduling," *Nav. Res. Log. Quart.,* **4,** 297–320 (1957).

Klein, M., "Some Production Planning Problems," *Nav. Res. Log. Quart.,* **4,** 269–286 (1957).

Koopmans, T. C., "Water Storage Policy in a Simplified Hydroelectric System," in *Proceedings of the International Conference on Operational Research,* John Wright and Sons, Bristol, England, 1958.

Levary, G., "A Pocket-Sized Case Study in Operations Research Concerning Inventory Markdown," *Opns. Res.,* **4,** 738–739 (1956).

Levinson, H. C., "Experiences in Commercial Operations Research," *Opns. Res.,* **1,** 220–239 (1953).

Levy, J., "Loss Resulting from the Use of Incorrect Data in Computing an Optimal Inventory Policy," *Nav. Res. Log. Quart.,* **5,** 75–82 (1958).

———, "Further Notes on the Loss Resulting from the Use of Incorrect Data in Computing an Optimal Inventory Policy," *Nav. Res. Log. Quart.,* **6,** 25–32 (1959).

Lieberman, G. J., "Lifo Versus Fifo in Inventory Depletion Management," *Mgmt. Sci.,* **5,** 102–105 (1958).

Little, J. D. C., "The Use of Storage Water in a Hydroelectric System," *Opns. Res.,* **3,** 187–197 (1955).

Magee, J. F., *Production Planning and Inventory Control,* McGraw-Hill, New York, 1958.

Manne, A. S., "A Note on the Modigliani—Hohn Production Smoothing Model," *Mgmt. Sci.,* **3,** 371–379 (1957).

———, "Programming of Economic Lot Sizes," *Mgmt. Sci.,* **4,** 115–135 (1958).

Mansfield, E., and Wein, H. H., "A Model for the Location of a Railroad Classification Yard," *Mgmt. Sci.,* **4,** 292–313 (1958).

Marshall, B. O., Jr., and Boggess, W. P., II, "The Practical Calculation of Reorder Points," *Opns. Res.,* **5,** 513–517 (1957).

Mills, E. S., "A Note on the Asymptotic Behavior of an Optimal Procurement Policy," *Mgmt. Sci.,* **5,** 204–209 (1959).

Minas, J. S., and Mitten, L. G., "The Hub Operation Scheduling Problem," *Opns. Res.,* **6,** 329–345 (1958).

Modigliani, F., and Hohn, F. E., "Production Planning over Time and the Nature of the Expectation and Planning Horizon," *Econometrica,* **23,** 46–66 (1955).

———, and Muth, J. F., *Optimum Lot Size under Uncertainty and Joint Costs,* O.N.R. Res. Memo. No. 21, Grad. School of Industr. Adm., Carnegie Inst. of Tech., July 1954.

Moran, P. A. P., "A Probability Theory of a Dam with a Continuous Release," *Quart. J. of Math.,* **7,** 130–137 (1956).

Morse, P. M., "Solutions of a Class of Discrete-Time Inventory Problems," *Opns. Res.,* **7,** 67–78 (1959).

———, *Queues, Inventories and Maintenance,* John Wiley and Sons, New York, 1958.

Naddor, E., "Some Models of Inventory and an Application," *Mgmt. Sci.,* **2,** 299–312 (1956).

———, and Saltzman, S., "Optimal Reorder Periods for an Inventory System with Variable Costs of Ordering," *Opns. Res.,* **6,** 676–685 (1958).

Page, E. S., and Muris, S., "The Effect of Departures from Assumption When Manufacturing to a Specification," *Opns. Res.,* **5,** 68–74 (1957).

Petersen, J. W., and Geisler, M. A., "The Costs of Alternative Air Base Stocking and Requisitioning Policies," *Nav. Res. Log. Quart.,* **2,** 69–82 (1955).

Petersen, J. W., and Steger, W. A., "Design Change Impacts on Airframe Parts Inventories," *Nav. Res. Log. Quart.,* **5,** 241–256 (1958).

Pinkham, R., "An Approach to Linear Inventory—Production Rules," *Opns. Res.,* **6,** 185–189 (1958).

Prager, W., "On the Caterer Problem," *Mgmt. Sci.,* **3,** 15–23 (1956).

Rogers, J., "A Computational Approach to the Economic Lot Scheduling Problem," *Mgmt. Sci.,* **4,** 264–291 (1958).

Salveson, M. E., "A Problem in Optimal Machine Loading," *Mgmt. Sci.,* **2,** 232–260 (1956).

Schild, A., "On Inventory, Production and Employment Scheduling," *Mgmt. Sci.,* **5,** 157–168 (1959).

Schneider, E., "Absatz, Produktion und Lagerhaltung bei einfacher Produktion," *Archiv fuer mathematische Wirtschofts und sozial Forschung,* Band IV, Heft 1, Leipzig, 1938.

Schupack, M. B., "Economic Lot Sizes with Seasonal Demand," *Opns. Res.,* **7,** 45–57 (1959).

Simon, H. A., "On the Application of Servomechanism Theory in the Study of Production Control," *Econometrica,* **20,** 247–268 (1952).

———, and Holt, C. C., "The Control of Inventory and Production Rates—A Survey," *Opns. Res.,* **2,** 289–301 (1954).

Simpson, J. R., "A Formula for Decisions on Retention or Disposal of Excess Stock," *Nav. Res. Log. Quart.,* **2,** 145–156 (1955).

Simpson, K. F., Jr., "In-Process Inventories," *Opns. Res.,* **6,** 863–873 (1958).

Solomon, M. J., "A Scientific Method for Establishing Reorder Points," *Nav. Res. Log. Quart.,* **1,** 289–294 (1954).

———, "Optimum Operation of a Complex Activity under Conditions of Uncertainty," *Opns. Res.,* **2,** 419–432 (1954).

Sutherland, W. H., "Graphical Selection of Military Supply Tables," *Opns. Res.,* **6,** 775–777 (1958).

Vassian, H. J., "Application of Discrete Variable Servo Theory to Inventory Control," *Opns. Res.,* **3,** 272–282 (1955).

Vazsonyi, A., "Economic Lot Size Formulas in Manufacturing," *Opus. Res.,* **5,** 28–44 (1957).

Wagner, H. M., and Whitin, T. M., "Dynamic Problems in the Theory of the Firm," *Nav. Res. Log. Quart.,* **5,** 53–74 (1958).

———, "Dynamic Version of the Economic Lot Size Model," *Mgmt. Sci.,* **5,** 89–96 (1958).

Whitin, T. M., *The Theory of Inventory Management,* Princeton University Press, Princeton, N. J., 1953.

———, "Erich Schneider's Inventory Control Analysis," *Opns. Res.,* **2,** 329–334 (1954).

———, "Inventory Control Research: A Survey," *Mgmt. Sci.,* **1,** 32–40 (1954).

———, "Inventory Control and Price Theory," *Mgmt. Sci.,* **2,** 61–68 (1955).

———, and Youngs, J. W. T., "A Method for Calculating Optimal Inventory Levels and Delivery Time," *Nav. Res. Log. Quart.,* **2,** 157–174 (1955).

Classified Bibliography

Books and general articles

Arrow, Karlin, and Scarf (1958)
Bellman (1957)
Bowman and Fetter (1957)
Case Institute of Technology (1954)
Churchman, Ackoff, and Arnoff (1957)
Dvoretzky, Kiefer, and Wolfowitz (1952)
Gourary, Lewis, and Neeland (1956)
Magee (1958)
Simon and Holt (1954)
Whitin (1953)
Whitin (1954)
Whitin (1955)

Static deterministic models

Derman and Klein (1958)
Derman and Klein (1959)

Lieberman (1958)
Whitin (1955)

Static probabilistic models

Arrow, Harris, and Marschak (1951)
Beckman and Muth (1956)
Bellman, Glicksberg, and Gross (1955)
Dvoretzky, Kiefer, and Wolfowitz (1953)
Freeman (1957)
Karush (1957)
Levy (1958)
Levy (1959)
Modigliani and Muth (1954)
Morse (1958)
Morse (1959)
Naddor (1956)
Pinkham (1958)
Simon (1952)
Simpson (1955)
Solomon (1954)
Vassian (1955)
Whitin and Youngs (1955)

Dynamic models

Antosiewiez and Hoffman (1954)
Bellman (1956)
Bellman (1957)
Bishop (1957)
Bonini (1958)
Bowman (1956)
Charnes, Cooper, and Mellon (1955)
Charnes, Cooper, and Symonds (1958)
Dannerstedt (1955)
Danskin (1955)
Dreyfus (1956)
Eastman (1959)
Gaddum, Hoffman, and Sokolowsky (1954)
Gessford (1959)
Hanssmann (1957)
Hoffman and Jacobs (1954)
Holt and Simon (1954)
Holt, Modigliani, and Simon (1955)
Holt, Modigliani, and Muth (1956)
Hu and Prager (1959)
Johnson (1957)
Karush (1958)
Karush and Vazsonyi (1957)
Klein (1957)
Koopmans (1958)
Little (1955)

Manne (1957)
Mills (1959)
Modigliani and Hohn (1955)
Moran (1956)
Prager (1956)
Schild (1959)
Schneider (1938)
Schupack (1959)
Simon (1952)
Vassian (1955)
Wagner and Whitin (1958)
Whitin (1954)

Models of parallel stations

Allen (1958)
Baumol and Wolfe (1958)
Dantzig (1955)
Gourary (1958)
Karr (1958)
Naddor and Saltzman (1958)
Rogers (1958)
Salveson (1956)
Vazsonyi (1957)

Models of series of stations

Bryan, Wadsworth, and Whitin (1955)
Hanssmann (1959)
Simpson (1958)

Static problems

Arnoff and Chambers (1956)
Arnoff, Kania, and Small Day (1958)
Beckman (1959)
Beckman and Bobkoski (1958)
Chambers, Bond, and Leake (1958)
Clark (1957)
Feeney (1955)
Heyvaert and Hurt (1956)
Hurst (1955)
Isaac (1956)
Levary (1956)
Marshall and Boggess (1957)
Page and Muris (1957)
Petersen and Geisler (1955)
Petersen and Steger (1958)

Dynamic problems

Charnes, Cooper, and Symonds (1958)
Fabian, Fisher, Sasieni, and Yardeni (1959)
Holt, Modigliani, and Simon (1955)
Little (1955)

Problems of parallel stations

Baumol and Wolfe (1958)
Bowman (1958)
Dantzig and Ferguson (1956)
Eagle (1957)
Friedman (1956)
Geisler and Karr (1956)
Hanssmann and Rivett (1959)
Karr and Geisler (1956)
Manne (1958)
Salveson (1956)
Sutherland (1958)

Problems of series of stations

Ackoff (1955)
Dillon (1956)
Minas and Mitten (1958)

Pipeline-inventory problems

Levinson (1953)
Mansfield and Wein (1958)

Chapter 4

MATHEMATICAL PROGRAMMING

E. Leonard Arnoff and
S. Sankar Sengupta
Case Institute of Technology, Cleveland, Ohio

Contents

1. BACKGROUND

Man has long been interested in, and intrigued by, optimization problems. Euclid, for example, in the third century B.C., set forth a number of optimization problems in his *Elements* (13 books) such as that of finding the longest and shortest straight line segment that can be drawn from a given point to the circumference of a given circle (Book III). For centuries, most optimization problems defied rigorous solution—in fact, until the development of the infinitesimal calculus (Leibnitz, 1646–1716; Newton, 1642–1727; et al.) and the calculus of variations (Jacob Bernoulli, 1654–1705; John Bernoulli, 1667–1748; et al.) in the seventeenth and eighteenth centuries. These brought about a great advance in one's ability to describe nature and, thereafter, enabled one to solve a wide range of optimization problems—both theoretical, as evidenced by the great variety of maximization and minimization problems one now encounters in college calculus courses, and applied, as evidenced by classical problems of physics and engineering.

In recent years, with the development of large organizations composed of many subfunctional units or echelons, a new class of optimization problems has emerged—problems involving the interaction of the various components of the organization and requiring the determination of the best solution in terms of the over-all interests of the organization as a whole (Churchman, Ackoff, and Arnoff, 1957, p. 3 ff.). Such problems, arising in the study of the complex organizational structures of today's business, industry, and government, are usually characterized by a large number of variables and many interactions among these variables—expressed in the form of constraints or restrictions.

Conceptually, problems of maximizing a function of any number of variables subject to a set of restrictions can be solved by classical methods such as those which make use of Lagrangian multipliers.[1] However, most organizational problems of today are very large (i.e., large number of variables), involve restrictions in the form of inequalities (rather than equalities), and constrain all of the solution

[1] See, for example, Chapter 5 in Saaty (1959*a*).

variables to be non-negative. These more complex problems require the development of new and more practical optimization methods and techniques for their solution.[2] One of the most powerful classes of optimization techniques developed to solve such problems is that of *mathematical programming.*

Mathematical programming refers to techniques for solving a general class of optimization problems dealing with the interaction of many variables, subject to a set of restraining conditions. Such problems are called allocation problems and arise when:

a. There are a number of activities to be performed and there are alternative ways of doing them, *and*—

b. Resources or facilities are not available for performing each activity in the most effective way.

The allocation problem, then, is to combine activities and resources in such a way as to maximize over-all effectiveness. (See Churchman, Ackoff, and Arnoff, 1957, p. 275.)

Generally speaking, allocation problems—and, hence, the problems of mathematical programming—may be expressed as that of maximizing a given effectiveness function, subject to a given set of restrictions; that is:[3]

To determine values of x_j which maximize (minimize)

$$z=f(x_1,x_2,\cdots,x_n) \tag{4.1}$$

subject to:

$$g_i(x_1,x_2,\cdots,x_n)=0 \qquad (i=1,2,\cdots,m) \tag{4.2}$$

$$x_j\geq 0 \qquad (j=1,2,\cdots,n) \tag{4.3}$$

To date, limited progress has been made in developing methods for solving the *general* allocation problem. However, significant success has been achieved in developing techniques for solving a subclass—namely, those involving linear effectiveness functions (to be maximized

[2] Extensions of the Lagrangian-multiplier method for resolving—*in concept*—the requirements of non-negativity of the variables in problems with inequality restrictions have been developed, e.g., that due to Klein (1955). However, as noted by Charnes and Cooper (1955*a*), such methods are most impractical except for the solution of very small "toy" problems. See, also, Slater (1951) and Chapter 10 in Churchman, Ackoff, and Arnoff (1957).

[3] The restrictions will usually appear as *in*equations of the forms: "no more than," "at least," "less than or equal to," "greater than or equal to," etc. These inequalities can, of course, be converted to equalities by the insertion of appropriate slack and artificial variables. (See Churchman, Ackoff, and Arnoff, 1957.)

or minimized) *and* linear restrictions. These are the techniques of *linear programming*—simple in structure but exceedingly powerful in their wide range of applicability.

Extensions of linear-programming techniques to problems involving non-linear effectiveness functions (and linear restrictions) have been made, although with somewhat less success from a practical (applicability) viewpoint, while problems involving non-linear effectiveness functions and/or non-linear restriction systems have been solved in only special cases. In all cases, such extensions will be referred to as *non-linear programming.*

In this chapter, mathematical programming will be discussed—in the main, for the special case of *linear* programming and, only briefly, for extensions to non-linear programming. Linear programming will be discussed for both the *static* (single time period) and *dynamic* (multistage or many time periods) cases, and, additionally, for the cases in which the given coefficients in the effectiveness function and the restriction relationships are: (1) known and fixed, (2) allowed to vary, or (3) subject to statistical variation. Such problems are called (1) deterministic, (2) parametric, or (3) stochastic, respectively, and, in the latter two cases, one speaks more particularly of *parametric programming* and *stochastic programming.* In all cases, progress will be discussed in terms of:

1. Theoretical development.
2. Computational development.
3. Applications.
4. Unsolved problems.

There is a significant interaction and relationship between mathematical programming and the mathematical theory of games. However, a discussion of this relationship will not be given in this chapter. Rather, the reader is referred to McKinsey (1952, Chapter 14) and the references contained therein.

Similarly, the relationship of mathematical programming with input-output analysis will not be discussed here, the reader being referred to Dorfman, Samuelson, and Solow (1958).

In this chapter, it is assumed that the reader has previously had some basic exposure to linear programming—in particular, some knowledge of (1) the simplex and transportation techniques and, possibly, also of the assignment technique for solving the corresponding problems of linear programming, along with (2) the associated basic terminology (e.g., *basis, iteration, tableau, slack variable, artificial variable,* etc.).[4]

2. LINEAR PROGRAMMING

2.1. Introduction

The general problem of *linear* programming is that of maximizing (minimizing) a linear function, subject to a set of linear restrictions (in the form of equations and/or inequations). Thus, the problem of linear programming is: [5]

To determine values of x_j which maximize (minimize)

$$f = \sum_{j=1}^{n} c_j x_j$$

subject to (P.1)

$$\sum_{j=1}^{n} a_{ij} x_j = b_i \qquad (i=1,2,\cdots,m)$$

$$x_j \geq 0 \qquad (j=1,2,\cdots,n)$$

where a_{ij}, b_i, and c_j are given constants.

[4] Throughout the chapter, references for particular topics are cited extensively. These consist, in the main, of fundamental research papers in the field of mathematical programming. For outstanding textbooks on the subject, the reader is referred to Gass (1958) and Vajda (1958), among others. The mathematically oriented economist is also referred to the excellent text of Dorfman, Samuelson, and Solow (1958).

For basic reading on the solution of the general linear-programming problem by the simplex technique, see the excellent elementary presentations (at high-school algebra level) by Dantzig (1956*a*) and Wagner (1958), and the lucid exposition by Charnes, Cooper, and Henderson (1953).

For basic reading about the transportation problem and the transportation technique, the reader is referred to Charnes and Cooper (1954*a*) and Churchman, Ackoff, and Arnoff (1957, Chapter 11). For the assignment problem, see Flood (1955) and Churchman, Ackoff, and Arnoff (1957, Chapter 12).

Finally, particular mention should be made of the monumental and exceptional annotated bibliography on mathematical programming by Riley and Gass (1958), and an acknowledgment is made here of the great value of this volume to the present writers in the preparation of this chapter.

[5] The symbol (P.1) is used to denote the general problem of linear programming. Other problems discussed in this chapter will be denoted by (P.2), (P.3), and so forth. The restrictions in (P.1) will usually appear as *in*equations of the forms: "no more than," "at least," "less than or equal to," "greater than or equal to," etc. These inequalities can, of course, be converted to equalities by the insertion of appropriate slack and artificial variables. (See Churchman, Ackoff, and Arnoff, 1957.)

Although problems of optimizing a linear function subject to a set of linear constraints had previously been considered in one form or another, it was not until 1947 that the general problem of linear programming was formulated. At that time, Marshall K. Wood, George B. Dantzig, and other associates of the United States Department of the Air Force had been called upon to study the possibility and feasibility of applying scientific and mathematical methods and techniques to the solution of problems of allocating and programming the conduct of war and the organization of national defense. Dantzig proposed that interrelationships between activities of a large organization be viewed as a linear-programming type of model and the optimizing program determined by minimizing a linear objective function. This led to the formation, by the Air Force, of a research group called Project SCOOP (Scientific Computation of Optimum Programs) under the direction of Marshall K. Wood. In 1947, while a member of Project SCOOP, Dantzig made the initial mathematical statement of the linear-programming problem. Also, in 1947, Dantzig developed one of the most outstanding contributions of Project SCOOP, namely: the simplex technique for solving the general linear-programming problem. The fundamental paper in which Dantzig set forth the simplex technique was circulated privately until it was finally published in 1951 (Dantzig, 1951*a*). The simplex technique was first presented in comprehensive form in 1953—by Charnes, Cooper and Henderson in their *Introduction to Linear Programming.*

There are a number of examples of linear-programming problems that had been considered prior to 1947. Probably the most important of these are (1) the *diet problem* formulated and approximately proposed in 1941 by Jerome Cornfield in an unpublished memorandum and treated by George Stigler (1945) by what he calls an "experimental procedure," and (2) the *transportation problem* formulated by Hitchcock in 1941 and, independently, by Kantorovich in 1942 and by Koopmans in 1947.

The diet problem is that of determining the optimum (least-cost) mixture of available foods that will satisfy certain minimum nutritional requirements. Stigler considered seventy-seven different foods that could be used to satisfy nine nutritional requirements. By means of his experimental procedure (trial and error), Stigler obtained a feasible solution of $39.93 as the "minimal" *annual* cost (based on 1939 prices) of satisfying one's nutritional requirements.

In 1947, Dantzig and Laderman solved the Stigler diet problem by use of the linear-programming simplex procedure and obtained an optimum solution of \$39.639. Their results, although unpublished, are discussed by Vajda (1958, pp. 55–56). Despite the large size of the problem, Stigler's solution was only *one* iteration away from the optimum solution later obtained by Dantzig and Laderman.

It is interesting to note Stigler's comment (1945) that "the procedure (Stigler's) is experimental because there does not appear to be any direct method of finding the minimum of a linear function subject to linear conditions." The presentation of the simplex procedure only two years later, is, with no discredit to Stigler, another indication of the great and significant contributions that have been made by Dantzig in the field of linear programming.

The diet problem is the first economic problem ever solved by the explicit use of Dantzig's simplex technique. Furthermore, originally intended to serve only as a test and illustration of the simplex technique, it has focused attention on, and stimulated the development of, a wide range of important, practical applications—not only in diet or food-mix problems, but also in abstractly similar problems of blending raw and in-process materials in the manufacture of steel (ores, blast-furnace, open-hearth, etc.), gasoline products, and so forth.

The transportation problem of linear programming can be thought of as that of minimizing the cost of distributing a product from several factories to a number of cities (warehouses). In 1951, Dantzig (1951*b*) formulated the transportation problem as a special linear-programming problem and then developed a special form of the simplex technique—called the transportation technique—for solving such problems. The transportation problem is probably the most important special linear-programming problem—in terms of the relative frequency with which it appears in applications and, also, the simplicity of the procedure developed for its solution. Specifically, the *transportation problem* may be stated as:

Determine $x_{ij} \geq 0$ which minimize

$$K = \sum_{i,j} c_{ij} x_{ij}$$

subject to:

$$\begin{aligned} &\sum_{j=1}^{n} x_{ij} = a_i \qquad (i = 1,2,\cdots,m) \\ &\sum_{i=1}^{m} x_{ij} = b_j \qquad (j = 1,2,\cdots,n) \\ &\sum_{i} a_i = \sum_{j} b_j \end{aligned} \tag{P.2}$$

where a_i, b_j, and c_{ij} are given constants $(i = 1,2,\cdots,m;\ j = 1,2,\cdots,n)$.

An important variant of the transportation problem is the so-called *assignment problem*, namely:

Determine $x_{ij} \geq 0$ which minimize

$$K = \sum_{i,j} c_{ij} x_{ij}$$

subject to

$$\begin{aligned} \sum_{i=1}^{n} x_{ij} &= 1 \qquad (j=1,2,\cdots,n) \\ \sum_{j=1}^{n} x_{ij} &= 1 \qquad (i=1,2,\cdots,n) \\ x_{ij} &= x_{ij}^2 \end{aligned} \tag{P.3}$$

where c_{ij} are given constants $(i,j=1,2,\cdots,n)$.

Thus, the general linear-programming problem (P.1) reduces to the transportation problem (P.2) when $a_{ij}=1$ for all i and j. Similarly, one obtains the assignment problem (P.3) when, in P.1, $a_{ij}=1$ and $b_i=1$ for all i and j.

The early results, problems, and potential applications of linear programming were presented and discussed at two important conferences held in 1949 and 1951, namely, the Conference on Linear Programming held at the University of Chicago (June, 1949) and the Symposium on Linear Programming held in Washington, D. C. (June, 1951). The papers presented at these conferences were later published in the proceedings of each conference and constituted, for a number of years, practically the only generally available formal sources of information on linear programming (see Koopmans, 1951*a*, and Orden and Goldstein, 1952). These proceedings provided a great stimulus to researchers in the further development and extension of linear programming, and in the application of linear-programming techniques (e.g., the simplex technique) to complex problems of business, industry, and government. The Charnes-Cooper-Henderson book (1953) focused further attention on linear programming and aroused the interest of an even larger group of researchers and managers.

A third major stimulus to the research, development, and application of linear-programming techniques was provided by a number of professional societies in the areas of applied mathematics and econometrics and by newly founded societies (such as the Operations Research Society of America, The Institute of Management Sciences, and The Society for Industrial and Applied Mathematics) and newly formed journals (such as the *Naval Research Logistics Quarterly*). Additionally, popularized articles on linear programming and its potential applications appeared in a number of publications such as *Business Week* and *Factory Management and Maintenance*. The net result was that linear programming was brought to the widespread attention of management, and scientific and technical personnel—especially in industry—and, in turn, the interaction and cross-stimulation between the researcher and the consumer—between the theoretical and the practical—resulted in an almost phenomenal development of linear programming in recent years.

The remarkable development of the simplex and transportation techniques has provided routine, clerical procedures for obtaining the optimum solution of a general class and subclass of problems.[6] These procedures are much easier to use and to demonstrate than the analytic optimization methods that have been proposed. Furthermore, in proceeding from a feasible solution to a "better" feasible solution (i.e., from one iteration to the next), the uninitiated, at least, can get a "feeling" of savings being achieved almost right on-the-spot.

Unfortunately, following the availability of these procedures, linear programming became oversold, misused, and often abused by opportunists and the uninformed.[7] Too often, problems were "formulated" according to preconceived notions so as to make possible a "solution" by linear-programming techniques. Too often, problems which had little resemblance to reality were "solved" by linear programming and demonstrations (claims) made, for example, that "the optimum matrix for *last* June is \$25,000 better than the actual performance—therefore, we can save (\$25,000) × (12) or \$300,000 per year." [8]

Soon, industrial personnel—many with non-technical backgrounds (production clerks, purchasing clerks, etc.)—were attending training programs in linear programming ("Come take our course in linear programming and learn to solve all of management's problems"). Too frequently, these courses encouraged operators to do little more than apply clerical procedures to a given matrix of numbers—be it the simplex procedure or the even-simpler transportation procedure. Thus one frequently encountered "management mechanics," equipped with only a fancy "screwdriver" (called linear programming), wandering around looking for "screws" to turn. When confronted with a nail,

[6] In fact, the routine, clerical nature of the simplex and transportation algorithms makes their development all the more remarkable.

[7] See, for example, Rinehart (1954).

[8] See, for example, Orden (1955, p. 172), in which he admonishes that "the claims of successful applications must be accepted with caution since claims have a rather natural tendency to get ahead of facts."

rather than a screw, persons with such background would be inclined to cut a slot into the head of the nail so as to be able to use the screwdriver.[9]

In spite of these unfortunate circumstances—which one can charitably attribute to "overenthusiasm"—the field of linear programming was developed by the professional scientist and researcher at what was earlier referred to as a phenomenal rate. As the researcher (and practitioner) devoted greater efforts to finding *appropriate* applications of linear programming, he soon realized that the problems of modern business, industry, and government were of such size and complexity that solutions by manual computation were often highly impractical (e.g., in production problems involving short customer-delivery lead times, where the solution time exceeds the total available delivery time) and, in some instances, virtually impossible.

Consequently, the next stage of development of linear programming was concerned with the development of codes and programs for the solution of general linear-programming problems—by the simplex technique—on electronic digital computers. The first successful solution of a linear-programming problem on a high-speed electronic computer was obtained in January, 1952—on the SEAC (Bureau of Standards Eastern Automatic Computer)—and represents another major contribution of Project SCOOP. However, it was not until several years later that the solution of the general linear-programming problem (by the simplex technique) was readily available on high-speed computers (such as the IBM-701, for example).

Despite the great strides taken through the use of electronic computers, the increasingly large scope and size of problems attacked by these techniques prevented a major breakthrough in the widespread use of the basic simplex technique. For many problems, the computational cost and time requirements (even on very high-speed computers) were of such magnitude that they prevented serious consideration of the problem (especially when one wished to obtain a number of solutions which reflect possible changes in requirements, restrictions, prices, customer demand, etc.). Furthermore, the use of electronic computers required the rounding-off of numbers and, accordingly, introduced large round-off errors which, in turn, often led to false solutions

[9] Although we have indicated the nature of some of the abortive uses of linear programming, it is not our intent to be in any way critical of the excellent work performed by researchers who used linear-programming approaches (and corresponding simplifications and assumptions) for a number of problems, in order to gain further insight into these problems and to develop *appropriate* solution-techniques for practical and valid applications.

(see Section 3.4). Additionally, even where high-speed computers (such as the IBM-701) could be used to solve a given linear-programming problem, such computers were not readily available (timewise and geographically) to more than just a few companies.

Accordingly, the next major efforts were directed towards developing revisions to the simplex technique and, also, new computational procedures for more efficient solution of the general linear-programming problem, and, simultaneously, developing techniques for linear-programming problems of special form or structure. Among the revised and new computational techniques developed were:

1. The dual simplex technique.
2. The revised simplex technique.
3. The composite simplex technique.
4. The primal-dual algorithm.
5. The Frisch multiplex method.

The dual simplex technique is based on the important Gale-Kuhn-Tucker dual theorem of linear programming discussed in Section 2.2. It, and the other revised or new computational techniques, are discussed in Section 7. However, it might be noted here that there is general agreement that the simplex technique still is probably the best procedure for the *manual* solution of the general linear-programming problem, and that the *revised* simplex technique is probably the best procedure for the solution of large linear-programming problems by means of electronic computers.

Special computational techniques have been developed for the transportation and assignment problems and also for the specialized warehouse problem, in particular, and more generally for the class of so-called block-triangular problems. Finally, in what might be called the current stage of development of linear programming, there is a concerted effort to develop techniques for solving variations of the basic linear-programming problem: dynamic linear programming, parametric programming, stochastic programming, and integer-valued programming.

2.2. *The Dual Theorem of Linear Programming*

One of the most important fundamental developments in mathematical programming is the *dual theorem of linear programming,* due to Gale, Kuhn, and Tucker (1951), which states, basically, that, for every maximization problem (the *primal* problem), there is a corresponding minimization problem (the *dual* problem) such that $f_{\max}$, the maximum value of the first (the primal problem), is equal to $g_{\min}$, the minimum value of the latter. This dual theorem has provided the basis for a large number of significant developments and advancements in mathematical programming and, also, for that matter, in several seemingly totally unrelated areas.

The duality theorem for linear programming has been developed, in a number of forms and variations, by von Neumann (1947), Gale, Kuhn, and Tucker (1951), Dantzig and Orden (1952), Motzkin (1952*a*), Tucker (1956), Goldman and Tucker (1956), and others.

The dual theorem of linear programming may be stated as follows:

If either the primal or the dual problem has a finite optimum solution, then the other problem also has a finite optimum solution and the extremes (optimum values) of the linear functions are equal (that is, $f_{\max}=g_{\min}$). If either problem has an unbounded optimum solution, then the other problem has no feasible solutions.

Depending upon the exact nature of the primal problem, there will be a corresponding dual problem for which the dual theorem applies. The most common dual problem is the *symmetric dual* problem, first stated by von Neumann (1947):

Primal Problem	*Symmetric Dual Problem*
Maximize	Minimize
$f=\sum_{j=1}^{n} c_j x_j$	$g=\sum_{i=1}^{m} b_i y_i$
subject to: (P.4*a*)	subject to: (P.4*b*)
$\sum_{j=1}^{n} a_{ij} x_j \leq b_i$	$\sum_{i=1}^{m} a_{ij} y_i \geq c_j$
$x_j \geq 0$	$y_i \geq 0$

The *unsymmetric dual problem* (see Dantzig and Orden, 1952 is given) by:

Primal Problem	*Unsymmetric Dual Problem*
Maximize	Minimize
$f=\sum_{j=1}^{n} c_j x_j$	$g=\sum_{i=1}^{m} b_i y_i$
subject to: (P.5*a*)	subject to: (P.5*b*)
$\sum_{j=1}^{n} a_{ij} x_j = b_i$	$\sum_{i=1}^{m} a_{ij} y_i \geq c_j$
$x_j \geq 0$	and *no* constraints (as to non-negativity) on the y_i.

Dual problems can also be determined for linear-programming problems involving mixed constraints; for example:

Primal Problem		*Dual Problem*	
Maximize $f=\sum_{j=1}^{n} c_j x_j$		Minimize $g=\sum_{i=1}^{m} b_i y_i$	
subject to:		subject to:	
$\sum_{j=1}^{n} a_{ij}x_j \leq b_i$	$(i=1,2,\cdots,r)$	$\sum_{i=1}^{m} a_{ij}y_i \geq c_j$	$(j=1,2,\cdots,s)$
	(P.6a)		(P.6b)
$\sum_{j=1}^{n} a_{ij}x_j = b_i$	$(i=r+1,\cdots,m)$	$\sum_{i=1}^{m} a_{ij}y_i = c_j$	$(j=s+1,\cdots,n)$
$x_j \geq 0$	$(j=1,2,\cdots,s)$	$y_i \geq 0$	$(i=1,2,\cdots,r)$
x_j unrestricted	$(j=s+1,\cdots,n)$	y_i unrestricted	$(i=r+1,\cdots,m)$

Similarly, one can state the following dual-matrix problems:

Primal Problem		*Dual Problem*	
Maximize $C_1X_1+C_2X_2$		Minimize $Y_1B_1+Y_2B_2$	
subject to:		subject to:	
$A_{11}X_1+A_{12}X_2 \leq B_1$		$Y_1A_{11}+Y_2A_{21} \geq C_1$	
	(P.7a)		(P.7b)
$A_{21}X_1+A_{22}X_2 = B_2$		$Y_1A_{12}+Y_2A_{22} = C_2$	
$X_1 \geq 0$		$Y_1 \geq 0$	
X_2 unrestricted		Y_2 unrestricted	

These, and a number of other types of elementary transformations from a primal problem to the corresponding dual problem are given in Goldman and Tucker (1956).

Gale, Kuhn, and Tucker (1951) have also stated the dual theorem, more generally, in terms of both vector and matrix linear-programming problems, as follows:

Primal Vector Problem		*Dual Vector Problem*	
Find a *maximal* vector d having the property that		Find a *minimal* vector d having the property that	
$Cx \geq d$	(P.8a)	$b'u \leq d'v$	(P.8b)
for some $x \geq 0$ such that		for some $u \geq 0, v > 0$ such that	
$Ax \leq b$		$A'u \geq C'v$	

Primal Matrix Problem	*Dual Matrix Problem*
Find a *maximal* matrix D having the property that	Find a *minimal* matrix D having the property that
$Cx \geq Dy$ (P.9*a*)	$B'u \leq D'v$ (P.9*b*)
for some $x \geq 0, y > 0$ such that	for some $u \geq 0, v > 0$ such that
$Ax \leq By$	$A'u \geq C'v$

For the matrix problem, for example, the dual theorem may be stated, very simply (see Gale, Kuhn, and Tucker, 1951):

A Matrix D is a solution for the primal problem if, and only if, it is a solution for the dual problem.

Charnes, Cooper, and Mellon (1954) have developed a very simple and useful schematic procedure for transforming from the primal to the *symmetric* dual problem (and vice versa),[10] which can be represented as follows (see also Goldman and Tucker, 1956):

$$
\begin{array}{r|cccc|l}
(\geq 0) & x_1 & x_2 & \cdots & x_n & (\leq) \\
\hline
y_1 & a_{11} & a_{12} & \cdots & a_{1n} & b_1 \\
y_2 & a_{21} & a_{22} & \cdots & a_{2n} & b_2 \\
\vdots & \vdots & \vdots & & \vdots & \vdots \quad \text{max} \\
y_m & a_{m1} & a_{m2} & \cdots & a_{mn} & b_m \\
\hline
(\geq) & c_1 & c_2 & \cdots & c_n & \\
 & & & \text{min} & &
\end{array}
$$

Referring, then, to the symmetric dual problems stated earlier, one can see that the primal problem can be formed from the rows of the matrix [using the inner product of $A = \{a_{ij}\}$ with $X = (x_1, x_2, \cdots, x_n)$], while the symmetric dual problem can, in turn, be formed from the columns of the matrix.

One of the first uses (exploitations) of the dual theorem of linear programming was the development of the dual-simplex algorithm by Lemke (1954), by which one is able to solve the primal problem by

[10] While the primal problem has been described here as a maximization problem, the minimization problem could—alternatively—have been so designated (with the maximization problem then being the corresponding dual problem).

first solving its dual problem. The difficulty first encountered in transforming from the dual solution to the corresponding primal solution (calculating an inverse matrix, etc.) was then removed by Charnes and Cooper (1954*b*) and Charnes, Cooper, and Mellon (1954), who developed the "regrouping principle" (namely, the schematic procedure described above), which enables one to transform quickly from one solution to the other (see Section 7; also Churchman, Ackoff, and Arnoff, 1957, Appendix 11C).

An immediate gain to be made as a consequence of the dual theorem is that one can choose to solve either the problem as given, or its corresponding dual problem. Since the amount of computation required to solve a linear-programming problem is, in a sense, proportional to the number of rows (restrictions) in the matrix, one has the option of solving a corresponding problem which may entail much less computation than the original problem (see Section 3.3). In fact, in some extremely large problems, the ability to solve the dual problem may even enable one to solve, by electronic computers, problems otherwise too large for the computer.

The economic implications and benefits arising out of primal-dual problems are most significant, especially in terms of enabling one to discuss the sensitivity of solutions to variations in the "prices," c_j, and also the resource restrictions, b_i.[11]

A number of linear-programming problems have arisen which, in principle, can be solved by means of such computational procedures as the simplex technique, but for which these means are impractical because of the large size of the matrix involved. Several classes of such problems have been found to have special structures which can be exploited to great advantage by means of their *dual* problem, so that one is now able to solve such problems by means of the special techniques that were developed to take advantage of such special structures. The warehousing problem to be discussed in Section 8 is an example of a class of problems that exhibits special structures (e.g., block-triangularity, sparseness of the matrix, etc.) which can be exploited most advantageously by means of the dual formulation (see Charnes and Cooper, 1954*b*).

The dual theorem of linear programming has also led to consider-

[11] For a discussion of the economic implications, see, for example, Dorfman, Samuelson, and Solow (1958), Dorfman (1951), and Charnes, Cooper, and Henderson (1953).

For a discussion of the analysis of the sensitivity of solutions, see Section 9.

able simplification of the solution procedure for the transportation problem and, furthermore, has made possible the computational algorithm for solving the generalized transportation problem, discussed in Section 4.3 (see also Ferguson and Dantzig, 1956, and Vazsonyi, 1958).

Another example of the importance of the dual theorem of linear programming is the proof by Hoffman and Dantzig (1955) of a theorem due to Dilworth (1950) on partially ordered sets. Dilworth proved that the smallest number of disjoint chains contained in a partially ordered set, such that every element of the set belongs to one of the chains, is the largest number of mutually unrelated elements in the partially ordered set. Hoffman and Dantzig show that the finite case of Dilworth's theorem is really the dual theorem of linear programming.

Similarly, the dual theorem of linear programming was used to "prove" a Ford-Fulkerson theorem on maximal flow in networks and, also, other theorems for problems in mathematical areas which, at first glance, seem to be totally unrelated (see Dantzig, 1956*b*).

Finally, the dual theorem of linear programming has provided the basis for a number of developments in the mathematical theory of games, for example, by Dorfman (1951) in computing the optimal strategies for *both* players simultaneously in a zero-sum, two-person game.

2.3. Degeneracy and Cycling in Linear-Programming Problems

In the development of the simplex algorithm, it is assumed that all basic feasible solutions (of the linear-programming problem) are non-degenerate; that is—given the basis vectors $P_1,P_2,\cdots,P_m$ for which

$$P_0=x_1P_1+x_2P_2+\cdots+x_mP_m$$

then $x_i>0$ for each and every $i=1,2,\cdots,m$. (If at least one $x_i=0$, the basic feasible solution is said to be *degenerate*.) More specifically, the non-degeneracy assumption is that "every subset of m points from the set $(P_0;P_1,P_2,\cdots,P_n)$ is linearly independent" (see Dantzig, 1951*a*).

The assumption of non-degeneracy is necessary in order to show that, for each successive admissible basis, the corresponding value of the objective function is (for a maximation problem) strictly monotonic increasing so that, in turn, having only a finite number of admissible bases, one will reach an optimum solution in a finite number of iterations.

Should degeneracy appear (as, in fact, it does in many linear-programming problems), it is possible for the value of the solution to remain unchanged from one iteration to the next (using the simplex technique). In this case it would then be possible for a basis to reappear—that is, for the problem to "cycle" with respect to a sequence of admissible bases so that, as a consequence, one could never arrive at an optimum solution.

To resolve the problem of degeneracy from both theoretical and computational points of view, Dantzig (1951*a*) suggested and Charnes (1952) developed "perturbation" procedures in which, whenever P_0 is linearly dependent on *less* than m of the P_i, the values of the components of P_0 are altered slightly, so that P_0 is moved from the face to the interior of the simplex (see also Charnes, Cooper, and Henderson, 1953). As noted in Vajda (1956, p. 68), Dantzig's suggested procedure can be made computationally equivalent to Charnes' perturbation procedure. However, the procedure first suggested by Dantzig, while convenient for obtaining a feasible solution, is itself subject to possible degeneracy (Charnes, 1952, p. 160, footnote 3). On the other hand, Charnes' procedure automatically removes any possibility of degeneracy at any stage; hence, the possibility of recycling is completely eliminated. Furthermore, initial knowledge of the linear dependence or independence of the equations is not required (Charnes, Cooper, and Henderson, 1953, p. 63).

In order to be able to completely remove the restrictive assumptions regarding "degeneracy" [i.e., assumptions about either the rank of the matrix of coefficients and constant elements or about the linear independence of every subset of m points from the set $(P_0;P_1,P_2,\cdots,P_n)$], Dantzig, Orden, and Wolfe (1954) developed a "generalized" simplex technique. However, just as a perturbation procedure is needed for the simplex technique to insure non-degeneracy and, hence, justify the non-degeneracy assumption of the simplex technique, so is a perturbation procedure (or similar scheme) necessary to insure non-degeneracy in the *revised* simplex technique. This procedure is provided by Dantzig (1953) and includes a rule for uniquely resolving ties, so that the admissible solutions always converge to the optimum solution. Dantzig's procedure is quite similar to that of Charnes (1952), but uses the *inverse* of the current basis (see also Dantzig, Orden, and Wolfe, 1954). Revised simplex techniques are discussed further in Section 7.

In practice, the problem of degeneracy is not an important one. In fact, Hoffman (1955) strongly urges that, in reading literature on linear programming, one ignore (certainly on the first reading) all references to, and discussions of, the problem of degeneracy. While degeneracy is an important *theoretical* consideration (as noted later in this section), it can virtually be completely ignored in all practical problems since, with the current "history" of hundreds of simplex computations arising out of practical (e.g., industrial) problems, not one of them has been known to have recycled (i.e., the simplex technique has worked in each and every case!). While examples have been given to demonstrate cycling and, hence, the failure of the simplex technique, the only available examples were *artificially* constructed for that purpose—for example those by Hoffman (1953) and Beale (1955).[12] Accordingly, the procedures developed to handle degeneracy have been virtually ignored in actual application—for example, in most computer programs. In practice, degenerate solutions are handled in the regular manner if they arise simply because one or more of the $x_i=0$. Ties in the value of $\theta=\min_i(x_{i0}/x_{ik})$, which lead to degeneracy in the next iteration, are usually resolved by choosing the smallest index i or by calculating and comparing the ratios x_{ij}/x_{ik} across the rows in which the ties occurred, until the time (column) at which the ties are broken (see Cooper, Charnes, and Henderson, 1953, p. 23 ff.; Charnes, 1952; and Saaty, 1959*a*, p. 185). For the former (i.e., choosing the smallest index i), cycling *can* (but is not likely to) occur, as evidenced by Beale's example. In the latter case, the rule for breaking the tie results from Charnes' perturbation procedure and, furthermore, the possibility of cycling is completely eliminated (Charnes, Cooper, and Henderson, 1953, p. 63).

While degeneracy procedures have not been needed in actual practice, these procedures have been most important in theoretical and computational considerations where linear-programming theorems and algorithms have been used to prove theorems, and show equivalence to problems in seemingly totally unrelated areas of mathematics.

3. COMPUTATIONAL ASPECTS OF LINEAR PROGRAMMING

As noted earlier, the simplex technique was developed by Dantzig for solving the general linear-programming problem. In practice—in

[12] Beale's example is discussed in terms of its dual, since Beale felt that "the geometric interpretation of the changes in basis when degeneracy occurs is easier to follow in the dual method (due to Lemke, 1954) than in the simplex method" (Beale, 1955). The cycling problem in terms of its primal problem is illustrated and discussed by Gass (1958) in terms of an unpublished example due to Beale.

applying the simplex technique, a number of important questions arise, namely, questions concerned with:

a. Estimates of the optimum value of the objective function and, hence, estimates of the potential payoff to be expected from a given study.

b. The number of iterations required to obtain an optimum solution and, hence, the amount of computation and time required.

c. Round-off errors and, hence, the possibility of incorrect results, introduced by use of electronic computers.

In order to facilitate computation, a number of revisions and alternatives to the simplex technique were developed for more efficient solution of the general linear-programming problem. We will also consider the bounded-variable problem in which some of the variables are subject to upper-limit constraints, and linear-programming problems in which the solution-variables are restricted to integer values.

3.1. Geometric Interpretation of the Linear-Programming Problem

The problem of linear programming is that of maximizing or minimizing a linear objective function subject to a set of linear constraints. These linear constraints (including those requiring the solution variables to be non-negative) form a *convex set,*[13] and, as has been shown by Dantzig and others, an optimum solution of the linear-programming problem will always lie at one of the *extreme points*[14] of the given convex set.

The simplex technique is—very briefly—a finite, converging iterative procedure which successively (iteration by iteration) translates—parallel to itself—the hyperplane representing the objective (optimizing) function. Since this hyperplane is translated from extreme point to extreme point of the convex set defined by the given restrictions, the optimum solution is reached in a finite number of iterations (see Charnes, Cooper, and Henderson, 1953, Part II).

The general problem of linear programming has been illustrated graphically in a number of textbooks and papers—to show (1) how the optimum solutions appear at extreme points of the convex set of re-

[13] A *convex set* is a collection of points such that, if x and y are any two points in the collection, the straight line segment joining them is also in the collection.

[14] An *extreme point* of a convex set is one which does *not* lie on a line segment joining some two other points of the set (for example, points O, A, B, C, and D in Fig. 4.1).

strictions, (2) how one converges from a *basic feasible solution* to the optimum (extreme-point) solution, (3) multiplicity of optimum solutions, (4) relationship of the dual problem to the primal problem, and so forth.

The general geometric interpretation of the linear-programming problem and of the simplex technique was first presented by Dantzig (1951*a*) and described in greater detail by Hoffman, Mannos, Sokolowsky, and Weigmann (1953). The geometric interpretation may be shown by means of the following simple linear-programming problem, taken from Churchman, Ackoff, and Arnoff (1957, Appendix 11B):

Determine: values of x and y which maximize

$$z = 2x + 5y$$

subject to: $x \leq 4$, $y \leq 3$, $x + 2y \leq 8$, $x \geq 0$, and $y \geq 0$.

The given set of restrictions are linear inequalities which define a convex set of points, namely, all points on or within the polygon *OABCD* of Fig. 4.1. A feasible solution to the linear-programming problem, that is, one that satisfies all of the given restrictions, will then be any of the infinity of points lying on or within the polygon *OABCD*.

As indicated in Fig. 4.2, the function $z = 2x + 5y$ is a one-parameter family of parallel straight lines such that the value of z increases as the line is displaced farther from the origin. The linear-programming problem, then, is to determine, from among the infinity of feasible points, the one or more points that will maximize $z = 2x + 5y$, that is, to determine that line segment of the family $z = 2x + 5y$ which is farthest

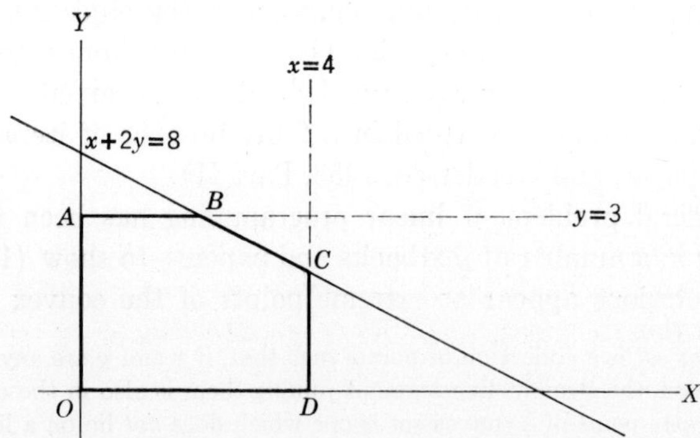

Fig. 4.1. Region satisfying restrictions.

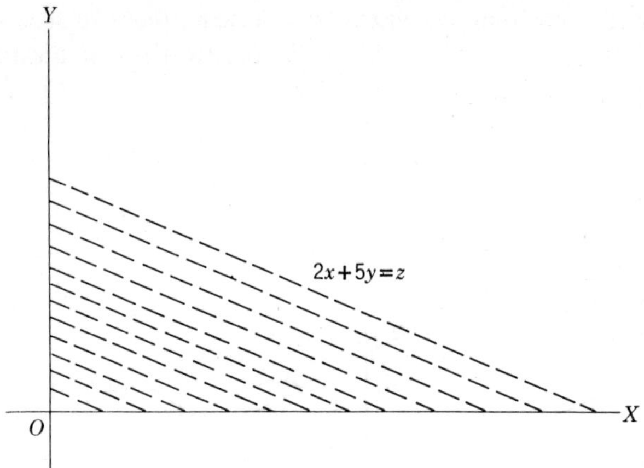

Fig. 4.2. Family of parallel straight lines, $z=2x+5y$.

from the origin but still contains at least one point of the polygon $OABCD$. The optimum solution is indicated in Fig. 4.3, namely, point $B(2,3)$.

If, in this illustrative problem, one wished to maximize $z=x+2y$ subject to the given set of restrictions, Fig. 4.4 shows how the optimum solution is then given by *either* of the extreme points B or C. This occurs because $x+2y=8$ is both a boundary line of the polygon $OABCD$ and a member of the family of parallel lines $z=x+2y$. In such cases, the points $B(2,3)$ and $C(4,2)$ both constitute solutions and, furthermore, any point on the line segment BC will also be an optimum solution. These points can be obtained by forming *convex linear combinations*[15] of B and C. That is, given $B=(2,3)$ and $C=(4,2)$, the set of optimum solutions will be given by all points (X,Y) such that

$$X=a(2)+(1-a)(4)$$

$$Y=a(3)+(1-a)(2)$$

for all a such that $0\leq a\leq 1$.

More generally, one can see that the optimum solution will always be found at an extreme point of the convex set. The simplex technique is based on this fact and, accordingly, enables one to converge (from

[15] A *convex linear combination* of $X_1,X_2,\cdots,X_n$ is given by

$$X = a_1X_1 + a_2X_2 + \cdots + a_nX_n$$

where $a_1,a_2,\cdots,a_n$ are any non-negative real numbers whose sum is unity.

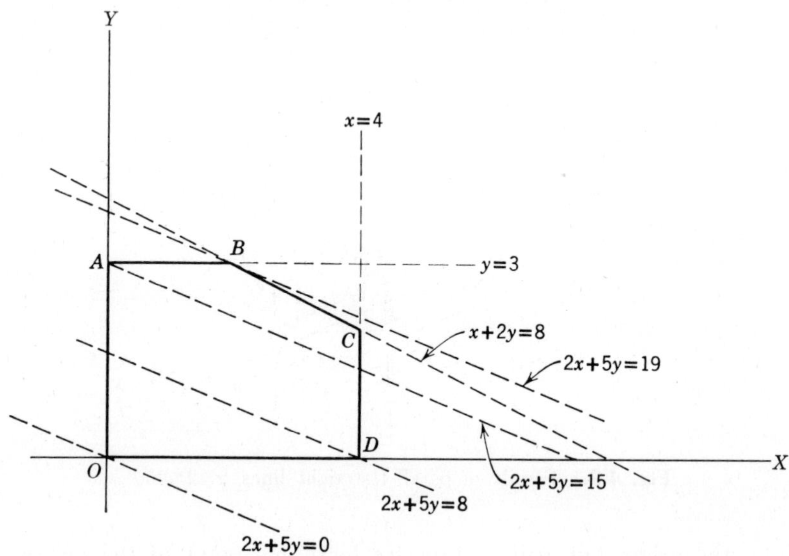

Fig. 4.3. Figure for geometric solution of linear-programming problem.

one extreme point to a "better" one) to the optimum solution in a finite number of steps.

For further discussion of the geometry of linear programming, see Churchman, Ackoff, and Arnoff (1957, Appendix 11B) and the exceptional "three-dimensional" drawings that appear in Vazsonyi (1958, Chapter 6).

3.2. Bounds on the Value of the Objective Function: Method of Partitions

One of the most important aspects of any operations research problem consists of obtaining order-of-magnitude estimates of the appropriate optimization functions. For example, in considering a particular problem area, one must have some knowledge of the potential gross gains to be realized as compared with the costs of obtaining these gains (namely, solving the problem). In many instances, the magnitude of the problem is such that the ability to obtain accurate estimates of the minimum cost, for example, might enable one to derive near-optimum decision rules by so-called "quick-and-dirty" methods. Furthermore, the marginal cost of deriving "optimum" decision rules (e.g., by the simplex technique) might very well exceed the corresponding added benefits!

For the linear-programming problem, Saaty (1955*a*, 1956, and 1959*a*) has developed a *method of partitions* whereby one is able to derive upper and lower bounds on the value of an objective function by solving a given linear-programming problem relative to subsets of the given constraints.

Saaty observes that increasing the number of constraints in a linear-programming problem monotonically increases the minimum value of the objective function. This follows from the fact that, given a set, S, of inequalities, and a larger (augmented) set, S', which is obtained by adding additional constraints to the original set (S), then the convex region determined by S will *contain* the convex region determined by S'. Hence, the minimum associated with S must be less than or equal to the minimum corresponding to S'. Similarly, the maximum value of the objective functions monotonically decreases as the number of constraints is increased. In other words, if P refers to the value of the objective function of the original problem, and P_i, to the value of the objective function for the ith subset of constraints, then:

$$\min P \geq \max_i (\min P_i) \tag{4.4}$$

and

$$\min (\max P_i) \geq \max P \tag{4.5}$$

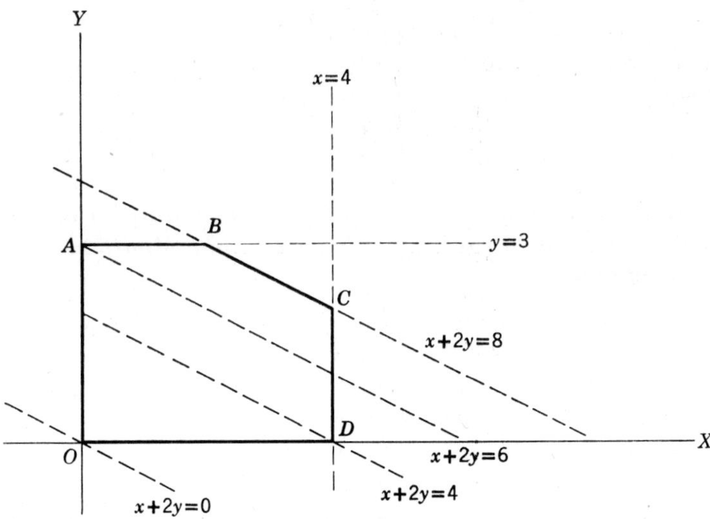

Fig. 4.4. Geometric solution of linear-programming problem with more than one optimum solution.

Saaty (1956) then suggests the following algorithm:

When minimizing, solve the linear-programming problems corresponding to subsets (partitions) of the constraints with the objective function of the original problem. For a lower bound to the minimum of the original problem, take the maximum of the minima obtained.

The sharpness of these bounds may, of course, be increased by considering a greater number of subsets. Furthermore, the "method of partitions" may be applied to the dual problem, thus possibly yielding further refinement.

3.3. The Number of Iterations in Simplex Solutions of the Linear-Programming Problem

An important question which continually arises—both in formulating a problem and stating the set of restrictions and also in solving the resulting linear-programming problem—concerns the number of iterations required to reach an optimum solution.

The number of iterations involved is, of course, a function of the particular problem being solved (e.g., the nature of the coefficients in the given restriction-matrix). However, an accepted rule-of-thumb is that the number, N, of iterations will be given approximately by

$$1.5m \leq N \leq 2m$$

where m is the number of restrictions.

Further insight into the number of iterations needed to solve a linear-programming problem by the simplex technique is provided by Saaty (1955*b*), who has determined upper bounds for the number of vertices of a polyhedron in n-dimensional space.

3.4. Round-Off Errors Arising in Computer Solutions of Linear-Programming Problems: Charnes-Lemke Modified Simplex Technique

In the simplex technique, *every* element of the simplex tableau is transformed (by means of the elimination formulas)—from one tableau (iteration) to the next. Thus, in the use of electronic computers, any error due to rounding-off a particular number can be greatly magnified in subsequent transformations, to the point where round-off errors accumulate and become so significant as to yield false results. For example, a non-optimum solution may appear to be optimum (due to errors in the criterion function $z_j - c_j$) while, on the other hand, an optimum solution may show up as non-optimum and, furthermore, additional iterations may result in a divergent value of the objective function. (For further discussion of how errors propagate, and the significance of such errors, see Jacobs, 1957.)

One can, of course, *start* with any solution as obtained from the computer solution, regenerate the correct elements of the tableau, and then proceed to further iterations, if needed. However, this is not always convenient or practical (see Churchman, Ackoff, and Arnoff, 1957, Appendix 11D).

To resolve the problem of round-off error, Charnes and Lemke (see Charnes and Lemke, 1952; Lemke and Charnes, 1953; and Lemke, 1954) developed a *modified simplex technique* which consists of using, at each stage, only (1) the inverse matrix of the *current* basis *and* (2) the *original* data (the P_j and c_j). The transformation formulas used in the modified simplex technique are the same as those in the original simplex technique. (However, again, these transformations are performed only on the current inverse matrix, and the original data.)

By means of the Charnes and Lemke modified simplex technique, control of round-off error is thus localized to control of errors in the inverse of the matrix of the basis at each stage. Furthermore, while round-off errors can accumulate in the current inverse matrix, standard methods are available for improving the accuracy of this matrix (that is, one can reduce the error at any given stage to an acceptable value, before proceeding further). Finally, in the modified simplex procedure, an initially sparse matrix (one with many zero elements) does not fill up with non-zero entries as one proceeds from iteration to iteration (as it does in the simplex procedure)—thus the amount of computation required here is generally less than that required for the simplex technique (see Lemke, 1954).

Modified simplex procedures quite similar to that of Charnes and Lemke were also suggested, discussed, and/or developed by others (Dantzig and Orden, 1952; Dantzig, 1953; Dantzig and Orchard-Hays, 1953; and Dantzig, Orden, and Wolfe, 1954). However, their initial interest in modifications to the simplex technique was apparently motivated by the question of degeneracy, rather than any consideration of control of round-off error.

3.5. *The Bounded-Variable Problem*

In a number of linear-programming problems, one is confronted by constraints on the variables of the form

$$x_j \leq d_j$$

Upper-limit constraints occur very frequently in problems involving, for example, capacity and/or sales limitations. Such constraints can, of course, be handled by the simplex procedure—simply by adding appropriate slack variables, y_j, to form a corresponding set of equations, $x_j + y_j = d_j$. However, in such cases, the size of the matrix and, hence, the computational requirements, can be greatly increased.

Charnes and Lemke (1954*a*) and Dantzig (1954*a* and 1955*a*) have developed a more efficient technique, which involves only a slight modification of either the regular simplex algorithm or the revised simplex algorithm and which enables one to solve the problem without explicitly including the upper-bound constraints in the restriction matrix.

Dantzig (1955*a*) notes that his procedure was developed by first solving the original problem (with upper bounds $x_j \leq d_j$ represented by $x_j + y_j = d_j$; x_j and y_j non-negative) by the simplex technique and then observing that certain computational simplifications could be obtained because the vector associated with each slack variable (y_j) is a unit vector.[16]

Based upon Dantzig's experience and other similar experiences, Gass suggests that "whenever one is faced with a new linear-programming model, one should construct numerical examples, arrange them in the simplex tableau, and solve the problems. An investigation of the computational tableaus might reveal hidden characteristics of the equations which could possibly lead to a special computing method" (Gass, 1958, p. 173).

The transportation problem with upper-bound constraints ($x_{ij} \leq d_{ij}$) has also received special treatment—by Dantzig (1956*b*), Ford and Fulkerson (1957) and Prager (1957*a*). This problem, called the *capacitated transportation*, or *capacitated Hitchcock problem*, is discussed in Section 4.4.

A full account of procedures to handle the bounded-variable linear-programming problem is also given in Charnes and Lemke (1954*a*).

[16] The upper-bound constraints are a special case of "block-triangularity." Dantzig, Charnes, Lemke, and others have developed a number of short-cut computational methods for solving block-triangular problems. These are discussed in Section 8.

4. TRANSPORTATION PROBLEMS

As noted earlier, the *transportation problem* is one of the subclasses of linear-programming problems for which simple and practical computational procedures have been developed that take advantage of the special structure of the problem. Several variations and generalizations in the formulation of transportation problems and methods which have been developed for solving them are presented here.

The transportation problem was presented in its standard or basic form in (P.2).

In formulating the transportation problem, the assumption $\sum_i a_i = \sum_j b_j$ may be satisfied indirectly because one can always arrive at the equality by adding either a "dummy origin" (for example, for the case: $\sum_i a_i < \sum_j b_j$) or a "dummy destination" (when $\sum_i a_i > \sum_j b_j$), as the case may be (Gass, 1958, p. 150). However, the assumption is required before one can apply any of the transportation algorithms.

Although in many formulations of the transportation problem, it is assumed that a_i, b_i, and c_{ij} are *all* non-negative integers, these assumptions are not really necessary. For example, Charnes and Cooper (1954*a*) exhibit and solve a simple transportation problem in which $c_{25} = -1$. However, by a simple linear transformation, one can obtain an associated cost K' for which all c_{ij}' are non-negative integers and for which the optimum solution for K' (i.e., those values of x_{ij} which yield the minimum cost for K') will also be the optimum solution for K. Furthermore, negative a_i or b_j simply mean that no feasible solutions exist, since all $x_{ij} \geq 0$, while non-integer values of a_i or b_j mean that non-integer values of x_{ij} are permissible. Usually one is interested only in integer values of x_{ij}, in which case the assumption that a_i, b_j, and c_{ij} are non-negative integers is *not* restrictive. This assumption is made for convenience and in order to be able to show that, for the standard transportation problem, one will always obtain integer solutions. Note, however, that in the generalized transportation problem, for example, non-integer solutions can result. However, as shown by Ferguson and Dantzig (1955), non-integer solutions can sometimes make sense—at least, such is the case in their particular aircraft-allocation example (see Section 4.3).

The transportation problem, often referred to as the Hitchcock-Koopmans transportation problem, was first formulated by Hitchcock (1941) and, later, independently, by Kantorovitch (1942) and Koopmans (1947). Hitchcock considered the problem of minimizing the cost of distributing a product from several factories to a number of cities. To solve this problem, Hitchcock outlined a constructive procedure (geometric approach) that closely resembles the simplex technique later developed by Dantzig in 1947 (see Dantzig, 1951*a*). During World War II, Koopmans (1947) and Koopmans and Reiter (1951) independently formulated (and solved—through a consideration of networks) the transportation problem in developing and discussing, in detail, a model of transportation—in the context of transporting cargoes on ocean-going ships.

In 1951, Dantzig (1951*b*) formulated the transportation problem as a special linear-programming problem and then developed a special form of the simplex technique for solving such problems. Now known as the transportation technique, Dantzig's solution procedure takes advantage of the special nature (structure) of the coefficient matrix and provides a procedure for readily solving transportation-type problems involving hundreds of equations (restrictions) in thousands of unknowns. An excellent exposition of Dantzig's transportation technique, using what has been called the "row-value, column-value approach" or the "row-column sum calculation method," may be found in Gass (1958), Henderson and Schlaifer (1954), and Vazsonyi (1958) (see also Section 4.3).

An alternative method for solving transportation problems, often referred to as the "stepping-stone method," was developed by Charnes and Cooper (1954*a*) and has special merit in explaining both the structure of the problem and the relationship of the transportation technique to the general simplex technique (see appendix in Charnes and Cooper, 1954*a*). Charnes and Cooper (1954*a*) also formalized the procedure suggested by Dantzig (1951*b*) for obtaining an initial feasible solution to the problem by developing what they call the "northwest-corner rule."

Considered separately, Dantzig's procedure has certain advantages for large-scale hand computations; however, a *combination* of the two procedures makes possible greater speed in obtaining an optimal solution.

In 1955, there appeared several papers by Kuhn (1955*a* and 1955*b*) and Flood (1955) on solving the assignment problem by the so-called "Hungarian method"—namely one utilizing a procedure of matrix reduction in which successive transformations (subtraction of constants) on the rows and columns of the matrix of coefficients yield a completely reduced matrix in which a set of zeros identifies the optimal solution (see Section 5). Shortly after these papers appeared, a number of persons readily recognized the ability to generalize and extend the "Hungarian method" to one which would solve the Hitchcock-Koopmans transportation problem. Friedman (1955), for example, combined a method for reducing matrices (quite similar to that used by Flood, 1955) with the notion of a covering of zeros by *weighted* lines, in which the transportation problem is essentially *visualized* as an $N \times N$ assignment problem, where $N = \sum_i a_i = \sum_j b_j$. Other developers of reduced-matrix methods of solution include Dwyer (1955), who, with Galler (Galler and Dwyer, 1957), also considered the application of reduced-matrix methods to multi-index transportation problems (see Section 4.6).

All reduced-matrix procedures for solving the transportation problem are alike in their notion of reducing the coefficient matrix to one in which a set of zeros identifies the optimal solution. However, they differ with respect to the criterion of optimality—that is, the specific criteria to be used to determine whether or not the set of zeros at any given stage will yield the optimum solution.[17] Friedman's condition of optimality is quite similar to that used in solving the assignment problem—namely, it is based upon the König-Egerváry theorem (see König, 1916, and Egerváry, 1931) regarding the minimum number of covering lines (see also, Kuhn, 1955*a*). However, a criterion of optimality which seems easiest to use is one that does *not* use any lines and, hence, avoids the problem (discussed by Friedman) of how one goes about drawing a minimum number of such lines. Rather, it uses the notion of "weighted zeros" which might be illustrated by the following example (next page) (taken from Churchman, Ackoff, and Arnoff, 1957, p. 284), in which the matrix elements ($c_{11} = 9$, $c_{12} = 10$, $c_{13} = 0$, etc.) represent the cost matrix resulting from one matrix reduction (by columns).

[17] Note that, unlike the standard linear-programming procedures, which consider improvements from one *feasible* solution to another (until the optimal solution is reached), the method of reduced matrices does *not* concern itself with intermediate feasible solutions but, rather, concentrates on matrix transformations which introduce additional zero terms until the desirable set of zeros is reached.

Origins	Destinations					Availa-bilities a_i	Zero Weights r_i
	D_1	D_2	D_3	D_4	D_5		
S_1	9	10	0	0	6	9	10
S_2	1	0	3	21	2	4	5
S_3	0	10	2	1	0	8	6
Requirements c_j	3	5	4	6	3		
Zero Weights k_j	8	4	9	9	8		

After having introduced at least one zero into each row and each column, and at any stage thereafter, compute, for each row and column, zero-weights r_i and k_j, respectively. For each row, determine r_i by [18]

$$r_i = \sum_{j \in J} b_j \tag{4.6}$$

where $J = \{j \mid c_{ij}' = 0 \text{ for the given } i\}$ and c_{ij}' are the coefficients at that stage.

For example, when $i=1$, $c_{13}'=c_{14}'=0$. Hence:

$$r_1 = b_3 + b_4 = 4 + 6 = 10$$

Similarly:

$$r_2 = b_2 = 5$$

and

$$r_3 = b_1 + b_5 = 3 + 3 = 6$$

For each column, determine k_j by

$$k_j = \sum_{i \in I} a_i \tag{4.7}$$

[18] J is the set of all j such that $c_{ij}'=0$, for the given i. Furthermore, the symbol "$\in$" denotes "belongs to."

where $I = \{i \mid c_{ij}' = 0$ for the given $j\}$ and c_{ij}' are the coefficients at that stage. Hence:

$$k_1 = a_3 = 3$$

$$k_2 = a_2 = 4$$

$$k_3 = a_1 = 9$$

$$k_4 = a_1 = 9$$

and

$$k_5 = a_3 = 8$$

Having computed these zero weights for each row and column, one can now determine whether or not one has an optimum solution, since *any given set of zeros will identify the optimum solution if and only if:*

1. $r_i \geq a_i$ $(i = 1, 2, \cdots, m)$,
2. $k_j \geq b_j$ $(j = 1, 2, \cdots, n)$,
3. at least one of the above inequalities is a *strict* inequality, *and*
4. the "solution" does not contain any non-feasible partitions.

If one does not have an optimum solution at any stage, that is, if $(a_i - r_i) > 0$ and/or $(b_j - k_j) > 0$ for some i and/or j, one can proceed towards the optimum solution by next introducing additional zeros into that row or column which has the greatest deficiency [that is, into that row i or column j for which $(a_i - r_i)$ or $(b_j - k_j)$ is greatest].

For obtaining optimum solutions to transportation problems "by hand," this method of reduced matrices is by far the simplest of all developed to date, and is much quicker than either the Dantzig or Charnes-Cooper procedures, used separately or jointly. However, the latter procedures must still be used in any full treatment of transportation problems where one seeks, not only optimum solutions, but also opportunity costs, costs associated with alternative choices, and so forth.

A number of other procedures for solving the Hitchcock-Koopmans transportation problem were developed by Vidale (1956), Camp (1957), Gleyzal (1955), Suzuki (1955), Ford and Fulkerson (1956), Gerstenhaber and Kelley (1956), Kelley (1957), Prager (1957*a*), and others.

Ford and Fulkerson (1956) developed a procedure for solving the transportation problem by extending a simple algorithm that they had first developed to determine maximal flows in a network (Ford and Fulkerson, 1955). Their procedure is based upon (1) a combinatorial method developed by Kuhn (1955*a* and 1955*b*) for solving the assignment problem (discussed in Section 5), (2) what Ford and Fulkerson called a "labeling process" for solving maximal flow network problems (see Ford and Fulkerson, 1955, and Fulkerson and Dantzig, 1955), and (3) the *dual* transportation problem, namely:

Given:

$$a_i,\ b_j,\ \text{and}\ c_{ij} \qquad (i=1,2,\cdots,m;\ j=1,2,\cdots,n)$$

Determine:

$$\alpha_i, \beta_j \quad \text{which}$$

maximize: (P.10)

$$W=\sum_{i=1}^{m} a_i\alpha_i+\sum_{j=1}^{n} b_j\beta_j$$

subject to:

$$\alpha_i+\beta_j \leq c_{ij} \qquad (i=1,2,\cdots,m;\ j=1,2,\cdots,n)$$

The Ford-Fulkerson "network" procedure is very efficient for "hand solution" of the transportation problem, although not quite as efficient as the method of reduced matrices discussed above. For a good illustration of this procedure, see Vajda (1958, p. 36), in addition to Ford and Fulkerson (1956) (see also Section 4.4).

Vidale (1956) presents a simple graphical procedure which yields a solution "as accurate as required" for the special transportation problem in which the unit transportation costs are monotonically increasing as one moves out from a given production center. (The *rate of increase*, however, need not be constant or uniform in all directions.)

Camp (1957) presents a set-theoretical generalization of the graphical method of Vidale which "eliminates his (Vidale's) topological difficulties and his restriction to unit costs which depend only on the geographical locations of customers and stations" (p. 297).

Suzuki (1955) developed a procedure—based on Dantzig's simplex technique—that is readily adaptable to high-speed digital computers and which, in fact, is now being used for the solution of the Hitchcock-Koopmans transportation problem on the Univac I and Model 1103 computers.

4.1. Approximation Procedures

Starting with a good first approximation to the solution significantly reduces the amount of computation required to obtain a solution and, fortunately, research has yielded a number of excellent approximation procedures to accomplish this gain. All are alike in that, once having obtained a "good" approximation, one then proceeds to the optimum solution by one of the now-standard transportation techniques.

A very fast approximation method involves selecting, first, the cell with lowest unit cost (in the entire cost matrix) and inserting the largest permissible number of units into that cell, that is, the smaller of the amount available and the amount required. One then proceeds along that same row, if the total amount available has not been used (or column, if the requirement has not been fully met) to the second lowest cost, and so forth. While usually quite efficient, this procedure completely ignores the essential fact that one must consider the *differences* in unit costs between alternative allocations in any row or any column, rather than the costs themselves (this is dramatized so effectively by the method of reduced matrices).

Houthakker (1955) developed a systematic trial-and-error procedure for obtaining a good first approximation to the solution and then improving it by successive adjustments.

A very effective and efficient approximation method—one that will very often yield the optimum solution immediately—is one in which one begins by considering the "first differences" in each row and column, that is, the differences between the lowest available unit cost and second lowest available unit cost in each row and column. Then, one selects that cell which has the least unit cost in the row or column with the *greatest* first difference, and proceeds to repeat this procedure for what is, in effect, a matrix of reduced dimensions. For a full explanation and illustration, see Sasieni, Yaspan, and Friedman (1959, pp. 198–201).

4.2. Transportation Problems with Non-Constant Unit Costs

In the classical Hitchcock-Koopmans transportation problem, it is assumed that unit transportation costs are independent of the amount shipped over any given route. Prager (1956*a*) has considered the case where the specific shipping cost for a route increases linearly with the amount shipped over this route and discusses the optimum solution in terms of either flows along the routes or accounting prices at the centers of production and consumption. Prager also establishes a maximum principle for the accounting prices which leads to a maximum characterization of the cost of the optimum program.

Vidale (1956) has outlined a non-converging successive-approximation procedure for the cases where:

1. Unit production cost varies with the source, but not with the *level* of production.

2. Unit production cost varies with the source, *and* with the level of production.

Shetty (1959) has considered the transportation problem with *non*-linear costs and developed criteria for an optimum solution and an iterative procedure for moving towards an optimal solution. Shetty also considers the case where the availability at each of the sources is fixed, but the demands are not known except by a probability distribution.

Variations in the transportation problem of the foregoing types are, of course, very realistic and of frequent occurrence in industry; hence, much more needs to be accomplished in this particular area (i.e., non-constant unit costs).

4.3. The Generalized Transportation Problem

Ferguson and Dantzig (1955) have considered the following *generalized* transportation problem:

Given:

$$a_i, b_j, c_{ij}, p_{ij} \qquad (i=1,2,\cdots,m;\ j=1,2,\cdots,n)$$

Determine:

$$x_{ij} \geq 0 \quad \text{which}$$

minimize:

$$K = \sum_{i,j} c_{ij} x_{ij} \tag{P.11}$$

subject to:

$$\sum_{j=1}^{n} x_{ij} = a_i \qquad (i=1,2,\cdots,m)$$

$$\sum_{i=1}^{m} p_{ij} x_{ij} = b_j \qquad (j=1,2,\cdots,n)$$

This problem (which obviously reduces to the Hitchcock-Koopmans transportation problem when all $p_{ij}=1$) is treated by Ferguson and Dantzig in the context of allocating passenger aircraft (i) to routes (j), where the p_{ij} are the number of passengers that the ith plane can carry on the jth route, a_i are the number of available aircraft of the ith type, b_j are the passenger demands (requirements) for the jth route, x_{in} denotes the surplus aircraft of the ith type, and x_{mj} denotes the number of passengers turned away on the jth route.

For the *standard* Hitchcock-Koopmans transportation problem, Dantzig (1951*b*) determines row values u_i and column values v_j for the feasible solution corresponding to each iteration such that

$$u_i + v_j = c_{ij} \tag{4.8}$$

for "basic" cells, that is, for (i,j) cells corresponding to $x_{ij}>0$. He then evaluates the "opportunity costs," e_{ij}, for all other cells by [19]

$$e_{ij}=c_{ij}-(u_i+v_j) \tag{4.9}$$

Then, the feasible solution is optimal if and only if $e_{ij}\geq 0$.

In the *generalized* transportation problem, row values u_i and column values v_j are computed such that [20]

$$\begin{aligned} u_i+p_{ij}v_j&=c_{ij} \\ u_m&=0 \\ v_n&=0 \end{aligned} \tag{4.10}$$

for basic cells, and the evaluations, e_{ij}, are computed for all other cells by [21]

$$e_{ij}=c_{ij}-(u_i+p_{ij}v_j) \tag{4.11}$$

The solution is then optimal if and only if $e_{ij}\geq 0$.

Ferguson and Dantzig have then extended their procedure to consider the case where there is *uncertain customer demand* (represented by the b_j), but where the frequency distribution of demand is known. The computational procedure is similar to the fixed-demand case, with only slightly more computational effort required. The theoretical development of their procedure is given in Ferguson and Dantzig (1955), while the illustration of linear programming under uncertain demand for the particular example of allocating aircraft to passenger routes is given in Ferguson and Dantzig (1956) (see also Section 12).

Markowitz (1954) has considered and developed computational procedures for a "slightly-generalized" transportation problem which turns out to be a special case of the generalized transportation problem. Called the "metal-processing" problem (see Dantzig, 1956*b*), it results from the generalized transportation problem when $c_{ij}=c_i$. More specifically, in this special problem, involving the use of the ith machine to produce the jth task, the cost of using one unit of the ith machine

[19] If, as in some references, the costs are expressed as $-c_{ij}$, where $c_{ij}\geq 0$, then the evaluations will be given by $e_{ij}'=-e_{ij}$, so that the conditions of optimality remain unchanged.

[20] How these formulas follow directly from the *dual* formulation of the generalized transportation problem is shown in Vazsonyi (1958, p. 161 ff.).

[21] If, as in some references, the costs are expressed as $-c_{ij}$, where $c_{ij}>0$, then the evaluations will be given by $e_{ij}'=-e_{ij}$ so that the conditions of optimality remain unchanged.

is (assumed to be) independent of the task, j, to be performed on that machine.

As Dantzig (1956*b*) notes, a special electronic computer code has been developed at the RAND Corporation which can solve a metal-processing problem of three-hundred equations in approximately one hour.

4.4. The Capacitated Transportation Problem

An important transportation-type problem is one in which there exist capacity constraints on the given routes. Such a problem is called the *capacitated transportation* or *capacitated Hitchcock problem* and may be formulated mathematically as:

Given:

$$a_i,\ b_j,\ c_{ij},\ \text{and}\ d_{ij} \qquad (i=1,2,\cdots,m;\ j=1,2,\cdots,n)$$

Determine:

$$x_{ij} \quad \text{which}$$

minimize:

$$K=\sum_{i\ j} c_{ij}x_{ij}$$

subject to: (P.12)

$$\sum_{j=1}^{n} x_{ij}=a_i \qquad (i=1,2,\cdots,m)$$

$$\sum_{i=1}^{m} x_{ij}=b_j \qquad (j=1,2,\cdots,n)$$

$$\sum_i a_i=\sum_j b_j=N$$

and

$$0\leq x_{ij}\leq d_{ij}$$

That is, the *capacitated* transportation problem is a transportation problem in which one must *also* satisfy the restrictions

$$x_{ij}\leq d_{ij} \tag{4.12}$$

on the solution-variables.

Capacitated transportation problems can be solved by standard transportation techniques—by introducing non-negative slack variables y_{ij} and adding extra equations of the form

$$x_{ij}+y_{ij}=d_{ij} \tag{4.13}$$

to represent the upper-bound constraints. However, as Dantzig (1956*b*) points out, this greatly enlarges the size of the problem. For example, a problem with 18 sources (availabilities) and 10 sinks (requirements) has a total of 28 equations in 180 unknowns. However, after adding upper-bound constraints on the x_{ij}, the problem "explodes" into one of 208 (28+180) equations in 360 (2×180) unknowns.

By means of Orden's transshipment device (see Section 4.5), Dantzig (1956*b*) proved that capacity constraints on routes (given by $x_{ij} \leq d_{ij}$) do *not* alter the character of the problem, that is, that the problem is still a transportation problem. Dantzig then developed a simple modification of the transportation algorithm to solve the constrained problem. Specifically, Dantzig (1956*b*) divides the variables x_{ij} into three classes:

1. Basic variables ($m+n-1$ in number) whose determinant is non-vanishing (that is, those x_{ij} for which $0 < x_{ij} < d_{ij}$).
2. Non-basic variables, x_{ij}, such that $x_{ij}=0$ (lower limit).
3. Non-basic variables, x_{ij}, such that $x_{ij}=d_{ij}$ (upper limit).

The "prices" u_i and v_j associated with any feasible solution are then computed as for the Hitchcock transportation problem, namely:

$$u_i+v_j=c_{ij} \tag{4.8}$$

for all basic variables. The criterion for optimality then becomes:

i. $u_i+v_j \geq c_{ij}$ for all non-basic variables x_{ij} at the lower limit (i.e., Class 2 variables).

ii. $u_i+v_j \leq c_{ij}$ for all non-basic variables x_{ij} at the upper limit (i.e., Class 3 variables).

If any x_{ij} does not satisfy the optimality criterion, an improved solution may be obtained by increasing or decreasing that value of x_{ij} until some variable (including, possibly, that particular x_{ij}) reaches either a lower or an upper bound. This latter variable is then dropped from the basis.

Ford and Fulkerson (1957) have developed a computationally efficient primal-dual algorithm for solving the capacitated transportation problem. The primal-dual algorithm was first proposed by Dantzig, Ford, and Fulkerson (1956) for solving the general linear-programming problem. (This latter primal-dual algorithm is, in turn, an extension and generalization of the Ford-Fulkerson "network" procedure initially devised for the Hitchcock transportation problem. See Sections 4 and 7). For the general linear-programming problem, one starts with a feasible solution to the *dual* problem. Then, associated with the dual solution is a "restricted" primal problem that requires optimization by the simplex technique. When accomplished, an improved solution to the dual system can then be obtained. This, in turn, gives rise to a new restricted problem to be optimized. After a finite number of improvements of the dual, an optimal solution is obtained for both the primal and dual systems (see Dantzig, Ford, and Fulkerson, 1956).

For the transportation problem, the optimization of the restricted primal problem can be accomplished without using the simplex procedure. Furthermore, the *capacitated* transportation problem can readily be handled in a manner quite similar to that for the regular (i.e., uncapacitated) transportation problem, the main difference being that one now considers the following dual problem (instead of that given in Section 4 for the standard transportation problem):

Given:

$$a_i,\ b_j,\ c_{ij},\ \text{and } d_{ij}$$

Determine:

$$\alpha_i,\ \beta_j,\ \text{and } \delta_{ij} \quad \text{which}$$

maximize: (P.13)

$$W=\sum_{i=1}^{m} a_i\alpha_i+\sum_{j=1}^{n} b_j\beta_j+\sum_{i,j} d_{ij}\delta_{ij}$$

subject to:

$$\delta_{ij}+\alpha_i+\beta_j\leq c_{ij}$$

$$\delta_{ij}\leq 0$$

The algorithm for the capacitated transportation problem is given in Ford and Fulkerson (1957).

Prager (1957*a*) has considered a capacitated transportation problem concerned with the "steady flow" of a homogeneous product from several production centers to numerous consumption centers. Specifically, Prager's problem may be stated as follows:

Given: either the price *or* the rate of production or consumption at each center,
Determine: the other prices and rates at the centers and the flow rates along the routes such that:

i. No route carries a negative flow or a flow in excess of its capacity.

ii. The total amount shipped from each production center per unit of time, or received at each consumption center per unit of time, equals the rate of production or consumption at this center.

iii. The price differential for a given shipping route is not larger than, equal to, or not smaller than the specific shipping cost for this route, according to whether the route carries zero flow, positive flow below capacity, or capacity flow.

Prager then develops a numerical method for solving such problems which is similar to, and a generalization of, the Ford-Fulkerson "network" method for solving the Hitchcock transportation problem.

4.5. *The Transshipment Problem*

The Hitchcock-Koopmans transportation problem is basically one of determining the optimum allocation or shipment of commodities from given origins to given destinations. In such problems, the possibility of transshipment (that is, permitting any origin or destination to also act as an intermediate point) is precluded—at least, with respect to the computational algorithms and procedures discussed so far.

Orden (1956) has extended the Hitchcock transportation problem to include the possibility of transshipment and shows how to solve the transshipment problem by a very simple extension to the method for solving the direct-shipment (i.e., non-transshipment) transportation problem. Basically, this involves, first, setting up the transshipment "unit cost" matrix, which can be thought of as an *augmented* transportation problem matrix where one adds to the rows (columns) those destinations (origins) which can also serve as intermediate stops. Then, secondly, since such intermediate stops, as such, have no requirements, one insures the *possibility* of transshipment by adding to all source availabilities and destination requirements a number large enough to cover all possible transshipments. (The solution will not be changed by adding these availabilities and requirements since $c_{ii}=0$).

An excellent and brief illustration of Orden's transshipment device is given in Vajda (1958).

Orden (1956) has proved that the transshipment problem requires no additional paths than would be required if only direct shipment were permitted (that is, both problems use $m+n-1$ paths, for m origins and n destinations in the original direct-shipment problem).

Orden (1956) has also shown how, by using the transshipment technique, one can find the shortest route from one point in a network to another, so that one can insert appropriate *minimal* unit costs in the coefficient (cost) matrix and transform the transshipment problem of size $(m+n)\times(m+n)$ into an equivalent one of size $m\times n$.

4.6. *Multi-Index Transportation Problems*

The Hitchcock-Koopmans transportation problem is usually conceived of as a *two*-dimensional problem. Schell, Galler, Dwyer and others have considered the *multi-index* transportation problem, which can be thought of as an n-dimensional problem, where $n\geq 3$. In such problems, the central variables are of the form $x_{ij\cdots k}$, rather than x_{ij} as in the Hitchcock transportation problem. Schell (1955) has considered the three-dimensional transportation problem in the context of a soap manufacturer with l factories (index i), m types of soap (index k), and n non-overlapping sales areas (index j), and considers unit costs, c_{ijk}, which might include such items as raw-materials costs (if different from plant to plant), variable manufacturing costs, shipping costs to the jth area, and local-advertising costs.

Schell considers four cases of the three-dimensional problem, as represented by the nature of the given restrictions, namely:

1. Three planar sums.
2. Two planar sums.
3. One planar and one axial sum.
4. Three axial sums.

For the case of *three planar sums*, the problem may be stated:

Determine:

$$x_{ijk} \geq 0 \qquad \begin{cases} i=1,2,\cdots,l \\ j=1,2,\cdots,n \\ k=1,2,\cdots,m \end{cases}$$

which minimize:

$$K = \sum_{i,j,k} c_{ijk} x_{ijk} \tag{P.14}$$

subject to:

$$\sum_i x_{ijk} = a_{jk}, \quad \sum_j x_{ijk} = b_{ik}, \quad \sum_k x_{ijk} = d_{ij}$$

$$\sum_k b_{ik} = \sum_j d_{ij}, \quad \sum_i d_{ij} = \sum_k a_{jk}, \quad \sum_j a_{jk} = \sum_i b_{ik}$$

where a_{jk}, b_{ik}, d_{ij}, and c_{ijk} are given non-negative integers.

Schell shows that the above-stated three-dimensional transportation problem will have at most $lmn-(l-1)(m-1)(n-1)$ independent relations and, accordingly, the minimum number of zero entries will be given by the symmetric functions with alternating signs:

$$lmn-(mn+nl+ml)+(l+m+n)-1$$

and states that these results can be generalized to higher dimensional problems. Schell further shows that, unlike the two-dimensional case, feasible solutions do not always exist, but develops a procedure for constructing an initial basic feasible solution, *if one exists.* Finally, for a *particular* example, Schell shows how to proceed from a basic feasible solution to the optimum feasible solution, using a slight generalization of the Dantzig transportation technique (see Dantzig, 1951*b*, and Section 4.3).

By means of his example, Schell illustrates quite dramatically that the greater the number of restrictions, the greater will be the minimum value of the objective function.

A *general* technique for solving this k-dimensional transportation problem ($k \geq 3$) is not available as yet. Furthermore, little is known about the properties of solutions to the k-dimensional problem other than, as shown by Motzkin (1952*b*), one cannot be assured of integral solutions even though the given constants a_{jk}, b_{ik}, and d_{ij} are integer-valued (see Gass, 1958, p. 178).

The problem with *three axial sums* is to:

Determine:

$$x_{ijk} \geq 0 \qquad \begin{cases} i=1,2,\cdots,l \\ j=1,2,\cdots,n \\ k=1,2,\cdots,m \end{cases}$$

which minimize:

$$K = \sum_{i,j,k} c_{ijk} x_{ijk} \tag{P.15}$$

subject to:

$$\sum_{j,k} x_{ijk} = a_i, \quad \sum_{i,k} x_{ijk} = b_j, \quad \sum_{i,j} x_{ijk} = d_k$$

$$\sum_i a_i = \sum_j b_j = \sum_k d_k = N$$

Schell (1955) shows how one can proceed to an optimum solution of this problem by a procedure quite similar to that used in two-dimensional problems.

For the problem with *two planar sums,* Schell shows how it reduces to l separate two-dimensional problems which are, of course, easily solved. Similarly, Schell shows that the problem with *one planar and one axial sum* reduces to one two-dimensional problem of dimensions $m \times ln$.

Galler and Dwyer (1957) have translated Dwyer's method of reduced matrices (Dwyer, 1955) for the solution of the Hitchcock transportation problem into a workable electronic computer program. They then propose a procedure for solving the special class of k-dimensional multi-index problems ($k \geq 2$) which, for $k=3$, yields the above three-dimensional axial-sum transportation problem. Furthermore, they state that the machine process that they have developed is the same for $k=2,3,4,\cdots$.

Galler and Dwyer concentrate their discussion on the three-dimensional axial-sum problem and first observe that an *algebraic* solution of the given constraints might yield negative values. They then show how one can eliminate negative solutions and arrive at a non-negative—but not necessarily integral—solution of the given problem.

They then set forth a suggested procedure for eliminating fractional solutions; that is, for obtaining non-negative integer-valued solutions. However, counter-examples have since been developed to show that the Galler-Dwyer procedure (which has been programmed for the IBM-704) does not always yield integer solutions. However, on the other hand, it now appears that one *can* obtain non-negative integer-valued solutions by combining the Galler-Dwyer reduced-matrix procedure with the Gomory (1958*a*) integer-value algorithm (see Section 11).

4.7. Multistage Transportation Problems

Another very important class of linear-programming problems is the multistage transportation problem in which one includes the effect of *time* into the statement and solution of the problem, thus giving rise to what has also been called *dynamic* transportation problems. Special multistage linear-programming problems include (1) the caterer problem, (2) the warehouse problem, and (3) the production-smoothing problem. These three classes of multistage linear-programming problems are especially significant in that they have been shown to be equivalent to, or special cases of, the Hitchcock-Koopmans transportation problem and, furthermore, computational techniques or procedures have been developed to take advantage of the special form or structure of the coefficient matrix.

Multistage linear-programming problems are discussed in detail in Section 8. See also Dantzig (1959).

Another type of multistage (or dynamic) transportation problem is that formulated by Heller (1952) and extended by Kelley (1955). The problem, which arose in connection with routing Navy tankers, differs from the classical Hitchcock-Koopmans problem in that there are *two* sets of port requirements to be satisfied—one associated with a short period of time, the other with a longer period of time containing the first.

The Heller problem may be stated as:

Determine:

$$x_{ij} \geq 0 \text{ and } y_{ij} \geq 0 \qquad (i=1,2,\cdots,m;\ j=1,2,\cdots,n) \quad \text{which}$$

minimize:

$$K=\sum_{i\,j} c_{ij}(x_{ij}+y_{ij})$$

subject to:

$$\sum_j y_{ij} \geq a_i \tag{P.16}$$

$$\sum_i y_{ij} \leq b_j$$

$$\sum_j (x_{ij}+y_{ij}) = A_i$$

$$\sum_i (x_{ij}+y_{ij}) = B_j$$

Kelley notes that the method proposed by Heller appears to be computationally infeasible for most problems, and then develops his own method for solving what he calls "an extension of the Heller problem," namely, where the m conditions $\sum_j y_{ij} \geq a_i$ are replaced by the m equalities $\sum_j y_{ij} = a_i$, for each $i = 1,2,\cdots,m$. Kelley then shows how all of the restrictions can be transformed to yield a problem equivalent to a subsystem of the Hitchcock-Koopmans transportation problem and, hence, one solvable by one of the many available solution methods.

5. THE ASSIGNMENT PROBLEM

The *assignment problem*, sometimes called the *personnel-assignment problem*, is another special case of the transportation problem. Mathematically, this problem has been stated in P.3.[22] We observe that the assignment problem is the special case of the transportation problem which arises when $a_i = b_j = 1$, for all i and all j.

Although the assignment problem can be solved as a transportation problem, special, and preferable, computational procedures have been developed for this particular class of problems. Dwyer (1954) and Votaw and Orden (1952) have developed rapid, not necessarily optimal methods for solving the assignment problem. Von Neumann (1953) treated the assignment problem by an equivalent zero-sum two-person game. Here, von Neumann showed that the $n \times n$ assignment problem is equivalent to a $2n \times n^2$ zero-sum (two-person) game, and suggested that one obtain significant approximate solutions by the differential-equation method of Brown and von Neumann (1950).

Flood (1952) has solved the degenerate case of the transportation problem and, hence, also the assignment problem as a special case of

[22] The restrictions $x_{ij} = x_{ij}^2$ are included to insure that the solution is integer-valued, namely, in this case, either 0 or 1. However, the solution techniques are such that integer solutions are always obtained.

degeneracy, as an extension of the graph-theoretic methods of Koopmans and Reiter (1951) for the non-degenerate case.

Robinson (1949) solved the assignment problem while seeking a solution to the traveling-salesman problem (see Section 6).

Dantzig (1951*b*), Flood (1952), and von Neumann (1953) have all stressed the computational advantages to be gained in considering the assignment problem in combination with the dual linear-programming problem. Kuhn (1955*a*) has developed a computational method—called the "Hungarian method"—that uses this duality in a particularly effective manner.

Kuhn first treated the assignment problem for the case of only two ratings, 1 and 0 (indicating, respectively, that a worker is, or is not, qualified)—using a proof due to König (1916). Then, using results due to Egerváry (1931), he showed that the general assignment problem can be very easily reduced to this special case. Using the dual problem formulation, he also derived the "Hungarian method" algorithm for solving the assignment problem. Flood (1956) later expressed the Hungarian method of Kuhn in terms of a reduced matrix algorithm which utilizes König's theorem regarding the minimum number of covering lines (i.e., horizontal or vertical lines that include all zero elements of a given reduced matrix). The Hungarian method remains today the best procedure for solving the assignment problem. For an excellent illustration and application of the "Hungarian method," see Friedman and Yaspan (1957).

If, in the assignment problem, different individuals have essentially similar "efficiency" ratings, c_{ij}, so that these men can be grouped into personnel categories, and if there are identical or sufficiently similar jobs, demanding essentially the same qualifications, which can be grouped into job categories, then the resulting problem is a "general" personnel-assignment problem that is *exactly* a transportation problem. Here, a_i denotes the number of men in the ith personnel category and b_j denotes the number of jobs in the jth category. Matrix-reduction methods for solving the transportation problem have already been discussed in Section 4. Hence, the extensions of the Kuhn "Hungarian method," discussed in Section 4, can also be used to solve the "general" personnel-assignment problem.

6. THE TRAVELING-SALESMAN PROBLEM

Still another important special form of the linear-programming problem appears as the *traveling-salesman problem.* This problem takes its name from the often cited illustration of the traveling salesman who, starting from home, must visit each of $n-1$ specified cities before returning home, and at the same time must "optimize" the *tour,* or sequence of cities visited. For example, he must determine that tour which will minimize some quantity such as distance traveled or total travel time.

The traveling-salesman problem may be stated as follows:

Determine:

$$x_{ij} \qquad (i,j=1,2,\cdots,n) \quad \text{which}$$

minimize:

$$T=\sum_{i\,j} a_{ij}x_{ij}$$

subject to:

$$\begin{aligned} x_{ij}&=x_{ij}^2 \\ \sum_i x_{ij}=\sum_j x_{ij}&=1 \qquad \text{(P.17)} \\ x_{i_1i_2}+x_{i_2i_3}+\cdots+x_{i_{r-1}i_r}+x_{i_ri_1}&\leq r-1 \\ x_{ii}&=0 \end{aligned}$$

where a_{ij} are given real numbers, and $(i_1,i_2,\cdots,i_r)$ is a permutation of the integers 1 through r.

Stated another way, the traveling-salesman problem is one of finding a permutation $P=(1,i_2,i_3,\cdots,i_n)$ of the integers from 1 through n such that, given a set of real numbers $a_{\alpha\beta}$ (representing distances or travel times between pairs of cities, α and β), the quantity

$$a_{1i_2}+a_{i_2i_3}+\cdots+a_{i_n1}$$

is minimized. In the traveling-salesman problem, the permutation P must be cyclic, while in the assignment problem P may also be non-cyclic. Furthermore, a solution of the assignment problem will also be a solution of the traveling-salesman problem if and only if there is a symmetric permutation of the rows and columns of the coefficient matrix such that the slant elements are all zero (see Flood, 1956). For example, the solution $x_{12}=x_{21}=x_{34}=x_{43}=1$ for a 4×4 assignment problem is *not* a solution of the four-city traveling-salesman problem. In the latter case, the "solution" gives two subtours, (1,2) and (3,4), rather than one complete tour, as required.

Since there are a *finite* number of possibilities [$\frac{1}{2}(n-1)!$ for the symmetric ($a_{ij}=a_{ji}$) traveling-salesman problem, and $(n-1)!$ for the non-symmetric case], the computational problem is really one of devising an *efficient* method for selecting the optimum sequence, or permutation, for large values of n.[23]

The origin of the traveling-salesman problem is rather obscure, with mathematicians apparently having discussed it informally for many years. The problem is closely related to several problems considered by Hamilton, including what Ball (1939) termed the "Hamiltonian game," where one wishes to determine the number of different tours that are possible over a specified network (see also, Flood, 1956; Robinson, 1949; and Dantzig, Fulkerson, and Johnson, 1954). Furthermore, as Dantzig, Fulkerson, and Johnson (1954) observe, the Hamiltonian game is, in turn, closely related to group theory and the four-color problem.

Flood (1956) notes that the traveling-salesman problem was posed by Hassler Whitney in a seminar talk given at Princeton University in 1934. In 1937, Flood attempted to obtain near-optimal solutions to this problem in connection with a study of routing school buses in New Jersey. For this effort and subsequent work on the traveling-salesman problem, Flood is credited with stimulating much of the great interest that exists with respect to this problem (see footnote, p. 393, in Dantzig, Fulkerson, and Johnson, 1954).

A number of persons have investigated the traveling-salesman problem and its relationship to other linear-programming problems. In addition to Flood (1956) and Dantzig, Fulkerson, and Johnson (1954), these include Robinson (1949), Koopmans (1947), and Heller (1953 and 1954). Robinson (1949), for example, solved the assignment problem while searching for a means of solving the traveling-salesman problem, and first demonstrated the nature of the relationship between the two problems. Flood (1956) points out the connections of the traveling-salesman problem with various other mathematical programming problems, and also cites important industrial and management applications (see, for example, Chapter 7 on "Sequencing").

To date, although methods and procedures have been developed

[23] While it is true that there are "only" a finite number of possibilities to consider, it should be noted that even for the relatively small symmetric traveling-salesman problem involving 15 cities, there are 653,837,184,000 different tours. The problem, then, is to select, of these 653,837,184,000 possibilities, one (or more) which will be optimum. In fact, given 20 cities and a computer that could evaluate each possible tour in 1 microsecond, it would take over 38,000 years to evaluate all of the $\frac{1}{2}(20!)$ possibilities. Obviously, one seeks and requires an *efficient* procedure for arriving at such an optimum solution, without having to consider very many of these possibilities.

for problems of a similar nature (e.g., the transportation and assignment problems), relatively little is known about efficient methods for solving the traveling-salesman problem. There are few mathematical results relative to this problem, and, as yet, no general method for obtaining a solution has been found. However, Flood (1956) has stated a very useful theorem, namely:

In the Euclidean plane, the minimal tour does not intersect itself.

Furthermore, as Flood notes, this intersection condition generalizes easily for arbitrary $a_{\alpha\beta}$, where $a_{\alpha\beta}$ represents the distances (or travel times) between each pair of cities α and β.

Heller (1953 and 1954) and Dantzig, Fulkerson, and Johnson (1954) have demonstrated the complexity of the traveling-salesman problem, while Flood (1956) has pointed out how "open" the traveling-salesman problem really is, in that a prize offered by the RAND Corporation for another significant theorem (pertaining to this problem) was still unawarded—countless conjectures each having fallen victim to counterexamples. Flood further observes that "it seems very likely that quite a different approach from any yet used may be required for successful treatment of the problem. In fact, there may be no general method for solving the problem and impossibility results would also be valuable" (Flood, 1956, p. 64).

While no general method has as yet been developed for solving the traveling-salesman problem, several procedures have recently been developed which enable one to obtain "near-optimal solutions" and, in some instances, optimal solutions. While these procedures are still somewhat tedious and somewhat intuitive, and can involve a significantly large amount of computation, nevertheless they do provide fairly practical means for computing solutions (i.e., tours) for problems of moderate size.

Dantzig, Fulkerson, and Johnson (1954), while not resolving any of the theoretical questions, have outlined a linear-programming approach to the symmetric ($a_{ij}=a_{ji}$) traveling-salesman problem that, in some instances, enables one to find an optimum route and prove it so. Observing that, as illustrated by the work of Heller (1953) and Kuhn (see ref. 6, p. 410 in Dantzig, Fulkerson, and Johnson, 1954), it is extremely difficult to describe tours *completely* by linear restrictions (even though such relations always exist), Dantzig, Fulkerson, and Johnson formulate a linear-programming problem—related to the traveling-salesman problem—in which not all of the required linear constraints are included. Their approach is to start with a tour and a small number of linear equality and inequality constraints that are satisfied by all tours. Then, this linear-programming problem is solved (by the simplex technique) to provide a new basic solution. If the new solution is not a tour, additional constraints on the problem are imposed which eliminate this solution, but no tours. Then, with the corresponding new problem, a new basic solution is determined (by the simplex technique) and so forth. Finally, once a "near-optimal" solution has been found, Dantzig, Fulkerson, and Johnson suggest a combinatorial approach, using a map of the cities and listing possible tours that have not yet been eliminated by the various conditions imposed on the problem.

Dantzig, Fulkerson, and Johnson illustrate their procedure for several small problems and, also, for a 42-city problem and an associated 49-city problem, all for which optimum solutions are obtained.

Heller (1955) has examined the procedure due to Dantzig, Fulkerson, and Johnson and provides a partial justification for their particular choice of constraints to be included in the linear-programming calculations. Further, as noted by Dantzig (1957) and Dantzig, Fulkerson, and Johnson (1959), experiments by Robacker (1955) with a number of randomly chosen traveling-salesman problems involving nine cities, simple upper bounds, and "loop conditions" on the variables were sufficient to yield the desired solution, indicating that the probability is very low that the more subtle and complicated restrictions (completely describing tours) will be needed in any particular problem.

Recently, Dantzig, Fulkerson, and Johnson (1959) further discussed their linear-programming approach to the traveling-salesman problem, along with giving another illustration of their procedure using the ten-city example discussed by Barachet (1957). Here, the authors note that, in solving the traveling-salesman problem, a *routine* procedure is still required for the combinatorial approach that they suggest be used once one has a "near-optimal solution." However, they further state that, based on their experience, their linear-programming method "does afford a practical means of computing optimal tours in problems that are not too huge" (1959, p. 66).

Barachet (1957) has developed an intuitive procedure in which, starting with an initial feasible solution (for the N-city problem), a series of ever-shorter routes are derived—first, one for which each of the N groups of three consecutive sections that constitute it would form a route the length of which would be minimum, next, one for the N groups of four consecutive sections, and so on, until (possibly) one obtains the desired solution, namely for the N groups of N consecutive sections. In other words, for the case of k consecutive sections, one starts with the route obtained for the case of $k-1$ consecutive sections and makes whatever adjustments are necessary so that the length of the k-section unit between any city and the kth next city (on that route) will be shorter than the length of any other k-section unit between these same two cities. Where adjustments are made, one must then start over to make certain that one still has minimal lengths for $3,4,\cdots,k-1$ consecutive sections, before proceeding to the $(k+1)$-case, and beyond.

To determine if a point should be joined to a "given" point to form a section of the minimum-length route, Barachet (1957) applies the following theorems:

Theorem 1: A route of a minimum length does not cross itself.

Theorem 2: If the protruding angles formed by three consecutive sections are obtuse angles, these three sections make up a route of minimum length.

Theorem 3: If all of the points make up a convex polygon, the route of minimum length corresponds to this convex polygon.

Theorem 4: A circuit including $N-k$ consecutive sections which are common with a minimum circuit obtained for the case of k-consecutive sections (as defined above) is longer than the latter or at the most equal to it.

As Barachet notes, "The essentially intuitive nature of the solution does not permit one to ascertain without doubt that the circuit of minimum length will be obtained" (1957, p. 845). For a full statement and illustration of this intuitive procedure, see Barachet (1957).

Croes (1958) has developed an iterative procedure for solving the traveling-salesman problem which consists of the following three phases:

1. Select an initial feasible solution.
2. Improve (by Croes' procedure) the initial solution by simple transformations which Croes calls "inversions."
3. Consider all further transformations (inversions) to obtain an optimum solution.

These phases are, of course, similar to those contained in the procedure developed by Dantzig, Fulkerson, and Johnson and in the intuitive approach due to Barachet. As Croes observed (1958, p. 791), his method has the following properties:

1. It is applicable to both symmetric and asymmetric problems with random elements.
2. It does not use subjective decisions, so that it can be completely mechanized.
3. It is appreciably faster than any other method proposed.
4. It can be terminated at any point where the "solution" obtained so far is deemed sufficiently accurate.

Croes' iterative procedure, however, is a laborious one and, while he states that the procedure can be mechanized, he observes that "it remains dubious whether it is efficient to use an electronic computer for these calculations, as they involve mostly inspectional work" (1958, p. 811).

The procedures developed by Dantzig, Fulkerson, and Johnson (1954), Barachet (1957), and Croes (1958) all require the selection of an initial, feasible solution. Flood (1956) has shown how the reduced-matrix method for solving the assignment problem may be used effectively in the initial preparation of a traveling-salesman problem for subsequent computations. Furthermore, he has presented techniques for obtaining good approximate solutions, especially for the symmetric case. Dacey (1960) has developed a procedure for obtaining an initial, *near-optimal* feasible solution which he has found will also yield the optimal solution in a number of instances. (If such a solution is not optimal, one can then proceed toward an optimum solution by one of the procedures cited above.)

A number of comparisons have been made among the various approaches and procedures suggested for the solution of the traveling-salesman problem.

Robacker (1955) generated ten random, symmetric, nine-city, traveling-salesman problems which were then solved by the method due to Dantzig, Fulkerson, and Johnson in an average time of three hours per problem, with each one requiring, on the average, less than four iterations to reach the *optimum* tour. Croes (1958) tried his method on several of Robacker's problems, and required an average solution time of twenty-five minutes per problem. Dacey (1960) used his procedure to obtain *near-optimal* initial solutions for all ten of Robacker's problems. To obtain initial solutions, Dacey required an average of five minutes per problem. Five of his initial solutions were, in fact, optimal, while, for all ten problems, his initial solutions were, on the average, 4.8 per cent greater than the optimum solutions.

Croes (1958) solved the 42-city problem of Dantzig, Fulkerson, and Johnson, by his procedure, and required 70 hours for complete solution, although he had arrived at what turns out to be the optimum solution after 10 hours. Dacey (1960) obtained in 90 minutes an initial solution to this problem that was only 4 per cent greater than the optimum distance.

Finally, Dacey also obtained an initial solution to the problem given by Croes (1958) which was 7.2 per cent greater than the optimum solution.

A rule of thumb for obtaining approximate solutions to the traveling-salesman problem has been stated by George Feeney [24] and is often referred to as the "nearest-city approach." Feeney determined this rule while studying a production problem in which the setup costs were dependent upon the sequence in which the products were made (see Chapter 7 on "Sequencing"). In this case, one determines the next product to be made by selecting the one requiring least setup time at that operation. This is analogous to the salesman selecting—as his next city to visit—the nearest city as yet unvisited. Flood (1956) has compared the result of applying the "nearest-city" approach to the 49-city problem of Dantzig, Fulkerson, and Johnson (1954) with their solution and finds that it yields a total distance of 904 units as compared with 699 units—an excess of approximately 30 per cent. However, in a number of industrial applications of the nearest-city approach, the resulting approximation has quickly yielded substantially good results as compared with other much slower computational (approximation) approaches then available.

Finally, attention should be called to the excellent case study by Hare and Hugli (1955) dealing with the production of kitchen units (cabinets and sinks) at the Mullins Manufacturing Company. Here the sequencing (traveling-salesman) problem was greatly complicated by its interrelationship with the production scheduling (lot size, etc.) and inventory problem—especially since a number of the final products (cabinets, sinks, etc.) had common parts. The particular problem of sequencing was handled by using the "nearest-city approach."

For further discussion of the traveling-salesman problem, see Chapter 7.

[24] Given, in 1954, during a talk at a seminar at Columbia University.

7. REVISED SIMPLEX PROCEDURES

The general problem of linear programming as given in P.1 can be restated as follows:

Determine numbers x_j $(j=1,2,\cdots,n)$ such that the linear function

$$f=\sum_{j=1}^{n} c_j x_j = c\cdot x = \max\ (\min)$$

subject to the m linear relations

$$\sum_{j=1}^{n} a_{ij}x_j \leq b_i \qquad (i=1,2,\cdots,m) \qquad \text{(P.18)}$$

$$(\text{i.e., } Ax\leq b)$$

and the n restrictions on the x_j, namely,

$$x_j \geq 0 \qquad (j=1,2,\cdots,n)$$

$$(\text{i.e., } x\geq 0)$$

in which the "parameters" c_j, a_{ij}, and b_i are given constants.

Solution of this class of problems requires (1) methods of obtaining the set of solutions of the system $Ax\leq b$ in terms of a finite number of fundamental basis vectors (see Gale, 1951, Tucker, 1955, Goldman and Tucker, 1956, and Goldman, 1956), and (2) an assurance that, on this solution set, the function $f=c\cdot x$ will obtain an extremum (Gale, Kuhn, and Tucker, 1951, and Tucker, 1956). This assurance is furnished by the principle of duality, which lays down the conditions under which $Ax\leq b$ will have positive or non-negative solutions (Gale, 1956). In the following presentation, the duality principle will be discussed first, and then some aspects of the properties of the solution space of $Ax\leq b$ will be discussed with a view to explaining the logic of the simplex procedure.

7.1. Principle of Duality

As in the theory of a system of linear differential equations, we can conveniently imbed the initial problem, namely, seeking solutions to $Ax\leq b$, in a wider class of problems by considering, in addition, two other associated systems, namely:

$$\begin{matrix} Ax\leqq 0 \\ x\geqq 0 \end{matrix} \quad (4.14a) \qquad\qquad \begin{matrix} Ax=0 \\ x\geqq 0 \end{matrix} \quad (4.14b)$$

Gordan (1873) and Gale (1956) proved that the system 4.14*b* possesses a solution $x \geq 0$ (i.e., non-trivial, non-negative) if and only if there exists no vector w, where $w^* = (w_1, w_2, \cdots, w_m)$, satisfying the inequalities (strict)

$$A^*w > 0$$

where A^* is the transpose of the matrix A. The sufficiency part of this result is the contranegative form of Theorem 1 of Tucker (1956), which states that the *combined* system of $n+m$ relations

$$Ax = 0, \quad x \geq 0, \quad A^*w \geq 0 \tag{4.14c}$$

possesses a solution $(\bar{x}; \bar{w})$ such that $\bar{x} + A^*\bar{w} \geq 0$. In other words, if $Ax = 0$ has only a trivial solution $x = 0$, then, the solution of the combined system 4.14*c* will be one in which $\bar{x} = 0$ and $\bar{w}$ is a vector for which $A^*\bar{w} > 0$. Thus, if $A_1, A_2, \cdots, A_n$ are n m-dimensional vectors (column vectors of the original matrix A), this theorem says that there exist n scalars $\bar{x}_1, \cdots, \bar{x}_n$ and a vector $\bar{w}$ such that

$$\begin{aligned} A_1\bar{x}_1 + \cdots + A_n\bar{x}_n &= 0 \\ \bar{x}_1 \qquad &\geqq 0 \\ &\;\vdots \\ \bar{x}_n &\geqq 0 \\ \bar{w}\cdot A_1 \geqq 0; \cdots ; \bar{w}\cdot A_n &\geqq 0 \\ \bar{x}_1 + \bar{w}\cdot A_1 > 0; \cdots ; \bar{x}_n + \bar{w}\cdot A_n &> 0 \end{aligned} \tag{4.15}$$

The vectors x and w defined by the system 4.14*c* are called *dual* vectors, and the problems

$$\text{(P)} \quad Ax = 0 \qquad \text{(D)} \quad A^*w \geq 0$$
$$x \geq 0$$

are said to be dual to each other.

The significance of this theorem is twofold. In the *first* place, if $-A_0, A_1, \cdots, A_n$ are $n+1$ m-dimensional vectors, then there exist non-negative scalars $\bar{x}_0, \bar{x}_1, \cdots, \bar{x}_n$ and a vector $\bar{w}$ such that

$$\begin{gathered} -A_0\bar{x}_0 + A_1\bar{x}_1 + \cdots + A_n\bar{x}_n = 0 \\ \bar{w}\cdot(-A_0) \geq 0; \quad \bar{x}_0 - \bar{w}\cdot A_0 > 0 \\ \bar{w}\cdot A_k \geq 0; \quad \bar{x}_k + \bar{w}A_k > 0 \qquad (1 \leq k \leq n) \end{gathered} \tag{4.16}$$

Therefore, if $\bar{x}_0=0$, then $\bar{w}A_0<0$ and $\bar{w}A_k\geq 0$ $(1\leq k\leq n)$; if $\bar{x}_0\neq 0$, it is possible to express A_0 as

$$A_0=A_1\xi_1+\cdots+A_n\xi_n \qquad \left(\xi_k=\frac{\bar{x}_k}{\bar{x}_0}\right) \tag{4.17}$$

This is a contranegative form of the important result due to Farkas (1902), viz., if $A_0,A_1,\cdots,A_n$ be $n+1$ vectors in m-space, and if $w\cdot A_0\geq 0$ for every w satisfying inequalities

$$w\cdot A_1\geqq 0,\cdots,w\cdot A_n\geqq 0$$

then A_0 is the non-negatively weighted sum of $A_1,\cdots,A_n$; that is,

$$A_0=A_1y_1+\cdots+A_ny_n \qquad (y_k\geq 0) \tag{4.18}$$

This result means that, if a set of non-negative numbers can be found such that the linear combination of column vectors of A with these weights equals the vector b of the system $Ax\leqq b$, then this set of numbers is an admissible solution.

Secondly, this theorem can be used to prove [25] a sharpened form of the "theorem of alternatives" due to von Neumann and Morgenstern (1953), namely: the dual systems

$$\text{(P)}\quad \begin{aligned} Ax&\leqq 0\\ x&\geqq 0\end{aligned} \qquad \text{(D)}\quad \begin{aligned} A^*y&\geqq 0\\ y&\geqq 0\end{aligned}$$

possess solutions $\bar{x}$ and $\bar{y}$ such that

$$\bar{y}-A\bar{x}>0; \qquad A^*y+\bar{x}>0 \tag{4.19}$$

This theorem can be applied in the following manner: Suppose S is a skew-symmetric matrix; then the theorem implies that the dual systems

$$\begin{aligned} Sw&\geqq 0\\ w&\geqq 0\end{aligned} \qquad \begin{aligned} Sx&\leqq 0\\ x&\geqq 0\end{aligned}$$

which are identical, possess solutions $\bar{w}$ and $\bar{x}$ such that

$$\bar{w}-S\bar{x}>0; \qquad \bar{x}-S\bar{w}>0 \tag{4.20}$$

Therefore,

$$\bar{w}+\bar{x}\geqq 0; \quad S(\bar{w}+\bar{x})\leqq 0; \quad (\bar{w}+\bar{x})-S(\bar{w}+\bar{x})>0 \tag{4.21}$$

The matrix $M=-S$ is also skew-symmetric, and setting $\bar{Z}=\bar{w}+\bar{x}$, we

[25] Suggested by the treatment given in Tucker (1956).

arrive at the "skew-symmetric matrix theorem" of Tucker (1956): If M is a skew-symmetric matrix, the self-dual system

$$Z \geqq 0; \quad MZ \geqq 0$$

has a solution $\bar{Z}$ such that $\bar{Z}+M\bar{Z}>0$. In other words, any component of one of the vectors (i.e., $\bar{Z}$ and $M\bar{Z}$) is positive if and only if the corresponding component of the other is zero.

Now consider the dual linear problems

$f=\sum_{j=1}^{n} c_j x_j = \max$	$\phi=\sum_{i=1}^{m} b_i u_i = \min$
$a_{11}x_1+\cdots+a_{1n}x_n \leqq b_1$	$a_{11}u_1+\cdots+a_{m1}u_m \geqq c_1$
$\cdots\cdots\cdots\cdots$	$\cdots\cdots\cdots\cdots$
$\cdots\cdots\cdots\cdots$	$\cdots\cdots\cdots\cdots$
$a_{m1}x_1+\cdots+a_{mn}x_n \leqq b_m$ (P.19*a*)	$a_{1n}u_1+\cdots+a_{mn}u_m \geqq c_n$ (P.19*b*)
$x_1 \geqq 0$	$u_1 \geqq 0$
$\vdots$	$\vdots$
$x_n \geqq 0$	$u_m \geqq 0$

For either program, a *feasible vector* is a solution that satisfies the constraints, while an *optimal vector* is one that extremizes the function f or ϕ. It should be noted at this stage that if $\bar{X}$, where $\bar{X}^*=(\bar{x}_1,\bar{x}_2,\cdots,\bar{x}_n)$, and $\bar{U}=(\bar{u}_1,\cdots,\bar{u}_m)$ are feasible vectors for their respective programs, then

$$\sum_{j=1}^{n} c_j \bar{x}_j \leq \sum_{i=1}^{m} \bar{u}_i b_i \tag{4.22}$$

If the equality holds, then each of the vectors is optimum in its program. Defining the skew-symmetric matrix M as

$$M=\begin{pmatrix} 0 & -A & b \\ A^* & 0 & -c \\ -b^* & c^* & 0 \end{pmatrix} \tag{4.23}$$

and the inequality system

$$M\xi = M\begin{pmatrix} U^* \\ x \\ t \end{pmatrix} \geq 0 \qquad \text{(where } t \text{ is a scalar)} \tag{4.24}$$

and applying the skew-symmetric matrix theorem, we note that, if $M \geq 0$ has a solution with $\bar{t}=0$, then *at least one of the programs is not feasible.* Further analysis of the implications of $\bar{t}=0$ leads to a *fundamental theorem of linear programming*, which can be stated as:

a. A feasible vector $\overline{X}$ for the maximum problem is optimal if and only if the dual minimum problem has a feasible vector $\overline{U}$ for which

$$\overline{U} \cdot b = c \cdot \overline{X}$$

b. One of the dual problems can have optimum vectors if and only if both possess feasible vectors.

7.2. The Solution Space

The general theory of solution space for linear inequality systems has been synthesized by Gale (1951) and Gerstenhaber (1951) in algebraic and geometric terminology. A simple and constructive treatment is to be found in Tucker (1955), Goldman (1956), and Goldman and Tucker (1956).

For the special purpose of linear programming, however, two features have to be incorporated in this theory. These are: (1) obtaining *non-negative* solutions, and (2) choosing some non-negative solution so as to extremize the linear form $\sum_{j=1}^{n} c_j x_j$. Clearly, by introducing so-called slack variables, it is possible to reduce $Ax \leq b$ to $B \cdot y = b$, say. The general theory, then, assures that the solution of $\binom{n+m}{m}$ subsystems of the system $By=b$ will give the minimal number of solution vectors—the so-called "vertex" solutions (see Tucker, 1955, and Goldman, 1956)—required to span the solution space. In principle, it is now possible to select in the first instance only the non-negative vectors (called feasible solutions), and then to select out of these the one that extremizes the given linear form. However, the amount of effort required by this procedure is almost prohibitive and, consequently, search has been directed towards efficient computation.

Techniques of efficient computation are all concerned with three major problems: (*a*) how to obtain an initial non-negative vertex solution, (*b*) how to obtain a chain of non-negative vertex solutions with the least effort such that, each time a new solution is obtained, there is an improvement in the value of $\sum_{j=1}^{n} c_j x_j$, and (*c*) how to know when the extremizing solution has been obtained. The first of these problems is solved trivially when the constraints are given as inequalities of the form $\Sigma a_{ij}x_j \leq b_i$, for, then, a first solution can be obtained by setting equal to zero all variables except the "slacks." However, when the constraints are given as equations or are of the form $\Sigma a_{ij}x_j \geq b_i$, a different procedure is called for; this is known as the method of artificial variables. The second and third problems were treated for the first time by Dantzig (1951), who also obtained a sufficient condition that a feasible solution shall not exist. This forms the cornerstone of the simplex technique.

7.3. The Simplex Algorithm

Let us write A_0 for the vector $b \geq 0$, and $A_i (i=1,2,\cdots,n)$ for the ith column of A; let us also suppose that the constraints are given initially as equations, so that we shall consider the problem: To find $x_1,\cdots,x_n$ such that $x_1A_1+\cdots+x_nA_n=A_0$ and $z=x_1c_1+\cdots+x_nc_n$ maximum. The principle of the simplex algorithm may now be stated in terms of these symbols.

1. Assuming that every subset of m of the m-dimensional vectors $A_0,A_1,\cdots,A_n$ is linearly independent, any vector A_j can be written as a linear combination:

$$A_j=\eta_{0j}A_0+\eta_{1j}A_1+\cdots+\eta_{m-1,j}A_{m-1} \qquad (j=1,2,\cdots,m) \quad (4.25)$$

If a feasible solution exists, then $\eta_{0j}>0$ for at least one index j.

2. If with arbitrary $\theta_0>0$ and $\mu_i>0$ $(i=1,2,\cdots,m-1)$ a reference vector S is defined as

$$S=-\theta_0A_0+\mu_1A_1+\cdots+\mu_{m-1}A_{m-1} \qquad (4.26)$$

and if wA_j (where A_j is given by Eq. 4.25) is subtracted from Eq. 4.26, then, the expression so obtained, namely

$$S+(\theta_0+w\theta_{0j})A_0$$
$$=wA_j+(\mu_1-w\eta_{ij})A_1+\cdots+(\mu_{m-1}-w\eta_{m-1,j})A_{m-1} \quad (4.27)$$

shows that if at least one $\eta_{ij}>0$ $(i=1,2,\cdots,m-1)$, there is a maximum value of w, say, $w_0=\min_i(\mu_i/\eta_{ij})$, which will make at least one coefficient in the right-hand side of Eq. 4.27 vanish. Further, a new vector $S+\theta_1A_0$ will be generated as a positive linear combination of $m-1$ of the A_i; the number θ_1 is given by $\theta_1=\theta_0+w_0\cdot\eta_{0j}>\theta_0$. After expressing each A_j in terms of the new basis, the process may be repeated, each time obtaining a higher value of θ.

3. This process terminates after a finite number of steps. (This is assured by the assumption about the rank of $[A,b]$). In particular, the

process terminates when *either* $\eta_{0j} \leq 0$ for all $j=1,2,\cdots,n$ (in which case there is no feasible solution) *or* when for some fixed j we have $\eta_{ij} \leq 0$ for all $i=1,2,\cdots,m$.

4. The process described in statement 2 shows that if a feasible solution exists then it is possible to construct one such solution consisting of exactly m vectors $A_1,\cdots,A_m$ with positive weights ξ_i, i.e.,

$$A_0=\xi_1 A_1+\cdots+\xi_m A_m \qquad (\xi_i>0) \tag{4.28}$$

and

$$\xi_1 c_1+\cdots+\xi_m c_m=f(\xi)=z_0 \tag{4.29}$$

Let all vectors A_j be expressed in terms of these m vectors as

$$A_j=\lambda_{1j}A_1+\cdots+\lambda_{mj}A_m \qquad (j=1,2,\cdots,n) \tag{4.30}$$

and the corresponding value of the linear form z be written as

$$z_j=\lambda_{1j}c_1+\cdots+\lambda_{mj}c_m \qquad (j=1,2,\cdots,n) \tag{4.31}$$

If now for some fixed index j, we have $c_j-z_j>0$, then a set $\bar{S}$ of feasible solutions can be constructed so that $z=f(x \mid x \in \bar{S})>z_0$. The upper bound of $z=f(x)$ is either (*a*) *finite*, in which case a feasible solution can be constructed with exactly m vectors A_i with positive weights, or (*b*) *infinite*, in which case a feasible solution can be constructed with exactly $m+1$ vectors A_i with positive weights such that the upper bound of $f(x)=+\infty$. The final basis will always have the property that $c_j-z_j \leq 0$ for all $j=1,2,\cdots,m$, unless $z=f(x \mid x \in \bar{S})$ is unbounded. The feasible solution associated with the final basis is also the maximum feasible solution.

7.4. Improvements on the Standard Simplex Technique

Extensive application of the standard simplex procedure has called for improvements in several directions, the more important of which are the following:

1. It is necessary to obtain, as simply as possible, an initial basic feasible solution in order to generate the chain of basic feasible solutions;
2. Some device has to be built into the solution procedure so that the value of the objective function $f(x)=\sum_{j=1}^{n} c_j x_j$ will not remain unchanged from one iteration to the other (i.e., no basis will be repeated in the course of iterations); and, intimately associated with this question,
3. Some method must be designed to secure an efficient choice of vectors to be brought into and removed from the basis in each iteration.

The first and second problems are the principal concern of Dantzig, Orden, and Wolfe (1954, 1955) relative to their generalized simplex method; the second problem has been alternatively treated by the perturbation methods due to Charnes, Cooper, and Henderson (1953). The third problem is treated by the so-called primal-dual methods and composite algorithms which also serve to reduce the number of iterations. All these modifications make extensive use of a special technique for obtaining a basis for the $(k+1)$th iteration directly from the one obtained for the kth iteration. A special algorithm has been developed by Frisch (1958) to reduce the number of iterations and to guard against the emergence of degeneracy through successive transformation of the vectors.

7.5. The Generalized Simplex Method

This method, due to Dantzig, Orden, and Wolfe (1954, 1955), imbeds the original problem as a component of a *generalized matrix problem* (Gale, Kuhn, and Tucker, 1951) by substituting lexicographically ordered vectors in place of non-negative variables x_j. Thus, the original problem is transformed into:

Determine numbers $x_0, x_1, \cdots, x_n$ such that

$$x_0 = \max$$

subject to

$$x_j \geq 0$$

$$x_0 + \sum_{j=1}^{n} a_{0j} x_j = 0 \tag{P.20}$$

$$\sum_{j=1}^{n} a_{1j} x_j = b_1 \qquad \left(a_{1j} = -\sum_{k=2}^{m} a_{kj};\ b_1 = -\sum_{k=2}^{m} b_k\right)$$

$$\sum_{j=1}^{n} a_{kj} x_j = b_k \qquad (k = 2, 3, \cdots, m)$$

The generalized problem is now one of finding a set of lexicographic vector-variables $\bar{x}_0, \bar{x}_1, \cdots, \bar{x}_n$ and auxiliary variables $\bar{x}_{n+1}, \cdots, \bar{x}_{n+m}$ satisfying the matrix equations

$$\bar{x}_0 + \sum_{j=1}^{n} a_{0j} \bar{x}_j = (0,1,0,\cdots,0)$$

$$\bar{x}_{n+k} + \sum_{j=1}^{n} a_{kj} \bar{x}_j = (b_k,0,0,\cdots,1,0,\cdots,0) \tag{4.32}$$

$$\bar{x}_j \geq 0 \qquad (j = 1, \cdots, n, n+2, \cdots, n+m)$$

In the first phase of the computational procedure (Dantzig, Orden, and Wolfe, 1955), $\bar{x}_{n+1}$ is maximized without any restriction on $\bar{x}_0$; this serves to show if the original problem can at all have a feasible solution. In the second phase, $\bar{x}_0$ is maximized under the additional constraint that $\bar{x}_{n+1} \geq 0$.

7.6. The Composite Simplex Algorithm

Lemke's dual-simplex method has been extended in several forms to suit the standard simplex and the revised simplex formats, the principal *motivation* being, in each case, *to reduce the number of iterations* in those cases where it is necessary to first find a basic feasible solution (i.e., in the case of artificial variables).

The first attempt of this kind is due to Beale (1954), who considered the problem in the format of the standard simplex and introduced a parameter, α, to perturb the original system of equations.

Beale's technique of introducing an α was the starting point for Dantzig (1954*b*), who considered the problem in the format of the revised simplex. While the revised simplex criterion is retained for selecting the vector to be brought into basis, a considerable modification is made in the criterion for selecting the one to be thrown out of the basis, so that α may be decreased. If a solution is optimal for $\alpha > 0$, then such a solution is a basic feasible solution to the *dual* problem and, from this point on, Lemke's method takes over.

Orchard-Hays (1954) simplified and improved upon the method of Dantzig (1954*b*) and thereby modified and refined the whole revised simplex procedure. In the first place, the (equated) constraints

$$\sum_{j=1}^{n} a_{ij}x_j = b_i \qquad (i=1,2,\cdots,m) \tag{4.33}$$

are replaced by the modified set

$$\Sigma a_{ij}x_j = b_i - u_i, \qquad u_i \geq 0 \tag{4.34}$$

which indicates that setting $u_i = b_i$ provides a solution to the modified equation

$$Px = Q - U \tag{4.35}$$

where

$$x = \begin{pmatrix} x_0 \\ x_1 \\ \cdot \\ \cdot \\ \cdot \\ x_n \end{pmatrix}; \qquad Q = \begin{pmatrix} 0 \\ b_1 \\ \cdot \\ \cdot \\ \cdot \\ b_m \end{pmatrix}; \qquad U = \begin{pmatrix} 0 \\ u_1 \\ \cdot \\ \cdot \\ \cdot \\ u_m \end{pmatrix} \tag{4.36}$$

$$P = (P_0, P_1, \cdots, P_m)$$

Then x_0 is sought to be maximized by reducing U to zero while maintaining feasibility ($x_j \geq 0$) and continuing to provide a basis with which to operate. As a result of this procedure, modifications are made in the rules for deciding which vector is to enter the basis and which vector is to leave the basis.

7.7. The Primal-Dual Algorithm

This is an extension and generalization of a technique initially devised for solving a class of transportation problems (Dantzig, 1951, and Ford and Fulkerson, 1955) to make it applicable to the general linear programming problem.

1. Given a linear programming problem (primal form)

$$\sum_{j=1}^{n} c_j x_j = \bar{z} = \min \qquad (4.37)$$

subject to: (P.21)

$$\text{(a)} \quad \sum_{j=1}^{n} a_{ij} x_j = b_i \qquad (i = 1, \cdots, m) \qquad (4.38)$$

$$\text{(b)} \quad x_j \geq 0$$

a *modified primal* is constructed by augmenting Eq. 4.38 by

$$x_0 + x_1 + \cdots + x_n = b_0; \quad x_0 \geq 0 \qquad (4.39)$$

and the *dual to the modified primal* is set up:

$$\sum_{j=0}^{m} b_j u_j = y = \max \qquad (4.40)$$

subject to: (P.22)

$$\text{(a)} \quad u_0 \leq 0 \qquad (4.41)$$

$$\text{(b)} \quad u_0 + \sum_{j=1}^{m} a_{ji} u_j \leq c_i$$

A feasible solution of this modified dual is obtained and employed to define the restricted primal problem (an alteration of the original problem) which is identical with the following *extended* primal problem:

$$\begin{aligned} \epsilon_0 + \epsilon_1 + \cdots + \epsilon_m &= \bar{w} = \min \\ x_0 + x_1 + \cdots + x_n + \epsilon_0 &= b_0 \\ a_{11}x_1 + \cdots + a_{1n}x_n + \epsilon_1 &= b_1 \\ \cdots\cdots\cdots\cdots & \\ a_{m1}x_1 + \cdots + a_{mn}x_n + \epsilon_m &= b_m \\ x_j \geq 0; \quad \epsilon_i &\geq 0 \end{aligned} \qquad \text{(P.23}$$

except that it contains a smaller number of x_j's because the extended primal is solved subject to the further restrictions; namely,

$$x_j = 0 \quad \text{when } \delta_j < 0$$

$$[\delta_0 = u_0; \quad \delta_j = u_0 + \sum_{i=1}^{m} a_{ij} u_i - c_j] \tag{4.42}$$

The purpose of solving the restricted primal problem is to find a solution as nearly feasible as possible. The method of solution is the revised simplex of Dantzig, Orden, and Wolfe (1955).

2. Optimal solutions of the restricted primal are employed to improve the feasible solution to the dual program. (In a transportation problem, this step can be performed without using the simplex technique.)

3. After a finite number of repetitions, the optimal solutions of the restricted primal coincide with those of the original primal problem.

An important computational device is to obtain a basis for the $(k+1)$th iteration directly from the one obtained for the kth iteration. Two methods have so far been suggested for deriving B_{k+1} from B_k:

a. The Product-Form of the Inverse (Dantzig, 1953, and Dantzig and Orchard-Hays, 1953) which writes the inverse of the $(k+1)$th basis as

$$[B_{k+1}]^{-1} = E_{k+1} \cdot [B_k]^{-1} \tag{4.43}$$

where E_{k+1} is an identity matrix, except for the column r (corresponding to the vector that has replaced P_{j_s} in B_{k+1}) whose components are

$$\xi_r = \frac{1}{y_r}, \quad \xi_i = -\frac{y_i}{y_r} \qquad (i = 0, 1, \cdots, m; i \neq r), \qquad \xi_s = [B_k]^{-1} P_s \tag{4.44}$$

The special advantage of this procedure is that only one additional column of information need be recorded with each iteration.

b. The Elimination-Form of the Inverse (Markowitz, 1955, 1957) which represents the inverse of a matrix M as

$$M^{-1} = C_1 \cdot C_2 \cdots C_m \cdot R_{m-1} \cdot R_{m-2} \cdots R_1 \tag{4.45}$$

where R_k is an identity matrix with its kth column replaced by the *column*-vector

$$\left\{0, 0, \cdots, 1, -\frac{v_{k+1,k}}{v_{kk}}, \cdots, -\frac{v_{mk}}{v_{kk}}\right\}$$

and C_k is an identity matrix with its kth row replaced by the row-vector

$$\left(0, 0, \cdots, 0, \frac{1}{v_{kk}}, -\frac{v_{k,k+1}}{v_{kk}}, \cdots, -\frac{v_{km}}{v_{kk}}\right)$$

The special feature of this representation is that it effectively uses the Gaussian method of solving a linear equations system. It becomes particularly useful when, as it happens after a sufficient number of iterations in the product-form method has been made, one likes to reinvert the current basis B_{k_0} as

$$[E_{k_0+k-1}]^{-1}\cdots[E_{k_0}]^{-1}[B_{k_0}]^{-1}$$

The elimination-form of the inverse is undoubtedly simpler when the matrix has a large number of zeros.

7.8. The Multiplex Method

Frisch (1957, 1958) has developed the multiplex method, which takes care of the same complications—(*a*) rounding-off errors due to successive transformations of the entire matrix, (*b*) possibility of expressing the *b*-vector as a linear combination of less than *m* vectors (degeneracy)—that motivated the generalized simplex method of Dantzig, Orden, and Wolfe (1955). The special feature of the multiplex method is, however, to arrive at an estimate of as many components of the optimizing vector as possible, and then to apply the simplex technique or *general adjacent extreme point methods* to arrive at the complete vector.

This method of estimation of the critical restrictions and, hence, of the critical variables proceeds in three steps:

1. The tangential move, which determines the constraint planes that are most nearly normal to the preference direction.
2. The conditional preference move, which determines how far the values of variables can be increased in the restraints determined by the tangential move; at the end of this step, we obtain the "candidate" constraints which define either the optimum or some corner very near to it.
3. The method of regression, which is essentially a step to move to the intersection of these "candidates."

8. DYNAMIC LINEAR PROGRAMMING

One of the earliest extensions of the basic linear-programming problem was the inclusion of the effect of *time* into the statement and solution of the problem, thus giving rise to what one might call "dynamic linear programming." The dynamic linear-programming problem is basically an extension, over a number of time periods, of the static linear-programming problem for one time period.

Dynamic linear-programming problems are characterized by (1) a set of linear restriction-equations which are *repetitive* in nature—hence, certain coefficients will be the same from one time period to the next, and (2) the sparseness of the coefficient matrix, that is, the very small number of *non*-zero elements which appear in the matrix.

Particular attention has been directed to the class of dynamic linear-programming problems in which the activities in any given time period are related only to activities in that and preceding (but not later) time periods. Such problems may be represented as:

Minimize:

$$C^{(1)}X_1+C^{(2)}X_2+\cdots+C^{(n)}X_n$$

subject to:

$$\begin{aligned} &A_{11}X_1 &&= b^{(1)} \\ &A_{21}X_1+A_{22}X_2 &&= b^{(2)} \\ &\cdots\cdots\cdots\cdots\cdots\cdots \\ &A_{n1}X_1+A_{n2}X_2+\cdots A_{nn}X_n &&= b^{(n)} \end{aligned} \qquad \text{(P.24)}$$

where the A_{ij} are submatrices (or *blocks*) of the original matrix of coefficients. The A_{ij} form a triangular system

$$\begin{bmatrix} A_{11} & & & \\ A_{21} & A_{22} & & \\ \cdot & \cdot & \cdot & \cdot \\ A_{n1} & A_{n2} & \cdots & A_{nn} \end{bmatrix}$$

where all non-block entries are zero. Problems whose matrices are of this form are called *block-triangular* (see Dantzig, 1956*b* and 1959).

Every dynamic linear-programming problem can be handled by certain standard algorithms. However, it is not always practical to do this—especially because of the very large-size matrices that are usually involved.[26] Fortunately, however, in addition to the properties listed above (i.e., repetitive nature and sparseness), transportation-type submatrices and block-triangular submatrices will usually be encountered (see Dantzig, 1956*b*). Accordingly, particular classes of dynamic linear-programming problems can be handled quite readily by using computational procedures that have been developed for these special cases. We will consider the most notable among these particu-

[26] See, for example, Dantzig's example of a "detailed" model which involves a matrix of size 164×336 and which is, at best, useful only as an over-all *guide* for planning (Dantzig, 1956*b*).

lar classes of problems: (1) the caterer problem, (2) the production-smoothing problem, and (3) the warehousing problem. For discussion of other dynamic (or multistage) linear-programming problems, see Dantzig (1956*b* and 1959) and Vazsonyi (1958, Chapter 8).

8.1. The Caterer Problem

The *caterer problem* was formulated by Jacobs (1954) as a paraphrase of a practical military problem that arose in estimating the number of spare aircraft engines required for various specified levels of performance of a fleet of aircraft. Jacobs stated the problem as follows:

> A caterer knows that, in connection with the meals he has arranged to serve during the next n days, he will need $r_j(\geq 0)$ fresh napkins on the jth day, $j=1, 2, \cdots, n$. Laundering normally takes p days; that is, a soiled napkin sent for laundering immediately after use on the jth day is returned in time to be used again on the $(j+p)$th day. However, the laundry also has a higher-cost service which returns the napkins in $q<p$ days (p and q integers). Having no usable napkins on hand or in the laundry, the caterer will meet his early needs by purchasing napkins at a cents each. Laundering costs b and c cents per napkin for normal and high-cost service, respectively. How does he arrange matters to meet his needs and minimize his outlays for the n days? (p. 155).

Mathematically, the caterer problem may be stated as:

Minimize:

$$C=a\sum_{i=1}^{n}x_i+b\sum_{i=1}^{n-p}y_i+c\sum_{i=1}^{n-q}z_i$$

subject to: (P.25)

$$x_j+y_{j-p}+z_{j-q}=r_j$$

$$y_j+z_j+s_j-s_{j-1}=r_j$$

$$x_j\geq 0; \quad y_j\geq 0; \quad z_j\geq 0; \quad s_j\geq 0$$

Having formulated the problem as one in linear programming, Jacobs then developed a procedure to handle the specific case where $q=p-1$. This procedure consists of simplifying the original problem, by means of several linear transformations, to such a degree that an explicit solution can be given. Specifically, the caterer problem is one of minimizing a linear function subject to an original convex set, A, of linear restrictions. Jacobs constructs a larger convex set, B, which contains A, but which is described by a smaller number of variables and inequalities than the original set. The transformed problem (for B) is then shown to be related to the original problem (for A) as follows: The *optimal* solutions of the transformed problem always correspond directly to optimal solutions of the original problem, even though there are *feasible* solutions of the transformed problem corresponding to which there are no feasible solutions of the initial problem. Finally, Jacobs develops an algorithm for determining the values of the missing variables.

Gaddum, Hoffman, and Sokolowsky (1954) have developed an algorithm for a slightly more general caterer problem, of which that due to Jacobs is a special case. This algorithm also provides a straightforward procedure for computing solutions to the Jacobs problem for any value of $q \leq p-1$.

Prager (1956*b*) has shown that the caterer problem is equivalent to a Hitchcock distribution (transportation) problem with a very special cost matrix.[27] He has also developed a simple procedure for solving the special case of $q=p-1$ and illustrates, by a numerical example, a possible extension of the procedure to the case $q<p-1$.

For further discussion of the caterer problem and corresponding methods of solution see Dantzig (1956*b*), Hoffman (1955), Prager (1956*b*), and Vajda (1958).

8.2. The Warehousing Problem

The warehousing problem is an example of another class of dynamic linear-programming problems where procedures have been developed which take advantage of special characteristics of the problem. This problem was formulated by Cahn (1948) as follows:

> Given a warehouse with a fixed capacity and an initial stock of a certain product, which is subject to known seasonal price and cost variations, what is the optimal pattern of purchasing (or production), storage and sales?

Mathematically, the warehouse problem can be stated as: [28]

Maximize:

$$\sum_{j=1}^{n}(p_j y_j - c_j x_j)$$

[27] This was also indicated earlier by Dantzig (1956*b*, footnote on p. 139).

[28] Again, we consider *structure* and not the definitions of the actual symbols. For full definitions and development of the mathematical statement of the problem, see Charnes and Cooper (1954*b*).

subject to:

$$A+\sum_{j=1}^{i}(x_j-y_j)\leq B \qquad (i=1,2,\cdots,n)$$

$$y_1\leq A \qquad \text{(P.26)}$$

$$y\leq A+\sum_{j=1}^{i-1}(x_j-y_j) \qquad (i=2,3,\cdots,n)$$

$$x_j\geq 0$$

$$y_j\geq 0$$

where A, B, c_j, and p_j are given constants.

The warehousing problem as thus formulated can, of course, be solved by the simplex technique (or its variations). Furthermore, the structure of the warehouse-type problem is such that we can more readily take advantage of its special characteristics through the dual rather than the primal statement of the problem. Charnes, Cooper, and Mellon (see Charnes and Cooper, 1954*b*, and Charnes, Cooper, and Mellon, 1954) developed the "regrouping principle," which enables one to transform quickly from the dual solution to the direct solution of the primal problem, and which avoids calculating an inverse matrix as formerly required. They also present a simple schematic device for facilitating the transformation of the primal problem into its dual problem, and vice versa (see Section 2.2).

The single-product warehousing problem due to Cahn was then extended by Charnes and Cooper (1955*b*) to the case of multiple products, multiple warehouses, and varying prices. A solution was effected, here, too, by use of the dual theorem, and the "regrouping principle." In this extension, they present an excellent exposition of the warehousing problem, its special structure, and the method of solution, as well as several numerical examples. They also point out that the warehousing problem is important—not only because of its application value, but also because it (1) represents a generalization of simpler transportation models, and (2) is the simplest example of a large and important class of dynamic models.

Bellman (1956*a*) has shown how warehouse-type problems can be approached by means of the functional-equation technique of the theory of dynamic programming and compares the corresponding computational implications with those of the Charnes-Cooper approach.

Finally, Prager (1957*b*) has shown that the warehousing problem can be transformed into a modified type of transportation problem (see also Dantzig, 1959, and Vajda, 1958).

8.3. The Production-Smoothing Problem

The *production-smoothing problem* is an example of a type of dynamic linear-programming problem where the developed computational procedures take advantage of the simple repetitive structure of the problem. The problem is a commonly occurring one in which one seeks to determine a production-inventory plan for a single-type product with, say, seasonal demand, such that the sum of costs due to storage and changing the production level will be minimized.

The production-smoothing problem may be stated symbolically as follows:

Minimize:

$$\sum_{t=1}^{n} s_t + \tfrac{1}{2}\lambda \sum_{t=1}^{n} \{x_t - x_{t-1} + |x_t - x_{t-1}|\}$$

subject to:

$$\sum_{=1}^{t} x_j - \sum_{j=1}^{t} r_j = s_t \qquad (t=1,2,\cdots,n) \qquad \text{(P.27}$$

$$x_j \geq 0$$

$$s_j \geq 0$$

where $r_1, r_2, \cdots, r_n$ are given constants (shipping requirements) and λ is the ratio of the cost of a unit change in production to the unit cost of storage.

Hoffman and Jacobs (1954) transform this problem to an equivalent one *with reduced dimensions* of minimizing

$$\sum_{t=1}^{n} s_t + \lambda \sum_{t=1}^{n} y_t \qquad (4.46)$$

which they then solve, for λ known, by the simplex technique (see also, Gass, 1958, p. 158).

For the case where the cost function involves a linear parameter, Hoffman and Jacobs refer to a method by Gass, Goldstein, Jacobs, and Saaty which will solve such problems for all values of the parameter (see Hoffman and Jacobs, 1954, p. 87). They also describe some interesting properties of the solution to the problem and also develop a formula for the solution in the special case where the r_t (shipping requirements) are increasing.

Bellman (1956*b*) considers the production-smoothing problem of Hoffman and Jacobs in the form

Minimize:

$$L(x)=\sum_{i=1}^{n} c_i x_i$$

subject to: (P.28)

$$\sum_{i=1}^{k} x_i \geq r_k$$

$$x_i \geq 0$$

where the r_k constitute a given sequence of numbers.

By the functional-equation approach of the theory of dynamic programming, Bellman solves the more general problem of minimizing

$$R(x)=\sum_{i=1}^{N} \phi_i(x_i)$$

where each $\phi_i(x_i)$ is a monotone increasing functions of x_i for $x_i \geq 0$.

The production-smoothing problem has also been formulated as a transportation problem by Bowman (1956). Dantzig and Johnson (1955) have developed a quick, systematic graphical procedure for obtaining optimal solutions to a problem (similar to the one studied by Jacobs and Hoffman) in which production costs, storage costs, and costs of changing production rates are given functions of time. They also solve directly a convex requirement scheduling problem in which production is required to be non-decreasing. Finally, they outline an (non-necessarily optimal) iterative procedure for the general production-smoothing problem.

9. SENSITIVITY ANALYSIS: PARAMETRIC LINEAR PROGRAMMING

In the formulation and solution of linear-programming problems, one essentially assumes, at least initially, that all values of the coefficients are given and exact. Actually, such coefficients are derived from analyses of data and usually represent *average* values or *best-estimate* values. Accordingly, it is most important to analyze the sensitivity of the solution to variations in these coefficients or in the estimates of these coefficients. Stated still another way, one seeks to determine the ranges of variation of the coefficients over which the solution will remain optimal. Sensitivity studies of this sort are known as *parametric linear programming.*

Without a knowledge of the probability distributions of the coefficients, questions regarding sensitivity of solutions can presently be "answered" only in a limited sense. As noted by Gass (1958, p. 109), not much has been accomplished to date with respect to sensitivity analyses for variations in the coefficients in the matrix of a_{ij}, and detailed study of the effects of variation of either the objective function cost coefficients or the constants on the right-hand side has been limited to the one special case discussed below. Needless to say, much research remains to be done in the area of parametric linear programming.

9.1. Variation of Coefficients of the Matrix of a_{ij}

A pair of dual problems, for example:

Maximum Problem	*Minimum Problem*
$a_{00}+\sum_i a_{i0}x_i=\max$	$a_{00}+\sum_j a_{0j}y_j=\min$
subject to: (P.29*a*)	subject to: (P.29*b*)
(a) $a_{0j}+\sum_i a_{ij}x_i \geq 0$	(a′) $a_{i0}+\sum_j a_{ij}y_j \leq 0$
(b) $x_i \geq 0$	(b′) $y_j \geq 0$

can be combined (see McKinsey, 1952, pp. 34–37) into a single saddle-point problem, viz., that of finding a pair of values (x^0,y^0) for the function

$$\psi(x,y,A)=a_{00}+\sum_{i=1}^{m}x_i a_{i0}+\sum_{j=1}^{n}a_{0j}y_j+\sum_{i,j}x_i a_{ij}y_j \tag{4.47}$$

where

$$A=\begin{pmatrix}a_{00}, & a_{0j}\\ a_{i0}, & a_{ij}\end{pmatrix} \qquad \begin{cases}i=1,\cdots,m\\ j=1,\cdots,n\end{cases}$$

such that, for all $x\geq 0, y\geq 0$, it is true that

$$\psi(x,y^0,A)\leq\psi(x^0,y^0,A)\leq\psi(x^0,y,A) \tag{4.48}$$

Then, x^0 and y^0 will also be solutions to the respective maximum and minimum problems.

Let $\psi(x^0,y^0,A)\equiv\psi(A)$ denote the common optimum value of the primal and dual objective functions. Kuhn and Tucker (1951) have shown that either problem has a solution if and only if there is a number, $\psi(A)$, and there are non-empty sets, $x^0(A)$ and $y^0(A)$, such that

$$\begin{aligned}x^0(A)&=\{x\geq 0\,|\,\psi(x,y,A)\geq\psi(A)\text{ for }y\geq 0\}\\ y^0(A)&=\{y\geq 0\,|\,\psi(x,y,A)\leq\psi(A)\text{ for }x\geq 0\}\end{aligned} \tag{4.49}$$

Mills (1956) uses these results (1) to find an expression for the variation in $\psi(A)$ due to variations in the elements of A, namely:

$$\frac{\partial\psi(A)}{\partial H}=\max_{x\in x^0(A)}\ \min_{y\in y^0(A)}\psi(x,y,H) \tag{4.50}$$

and (2) to find relationships between solutions based on A and solutions based on the perturbed matrix $[A+\alpha H]$, namely

$$x^0(A,H)\subset x^0(A);\quad y^0(A,H)\subset y^0(A) \tag{4.51}$$

where

$$x^0(A,H)=\left\{x\,|\,x \text{ is a limit point of } \{x^{(k)}\},\ \text{where } x^{(k)}\in x^0(A+\alpha^{(k)}H) \text{ and } \{\alpha^{(k)}\}\to 0^+\right\} \tag{4.52}$$

and $y^0(A,H)$ is similarly defined. It should be observed that the result (2) has a meaning only if $\psi(A+\alpha H)$ exists for $0\leq\alpha<\alpha_0$, where α_0 is some prescribed number.

9.2. *Variation of Coefficients of the Objective Function*

As noted by Gass (1958, p. 109), the investigation of parametric programming as applied to the variation of the coefficients of the objective function originated in the study of a dynamic (multiperiod) production-inventory problem in which a manufacturer of a seasonal item must determine optimum monthly production schedules, so that customer demand can always be satisfied by a combination of current production and overproduction (i.e., inventory) from previous months. Here, one seeks to minimize the sum of costs due to output fluctuations (e.g., overtime, hiring and layoff, etc.) and to inventories (see Gass, 1958, p. 158 ff.).

One-parameter problem. As considered by Gass and Saaty (1955*a*), the one-parameter linear-programming problem may be stated mathematically as:

Let $\delta\leq\lambda\leq\phi$, where δ is any arbitrary, algebraically small, but finite, number and ϕ is any arbitrary, algebraically large, but finite number. For each λ in this interval, find a vector $x=(x_1,x_2,\cdots,x_n)$ such that

$$\sum_{j=1}^{n}(c_j+\lambda c_j')x_j=\text{minimum} \tag{4.53}$$

subject to: (P.30)

$$\sum_{j=1}^{n}a_{ij}x_j=b_i \qquad (i=1,2,\cdots,m)$$
$$x_j\geq 0 \qquad (j=1,2,\cdots,n) \tag{4.54}$$

where c_j, c_j', a_{ij}, and b_i are given constants.

Gass and Saaty then assume, by virtue of the work of Charnes (1952) and Dantzig, Orden, and Wolfe (1954), that this problem is non-degenerate and that a basic feasible solution of Eq. 4.54 is already available (see also, Section 2.3). Then, solving their problem, by the simplex technique, for $\lambda = \delta$, one obtains either a solution (Case A), or the information that the objective function (Eq. 4.53), with $\lambda = \delta$, has no finite minimum on the convex set of restrictions (Eq. 4.54) (Case B).

Case A (solution exists for $\lambda = \delta$*).* The optimality-criterion function $z_j - c_j$ can be represented as a linear function of λ, namely

$$z_j - c_j = \alpha_j + \lambda\beta_j \tag{4.55}$$

Hence, for an optimum solution for $\lambda = \delta$, one must have

$$\alpha_j + \delta\beta_j \leq 0 \qquad (j = 1, 2, \cdots, n) \tag{4.56}$$

Defining

$$\underline{\lambda} = \max_{\beta_j < 0} \frac{-\alpha_j}{\beta_j}, \quad \text{or} \quad -\infty, \text{ if all } \beta_j \geq 0 \tag{4.57}$$

and

$$\bar{\lambda} = \min_{\beta_j > 0} \frac{-\alpha_j}{\beta_j}, \quad \text{or} \quad +\infty, \text{ if all } \beta_j \leq 0 \tag{4.58}$$

the minimum solutions will then be obtained for all λ such that

$$\underline{\lambda} \leq \lambda \leq \bar{\lambda} \tag{4.59}$$

If $\bar{\lambda} = +\infty$, then the solution is optimum over all admissible values of λ, $\delta \leq \lambda \leq \phi$. If, however, $\bar{\lambda}$ is finite, then, in particular, $\bar{\lambda} = -\alpha_k/\beta_k$ for some particular $\beta_k > 0$. If all of the corresponding $x_{ik} \leq 0$, then no minimum (optimum) solution will exist for $\lambda > \bar{\lambda}$. If, however, at least one $x_{ik} > 0$, then one can introduce a new vector P_k into the basis (by the simplex technique). This new basis will result in a new range of optimality on λ, namely:

$$\bar{\lambda} = \underline{\lambda}' \leq \lambda \leq \bar{\lambda}' \tag{4.60}$$

Thus, by successive iterations, one can proceed from one range of values of λ to the next, and completely cover all admissible value of λ, $\delta \leq \lambda \leq \phi$.

As noted by Gass (1958, p. 112), the various $\underline{\lambda}$ and $\bar{\lambda}$ that arise are called *characteristic values of* λ, while the corresponding optimum solutions are called *characteristic solutions.*

Case B (no finite optimum solution exists for $\lambda = \delta$*).* Here, in attempting to determine an optimum (minimal) solution when $\lambda = \delta$, one has a column, k, such that $\alpha_k + \delta\beta_k > 0$. However, one cannot introduce a new vector into the basis because all $x_{ik} \leq 0$.

1. If $\beta_k \geq 0$, then no finite minimum solutions exist for any λ.
2. If $\beta_k < 0$, then $\alpha_k + \lambda\beta_k > 0$ will hold for all

$$\lambda < \lambda_1' = -\frac{\alpha_k}{\beta_k}$$

Hence, no finite minimum solutions will exist for $\delta \leq \lambda \leq \lambda_1'$.

If all $\alpha_j + \lambda_1'\beta_j \leq 0$, then an optimum solution will exist for λ_1', and λ_1 can be determined by $\lambda_1 = \min_{\beta_j > 0}(-\alpha_j/\beta_j)$. The characteristic solution holds for $\lambda_1' \leq \lambda \leq \lambda_1$, and one can then proceed as in Case A.

If $\alpha_j + \lambda_1'\beta_j > 0$ for at least one value of j, then a new basis can be obtained, and one can continue, finally obtaining a solution as in Case A, or the knowledge that there are no values of λ for which a finite minimum solution exists.

For further discussion and examples of the one-parameter problem, see Gass (1958), Gass and Saaty (1955*a*), Manne (1953), Charnes, Cooper, and Henderson (1953), and Saaty and Gass (1954).

n-*Parameter problem.* The generalization of the one-parameter linear-programming problem to the case of the parameterization of the objective function with n parameters has been outlined by Gass and Saaty (1955*b*).

For the case of $n=2$, one seeks to minimize

$$\sum_{j=1}^{n} (c_j + \lambda_1 c_j' + \lambda_2 c_j'')x_j \qquad (4.61)$$

and, generalizing on the method for the one-parameter problem, one must determine the convex region in the (λ_1,λ_2)-plane whose points satisfy

$$\alpha_j + \lambda_1\beta_j + \lambda_2\gamma_j \leq 0 \qquad (j=1,2,\cdots,n) \qquad (4.62)$$

Gass and Saaty consider two methods for so doing, namely, the double descriptive method (see Motzkin, 1952*c*) and the two-dimensional graph of the inequalities, and illustrate their parametric programming procedure by the latter process.

Finally, Gass and Saaty outline the further generalization to $n > 2$ parameters, observing, at the same time, the increasing complexity and immensity of the problem.

9.3. Variation of Coefficients of the Right-Hand Side

The parametric-programming problem involving the right-hand-side coefficients can be stated mathematically as (see Gass, 1958, p. 115):

Let $\sigma \leq \theta \leq \beta$. For each θ in this interval, find a vector $x=(x_1,x_2,\cdots,x_n)$ such that

$$\sum_{j=1}^{n} c_j x_j = \text{minimum}$$

subject to: (P.31)

$$\sum_{j=1}^{n} a_{ij} x_j = b_i + \theta b_i \qquad (i=1,2,\cdots,m)$$

$$x_j \geq 0 \qquad (j=1,2,\cdots,n)$$

This problem, however, can be considered in its *dual* formulation, in which case one obtains a parametric objective-function problem of the form considered in Section 9.2, which can then be solved by the procedure described therein. Specific results for the direct problem are given in Gass (1958, pp. 115–117).

9.4. General Case: All Coefficients Parameterized

Saaty (1959*b*) considers a more general parametric-programming problem in which all coefficients a_{ij}, c_j, and b_i are functions of time. His procedure requires solving sets of simultaneous general (not necessarily linear) inequalities in t, resulting from the condition $z_j - c_j \leq 0$ and, as Saaty observes, is generally cumbersome except for problems involving the parameterization of the coefficients of only a few of the basis vectors.

10. COMPUTATION OF SOLUTIONS TO LINEAR-PROGRAMMING PROBLEMS

After a linear-programming problem has been formulated mathematically for a given set of data, the computational problem must be solved—namely, how to obtain a solution in the most efficient manner. In this section, the computational aspects will be reviewed from the viewpoint of "hand" solutions and also those obtained through the use of electronic computers.

10.1. Computational Problems of Linear Programming

Any linear-programming problem can, of course, be solved by the simplex technique or one of the revised simplex techniques (see Section 7; also Chapters 4 and 6 in Gass, 1958). However, in a number of instances, simplified and more efficient computational procedures have been devised which take advantage of the special form or structure of the problem—as, for example, in the cases of the transportation and assignment problems (Sections 4 and 5), and the warehousing, catering and production-smoothing problems (Sections 4.7 and 8). In other instances, attempting to devise a special computational procedure to solve a particular problem may sometimes be exceedingly time-consuming and even unproductive so that, in the last analysis, using the simplex technique might be the most efficient approach.[29] However, it should be noted that the efficient short cuts and simplifications developed by Charnes and Cooper have made possible resolution of certain large-scale systems.

Most of the computational problems of linear programming arise in trying to solve the *general* linear-programming problem (i.e., one which cannot be solved by the much easier transportation and assignment techniques). Hence, most of the research into developing more efficient computational procedures has been, and is being, concentrated on attempts to overcome certain difficulties or inadequacies arising in the use of the simplex technique. For example, in discussing multistage linear-programming problems, Dantzig notes, "Experience with many large linear programming systems of the order of 20 equations in 500 to 1,000 unknowns indicates that they tend to go to hundreds of iterations (using the simplex technique) before an optimum is reached" (1959, p. 68). As Dantzig also notes, the number of operations required, per iteration, to use the inverse of a basis increases roughly as the square of the number of equations, and more decimal places are necessary to maintain the required accuracy. Accordingly, a number of variations to the simplex technique were developed—all designed to reduce the amount of computation by:

1. Decreasing the size of the matrix (e.g., by solving the dual problem) (see Section 2.2).
2. Decreasing the total number of iterations required to reach the optimum solution.
3. Resolving the problem of round-off errors, which arise when using the simplex technique (see Section 3.4).
4. Finding a compact form for the inverse of the basis.

In some cases, where the original problem is of a size within the capabilities of electronic computers, such simplifications enable one to obtain the optimum solution more readily. However, in other cases, the problem is of such large size that it exceeds the current computer

[29] In a sense, this is analogous to solving an "operations research" problem by "quick-and-dirty" or near-optimal procedures, where the *cost* of obtaining the *mathematically* optimum solution may very well exceed the added gains (over the near-optimum solution).

capabilities (due to solution-time and/or the increased accuracy requirements), so that simplifications are necessary to enable one to solve the problem in any manner, practical or otherwise [30] (see also, Section 3).

As noted earlier (Section 7), the general simplex technique is divided into two distinct computational phases: Phase I, concerned with determining a basic feasible solution (by eliminating the artificial variables from the basis), and Phase II, which starts with this basic feasible solution and proceeds to obtain an optimum (minimum) feasible solution. Much research has been devoted to developing variations of the simplex technique that will either replace Phase I entirely (by directly yielding an initial basic feasible solution) or, at worst, reduce the initial number of artificial variables in the basis (in Phase I). Some of the corresponding variations proposed for this purpose include:

1. Dual-simplex technique—Lemke (1954).
2. Composite simplex algorithm—Orchard-Hays (1954) and Dantzig (1954*b*).
3. Primal-dual algorithm—Dantzig, Ford, and Fulkerson (1956).
4. Method of leading variables—Beale (1954).
5. Maximum decrease of objective form per decrease of infeasibility form—Markowitz (see Dantzig, 1959).

Some of these variations are discussed in Section 7. See also, Dantzig (1959).

There are other methods which can be used for solving linear-programming problems. These include:

1. Relaxation method—Motzkin (1952*c*), Agmon (1954), Motzkin and Schoenberg (1954).
2. Fictitious-play method—Brown (1951), von Neumann (1954).
3. Projection method—Tompkins (1955).
4. Double-description method—Motzkin (1952*c*), Raiffa, Thompson, and Thrall (1952), Motzkin, Raiffa, Thompson, and Thrall (1953), and Pollack (1953).

However, as noted by Hoffman, Mannos, Sokolowsky, and Weigmann (1953) and Hoffman (1955), these latter methods have not proved as effective in solving linear-programming problems as the

[30] As noted by Dantzig (1959), the ability to significantly reduce the number of iterations may well make the difference between success and failure in the solution of a large system.

simplex technique or some version of the simplex technique—mainly because of the slowness in convergence and the very large number of steps (iterations) required.

Proposals for finding a compact form for the inverse of the basis are summarized and discussed in Dantzig (1959) and include those due to:

1. Markowitz (1955). Markowitz has developed a procedure which is particularly applicable to problems in which the coefficient matrix is composed largely of zeros. Here, one selects, for the pivotal element, a column with as many zeros as possible, and which results in the inverse of the matrix being represented as a product of "elementary" matrices (namely, matrices that differ from the identity matrix by only one row or column).
2. Dantzig (1955*a*). This proposal is designed for block-triangular structures and is efficient where the number of columns exceeds the number of rows by only a relatively small amount. It consists mainly of modifying the columns of the matrix to produce square submatrices down the diagonal.
3. Dantzig and Wolfe (1958, 1960). This is an iterative procedure, designed primarily as an electronic-computer routine, which is particularly applicable to angular systems[31] and to certain multistage problems of the staircase type, such as are found in the warehousing problem.

For further discussion, see Dantzig (1959). See also, Hoffman (1955).

Hoffman (1955) also discusses the computational problems of linear programming and, in particular, four features that are likely to arise in most linear-programming problems, namely:

1. Large size of the problem.
2. Sparseness of the coefficient matrix.
3. Time-phasing or multiperiodicity in the problem.
4. Inactive constraints.

Hoffman also discusses the problems of degeneracy and round-off error, as well as computational devices which may be used for special situations.

[31] *Angular systems* are block-triangular systems in which the blocks are vacuous except along the diagonal and the bottom rows of the matrix (see Dantzig, 1959, footnote on p. 67).

TABLE 4.1

COMPUTER SOLUTION OF THE GENERAL LINEAR-PROGRAMMING PROBLEM *

Company	Computer	Problem Capacity	Technique Used
Burroughs	Datatron	$m \leq 40$; $n \leq 200$ $mn \leq 3000$	Simplex—with artificial basis
Ferranti Ltd.	Pegasus	$m \leq 30$; $n \leq 95$	Simplex—with artificial basis
IBM	650	a) $m \leq 30$; $n \leq 50$ $m(n+1) < 1400$	Simplex—with artificial basis
		b) $n \leq 40$; n unlimited	Revised simplex
		c) $m \leq 33$; $n \leq 1000$ [Routine due to Graves (1956)]	Revised simplex, modified to use the dual algorithm to initiate a solution when possible
		d) $m \leq 97$; n unlimited	Revised simplex—product form of the inverse
	701	$m \leq 99$; n unlimited	Revised simplex—product form of the inverse
	702	$m \leq 200$; $n \leq 250$	Revised simplex—product form of the inverse
	704	$m \leq 255$; n unlimited	Revised simplex—see Gass (1958, p. 132)
	705	$m \leq 60$; n unlimited	Revised simplex
Sperry Rand (Univac Division)	Univac I	a) Variable, depending on both m and n $1 \leq m \leq 57$; $n < 2000$ $58 \leq m \leq 117$; $n < 1000$ $118 \leq m \leq 177$; $n < 660$ $178 \leq m \leq 237$; $n < 500$	Simplex—artificial basis
		b) $m \leq 178$; $n \leq 999$	Revised simplex—full inverse form
	1103	$m \leq 106$; $n \leq 140$ $(m+n) \leq 246$	Revised simplex—product form of the inverse
	1103A	$m \leq 242$; n unlimited	Revised simplex—modified for the upper-bound technique

* Reprinted, in slightly modified form, from Gass (1958, pp. 131–133.)

10.2. *Computer Solution of Linear-Programming Problems*

As noted in Section 2.1, a high-speed electronic computer was first successfully used in solving a linear-programming problem in January, 1952—by the Project SCOOP staff on the SEAC (Bureau of Standards Eastern Automatic Computer). Since that time, the simplex technique, or modifications of the simplex technique, has been coded for almost all of the medium- and large-scale electronic computers, both in the United States and abroad. Additionally, a number of computers are programmed to solve the transportation problem.

Gass (1958) has provided what is probably the best available résumé of computer programs for solving the general linear-programming problem and the transportation problem. Gass' résumé is reprinted here in tabular form as Tables 4.1 and 4.2, respectively.[32]

11. INTEGER SOLUTIONS

11.1. *The Linear Case*

When solutions are required to be non-negative *integers*, the ordinary linear-programming problem (P.1) can be transformed into the [0–1] (i.e., yes-no) form, where $x_j=0$ or 1, *provided that* the variables x_j have known upper bounds (see Dantzig, 1957). Thus, if $x_j \leq k$, then this transformation becomes

$$x_j = y_{1j} + y_{2j} + \cdots + y_{kj}$$

$$y_{ij} = \begin{cases} 0 \\ 1 \end{cases} \qquad (i=1,2,\cdots,k) \tag{4.63}$$

Solution techniques generally make use of the obvious proposition that the set C' of points satisfying $x_j = (0,1)$, where

$$C' = \{x_j \mid \Sigma c_j x_j = \min; \quad Ax=b; \quad x_j = 0 \text{ or } 1\} \tag{4.64}$$

is a *subset* of the set

$$C = \{x_j \mid \Sigma c_j x_j = \min; \quad Ax=b; \quad 0 \leq x_j \leq 1\} \tag{4.65}$$

Techniques of solution of *linear* integer programming are based either on an extension and modification of the simplex procedure, or

[32] See, also, the excellent discussion of the evolution of linear-programming computing techniques in Orchard-Hays (1958).

TABLE 4.2

COMPUTER SOLUTION OF THE TRANSPORTATION PROBLEM *

Company	Computer	Problem Capacity	Technique Used †
Ferranti Ltd.	Pegasus	$m+n \leq 128$ $mn \leq 1024$	
IBM	650	Variable, depending on m and n. Approximate: $5m+6n \leq 2300$ $n \leq 100$	
	701	$m \leq 199$; $n \leq 399$ $m+n \leq 426$ $n(m+3) \leq 16{,}384$	
	702	$m \leq 349$ $m+n \leq 700$	
	704	$n \leq 800$ $m+n \leq 5500$ $mn \leq 700{,}000$	
	705	$m \leq 500$ $m+n \leq 2500$	
Sperry Rand (Univac Division)	Univac I	a) $m+n \leq 600$	
		b) Variable, depending on m and n $1 \leq m \leq 30$; $m+n<2000$ $31 \leq m \leq 60$; $m+n<1000$ $61 \leq m \leq 90$; $m+n<677$ $91 \leq m \leq 119$; $m+n<500$	Revised procedure adapted for transportation technique by Suzuki (1955)
		c) $m \leq 180$ $n \leq 2000$	Threshold technique by Gerstenhaber and Kelley (1956)
	1103	$m+n<8000$	Revised procedure due to Suzuki (1955)

* Reprinted, in slightly modified form, from Gass (1958, pp. 133–134).

† The transportation technique due to Dantzig (1951*b*) or the "stepping-stone method" of Charnes and Cooper (1954*a*) is used, unless otherwise indicated.

on the use of functional equations (which serves to reduce the number of variables). For *non-linear* integer programming, computational solutions have been found for the case where the objective function is of separable convex form.

Extension and modification of the simplex procedure. If one replaces the requirements that $x_j=0$ or 1 by the requirement that $0\leq x_j\leq 1$, then, one can apply the simplex procedure and obtain a solution, and then seek an efficient means for discarding the fractional solutions to obtain the optimum integer solution (see Dantzig, 1957 and 1958). To do this, *one must impose additional linear inequality constraints* (somewhere in the simplex process) *so that* the *fractional extreme points of the set* C *are modified,* while the set C' of admissible solutions remains unchanged.

Gomory (1958*b*) gives a method of automatically generating such additional inequalities. For the integer linear-programming problem, his method is to set up the following *maximization* problem:

Find non-negative integers x_j so that

$$z=a_{00}+\sum_{j=1}^{n}a_{0j}(-x_j)=\max$$

subject to: (P.32)

$$\sum_{j=1}^{n}a_{ij}x_j\leq a_{i0} \qquad (i=1,2,\cdots,m)$$

Transform P.32 into the form:

$$z=a_{00}+\sum_{j=1}^{n}a_{0j}(-x_j)=\max$$

subject to: (P.33)

$$\bar{x}_i=a_{i0}+\sum_{j=1}^{n}a_{ij}(-x_j) \qquad (i=1,2,\cdots,m)$$

$$x_s=\sum_{j=1}^{n}(-\delta_{sj})(-x_j) \qquad \delta_{sj}=\begin{cases}0 \text{ for } s\neq j\\ 1 \text{ for } s=j\end{cases} \quad (s=1,2,\cdots,n)$$

where the $\bar{x}_i$ are the slack variables resulting from the inequalities in P.32. The maximand together with the restrictions are then written as

$$X=A^0T^0$$

where

$$X=\begin{bmatrix} z \\ \bar{x}_1 \\ \cdot \\ \cdot \\ \cdot \\ \bar{x}_m \\ x_1 \\ \cdot \\ \cdot \\ \cdot \\ \bar{x}_n \end{bmatrix}; \quad T^0=\begin{bmatrix} 1 \\ -x_1 \\ -x_2 \\ \cdot \\ \cdot \\ \cdot \\ -x_n \end{bmatrix}; \quad A^0=\begin{bmatrix} a_{00}, & a_{01}, & \cdots, & a_{0n} \\ a_{10}, & a_{11}, & \cdots, & a_{1n} \\ \cdot & \cdot & \cdot & \cdot \\ a_{m0}, & a_{m1}, & \cdots, & a_{mn} \\ 0, & -1, & \cdots, & 0 \\ \cdot & \cdot & \cdot & \cdot \\ 0, & 0, & \cdots, & -1 \end{bmatrix} \tag{4.66}$$

If the problem is primally feasible, that is, if $a_{i0}\geq 0$ $(i\geq 1)$ for all i, choose a column, k, with first element a_{0k} negative. From among the *positive* elements in this column, select the one for which $a_{i0}/a_{ik}=\min$. Call this the rth row; then the pivotal element is a_{rk}.

With this pivotal element, a_{rk}, we transform the matrix by the following rule:

$$a_{ij}'=a_{ij}-a_{ik}\left(\frac{a_{rj}}{a_{rk}}\right) \qquad (i\neq r, \quad j\neq k)$$
$$a_{ik}'=\frac{-a_{ik}}{a_{rk}}\ (i\neq r); \quad a_{rj}'=\frac{a_{rj}}{a_{rk}}\ (j\neq k); \quad a_{rk}'=\frac{1}{a_{rk}} \tag{4.67}$$

The solution to an ordinary linear-programming problem is obtained when some kth iterate, A^k, is found to satisfy:

$$\begin{aligned} &\text{(primal feasibility)} \qquad a_{i0}\geq 0, \quad \text{all } i \\ &\text{(dual feasibility)} \qquad a_{0j}\geq 0, \quad \text{all } j \end{aligned} \tag{4.68}$$

$$X=\alpha_0=\{a_{i0}\}, \text{ (first column of } A^k\text{), non-negative integers}$$

When $X=\alpha_0$ are not all integers, one or more equations (each representing an inequality and the corresponding slack variable) are added to the set A^k in the form

$$s=-f_0-\sum_{j=1}^{n} f_j(-t_j) \tag{4.69}$$

where the f_j are the fractional parts of some row and the t_j are the current non-basic variables. The addition of these equations does *not* eliminate any non-negative integer solution to the original problem

(P.32); on the other hand, the now-enlarged matrix (enlarged because of addition of another group of equations) does *not* remain in the form of Eq. 4.68.

The simplex technique is now applied to the enlarged matrix until conditions 4.68 are satisfied. Somewhere in the process, *a newly added row can be dropped as soon as its slack variable becomes strictly positive.* In a finite number of steps, the final matrix $A^{k'}$ is obtained which satisfies Eq. 4.68 and which contains all integer entries.

Dantzig (1957, 1958) has furnished some alternative rules for generating additional constraints. These stem from the consideration that if a linear-programming problem in n variables $x_1,x_2,\cdots,x_n$ has a basic feasible solution for basic variables $x_1,x_2,\cdots,x_m$ $(m<n)$ which is inadmissible for some reason, then any admissible non-basic solution that has integral values must satisfy the partial-sum condition

$$x_{m+1}+x_{m+2}+\cdots+x_n\geq 1$$

If n is not very large, solving the dual program will be easier, because additional constraints take the form of adding new columns to the matrix. These constraints are automatically generated by forming sums of the columns in the basis, except for the component in the cost row, where the sum is increased by unity.

Functional-equation approach. Gross (1955) considers the linear-programming problem

$$\sum_{i=1}^{n} u_i=\min$$

subject to:

$$\begin{gathered} u_i\geq 0 \qquad (i=1,2,\cdots,n) \\ u_1+u_2\geq \alpha_1;\quad u_2+u_3\geq \alpha_2;\cdots; \\ u_{n-1}+u_n\geq \alpha_{n-1}; \\ u_n+u_1\geq \alpha_n \end{gathered} \tag{P.34}$$

which, after setting $x_i=\sum_{j=1}^{i} u_j$ $(i=1,2,\cdots,n)$, reduces the given problem to

$$x_n=\min$$

subject to:

$$\begin{gathered} x_n\geq x_{n-1}\geq\cdots\geq x_1\geq 0 \\ x_{j+1}\geq \alpha_j+x_{j-1} \qquad (j=1,2,\cdots,n-1;\quad x_0=0) \\ x_n-x_{n-1}+x_1\geq \alpha_n \end{gathered} \tag{P.35}$$

The inequalities of the transformed problem imply that

$$x_{j+1} \geq \max[x_j; x_{j-1}+\alpha_j] \qquad (j=1,2,\cdots,n-2)$$

and (4.70a)

$$x_n = \max[x_{n-1}; x_{n-1}-x_1+\alpha_n; x_{n-2}+x_{n-1}]$$

Therefore, the original minimization problem is equivalent to solving the last line of Eq. 4.70a subject to the rest of the inequalities of Eq. 4.70a, that is, subject to

$$\begin{aligned} x_1 &= x \geq 0 \\ x_2 &= \max\,[x, \alpha_1] \\ &\cdots\cdots\cdots \\ x_{n-1} &= \max\,[x_{n-2}; \alpha_{n-2}+x_{n-3}] \end{aligned} \tag{4.70b}$$

Thus, if x is assigned a chosen value, then, for this chosen value, it is possible to maximize x_n by considering the inequalities 4.70b as strict equalities. In other words, the problem is reduced to one of expressing x_{n-1} and x_{n-2} in terms of x, which is the only minimizing variable.

The method of functional equations has been extended to the case of a convex separable objective function. Gross (1956) gives the following treatment for the minimization problem:

$$\sum_{j=1}^{n} \phi_j(x_j) = \min$$

subject to: (P.36)

(1) $x_j \geq 0$, integers

(2) $\sum_{j=1}^{n} x_j = m > 0$

The convexity of each $\phi_j(x_j)$ and non-negativity of x_j are employed to reduce the problem to the following equivalent problem:

$$\sum_{j=1}^{n} u_j = \min$$

subject to:

(1) $x_j \geq 0$ (P.37)

(2) $\sum_{j=1}^{n} x_j = m > 0$

(3) $u_j - \phi_j(k) \geq (x_j - k)[\phi_j(k+1) - \phi_j(k)] \qquad (k=0,1,\cdots,m-1)$

A necessary and sufficient condition for a feasible solution, x, of P.37 to furnish a minimum of problem P.36 is shown to be

$$\min_{j \in \sigma} [\phi_j(x_j+1)-\phi_j(x_j)] \geq \max_{j \in S^+(x)} [\phi_j(x_j)-\phi_j(x_j-1)] \tag{4.71}$$

where σ is the set of integers, 1 to n, and $S^+(x)$ is the subset of σ for which $x_j>0$, x being a feasible solution.

11.2. The Non-Linear Case

It has been mentioned earlier that a *convex* objective function $f(x)$ can be "approximated" by polygonal line segments lying above the curve $f(x)$. In such cases, the Charnes and Lemke (1954*b*) method of approximating the original problem by a linear problem is valid because the maximization of a linear function on a convex constraint set always assures that a local maximum is also an absolute or global maximum. However, if the objective function expresses the quantity of resource required as a function of the quantity of output, and if there are economies of scale, then, as Markowitz and Manne (1957) point out—the linear approximation introduces an awkward problem: since the slopes, a_i, between two points are a diminishing sequence $a_i<a_{i-1}$, the constraint set becomes non-convex and, consequently, a local optimum ceases to be necessarily an absolute optimum. Markowitz and Manne (1957) suggest, for such cases, an *equivalent linear* programming problem in which 0–1 solutions are sought for a class of variables which are defined in terms of the end-points of intervals over which the polygoned approximations are made. Thus, if $r=r(q)$ is a function expressing resource required as a function of the quantity, q, of output, then a polygonal approximation is given over some range $0 \leq q \leq v_n$ by

$$\bar{r}=\sum_{i=1}^{n} a_i q_i \tag{4.72}$$

where a_i are the slopes from v_{i-1} to v_i and where $a_i>a_{i-1}$. Further, we have,

$$q=\sum_{i=1}^{n} q_i; \quad 0 \leq q_i \leq v_i - v_{i-1} \tag{4.73}$$

Now, from the nature of the function $r(q)$, it follows that in an optimal solution some q_i is to be more "economical" than q_{i+1}, so that if $q_i<v_i-v_{i+1}$, then q_{i+1} has to be zero. Thus, new variables x_i, equal to 0 or 1 are defined as:

$$x_i \geq \frac{q_i}{v_i - v_{i-1}} \quad (i=1,2,\cdots,n); \qquad x_{i+1} \leq \frac{q_i}{v_i - v_{i-1}} \quad (i=1,2,\cdots,n-1) \tag{4.74}$$

The conditions on x_i insure that if q_i is to be positive, x_i will have to be equal to 1, and that if q_i has not attained its maximum value it will be impossible to assign a positive value to q_{i+1}.

Thus the non-linear problem is reduced to a discrete linear-programming problem of the form

$$P(X,Y) = \sum_{j=1}^{n_1} c_j x_j + \sum_{j=1}^{n_2} \bar{c}_j y_j = \max$$ [over $D(0)$, namely, a set wherein some or all the variables take integer values]

subject to: (P.38)

(1) $\sum_{j=1}^{n_1} a_{ij} x_j + \sum_{j=1}^{n_2} \bar{a}_{ij} y_j = b_i \qquad (i=1,2,\cdots,m)$

(2) x_j = a non-negative integer

(3) $y_j \geq 0$

One may now arrive at a complete solution by applying the technique of Dantzig, Fulkerson, and Johnson (1954), as discussed in Section 6.

12. STOCHASTIC PROGRAMMING

12.1. Risk, Uncertainty, and Decisions over Time

A common feature of the classes of problems discussed so far is that *anticipations* about future data were not considered to be relevant to the determination of optimal programs. In particular, the programs were implicitly interpreted as "one-shot" decisions, relative to one or more time periods. If these decisions are made on the basis of a set of *fixed* data, one refers to this type of programming as *static, deterministic* programming. When decisions are made on the basis of given data whose values do not remain fixed over the time periods, the programming involved is said to be *dynamic, deterministic* programming.

We shall consider here a class of *stochastic* programming problems, where decisions are based, at each stage, on the *anticipations* about probable values of relevant parameters (e.g., unit costs, selling price, demands, etc.) in unchanging probability distributions. Such anticipations may or may not be unique. If unique, the problem is not conceptually different from deterministic programming. It is only when anticipations or probable values are not unique (i.e., drawn from a fixed distribution) that programming begins to acquire a "stochastic" character.

Earliest analysis of this class of problems can be traced to the work of a few mathematical economists associated with the Cowles Commission (Foundation). Hart (1941) and Tintner (1941) distinguished between two broad types of situations: (*a*) those in which the parameters have known probability distribution functions—*risky* situations, and (*b*) those in which the nature of the distribution functions is not known—the *uncertain* situations.

The distinction may appear to be rather artificial because, when one has a probability distribution of probability distributions, one can multiply each individual distribution by its probability, sum (integrate) the products, and obtain a single probability distribution. However, merging various contingent probability distributions means merging the likelihoods and probabilities by multiplication, so that the resulting total distribution may conceal some of the data relevant for planning activity levels (see Hart, 1941).

The basic considerations that enter into the analysis of *uncertain situations* are twofold: (*a*) anticipation of a change in anticipation and (*b*) possibility of deferring decisions with or without loss or some additional cost. Consequently, planning under uncertainty may be worked out by hypothetically constructing the situation likely to prevail in the latest period of the planning horizon at which decisions affecting output of a given date will be taken, and then developing the plan backwards to the present. Giving hypothetical values to the inputs to be determined earlier makes it possible to say (hypothetically) what will be the input scheme offering the greatest expectation of profit in the light of each price-probability distribution for outputs now considered possible. This hypothetical decision will depend merely on the expected value of each such distribution taken as a whole (i.e., not on the specific parameters of the distribution). For each contingency, there is thus a profit expectation; and multiplying each such expectation by the likelihood ascribed to the corresponding probability distribution at the date of planning gives a combined, or weighted, expectation.

The process may now be extended by reconstructing the next-to-the-last input decisions and choosing that one which has highest profit expectation. Thus, *decisions at each stage can be formulated in the light of their effects on the setting of later decisions.* This method of programming has been characterized as *stochastic programming.*

12.2. Earlier Methodology and Mathematical Formulations

For a finite planning horizon $(t=1,2,\cdots,n)$, let us suppose that there is a technological transformation function

$$g(x_{11},\cdots,x_{m1};\cdots;x_{1n},\cdots,x_{mn})=0 \tag{4.75}$$

where the x_{ij} stands for the ith input (or output) at jth period. If q_{ij} represents the anticipated *discounted* price, then the anticipated discounted profit is

$$W=\sum_{i=1}^{m}\sum_{j=1}^{n}x_{ij}q_{ij} \tag{4.76}$$

which, in the continuous case, becomes the sum of integrals:

$$W=\sum_{i=1}^{m}\int_{0}^{n}x_i(t)q_i(t)\,dt \tag{4.77}$$

Let us now assume, for the *risky* situation, that the joint probability distribution, P, of prices $p_{11},\cdots,p_{mn}$ and of accumulation rates $r_1,\cdots,r_n$ is *known* and characterized by, say, a parameters:

$$\begin{aligned}P\,dp_{11}\cdots dp_{mn}dr_1\cdots dr_n\\ =P(p_{11},\cdots,p_{mn};r_1,\cdots,r_n;k_1,\cdots,k_a)\,dp_{11}\cdots dp_{mn}dr_1\cdots dr_n\end{aligned} \tag{4.78}$$

This distribution defines a distribution, Q, for the anticipated discounted profit W:

$$Q\,dW=Q(W;x_{11},\cdots,x_{mn};k_1,\cdots,k_a)\,dW \tag{4.79}$$

where the decision variables x_{ij} appear as ordinary variables without any probability distributions. It is convenient to introduce the notion of a *risk preference functional*, Φ, which expresses the manner in which the decision maker evaluates [33] the probabilities associated with specific amounts of W. Symbolically, we assume known

$$\Phi=\Phi[Q(\overset{\infty}{\underset{-\infty}{W}})] \tag{4.80}$$

The functional Φ is to be maximized subject to the restriction 4.75 on the technology. Using the functional derivative of Φ with respect to Q, evaluated at $W=W_0$, we get the first-order conditions:

[33] A *special instance* of Φ is the mathematical expectation, i.e., $\int_{-\infty}^{\infty}WQ(W)\,dW$.

$$g(x_{11},\cdots,x_{m1};\cdots;x_{1n},\cdots,x_{mn})=0$$
$$\int_{-\infty}^{\infty}\Phi'[Q(W);W_0]\frac{\partial Q(W_0)}{\partial x_{ij}}\,dW_0=\lambda\frac{\partial g}{\partial x_{ij}}=\lambda q_{ij} \tag{4.81}$$

where λ is a Lagrange multiplier.[34] The substantive problem, however, is to investigate the effect of changes in the probability distribution P upon the decisions about the expected levels of x_{ij}. This involves differentiating the first-order conditions with respect to the parameters $k_1,\cdots,k_a$ (of the P-distribution) that may be of practical interest, and thus obtaining an expression for $\partial x_{ij}/\partial k_\alpha$.

For the *uncertain* situation, we assume a *likelihood function*

$$L\,dk_1\cdots dk_a=L(k_1,\cdots,k_a;h_1,\cdots,h_b)\,dk_1\cdots dk_a \tag{4.82}$$

to represent the decision maker's knowledge of the parameters $k_1,\cdots,k_a$ of the distribution P. With this likelihood function, the likelihood of the anticipated discounted profits, W, is written as

$$\begin{aligned}M\,dW&=\int_{(k_1)}\cdots\int_{(ka)}QL\,dW\,dk_1\cdots dk_a\\&=M(W;h_1,\cdots,h_b)\,dW\end{aligned} \tag{4.83}$$

Corresponding to this likelihood of W, we define a preference functional

$$\psi=\psi[M(W)]$$

and this is maximized subject to the technological restriction of Eq. 4.75. The first-order conditions

$$\int_{-\infty}^{\infty}\psi'[M;W_1]\frac{\partial M(W_1)}{\partial n_{ij}}dW_1=\lambda\frac{\partial g}{\partial n_{ij}};\quad g=0 \tag{4.84}$$

are then solved to obtain x_{ij} as functions of the parameters $h_1,\cdots,h_b$ of the likelihood function.

A simple extension of this logical structure is made to the situation where the decision maker likes to make provision for possible future changes in plans. This consists in introducing a *second-order likelihood function* for the parameters of L, say,

$$N=N(h_1,\cdots,h_b;\theta_1,\cdots,\theta_c)$$

which gives the likelihood of expected discounted net profits $B\,dW$

[34] These equations are now solved to obtain x_{ij} as a function of the parameters $k_1,\cdots,k_a$.

$$B\,dW = \int_{(h_1)} \cdots \int_{(h_b)} MN\,dW\,dh_1 \cdots dh_b \tag{4.85}$$

in place of $M\,dw$. Similarly, a new preference-functional, Ω, is defined for the second-order likelihood of B:

$$\Omega = \Omega[B(W)]$$

then Ω is maximized subject to Eq. 4.75, and the x_{ij} are then solved for functions of the parameters $\theta_1, \cdots, \theta_c$ of the second-order likelihood function.

12.3. Contemporary Methodology and Formalism (mainly conceptual)

Dantzig (1955), Radner (1955), and Charnes and Cooper (1959*a*) have given abstract formulations without the above distinction between "risk" and "uncertainty." However, even for the assumption of *known* distributions (therefore, in the classical sense, signifying risky situations), they reach a high degree of generality by considering the distribution functions as a whole rather than the specific parameters only. The problem of uncertainty has, therefore, been recognized insofar as approximations are sought in "policy-space."

The basic description of the problem can be given as follows (see Radner, 1955 and 1959): There is a probability-space X, with *states*, x, of nature. Corresponding to each x, there is an *information variable* y

$$y_i = \eta_i(x) \qquad (i = 1, 2, \cdots, n) \tag{4.86}$$

which describes some aspect of the environment (from the viewpoint of the decision maker); the set of y's and the corresponding η's constitute an *information structure.* Rates of return, c_i, are random variables depending on the states x; $c_i = \gamma_i(x)$. Decisions α_i about activity levels are set up in terms of the y's; thus $\alpha_i = \alpha_i(y_i)$. Then, where $\gamma_i(y_i) = E\{\gamma_i(x) \mid y_i\}$, the expected payoff, that is, the quantity

$$E\left\{\sum_{i=1}^{n} \alpha_i(y_i)\gamma_i(x)\right\} = E\{\Sigma \alpha_i(y_i)\bar{\gamma}_i(y_i)\} \tag{4.87}$$

is to be maximized by appropriate choice of the decision functions α_i, given an information structure, and given some constraints on the α_i. Clearly, these constraints are also to be obtained as functions of x, the state of nature. Since the form of the payoff function is linear in decision variables, this statement of the problem can be interpreted as a problem of linear programming in the space of decision variables. The decisions may refer to those of one decision maker over several time periods or several decision makers (as in a team) for one period; mathematical formalism is the same in both cases.

Conceptually, therefore, the "solutions" to a stochastic programming problem are stochastic decision rules, and solving such a problem means selecting certain random variables as functions of some other random variables having known distributions, so as to maximize a functional of both classes of variables, subject to constraints on these variables which must be maintained at preassigned levels of probability (see Charnes and Cooper, 1959*a*). For the linear case, the current procedure is to choose optimal information structure *and* optimal decisions. This, however, requires a separation of the problem into two parts: (1) determine the distribution (or discrete probabilities) which solve the maximizing problem, and (2) find a "best" approximation to this probability distribution by functions of the known random variables.

Example No. 1 (see Dantzig, 1955*b* and 1956*b*; and Ferguson and Dantzig, 1956). Suppose m products (index i) are to be allocated to n destinations (index j) where the demand is uncertain, and that the "cost" has two components: (a) the cost of assigning a product to a location, c_{ij}, and (b) the revenue lost (α_j per unit) due to failure to meet unknown demands. The problem is one of *two-stage decision.* For the one-stage situation, we have [35]

$$\sum_{j=1}^{n} x_{ij} = a_i; \quad \sum_{i=1}^{m} b_{ij} x_{ij} = u_j \tag{4.88}$$

where x_{ij} = amount of ith product (aircraft type) assigned to jth location (passenger route), and b_{ij} = units of demand at j that can be satisfied by a unit of ith resource. However, for the two-stage case, we have the possibility of shortages (v_j) or excesses (s_j); hence *demand* is $d_j = u_j + v_j - s_j$. Further, the total cost is assumed to be of the form $C = \Sigma\Sigma c_{ij} x_{ij} + \Sigma \alpha_j v_j$. If we define $\phi_j(u_j | d_j)$ = minimum cost if, at j, the demand is d_j and the supply is u_j, then

$$\phi_j(u_j | d_j) = \begin{cases} \alpha_j(d_j - u_j) & d_j \geq u_j \\ 0 & d_j < u_j \end{cases} \tag{4.89}$$

[35] In the context of the example given in Ferguson and Dantzig (1956), the problem is one of assigning the ith type of aircraft to the jth passenger route. Further, a_i is the availability of the ith aircraft type, b_{ij} is the number of passengers that can be carried on the ith-type aircraft over the jth route, and u_j is the passenger demand over the jth route.

and the expected total cost becomes

$$E(C)=\sum_{i,j}\alpha_{ij}x_{ij}+\sum_{j}\alpha_j\phi_j(u_j) \tag{4.90}$$

Since the functions $\phi_j(u_j)$ are convex in u_j, the minimization of $E(C)$ can be done by the methods applicable to the "convex separable" case.

A special feature of the problem is that activity levels in time t are to be determined, while those in time $t+h$ ($h=1,2,\cdots$) cannot be fixed in advance because they depend on earlier stages and because uncertain requirements have to be fulfilled. Problems involving probabilistic demands at the destinations have been analyzed in this fashion by Dantzig (1956*b*) and Ferguson and Dantzig (1956).

Example No. 2 (see Charnes and Cooper, 1959*a*). Consider the operation over N periods of time of an oil refinery which sends heating oil to terminal tanks, from which, in turn, tankers pick up deliveries in a non-predictable manner. Decisions about production rate in any planning period have to be made *before* the sales demand for the period can be observed. For simplicity, then, it may be assumed that decisions about production rate or about the total quantity to produce and hold in inventory (the level of "preparedness") depend on the whole course of sales-demand up to the previous period, i.e., on a sequence of random variables. If, furthermore, each element in the sequence is statistically independent, we may regard the level of preparedness and the level of demand as statistically independent. *The problem* is to choose the production rates to be scheduled so that the expected net profits may be maximized, subject to preassigned probabilities that the sum of sales and minimum inventory shall not fall below the sum of inventory at the beginning of, and production during each of, the planning periods. Solution is accomplished in two stages: first, determining the unknown relative frequencies (in the discrete case) of the random variables possessing these preassigned probabilities, and, then, using a linear decision rule to approximate the distribution function of these random variables.

If the demand densities are assumed known, it is possible to solve this problem in a different manner (see Charnes, Cooper, and Symonds, 1958). A decision rule, say, linear, may be assumed, and then this may be substituted in the constraints to yield bounds on the decision variables. (These are called *certainty equivalents.*) Again, substituting the rule in the cost expression and minimizing this with respect to the coefficients of the decision rule, one can obtain optimizing values of these coefficients which would minimize the cost of meeting stated requirements on the performance of the system.

12.4. Problem Areas and Suggestions

We have already seen that a stochastic programming problem consists of deriving decision rules, x, as functions of known (or unknown) probability distributions, $p(y)$, about states of nature, y. Mathematically, this was seen to be equivalent to minimizing an integral of the form

$$\int_{(y)} f(x,y)\,dp(y)$$

where $f(x,y)$ describes the outcome of an action associated with some assumed state of nature.

Reiter (1957) has indicated how it may be possible, under not too severe restrictions, to obtain decision rules for a *subproblem* which will be *approximately optimal* in the original problem, in the sense that the loss due to a decision obtained by solving the subproblem will not exceed a controllable margin. This technique is called the *method of surrogates.* The use and development of this technique indicates that it may be possible to set up a theory of minimal information for decision making.

The search for duality is not merely a question of theoretical refinement, for, as Koopmans (1951*b*), Samuelson (1955), and Dorfman, Samuelson, and Solow (1958) have demonstrated, the principle of duality reveals clearly the possibility of maintaining an optimum set of activities through a price mechanism.

Radner (1955, 1959) has shown that the problem of multicomponent decisions under uncertainty (where each component may depend upon different aspects of information structure) has the formal structure of a linear program. In principle, it should be possible, therefore, to define and interpret a dual problem. Radner (1955) has given a simple construction of the dual with the help of the Kuhn-Tucker theorem, and has indicated that the solution to the dual which appears as a set of Lagrange multipliers for the primal problem is, in the stochastic case, a set of random prices (see Kuhn and Tucker, 1950*b*).

It still remains to bring out the precise role of these probabilistic price coefficients in the temporal stability of decision processes.

Tintner (1955) has worked out the case where the elements of the constraint matrix A in the linear-programming problem

$$cx = \min$$

subject to: (P.39)

$$Ax \leq b$$

$$x \geq 0$$

are jointly normally distributed. Charnes and Cooper (1959*b*) had worked out the case where A, b, and c are normal deviates and, for the case of an assignment problem, Ferguson and Dantzig (1956) have given the solution for the case where the objective function is an "expectation" with respect to the probability measure of customer demand. It is only in this last case that we find a comparison of the numerical solutions for stochastic and deterministic formulations of a given problem.

In any event, when the data of the problem are distributed variables, we have to consider the "preference" functional which, in the simplest case, is the expected value $E(cx)$. Consider the simplest situation, where only stochastic elements are the components of the vector, b. Since b cannot be replaced by $E(b)$ to obtain an optimum solution, the value of the objective function corresponding to the approximation due to replacing the distribution of b by $E(b)$ will not in general be the same as $E(cx)$. The errors due to this replacement have been explicitly derived by Madansky (1960). Such results have yet to be derived for more general situations.

13. APPLICATIONS OF LINEAR PROGRAMMING

In the 1940's and early 1950's, the applications of linear-programming techniques were limited to three main classes of problems: (1) military applications arising from the Air Force's Project SCOOP, (2) Leontief input-output analysis of interindustry economic problems, and (3) problems involving the relationship between linear programming and two-person zero-sum games (see Riley and Gass, 1958, p. 213). Industrial applications of linear-programming techniques were practically non-existent in these early years. In fact, as recently as 1955, a panel of linear-programming experts from all over the United States could cite no more than twenty industrial applications, with a significant contribution to management being attributed to less than half of these (Smith, 1956). However, since that time, a considerable emphasis has been placed on applying linear-programming techniques to the solution of industrial problems—and the result has been a phenomenal growth in the number of such applications. Especially successful have been the applications to strategic (planning) problems but, on the other hand, only a limited success has been obtained in the case of tactical ("day-to-day") problems. In the latter case, successful solutions presuppose accurate knowledge, on a day-to-day basis, of the values of parameters [such as (1) actual productive hours available in a machine center, (2) productive backlog at each work station from previous allocations, that is, productive hours previously committed and still unused, (3) day-to-day customer requirements, etc.]. Furthermore, the situation is complicated by difficulties in handling problems in which the values of the parameters must be forecasted and which are subject to significant statistical variation.

Applications of the general linear-programming problem have been divided by Gass (1958) into three categories: (1) production-scheduling and inventory control problems, (2) interindustry problems, and (3) diet problems, where the latter two are forms of the "product mix" problems. Riley and Gass (1958, p. 213 ff.) also discuss problems of equipment replacement, as well as a number of other classifications.

The applications of non-linear programming techniques are few in number because of the lack of general algorithms or solution procedures for solving such problems. Of the few applications that have been made to date, the most significant have been concerned with solving certain blending problems in the oil industry.

By far the most complete compilations, classification, and summaries of the applications of both linear and non-linear programming are the outstanding annotated bibliography of Riley and Gass (1958) and the textbook on linear programming by Gass (1958). In both of these excellent sources, applications are listed by *category* (e.g., industrial applications, by industry; contract awards; military applications; agricultural applications; production scheduling and inventory control; equipment replacement; etc.) as well as by *problem type* (e.g., transportation, assignment, etc.).

Applications of non-linear programming and dynamic programming (both linear and non-linear) are discussed in Riley and Gass (1958).

BIBLIOGRAPHY

Agmon, Shmuel, "The Relaxation Method for Linear Inequalities," *Canadian J. of Math.*, **6**, 382–392 (1954).

Antosiewicz, H. A. (ed.), *Proceedings of the Second Symposium in Linear Programming* (2 volumes), Directorate of Management Analysis and National Bureau of Standards, Washington, D. C., 1955.

Arrow, K. J., and Hurwicz, L., "Reduction of Constrained Maxima to Saddle-Point Problems," in Neyman (ed.), *Proc. of the Third Berkeley Symposium on Math. Stat. and Probability,* U. of California Press, Berkeley, **5,** 1–20 (1956).

———, "Gradient Methods for Concave Programming—Local Results," in Arrow, Hurwicz, and Uzawa (1958), pp. 117–125, 1958*a*.

———, "Gradient Methods for Concave Programming—Further Global Results and Applications to Resource Allocation," in Arrow, Hurwicz, and Uzawa (1958), pp. 133–138, 1958*b*.

Arrow, K. J., Hurwicz, L., and Uzawa, H., *Studies in Linear and Non-Linear Programming,* Stanford U. Press, Stanford, Calif., 1958.

Ball, W. W. R., *Mathematical Recreations and Essays,* revised by H. S. M. Coxeter (11th ed.), Macmillan, New York, 1939.

Barachet, L. L., "Graphic Solution of the Traveling-Salesman Problem," *Opns. Res.,* **5,** 841–845 (1957).

Beale, E. M. L., "An Alternative Method for Linear Programming," *Proc. Cambridge Philos. Soc.,* **50,** 513–532 (1954).

———, "Cycling in the Dual Simplex Algorithm," *Nav. Res. Log. Quart.,* **2,** 269–275 (1955).

Bellman, Richard, "On the Theory of Dynamic Programming," *Mgmt. Sci.,* **2,** 272–275 (1956*a*).

———, "Dynamic Programming and the Smoothing Problem," *Mgmt. Sci.,* **3,** 111–113 (1956*b*).

———, *Dynamic Programming,* Princeton University Press, Princeton, 1957.

Bowman, Edward H., "Production Scheduling by the Transportation Method of Linear Programming," *Opns. Res.,* **4,** 100–103 (1956).

Brown, George W., "Iterative Solution of Games by Fictitious Play," 1951, Ch. 24 in Koopmans (1951*a*), pp. 374–376.

Brown, G. W., and von Neumann, J., "Solutions of Games by Differential Equations," in Kuhn and Tucker (1950), pp. 73–79.

Cahn, A. S., "The Warehouse Problem," *Bull. Am. Math. Soc.,* **54,** 1073 (1948).

Camp, Glen D., "Application of Set Theory to a Class of Allocation Problems," *Opns. Res.,* **5,** 296–297 (1957).

Charnes, A., "Optimality and Degeneracy in Linear Programming," *Econometrica,* **20,** 160–170 (1952).

Charnes, A., and Cooper, W. W., "The Stepping Stone Method of Explaining Linear Programming Calculations in Transportation Problems," *Mgmt. Sci.,* **1,** 49–69 (1954*a*).

———, "Duality, Regrouping and Warehousing," ONR Research Memo. 19, Carnegie Institute of Technology, June, 1954*b*.

———, "Such Solutions Are Very Little Solved," *J. Opns. Res. Soc. Am.,* **3,** 345–346 (1955*a*).

———, "Generalizations of the Warehousing Model," *Opnal. Res. Quart.,* **6,** 131–172 (1955*b*).

———, "Chance-Constrained Programming," *Mgmt. Sci.,* **6,** 73–80 (1959*a*).

———, "Chance-Constrained Programs with Normal Deviates and Linear Decision Rules," The Technological Institute, Northwestern University, 1959*b*.

Charnes, A., Cooper, W. W., and Henderson, A., *An Introduction to Linear Programming,* Wiley, New York, 1953.

Charnes, A., Cooper, W. W., and Mellon, Bob, "A Model for Programming and

Sensitivity Analysis in an Integrated Oil Company," *Econometrica,* **22,** 193–217 (1954).

Charnes, A., Cooper, W. W., and Symonds, G. H., "Cost-Horizons and Certainty Equivalents: An Approach to Stochastic Programming of Heating Oil," *Mgmt. Sci.,* **4,** 235–263 (1958).

Charnes, A., and Lemke, C. E., "A Modified Simplex Method for Control of Round-Off Error in Linear Programming" (mimeographed), Carnegie Institute of Technology, May 7, 1952.

———, "Computational Theory of Linear Programming, Part I—The 'Bounded Variables' Problem," ONR Research Memo. No. 10, Carnegie Institute of Technology, January 7, 1954*a*.

———, "Minimization of Non-Linear Separable Convex Functionals," *Nav. Res. Log. Quart.,* **1,** 301–312 (1954*b*).

Churchman, C. West, Ackoff, Russell L., and Arnoff, E. Leonard, *Introduction to Operations Research,* Wiley, New York, 1957.

Croes, G. A., "A Method for Solving Traveling-Salesman Problems," *Opns. Res.,* **6,** 791–812 (1958).

Dacey, Michael F., "Selection of an Initial Solution for the Traveling-Salesman Problem," *Opns. Res.,* **8,** 133–134 (1960).

Dantzig, George B., "Maximization of a Linear Function of Variables Subject to Linear Inequalities" (1951*a*), Chapter 21, in Koopmans (1951*a*), pp. 339–347.

———, "Application of the Simplex Method to a Transportation Problem" (1951*b*), Chapter 23, in Koopmans (1951*a*), pp. 359–373.

———, "Computational Algorithm of the Revised Simplex Method," *Notes on Linear Programming: Part III,* RAND Memo RM-1266, October 26, 1953.

———, "Variables with Upper Bounds in Linear Programming," RAND Memo RM-1271 (1954*a*).

———, "Composite Simplex-Dual Simplex Algorithm—I," *Notes on Linear Programming: Part XI,* RAND Memo RM-1274, April 26, 1954*b*.

———, "Upper Bounds, Secondary Constraints, and Block Triangularity in Linear Programming," *Econometrica,* **23,** 174–183 (1955*a*). Also published as RAND Memo RM-1367, and as RAND Report P-576, October 4, 1954.

———, "Linear Programming under Uncertainty," *Mgmt. Sci.,* **1,** 197–206 (1955*b*). Also published as RAND Report P-596, November 30, 1954.

———, "The Simplex Method," RAND Report P-891, July 9, 1956*a*.

———, "Recent Advances in Linear Programming," *Mgmt. Sci.,* **2,** 131–144 (1956*b*).

———, "Discrete-Variable Extremum Problems," *Opns. Res.,* **5,** 266–276 (1957). Also published as RAND Memo RM-1832, December 6, 1956, and as P-876.

———, "Solving Linear Programs in Integers," RAND Memo RM-2209, July 11, 1958.

———, "On the Status of Multistage Linear Programming Problems," *Mgmt. Sci.,* **6,** 53–72 (1959).

Dantzig, G. B., Ford, L. B., Jr., and Fulkerson, D. B., "A Primal-Dual Algorithm," *Notes on Linear Programming: Part XXXI,* RAND Memo RM-1709, May 9, 1956.

Dantzig, G. B., and Fulkerson, D. R., "Computation of Maximal Flows in Networks," *Nav. Res. Log. Quart.,* **2,** 277–283 (1955).

Dantzig, G. B., Fulkerson, D. R., and Johnson, S. M., "Solution of a Large-Scale Traveling-Salesman Problem," *J. Opns. Res. Soc. Am.*, **2,** 393–410 (1954).

Dantzig, G. B., Fulkerson, D. R., and Johnson, S. M., "On a Linear-Programming, Combinatorial Approach to the Traveling-Salesman Problem," *Opns. Res.*, **7,** 58–66 (1959).

Dantzig, G. B., and Hoffman, Alan J., "Dilworth's Theorem on Partially Ordered Sets," in Kuhn and Tucker (1956), pp. 207–214.

Dantzig, G. B., and Johnson, S. M., "A Production Smoothing Problem," in Antosiewicz (1955), pp. 151–176.

Dantzig, G. B., and Orchard-Hays, W., "Alternate Algorithm for the Revised Simplex Method," *Notes on Linear Programming: Part V,* RAND Memo RM-1268, Nov. 19, 1953*a*.

———, and ———, "Product-Form for the Inverse," RAND Report P-440, October, 1953*b*.

Dantzig, G. B., and Orden, A., "A Duality Theorem Based on the Simplex Method," in Orden and Goldstein (1952), pp. 51–55.

Dantzig, G. B., Orden, A., and Wolfe, P., "The Generalized Simplex Method for Minimizing a Linear Form under Linear Inequality Restraints," *Notes on Linear Programming: Part I,* RAND Memo RM-1264, April 5, 1954. Also published in *Pacific J. of Math.*, **5,** 183–195 (1955).

Dantzig, G. B., and Wolfe, P., "A Decomposition Principle for Linear Programs," RAND Report P-1544, Nov. 10, 1958.

———, "Decomposition Theorems for Linear Programs," *Opns. Res.*, **8,** 101–111 (1960).

Dennis, J. B., *Mathematical Programming and Electrical Networks,* The Technology Press, MIT, Cambridge, 1959.

Dilworth, R. P., "A Decomposition Theorem for Partially Ordered Sets," *Annals of Mathematics,* **51,** 161–166 (1950).

Dorfman, R. P., *Application of Linear Programming to the Theory of the Firm, Including an Analysis of Monopolistic Firms by Nonlinear Programming,* University of California Press, Berkeley, 1951.

Dorfman, R. P., Samuelson, P., and Solow, R. M., *Linear Programming and Economic Analysis,* McGraw-Hill, New York, 1958.

Dwyer, Paul S., "Solution of the Personnel Classification Problem with the Method of Optimal Regions," *Psychometrika,* **18,** 11–26 (1954).

———, "The Solution of the Hitchcock Transportation Problem with a Method of Reduced Matrices" (hectographed), University of Michigan, Ann Arbor, December, 1955.

Egerváry, E., "Matrixok Kombinatorius Tulajdonsagairol," *Matematikai es Fizikai Lapok,* **38,** 16–28 (1931). Translated by H. W. Kuhn as "Combinatorial Properties of Matrices" (mimeographed), ONR Logistics Project, Princeton, 1953.

Ferguson, A. R., and Dantzig, G. B., "The Problem of Routing Aircraft—A Mathematical Solution," *Aero. Eng. Review,* **14,** 51–55 (1955). Also published in *Notes on Linear Programming: Part XVI,* RAND Memo RM-1369, Sept. 1, 1954.

———, "Allocation of Aircraft to Routes—An Example of Linear Programming under Uncertain Demand," *Mgmt. Sci.,* **3,** 45–73 (1956). Also published as RAND Memo RM-1833, Dec. 7, 1956.

Flood, M. M., "On the Hitchcock Distribution Problem," in Orden and Goldstein (1952), pp. 74–99. Also published in *Pac. J. of Math.*, **3**, 369–386 (1953).

———, "The Traveling-Salesman Problem," Seminar Paper No. 13, The Johns Hopkins University, Baltimore, February 16, 1955. Also published in *Opns. Res.*, **4**, 61–75 (1956) and in McCloskey and Coppinger (1956), pp. 340–357.

———, "The Traveling-Salesman Problem," *Opns. Res.*, **4**, 61–75 (1956).

Ford, L. R., and Fulkerson, D. R., "A Simple Algorithm for Finding Maximal Network Flows and an Application to the Hitchcock Problem," RAND Report P-743, Dec. 29, 1955; and also, *Notes on Linear Programming: Part XXIX*, RAND Memo RM-1604, Dec. 29, 1955.

———, "Solving the Transportation Problem," *Mgmt. Sci.*, **3**, 24–32 (1956).

———, "A Primal-Dual Algorithm for the Capacitated Hitchcock Problem," *Nav. Res. Log. Quart.*, **4**, 47–54 (1957).

Friedman, L. F., "A Reduced Matrix Solution to the Transportation Problem" (mimeographed), Operations Research Group, Case Institute of Technology, November 11, 1955.

Friedman, L. F., and Yaspan, A. J., "An Analysis of Stewardess Requirements and Scheduling for a Major Domestic Airline—Annex A. The Assignment Problem Technique," *Nav. Res. Log. Quart.*, **4**, 193–197 (1957).

Frisch, R., *The Multiplex Method for Linear Programming*, Memorandum of Social-Economic Institute, University of Oslo, Oslo, Norway, September, 1958.

Fulkerson, L. R., and Dantzig, G. B., "Computation of Maximal Flows in Networks," *Nav. Res. Log. Quart.*, **2**, 277–283 (1955).

Gaddum, J. W., Hoffman, A. J., and Sokolowsky, D., "On the Solution of the Caterer Problem," *Nav. Res. Log. Quart.*, **1**, 223–229 (1954).

Gale, D., "Convex Polyhedral Cones and Linear Inequalities," in Koopmans (1951*a*), pp. 287–297.

———, "The Basic Theorems of Real Linear Equations, Inequalities, Linear Programming and Game Theory," *Nav. Res. Log. Quart.*, **3**, 193–200 (1956).

Gale, D., Kuhn, H. W., and Tucker, A. W., "Linear Programming and the Theory of Games" (1951), Ch. 19, in Koopmans (1951*a*), pp. 317–329.

Galler, Bernard, and Dwyer, Paul S., "Translating the Method of Reduced Matrices to Machines," *Nav. Res. Log. Quart.*, **4**, 55–71 (1957).

Gass, Saul I., *Linear Programming*, McGraw-Hill, New York, 1958.

Gass, Saul I., and Saaty, Thomas, "The Computational Algorithms for the Parametric Objective Function," *Nav. Res. Log. Quart.*, **2**, 39–45 (1955*a*).

———, "Parametric Objective Function (Part 2)—Generalization," *J. Opns. Res. Soc. Am.*, **3**, 395–401 (1955*b*).

Gerstenhaber, Murray, "Theory of Convex Polyhedral Cones," in Koopmans (1951*a*), pp. 298–316.

Gerstenhaber, Murray, and Kelley, James E., Jr., "Threshold Methods in Linear Programming," Applications Research Center Report, Remington RAND Univac, Philadelphia, December 20, 1956.

Gleyzal, Andre N., "An Algorithm for Solving the Transportation Problem," Research Paper No. 2583, *J. of Res. of N. B. S.*, **54**, 213–216 (1955).

Goldman, A. J., "Resolution and Separation Theorems for Polyhedral Convex Sets," in Kuhn and Tucker (1956), pp. 41–52.

Goldman, A. J., and Tucker, A. W., "Theory of Linear Programming" in Kuhn and Tucker (1956), pp. 53–98.

Gomory, Ralph E., "Outline of an Algorithm for Integer Solutions to Linear Programs," *Bull. Amer. Math. Soc.,* **64**, 275–278 (1958*a*).

———, "An Algorithm for Integer Solutions to Linear Programs," Princeton-IBM Mathematics Research Project, Technical Report, No. 1, Princeton, N. J., 1958*b*.

Graves, R. L., "A 650 Floating Decimal Code for Linear Programming," Engineering Research Department, Standard Oil Company (Indiana), 1956.

Gross, Oliver A., "A Simple Linear Programming Problem Explicitly Solvable in Integers," *Notes on Linear Programming:* Part XXVIII, RAND Memo RM-1560, Sept. 30, 1955.

———, "A Class of Discrete-Type Minimization Problems," *Notes on Linear Programming: Part XXX,* RAND Memo RM-1644, Feb. 24, 1956.

Hare, Van Court, Jr., and Hugli, Wilfred C., "Applications of Operations Research to Production Scheduling and Inventory Control, II," *Proceedings of the Conf. on "What is Operations Research Accomplishing in Industry?",* 56–62, Case Institute of Technology, Cleveland, 1955.

Hart, A. G., "Risk, Uncertainty and the Unprofitability of Compounding Probabilities," in *Studies in Mathematical Economics and Econometrics,* Oscar Lange, Frances McIntyre, and Theodore O. Yntema (eds.), U. of Chicago Press, Chicago, 1941.

Heller, Isidor, "Least Ballast Shipping Required to Meet a Specified Shipping Program," in Orden and Goldstein (1952), pp. 164–171.

———, "On the Problem of the Shortest Path Between Points" (Abstract), *Bull. Am. Math. Soc.,* **59,** 551 (1953).

———, "The Traveling-Salesman Problem, Part I: Basic Facts," The George Washington U. Logistics Research Project, 1954.

———, "On the Traveling-Salesman's Problem," in Antosiewicz (1955), pp. 643–665.

Henderson, Alexander, and Schlaifer, Robert, "Mathematical Programming—Better Information for Better Decision Making," *Harvard Business Review,* **32,** 73–100 (1954).

Hitchcock, F. L., "The Distribution of a Product from Several Sources to Numerous Localities," *J. Math. and Phys.,* **20,** 224–230 (1941).

Hoffman, Alan J., "Cycling in the Simplex Algorithm," National Bureau of Standards Report No. 2974, Washington, D. C., 1953.

———, "How to Solve a Linear Programming Problem," in Antosiewicz (1955), pp. 397–424.

Hoffman, Alan J., and Dantzig, G. B., "Dilworth's Theorem on Partially Ordered Sets," *Notes on Linear Programming: Part XXVII,* RAND Memo RM-1553, Aug. 26, 1955. See, also, Dantzig and Hoffman (1956).

Hoffman, A. J., and Jacobs, Walter, "Smooth Patterns of Production," *Mgmt. Sci.,* **1,** 86–91 (1954).

Hoffman, A., Mannos, M., Sokolowsky, D., and Wiegmann, N., "Computational Experience in Solving Linear Programs," *J. of the Soc. for Ind'l. and Applied Math.,* **1,** 17–34 (1953).

Houthakker, H. S., "On the Numerical Solution of the Transportation Problem," *J. Opns. Res. Soc. Am.,* **3,** 210–214 (1955).

Jacobs, Walter, "The Caterer Problem," *Nav. Res. Log. Quart.,* **1,** 154–165 (1954).

———, "Loss of Accuracy in Simplex Computations," *Nav. Res. Log. Quart.,* **4,** 89–94 (1957).

Kantorovitch, L., "On the Translocation of Masses," *Comptes Rendus (Doklady) de l'Academie des Sciences de l'URSS,* **37,** 199–201 (1942). Also published in *Mgmt. Sci.,* **5,** 1–4 (1958).

Kelley, J. E., Jr., "A Dynamic Transportation Model," *Nav. Res. Log. Quart.,* **2,** 175–180 (1955).

———, "A Threshold Method for Linear Programming," *Nav. Res. Log. Quart.,* **4,** 35–45 (1957).

Klein, Bertram, "Direct Use of Extremal Principles in Solving Certain Optimizing Problems Involving Inequalities," *J. Opns. Res. Soc. Am.,* **3,** 168–175 (1955).

König, D., "Uber Graphen und ihre Anwendung auf Determinatentheorie und Mengenlehre," *Math. Ann.,* **77,** 453–465 (1916).

Koopmans, T. C., "Optimum Utilization of the Transportation System," *Proceedings of the International Statistical Conferences,* Washington, D. C., 1947. Also, published in a Supplement to *Econometrica,* **17,** 136–146 (1949).

——— (ed.), *Activity Analysis of Production and Allocation,* Cowles Commission Monograph No. 13, Wiley, New York, 1951*a*.

———, "Analysis of Production as an Efficient Combination of Activities," 1951*b*, in Koopmans (1951*a*), pp. 33–97.

Koopmans, T. C., and Reiter, Stanley, "A Model of Transportation" (1951), Chapter 14 in Koopmans (1951*a*), pp. 222–259.

Kuhn, H. W., "The Hungarian Method for the Assignment Problem," *Nav. Res. Log. Quart.,* **2,** 83–97 (1955*a*).

———, "A Combinatorial Algorithm for the Assignment Problem," Issue 11 of *Logistics Papers,* George Washington U. Logistics Research Project, 1955*b*.

Kuhn, H. W., and Tucker, A. W. (eds.), *Contributions to the Theory of Games, I,* Annals of Math. Studies, No. 24, Princeton U. Press, Princeton, 1950.

———, "Non-Linear Programming," in *Proceedings of the Second Symposium on Mathematical Statistics and Probability* (Jerzy Neyman, ed.), U. of California Press, Berkeley, 1951, pp. 481–492.

——— (eds.), *Contributions to the Theory of Games, II,* Annals of Math. Studies, No. 28, Princeton U. Press, Princeton, 1953.

——— (eds.), *Linear Inequalities and Related Systems,* Annals of Mathematics Studies, No. 38, Princeton University Press, Princeton, N. J., 1956.

Lemke, C. E., "The Dual Method of Solving the Linear Programming Problem," *Nav. Res. Log. Quart.,* **1,** 36–47 (1954).

Lemke, C. E., and Charnes, A., "Control of Round-Off Error in Linear Programming," 35–38, in *Extremal Problems in Linear Inequalities,* Technical Report No. 36, Carnegie Institute of Technology, Pittsburgh, 1953.

McKinsey, John C. C., *Introduction to the Theory of Games,* McGraw-Hill, New York, 1952.

Madansky, A., "Inequalities for Stochastic Linear Programming," *Mgmt. Sci.,* **6,** 197–205 (1960).

Manne, A. S., "Notes on Parametric Linear Programming," RAND Report P-468, Dec. 15, 1953.

Markowitz, Harry, "Concepts and Computing Procedures for Certain X_{ij} Programming Problems," RAND Report P-602, November 19, 1954. Also published in Antosiewicz (1955), pp. 509–565.

———, "The Elimination Form of the Inverse and its Application to Linear Programming," RAND Memo RM-1452, April 8, 1955.

Markowitz, Harry M., and Manne, A. S., "On the Solution of Discrete Programming Problems," *Econometrica,* **25,** 84–110 (1957). Also published as RAND Report P-711, 1955 (revised Feb. 9, 1956).

Mills, Harlan D., "Marginal Values of Matrix Games and Linear Programs," in Kuhn and Tucker (1956), pp. 183–193.

Motzkin, T. S., "Remarks on the History of Linear Inequalities" (1952*a*) (abstract), in Orden and Goldstein (1952), p. 179.

———, "The Multi-Index Transportation Problem" (abstract), *Bull. Amer. Math. Soc.,* **58,** 494 (1952*b*).

———, "New Techniques for Linear Inequalities and Optimization" (1952*c*), in Orden and Goldstein (1952), pp. 15–27.

Motzkin, T. S., Raiffa, H., Thompson, G. L., and Thrall, R. M., "The Double Description Method," in Kuhn and Tucker (1953), pp. 51–73.

Motzkin, T. S., and Schoenberg, I. J., "The Relaxation Method for Linear Inequalities," *Canadian J. of Math.,* **6,** 393–404 (1954).

Orchard-Hays, W., "A Composite Simplex Algorithm—II," *Notes on Linear Programming—Part XII,* RAND Memo RM-1275, May 7, 1954*a*.

———, "Background, Development and Extension of the Revised Simplex Method," RAND Memo RM-1433, April, 1954*b*.

———, "Evolution of Linear Programming Computing Techniques," *Mgmt. Sci.,* **4,** 183–190 (1958).

Orden, Alex, "Transhipment and Storage in the Hitchcock-Koopmans Transportation Problem," Director of Management Analysis Service; Controller, USAF, March 15, 1951.

———, "Survey of Research on Mathematical Solutions of Programming Problems," *Mgmt. Sci.,* **1,** 170–172 (1955).

———, "The Transhipment Problem," *Mgmt. Sci.,* **2,** 276–285 (1956).

Orden, A., and Goldstein, L. (eds.), *Symposium on Linear Inequalities,* Project SCOOP Publication No. 10, Directorate of Management Analysis Service, Washington, D. C., 1952.

Pallack, S., "The Double Description Method on the SEAC," Nat'l. Bur. Standards Report No. 2961, Dec. 9, 1953.

Prager, William, "On the Role of Congestion in Transportation Problems" (abstract), *Mgmt. Sci.,* **2,** 190 (1956*a*). Complete article published in *Zeitschrift fur Angewandte Mathematik und Mechanik,* 264–268 (1955).

———, "On the Caterer Problem," *Mgmt. Sci.,* **3,** 15–23 (1956*b*).

———, "Numerical Solution of the Generalized Transportation Problem," *Nav. Res. Log. Quart.,* **4,** 253–261 (1957*a*).

———, "On Warehousing Problems," *Opns. Res.,* **5,** 504–512 (1957*b*).

Radner, R., "The Linear Team: An Example of Linear Programming under Uncertainty," in Antosiewicz (1955), pp. 381–396.

———, "The Application of Linear Programming to Team Decision Problems," *Mgmt. Sci.,* **5,** 143–150 (1959).

Raiffa, H., Thompson, G. L., and Thrall, R. M., "An Algorithm for the Determination of All Solutions of a Two-Person Game with a Finite Number of Strategies (Double Descriptive Method)," in Orden and Goldstein (1952), pp. 100–114.

Reiter, Stanley, "Surrogates for Uncertain Decision Problems," *Econometrica,* **25,** 339–345 (1957).

Riley, Vera, and Gass, S. I., *Linear Programming and Associated Techniques: A Comprehensive Bibliography on Linear, Nonlinear and Dynamic Programming,* The Johns Hopkins Press, Baltimore, 1958.

Rinehart, Robert F., "Threats to the Growth of Operations Research in Business and Industry," *J. Opns. Res. Soc. Am.,* **2,** 229–233 (1954).

Robacker, J. T., "Some Experiments on the Traveling-Salesman Problem," RAND Report RM-1521, July 28, 1955.

Robinson, Julia, "On the Hamiltonian Game (A Traveling-Salesman Problem)," RAND Memo RM-303, December 5, 1949.

Saaty, Thomas L., "Partitions of a Linear Programming Problem" (abstract), *Opns. Res.,* **3,** 35 (1955*a*).

———, "The Number of Vertices of a Polyhedron," *Amer. Math. Monthly,* **62,** 326–331 (1955*b*).

———, "Approximation to the Value of the Objective Function in Linear Programming by the Method of Partitions," *Opns. Res.,* **4,** 352–353 (1956).

———, *Mathematical Methods of Operations Research,* McGraw-Hill, New York, 1959*a*.

———, "Coefficient Perturbation of a Constrained Extremum," *Opns. Res.,* **7,** 294–302 (1959*b*).

Saaty, T., and Gass, Saul, "Parametric Objective Function (Part I)," *J. Opns. Res. Soc. Am.,* **2,** 316–319 (1954).

Samuelson, Paul A., "Linear Programming and Economic Theory," in Antosiewicz (1955), pp. 251–272.

Sasieni, M. W., Yaspan, A., and Friedman, L., *Operations Research: Methods and Problems,* Wiley, New York, 1959.

Schell, Emil D., "Distribution of a Product of Several Properties," in Antosiewicz (1955), pp. 615–642.

Shetty, C. M., "A Solution to the Transportation Problem with Non-Linear Costs," *Opns. Res.,* **7,** 571–580 (1959).

Slater, Morton, "Lagrange Multiplier Revised: A Contribution to Non-Linear Programming," RAND Memo RM-676, August, 1951.

Smith, L. Wheaton, Jr., "Current Status of the Industrial Use of Linear Programming," *Mgmt. Sci.,* **2,** 156–158 (1956).

Stigler, George J., "The Cost of Subsistence," *J. Farm Economics,* **27,** 303–314 (1945).

Suzuki, George, "A Transportation Simplex Algorithm for Machine Computation Based on the Generalized Simplex Method," Report No. 959, David W. Taylor Model Basin, 1955.

Tintner, G., "A Contribution to the Non-Static Theory of Production," in *Studies in Mathematical Economics and Econometrics,* Oscar Lange, Frances McIntyre, and Theodore O. Yntema (eds.), U. of Chicago Press, Chicago, 1941.

———, "Stochastic Linear Programming with Applications to Agricultural Economics," in Antosiewicz (1955), pp. 197–228.

Tompkins, C., "Projection Methods in Calculation," in Antosiewicz (1955), pp. 425–447.

Tucker, A. W., "Linear Inequalities and Convex Polyhedral Sets," in Antosiewicz (1955), pp. 569–602.

———, "Dual Systems of Homogeneous Linear Relations," pp. 3–18 in Kuhn and Tucker (1956).

Uzawa, H., "The Kuhn-Tucker Theorem in Concave Programming" (1958*a*), in Arrow, Hurwicz, and Uzawa (1958), pp. 32–37.

———, "Gradient Methods for Concave Programming—Global Stability in the Strictly Concave Case" (1958*b*), in Arrow, Hurwicz, and Uzawa (1958), pp. 127–132.

Vajda, S., *The Theory of Games and Linear Programming,* Wiley, New York, 1956.

———, *Readings in Linear Programming,* Wiley, New York, 1958.

Vazsonyi, Andrew, *Scientific Programming in Business and Industry,* Wiley, New York, 1958.

Vidalle, M. L., "A Graphical Solution of the Transportation Problem," *Opns. Res.,* **4**, 193–203 (1956).

von Neumann, John, "Discussion of a Maximum Problem," Institute for Advanced Study, Princeton, N. J., 1947.

———, "A Certain Zero-Sum Two-Person Game Equivalent to the Optimal Assignment Problem," in Kuhn and Tucker (1953), pp. 5–12.

———, "A Numerical Method to Determine Optimum Strategy," *Nav. Res. Log. Quart.,* **1**, 109–115 (1954).

Votaw, D. F., and Orden, A., "The Personnel Assignment Problem," in Orden and Goldstein (1952), pp. 155–163.

Wagner, H. M., "A Two-Phase Method for the Simplex Tableau," *Opns. Res.,* **4**, 443–447 (1956).

———. "A Linear Programming Solution to Dynamic Leontief Type Models," *Mgmt. Sci.,* **3**, 234–254 (1957*a*).

———, "A Comparison of the Original and Revised Simplex Methods," *Opns. Res.,* **5**, 361–369 (1957*b*).

———, "A Supplementary Bibliography on Linear Programming," *Opns. Res.,* **5**, 555–562 (1957*c*).

———, "The Simplex Method for Beginners," *Opns. Res.,* **6**, 190–199 (1958).

———, "On a Class of Capacitated Transportation Problems," *Mgmt. Sci.,* **5**, 304–318 (1959).

Chapter **5**

DYNAMIC PROGRAMMING

Stuart Dreyfus

The RAND Corporation, Santa Monica, California

Contents

1. INTRODUCTION

The purpose of this chapter is to acquaint the reader with the dynamic-programming viewpoint; to familiarize him with the salient features that determine the applicability of dynamic programming to a problem; to develop the basic computational algorithms and to present the more important new special techniques that simplify and render practical numerical solution; to give the reader some examples of problem formulation; and to make references to recent interesting uses of dynamic programming.

Dynamic programming is a way of viewing a problem. The problem need not be characterized by a set of equations of a particular form, as is the case with linear programming. Nor, unfortunately, does there exist a general-purpose preprogrammed computational algorithm, again as is the case in linear programming. While, from the point of view of some industrial users, this lack of a well-defined formulation and of quick numerical results may appear discouraging, the true operations *researcher* will be pleased to find each problem an interesting challenge. What is most important, once the initial formulational and computational obstacles have been surmounted, many imposing problems with non-linear, stochastic, and adaptive features will yield before the powerful coalition of mathematician and computer.

As the reader will discover below, the essential idea of dynamic programming is the characterization of the problem by means of a functional equation or its discrete analogue, the recurrence relation.

Recurrence relations have long been used to describe sequential phenomena in mathematical physics. The same idea is an important, and standard, technique in queuing-theory analysis. In both of these cases, however, recurrence is used as a descriptive device, rather than as a technique for decision making.

The new ideas of dynamic programming are concerned with the recurrent characterization of decision processes, and with the subsequent analysis of the resulting functional equations containing a maximum operator.

The use of recurrence relations in decision theory seems to have had its beginning during the 1940's, when considerable interest developed among statisticians in statistical decision theory. A book by Abraham Wald (1950) uses the technique for the testing of hypotheses.

About 1951 Dr. Richard Bellman became interested in the functional-equation approach to decision problems, both of deterministic and stochastic types, and coined the term "dynamic programming" to describe the approach. Most of his early research concerned the existence and uniqueness of solutions to this new type of functional equation. His many theoretical papers of the early 1950's led to a book, *Dynamic Programming,* published in 1957.

In 1955 the author joined Dr. Bellman at the RAND Corporation, and emphasis was placed upon problem formulation and computational solution. Special devices were developed to reduce the amount of computation necessary for the solution of important classes of problems. Several of these techniques will be discussed below. The work has led to a book on computational aspects of dynamic programming to be published in 1961.

This new emphasis on practical dynamic programming has led to wide interest in the subject with additional research being performed at Harvard, MIT, Carnegie Tech, Pittsburgh, Case, Purdue, Stanford, and UCLA, to mention a few universities. By 1958 dynamic programming had aroused sufficient interest to become the subject of an entire session of the annual meeting of the Operations Research Society in Boston.

A fairly complete bibliography of papers up to 1954 can be found in Bellman's expository address presented before the American Mathematical Society in September 1954 and published later that year (Bellman, 1954). Later references appear in Bellman's book (1957) as well as in the bibliography on linear programming and associated techniques (Riley and Gass, 1958). Current references will appear in the forthcoming book by Bellman and Dreyfus.

2. MULTISTAGE DECISION PROCESSES

Since dynamic programming was developed to facilitate the study of multistage decision processes, it seems appropriate to explain the nature of such a process here. However, as the reader has been forewarned, there are few unqualified truths in dynamic programming. It cannot be categorically stated either that (1) all multistage decision processes can be solved by dynamic programming, or (2) all dynamic-programming problems are multistage decision processes.

As will be seen subsequently, the very size and complex structure of some problems makes dynamic programming inapplicable in any practical sense. (Perhaps one can correctly say that all multistage-decision-process problems can be *formulated* in terms of dynamic programming.) Conversely, it is possible to treat some problems characterized by *no* multistage aspects in such a way that dynamic programming offers a practical means of solution.

In a multistage decision process, a sequence of decisions is sought which maximizes (or minimizes) some predefined *objective function* or *criterion function.*

As an example of a multistage decision process, consider the automobile-replacement problem so familiar to most Americans. The sequence of decisions sought is a *policy,* which perhaps has the form: replace the car every N years with an M-year-old model.[1] The criterion function should reflect a combination of minimum-cost considerations (purchase cost plus upkeep) and a subjective sociological worth. Since individuals differ greatly in the relative weight they attach to these factors, there is no universal *optimal policy.* However, given numerical estimates of the utilities for a *particular* person, there does exist an optimal replacement policy, easily determined by dynamic programming. This is all that can ever be asked from a mathematical theory. The determination of the criterion function and the possible policies is a metamathematical, and often, metaphysical problem.

Let us examine the automobile-replacement problem in more detail, to extract the essence of a multistage-decision-process problem.[2] Observe that the optimal policy will depend on the length of the process. An individual who has been told he only has one more year to live will behave differently from a taxicab-fleet owner with an essentially infinite planning horizon. Secondly, the best policy will depend on the current *state* of the system. By "state," a term to be much used in subsequent pages, we mean the sum total of all relevant information about the situation under consideration. For example, the state of a car, for a simplified analysis, would be its *age.* For more detailed analyses, its *condition* would also be considered. Hence, "state" is a relative term depending on the depth of analysis, and it is the job of the operations researcher to balance properly realism of state description against mathematical solvability.

[1] More generally: replace a model of type i every N_i years by a model of type j.

[2] For some examples of the application of dynamic programming to equipment-replacement problems, see Bellman (1955), Dreyfus (1960), and Howard (1960).

We have established the point that in studying a multistage process one must consider the length of the process and the state of the system. Let us now consider the effect of a decision at a particular *stage* (time) and state.

In general, a decision will change both the state and the stage of a multistage process. Returning to the automobile-replacement example, a decision to purchase a new car at year N where the old car is of age M will result in the possession of a one-year-old car at year $N+1$. The decision to "keep the old buggy" another year will result in an $M+1$-year-old car at year $N+1$. The purchase of a used car will result in the ownership of a car of some intermediate age.

The *optimal decision* is one that properly balances the current cost of the decision against the future value of the new state resulting from the decision. Therefore, one needs to know certain properties of the future—the long-term value of any particular state—in order to act correctly during the present. This important observation is exploited fully by dynamic programming.

In the first section of this chapter, we said that dynamic programming was a point of view. In our discussion of multistage processes we have begun to acquaint the reader with this new viewpoint. We have introduced the concepts of stage and state, policy and decision. We have discussed how an optimal decision at a particular time depends only on the length of the process and on the state of the system in certain important processes.[3]

Before continuing to the next sections, where mathematical substance shall be given to the above ideas, the reader should reflect upon the differences between the conventional and the dynamic programming approaches. Both conventional calculus and linear programming would describe the entire multistage process in one massive set of equations and optimize, if sufficient assumptions of "good behavior" were present, by a mechanical algorithm that makes no use of the actual physical process underlying the equations. When the necessary simplifying assumptions are warranted this leads to very efficient algorithms. In general, the multistage aspects introduce grave dimensionality difficulties. However, by studying the process on its own terms—multistage terms—dynamic programming has succeeded in producing answers to a wide variety of problems of surprisingly diverse mathematical and physical nature.

[3] In mathematical parlance, this is called a Markovian property.

3. THE PRINCIPLE OF OPTIMALITY

The principle of optimality justifies the linking of the N-stage decision process to the $(N-1)$-stage process. If we should find ourselves in a certain state at a certain stage of a process, and if we know the optimal attainable return from each state possible at the next stage, assuming that the process is then continued until its termination, we would make the decision which maximized the total of:

1. The immediate return.
2. The optimal return from the $(N-1)$-stage process starting in the new state.

The principle of optimality merely states that this reasoning does indeed yield the optimal return. To quote Bellman:

An optimal policy has the property that whatever the initial state and initial decision are, the remaining decisions must constitute an optimal policy with regard to the state resulting from the first decision.

If the state description is sufficiently complete, the optimal policy starting in a given state depends only on that state and not upon how one got to the state.[4] For dynamic programming to be applicable, the state-description variables must contain all necessary information to accomplish this separation. In addition, there must not be too many state variables.

4. THE FUNCTIONAL EQUATION

Since we have observed that a multistage process can be characterized by the initial state of the system and by the length of the process, let us define:

$f_N(x) =$ the total return from an N-stage process starting in state x where an optimal policy is used

Also let us define:

$P =$ the set of admissible policies

$R_N(x,p) =$ the return from the first stage of a process of length N starting in state x using decision $p \in P$

$x'(N,x,p) =$ the new state resulting from decision p

[4] This is the Markovian property mentioned above.

Then

$$f_N(x) = \max_{p \in P} \{R_N(x,p) + f_{N-1}[x'(N,x,p)]\} \tag{5.1}$$

This equation states mathematically what has been stated above verbally. Namely, that the total return from an N-stage process is the sum of the first-stage return plus the optimal return from the $(N-1)$-stage process, where the decision $p \in P$ is chosen so as to maximize the sum.

It should be noted that for the sake of generality the single-state return R and the new state x' are allowed to be functions of N, the time variable, as well as the decision and state variables. Usually, the same return and transformation functions apply throughout the process.

4.1. *Solution of the Functional Equation*

Here we come to the initial fork in what shall become an ever-dividing path—but who finds straight roads and flat land interesting? There are two basic approaches to the solution of the above functional equation or recurrence relation.

One, which we shall call "approximation in function space," involves the optimal solution of successively longer and longer processes until the full-length process has been solved. This technique will be illustrated in subsequent sections, culminating with a discussion of a recently finished program for the analysis of a logistic-replacement problem.

The second approach to numerical solution uses "approximation in policy space." The idea of this approach is to consider from the very start the problem in its entirety. An initial guess of the optimal policy is successively improved at each step until the optimal policy is found. One example of this general method is the simplex algorithm of linear programming. An efficient new algorithm of this type, developed by Ronald Howard, will be presented and illustrated.

4.2. *An Example*

In order to illustrate the function-space-approximation technique, we shall formulate and solve a very simple multistage-decision-process problem. We shall then show how one can solve, with almost no additional mathematical effort, generalizations of the problem which include stochastic and adaptive elements.

Suppose we are asked to find the path between the vertical lines A

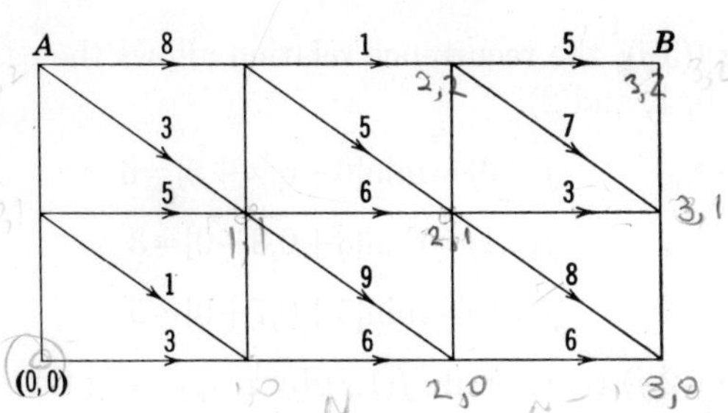

Fig. 5.1.

and B such that the sum of the numbers along the path is minimum.[5] See Fig. 5.1. This is a multistage process. There are three stages. Each decision has two effects. It incurs a cost equal to the number on the line segment and it results in a change of state—to some new vertex one stage on.

Assigning the origin to the lower-left-hand vertex and using the obvious rectangular-coordinate system, one can write a functional-equation representation for the problem. Defining

$$f(i,j) = \text{the minimum sum starting at the point } (i,j) \text{ and using an optimal path to the line } B$$

the principle of optimality yields

$$f(i,j) = \min \begin{bmatrix} n(i,j;i+1,j) + f(i+1,j) \\ n(i,j;i+1,j-1) + f(i+1,j-1) \end{bmatrix} \tag{5.2}$$

where

$$n(i,j;k,l) = \text{the number on the line segment joining } (i,j) \text{ to } (k,l)$$

and

$$n(i,j;k,l) = \infty \qquad \text{for } i,j,k \text{ or } l < 0$$

The latter stipulation makes it unnecessary to treat the x-axis, where no downward decision is possible, as a special case.

We see that $f(3,j) \equiv 0$ since this is the line B, and the best path *from* the line B *to* the line B has no cost.

As we have indicated above, the method of solution is to solve first a one-stage problem, then the two-stage problem, and finally the entire three-stage process.

[5] An example of a practical application of this model can be found in Cartaino and Dreyfus (1957).

Knowing $f(3,j)$, the recurrence relation allows the easy computation of $f(2,j)$ ($j=0$, 1, and 2).

$$f(2,0)=\min[6+0,\infty+0]=6$$

$$f(2,1)=\min[3+0,8+0]=3$$

$$f(2,2)=\min[5+0,7+0]=5$$

Now, we use $f(2,j)$ to compute $f(1,j)$ by reapplying the same recurrence relation.

$$f(1,0)=\min[6+6,\infty\quad]=12$$

$$f(1,1)=\min[6+3,9+6]=9$$

$$f(1,2)=\min[1+5,5+3]=6$$

Finally, a third application of the recurrence relation yields

$$f(0,0)=\min[3+12,\infty\quad]=15$$

$$f(0,1)=\min[5+9,1+12]=13$$

$$f(0,2)=\min[8+6,3+9\ ]=12$$

What we can assert, now, is that the best path starts from the point (0,2) and has cost 12. If, at the time the above function was computed we had also noted the direction of the best decision, we would have the best path as well as the best sum. Figure 5.2 summarizes this information.

Let us record some observations about the foregoing numerical solution which are valid for all dynamic-programming calculations of this type.

1. A multistage process *cannot*, in general, be treated as a sequence of single-stage problems by starting from the beginning and at each

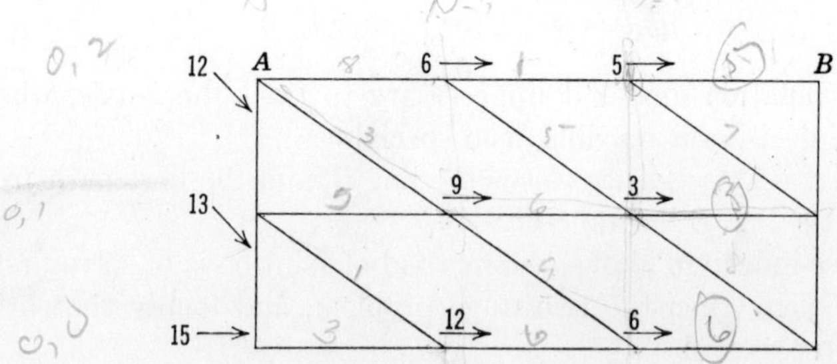

Fig. 5.2.

stage optimizing the single-stage return. Such a policy would have started at (0,1), incurring an initial cost of 1, but a total cost of 13.

2. The computation yields the solution for the totality of possible initial points. This is useful for *sensitivity analysis.* It is the above property that allows the problem of unspecified end-points to be treated as mechanically and easily as a two-point boundary-value problem.

3. The computational effort depends linearly on the number of stages. To solve a twelve-stage problem involves exactly four times the work necessary to solve a three-stage problem. In linear-programming formulations of multistage processes, additional stages lead to additional equations and variables, with the result that the computational effort increases geometrically with time: for example, like r^N for some $r>1$, or at the very least in a non-linear fashion such as N^2 or N^3.

4. The computation is repetitive, which means that only a computer program capable of getting from the k- to the $k+1$-stage problem is necessary. This program is then repeated as many times as there are stages.

5. To compute $f_{k+1}(x)$, only the function $f_k(x)$ is needed. Hence computer memory requirement depends only on the number of states and *not* on the number of stages.

6. The same answer could be obtained by working forward from line A and then tracing the best policy back from line B. At each stage we would ask the question: "What is the best path *to* this point?" rather than "What is the best path *from* this point?"

5. A STOCHASTIC VERSION

To illustrate the natural way that the function-space-approximation technique generalizes to stochastic problems, let us reconsider the above numerical example. This time, however, instead of allowing two decisions in each state (across, or diagonally down), let us suppose that several decisions are possible, but that a decision does not determine a direction, but only a set of *probabilities* for pursuing the various directions.

This is an example of one of several types of stochastic problems often encountered in operations research. We might call this a *stochastic-policy* problem, since we cannot make our decisions with certainty.

Other types of stochastic problems are those in which:

1. The immediate return is only statistically known, but the new state is determined.
2. The new state is stochastic but the return is deterministic.

In all such problems, the initial step is the choice of a criterion function. Usually, *expected value* is acceptable. In rare cases we wish to introduce a more complicated criterion such as "maximize the probability that return exceeds some fixed amount."

In all cases, we are using the expected value of some criterion function.

Suppose that the previous numerical problem was given a stochastic twist by introducing decisions that determine only the probability of various transitions. If we let p_k denote the probability of moving horizontally under decision k, and $(1-p_k)$ the probability of moving diagonally, the new recurrence relation is

$$f(i,j)=\min_k\{p_k[n(i,j;i+1,j)+f(i+1,j)] \\ +(1-p_k)[n(i,j;i+1,j-1)+f(i+1,j-1)]\} \quad (5.3)$$

where the function $f(i,j)$ is now defined as: the minimum *expected* sum starting at the point (i,j) and using an optimal policy to the line B.

Computationally, matters proceed exactly as before. We compute $f(3,j)$, then $f(2,j)$, $f(1,j)$, and finally $f(0,j)$.

Our optimal policy now has a slightly different interpretation. Instead of the entire optimal path being specified, the computation tells us where, along the line A, to start and what decision to choose.[6] After a stage has passed and a new state has occurred as a result of chance and our decision, we then consult the table of policies to determine the new decision. Such a process makes full use of the plethora of data generated by any dynamic programming calculation. It should be noted that no longer does one have the dual option of starting at the beginning, as discussed in observation 6 of Section 4.2.

6. ADAPTIVE PROCESSES

We come now to a new and exciting field of application of dynamic programming, *adaptive processes*. By adaptive processes we mean those processes in which the precise rules of the game are not completely known to the decision maker in advance. This means that

[6] The reader should convince himself that if $p_1=\frac{1}{2}$ and $p_2=\frac{3}{4}$ (except for the bottom line where one must go across) the optimal starting point is now (0,1) with expected cost of 471/32.

knowledge of the process must be used as it becomes available. Often, the best policy will dictate that first one should make decisions designed to improve the state of knowledge of the situation, then one should adjust the state of the system, and finally one can act so as to accrue the return originally sought after.

Note that if, in a stochastic model, the relevant distribution functions are assumed known in advance, we do not consider this an adaptive problem. However, if distribution functions are assumed to have a particular form, but the parameters, such as mean and variance, are unknown, we have a simple example of an adaptive process.

To fit these remarks into a familiar format, let us once more reexamine the minimum-sum-path problem from the adaptive point of view. Let us assume that decisions lead to stochastic path choices. Let decision 1 have probability p_1 of moving horizontally and $(1-p_1)$ of moving diagonally, and let the similar probabilities for decision 2 be p_2 and $(1-p_2)$. We now assume that p_1 and p_2 are initially unknown. Let us make the important additional assumption that a Laplace-Bayes formula applies, which means that if n choices of decision 1 result in a total of m horizontal moves, we agree to act as if $p_1=(m+1)/(n+2)$, and similarly for decision 2.

Under this assumption we can solve the problem by imbedding the transition probabilities in the state description. Let us define:

$f(i,j,n_1,m_1,m_2)=$ expected minimum cost of the optimal policy starting at point (i,j), where, previously, decision 1 has been chosen n_1 times resulting in m_1 horizontal moves and decision 2 has been chosen $i-n_1$ times resulting in m_2 horizontal moves

Then

$$f(i,j,n_1,m_1,m_2)$$

$$=\min\left[\begin{array}{l}\left(\dfrac{m_1+1}{n_1+2}\right)[n(i,j;i+1,j)+f(i+1,j,n_1+1,m_1+1,m_2)] \\ \quad +\left(1-\dfrac{m_1+1}{n_1+2}\right)[n(i,j;i+1,j-1)+f(i+1,j-1,n_1+1,m_1,m_2)] \\ \left(\dfrac{m_2+1}{i-n_1+2}\right)[n(i,j;i+1,j)+f(i+1,j,n_1,m_1,m_2+1)] \\ \quad +\left(1-\dfrac{m_2+1}{i-n_1+2}\right)[n(i,j;i+1,j-1)+f(i+1,j-1,n_1,m_1,m_2)]\end{array}\right] \tag{5.4}$$

The problem is solved by recurrently computing $f(0,j,0,0,0)$, minimizing this function over the starting point j, and using as the initial decision that decision that led to the computation of the value of $f(0,j,0,0,0)$. Whatever happens, one will be in a new state at $i=1$ for which an optimal decision has been already determined.

While, admittedly, the size of the problem—as measured by the number of state variables—has increased, the original formalism has remained unchanged.

Research remains to be done on the best method of determining what information is to be assumed and by what rules the relevant parameter estimates are to be adjusted.[7]

7. SPECIAL TECHNIQUES—I: THE LAGRANGE MULTIPLIER

A great many special devices have been developed that have proven useful in certain areas of dynamic-programming application. However, two are of such general usefulness that a discussion of their use should be included here.

As the reader has by now recognized, the chief obstacle to the general use of dynamic programming is the size of the state description vector. If ten variables are necessary to describe adequately the state of the system, and if each variable can assume, say, ten values, then a sequence of functions of $10^{10} = 10{,}000{,}000{,}000$ values must be computed and stored. This is beyond the range of available computers. Therefore, as far as any direct routine approach is concerned, we must confine our attention to problems involving two, three, or four state variables, each assuming ten or twenty values. Clearly, the elimination of even one state variable from a problem represents a tremendous saving. This is the purpose of the Lagrange multiplier, as used in conjunction with dynamic programming.[8]

Suppose that we are asked to allocate a scarce commodity to several activities. If we consider this to be a multistage problem in which we allocate to the activities one at a time—here is an example of a static

[7] For further remarks on stochastic and adaptive control problems, see Kalaba (to be published).

[8] This unusual computational use of a familiar analytic device was first announced by Bellman in the *Proc. Nat. Acad. Sci.,* **42,** 767–769 (1956) and illustrated numerically by Dreyfus in a paper, "Dynamic Programming Solution of Allocation Problems," delivered at the Operations Research Seminar at IIT in June 1957.

problem artificially made dynamic—the state description at a particular stage would naturally need to include the quantity of the scarce commodity available and unallocated as well as any other information necessary to the problem. However, by attaching a "cost" to the use of the scarce commodity and by including this cost in the objective function, one can control the amount of scarce commodity allocated, without *explicitly* including the constraint in the formulation. The problem then reduces to a search for the "cost" that results in an optimal policy satisfying the constraint. The artificial "cost," usually denoted λ, reduces to the Lagrange multiplier of classical calculus, in problems involving continuous variation.

That this cost can be successfully automatically adjusted by the computer during a calculation has been recently demonstrated. A very simple variational problem with constraints (for which the analytic result had been determined by Magnus Hestenes) was solved, entirely automatically on an IBM-704 computer in only a few minutes, using the functional-equation approach. The entire procedure, including the adjustment of the multiplier until a constraint equation was satisfied, was accomplished without human intervention. The answers proved to be as accurate as possible in a problem involving discretization of continuous variables.

8. SPECIAL TECHNIQUES—II: SUCCESSIVE REFINEMENT

The iterative technique of dynamic programming is an example of the powerful analytical and computational tool called *successive approximations*. It is interesting that in the case of dynamic programming, a second level application of the same idea leads to striking results. While this concept can be applied in several ways, we shall discuss here only one such application. We shall illustrate the use of successive refinement of the grid to produce extremely accurate results.

Suppose that we are confronted with an allocation problem of the form

$$\min_{\{x_i\}} \left[\sum_{i=1}^{N-1} g_i(x_i, x_{i+1}) \right]$$

and are asked to find the set of minimizing x_i where $0 \le x_i \le 1$, to six significant decimal places. This demand recently occurred in a crystal-structure problem of mathematical physics studied by John Cahn of General Electric and Ryoichi Kikuchi of Hughes Aircraft Company.

Defining

$$f_k(x_k) = \min_{x_1, x_2, \cdots, x_{k-1}} \left[\sum_{i=1}^{k-1} g_i(x_i, x_{i+1}) \right]$$

we have the recurrence relation

$$f_k(x_k) = \min_{x_{k-1}} [g_k(x_{k-1}, x_k) + f_{k-1}(x_{k-1})] \tag{5.5}$$

This equation states that the cost of the best set of k x's ending with x_k is the sum of (1) the cost of the best set of $(k-1)$ x's ending with x_{k-1}, plus (2) the cost of the last term, $g_k(x_{k-1}, x_k)$. The quantity x_{k-1} is then chosen to minimize the sum. It should be noted that the pairwise interlinking of the x's makes any single-stage approach non-optimal.

If we are asked for six-place accuracy in the x's, we could construct successive tables of 10^6 values. If $N = 20$, for example, we would compute 20×10^6 numbers, no small task even for present-day computing giants.

Suppose we were to divide the interval $0 \leq x_k \leq 1$ into ten parts and determine the optimal solution using this coarse grid. This would require ten computations per stage and $20 \times 10 = 200$ computations in all. If there are no relative extrema to mislead us, we now have the answer correct to $\pm 10^{-1}$. Dividing the interval $x_k \pm 10^{-1}$ into ten parts, where x_k is the optimal result given by the first calculation, we perform 200 more calculations and have results to accuracy $\pm \dfrac{(2)(0.1)}{10} = 0.02$. Eight successive refinements give six-place accuracy at a cost of only $8 \times 200 = 1600$ computations, a considerable saving over 20×10^6.

There are many combinations of grid sizes and successive refinements that give six-place accuracy. Eight iterations of ten grid points is not necessarily optimal, but was used to show the immense saving possible. The optimal grid size for given accuracy is easily determined.

As in the Lagrange multiplier case, recent experience indicates that the entire sequence of calculations can be carried out efficiently and rapidly on a high-speed digital computer.

Naturally, a technique of successive refinement such as that described above can theoretically converge to a relative extremum. Detailed mathematical analysis of the objective function can usually disclose the possibility of this situation. For most physical problems, such as trajectory problems, sensible relative extrema close to the true optimum do not exist. At any rate, the technique is a useful one for improving upon previous "best" results. This is often the goal of an operations research study.

9. A LOGISTIC-REPLACEMENT PROBLEM

As a final exercise in problem formulation, and as an example of current capabilities of dynamic programming, we shall discuss in some detail the formulation and solution of an interesting problem involving the replacement of unreliable equipment. The problem was formulated and programmed at RAND by Dale Jorganson, Roy Radner, Nancy Proger, and the author.

It is interesting to note that while the problem seems amenable to solution by both Alan Manne's stochastic programming technique and Ronald Howard's Markov-decision-process approach, to be discussed below, each leads to sets of several thousand equations.

Suppose that a machine consists of N unreliable components and that the machine is usable only if all N components are working. Furthermore, only by examination can the condition of a part be determined. Let us further assume that the component parts wear out exponentially, i.e., that the probability of a *good* part failing during the next time interval after examination is a constant, p, regardless of age. (Light bulbs, for example, seem to exhibit this property.) Failure of a part, or replacement or checkout of a suspect part, result in a period of machine inactivity, called *"downtime."* We suppose that parts do not age during downtime. We shall seek a parts-replacement policy that will minimize the long-term expected discounted downtime.

Many decisions are at the disposal of the repairman. Any or all of the components may be replaced as they become sufficiently old to be of doubtful value. There are economies of scale that render the simultaneous replacement of several parts more desirable than separate replacement. Furthermore, at a comparatively small cost in inoperative time, parts may be checked for usability. Again, simultaneous checking is more efficient than individual checking. Finally, if checking shows one or more failures, some unchecked parts may be replaced as well as the known bad components. Hence, the replacement policy, as a function of ages of parts since last checkout or replacement, should be expected to possess a very complex structure.

Viewed as a dynamic programming process, this problem has as many state variables as there are components, and each state variable may take on as many values as there are possible part ages—by ages we shall always mean time since last checkout or replacement. The exponential-decay assumption makes these two events indistinguishable.

An interesting feature of the problem is the fact that a replacement or multiple checkout decision may invoke several time periods of delay. Consequently, the new state will occur, not at the next stage, but several stages removed. This results in the need for the storage of several, rather than one, function tables, but entails no additional computing time.

Furthermore, since we are interested in the long-term, essentially infinite, process, the optimal policy dictates an action for each state, which is independent of the stage. The discount factor assures us that the total downtime, even for an infinite process, will be finite.

The solution was obtained by successively iterating a recurrence relation representing longer and longer processes until both the optimal policy and discounted downtime stabilized. Stabilization was defined as no change in policy for L iterations and a change in expected downtime per iteration of at most ϵ. Typically, L would equal 10, and $\epsilon = 0.001$. With a discount factor of 0.9, about 50 iterations sufficed for "convergence." The problem was programmed to allow up to three components. With maximum ages of 10 per component, this resulted in tables of up to 1,000 values. Actually, any combination of number of components and maximum ages such that the tables generated were of size $\leqq 1800$ would be allowable. Allowing for as many as 13 time periods to check and then replace all components, the function tables used 23,400 of the IBM 704's 32,000 high-speed memory cells. The remaining space was occupied by the policy table and the program of about 5,000 instructions.

The actual functional equation used is too complex to write out in its entirety here. It involved one policy called N, "do nothing," seven policies involving all possible replacement combinations, and innumerable more complex decisions involving checkout, with further checkout and replacement depending on the initial checkout results. The largest allowable problem involving only replacement requires about fifteen minutes of computing time. With all checkout options, about three to four hours could be used.

To illustrate the formulation, we shall write a portion of the recurrence relation for two parts, where it is desired to maximize expected "goodtime," or "uptime." The quantities $R_1,R_2,R_{12},C_1,C_2,C_{12}$ are the replacement and checkout times for the two parts (e.g., R_{12} means time to replace 1 and 2 simultaneously). By p_i we denoted the probability of the ith component surviving one period. The quantity $0 < a < 1$ is the discount factor. We define

$f_n(i,j)$ = expected goodtime for an n-period process starting with components 1 of age i and 2 of age j

$$f_n(i,j) = \max \begin{bmatrix} N: & p_1{}^i p_2{}^j + a\, f_{n-1}(i+1,j+1) \\ R_1: & a^{R_1} f_{n-R_1}(0,j) \\ R_2: & a^{R_2} f_{n-R_2}(i,0) \\ R_{12}: & a^{R_{12}} f_{n-R_{12}}(0,0) \\ C_1: & p_1{}^i a^{C_1} f_{n-C_1}(0,j) \\ & +(1-p_1{}^i) a^{C_1} \max \begin{bmatrix} R_1: & a^{R_1} f_{n-C_1-R_1}(0,j) \\ R_{12}: & a^{R_{12}} f_{n-C_1-R_{12}}(0,0) \\ C_2: & p_2{}^j a^{C_2+R_1} f_{n-C_1-C_2-R_1}(0,0) \\ & +(1-p_2{}^j) a^{C_2+R_{12}} \\ & \quad f_{n-C_1-C_2-R_{12}}(0,0) \end{bmatrix} \\ \text{etc., for } C_2 \text{ and } C_{12} & \end{bmatrix} \tag{5.6}$$

The reader cannot but be struck with awe that:

1. Such a simple problem can actually be so complicated.
2. Such a complicated problem can actually be solved!

It should be stressed that we are considering here a multistage, multicomponent, multidecision, stochastic problem. Conventional equipment-replacement problems now fall before dynamic programming with ease and regularity.

10. MARKOV PROCESSES

The above problem, which could be characterized as a *Markovian decision process,* serves as a good introduction to a new and important technique due to Ronald Howard. Howard's work is particularly significant in that it represents an interesting synthesis of the ideas of linear and dynamic programming. Like the simplex method, it involves a successive improvement of policy and return. Also, convergence is easily proved when the solution is optimal. The price one pays for these niceties is a fairly rigorous body of assumptions. Linearity is the essential assumption, so we have here, in a sense, the dynamic-programming approach to the linear-programming problem.

Before talking about Markovian decision processes, the particular types of sequential decision processes we wish to discuss in this section, it is necessary for us to discuss what we mean by a *Markov process.*

Consider a system which at any particular time is in one of a finite number of states, which we number $i=1,2,\cdots,N$, and assume that at the discrete times $t=0,1,\cdots$ the system changes from one of these admissible states to another. In place of supposing that this change is deterministic, we assume that it is stochastic, ruled by a transition matrix $P = (p_{ij})$, where

(1) p_{ij} = the probability that given the system is in state i at time t it will be in state j at time $t+1$

We consider here the important case where the transition matrix P is independent of time. This is the most interesting case.

Let us then introduce the following functions:

(2) $x_t(i)$ = the probability that the system is in state i at time t, $i = 1,2,\cdots,N$

with t assuming only the values $0,1,\cdots$. The elementary rules of probability theory then yield the equations

(3)
$$x_{t+1}(j) = \sum_{i=1}^{N} p_{ij} x_t(i) \qquad (j = 1,2,\cdots,N) \tag{5.7}$$
$$x_0(j) = c_j$$

The theory of Markov processes is devoted to the study of the asymptotic behavior of the functions $x_t(j)$ as $t \to \infty$. If all of the transition probabilities p_{ij} are positive, it is not too difficult to show that these functions converge as $t \to \infty$ to quantities $x(j)$ which satisfy the "steady-state" equation

(4)
$$x(j) = \sum_{i=1}^{N} p_{ij} x(i) \qquad (j = 1,2,\cdots,N) \tag{5.8}$$

That these functions converge as $t \to \infty$ is perhaps not too surprising, in view of the mixing property involved in the assumption that all of the p_{ij} are positive. What is surprising is that in this case, the limiting values are independent of the initial state of the system, the values of $x_0(j)$.

11. MARKOVIAN DECISION PROCESSES

We now wish to extend the concept of a Markov process to more general situations in which decisions are made at each stage. Let us suppose that at each stage the transition matrix can be chosen from one of a set of such matrices, and denote the matrix corresponding to policy decision q by $P(q) = [p_{ij}(q)]$.

Let us further suppose that not only is there a change of state involved at each stage, but also a return, which is a function of the initial and terminal state, and the decision.

Let $R(q) = [r_{ij}(q)]$ represent the return matrix defined in this fashion.

A process of this type we call a *Markovian decision process.* The problem that we wish to consider is that of choosing the sequence of decisions which will maximize the expected return obtained from an N-stage process, given the initial state of the system.

11.1. Example—A Taxicab Problem

Before entering into any analytic discussion of this type of problem, let us see how problems of this nature enter in a very natural way. To illustrate, Howard presents a simplified version of the operation of a fleet of taxicabs.

The advantage of an example of this nature is that it enables us to give concrete meanings to such terms as "transition matrix," "alternative decisions," and so on.

Suppose that a taxi driver has an area of operation encompassing three towns. If he is in town 1, he has three alternatives:

1. He can cruise in the hope of picking up a passenger by being hailed.
2. He can drive to the nearest cab stand and wait in line.
3. He can pull over to the curb and wait for a radio call.

In town 3, he has the same alternatives, but in town 2, the last alternative is not available since there is no radio cab service in that town.

For any given town and any given alternative within this town, there is a probability that the next trip will go to each of the towns 1, 2, and 3, and a corresponding known return in monetary units associated with each such trip. The probabilities of transition and the returns depend upon the alternative because different customer populations will be contacted under each alternative.

Assigning hypothetical numbers, the data for the problem can be shown in Table 5.1. As an example of the interpretation of Table 5.1, we see from the next to last row that, if the driver is in city 3 and chooses to drive to a cab stand, there is a $\frac{1}{8}$th chance he will get a customer who wants to go to city 1, the profit being 6; $\frac{3}{4}$th chance of a trip to city 2 yielding a profit of 4; and $\frac{1}{8}$th chance of a trip within city 3, with a profit of 2 units.

TABLE 5.1

State (city)	Alternative	Transition Probability $j=1$	2	3	Return $i=1$	2	3
1	1	$\frac{1}{2}$	$\frac{1}{4}$	$\frac{1}{4}$	10	4	8
	2	$\frac{1}{16}$	$\frac{3}{4}$	$\frac{3}{16}$	8	2	4
	3	$\frac{1}{4}$	$\frac{1}{8}$	$\frac{5}{8}$	4	6	4
2	1	$\frac{1}{2}$	0	$\frac{1}{2}$	14	0	18
	2	$\frac{1}{16}$	$\frac{7}{8}$	$\frac{1}{16}$	8	16	8
3	1	$\frac{1}{4}$	$\frac{1}{4}$	$\frac{1}{2}$	10	2	8
	2	$\frac{1}{8}$	$\frac{3}{4}$	$\frac{1}{8}$	6	4	2
	3	$\frac{3}{4}$	$\frac{1}{16}$	$\frac{3}{16}$	4	0	8

In this problem we have 3 states, i.e., $N=3$; there are 3 alternatives in states 1 and 3, and 2 in state 2; i.e., $n_1=3$, $n_2=2$, $n_3=3$. There are $3\times2\times3=18$ possible policies.

If the taxi driver knows that he has time for n more trips during a particular day (i.e., n stages remain) he can use an algorithm such as that given below to determine his optimal policy via successive approximation in function space.

However, if we look upon this as an infinitely continuing process, the policy-space algorithm of Howard, to be presented further below, becomes attractive.

After the tools of solution have been developed, we will return to this problem and show its numerical solution.

11.2. Analytic Formulation

Let us now use functional-equation techniques to obtain an analytic formulation of the problem characterized above. Let, for $i=1,2,\cdots,N$, $n=0,1,\cdots$

(1) $f_n(i)=$ expected return obtained from an n-stage process, starting in state i and using an optimal policy

Note that n represents the *length* of a process, whereas t, used in earlier sections, denoted *time*. The principle of optimality then yields the recurrence relations

$$(2) \qquad f_n(i)=\max_q\left[\sum_{j=1}^{N} p_{ij}(q)(r_{ij}(q)+f_{n-1}(j))\right] \qquad (i=1,2,\cdots,N) \quad (5.9)$$

for $n=1,2,\cdots$, with $f_0(i)=0$.

An optimal policy consists of a vector $(q_n(1),q_n(2),\cdots,q_n(N))$, giving the choice to be made in the ith state when n stages remain.

It can be established rigorously from this equation that for such a process, as $n \to \infty$, the optimal policy depends upon the state and not the stage. This becomes the basis of Howard's technique.

12. HOWARD'S POLICY-SPACE TECHNIQUE

The details of a policy-space iterative technique applicable to infinite processes and based on the foregoing ideas have been worked out by Dr. Ronald Howard. We shall discuss his technique, which furnishes the optimal policy for very long processes (i.e., "steady-state processes") where decisions depend only on the state, and not on the stage. Furthermore, we shall adopt his notation, in order to allow easy reference to his writings.

Defining

(1) V_i^n = total expected return from an n-stage process starting in state i using a *fixed policy*

one easily sees that V satisfies the recurrence relation

(2) $$V_i^n = \sum_{j=1}^{N} p_{ij}(r_{ij} + V_j^{n-1}) \tag{5.10}$$

Also, for large n,

(3) $$V_i^n = v_i + ng \tag{5.11}$$

if all states belong to the same chain. This will certainly be the case if all $p_{ij} > 0$.[9] This equation asserts that return will, in general, be composed of two parts, a steady-state part, ng, resulting from the behavior as $n \to \infty$, and a transient part v_i which depends only on the starting state.

Substitution of the limiting expression (3) in relation (2) yields

(4) $$v_i + ng = \sum_{j=1}^{N} p_{ij}[r_{ij} + v_j + (n-1)g] \tag{5.12}$$

Since $\sum_{j=1}^{N} p_{ij} = 1$ by definition, this relation simplifies to

(5) $$g + v_i = \sum_{j=1}^{N} p_{ij}(r_{ij} + v_j) \qquad (i = 1, 2, \cdots, N) \tag{5.13}$$

[9] The concepts of *chains* are discussed in extenso in Howard (1960), and may also be found in any comprehensive account of Markov chains.

13. THE VALUE-DETERMINATION OPERATION

The above is a system of N equations in $N+1$ unknowns, the Nv_i's and g. Observe, however, that the addition of a constant to all the v_i's does not change the equations. This means that only the relative values of the v_i's, rather than their absolute values, are important. Hence one v_i can be arbitrarily designated, leaving N equations in N unknowns. Setting $v_N=0$, solution of the equations gives the average long-term gain, g, and relative values of various starting states, v_i, for a fixed policy.

Howard calls the above generation of the gain and values under a given policy the *value determination operation* (VDO).

14. THE POLICY-IMPROVEMENT ROUTINE

We come now to the central problem. Having guessed a policy, a choice of alternatives for each state, we have shown how to evaluate this policy. On the basis of this information, how are we to generate a better policy? By "better," we mean one possessing a larger expected gain, g.

Returning to Eq. 5.13, we can solve for g:

$$(1) \qquad g=\sum_{j=1}^{N} p_{ij}(r_{ij}+v_j)-v_i \qquad (i=1,2,\cdots,N) \qquad (5.14)$$

Recall that p_{ij} and r_{ij} depend on the particular policy we have chosen to pursue.

Using the v's associated with the old policy, we can choose a new policy which maximizes the right-hand side of Eq. (1). Calling this new policy k, we choose k which maximizes $\sum_{j=1}^{N} p_{ij}^{(k)}(r_{ij}^{(k)}+v_j)-v_i$, where $p_{ij}^{(k)}$ denotes the transition probabilities associated with alternative k in state i.

Once g and v have been determined for a given policy, the use of the above rule for generating the new policy is called the *policy-improvement routine* (PIR).

One can prove that this rule:

1. Leads at each application to a policy of higher, or at least as large, gain.
2. Will eventually lead to the optimal policy.

These proofs depend strongly on the linearity of this simple model. It is, however, not intuitive that a decision dictated by gain and values of one policy will yield a policy with a larger gain.

15. SOLUTION OF THE TAXICAB PROBLEM

Let us return to the taxicab problem and apply the above rules. As an initial guess, we choose the policy vector

$$D=\begin{bmatrix}1\\1\\1\end{bmatrix}$$

which means we cruise in all cities. This is the policy that maximizes the expected immediate return. For this policy we have the transition-probability matrix

$$[p_{ij}]=\begin{bmatrix}\frac{1}{2} & \frac{1}{4} & \frac{1}{4}\\ \frac{1}{2} & 0 & \frac{1}{2}\\ \frac{1}{4} & \frac{1}{4} & \frac{1}{2}\end{bmatrix}$$

and immediate-return vector

$$\left[\sum_{j=1}^{N} p_{ij}r_{ij}\right]=\begin{bmatrix}8\\16\\7\end{bmatrix}$$

Let us denote $\sum_{j=1}^{N} p_{ij}r_{ij}$ by q_i, since the expected return depends only upon i. The value-determination equations, with v_3 set equal to 0, are

$$g+v_1=8+\tfrac{1}{2}v_1+\tfrac{1}{4}v_2$$

$$g+v_2=16+\tfrac{1}{2}v_1$$

$$g=7+\tfrac{1}{4}v_1+\tfrac{1}{4}v_2$$

yielding the solution

$$v_1=1.33$$

$$v_2=7.47$$

$$v_3=0$$

$$g=9.2$$

Using a policy of "always cruise," the driver will make 9.2 units per trip on the average.

Returning to the PIR, we calculate the quantities $q_i^k + \sum_{j=1}^{N} p_{ij}^k v_j$ for all i and k:

i	k	$q_i^k + \sum_{j=1}^{N} p_{ij}^k v_j$
1	1	10.50 *
	2	8.43
	3	5.51
2	1	16.67
	2	21.75 *
3	1	9.20
	2	9.66 *
	3	6.75

* Maximum. See following paragraph.

We see that for $i=1$, the quantity in the right-hand column is maximized when $k=1$. For $i=2$ or 3, it is maximized when $k=2$. In other words, our new policy is

$$D=\begin{bmatrix}1\\2\\2\end{bmatrix}$$

This means that if the cab is in town 1, it should cruise; if it is in town 2 or 3, it should drive to the nearest stand.

We now have

$$[P_{ij}]=\begin{bmatrix}\frac{1}{2} & \frac{1}{4} & \frac{1}{4}\\ \frac{1}{16} & \frac{7}{8} & \frac{1}{16}\\ \frac{1}{8} & \frac{3}{4} & \frac{1}{8}\end{bmatrix}, \qquad [q_i]=\begin{bmatrix}8\\15\\4\end{bmatrix}$$

Returning to the VDO, we solve the equations

$$g+v_1=8+\tfrac{1}{2}v_1+\tfrac{1}{4}v_2+\tfrac{1}{4}v_3$$

$$g+v_2=15+\tfrac{1}{16}v_1+\tfrac{7}{8}v_2+\tfrac{1}{16}v_3$$

$$g+v_3=4+\tfrac{1}{8}v_1+\tfrac{3}{4}v_2+\tfrac{1}{8}v_3$$

Again with $v_3=0$ we obtain

$$v_1=3.88$$

$$v_2=12.85$$

$$v_3=0$$

$$g=13.15$$

Note that g has increased from 9.2 to 13.15 as desired, so that the cab earns 13.15 units per trip on the average. Entering the PIR with these values,

i	k	$q_i^k + \sum_{j=1}^{N} p_{ij}^k v_j$
1	1	9.27
	2	12.14 *
	3	4.91
2	1	14.06
	2	26.00 *
3	1	9.26
	2	12.02 *
	3	2.37

* Maximum.

The new policy is thus

$$D = \begin{bmatrix} 2 \\ 2 \\ 2 \end{bmatrix}$$

The cab should drive to the nearest stand regardless of the town in which it finds itself.

With this policy

$$[p_{ij}] = \begin{bmatrix} \frac{1}{16} & \frac{3}{4} & \frac{3}{16} \\ \frac{1}{16} & \frac{7}{8} & \frac{1}{16} \\ \frac{1}{8} & \frac{3}{4} & \frac{1}{8} \end{bmatrix}, \qquad [q_i] = \begin{bmatrix} 2.75 \\ 15 \\ 4 \end{bmatrix}$$

Entering the VDO,

$$g + v_1 = 2.75 + \tfrac{1}{16}v_1 + \tfrac{3}{4}v_2 + \tfrac{3}{16}v_3$$

$$g + v_2 = 15 + \tfrac{1}{16}v_1 + \tfrac{7}{8}v_2 + \tfrac{1}{16}v_3$$

$$g + v_3 = 4 + \tfrac{1}{8}v_1 + \tfrac{3}{4}v_2 + \tfrac{1}{8}v_3$$

With $v_3 = 0$,

$$v_1 = -1.18$$

$$v_2 = 12.66$$

$$v_3 = 0$$

$$g = 13.34$$

Note that there has been a small but definite increase in g from 13.15 to 13.34.

Trying the PIR,

i	k	$q_i^k + \sum_{j=1}^{N} p_{ij}^k v_j$
1	1	10.57
	2	12.16 *
	3	5.53
2	1	15.41
	2	26.00 *
3	1	9.86
	2	13.33 *
	3	5.40

* Maximum.

The new policy is

$$D = \begin{bmatrix} 2 \\ 2 \\ 2 \end{bmatrix}$$

but this is equal to the last policy, so that the process has converged and g has attained its maximum, namely, 13.34. The cab driver should drive to the nearest stand in any city. Following this policy will yield a return of 13.34 units per trip on the average, almost half as much again as the policy of always cruising, found by maximizing immediate return.

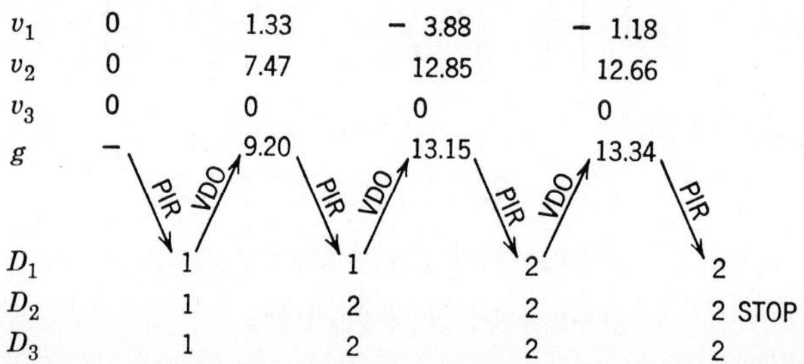

Notice that the optimal policy of always driving to a stand is the *worst* policy in terms of immediate return. It often happens in the sequential decision process that the birds in the bush are worth more than the one in the hand.

16. THE MORE GENERAL PROBLEM

In the discussion thus far we have required that there be a unique gain, g, associated with the problem. This means that there is only one chain and no matter what policy we choose it is possible to get from any persistent state to any other. Taking all the p_{ij} positive is one way of assuring this result.

We would, however, like our technique to be valid for the more general case involving several chains. A transition matrix having this property is shown below:

$$[p_{ij}] = \begin{bmatrix} \frac{1}{2} & \frac{1}{2} & 0 & 0 \\ \frac{1}{2} & \frac{1}{2} & 0 & 0 \\ 0 & 0 & \frac{1}{4} & \frac{3}{4} \\ 0 & 0 & \frac{1}{8} & \frac{7}{8} \end{bmatrix}$$

Here if we start in state 1 or 2, there is no possibility of transition to states 3 or 4, and conversely. If we have an accompanying return matrix, there will be one long-term average gain associated with starting in state 1 or 2, another for state 3 or 4. This leads to a subscripting of gain, g_1 meaning gain in chain 1, g_2 for chain 2, and so on, in general. With this notation, Howard proceeds to a more general algorithm, which we show schematically (see next page).

16.1. The General Solution

Using the p_{ij} and q_i for a given policy, solve the double set of equations

$$g_i = \sum_{j=1}^{N} p_{ij} g_j \tag{5.15}$$

$$v_i + g_i = q_i + \sum_{j=1}^{N} p_{ij} v_j \tag{5.16}$$

for all v_i and g_i. The solution will involve as many arbitrary constants as there are independent Markov chains; these constants may be set equal to zero.

For each state i, determine the alternative k which maximizes $\sum_{j=1}^{N} p_{ij}^k g_j$ and make it the new decision in the ith state. If $\sum_{j=1}^{N} p_{ij}^k g_j$ is the same for all alternatives, the decision must be made on the basis of values rather than gains. Therefore, if the gain-test fails, determine the alternative k which maximizes $q_i^k + \sum_{j=1}^{N} p_{ij}^k v_j$ and make it the new decision in the ith state.

Regardless of whether the policy-improvement test is based on gains or values, if the old decision in the ith state yields as high a value of the test quantity as any other alternative, leave the old decision unchanged. This rule assures convergence in the case of equivalent policies.

When this procedure has been repeated for all states, a new policy has been determined and new $[p_{ij}]$ and $[q_i]$ matrices have been obtained. If the new policy is equal to the previous one, the calculation process has converged and the best policy has been found.

17. RECENT APPLICATIONS OF DYNAMIC PROGRAMMING

To give the reader an idea of the range of applicability of dynamic programming, we shall state briefly some problems that have been recently attacked by dynamic-programming techniques. Details of solution can be found in the references cited. For further references on the basic techniques, see Bellman (1957) and Howard (1960).

1. *Optimal satellite trajectory.* Ascertain the thrust-control policy and fuel-consumption regime which will put a satellite into orbit at a specified altitude with maximum horizontal component of velocity. See Bellman and Dreyfus (1959).

2. *Subprogram storage within a digital computer.* A program written for a digital computer contains many subprograms, some of which must be permanently stored in auxiliary memory because of space limitations in high-speed memory. The length of each subprogram is known, as is the transfer time that would be required if the subprogram were stored in auxiliary memory. Also known is the number of available high-speed registers. Which subprograms should be stored in high-speed memory in order to minimize the resulting operating time of the program? See Grometstein (1959).

3. *Manganese problem.* Manganese can be either imported or produced domestically. Domestic production involves the gradual build-up of American industrial capacity. Costs of importation and domestic build-up and production depend on the international political situation. Given a stochastic political future, how best should we obtain manganese? See *Econometric Analysis* (1958).

4. *Optimum staging ratio for missiles.* How many booster stages and of what sizes result in most efficient missiles? See Ten Dyke (1958).

5. *Optimal inventory location and control.* Find optimal inventory control schemes for a system involving interacting inventories at different locations, and select that optimal inventory location. See Hanssmann (1959).

6. *Theory of the firm.* Von Thuenen's theory of the natural wage can form the basis for a theory of the firm for companies with deferred profit-sharing plans. Dynamic programming proves a useful tool in developing a long-range policy for a firm using the Van Thuenen theory. See Schlager (1959).

BIBLIOGRAPHY

Bellman, R., "The Theory of Dynamic Programming," *Bull. Amer. Math. Soc.*, **60,** 503–515 (1954).

———, "Equipment Replacement Policy," *J. of SIAM,* **3,** 133–136 (1955).

———, *Dynamic Programming,* Princeton University Press, Princeton, N.J., 1957.

———, and Dreyfus, S., "An Application of Dynamic Programming to the Determination of Optimal Satellite Trajectory Problems," *J. British Interplanetary Soc.,* **17,** 78–83 (1959).

Cartaino, T., and Dreyfus, S., "Application of Dynamic Programming to the Airplane Minimum Time-to-Climb Problem," *Aero. Engr., Rev.,* **16,** 74–77 (1957)

Dreyfus, S., "A Generalized Equipment Replacement Study," *J. of SIAM,* **8,** 425–435 (1960).

Econometric Analysis of the United States Manganese Problem, Econometric Research Program, RM 3, Princeton University, Princeton, N.J., Oct. 1958.

Grometstein, A. A., *Sub Program Storage within a Digital Computer: A Cargo Loading Problem,* Lincoln Laboratory Report 22G-0006, Aug. 1959.

Hanssmann, F., "Optimal Inventory Location and Control in Production and Distribution Networks," *Opns. Res.,* **7,** 483–498 (1959).

Howard, R., *Dynamic Programming and Markov Processes,* Technology Press and Wiley, 1960.

Kalaba, R., *Proceedings of the Symposium of Ordinary Differential Equations,* Mexico City, Sept. 1959, to be published.

Riley, V., and Gass, S. I., *Linear Programming and Associated Techniques,* Operations Research Office, The Johns Hopkins University, Chevy Chase, Md., 1958.

Schlager, K. J., *Optimization of a Von Thuenen Model of the Firm by Dynamic Programming,* Fifteenth National Meeting of the Operations Research Society, May 1959.

Ten Dyke, R. P., "Computation of Rocket Step Weights to Minimize Initial Gross Weight," *Jet Propulsion,* **28,** 338–340 (1958).

Chapter 6

DYNAMICS OF OPERATIONAL SYSTEMS: Markov and Queuing Processes

Philip M. Morse

Massachusetts Institute of Technology, Cambridge, Massachusetts

Contents

1. INTRODUCTORY DEFINITIONS

As experience in operations research grows, we can begin to classify operations according to their response patterns and begin to develop theories describing these patterns, much as classical dynamics was distilled from numerous observations of the response patterns of simple physical systems. We report here the elements of the dynamical theory of one class of operational systems. Lack of space will preclude the presentation of more than elementary examples of the theory, or with details of the mathematical proofs of the solutions; these can be found in the books and articles mentioned in the bibliography.

A large class of operational systems are amenable to description in terms of a denumerable set of *states*. The state of a simple inventory system, for example, can be given by enumerating the items on hand, those on order, and those on backorder. The state of a fleet of delivery trucks can be specified by giving the number of trucks being loaded, those on different delivery routes, those being repaired, and so on. The state need not describe all the details of the system; it need only include those characteristics which the *manager* of the operation *must know* in order to make his decisions regarding the next actions of the system. The manager is notified, periodically or continuously, of the state of the system, by means of some status report, on the basis of which he issues his orders. The class of systems discussed here is that for which all the possible different status reports form a denumerable set, categorized by one (or more) integers i (or j) which can run from 1 to s (s can be infinite).

The system will change its state from time to time, either because outside influences affect it (items are withdrawn from the inventory, trucks complete loading or break down, etc.) or else because of decisions of the manager (orders for more items are placed, trucks are assigned to other delivery routes, etc.). These influences, tending to change the state of the system, will be called respectively the *external* and *internal forces* acting on the operational system, by analogy with the physical systems of classical dynamics. The future behavior of the system depends on the interaction between these forces and the structure of the system.

Because of the stochastic nature of most operational forces, the motions of operational systems will not usually be completely reproducible; similar systems, acted on by similar forces, will not have similar histories. Thus we must usually be satisfied with probabilities and expected values. We can imagine an ensemble of similar systems, acted on by similar forces, from which we determine the relative frequency of a system being in state i at a given time. Corresponding to this, we desire our dynamical theory to provide means of evaluating the probabilities $p_i(t)$ that the system is in state i at time t. Corresponding to the position vector for the physical system in classical dynamics is the s-component *probability vector*

$$\mathbf{P}(t) = \{p_1(t), p_2(t), \cdots, p_s(t)\}; \quad 0 \leq p_j; \quad \sum_j p_j = 1 \tag{6.1}$$

which describes the distribution-in-states of the ensemble of operational systems and from which expected values of various properties of the system can be computed.

Our task, in operations research, often is to work out the consequences of various decisions which management might make. In many cases it is to calculate the consequences of a whole pattern or sequence of decisions, made according to some set of rules of decision, some doctrine of behavior for the manager. In connection with the simple systems we are discussing, a *doctrine of operation* is a complete set of rules which tells management what to do in each situation, which can be decided in advance, and which can be followed as long as the structure of the system is unchanged. It is often the task of operations research to work out which doctrine best meets some management criterion, which makes some subsystem operate appropriately as part of some larger system, for example. We thus desire our dynamical theory to enable us to compare expected values of variables of interest for systems subject to different internal forces, assuming the external forces are the same. The task is first to understand the relationship between the responses and the various doctrines which cause them; it may later be to determine which doctrine produces average results which correspond to managerial desires.

In many cases (at least for simple operational systems) it is desirable that the doctrine of operation be simple, a set of rules simple enough so that an inexperienced supervisor (or clerk) can run things with a minimum of supervision from higher authority. It is preferable, whenever possible, to make the set of rules be functions only of the present state of the system (for example, if the present state is j, then take the following action). Thus we will be primarily interested in doctrines which are functions of the latest state of the system (or, at most, of the last two states the system has occupied).

For the systems under consideration in this chapter, the effect of the internal and external forces on the system will be represented by *transition probabilities* M_{ij}, the conditional probabilities that the system will change from state i to state j in a specified period of time, or else by *transition rates* A_{ij}, the time rates of change of the system from state i to state j. We further will limit our discussion here to systems with external forces and choices of doctrine (internal forces) such that the *matrix elements* M_{ij} or A_{ij} are *independent of time*. This places a severe limitation on the nature of the forces acting (that they have a Poisson distribution in time, for example, or some related limitation), the implications of which will have to be worked out in the various cases studied. It does turn out that a large number of the simpler production, inventory, transportation, and small-group military operations are represented by this model, or correspond well enough so that the results can be used as a first-order approximation to the actual behavior.

These limitations placed on the model, and thus on the systems which it can represent, are analogous to the limitations usually placed on the model which represents many of the dynamical systems of classical physics. The forces acting on many physical systems are to good approximation dependent on the configuration of the system and on its rates of change, but not dependent explicitly on the time; likewise these forces affect only the accelerations of the system, so that the equations of motion involve the first and second time derivatives of the system but no higher derivatives. Put another way, the systems usually dealt with in classical dynamics are those whose future behavior can be predicted once the coordinates and velocities are specified at a given instant of time, and furthermore, this behavior is independent of the absolute value of the time at which these are specified.

As with classical dynamics, our operational dynamics should be capable of extension to other operational systems, not subject to all the limitations listed above. But for the purposes of exposition, and to develop techniques which can deal with many of the simpler systems, this chapter will consider only the dynamics of systems describable in terms of a denumerable set of states, with the temporal change in state probabilities controlled by transition probabilities which are independent of time.

2. EXAMPLES OF DISCRETE-TIME SYSTEMS

In many operations, status reports are presented to the manager, and the manager issues orders affecting the operation, at the ends of discrete periods of time. In these cases our dynamics may consider time as a discrete variable, with the probability vector

$$\mathbf{P}(n) = \{p_1(n), p_2(n), \cdots, p_s(n)\}; \quad 0 \leq p_j(n); \quad \sum_j p_j(n) = 1 \qquad (6.2)$$

having components $p_j(n)$ which are the probabilities that the system be in one or another of the states, represented by j, at the end of the nth period. If the effects of the external and internal forces depend only on the present state of the system, so that the probability of transition from state i to state j is independent of any previous state of the system, then the equation of motion for the probability vector is

$$\mathbf{P}(n+1) = \mathbf{P}(n) \cdot \mathfrak{M}, \quad \text{or} \quad P_j(n+1) = \sum_i P_i(n) M_{ij} \qquad (6.3)$$

where $\mathfrak{M}$ is the transition matrix

$$\mathfrak{M} = \begin{bmatrix} M_{11} & M_{12} & \cdots & M_{1s} \\ M_{21} & M_{22} & \cdots & M_{2s} \\ \cdot & \cdot & \cdot & \cdot \\ \cdot & \cdot & \cdot & \cdot \\ \cdot & \cdot & \cdot & \cdot \\ M_{s1} & M_{s2} & \cdots & M_{ss} \end{bmatrix}$$

with elements subject to the following restrictions

$$0 \leq M_{ij} \leq 1; \quad \sum_j M_{ij} = 1 \qquad (6.4)$$

A process satisfying Eq. 6.3 is termed a *simple Markov process* (see Feller and Bush) and a matrix satisfying the requirements of Eq. 6.4 is called a *stochastic matrix.* We note that if $\mathfrak{M}$ is stochastic, and if $\mathbf{P}(n)$ is a probability vector, then $\mathbf{P}(n+1)$ is a probability vector.

The matrix element M_{ij} is the conditional probability of transition from state i to state j in one time period, under the combined influence of the internal and external forces. A few examples will illustrate the nature of the relation between these elements and the forces they represent. Consider, for example, a simple inventory operation, that of receiving, storing, and supplying on demand a single type of item. We first assume that inventory may be replenished from the source of supply (factory, wholesaler, or other source) in any quantity and that the replenishment time, the time between the decision to place an order and the delivery of the items ordered to the inventory, is always time T. We also here assume that the operation is discrete in time, the inventory manager looking at the size of the inventory just after the preceding replenishment order has been received, deciding then the size of the next order and issuing the order. The demands for withdrawals from the inventory are supposed to be stochastic, the probability that j items are demanded in time T being $U_j(T)$ and, for the model we are discussing to be applicable, the values of the U's must be independent of the number of demands which arrived in previous periods. We also assume, for this simple example, that the U's are independent of the size of the inventory. This specifies the structure of the system and the nature of the external forces, which are represented by the U's.

We next must specify the internal forces, the replenishment doctrine to be followed by the manager, the set of rules which will tell him how much to order if his inventory contains i items at the end of a period; these rules must be a function only of the state of the inventory at the instant of issuing the order if the process is to a simple Markov process. We also must specify what is done if the inventory runs out, whether backorders are taken, to be filled when the next replenishment arrives, or whether "sales" are "lost" if stock is out (this decision is, of course, not entirely under the control of the manager but it must be estimated or assumed to make the model specific).

Consider the "lost-sales" case first. Let us assume that the replenishment doctrine is a simple one, to make up the inventory to some maximum figure M. In other words we specify that if the inventory, just after arrival of the last replenishment order, is I items, a replenishment order for $M-I$ items should be issued, which will arrive a time T later. The description of the system, and the form of the corresponding transition matrix follows.

Lost sales case:

State of system $=i$; $(0 \leq i \leq M) =$ difference between M and actual inventory after receipt of last replenishment

Prob. of j demands per period $T = U_j(T)$. $\sum_{j=k}^{\infty} U_j = W_k$; $W_0 = 1$

Inventory at beginning of period $I = M - i$
Size of replenishment order $= i$
Transition matrix is

$$\mathfrak{M} = \begin{bmatrix} U_0 & U_1 & U_2 & \cdots & U_{M-2} & U_{M-1} & W_M \\ U_0 & U_1 & U_2 & \cdots & U_{M-2} & W_{M-1} & 0 \\ \cdot & \cdot & \cdot & \cdot & \cdot & \cdot & \cdot \\ \cdot & \cdot & \cdot & \cdot & \cdot & \cdot & \cdot \\ \cdot & \cdot & \cdot & \cdot & \cdot & \cdot & \cdot \\ U_0 & W_1 & 0 & \cdots & 0 & 0 & 0 \\ 1 & 0 & 0 & \cdots & 0 & 0 & 0 \end{bmatrix} \tag{6.5}$$

For example, if the initial state is i, then no more than $M-i$ items can be withdrawn in the next period, and if $j(\leq M-i)$ items are withdrawn, then the number of items on hand at the end of the period, after the replenishment order for i items is received, is $(M-i)-j+i=M-j$ so that the final state is j. The reason for preferring $i=M-I$, over the inventory I, as state designation, will become apparent as the discussion progresses.

If, on the other hand, backorders are allowed and no "sales" are lost, the number of possible states is infinite and the transition matrix takes on a simpler form, as in the next case.

Backorder case:

State of system $=i \quad (0 \leq i)$
Prob. of j demands per period $= U_j(T)$
No. of items in inventory at start of period $= M-i \quad$ (if $i<M$)
$\qquad = 0 \quad$ (if $i \geq M$)
No. of backorders on hand at start $= 0 \quad$ (if $i \leq M$)
$\qquad = i-M \quad$ (if $i>M$)
Size of replenishment order $= i$
Transition matrix is

$$\mathfrak{M} = \begin{bmatrix} U_0 & U_1 & U_2 & \cdots \\ U_0 & U_1 & U_2 & \cdots \\ U_0 & U_1 & U_2 & \cdots \\ \cdot & \cdot & \cdot & \cdot \\ \cdot & \cdot & \cdot & \cdot \\ \cdot & \cdot & \cdot & \cdot \end{bmatrix} \tag{6.6}$$

If, however, single items cannot be ordered, but only integral multiples of Q items, so that the size of the replenishment order is kQ, where k is the largest integer no larger than (i/Q), then the transition matrix has the form.

Backorder case (order in multiples of Q items): State of system i, as before.

$$M_{kQ+l,j}=0 \quad (\text{if } j<l), \quad =U_{j-l} \quad (\text{if } j\geq l) \quad (l<Q)$$

$$\mathfrak{M}=\begin{bmatrix} U_0 & U_1 & U_2 & \cdots & U_{Q-2} & U_{Q-1} & U_Q & \cdots \\ 0 & U_0 & U_1 & \cdots & U_{Q-3} & U_{Q-2} & U_{Q-1} & \cdots \\ 0 & 0 & U_0 & \cdots & U_{Q-4} & U_{Q-3} & U_{Q-2} & \cdots \\ \cdot & \cdot & \cdot & \cdot & \cdot & \cdot & \cdot & \cdot \\ \cdot & \cdot & \cdot & \cdot & \cdot & \cdot & \cdot & \cdot \\ \cdot & \cdot & \cdot & \cdot & \cdot & \cdot & \cdot & \cdot \\ 0 & 0 & 0 & \cdots & U_0 & U_1 & U_2 & \cdots \\ 0 & 0 & 0 & \cdots & 0 & U_0 & U_1 & \cdots \\ U_0 & U_1 & U_2 & \cdots & U_{Q-2} & U_{Q-1} & U_Q & \cdots \\ 0 & U_0 & U_1 & \cdots & U_{Q-3} & U_{Q-2} & U_{Q-1} & \cdots \\ \cdot & \cdot & \cdot & \cdot & \cdot & \cdot & \cdot & \cdot \\ \cdot & \cdot & \cdot & \cdot & \cdot & \cdot & \cdot & \cdot \\ \cdot & \cdot & \cdot & \cdot & \cdot & \cdot & \cdot & \cdot \end{bmatrix} \tag{6.7}$$

Other generalizations, such as the introduction of variability into the replenishment time, are also possible (see Morse, 1959).

Another example can be that of the operation, breakdown, and repair of a piece of machinery. We are here considering examples which can be expressed in terms of discrete time periods, which might be the time required to do a single task (single trip for a plane or truck, unit operation for a piece of factory equipment, etc.). The simplest possible assumptions are that there is a certain probability b of breakdown during a period, independent of how long the machine has been running previously and that, if the machine has broken down and is being repaired, there is a probability α that it will be repaired and in running shape next period, independent of how long it has been under repair. In this case the system description and the transition matrix are

State 1. Productive.
State 2. Being repaired.

$$\mathfrak{M}=\begin{pmatrix} 1-b & b \\ \alpha & 1-\alpha \end{pmatrix} \tag{6.8}$$

This is usually too simple a model to describe many of the complications of actual maintenance operations; it is seldom that the breakdown or repair probabilities have such simple statistical behavior. For example, the machine may behave statistically as though it can break down in two ways; one needing only a single period to repair, the other perhaps needing several periods to fix. The description then could be

State 1. Productive, predestined for breakdown type A.
State 2. Productive, predestined for breakdown type B.
State 3. Breakdown type A (short repair job).
State 4. Breakdown type B (possibly long repair job).

$$\mathfrak{M}=\begin{pmatrix} 1-a & 0 & a & 0 \\ 0 & 1-b & 0 & b \\ \alpha & 1-\alpha & 0 & 0 \\ \beta & \gamma & 0 & 1-\beta-\gamma \end{pmatrix} \tag{6.9}$$

The quantities α, β, and γ measure the relative frequencies that breakdowns of type A or B occur the next time, after a short or a long repair job. We note that, since $M_{33}=0$, a short repair job (state 3) is always completed in one period, but that a long job (state 4) may take longer. States 1 and 2 may or may not be distinguishable before the next breakdown. By proper choice of a, b, α, β, and γ a wide variety of statistical situations may be simulated.

In the last two examples there was not much effect of alternate doctrines of operation, except indirectly in terms of decisions regarding the size of repair crews, which would affect the values of α and β. Another example will indicate how the relative advantages of preventive maintenance might be investigated. Suppose the breakdown statistics can be simulated by assuming that the machine goes through two phases in sequence; in the first phase the machine is in good shape, in the second phase it is still productive but if, during this phase, it is checked and adjusted it can be put back into good order again with the loss of only one period's time, whereas if it is allowed to go to final breakdown the repair time may be considerably longer.

Three doctrines are possible: I. Let the machine go to final breakdown, in which case the system and transition matrix are:

State 1. Productive, phase 1.
State 2. Productive, phase 2.
State 3. Breakdown, being repaired.

$$\mathfrak{M} = \begin{pmatrix} 1-a-c & a & c \\ 0 & 1-b & b \\ \alpha & 0 & 1-\alpha \end{pmatrix} \tag{6.10}$$

(the uses of phases in parallel or series in simulating various statistical behavior is discussed in Morse, 1958, Chapter 5). II. If it can be determined when the machine goes into phase 2, then it might be better, for some values of a, b, c, and α, to check and adjust the machine as soon as it gets to phase 2. In this case the model is:

State 1. Productive, phase 1.
State 2. Phase 2, under preventive maintenance.
State 3. Breakdown, being repaired.

$$\mathfrak{M} = \begin{pmatrix} 1-a-c & a & c \\ 1 & 0 & 0 \\ \alpha & 0 & 1-\alpha \end{pmatrix} \tag{6.11}$$

III. Even if it cannot be determined when the transition from phase 1 to phase 2 occurs, in some cases it may be best to use preventive maintenance every other period (unless a serious breakdown has already occurred). In this case the model is:

State 1. Productive.
State 2. Preventive maintenance applied.
State 3. Breakdown, under repair.

$$\mathfrak{M} = \begin{pmatrix} 0 & 1-c & c \\ 1 & 0 & 0 \\ \alpha & 0 & 1-\alpha \end{pmatrix} \tag{6.12}$$

These simple examples illustrate the relationship between the external and internal forces and the transition matrix. They also illustrate the nature of the restrictions on the type of operational system which can be represented by the Markov process of Eq. 6.3 and indicate how some of the restrictions can be relaxed, by suitable insertion of hypothetical substates. It should be pointed out that Eq. 6.3 (which is the analogue of a first-degree equation of motion) is but the simplest equation of motion for operational systems of this general class. Other patterns of operation may give rise to more complex equations. For example, if the manager does not get up-to-date information on the state of the system, he may have to make his decisions on the basis of one-period-old data. The equations of motion may then take on the form

$$\mathbf{P}(n+1)-\mathbf{P}(n)=\mathbf{P}(n-1)\cdot\mathfrak{A};\quad p_j(n+1)-p_j(n)=\sum_i p_i(n-1)A_{ij} \qquad (6.13)$$

which is analogous to a second-degree equation. The elements of the matrix $A_{ij}=M_{ij}-\delta_{ij}$ must satisfy the limitations

$$0\le A_{ij}\le 1 \quad (i\ne j);\quad \sum_j A_{ij}=0 \qquad (6.14)$$

Such matrices may be called *differential matrices.*

3. DISCRETE-TIME SYSTEMS, STEADY-STATE SOLUTIONS

Having given a few elementary examples of the sorts of operational systems which are subject to the equations of motion (6.3), it is appropriate to discuss techniques of solution. By analogy with classical mechanics, we should expect our ensemble of similar systems, acted on by similar internal and external forces, to exhibit the following general behavior. Just after the systems have been started their average behavior would be expected to change with time in a manner which depends on the *initial conditions,* i.e., on the relative distribution of state-occupations of the systems in the ensemble at the end of the zeroth period of time, represented by the components of the probability vector $\mathbf{P}(0)$. This initial behavior, by analogy, can be called the *transient behavior* of the ensemble.

After sufficient time has elapsed, however, the ensemble will usually settle down to a *steady-state motion,* which is independent of the initial conditions, depending only on the nature of the systems and the forces involved. This does not mean that all the systems of the ensemble end up doing the same thing, or that eventually no system will change its state. It does mean that, in the steady state, the different systems will change state in such a manner that as many leave a given state as enter it, so that the mean distribution-in-states of the ensemble, represented by the vector $\mathbf{P}(n)$, is independent of n [and also independent of $\mathbf{P}(0)$] when n is large enough. There are exceptions, matrices which represent ensembles which do not settle down to a steady state, just as there are idealized physical systems, with no friction, which have no steady-state motion. But these are usually overidealized models.

If we use the rule for matrix multiplication

$$(\mathfrak{A}\cdot\mathfrak{B})_{ij}=\sum_k A_{ik}B_{kj} \tag{6.15}$$

to compute the elements of the matrices for powers of the transition matrix $\mathfrak{M}$ of Eq. 6.3, we can see that a formal solution of Eq. 6.3 is

$$\mathbf{P}(n)=\mathbf{P}(0)\cdot(\mathfrak{M}^n);\quad p_j(n)=\sum_i p_i(0)(\mathfrak{M}^n)_{ij}$$
$$(\mathfrak{M}^n)_{ij}=\sum_k(\mathfrak{M}^{n-1})_{ik}M_{kj} \tag{6.16}$$

It is thus possible to compute the probability vector $\mathbf{P}(n)$ for the system at the end of the nth period, given the initial probability vector $\mathbf{P}(0)$. (We note that if $\mathfrak{M}$ is stochastic, $\mathfrak{M}^n$ is stochastic.) We emphasize again that although the vector $\mathbf{P}(n)$ is thus determined exactly for each n, this does not mean that the behavior of any individual system in the ensemble is exactly predictable. At the end of the nth period a given system can be in any state j for which the component $p_j(n)$ is not zero, but the relative frequency of occupation of state j is predicted, and the change of these frequencies from period to period is what can be computed from Eq. 6.16.

We will see later, when we come to compute the transient motion, that for most stochastic (see Eq. 6.4) matrices $\mathfrak{M}$ the matrix $\mathfrak{M}^n$ approaches a limiting form, independent of n, as n is increased without limit. This asymptotic form has identical rows; i.e., it is usually true that

$$(\mathfrak{M}^n)_{ij}\to P_j\quad(n\to\infty)\quad\text{for all } i \tag{6.17}$$

This means that (when the system has a steady state) no matter what the initial state of the system, the probability $p_j(n)$ will approach

$$p_j(n)=\sum_i p_i(0)(\mathfrak{M}^n)_{ij}\to P_j\quad(n\to\infty),\quad\text{or}$$
$$\mathbf{P}(n)\to\mathbf{P}(\infty)=\{P_1,P_2,\cdots,P_s\} \tag{6.18}$$

where the components $P_j=p_j(\infty)$ are called the steady-state probabilities for the system. The nature of the exceptional systems, which have no steady state, will be discussed when we come to calculate the transient behavior.

Values of the steady-state probabilities can be computed by taking advantage of the fact that, when steady state is reached, the probability distribution does not change further. In other words

$$\mathbf{P}(\infty)=\mathbf{P}(\infty)\cdot\mathfrak{M},\quad\text{or}\quad P_j=\sum_i P_iM_{ij} \tag{6.19}$$

This set of s homogeneous equations in s unknowns, the P's, has a non-trivial solution, since the determinant of the coefficients of the P's,

$$|M_{ij}-\delta_{ij}| \equiv \begin{vmatrix} M_{11}-1 & M_{12} & \cdots & M_{1s} \\ M_{21} & M_{22}-1 & \cdots & M_{2s} \\ \cdot & \cdot & \cdot & \cdot \\ \cdot & \cdot & \cdot & \cdot \\ \cdot & \cdot & \cdot & \cdot \\ M_{s1} & M_{s2} & \cdots & M_{ss}-1 \end{vmatrix} = 0 \qquad (6.20)$$

is zero for all stochastic matrices (from Eq. 6.4). The values are computed relative to an undetermined factor, and this factor is determined by the requirement that the sum of the P's be unity.

As examples, we write down the solutions of Eq. 6.19 for some of the systems discussed in Section 2. For the simple, backorder inventory system described in Eq. 6.6, the steady state is easily found, for in this case $\mathfrak{M}^n = \mathfrak{M}$, so from Eq. 3.3

$$\text{System of Eq. 6.6} \quad P_j = M_{ij} = U_j(T) \qquad (6.21)$$

For this system the probability that $M-j$ units are in stock at the end of a period is equal to the probability that j units are withdrawn in a period, a not surprising result.

It is not much more difficult to find the solution for the backorder system of Eq. 6.7, where items are ordered in batches of Q items, or multiples of Q (see Morse, 1959).

Backorder system of Eq. 6.7. Replenishment order for state i is for kQ items, where k is the largest integer not larger than (i/Q). Steady-state solution

$$P_j = \sum_{i=0}^{j}(U_{j-i}/Q) \quad (j<Q), \quad = \sum_{j=0}^{Q-1}(U_{j-i}/Q) \quad (j \geq Q) \qquad (6.22)$$

If (as often happens) the distribution U_j of demands in a period has a sharp maximum at $j=m$, where m is approximately the average demand per period, then if batch ordering is not required (and the order is for i items) the distribution-in-states also has a sharp maximum, but if batch ordering is necessary the distribution-in-states is more spread out and the inventory variance increases as Q increases (as will be shown in the next Section, Eq. 6.34).

The steady-state solution for the simple maintenance system of Eq. 6.8 is

$$\text{System of Eq. 6.8} \quad P_1 = \frac{\alpha}{\alpha+b}, \quad P_2 = \frac{b}{\alpha+b} \tag{6.23}$$

The probability the machine is out of commission and being repaired is proportional to the probability of breakdown, and the probability the machine is productively running is proportional to the probability of completion of repair in one period.

In the maintenance systems of Eqs. 6.10, 6.11, and 6.12, the steady-state solutions are

$$\text{Eq. 6.10} \quad P_1 = \frac{\alpha b}{Q}, \quad P_2 = \frac{\alpha a}{Q}, \quad P_3 = \frac{b(a+c)}{Q}, \quad Q = \alpha(b+a) + b(a+c)$$

$$\text{Eq. 6.11} \quad P_1 = \frac{\alpha}{R}, \quad P_2 = \frac{\alpha a}{R}, \quad P_3 = \frac{c}{R}, \quad R = \alpha(1+a) + c \tag{6.24}$$

$$\text{Eq. 6.12} \quad P_1 = \frac{\alpha}{S}, \quad P_2 = \frac{\alpha(1-c)}{S}, \quad P_3 = \frac{c}{S}, \quad S = \alpha(2-c) + c$$

To decide whether to use preventive maintenance or not we could compare the fraction of time the machine is productive when no preventive maintenance is used, $\alpha(a+b)/[\alpha(a+b)+b(a+c)]$ for Eq. 6.10, with the productive fraction when maintenance is applied whenever the machine is in phase 2, $\alpha/[\alpha(1+a)+c]$ for Eq. 6.11, or with the productivity when the machine is serviced every other time, $\alpha/[\alpha(2-c)+c]$ for Eq. 6.12. We note, for example, that if $[(b-c)/\alpha(a+b)]>1$ then the use of preventive maintenance will *reduce* the productive time of the machine; if $[(b-c)/\alpha(a+b)]<1$ then use of the preventive maintenance system of Eq. 6.11 (if this is possible) will result in the largest fraction of productive time.

Other examples of steady-state solutions can be found in the literature (Feller, Chapter 15, and also MIT, Chapter 3).

4. STEADY-STATE AVERAGES, AUTOCORRELATION FUNCTIONS

The measures of effectiveness, which can be used to test which operational doctrine conforms to some managerial requirement, often are time averages of quantities x_j which are functions of the state j of the system at the end of periods (such as the mean value of inventory or the fraction of periods the machine is productive, in our examples) or else are time averages of functions X_{ij} of the transitions made by the system (such as the mean time the inventory system is out of stock). If the system is to be run for a long time, so that steady-state conditions can be assumed, the time average over the behavior of one system will be the same as the ensemble average at any time, so we can compute our expected values by averaging over the steady-state probability distribution.

For example, if the quantity of interest is a *state function*, having value x_i when the system is in state i, the *expected value* of x under steady-state conditions is

$$E(x) = \sum_i x_i P_i \tag{6.25}$$

If, however, it is a *transition function*, taking on the value X_{ij} whenever the system goes from state i to state j in one period, then the steady-state expected value is

$$E(X) = \sum_{ij} X_{ij} P_i M_{ij} \tag{6.26}$$

The value x takes on for a given system varies from period to period, of course, as the system changes from state to state. Over the long run its average value will approach $E(x)$, but usually it will stochastically deviate above and below this value. A measure of the degree of fluctuation of x, and thus of the degree of stability which the system possesses in regard to x, is the *variance* of x (or of X)

$$\Delta^2(x) = \sum_i P_i x_i^2 - E^2(x); \quad \Delta^2(X) = \sum_{ij} P_i M_{ij} X_{ij}^2 - E^2(X) \tag{6.27}$$

The square root of the variance, $\Delta(x)$ or $\Delta(X)$, is called the *standard deviation* of x (or of X).

As an example, we return to the backorder inventory system of Eq. 2.6. We define the *net stock* of the system at the end of the mth period as being $N = M - i$ when the system is in state i; it is equal to the inventory if $M - i$ is positive, equal to minus the number of backorders if $M - i$ is not positive. If the demands for items are spaced at random in time, the probability that n demands arrive in a period T is given by the Poisson distribution,

$$U_n(T) = (S^n/n!)e^{-S}, \qquad S = \text{mean no. of demands in time } T \tag{6.28}$$

Then, since $P_j = M_{ij} = U_j$ for this system, we find that the expected value of net stock, at the end of a period (just after the previous replenishment order has been received, all outstanding backorders satisfied and the remainder, if any, placed in stock), and its variance are

$$E(N)=\sum_j (M-j)P_j=M-S;\quad \Delta^2(N)=\sum_j (S-j)^2 P_j=S \quad (6.29)$$

The net stock at period-end thus fluctuates about its mean value $M-S$ with a standard deviation of $\sqrt{S}$.

The average value of net stock over a period is a transition function, for if the initial state is i (net stock $M-i$, replenishment order for i) and j items are demanded in the succeeding period, the net stock just before the replenishment order for i is received is $M-i-j$, so the mean value of net stock over the period is $\overline{N}=M-i-\frac{1}{2}j$ and the expected value of this is

$$E(\overline{N})=\sum_{ij} P_i M_{ij}(M-i-\tfrac{1}{2}j)=\sum_{ij} U_i U_j (M-i-\tfrac{1}{2}j)=M-\tfrac{3}{2}S \quad (6.30)$$

(We have assumed that, on the average, the stock depletion is linear in time during the period; this is legitimate for Poisson demands.)

The number of backorders B_0 still on hand at the end of a period (just after a replenishment order is received), when the state is i, is zero if $i\leq M$ and is $i-M$ when $i>M$. This is the minimal number of backorders present during the next period, before the next replenishment order is received. The expected value of this quantity, for Poisson demands, is thus

$$E(B_0)=\sum_{i=M}^{\infty}(i-M)U_i(T)=S-M[1-D_{M-1}(S)]$$

where (6.31)

$$D_m(x)=\frac{1}{m+1}\sum_{n=0}^{m}(m+1-n)(x^n/n!)e^{-x}$$

is a tabulated function (see Morse, 1958; see also Eq. 6.75). On the other hand, if the final state is j, the maximal number of backorders B_m during the period (the number on hand just before the next replenishment order arrives) is zero if $M\leq i+j$ and is $i+j-M$ if $M<i+j$, and the expected value of this is

$$\begin{aligned} E(B_m)&=2S-M-\sum_{i=0}^{M}\sum_{j=0}^{M-1}(i+j-M)U_i(T)U_j(T) \\ &=2S-M[1-D_{M-1}(2S)] \end{aligned} \quad (6.32)$$

since, for the Poisson distribution,

$$\sum_{i=0}^{n} U_i(T)\,U_{n-i}(t) = U_n(T+t)$$

Incidentally, since net stock N equals actual inventory on hand I minus the number of backorders on hand B (see Eq. 6.6), the expected value of the stock on hand at the beginning of a period is $E(N)+E(B_0)$ and the minimal value of stock on hand, just before the replenishment order arrives, has expected value $M-2S+E(B_m)$.

Finally, the mean fraction of the period when the system is out of stock, when the transition is from state i to state j, is zero when $M\geq i+j$, is $(i+j-M)/j$ when $i<M<i+j$ and is unity when $i\geq M$ (assuming linearity in each time period). The expected fraction of time the system is out of stock is therefore

$$P_{\text{out}} = \sum_{i=0}^{M-1} \sum_{j=M-1}^{\infty} \frac{i+j-M}{j} U_i(T)\,U_j(T) + \sum_{i=M}^{\infty} U_i(T) \tag{6.33}$$

The same sort of calculations can be carried out for the system of Eqs. 6.23, with replenishments ordered in integral multiples of Q. For example, the expected value of net stock at the end of a period, and its variance, for Poisson demands, are

$$\begin{aligned} E(N) &= \sum_j (M-j)P_j = M-S-\tfrac{1}{2}(Q-1) \\ \Delta^2(N) &= \sum_j (M-j)^2 P_j - E^2(N) = S+\tfrac{1}{12}(Q-1)^2 \end{aligned} \tag{6.34}$$

We thus see that ordering in batches reduces the mean value of net stock and increases its variance (see discussion of Eq. 6.22).

Further details as to the nature of the variability of the system in its steady state can be obtained by computing the correlation function for one or more of the state or transition functions of the system. If x is a state function of the system, its *autocorrelation function* $\Psi_m(x)$ is defined as the expected value of the product of the deviation $x-E(x)$ at one period by the value of the deviation m periods later,

$$\Psi_m(x) = \sum_i P_i x_i (\mathfrak{M}^m)_{ij} x_j - E^2(x); \quad \Psi_0(x) = \Delta^2(x) \tag{6.35}$$

The change of this function, as m is increased, is a measure of how the value of x, during the history of a given system, tends to return to its average value after it has, by chance, fluctuated away from this value.

To put it another way, the rapidity with which Ψ_m returns to zero as m is increased is a measure of how rapidly the system "forgets" its past behavior.

For the inventory system of Eqs. 6.6 and 6.29, for example, the autocorrelation function for the net stock N is

$$\Psi_0(N) = S; \quad \Psi_m(N) = 0 \quad (m > 0) \tag{6.35a}$$

since, in this case $\mathfrak{M}^m = \mathfrak{M}$. Thus the inventory system, for which the replenishment order is exactly the number of items withdrawn in the previous period, "recovers" from a fluctuation in one period; it has no "memory." On the other hand, for the batch-ordering system of Eqs. 6.23,

$$\Psi_0(N) = S + \tfrac{1}{12}(Q-1)^2; \quad \Psi_1(N) = \sum_{k=0}^{\infty} \sum_{j=0}^{Q-1} (kQ+j)(j - \tfrac{1}{2}Q + \tfrac{1}{2}) P_{kQ+j} \tag{6.36}$$

Since the autocorrelation function Ψ_m does not go immediately to zero for $m > 0$, this system does not return to average as speedily as does the case for $Q = 1$; the larger Q is the more the system "remembers" its previous state. Consideration in detail of the effects of batch ordering will indicate why this is so.

5. TRANSIENT BEHAVIOR OF DISCRETE-TIME SYSTEMS

To compute the general solution (6.16) or the autocorrelation function (6.35) we need a means of computing the stochastic matrix which is the mth power of the Markov matrix $\mathfrak{M}$. Straightforward matrix multiplication is a possibility, but one neither elegant nor conducive to demonstration of the properties of $\mathfrak{M}^m$ as a function of m. More rewarding is an investigation of the transformation properties of matric functions (see Ferrar, for example). We will take advantage of the fact that, if we can find the appropriate, non-singular, transformation matrix $\mathfrak{T}$ and its inverse $\mathfrak{T}^{-1}$, such that it is easy to work with the transformed matrix

$$\mathfrak{D} = \mathfrak{T}^{-1} \cdot \mathfrak{M} \cdot \mathfrak{T}; \quad \mathfrak{M} = \mathfrak{T} \cdot \mathfrak{D} \cdot \mathfrak{T}^{-1} \tag{6.37}$$

we can then do our calculations with $\mathfrak{D}$ and only transform back to $\mathfrak{M}$ at the end. For example, the powers of $\mathfrak{D}$ are simply related to the powers of $\mathfrak{M}$,

$$\mathfrak{M}^m = (\mathfrak{T} \cdot \mathfrak{D} \cdot \mathfrak{T}^{-1})^m = \mathfrak{T} \cdot (\mathfrak{D}^m) \cdot \mathfrak{T}^{-1} \tag{6.38}$$

For most stochastic matrices the elements of the transformation matrix $\mathfrak{T}$ and its inverse $\mathfrak{T}^{-1}$ can be found in terms of the eigenvectors and eigenvalues of $\mathfrak{M}$. We define the s *eigenvalues* $\mu_\nu(\nu=1,2,\cdots,s)$ of the s-row, s-column matrix $\mathfrak{M}$ as the s roots of the *secular equation*

$$|M_{ij}-\mu\delta_{ij}| \equiv \begin{vmatrix} M_{11}-\mu & M_{12} & M_{13} & \cdots & M_{1s} \\ M_{21} & M_{22}-\mu & M_{23} & \cdots & M_{2s} \\ \cdot & \cdot & \cdot & \cdot & \cdot \\ \cdot & \cdot & \cdot & \cdot & \cdot \\ \cdot & \cdot & \cdot & \cdot & \cdot \\ M_{s1} & M_{s2} & M_{s3} & \cdots & M_{ss}-\mu \end{vmatrix} = 0 \qquad (6.39)$$

The νth *forward eigenvector* $\mathbf{X}(\nu)$ and the νth *rearward eigenvector* $\mathbf{Y}(\nu)$ of $\mathfrak{M}$ are then defined as the vectors with components $X_i(\nu)$ and $Y_j(\nu)$ which satisfy the following equations:

$$\sum_i X_i(\nu)M_{ij}=\mu_\nu X_j(\nu); \quad \sum_j M_{ij}Y_j(\nu)=\mu_\nu Y_i(\nu)$$

$$\sum_i X_i(\nu)Y_i(\lambda)=\delta_{\nu\lambda}; \quad \sum_\nu X_i(\nu)Y_j(\nu)=\delta_{ij}=\begin{cases}1(i=j)\\0(i\neq j)\end{cases} \qquad (6.40)$$

We then see that if the transformation matrix $\mathfrak{T}$ has the elements $(\mathfrak{T})_{j\nu}=Y_j(\nu)$, its inverse will have elements $(\mathfrak{T}^{-1})_{\nu i}=X_i(\nu)$, and the transformed matrix

$$(\mathfrak{D})_{\nu\lambda}=\sum_{ij} X_i(\nu)M_{ij}Y_j(\lambda)=\mu_\nu\delta_{\nu\lambda} \qquad (6.41)$$

is a *diagonal matrix*. The mth power of such a matrix is also a diagonal matrix, with elements $(\mathfrak{D}^m)_{\nu\lambda}=(\mu_\nu)^m\delta_{\nu\lambda}$; a matric function of $\mathfrak{D}$ which can be expressed as a power series in $\mathfrak{D}$ is also a diagonal matrix, with diagonal elements the corresponding function of μ_ν. Consequently the mth power of $\mathfrak{M}$ can be written as a sum of s matrices $\mathfrak{F}_\nu$,

$$\mathfrak{M}^m=\mathfrak{T}\cdot\mathfrak{D}^m\cdot\mathfrak{T}^{-1}=\sum_\nu(\mu_\nu)^m\mathfrak{F}_\nu; \quad (\mathfrak{M}^m)_{ij}=\sum_\nu Y_i(\nu)(\mu_\nu)^m X_j(\nu)$$

$$\mathfrak{F}_\nu=\begin{bmatrix} Y_1(\nu)X_1(\nu) & \cdots & Y_1(\nu)X_s(\nu) \\ Y_2(\nu)X_1(\nu) & \cdots & Y_2(\nu)X_s(\nu) \\ \cdot & \cdot & \cdot \\ \cdot & \cdot & \cdot \\ \cdot & \cdot & \cdot \\ Y_s(\nu)X_1(\nu) & \cdots & Y_s(\nu)X_s(\nu) \end{bmatrix} \qquad (6.42)$$

The matrices $\mathfrak{F}_\nu$ are independent of m, and thus enter into the expression of any matric function of $\mathfrak{M}$.

When the eigenvalues μ_ν are all different, it is always possible to find the s forward and rearward eigenvectors, and thus to find the transformation of $\mathfrak{M}$ to a diagonal form $\mathfrak{D}$. When some of the eigenvalues are equal then occasionally it is not possible to find a transformation which will diagonalize $\mathfrak{M}$. In such cases a transformation can be found which results in a nearly diagonal form (called a canonical form, see Ferrar), from which the mth power of $\mathfrak{M}$ can be found, though not as easily as with Eq. 6.42. However, these special cases are not of much practical interest. As with the special case of critical damping of the damped harmonic oscillator of classical dynamics (to which they are analogues), they occur only when the elements of $\mathfrak{M}$ have very special interrelations. Even when the system is such that these special relations hold, the behavior of the system is not much different from the non-special cases where the elements of $\mathfrak{M}$ differ only slightly from the special values. In this chapter, therefore, we assume that the mth power of $\mathfrak{M}$ can be expressed in the form given in Eq. 6.42 and refer the reader interested in the special cases to the voluminous literature on the subject (as, for example, Ferrar and Feller and Bellman).

If $\mathfrak{M}$ is a stochastic matrix (see Eq. 6.4) it turns out that none of its eigenvalues has amplitude greater than unity, but that at least one eigenvalue equals unity. We will call this eigenvalue $\mu_1=1$. Reference to Eqs. 6.19 and 6.20 shows that the corresponding forward eigenvector can be set equal to the steady-state probability vector for the system, and that the corresponding rearward eigenvector has a very simple form

$$\mu_1=1; \quad X_i(1)=P_i; \quad Y_i(1)=1 \tag{6.43}$$

In most cases (see below) no other eigenvalue equals unity, and usually no other eigenvalue has an amplitude as large as unity. Use of the equation $\mu_\nu\sum_j X_j(\nu)=\sum_{ij} X_i(\nu)M_{ij}=\sum_i X_i(\nu)$ (which holds when $\mathfrak{M}$ is stochastic) indicates that when

$$|\mu_\nu|<1, \quad \text{then} \quad \sum_i X_i(\nu)=0 \tag{6.44}$$

which usually holds for $\nu=2,3,\cdots,s$. Thus the forward eigenvector for $\nu=1$ is a probability vector; the other forward eigenvectors have components which add up to zero.

Returning to Eq. 6.42, we now can discuss the transient behavior of the system. If the system starts in state i, the probability that it will be in state j after m periods will be

$$(\mathfrak{M}^m)_{ij} = \sum_{\nu=1}^{s} Y_i(\nu)(\mu_\nu)^m X_j(\nu) = P_j + \sum_{\nu=2}^{s} (\mu_\nu)^m Y_i(\nu) X_j(\nu) \tag{6.45}$$

These quantities, as functions of j, are the components of a probability vector (see Eq. 6.1). The first term, P_j, is independent of m and of i and corresponds to the steady-state behavior of the system. In the usual case, all the other eigenvalues, μ_ν for $\nu > 1$, have amplitudes smaller than unity, so the second term, the summation, diminishes as m is increased. This second term, therefore, represents the transient behavior of the system, which usually damps out as time goes on. The analogy with the harmonic oscillator is even more clear in the cases where one or more of the eigenvalues $\mu_\nu(\nu > 1)$ is negative or complex; in these cases the transition probabilities will exhibit damped oscillations as functions of m.

Next it is possible to classify the different kinds of Markov matrices $\mathfrak{M}$ in terms of the nature of their eigenvalues μ_ν and their steady-state probabilities P_i (see Feller, Chapter 15, for a more complete discussion of the different possible behaviors). For example, in some cases P_j is zero for some values of j. These states are called *transient states;* they do not occur in the steady-state motion. In other cases there may be sets of states between which there is no chance of transition, the matrix $\mathfrak{M}$ being factorable, with zeros in the regions corresponding to all transitions between states of one set and states of the other set. For a matrix of this sort there are two (or more) eigenvalues equal to unity and the steady state involves either one set of states or else the other, depending on which state the system started in. In cases like this it is better to consider each set of states separately, in other words to factor the matrix and deal with each factor separately. In a few limiting cases some roots will be complex, with unit amplitude; in these cases the system will not settle down to the steady state, represented by the matrix $\mathfrak{F}_1$ of Eqs. 6.42 its probability distribution will oscillate continuously, as does the harmonic oscillator in the limiting case of zero friction. For the systems usually encountered in practice, the matrix is non-factorable and the amplitudes of all eigenvalues except μ_1 are less than unity, so that a steady state does develop; the systems we discuss in this chapter are of this type.

Returning to the definition of the autocorrelation function for the state function x, given in Eq. 6.35, we can use Eq. 6.45 to obtain an expression for Ψ_m in terms of the eigenvectors,

$$\Psi_m(x) = \sum_{i.j=1}^{s} x_i x_j \sum_{\nu=2}^{s} \mu_\nu{}^m X_i(1) Y_i(\nu) X_j(\nu) \tag{6.46}$$

Since this involves only the transient part of the solution ($\nu>1$), which usually damps out, this function will usually approach zero as m increases; it may execute damped oscillations if one or more eigenvalue μ_ν is negative or complex.

As an example we compute the transient behavior of the simple maintenance system of Eq. 6.8. The eigenvalues and eigenvectors are

$$\mu_1=1;\quad \mathbf{X}(1)=\left\{\frac{\alpha}{\alpha+b},\frac{b}{\alpha+b}\right\};\quad \mathbf{Y}(1)=\{1,1\}$$

$$\mu_2=1-\alpha-b;\quad \mathbf{X}(2)=\{1,-1\};\quad \mathbf{Y}(2)=\left\{\frac{b}{\alpha+b},\frac{-\alpha}{\alpha+b}\right\} \tag{6.47}$$

$$\mathfrak{M}^m=\frac{1}{\alpha+b}\begin{pmatrix}\alpha+b\mu_2{}^m & b(1-\mu_2{}^m)\\ \alpha(1-\mu_2{}^m) & b+\alpha\mu_2{}^m\end{pmatrix}$$

If we value (see Section 4) the productive state ($i=1$) as $x_1=1$ and the state of being repaired ($i=2$) as $x_2=-1$, the steady-state, expected value of x and its autocorrelation function are

$$E(x)=\frac{\alpha-b}{\alpha+b};\quad \Psi_m(x)=\frac{4\alpha b\mu_2{}^m}{(\alpha+b)^2} \tag{6.48}$$

If the probabilities b of breakdown and α of completing repair in one period are small enough, μ_2 will be positive and real, but smaller than unity. In this case there is no oscillation in the elements of $\mathfrak{M}^m$ or in $\Psi_m(x)$; they approach the steady-state values monotonically. Any individual system of the ensemble, which the solution represents, will of course oscillate between production and repair. But if, for example, we start all the machines of the ensemble in repair, a few will get out of order in the second period, more in the next and so on, so that before long the repair-production cycle of each machine is out of phase with all the others, and the initially homogeneous state of the ensemble has gradually dissolved into the heterogeneous disorder of the steady state where, in each period, $\alpha/(\alpha+b)$ of the machines are working and $b/(\alpha+b)$ of them are being repaired.

On the other hand, when α and b are large enough so that $0>\mu_2>-1$ then a certain periodicity will be apparent in the transient behavior. If the ensemble is started in working order, most of them will break down in the first period and most of these will be repaired in the second period, so that a sizable fraction of the machines will be in phase for the first few periods, though the preponderance of in-phase over out-of-phase machines in the ensemble will diminish. Of course, if $\alpha=b=1$, μ_2 will equal

-1 and the ensemble will stay in phase, all machines alternating between the in-working-order and being-repaired states simultaneously. This is the limiting case of complete periodicity.

The transient solutions for the other maintenance systems described in Section 2 can also be worked out with little more difficulty. Other examples have been worked out and reported in the literature (see, for example, MIT, Bush and Feller, for other types of examples).

Incidentally, more complex situations than those giving rise to simple Markov processes can be dealt with in terms of the analysis given here. For example, if there is a delay in the application of the control doctrine, it might be that the equation for the change in the probability vector with time may be (see Eqs. 6.13 and 6.14)

$$\mathbf{P}(m+1)-\mathbf{P}(m)=\mathbf{P}(m-1)\cdot\mathfrak{A} \tag{6.49}$$

where $\mathfrak{A}$ is a differential matrix. In this case we again set

$$\mathbf{P}(m)=\mathbf{P}(0)\cdot\mathfrak{M}^m$$

and obtain the equation for the unknown matrix

$$\mathfrak{M}^2-\mathfrak{M}=\mathfrak{A} \tag{6.50}$$

Transforming both $\mathfrak{A}$ and $\mathfrak{M}$ so that $\mathfrak{A}$ takes on its diagonal form, with eigenvalues α_ν and eigenvectors $\mathbf{X}(\nu)$ and $\mathbf{Y}(\nu)$, we can then solve for the corresponding diagonal terms of

$$\mu_\nu{}^2-\mu_\nu=\alpha_\nu; \quad \mu_\nu=\tfrac{1}{2}\pm\tfrac{1}{2}\sqrt{1+4\alpha_\nu{}^2} \tag{6.51}$$

There thus are a pair of values of μ_ν for each eigenvalue α_ν and thus a whole set of alternative matrices of the form

$$\mathfrak{M}=\sum_\nu \mu_\nu\mathfrak{F}_\nu; \quad (\mathfrak{F}_\nu)_{ij}=Y_i(\nu)X_j(\nu) \tag{6.52}$$

for the different choices of the roots μ_ν. The appropriate combination of these matrices is the one which makes $\mathfrak{M}$ a stochastic matrix (as it must be). Having obtained the appropriate form for matrix $\mathfrak{M}$, the determination of the behavior of the system is carried on as before. Systems with control delay exhibit more tendency to oscillate than do the ones obeying Eq. 6.4, where the control data is up-to-date.

6. DYNAMIC PROGRAMMING FOR MARKOV SYSTEMS

We have tacitly assumed that one of the reasons for setting up the Markov model for the system, and calculating its dynamic behavior, is to be able to compare consequences of various possible doctrines of operation, and thus to pick one having expected behavior satisfying managerial requirements. In some cases the possible choice of doctrines is not large and we can set up the corresponding Markov matrices (as in Eqs. 6.10, 6.11, and 6.12, for example) with adjustable parameters if necessary, solve, and make the comparison. If there are a large number of alternative doctrines this becomes a tedious process, and it would be desirable to have some regular system of arriving at the appropriate doctrine. Whenever the criterion for appropriateness can be expressed in terms of a state function x or transition function X (see Eq. 6.25 or 6.26) such that an increase in $E(x)$ or $E(X)$ is always desirable (i.e., so that the doctrine for which E is maximum is the "most appropriate" doctrine) then we can use the technique of sequential optimization known as dynamic programming.

We call the state function x_j, which is to measure the appropriateness of the system's behavior, the *return* from the state j. We want to adjust our doctrine (i.e., the elements of the Markov matrix) so that, if the system starts from state i and runs for N periods, the sum of the expected returns attained during the sequence of periods will be as large as possible. In many cases the different rows of the Markov matrix can be considered separately; we can ask, if the system is in state i, what orders should be issued so that the mean return, over the long run, is as large as possible. This does not necessarily mean that the transition should be made from state i directly to the state of highest return, for if that is done the subsequent states may not be high-return ones; we may thus sacrifice long-term gains for immediate gains. The transitions should be chosen so that the mean return over the whole N periods is maximal. In many cases we wish to extend N to infinity, to find the maximal doctrine for the steady state.

Starting from state i, the possible changes of state are governed by the components M_{ij} of the Markov matrix and these components are specified by the particular doctrine we decide to use. The components corresponding to the kth doctrine can be written $M_{ij}^{(k)}$. We then define the *value* V of state i, for doctrine k, for a run of N periods, by the equation

$$V_i^{(k)}(N) = x_i + \sum_j M_{ij}^{(k)} V_j^{(k)}(N-1) \tag{6.53}$$

This value is equal to the return from state i plus the values of the next states for runs of $N-1$ periods, weighted by the probabilities of transition. If the return is not a state function x_i but a transition function X_{ij}, then x_i in Eq. 6.53 is replaced by $\sum_j M_{ij}^{(k)} X_{ij} = q_i^{(k)}$.

We would expect this value $V_i^{(k)}(N)$ to equal N times some mean gain per period, plus a transient effect $v_i^{(k)}$, resulting from starting the system in state i,

$$V_i^{(k)}(N) = Ng^{(k)} + v_i^{(k)}, \quad \text{so that}$$

$$\begin{aligned} Ng^{(k)} + v_i^{(k)} &= x_i + \sum_j M_{ij}^{(k)}[(N-1)g^{(k)} + v_j^{(k)}] \\ &= x_i + (N-1)g^{(k)} + \sum_j M_{ij}^{(k)} v_j^{(k)}, \quad \text{or} \end{aligned}$$

$$g^{(k)} + v_i^{(k)} = x_i + \sum_j M_{ij}^{(k)} v_j^{(k)} \tag{6.54}$$

To show that g is indeed the steady-state expected return, we multiply Eq. 6.54 by the steady-state probability distribution $P_i^{(k)}$ (see Eq. 6.19) and sum over i. Because $\sum_i P_i = 1$ and $\sum_i P_i M_{ij} = P_j$ we have

$$\begin{aligned} g^{(k)} + \sum_i v_i^{(k)} P_i^{(k)} &= E(x) + \sum_i v_i^{(k)} P_i^{(k)}, \quad \text{or} \\ g^{(k)} = E(x) &= \sum_i x_i P_i^{(k)} \end{aligned} \tag{6.55}$$

This, of course, is one way to compute $g^{(k)}$, if we care to work out the P's for each possible doctrine. But we are at present developing a method of determining optimal doctrine *without* having to compute all the P's for all possible doctrines.

What we do is to compute the v's and g for some one trial doctrine, a much easier task. Since only the sum of g and v has significance we can add an arbitrary constant to all the v's and subtract it from g. In other words we can choose the value of one v arbitrarily (v_1, say) and then compute g and the other v's in terms of it. Having now computed the state values for a given choice of doctrine (doctrine k, for instance) we proceed stepwise to find whether some other doctrine (doctrine l, for example) is better. We do this by first computing the elements of the Markov matrix $M_{ij}^{(l)}$ for the new doctrine and then comparing the quantities

$$C_i = x_i + \sum_j M_{ij}^{(l)} v_j^{(k)} \quad \text{with the quantity} \quad g^{(k)} + v_i^{(k)} \tag{6.56}$$

which has already been computed. If the new quantity C_i is larger, then doctrine l is better than doctrine k. Note that the new quantity C_i uses the values $v_j^{(k)}$, previously computed for the kth doctrine. Note also that the comparison can be made row by row of the matrix, rather than having to compute the P's for the matrix as a whole and then compare the g's as computed from Eq. 6.55.

Going through, row by row, we can thus choose a new matrix with elements $M_{ij}^{(l)}$, such that for every row C_i is greater than (or no less than) $g^{(k)}+v_i^{(k)}$. We then use Eqs. 6.54 to compute a new set of mean and transient values, $g^{(l)}$ and $v_i^{(l)}$. To check whether the resulting doctrine is indeed the best, or whether the adjustment of one row requires a slight readjustment of other rows, we go through the comparison represented by Eqs. 6.56, using the new v's, to see whether there is another doctrine which is still better. In practice only a few such readjustments are needed before no C_i can be found larger than the final value of $g+v_i$, and we have found the optimal doctrine. For a more detailed discussion of this, with examples of its application, see MIT, Chapter 7.

7. CONTINUOUS-TIME SYSTEMS

So far we have considered that time is a discrete variable, that changes of state could occur only at the ends of finite periods of time. For operational systems where decisions are made only at the ends of time periods this is an appropriate representation. But if data on the state of the system is kept continually and if decisions are made *whenever* the system reaches predetermined states, it is more appropriate to consider time to be a continuous variable and recast our dynamical equations correspondingly. Since Eq. 6.3 can be written

$$\mathbf{P}(n+1)-\mathbf{P}(n)=\mathbf{P}(n)\cdot\mathfrak{A}; \quad A_{ij}=M_{ij}-\delta_{ij} \tag{6.57}$$

its limiting form is

$$\frac{d}{dt}\mathbf{P}(t)=\mathbf{P}(t)\cdot\mathfrak{A}; \quad \frac{d}{dt}P_j(t)=\sum_i P_i(t)A_{ij} \tag{6.58}$$

where A_{ij} is an element of the differential matrix (see Eq. 2.13), subject to the limitations

$$A_{ij}\geq 0 \quad (j\neq i); \quad \sum_j A_{ij}=0 \tag{6.59}$$

The operational systems, which these equations can be used to represent, are of course subject to the same limitations which we mentioned for discrete-time systems: the posture of the system can be described in terms of a denumerable set of states; transitions between the states can be expressed by transition probabilities which depend only on the initial and final states and are independent of time. For the continuous-time systems these are *rates of transition* and are the off-diagonal elements of the differential matrix $\mathfrak{A}$ which determines the rate of change of the probability vector $\mathbf{P}(t)$ for the system. By limiting the discussion to transition rates independent of time we are limiting ourselves to transitions which are distributed in time according to the Poisson distribution, but by suitable subdivision of states we can usually simulate sequences of events with other time distributions (see Morse, 1958, for example).

A few simple examples will illustrate the sorts of systems which can thus be represented. If, for example, equipment is repaired whenever it breaks down instead of at the beginning of a time period, as was assumed in Eqs. 6.8 to 6.12, then Eqs. 6.58 can be used. Suppose two similar machines each have exponential breakdown characteristics, such that the probability of one running a time t without breaking down is e^{-bt}, where the *breakdown rate* b is independent of time. (This is the same as saying that if the machine is running at time t, its chance of breaking down before $t+dt$ is $b\,dt$, where b is constant.) Suppose further that the repair operation for each machine, after it breaks down, also has exponential statistics, some repair jobs taking a short time and some a long time, such that the probability of the job taking longer than t is e^{-rt} where r is the *repair rate*, also independent of time. We can then characterize the states of the machines-repair system by the number n of machines in running order.

We assume first that there is but one repair crew. If both machines are down (state 0) one must wait while the other is being repaired; the rate of transition A_{01} from the state 0 to the state 1, where one machine is running, is therefore r. There is no transition from state 0 to state 2. When one machine is running (state 1) the other machine is being worked on and the transition rate A_{12} is also r; since the running machine may break down, the transition rate A_{10} is b. When both machines are running (state 2) either of them can break down, so that the rate A_{21} is $2b$, one b for each machine. Since the chance of both machines breaking down simultaneously is negligibly small, A_{20} is zero. Consequently the differential matrix embodying the external and internal forces, to use in Eq. 6.58 is

$$\mathfrak{A}=\begin{pmatrix} -r & r & 0 \\ b & -r-b & r \\ 0 & 2b & -2b \end{pmatrix} \tag{6.60}$$

The diagonal terms are negative, to satisfy Eq. 6.59; for example, the ways of leaving state 1 are either by breakdown (rate $-b$) or by repair of the down machine (rate $-r$), the minus sign indicating a reduction of the probability of being in state 1.

Having only one repair crew on hand makes for delay if two machines are down. If continued productivity is valuable enough it might pay to have two repair crews, even though they are often idle. In this case the repair rate A_{01} would be $2r$ rather than r, A_{02} would still be zero, since the chance of completion of repair of both machines in the same interval dt is proportional to $(dt)^2$, which is negligible compared to the $r\,dt$ or $b\,dt$ terms. In this case the matrix is

$$\mathfrak{A} = \begin{pmatrix} -2r & 2r & 0 \\ r & -r-b & b \\ 0 & 2b & -2b \end{pmatrix} \tag{6.61}$$

Another example is that of a truck (or a freight car or barge) which transports material between points A and B. Here the states could be designated as follows:

State 1. Traveling from A to B, plus unloading at B.
State 2. Traveling from B to A, plus unloading at A.
State 3. Waiting at A for next load, plus loading at A.
State 4. Waiting at B for next load, plus loading at B.

If each of these processes has exponential statistics (for example if the chance that the truck took longer than t to go from A to B plus unloading at B is e^{-ut}, the chance that it had to wait longer than t to get a load on board at A is e^{-vt} and similarly for the other two states) then the transition matrix is

$$\mathfrak{A} = \begin{pmatrix} -u & 0 & 0 & u \\ 0 & -u & u & 0 \\ v & 0 & -v & 0 \\ 0 & v & 0 & -v \end{pmatrix} \tag{6.62}$$

where $1/u$ can be called the mean transshipment time and $1/v$ the mean waiting time. This matrix assumes that both stations are statistically equivalent; if A differed from B the v's in the third row would differ from those in the fourth row and the u's in the first two rows might also differ.

Incidentally, this example shows the range of applicability of the models. The same matrix can be used to describe the operation of a machine which can do two different tasks. If state 1 corresponds to the machine doing job A (such as working at a mine face A, if the machine is a mining machine), state 2 the machine doing job B, state 3 the machine changing over from job B to job A, and state 4 the change-over from A to B then the same matrix would apply (if the job durations and change-over times were exponentially distributed).

Time intervals between transitions with distributions other than exponential can be simulated by increasing the number of states. For example, a breakdown characteristic such that the probability that the time between completion of repair and next breakdown is longer than t is $e^{-2bt} + 2bte^{-2bt}$ (which has the same average breakdown time as the distribution e^{-bt} but has half the variance) can be simulated by assuming that the machine goes through two exponential phases, each of mean rate $2b$, and does not break down until the end of the second phase. If the variance of the repair time is also about half the value r^2 it has for an exponential distribution, so that a similar two-phase simulation can be used for the repair job, the system can be described as

$$\left.\begin{array}{ll} \text{State 1.} & \text{Operative phase 1.} \\ \text{State 2.} & \text{Operative phase 2.} \\ \text{State 3.} & \text{Repair, phase 1.} \\ \text{State 4.} & \text{Repair, phase 2.} \end{array}\right\}; \qquad \mathfrak{A} = \begin{pmatrix} -2b & 2b & 0 & 0 \\ 0 & -2b & 2b & 0 \\ 0 & 0 & -2r & 2r \\ 2r & 0 & 0 & -2r \end{pmatrix} \tag{6.63}$$

If, on the other hand, the breakdown characteristic has greater variance than b^2 and may be given by the probability $\alpha e^{-2\alpha bt} + (1-\alpha)e^{-2(1-\alpha)bt}$ (where $0 \leq 2\alpha \leq 1$) the machine, when productive, may be thought of as either in state 1, having a long life $1/2\alpha b$, or else in state 2, having a short life $1/2(1-\alpha)b$, entering state 1, α of the time and state 2, $1-\alpha$ of the time (so that the mean life of the machine between breakdowns is $1/b$ as usual). Combining this with a small-variance repair operation, as in Eq. 6.63, we have a system description

State 1. Productive, long life.
State 2. Productive, short life.
State 3. Repair, phase 1.
State 4. Repair, phase 2.

$$\mathfrak{A} = \begin{pmatrix} -2\alpha b & 0 & 2\alpha b & 0 \\ 0 & -2(1-\alpha)b & 2(1-\alpha)b & 0 \\ 0 & 0 & -2r & 2r \\ 2\alpha r & 2(1-\alpha)r & 0 & -2r \end{pmatrix} \tag{6.64}$$

Many other combinations can be worked out so that, by the proliferation of states, each with exponential characteristic, we can simulate nearly any interval-length characteristic found in practice.

8. QUEUING OPERATIONS

A large class of operational situations, which can be described by Eqs. 6.58 are called *queuing operations*. They all are concerned with the flow of people or equipment or messages flowing through a "bottle-neck," where the arriving units sometimes pile up, waiting to get "serviced" before they can continue on their way. Airplanes arrive at an airport and sometimes have to wait in a "stack" over the field until the runway is clear to land. A telephone subscriber wishes to put in a call and may have to wait until a circuit is free. An incoming message may have to wait for transmittal; a record of a transaction may be delayed in processing or posting. A machine may break down and have to wait for a repair crew (the system of Eq. 6.60 is of this type). A customer arrives at a store, wishing to purchase some item, thus producing a blank space on the inventory shelves (or creating a backorder) which remains until the replenishment shipment arrives.

In all of these cases (and many more) *units* arrive desiring to be *serviced*, wait in a *queue* if the *service channel* is busy, eventually enter the service channel, are serviced, and then leave the system. Systems differ in the mean *rate* λ of *arrival*, the mean *rate* μ of *service*, the doctrine regarding how the units wait in queue (which of them wait and which enter service next), how many service channels there are, and how these channels are arranged with respect to each other (whether in parallel or series).

Consideration of the simplest sort of queuing system will indicate the connection between the parts of the system and the equation of motion 6.58. Suppose the arriving units are distributed at random in time (Poisson distribution) with a mean rate of arrival λ; so that the probability of another arrival occurring in an element of time dt (chosen at random) is $\lambda\, dt$ and the probability of two arrivals occurring in the same dt is proportional to dt^2. Suppose that there is a single service channel which can service only one unit at a time and that if a unit is in service the chance of the service being completed in time dt is $\mu\, dt$, where μ is the mean rate of service if the channel is never idle. We also assume that, if the service channel is busy servicing a unit, no other unit can enter but that as soon as the channel has discharged one unit it takes on the first unit in queue, if any units are waiting; otherwise the channel is idle until a unit arrives, when it goes immediately into service.

If the arriving unit does not find the service channel idle it always waits in queue and "first come first served" order is maintained. It is possible to work out the properties of systems with each of these restrictions relaxed or modified (see, for example, Morse, 1958) but our exposition will be more understandable with the simplest case.

The states of the system can be distinguished in terms of the total number n of units present, those in queue, if present, plus the one in service, if service is busy. The probability $p_n(t+dt)$ that n units are present at time $t+dt$ is equal to the sum of products of the probabilities $p_m(t)$ times the probabilities of transition from state m to state n in time dt. The probability of one unit arriving ($m=n-1$ goes to n) is $\lambda\,dt$; the probability of more than one arriving in dt is of higher order in dt and may be neglected. The probability of the servicing channel discharging one unit ($m=n+1$ goes to n) in time dt is $\mu\,dt$ unless $m=0$, when it is zero (no unit in service); probabilities of discharging more than one unit in time dt are negligible. The probability that the state is unchanged during dt ($m=n$) is $1-\lambda\,dt-\mu\,dt$ unless $m=0$, when the $\mu\,dt$ term is absent. Hence

$$p_n(t+dt)=p_n(t)+\frac{d}{dt}p_n(t)\,dt=\begin{cases}(1-\lambda\,dt)p_n+\mu\,dt\,p_{m+1} & (n=0)\\ [1-(\lambda+\mu)\,dt]p_n+(\mu p_{n+1}+\lambda p_{n-1})\,dt & \\ \quad (n>0)\end{cases}$$

or

$$\frac{d}{dt}p_n(t)=\begin{cases}\mu p_{n+1}(t)-\lambda p_n(t) & (n=0)\\ \mu p_{n+1}(t)+\lambda p_{n-1}(t)-(\lambda+\mu)p_n(t) & (n>0)\end{cases} \tag{6.65}$$

This has the form of Eq. 6.59 with

$$\mathfrak{A}=\begin{pmatrix}-\lambda & \lambda & 0 & 0 & \cdots\\ \mu & -\lambda-\mu & \lambda & 0 & \cdots\\ 0 & \mu & -\lambda-\mu & \lambda & \cdots\\ \cdot & \cdot & \cdot & \cdot & \cdot\\ \cdot & \cdot & \cdot & \cdot & \cdot\\ \cdot & \cdot & \cdot & \cdot & \cdot\end{pmatrix}$$

The steady-state distribution of probabilities $p_n(t)\underset{t\to\infty}{\longrightarrow}P_n$ can easily be found by setting the time derivatives equal to zero and solving the resulting simultaneous equations for the P's, adjusting their amplitudes so their sum equals unity,

$$P_n=(1-\rho)\rho^n,\quad \rho=(\lambda/\mu) \tag{6.66}$$

As long as the service rate μ is larger than the arrival rate λ $(\rho<1)$, the probabilities P_n diminish to zero as n increases. If ρ is quite small (i.e., if the service channel is more than adequate to accommodate the arrivals) the chance of there being a queue $(n>1)$ is quite small and few arriving units have to wait for service. If ρ is near unity (if the service channel can just barely keep ahead of the average rate of arrivals) the P_n's diminish slowly with n and there is a good chance of there being a long queue of waiting units. The mean number L of units in the system and the mean number in queue L_q are

$$L=\sum_{n=1}^{\infty} nP_n=\rho/(1-\rho); \quad L_q=\sum_{n=2}^{\infty}(n-1)P_n=\rho^2/(1-\rho)=\rho L \qquad (6.67)$$

The actual numbers present at any time may depart considerably from these mean values, for their variances are

$$\Delta^2(L)=\frac{\rho}{(1-\rho)^2}; \quad \Delta^2(L_q)=\frac{\rho^2+\rho^3-\rho^4}{(1-\rho)^2} \qquad (6.68)$$

which are larger than L^2 and $L_q^{\,2}$ respectively as long as $\rho<1$. The fraction of time the service channel is busy is $1-P_0=\rho$, so that $\rho=(\lambda/\mu)$ is called the *utilization factor*.

These formulas are valid as long as $\rho<1$ $(\lambda<\mu)$; when $\rho\geq 1$ the service channel cannot keep up with the arrivals, the solution diverges and no steady-state behavior is possible; the queue increases without limit.

A general characteristic of queuing systems is already apparent: that full utilization of the service facility is incompatible with speedy service for the units. In the simple system here considered (single-channel, Poisson arrivals and service, all units go through service, first come first served) as ρ is increased from $\frac{1}{2}$ to $\frac{3}{4}$ the mean number waiting in queue increases from $\frac{1}{4}$ to $2\frac{1}{4}$ and as ρ increases still nearer unity (as the mean fraction of time the service channel is idle is reduced from $\frac{1}{4}$ to zero) L_q goes rapidly to infinity. For this system, if the service facility is busy more than three quarters of the time, most of the arriving units will have to wait in queue more than twice the mean service time $(1/\mu)$ before service is started for them. If it is costly to keep these units waiting, ρ should never be this close to unity.

We can compute the probability $G(t)$ that a unit will have to remain in the system, queue or service channel, for longer than time t. If the unit arrives when the channel is idle, it goes immediately into service and the probability that it takes longer than t to be serviced is $e^{-\mu t}$ as mentioned earlier. If, however, there are m units ahead of it when it arrives then the probability that it will not yet be discharged from service by the end of time t is the probability that none, or one, or two, or any number up to and including m units are serviced, but not $m+1$ or $m+2$, etc. Since the spacing of service completions in time is Poisson when the channel is busy, this probability is

$$e^{-\mu t}+(\mu t)e^{-\mu t}+\tfrac{1}{2}(\mu t)^2e^{-\mu t}+\cdots(1/m!)(\mu t)^m e^{-\mu t}$$

Multiplying this conditional probability by the probability $(1-\rho)\rho^m$ that the arriving unit will find m units ahead of it when it joins the system and then summing over m, we obtain

$$G(t)=\sum_{m=0}^{\infty}(1-\rho)\rho^m\sum_{n=0}^{m}\frac{(\mu t)^n}{n!}e^{-\mu t}=e^{(\lambda-\mu)t} \tag{6.69}$$

for the probability that a unit will remain in the system longer than time t. A similar calculation obtains the result

$$G_q(t)=\rho e^{(\lambda-\mu)t} \quad (t>0,\mu>\lambda) \tag{6.70}$$

for the probability that an arriving unit will wait longer than t in the queue, before it enters service (there is a finite chance, $1-\rho$, that the unit will not have to wait in queue at all, consequently $G_q\to\rho$ as $t\to 0$). We note that as λ increases in value until it approaches μ these exponentials fall off more and more slowly with time.

The mean time spent in the system, W, and the mean wait in queue, W_q, are obtained by integrating the G's

$$W=\int_0^\infty G(t)\,dt=1/(\lambda-\mu)=L/\lambda;\quad W_q=\int_0^\infty G_q(t)\,dt=L_q/\lambda \tag{6.71}$$

These mean waits increase without limit as $\lambda\to\mu$, and the variance of the waits increases even faster. This characteristic, that waits increase indefinitely as the utilization of the service channels increases toward unity, is true of all queuing systems having any variability in arrivals or service.

9. MULTIPLE CHANNELS, ARRIVAL AND SERVICE DISTRIBUTIONS

One way to reduce the mean wait of a unit in the system is to increase the speed of the single service channel; another way would be to increase the number of service channels. Sometimes this is impossible; there is no room to add additional channels. But sometimes it is impossible to increase the speed of the single channel, so room has to be made for additional channels if the capacity of the service facility is to be increased. In other cases there is a choice as to how the capacity is to be increased. So it is useful to see whether multiplying the number of channels produces other results which differ from those produced by correspondingly multiplying the capacity of a single channel.

Let us examine the behavior of a system with M channels, each of the Poisson or exponential type discussed earlier, each of mean service rate μ (total service rate thus $M\mu$), each drawing from the queue as soon as previous service is completed (if there is a queue), an arriving unit going to the end of the queue if all channels are busy but choosing at random from the idle channels if there are some. The state of this system also can be specified by the total number n of units in the system: if $n \le M$ all units are in service channels; if $n > M$ all service channels are busy and there are $n-M$ units in queue. In considering the rate of change of a state $n<M$ there is a rate of arrival (change from state $n-1$ to state n) of λ as before, but a rate of change from state $n+1$ to n (because one of the $n+1$ busy channels has completed service) of $(n+1)\mu$, since any one of the $n+1$ busy channels could have completed service. As before, the chance of two arrivals or of two service completions in the same interval dt is negligible. If $n \ge M$ the rate of change from n to $n+1$ because of a unit arrival is λ, the rate of change because one of the M busy channels has finished service is $M\mu$. The equations of motion, analogous to Eqs. 6.65, are thus

$$\frac{d}{dt}p_n(t) = \begin{cases} (n+1)\mu p_{n+1} - \lambda p_n(t) & (n=0) \\ (n+1)\mu p_{n+1} + \lambda p_{n-1} - (\lambda + n\mu)p_n & (0<n<M) \\ M\mu p_{n+1} + \lambda p_{n-1} - (\lambda + M\mu)p_n & (M \le n) \end{cases} \quad (6.72)$$

The steady-state solution of this set of equations is $p_n(t) \underset{t\to\infty}{\longrightarrow} P_n$, where

$$P_n = \begin{cases} P_0(M\rho)^n/n! & (0 \le n \le M) \\ P_0\rho^n M^M/M! & (M \le n) \end{cases};$$

$$P_0 = \frac{(1-\rho)e^{-\rho M}}{D_{M-1}(\rho M)} \to \begin{cases} 1-\rho M & (\rho M \ll 1) \\ (1-\rho)M!/M^M & (\rho \to 1) \end{cases} \quad (6.73)$$

where $\rho M = \lambda/\mu$ is the mean number of busy channels and thus $\rho = \lambda/M\mu$ is again the utilization factor, the fraction of the time a channel is busy, on the average. The mean number in the queue, its variance, and the mean number in the system are

$$L_q=\sum_{m=1}^{\infty} mP_{M+m}=[\rho e_M(\rho M)/(1-\rho)D_{M-1}(\rho M)]\rightarrow\begin{cases}\rho(\rho M)^M/M & (\rho M\ll 1)\\ 1/(1-\rho) & (\rho\rightarrow 1)\end{cases}$$

$$\Delta^2(L_q)=\{\rho e_M(\rho M)[E_M(\rho M)-\rho^2E_{M-1}(\rho M)]/(1-\rho)^2D_{M-1}(\rho M)\} \quad (6.74)$$

$$L=L_q+\rho M;\quad W=L/\lambda;\quad W_q=L_q/\lambda$$

where the functions e, E, and D used in Eqs. 6.73 and 6.74 are

$$e_n(x)=(x^n/n!)e^{-x};\quad E_n(x)=\sum_{m=0}^{n} e_m(x)$$

$$D_n(x)=\sum_{m=0}^{n} E_m(x)/(n+1)=\sum_{m=0}^{n}(n+1-m)[e_n(x)/(n+1)] \quad (6.75)$$

(see also Eq. 6.31). The mean wait in queue W_q and the mean time spent in the system W are related to the corresponding L's by the factor λ as with the single-channel system.

We see that these mean numbers and mean waits also go to infinity as ρ approaches unity, so we cannot avoid the need for excess capacity, to keep down waiting time, by using multiple channels. However, it may be that we do not need as much excess capacity, that ρ can be brought closer to unity before W and W_q become unallowably large. Detailed numerical comparison between the behavior of a single-channel system with mean service rate λ/ρ and the behavior of a system of M channels each with rate $\lambda/M\rho$, for the same ρ, shows that for $\rho<\frac{1}{2}$ the variance $\Delta^2(L_q)$ for the multichannel system is considerably smaller than that for the single-channel system, but as $\rho\rightarrow 1$ the difference in variances is relatively negligible. The results do show, however (see Morse, 1958, Chapter 8), that the multichannel system involves *shorter* mean waits *in queue* but *longer* mean *total time* in the system than does the single-channel system with equal utilization factor. The multiple channels siphon off the arriving units into the many channels, so the queue is shorter, but the individual channels are $(1/M)$th as fast in completing service, so the total time is longer. The choice of single or multiple channels will thus depend on the details of the requirements placed on the system and on the relative costs; in some cases the multichannel system will be appropriate, in others the single, fast channel is better.

Some of the characteristics of queuing systems depend on the statistical distribution of interarrival and service times, as an examination of a very simple system will demonstrate. We assume a single service channel but, instead of allowing the queue to be of indefinite length, we consider the opposite limit where the arriving unit enters the system only if the service channel is idle; if the channel is busy the unit goes elsewhere. This case will be said to have a zero-length queue; it is a case not infrequently encountered in practice. We will now proceed to work out the behavior of this system and its dependence on the statistical nature of the arrival and service times.

We describe the service and arrival statistics by a service-time distribution $S(t)$, the probability that a unit will take longer than t to be serviced, and an interarrival distribution $A(t)$, the probability that the time between successive arrivals is greater than t. The mean service and arrival rates μ and λ are related to these by the equations

$$(1/\mu)=\int_0^\infty S(t)\,dt;\quad (1/\lambda)=\int_0^\infty A(t)\,dt \tag{6.76}$$

For Poisson arrivals $A(t)=e^{-\lambda t}$ and for exponential service $S(t)=e^{-\mu t}$, as has been mentioned before. The variance of these arrival and service times are $(1/\lambda^2)$ and $(1/\mu^2)$ respectively. A distribution which has less variance than this is the kth *Erlang distribution*

$$A(t)=E_{k-1}(k\lambda t)=\sum_{n=0}^{k-1}[(k\lambda t)^n/n!]e^{-k\lambda t} \tag{6.77}$$

and similarly for S, with μ instead of λ. The case $k=1$ is the exponential distribution. The sum has been arranged so that the mean rate, as computed from Eq. 6.76, is λ (or μ) for any k. The variance for the kth distribution, however, is $(1/\lambda^2 k)$, so that as k is increased the variance in interarrival (or service) times decreases, the distribution becoming more "steplike" until, for $k\to\infty$, the function equals unity for $t<(1/\lambda)$ and is zero for $t>(1/\lambda)$, which corresponds to regular arrivals, all spaced $(1/\lambda)$ apart. Thus the family of Erlang distributions can be used to represent arrivals (or services) more regularly spaced in time than is the Poisson distribution.

The reason we prefer to use the Erlang distributions to approximate actual arrival or service distributions, which are less variant than the Poisson case, is that these distributions can be simulated by a series of k exponential phases, each of rate $k\lambda$, so that, by subdivision of states, we can continue to use the equations of motion (6.58) for the system. For example (see discussion of Eq. 6.63) a zero-queue, single-channel system, with Poisson arrivals and one kth Erlang service channel can be represented as follows (see Morse, 1958, for more detailed discussion):

State 0. No unit, service idle.
State 1. Unit in 1st phase of service.
. . . .
State k. Unit in kth phase of service, just prior to ejection from service.

$$\mathfrak{A}=\begin{bmatrix} -\lambda & \lambda & 0 & 0 & \cdots & 0 & 0 \\ 0 & -k\mu & k\mu & 0 & \cdots & 0 & 0 \\ 0 & 0 & -k\mu & k\mu & \cdots & 0 & 0 \\ \cdot & \cdot & \cdot & \cdot & \cdots & \cdot & \cdot \\ \cdot & \cdot & \cdot & \cdot & \cdots & \cdot & \cdot \\ \cdot & \cdot & \cdot & \cdot & \cdots & \cdot & \cdot \\ 0 & 0 & 0 & 0 & \cdots & -k\mu & k\mu \\ k\mu & 0 & 0 & 0 & \cdots & 0 & -k\mu \end{bmatrix} \tag{6.78}$$

The steady-state solution is

$$P_0=\frac{1}{1+\rho}; \quad P_1=P_2=\cdots=P_k=\frac{\rho}{k(1+\rho)} \tag{6.79}$$

where ρ, as usual, is λ/μ. The fraction of the time, P_{idle}, the service channel is idle is in this case equal to the fraction of time P_{served} an arriving unit finds the channel idle and stays to be serviced,

$$P_{\text{idle}}=P_{\text{served}}=P_0=\frac{1}{1+\rho} \tag{6.80}$$

Of course the probability $P_{\text{busy}}=1-P_{\text{idle}}$ that the channel is busy also is equal, in this case, to $P_{\text{lost}}=1-P_{\text{served}}$, the fraction of arrivals which find the system busy and are thus lost to the system. We note that for this zero-queue system a steady state is possible for any value of ρ, not just for values less than 1.

To simulate an lth Erlang arrival distribution we can imagine that the next unit to arrive is going through an "arrival-timing channel" of l phases, each exponential, of rate $l\lambda$, such that when the unit is ejected from the lth phase it "arrives" at the system, to go into service or else leave, and another unit immediately starts through the arrival-timing channel. A zero-queue, single-channel system, with lth Erlang arrivals and exponential service would therefore be represented as,

State 1,0. 1st arrival phase, service idle.
State 2,0. 2nd arrival phase, service idle.

. . . .

State l,0. lth arrival phase, just prior to arrival, service idle.
State 1,1. 1st arrival phase, service busy.

. . . .

State l,1. lth arrival phase, just prior to arrival, service busy.

$$\mathfrak{A}=\begin{bmatrix} -l\lambda & l\lambda & \cdots & 0 & 0 & 0 & 0 & \cdots & 0 & 0 \\ 0 & -l\lambda & \cdots & 0 & 0 & 0 & 0 & \cdots & 0 & 0 \\ \cdot & \cdot & \cdot & \cdot & \cdot & \cdot & \cdot & \cdot & \cdot & \cdot \\ 0 & 0 & \cdots & -l\lambda & \lambda & 0 & 0 & \cdots & 0 & 0 \\ 0 & 0 & \cdots & 0 & -l\lambda & l\lambda & 0 & \cdots & 0 & 0 \\ \mu & 0 & \cdots & 0 & 0 & -\mu-l\lambda & l\lambda & \cdots & 0 & 0 \\ 0 & \mu & \cdots & 0 & 0 & 0 & -\mu-l\lambda & \cdots & 0 & 0 \\ \cdot & \cdot & \cdot & \cdot & \cdot & \cdot & \cdot & \cdot & \cdot & \cdot \\ 0 & 0 & \cdots & \mu & 0 & 0 & 0 & \cdots & -\mu-l\lambda & l\lambda \\ 0 & 0 & \cdots & 0 & \mu & l\lambda & 0 & \cdots & 0 & -\mu-l\lambda \end{bmatrix} \tag{6.81}$$

State s'0 can go only to state $s+1$,0, but state s,1 can go either to state $s+1$,1 (advance one phase in arrival-timing channel) or else to state s,0 (unit in service is discharged). The steady-state solution is

$$P_{m,0}=\frac{1}{l}\left[1-\left(1+\frac{\mu}{l\lambda}\right)^{-m}\right];\quad P_{m,1}=\frac{1}{l}\left(1+\frac{\mu}{l\lambda}\right)^{-m} \tag{6.82}$$

In this case the probability P_{idle} that the service channel is unoccupied is $\Sigma P_{m,0}$ but, since only expulsion from the lth phase of the arrival-timing channel corresponds to actual arrival at the service channel, the chance P_{served} of an *arriving unit* finding the channel idle and thus being served is $P_{l,0}/(P_{l,1}+P_{l,0})$,

$$\begin{aligned} P_{\text{idle}}&=1-\rho\left[1-\left(1+\frac{1}{l\rho}\right)^{-l}\right]\underset{l\to\infty}{\longrightarrow}1-\rho(1-e^{-1/\rho}) \\ P_{\text{served}}&=1-\left(1+\frac{1}{l\rho}\right)^{-l}\underset{l\to 8}{\longrightarrow}1-e^{-1/\rho} \end{aligned} \tag{6.83}$$

which are not equal except when $l=1$ (Poisson arrivals). P_{idle} is the probability that an observer, coming at a randomly chosen instant, would find the channel idle; the next arrival *does not occur* at a randomly chosen instant (for arrivals are not Poisson) but at an instant related to the service being carried out on the last arrival. Consequently the probability P_{served} of an *arriving unit* finding the channel idle is somewhat larger than P_{idle}, the difference being larger the greater the value of l (i.e., the more regular are the arrivals); as a function of ρ the difference is greater for $\rho=1$ than it is for ρ larger or smaller than 1.

Simulation of a distribution with greater than Poisson variance can be achieved by two or more exponential, alternative processes (see Eq. 6.64). For example the *hyperexponential* distribution

$$S(t)=\alpha e^{-2\alpha\mu t}+(1-\alpha)e^{-2(1-\alpha)\mu t} \quad (0<2\alpha<1) \tag{6.84}$$

which has a mean service time $1/\mu$ but a variance $[(1-2\alpha+2\alpha^2)/\mu^2(2\alpha-2\alpha^2)]$, which is larger than $1/\mu^2$, can be simulated by two alternative exponential service operations, the long-service one with rate $2\alpha\mu<\mu$, which is carried out on α of the arriving units (chosen at random) and the short-service one with rate $2(1-\alpha)\mu>\mu$, which is carried on the other $1-\alpha$ arrivals, which enter service. For Poisson arrivals, one-channel hyperexponential service we have

State 0. No unit, service idle.
State 1. Unit undergoing short service.
State 2. Unit undergoing long service.

$$\mathfrak{A}=\begin{pmatrix} -\lambda & \lambda\alpha & \lambda(1-\alpha) \\ 2\alpha\mu & -2\alpha\mu & 0 \\ 2(1-\alpha)\mu & 0 & -2(1-\alpha)\mu \end{pmatrix} \tag{6.85}$$

with steady-state solution

$$\begin{gathered} P_0=1/(1+\rho); \quad P_1=P_2=\rho/2(1+\rho); \quad \rho=\lambda/\mu \\ P_{\text{idle}}=P_{\text{served}}=P_0=1/(1+\rho) \end{gathered} \tag{6.86}$$

The expressions for P_{idle} and P_{served} are the same as in Eq. 6.76; indeed they are the same for *any* service distribution with mean rate μ, provided arrivals are Poisson with mean rate λ. For Poisson arrivals, whenever the service unit becomes empty, it will take a time $(1/\lambda)$, on the average, until the next unit arrives, after which it will take a time $(1/\mu)$, on the average (no matter what the service distribution is) to complete the service and start the next cycle. For non-Poisson arrivals it is not true that, whenever the service channel becomes empty, the expected time till next arrival is $(1/\lambda)$, so the simple relationship fails and differences between P_{idle} and P_{served} can be expected.

For hyperexponential arrivals, exponential, single-channel service, no queue, the parallel exponential processes are hypothetical "arrival timers," which release the next unit so it can arrive. The system can be represented as

State 1,0. Next unit in slow arrival timer, no unit in service.
State 2,0. Next unit in fast arrival timer, no unit in service.
State 1,1. Next unit in slow arrival timer, unit in service.
State 2,1. Next unit in fast arrival timer, unit in service.

$$\mathfrak{A} = \begin{pmatrix} -2\alpha\lambda & 0 & 2\alpha^2\lambda & 2\alpha(1-\alpha)\lambda \\ 0 & -2(1-\alpha)\lambda & 2\alpha(1-\alpha)\lambda & 2(1-\alpha)^2\lambda \\ \mu & 0 & 2\alpha^2\lambda-\mu-2\alpha\lambda & 2\alpha(1-\alpha)\lambda \\ 0 & \mu & 2\alpha(1-\alpha)\lambda & 2(1-\alpha)^2-\mu-2(1-\alpha)\lambda \end{pmatrix} \tag{6.87}$$

with steady-state solution

$$P_{11} = \frac{\alpha\rho}{1+2\alpha\rho} = 2\alpha\rho P_{10}; \quad P_{21} = \frac{(1-\alpha)\rho}{1+2(1-\alpha)\rho} = 2(1-\alpha)\rho P_{20}$$
$$P_{\text{idle}} = \frac{1+\rho}{Q}; \quad P_{\text{served}} = \frac{1+4\alpha(1-\alpha)\rho}{Q}; \quad Q = [1+2\alpha\rho][1+2(1-\alpha)\rho] \tag{6.88}$$

Comparison of Eqs. 6.83 and 6.88 shows that, for completely regular arrivals ($l \to \infty$) to an exponential service channel, the service facility is *less* often idle than it is for Poisson arrivals with the same mean arrival rate λ, and a *greater* fraction of the arriving units are served. This difference between P_{idle} and P_{served} diminishes as l is decreased (as interarrival variance is increased) until the two are equal for $l=1$ (Poisson arrivals). As we go to the hyperexponential arrivals, making arrival-time variance greater than Poisson, P_{idle} increases still further and P_{served} decreases still further. It can be shown in general that, without changing the ratio ρ between mean arrival and mean service rates, decreasing arrival variance will reduce idle time and increase the fraction of arrivals serviced, increasing arrival variance will increase idle time and diminish the fraction serviced. Increase in arrival variance means an increase in the chance that arrivals come in "bunches," with long waits between bunches. When a bunch arrives, the service channel can only serve the first of the bunch and the rest are turned away; by the time this unit is served the service facility has to wait till the next bunch comes along. Thus large arrival variance has a deleterious effect on the efficiency of the system, both in utilization of the service facility and on the fraction of arrivals which are serviced.

The subject of queuing problems is a large one. It is possible to calculate the effect of arrival and service distributions on more complex systems than the one described above; it is also possible to compute the effect of giving some units priority over others and of other arrangements of queues and of service channels. Lack of space precludes our even sketching the results here. They can be found in various books and journal articles (see, for example, Kendall, Brockmeyer, McCloskey, Appendix A, Vol. 2).

It should also be apparent that there are other ways of analyzing queuing systems than by the use of Eq. 6.59. For example, one can express the probability that a unit waits longer than a time t in terms of integrals of the probabilities of arrival of the next unit and probabilities of completion of the service, and thus obtain an integral equation for $G(t)$ for any specified arrival or service distribution. These and other special techniques, discussed in the literature (see Kendall and McCloskey) are useful in some applications, but appear not to have the range of computability which the analyses based on Eq. 6.59 turn out to have.

10. A CONTINUOUS-TIME INVENTORY SYSTEM

Instead, we turn to another, rather different, system, which gives rise to an equation of motion of the general Markov type. This is a continuous-time inventory system, in contast to the discrete-time systems of Eqs. 6.5 to 6.7. Suppose the manager of the inventory does not wait until the end of a period to make his decision about reordering; suppose he keeps continuous watch over the inventory level and sends in a replenishment order *whenever* the stock on hand reaches a certain level. If the probability that a given replenishment order is not yet received a time t after it was placed is $e^{-\mu t}$ and if the demands for the item are spaced at random in time, then the system has the structure of a queuing system, the equations can be set up in the form of Eqs. 6.58, and the steady-state solution can be found (see Galliher, 1959). But if the replenishment order is always received a time T after it is placed (constant replenishment time) then the formulation and the solution for the steady-state case is easier.

Suppose the doctrine is to place an order for Q items whenever the stock on hand diminishes to the level of R items. To put it another way, suppose we decide the maximum inventory is to be $M = R + Q$ items and that when the stock on hand is Q less than M we order Q. If less than Q items are demanded and withdrawn in the time T for the order to be delivered, then the stock just after receipt will be larger than $R = M - Q$ and we can order again when the stock level reaches R. But if more than Q items are withdrawn before the replenishment arrives, then, just after receipt, the level will still be less than R and we find that we should already have placed another order for Q items.

Consequently we make our operating doctrine that whenever the items on hand *plus* the items on order diminish to $M - Q$ we place another order for Q items. We allow backorders, so that net stock, when positive, equals stock on hand, when negative equals minus the number of backorders. The system is therefore described as follows:

Demands arrive at random (Poisson) with mean rate λ.
State of system i equals M minus net stock $(0 \leq i)$.
Q items are ordered whenever net stock plus items on order diminishes to $M - Q$. This order takes time T to be delivered. In the interval, the probability that n items are withdrawn or back-ordered is $U_n = (S^n/n!)e^{-S}$ where $S = \lambda T$ is the mean number withdrawn in replenishment time T. (6.89)

As before we let P_i be the steady-state probability that the net stock is $M - i$. Since replenishment orders are placed and delivered at randomly placed times we can determine the P's by requiring them to be the same at time t as they are at $t + T$, for every value of t. We choose the interval to be T because then we are sure that every replenishment order placed before time t will have been received before time $t + T$ and all orders placed after time t will not have been received by $t + T$. The probability P_j of having net stock $M - j$ at time $t + T$ is related to the probabilities P_i of having net stock $M - i$ at t via the conditional probabilities M_{ij} of transition from state i to state j in time T. If i is smaller than Q then there were no outstanding orders at time t. If n items are withdrawn or back-ordered between t and $t + T$ then the state of the system at $t + T$ is $i + n = j$; the probability of this occurring is U_{j-i}. If i is equal to or larger than kQ and smaller than $(k+1)Q$ (k an integer) then orders for kQ items are outstanding at time t and if n items are withdrawn or back-ordered between t and $t + T$ the net stock at $t + T$ is $M - i + kQ - n$, so that the state is $i - kQ + n = j$; the probability of this occurring is U_{j-i+kQ}.

Therefore the equations relating the state probabilities are

$$P_j=\begin{cases}\sum_{i=0}^{j} U_{j-i}\sum_{k=0}^{\infty} P_{i+kQ} & (j<Q)\\ \sum_{i=0}^{Q-1} U_{j-i}\sum_{k=0}^{\infty} P_{i+kQ} & (j\geq Q)\end{cases} \tag{6.90}$$

This set of equations is the same as those of Eq. 6.7 for the discrete-time inventory system with batch orders of size Q. We wrote down the solutions in Eq. 6.22 and will write them here again,

$$P_j=\begin{cases}(1/Q)\sum_{i=0}^{j} U_{j-i} & (j<Q)\\ (1/Q)\sum_{i=0}^{Q-1} U_{j-i} & (j\geq Q)\end{cases} \tag{6.91}$$

We also computed, for Poisson demands, the expected value of net stock and its variance (see Eqs. 6.34)

$$E(N)=M-S-\tfrac{1}{2}(Q-1);\quad \Delta^2(N)=S+\tfrac{1}{12}(Q-1)^2 \tag{6.92}$$

Since only the positive values of net stock N are equal to stock on hand, the negative values of N are equal to minus the number of backorders. Thus the expected value of stock on hand is equal to the expected value of net stock *plus* the expected number of backorders.

For the discrete-time system, these probabilities and mean values were valid only at the ends of each period; for the present continuous-time system they hold for any time, as long as the system is in steady-state motion. Therefore the fraction of time the system has stock on hand is

$$\sum_{j=0}^{M-1} P_j=(1/Q)[MD_{M-1}(S)-(M-Q)D_{M-Q-1}(S)] \quad (M>Q) \tag{6.93}$$

where the function D is defined in Eqs. 6.31 and 6.75. This fraction of time is very nearly unity when S is smaller than $M-Q-\sqrt{M-Q}$, diminishes approximately linearly toward zero as S goes from $M-Q$ to M, and for S larger than about $M+\sqrt{M}$ it is negligibly small. Consequently if we wish to be almost certain to have stock on hand we should have M somewhat larger than $Q+S+\sqrt{S}$. For this value of M the mean value of net stock is approximately $Q+\sqrt{S}$, roughly the standard deviation of N above zero. Of course this protection against being out of stock is attained at the price of having a fairly large amount of stock on hand most of the time, and if carrying stock is expensive the value of M should be reduced to where the "cost" of being out of stock roughly balances the cost of inventory. The formulas given above enable one to work out this solution and others, based on other possible management requirements.

11. CONTINUOUS-TIME SYSTEMS, TRANSIENT BEHAVIOR

To complete our discussion of simple, operational systems, subject to random external and internal forces, we should apply the methods of Section 5 to the continuous-time equations of motion (6.58),

$$\frac{d}{dt}p_j(t) = \sum_i p_i(t)A_{ij} \tag{6.94}$$

where A_{ij} are the elements of a differential matrix $\mathfrak{A}$ (see Eq. 6.59). We first compute the s eigenvalues of $\mathfrak{A}$ (the total number of states is s), the roots α_ν of the secular equation

$$|A_{ij} - \alpha\delta_{ij}| = 0 \tag{6.95}$$

where $\delta_{ij} = 0$ when $i \neq j$ and $= 1$ when $i = j$. At least one of these roots is zero, none of them have positive real parts (this follows from the results quoted earlier for the roots of stochastic matrices). Corresponding to the eigenvalue α_ν there are the forward and rearward eigenvectors $X(\nu)$ and $Y(\nu)$, satisfying the equations

$$\begin{gathered}\sum_i X_i(\nu)A_{ij} = \alpha_\nu X_j(\nu); \quad \sum_j A_{ij}Y_j(\nu) = \alpha_\nu Y_i(\nu) \\ \sum_i X_i(\nu)Y_i(\lambda) = \delta_{\nu\lambda}; \quad \sum_\nu X_i(\nu)Y_j(\nu) = \delta_{ij}\end{gathered} \tag{6.96}$$

We next set $\mathbf{P}(t) = \mathbf{P}(0)\cdot\mathfrak{M}(t)$, where the (i,j)th element of the stochastic matrix $\mathfrak{M}$ is the conditional probability that if the system is in state i at $t=0$ it will be in state j at time t. Inserting this in Eq. 11.1 we have

$$\frac{d}{dt}\mathfrak{M}(t) = \mathfrak{M}(t)\cdot\mathfrak{A}; \quad \frac{d}{dt}M_{ij}(t) = \sum_k M_{ik}(t)A_{kj} \tag{6.97}$$

By summing over j it can be shown that if $\mathfrak{A}$ is a differential matrix, since $\mathfrak{M}(0)$ is stochastic (it is the unity matrix, with $M_{ij} = \delta_{ij}$) therefore $\mathfrak{M}(t)$ is stochastic. By transforming $\mathfrak{A}$ and $\mathfrak{M}$ to their diagonal forms (as in Section 5) and then transforming $\mathfrak{M}$ back again, we can obtain the general solution for $\mathfrak{M}$ and therefore determine the dynamical behavior of the system. If the transformed forms of $\mathfrak{A}$ and $\mathfrak{M}$ are

$$\mathfrak{B}=\mathfrak{T}^{-1}\cdot\mathfrak{A}\cdot\mathfrak{T};\quad B_{\lambda\nu}=\alpha_\nu\delta_{\lambda\nu};\quad \mathfrak{D}=\mathfrak{T}^{-1}\cdot\mathfrak{M}\cdot\mathfrak{T}$$

$$D_{\lambda\nu}=\mu_\nu(t)\,\delta_{\nu\lambda};\quad (\mathfrak{T})_{j\nu}=Y_j(\nu);\quad (\mathfrak{T}^{-1})_{\lambda i}=X_i(\lambda)$$

then the equations of motion and their solution for the diagonal elements are

$$\frac{d}{dt}\mu_\nu(t)=\alpha_\nu\mu_\nu(t);\quad \mu_\nu(t)=e^{\alpha_\nu t} \tag{6.98}$$

and the matrix governing the time dependence of the probability vector for the system is

$$\mathfrak{M}(t)=\sum_\nu e^{\alpha_\nu t}\mathfrak{F}_\nu;\quad (\mathfrak{F}_\nu)_{ij}=Y_i(\nu)X_j(\nu) \tag{6.99}$$

as in Eq. 6.42 (except that now the coefficients are $e^{\alpha_\nu t}$ instead of μ^m). Exceptions to this equation are mentioned in Section 5.

As noted, the first eigenvalue α_1 is zero and, usually, the others have real parts less than zero. Consequently, as time goes on, all of the exponentials vanish except the first, which corresponds to the steady state. The steady-state matrix $\mathfrak{F}_1$ has each row identical, $(\mathfrak{F}_1)_{ij}=X_j(1)=P_j$, representing the fact that for the steady state the probability P_j of being in state j is independent of the initial state of the system (we assume here, as we did in Section 5, that we are not dealing with the factorable, periodic, or other exceptional cases).

As examples we can take the alternative maintenance systems of Eqs. 6.60 and 6.61 (to simplify the presentation we assume the repair rate r to be 6 times the breakdown rate b). The resulting eigenvalues and eigenvectors are

Single repair crew, $r=6b$:

$$\begin{aligned}
&\alpha_1=0; && \mathbf{X}(1)=\{\tfrac{1}{25},\tfrac{6}{25},\tfrac{18}{25}\}; && \mathbf{Y}(1)=\{1,1,1\}\\
&\alpha_2=-5b; && \mathbf{X}(2)=\{1,1,-2\}; && \mathbf{Y}(2)=\{\tfrac{18}{25},\tfrac{3}{25},-\tfrac{2}{25}\}\\
&\alpha_3=-10b; && \mathbf{X}(3)=\{1,-4,3\}; && \mathbf{Y}(3)=\{\tfrac{6}{25},-\tfrac{4}{25},\tfrac{1}{25}\}
\end{aligned} \tag{6.100}$$

$$\mathfrak{M}=\frac{1}{25}\begin{pmatrix}1&6&18\\1&6&18\\1&6&18\end{pmatrix}+\frac{e^{-5bt}}{25}\begin{pmatrix}18&18&-36\\3&3&-6\\-2&-2&4\end{pmatrix}+\frac{e^{-10bt}}{25}\begin{pmatrix}6&-24&18\\-4&16&-12\\1&-4&3\end{pmatrix}$$

Two repair crews, each $r=6b$:

$$\alpha_1=0; \quad \mathbf{X}(1)=\{\tfrac{1}{49},\tfrac{12}{49},\tfrac{36}{49}\}; \quad \mathbf{Y}(1)=\{1,1,1\}$$
$$\alpha_2=-7b; \quad \mathbf{X}(2)=\{1,5,-6\}; \quad \mathbf{Y}(2)=\{\tfrac{12}{49},\tfrac{5}{49},\tfrac{-2}{49}\} \qquad (6.101)$$
$$\alpha_3=-14b; \quad \mathbf{X}(3)=\{1,-2,1\}; \quad \mathbf{Y}(3)=\{\tfrac{36}{49},\tfrac{-6}{49},\tfrac{1}{49}\}$$

$$\mathfrak{M}=\frac{1}{49}\begin{pmatrix}1 & 12 & 36\\ 1 & 12 & 36\\ 1 & 12 & 36\end{pmatrix}+\frac{e^{-7bt}}{49}\begin{pmatrix}12 & 60 & -72\\ 5 & 25 & -30\\ -2 & -10 & 12\end{pmatrix}+\frac{e^{-14bt}}{49}\begin{pmatrix}36 & -72 & 36\\ -6 & 12 & -6\\ 1 & -2 & 1\end{pmatrix}$$

Therefore, if both machines are in good condition at $t=0$, the probabilities that 2, 1, or 0 machines will be operative at time t later are

Single crew:

$$M_{22}=\tfrac{1}{25}(18+4e^{-5bt}+3e^{-10bt})\rightarrow 1-2bt+8b^2t^2\cdots \qquad (bt\ll 1)$$
$$M_{21}=\tfrac{1}{25}(6-2e^{-5bt}-4e^{-10bt})\rightarrow 2bt-9b^2t^2\cdots \qquad (bt\ll 1)$$
$$M_{20}=\tfrac{1}{25}(1-2e^{-5bt}+e^{-10bt})\rightarrow b^2t^2\cdots \qquad (bt\ll 1)$$

(6.102)

Two crews:

$$M_{22}=\tfrac{1}{49}(36+12e^{-7bt}+e^{-14bt})\rightarrow 1-2bt+8b^2t^2\cdots \qquad (bt\ll 1)$$
$$M_{21}=\tfrac{1}{49}(12-10e^{-7bt}-2e^{-14bt})\rightarrow 2bt-9b^2t^2\cdots \qquad (bt\ll 1)$$
$$M_{20}=\tfrac{1}{49}(1-2e^{-7bt}+e^{-14bt})\rightarrow b^2t^2\cdots \qquad (bt\ll 1)$$

and the expected numbers $N(t)=2M_{22}+M_{21}$ in operation at time t are:

Single crew:

$$N(t)=\tfrac{1}{25}(42+6e^{-5bt}+2e^{-10bt})\rightarrow 2-2bt+7b^2t^2\cdots$$

(6.103)

Two crews:

$$N(t)=\tfrac{1}{49}(84+14e^{-7bt})\rightarrow 2-2bt+7b^2t^2\cdots$$

We see that the initial behavior of the two systems, near $t=0$, is identical; M_{22}, the chance that both machines are still running, decreases linearly; M_{21}, the chance that only one machine is running, increases linearly from zero; and M_{20}, the chance that both machines are down, increases quadratically with t (since state 0 cannot be reached directly from state 2, but only via state 1, this quadratical initial dependence is to be expected). We also see that, in steady state, the single-crew system has 1.680 machines in operation, on the average, whereas the two-crew system achieves 1.714 machine-weeks per week, not a great increase in productivity. But we have assumed that the crews can usually complete their repair job in one sixth of the mean life of a machine (between repairs). With crews that fast it is seldom that both machines are down simultaneously and the second crew is needed. In fact, in steady state, the second crew is working only $\frac{1}{49}$th of the time. If the repair rate were smaller than the assumed $6b$ the second crew would be needed more often and there would be a greater difference between the N's.

Finally we calculate the behavior of the shuttle-transport system of Eqs. 6.62, where, to simplify notation, we let $\mu = \beta v$(i.e., the mean wait for a load is β times the mean transport time). The eigenvalues and eigenvectors of the matrix $\mathfrak{A}$ are

$$\alpha_1 = 0; \quad \mathbf{X}(1) = \frac{}{1+\beta}\{1,1,\beta,\beta\}; \quad \mathbf{Y}(1) = \{1,1,1,1\}$$

$$\alpha_2 = -(1+\beta)v; \quad \mathbf{X}(2) = \{1,1,-1,-1\}; \quad \mathbf{Y}(2) = \frac{\frac{1}{2}}{1+\beta}\{\beta,\beta,-1,-1\}$$

$$\alpha_3 = -\tfrac{1}{2}(1+\beta)v - i\omega v; \quad \mathbf{X}(3) = \{1,-1,-\tfrac{1}{2}(1-\beta)-i\omega,\tfrac{1}{2}(1-\beta)+i\omega\};$$

$$\mathbf{Y}(3) = \frac{i}{8\omega}\{1-\beta-2i\omega,-1+\beta+2i\omega,2\omega,-2\omega\} \tag{6.104}$$

$$\alpha_4 = -\tfrac{1}{2}(1+\beta)v + i\omega v; \quad \mathbf{X}(4) = \{1,-1,-\tfrac{1}{2}(1-\beta)+i\omega,\tfrac{1}{2}(1-\beta)-i\omega\};$$

$$\mathbf{Y}(4) = \frac{i}{8\omega}\{-1+\beta-2i\omega,1-\beta+2i\omega,-2\omega,2\omega\}$$

where $\omega = \frac{1}{2}\sqrt{6\beta-\beta^2-1} = \sqrt{1-\frac{1}{4}(1-\beta)(5-\beta)}$ is real for $0.172 < \beta < 5.838$ and where

$$[\tfrac{1}{2}(1-\beta)+i\omega][\tfrac{1}{2}(1-\beta)-i\omega] = \beta$$

In this case two of the eigenvalues are complex, indicating that there is an initial oscillation of the state probabilities when ω is real.

When ω is real the matrix elements M_{ij}, the probabilities that if the system is initially in state i it will be in state j at time t, execute damped oscillations. The ensemble of systems goes initially from transshipping to waiting more or less in phase; but as time goes on some shuttlings go faster and some slower, so that the systems get more and more out of phase, the oscillations of the M's die out, and eventually the constant, steady-state distributions remain. After a long enough time the truck is as likely to be going from A to B as it is to be going from B to A, to be waiting at B as to be waiting at A. Initially because of the oscillations there will be a difference. If the system is run for a finite time (for the day, for example) and then is started over again next day, these transient solutions will be needed to find whether it matters if the truck is always started out from the same point.

If it starts from state 1 (going from A to B, then unloading at B), the probabilities M_{1j} of being in state j at time t are

$$M_{11}=\frac{1+\beta e^{-(1+\beta)vt}}{2(1+\beta)}+e^{-\frac{1}{2}(1+\beta)vt}\left[\tfrac{1}{2}\cos\omega vt+\frac{1-\beta}{4\omega}\sin\omega vt\right]\to 1-\beta vt\ldots$$

$$M_{12}=\frac{1+\beta e^{-(1+\beta)vt}}{2(1+\beta)}-e^{-\frac{1}{2}(1+\beta)vt}\left[\tfrac{1}{2}\cos\omega vt+\frac{1-\beta}{4\omega}\sin\omega vt\right]\to -\beta v^2t^2\ldots$$

$$M_{13}=\frac{\beta-\beta e^{-(1+\beta)vt}}{2(1+\beta)}-\frac{\beta}{2\omega}e^{-\frac{1}{2}(1+\beta)vt}\sin\omega vt\to -\beta^2v^3t^3\cdots \tag{6.105}$$

$$M_{14}=\frac{\beta-\beta e^{-(1+\beta)vt}}{2(1+\beta)}+\frac{\beta}{2\omega}e^{-\frac{1}{2}(1+\beta)vt}\sin\omega vt\to\beta vt\cdots \qquad (\beta vt\ll 1)$$

The probability of being in state 1 starts at 1, drops down linearly to a minimal value at $t\cong(\pi/\omega v)$ (about the time when the truck is more likely to be going back again to A), then rises again, but not as high as unity, and so on. The chance of being found waiting at B (state 4) starts up linearly from zero and then performs damped oscillations. The probability of having picked up a load and being in the act of returning to A starts up quadratically from zero, and the probability of being back at A and waiting for another load starts up with the cube of t for small t. This initial dependence would be different if the individual states had other than exponential distributions, of course.

But this discussion, and these oversimplified examples indicate the range of applicability of the dynamical model treated in this article; application to specific cases of interest must be made by the reader.

BIBLIOGRAPHY

Bellman, Richard, *Introduction to Matrix Analysis,* McGraw-Hill Book Co., New York, 1960.

Brockmeyer, E., Halstrom, H. L., and Jensen, Arne, "The Life and Works of A. K. Erlang," *Transactions of the Danish Academy Technical Sciences,* **2,** Copenhagen, 1948.

Bush, R. R., and Mosteller, Frederick, *Stochastic Models for Learning,* John Wiley and Sons, New York, 1955.

Feller, W., *Introduction to Probability Theory and Its Applications,* Second Edition, John Wiley and Sons, New York, 1957.

Ferrar, W. L., *Finite Matrices,* Clarendon Press, Oxford, 1951.

Galliher, H. P., Morse, Philip M., and Simond, M., "Dynamics of Two Classes of Continuous-Review Inventory Systems," *Opns. Res.,* **7,** 362–384 (1959).

Kendall, D. G., "Some Problems in the Theory of Queues," *J. Roy. Stat. Soc.,* **13,** 151 (1951); **24,** 338 (1953).

McCloskey, J. F., and Coppinger, J. M. (Eds.), *Operations Research for Management,* The Johns Hopkins Press, Baltimore, 1956, Appendix A, p. 415.

MIT Operations Research Center, *Notes on Operations Research, 1958,* The Technology Press, Cambridge, Mass., 1959.

Morse, Philip M., "Solutions of a Class of Discrete-Time Inventory Problems," *Opns. Res.,* **7,** 67–78 (1959).

———, *Queues, Inventories and Maintenance,* John Wiley and Sons, New York, 1958.

Chapter **7**

SEQUENCING THEORY

Roger L. Sisson

Autonutronic Division, Ford Motor Company, Newport Beach, California

Contents

1. INTRODUCTION

1.1. Definition of Sequencing

A number of operational situations exist in which certain facilities or machines are available. A number of commodities or jobs must be processed on some or all of these machines. As with other operational problems, the goal is to optimize the use of the facilities to effectively process the commodities, effectiveness being measured in terms of minimized cost, maximized profit, minimum processing time, meeting of due dates, etc., whichever is most appropriate. If it is assumed that the time required to perform the processing of a particular commodity at a specific machine is given, the question of optimizing becomes the question of ordering or *sequencing* the commodities at each facility. "Sequencing is used here to refer to the order in which units requiring service are serviced" (Churchman, 1957, p. 450).

The term "scheduling" is often used to describe the sequencing situation. "Scheduling" should be reserved for procedures which give the time of arrivals of units requiring service. Scheduling problems are approached by the application of queuing theory, and will not be considered further here. A more precise definition of sequencing will be given below.

The most common and frequently referred to example of a sequencing problem is the job shop. In a job shop there will be a requirement for processing J commodities (also referred to as job lots or jobs) on M facilities. The commodities are indexed by j and the facilities by m.

The processing of a commodity at a facility is called an *operation* or task. Other sequencing situations occur, as will be noted below.

1.2. Methods of Analysis

As is the case in analyzing other operational situations, a procedure such as suggested by Fig. 7.1 is followed. Thus, the actual sequencing problem or a set of such problems is studied. From these a model is abstracted. This model may involve a high level of abstraction, usually leading to simple models, or may be a model which attempts to represent the actual situation in great detail. It is also necessary to choose from the situation and its environment a criterion or objective function. The criterion may be defined as a measure of how close a solution comes

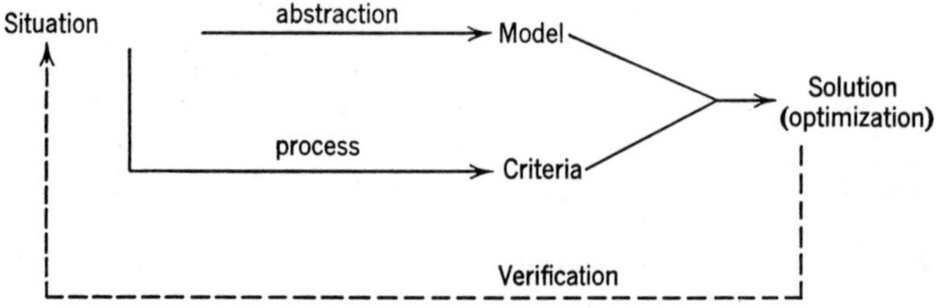

Fig. 7.1.

to meeting a decision maker's objectives, the decision maker being a part of the environment of the sequencing situation (Churchman, 1957, pp. 108–154). The model and criterion can often be expressed in terms of mathematical symbols. It is also possible to represent a situation in terms of a computer program (or clerical procedure) which is intended to simulate the situation. Simulation models are being used for studying sequencing situations.

The optimizing solution must now be derived by some definite procedure from the model. The solution may be obtained by analysis, that is, derived from the model by a set of logical procedures, or it may be at least tested by Monte Carlo. The latter procedure amounts to taking random samples of solutions of the model, in the hope (sometimes rigorously justified) that the sampling procedure will lead to a solution as close to the optimum as can be afforded.

Considerable progress has been made in the study of sequencing situations since 1957. (See Sisson, 1959, for a report of progress to that time. Below, references to this review are made in some cases rather than to list all papers prior to 1958.) Several relationships have been discovered which permit the reduction of the number of cases that must be considered relative to a brute-force approach. The latter amounts to examining all possible sequences or combinations, of which there are $(J!)^M$.

Probably the most significant conceptual advance is the recognition that many sequencing problems can be represented by an integer-linear-programming model (Wagner, 1959) and therefore a computational procedure to obtain the solution is available. However, the number of computational steps in such a solution is still extremely large. Therefore, there is an active, continuing interest in other analytic approaches to solution, as well as in simulation approaches. For some simpler cases, it can be shown that a Monte Carlo procedure will permit determining a solution as close to optimum as desired. That is, answer can be given to the question of how many samples to take in order to derive the least costly solution, where cost of computation as well as cost of non-optimum sequencing is taken into account.

From an "operations engineering" point of view, a handbook of techniques for sequencing problems has a few basic entries. Many others are not practical as they (*a*) require a very large number of computational steps, and (*b*) are not yet verified. Useful ideas for improving many sequencing procedures through simulation are available.

1.3. Typical Cases

As mentioned above, the principal situation to which sequencing models are applied is the job shop. Classically, this is a shop in which the commodities are brought to the machines; test operations, engineering work, and so on are equivalent. Another common sequencing situation occurs in the construction business, in which the machines are brought to the jobs. Neglecting minor transportation times, the problem is the same, that of sequencing the tasks to be accomplished by given facilities.

Sherman (1959) notes a related sequencing problem, which is that of sequencing students who wish to take certain courses into a number of class sections. Here the classes might be thought of as "machines" and the students as "commodities." Each commodity will have the same processing time, that is, the class time, on any machine. The problem is not only to sequence the students, but also to "load" the classes or machines so that they are nearly full but not oversubscribed.

Wyatt (1959) describes a situation in which there are fewer operators than machines. In his model "each job is allocated to the appropriate machines in the correct sequence. There are more machines in the workshop than there are men to operate them. Jobs wait in a queue at each machine and are dealt with on a 'first-come, first-served basis.' . . . Each time a man completes the processing of a job . . . a priority rule determines whether he should start on the next job in the queue or move to another machine" (p. 137). "The priority for each job is [obtained] by assessing the difference between the scheduled completion time for the job on its current machine and the time it joined the queue for that machine" (p. 139). Note that this is a priority for assigning men, not jobs, to machines. Studies were made of this problem on a Ferranti Pegasus computer.

Churchman (1957, pp. 468–470) makes note of other related sequencing problems, the assembly-line-balancing problem and the traveling-salesman problem. The assembly-line-balancing problem involves the notion of arranging the work steps performed at each station of an assembly line so as to balance the processing time at each station. The problem is to assign the work steps so that they are done in the proper sequence and so that the time at each station is as nearly equal as possible. The traveling-salesman problem "involves sequencing each of a set of jobs (e.g., visiting a location) for a facility (e.g., a salesman) so as to minimize some characteristic of movement from one job to the next" (Churchman, 1947, p. 468). These problems will not be discussed further.

2. MODELS

Every researcher abstracts or assumes his own model. First, we will present a model which is more general than any considered by many researchers active in the past two years from which logical (not simulation) deductions have been made. We can then discuss various simpler versions of this model, which have been analyzed, and also discuss the ways in which real sequencing situations are even more complex.

The principal assumptions made on the model are as follows (Sisson, 1959, p. 3, and Giffler, 1959, p. 1):

1. No machine may process more than one operation at a time.
2. Each operation, once started, must be performed to completion.
3. A commodity is an entity; that is, even though the commodity represents a lot of individual parts, no lot may be processed by more than one machine at one time.
4. A known, finite time is required to perform each operation and each operation must be completed before any operation which it must precede can begin.
5. The time intervals for processing are independent of the order in which the operations are performed.
6. Each commodity must be processed by a designated sequence of machines, this sequence being also called "the technological ordering" or "the routing."
7. There is only one of each type of machine.
8. A commodity is processed as soon as possible subject only to routing requirements given above.
9. All jobs are known and are ready to start processing before the period under consideration begins.

10. The time required to transport commodities between machines is negligible.

11. In-process inventory must be allowable (Wagner, 1959, p. 131).

2.1. *A General Model*

The model may be stated, finally, as follows:

a. Facilities are given and designated $1,2,3,\cdots,m,\cdots,M$.

b. Commodities or jobs are given and designated $1,2,3,\cdots,j,\cdots,J$.

c. A given sequence of jobs is designated $j_1,j_2,\cdots,j_k,\cdots$.

d. An operation is designated mj, a specific one being m_rj_s. The time to process an operation is t_{mj}. T is the time when the last operation is completed.

e. Two relationships can be defined following Giffler (1959, pp. 2, 3) and Heller (1959, p. 8): m_tj_u *"follows"* m_rj_s if (roughly) the start (or completion) of operation m_rj_s must always occur before the start (or completion) of m_tj_u. This is designated $m_rj_s \prec m_tj_u$.

f. m_tj_u *"next follows"* m_rj_s (1) if $m_rj_s \prec m_tj_u$ and (2) if no operation, say m_xj_y, can exist such that $m_rj_s \prec m_xj_y \prec m_tj_u$.

This is designated $m_rj_s \prec\prec m_tj_u$.

"Next follows" is defined only if the two operations have a commodity or a facility in common. See Fig. 7.2, which is a partial Gantt chart for examples of operations which next follow.

g. The required routing may be described in two ways: (1) by giving the routings, a sequence of machines for each job, also called a facility matrix:

$$\mathcal{G}_j = \{m_1j, m_2j, \cdots\} \qquad (j=1,2,\cdots)$$

or (2) by indicating a sequence of commodities for each machine, or a commodity matrix:

$$\mathfrak{M}_m = \{mj_1, mj_2, \cdots\} \qquad (m=1,2,3,\cdots)$$

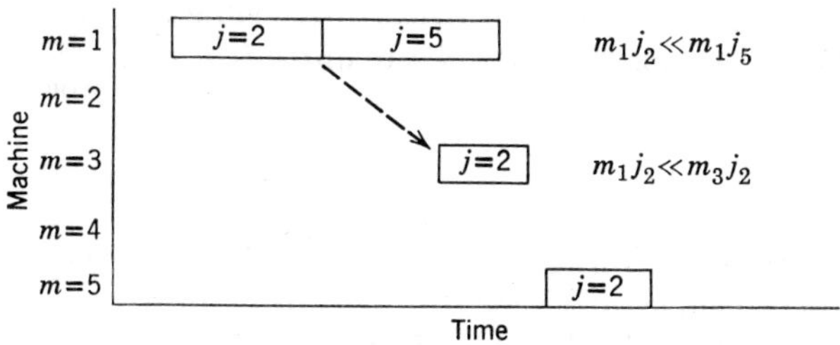

Fig. 7.2.

A complete sequence, that is, a solution to the problem, is given when both ordered sets are given. Usually $\mathcal{J}_j$ is given and it is desired to find the sequence of jobs on each facility $\mathfrak{M}_m$ which is optimal. Note that $\mathfrak{M}_m$ defines a queue served by machine m (Sisson, 1959, p. 17).

Three other notations related to this model have found use: the *next-follows* matrix, the *Gantt* chart, and a sequence notation.

The next-follows matrix P is an MJ square matrix, of the form of Fig. 7.3. In this matrix, the entries are:

$$p_{rs} = \begin{cases} t_{rs} \text{ if the } s\text{th operation "next follows" the } r\text{th} \\ 0 \text{ otherwise} \end{cases}$$

where t_{rs} is the interval of time that *must* be expended on the rth operation before the sth can be started.

For example (after Giffler, 1959, p. 24), such a matrix for two commodities and three machines, and all $t_{mj} = 1$:

$$\left\| \begin{array}{cc|cc|cc} 0 & 1 & 1 & 0 & 0 & 0 \\ 0 & 0 & 0 & 0 & 0 & 0 \\ \hline 0 & 0 & 0 & 1 & 1 & 0 \\ 0 & 1 & 0 & 0 & 0 & 0 \\ \hline 0 & 0 & 0 & 0 & 0 & 0 \\ 0 & 0 & 0 & 1 & 1 & 0 \end{array} \right\|$$

for which,

$$\mathfrak{M}_m = \begin{array}{r|cc|} m=1 & 1 & 2 \\ m=2 & 1 & 2 \\ m=3 & 2 & 1 \end{array} \qquad \mathcal{J}_j = \begin{array}{r|ccc|} j=1 & 1 & 2 & 3 \\ j=2 & 3 & 2 & 1 \\ & & & \end{array}$$

Note that the diagonal submatrices are determined by $\mathfrak{M}_m$. Giffler (1959) uses next-follows and related matrices formally to generate and determine the operating characteristics of schedules.

Assume time is measured in discrete units, $t_1, t_2, \cdots$. Then a "Gantt chart" G can be defined as follows:

$$G_m = \{g_{mt_1}, g_{mt_2}, \cdots, g_{mT}\} \qquad (m = 1,2,3,\cdots)$$

$$\text{where } g_{mt_1} = \begin{cases} j \text{ (the job index) if operation } mj \text{ is being processed on} \\ \text{machine } m \text{ at time } t_1 \\ 0 \text{ otherwise (machine idle)} \end{cases}$$

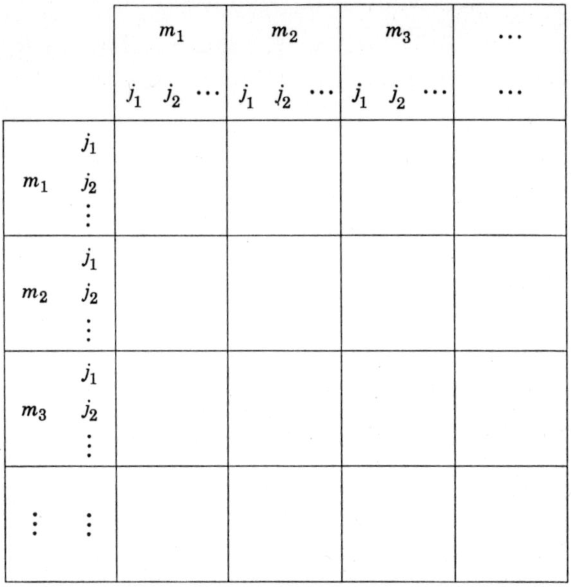

		m_1	m_2	m_3	$\cdots$
		j_1 j_2 $\cdots$	j_1 j_2 $\cdots$	j_1 j_2 $\cdots$	$\cdots$
m_1	j_1 j_2 $\vdots$				
m_2	j_1 j_2 $\vdots$				
m_3	j_1 j_2 $\vdots$				
$\vdots$	$\vdots$				

Fig. 7.3.

For the example above, the Gantt chart might be:

$$G=\begin{vmatrix} 1 & 1 & 0 & 0 & 0 & 0 & 0 & 2 & 2 & 2 \\ 0 & 0 & 1 & 1 & 1 & 2 & 2 & 0 & 0 & 0 \\ 2 & 2 & 2 & 2 & 0 & 1 & 1 & 0 & 0 & 0 \end{vmatrix}$$

$T=10$ for this sequence.

It is sometimes convenient to denote that item j is in the kth-order position on machine m by

$$x_{mj_k}=1$$

and, if not, $x_{mj_k}=0$. Also we can denote the time at which an operation begins as h_{mj_k}.

2.2. *Simpler Models*

Most researchers are working with models which are somewhat less complex than the one just described. Table 7.1*A* and *B* reviews various simplifying assumptions which can be made to arrive at a set of expressions that are amenable to analytic treatment. Case V of Table

TABLE 7.1*A*

SUMMARY OF SEQUENCING RESEARCH

	M	Assumptions 1	2	3	4	5	6	7	8	9	10	$N(\mathcal{J})$	$N(\mathfrak{M})$	
	No. of Machs.	One Job per Mach.	No Interrupted Opns.	No Split Lots	Well-Defined Opn. Times	Time Independent of Sequence	Routing Given	One Mach. per Type	Process Opn. as Soon as Possible	All Jobs Ready	Neglect Transportation Times	(if = 1, all jobs have same routing)	(if = 1, jobs in same order on all M)	Objective Function
I	1	✓	✓	✓	✓	✓	✓	✓	✓	no	✓	1	1	meet due date
II	2	✓	✓	✓	✓	✓	✓	✓	no (3)	✓	✓	1	1	min T
	2	✓	✓	✓	✓	✓	✓	✓	no (3)	✓	✓	1	any	min T
III	3	✓	✓	✓	✓	✓	✓	✓	✓	✓	✓	1	1 (1)	min T
IV	many	✓	✓	✓	✓	✓	✓	✓	not explicit	✓	✓	1	many	min T
	many	✓	✓	✓	✓	✓	✓	✓	✓	✓	✓	1	many	min T
	many	✓	✓	✓	✓	✓	✓	✓	not explicit	✓	✓	1	many (2)	min T
V	many	✓	✓	✓	✓	✓	partial	no	not explicit	✓	✓	many	many	min T
	many	✓	✓	✓	✓	✓	partial	✓	✓	✓	✓	many	many	min T
	many	✓	✓	✓	✓	✓	partial	✓	no (3)	✓	✓	many	many	min T or meet due date
VI	many	✓	✓	✓	✓	✓	✓	no	not explicit	no	✓	many	many	various
VII	many	usually	no	no	stochastic	no	partial	no	no (3)	no	✓	many	many	complex

(1) For m = 2,3 it can be shown that this causes no loss of optimality (under assumption 8) (Johnson, 1954).
(2) The case of $N(\mathfrak{M}) = 1$ is also explicitly considered.
(3) In these cases, specific interoperation delays can be included.

TABLE 7.1*B*

SUMMARY OF SEQUENCING RESEARCH

	Researcher	Method of arriving at Optimizing Procedures	Method of Executing the Procedure to Obtain Specific Solution
I	Jackson	statistical analysis (queuing)	none yet
II	Johnson (1959), Mitten	combinatorial analysis	solve algorithm on paper
	Johnson (1959)	combinatorial analysis	solve algorithm on paper
III	Wagner, Part IV	integer linear programming	paper or computer for small problems, $J<25$
IV	Wagner, Part III	integer linear programming	computer may be feasible for small problems
	Heller	combinatorial+statistical analysis	computer—Monte Carlo (*B*)
	Smith	statistical analysis	computer—Monte Carlo (*B*)
V	Wagner	integer linear programming	numerical analysis to judge economics not reported
	Giffler and Thompson	combinatorial analysis	computer-algorithm+ enumeration or Monte Carlo (*A*)
	Manne	integer linear programming	numerical analysis not reported
VI	Rowe	empirical rules	computer-simulated trials (*C*)
	Conway, Nelson	queuing approach	computer-simulated trials (*C*)
	Giffler and Thompson		computer-simulated trials (*C*)
VII	typical actual situation		computer-simulated trials (*C*)

(*A*), (*B*), (*C*)—see text, p. 311.

7.1 is the model described above. One direction of simplification is to reduce the number of machines considered to some small number. The one-machine case is not trivial; it has practical value. The problem of scheduling a computing center is essentially a one-machine problem. (Mr. Gerald Fine, of System Development Corporation, has done some work on the problem of scheduling one computer, where the jobs can be divided into two parts, those which are routine and are scheduled for periodic processing, and those which arrive at random and must be processed quickly, i.e., programs to be debugged.)

Another direction of simplification is to assume that all jobs have the same routing, $N(\mathcal{J}_j) = 1$. Since the machines may be numbered in any convenient way, this amounts to saying that all jobs will be processed on machines 1, 2, 3, and so on. With one routing, a further simplifying assumption can be made: let all jobs be processed in the same sequence, $N(\mathfrak{M}_m) = 1$. It can be shown that for $m \leq 3$, this does not restrict optimality (Johnson, 1954). Algorithms for solving this case, for situations with two machines, have been derived (Johnson, 1954, 1959; and see Sisson, 1959, p. 19) and the computational implications seem to be within reason. Jackson (1956) develops an algorithm for $m = 2$ where $N(\mathfrak{M}_m) > 1$.

Assumption 8, p. 298 (tasks performed as soon as possible), can be relaxed in the two-machine case (case II) and an algorithm still applies (Mitten, 1959). For problems with only two machines for which $\mathfrak{M}_1 \neq \mathfrak{M}_2$, and 8 is not assumed, no optimizing algorithms have been found.

Likewise, for $m > 3$, or even $m = 3$ and fewer restrictive assumptions, combinatorial analysis has not proven fruitful of optimizing algorithms. Case IV is quite general, being representative of an assembly line, the restriction being that all jobs have the same routing.

2.3. *Very General Models*

Case VI, Table 7.1, represents the more "realistic" cases in which assumptions 1 through 10 do not necessarily apply and where the objective function is more complex and may depend on several factors related to the commodities being processed and machine usage. Rowe (1959) presents a rather complete description of a complex sequencing situation. (Sequencing is referred to as "dispatching" in his report.)

It might be emphasized that in most real situations some of the assumptions 1 through 10 do not apply and in many, none do. Nevertheless, there is good indication that the model resulting from adopting these assumptions characterizes the heart of the sequencing problem.

3. OBJECTIVE FUNCTIONS

As in most operational situations which are a part of a larger entity (e.g., a business), the ultimate desire is to optimize an objective of the larger organization (e.g., profits). This requires knowing how the specific situation relates to the whole, knowledge which we do not have. Thus, for research purposes, one optimizes a lesser criterion chosen in some reasonable way.

Researchers in sequencing (Sisson, 1959, p. 12, and Sasieni, 1959, p. 264) are, in many cases, using the objective function: minimize T; that is, minimize the total time required to process all of a given set of jobs. This is a simple measure, easy to apply to a given schedule, and has some relation to other criteria, such as: minimize idle time, maximize facility utilization, minimize cost, etc. (Manne, 1959, p. 5).

Another important objective is to meet preset completion times for each job. A summary measure of this ability is the total tardiness. If $D(j)$ is the preset completion time or "scheduled due date" and $A(j)$ is the actual completion time, the total tardiness can be defined as:

$$\sum_j A(j) - D(j)$$

or

$$\sum_j \max[A(j) - D(j), 0] \tag{7.1}$$

For multimachine cases, more complex objectives have been considered only where simulation experiments were attempted. Some are: minimize in-process inventory costs, maximize machine utilization or throughput, minimize flow time, meet some prescribed distribution of completion time (relative to due times), minimize waiting time (time is queue) (Rowe, 1959).

(Jackson [letter, Oct. 15, 1959] points out that, when considered as queuing problems, some procedures are known for minimizing certain of these objectives individually.)

"It is not 'necessary' . . . to pick a criterion function. One can also—and . . . perhaps more intelligently, from a basic research point of view—seek to discover the relationships among sequencing procedures in general and consequent input-output characteristics of the system concerned" (J. Jackson, letter, Oct. 15, 1959). See Jackson, 1959.

4. OPTIMIZING PROCEDURES

"The objective of many previous investigations . . . is to find an arrangement that minimizes the processing time . . . as a function of given job times. . . . This objective is not the whole story. We must ask the question: Can we find an order relation that minimizes the processing time such that the number of arithmetic and logical operations to obtain this minimum order is *very* much smaller than the number of arithmetic and logical operations needed to enumerate all processing times and their corresponding order relations? . . . solutions to this problem will not exist [for three or more machines] if we define 'very much smaller' as sufficiently small" (Heller, 1959, p. 17).

Thus, the purpose of research in sequencing is to develop algorithms for arriving at optimum solutions. First, it is necessary to demonstrate that a solution which is optimum can be obtained and, second, it is necessary to show that the solution can be computed on an economic basis in practical situations.

4.1. Combinatorial Solutions

For the simpler models, specific algorithms are becoming available.

Johnson (1954) has solved a two-machine case, giving a simple algorithm. In this, he assumes all jobs are processed on machine 1 and then 2. He shows that, without loss of optimality, the job sequence on both machines may be the same. See Sasieni (1959) for a review and examples of these cases: two machines, three machines with one job sequence and two jobs on m machines. Jackson (1956) notes an algorithm which generalizes the two-machine case to include a mixture of jobs with any routings; that is, $J=[1]$ or $[2]$ or $[1,2]$ or $[2,1]$. Smith (1956) has given rules for sequencing jobs processed on one machine so as to minimize the sum of completion times.

For the more complex situations, some algorithms are available, which, however, lead to expensive computational procedures. Therefore, for these models, researchers have been resorting to simulation procedures in order to gain an insight into the sequencing situation, and through Monte Carlo to arrive at near-optimum solutions.

During the past year, algorithms have been obtained by Johnson (1959) and Mitten (1959) for case II, Table 7.1*A* and *B*, where the number of machines is restricted to two, and the routing for all jobs is the same. Mitten's procedure covers the case where assumption 8 does not apply, that is, to the case where certain prescribed lags between the time a job starts on machine 1 and can start on machine 2 (start-lag), or the time a job is completed on machine 1 and can be completed on machine 2 (stop-lag), can be included in the model. This optimizing algorithm has been derived through the shrewd logical analysis of the two-machine situation.

The problem of two machines, with start-lag and stop-lag included, has many practical applications. Assume that one has a process in which most jobs flow through a given sequence of machines in the same order. Suppose two machines create the most serious bottlenecks, and that after being run on machine 1, jobs may be routed over a variety of intermediate (non-bottleneck) machines before being started on machine 2. The start-lag may then represent the time to complete intermediate operations, plus time to accumulate any initial minimum backlog required to start processing on machine 2. Likewise, the stop-lag can include the time to complete intermediate operations, plus time to accumulate the minimum final backlog required. "By concentrating attention on the two most serious bottlenecks, the two-machine Gantt-chart problem may be used to provide an optimal scheduling framework for a facility employing a large number of machines" (Mitten, 1959, p. 133).

Start-lag and stop-lag can also be used to represent transportation times between machines, or to represent overlapping production procedures common in engineering and construction work.

The optimizing algorithm given by Mitten is as follows: If a_j = the start-lag and b_j = the stop-lag, then form

$$m_j = \max[a_j - t_{1j}, b_j - t_{2j}] \tag{7.2}$$

Consider the jobs in two sequences:

$\mathfrak{M}_{\mathrm{I}}$ such that $t_{1j} < t_{2j}$, ordered so that $m_{j_1} + t_{1j_1} < m_{j_2} + t_{1j_2} \cdots$.
$\mathfrak{M}_{\mathrm{II}}$ such that $t_{1j} \geq t_{2j}$, ordered so that $m_{j_1} + t_{2j_1} \geq m_{j_2} + t_{2j_2} \cdots$.

An optimum sequence is then $\mathfrak{M}_{\mathrm{I}}$ followed by $\mathfrak{M}_{\mathrm{II}}$. This can be demonstrated by showing that (*a*) any non-optimum sequence S' can be obtained from the optimum sequence S^* by a series of transpositions of adjacent jobs in S^*, and (*b*) that for any such transposition $T' \geqq T^*$.

Johnson has considered this case of two machines with lags where different job sequences are allowed for the two. He derives some rules which "reduce the problem in these cases down to a relatively small list of sequences whose total times can be compared in the optimal sequence found" (Johnson, 1959). Typically, he reduces the problem from $(J!)^2$ to $J!$ cases.

Even for the problem of sequencing one machine, if the criteria is to schedule jobs so as to meet specific due dates, e.g., to minimize total tardiness, no (published) algorithms exist. Dantzig (1956) uses linear programming to sequence work on one machine, where the priority of a job decays with time, providing a job does not have to be processed in its entirety at one time (restriction 2). Jackson has been performing simulations (on paper) for this situation and has observed the following: "Preliminary results include a startling lack of dependence of the upper tail of the tardiness distribution (with "mean flow time" as the time unit) upon the variance of the desired flow time distribution" (J. Jackson, UCLA, letter, June 2, 1959).

Others have also reported that ordinary statistics are not always useful when the objective is to find the maximum or minimum by sampling techniques. The statistical convergence depends upon the nature of the tails of the assumed distributions, whereas, the precise form of these tails is usually ignored in other statistical problems. (However, see Gumbel, 1957.)

Johnson notes, in regard to the problem of minimizing the total tardiness, "I have worked out a set of somewhat complicated implications which greatly reduce the number of possible optimal sequences. Thus, problems involving 15 or so items can be solved by hand computation with a little work" (S. Johnson, RAND, letter, July 1, 1959).

4.2. Integer-Linear-Programming Solutions

The other major approach to deriving an algorithm for solving a sequencing problem is to use integer linear programming (Gomory, 1958). The principle work of this has been developed by Wagner (1959), Bowman (1959), and Manne (1959). The importance of this work is noted by Jackson: "Since the integer programming advances permit the solution-in-principle of a huge class of sequencing problems, it seems to me that the interest in impractical theoretical results of the combinatorial type ought to die quickly" (J. Jackson, letter, June 2, 1959). On the other hand, Giffler and Thompson (1959) point out: "Scheduling problems have, in some recent work, been formalized as an integral linear program. We note, however, that this approach has not yet led (for problems of practical interest) to computationally practical methods of solution." Obviously, both statements have merit and depend in part on the power one wishes to attribute to currently available and future computing machines. Within ten years, computing machines which will solve large linear programs quickly and inexpensively will probably be available. At the present time, however, solutions through this technique (which leads to a large number of variables and equations) do not appear practically feasible and a continued search for other combinatorial approaches does seem to be in order.

About integer programming for sequencing, Wagner (1959, p. 131) says:

It is of interest to present the model, because (1) it shows that there is a single model which encompasses a wide variety of machine-scheduling situations, (2) the linear format establishes the existence of a finite algorithm which monotonically seeks an optimum solution to such sequencing problems, (3) although the model is now of very limited computational interest, future developments in integer linear programming and methods for efficiently handling "secondary constraints" may make numerical solutions of particular problems possible, and (4) there is an indication of the possibility of constructing special algorithms to exploit the structure of certain of the "classical" scheduling problems. Needless to say, the major justification for considering such an approach is that Gomory (1958) and others . . . have recently discovered promising methods for solving integer linear-programming problems; a related justification is that Dantzig, Fulkersen and Johnson (Dantzig, 1954) have achieved noteworthy success in using secondary constraint techniques for solving a problem which *a priori* contains a mammoth number of restrictions. As will be evident below, the model in its present form is computationally unwieldy except perhaps for situations with a very few machines and a limited number of items; in such cases, a frequently recurring sequencing problem or one involving a considerable financial sum might profitably be solved by the method herein.

Where computers are used, it is possible that many infeasible cases can be eliminated by intuition, if the proper coupling between the computer and the man is provided. Experiments along these lines may deserve consideration.

The integer-linear-programming model for sequencing was first developed by Wagner (1959). He considers the general model, case V, but does not need to assume that there is only one machine of a type (assumption 7). Manne (1959) shows that this approach may be modified so as to satisfy due-date constraints, as well as minimizing T. Wagner also analyzes cases where there is one routing for all jobs (Wagner, 1959, Part III) and the three-machine version of this situation (Part IV).

Very summarily, an integer-linear-programming approach involves the following sets of equations (after Wagner):

a. Constraints to insure that each commodity completes the necessary operations:

$$\sum_{k=1}^{N} x_{mj_k} = 1 \tag{7.3}$$

where N = maximum number of items that might ever be processed on m

b. Constraints to insure that no more than one item be assigned as the *k*th commodity to be processed on *m*:

$$\sum_{j\epsilon\mathcal{J}_j'} x_{mj_k} \leq 1 \qquad \text{for } k=1,2,\cdots,N \tag{7.4}$$

where $\mathcal{J}_j'$ = the subset of $\mathcal{J}$ such that some machine in $\mathcal{J}_j' = m$

c. Calculate $h_{mj_1} = S_{m_0}$, the time after the start of the sequencing period when the first commodity is processed on *m*, and the operation start time:

$$h_{mj_k} = \sum_{q=1}^{k-1} \sum_{j\epsilon\mathcal{J}_j'} t_{mj} x_{mj_q} + \sum_{q=0}^{k-1} S_{mq} \tag{7.5}$$

where S_{mq} = the *q*th idle period on machine *m*

d. Constraints to insure the proper routings J for a given job *j* in queue positions j_a for machine 1 and j_b for machine 2:

$$h_{m_1j_a} + t_{m_1j} x_{m_1j_a} \leq h_{m_2j_b} + B(1 - x_{m_1j_a}) + B(1 - x_{m_2j_b}) \tag{7.6}$$

where $j_a \simeq j_b$

B = some large positive integer

In general, for each commodity *j* and each machine pair (as m_1, m_2) and each order position, $k = 1, \cdots, N$, for each machine, there will be a constraint, Eq. 7.6, plus the constraints to insure integers (Gomory, 1958).

"Although the total number of such constraints [and variables] for the model is obviously enormous, only a relatively few of the relations will be binding in any solution. This fact suggests the technique of treating relations of the type [7.6] as secondary constraints (Dantzig, 1955) . . .; in other words we might attempt to solve a scheduling problem by a series of trial solutions in which constraints are introduced only as needed to eliminate infeasibilities" (Wagner, 1959, p. 135).

Manne (1959) has also given a formulation of the sequencing problem where all jobs have the same routing using a "discrete linear-programming" approach. "Thus far, no attempt has been made to establish the computational feasibility of the approach in the case of large-scale realistic problems. This formulation seems, however, to involve considerably fewer variables than two other recent proposals (Bowman, Wagner, 1959), and on these grounds, may be worth some computer experimentation" (Manne, 1959, p. 1). The principal difference from Wagner appears to be in the formulation of the restrictions which assure that two jobs do not occupy the same machine at the same time. Manne's formulation deals directly with start times h_{mj} and does not introduce a measure of order-position x_{mj_k}.

4.3. Solutions through Simulations

There are in the research three approaches toward the "Monte Carlo" solution of a sequencing problem. In approach A, one first applies combinatorial analysis to reduce the number of cases which must be studied. Through the proper recognition of given routings and the equivalence of various sequences, the total number of combinations can be reduced to a number of feasible cases which contain an optimum solution. One then selects (Monte Carlo fashion) at random from this number of cases instead of from the population of all possible schedules. Proofs that the sampling will indeed approach in some sense an optimum solution are given. In this case, one can find an economic solution, in the sense of minimizing the total cost, where the total cost is a function of the added cost of a non-optimum sequence, and of the cost of the computations involved in the Monte Carlo process. In case B, no algorithm is used to eliminate non-optimum cases, but proofs are given that the sampling procedure does permit the selection of a solution as near-optimum as desired. Finally, for the more complex models, researchers resort to approach C, a general simulation. Here, they are essentially modeling the situation with a computer program and then studying the latter. Since many trials are possible with the model, it is possible to find a sequencing procedure which is better than the rule-of-thumb techniques now used in an actual shop or other situations. That a "near-optimum" solution can be found by simulation has not been demonstrated.

One "type of simulation is exploratory in that the new design [e.g., of sequencing rules] will result. . . . The second type is a form of statistical sampling . . . [in which] a given design is subjected to many conditions in order to determine its suitability. This latter has been referred to as Monte Carlo sampling. . . . Although there is no known distribution for scheduling type combinatorial problems, Monte Carlo sampling seems to offer a basis for comparing various decision rules" (Rowe, 1959, p. 34).

Elimination of non-optimum sequences. Principal research using approach A (since the original work by Akers and Freidman (Akers, 1955) is being performed by Giffler and Thompson and others at IBM's Yorktown Research Laboratory. Assuming a model described as case V, "the approach, in this work, to solve the scheduling problem is twofold. First, instead of considering all feasible schedules, which respect the technological requirements to be potentially optimum, we consider only a particular sub-set of these schedules which can be shown to include the optimum schedule(s). Second, making use of several general mathematical formulizations of scheduling processes, we are able to develop direct numerical procedures, either to generate and evaluate all schedules in the sub-set or to random sample from this sub-set. A random sampling, or Monte Carlo approach, produces a schedule which can be shown to be optimum with a given probability. This probability, by increasing the size of the sample, can be brought as close to unity as desired" (Giffler, 1959, p. 4).

Giffler and Thompson consider two problems: (1) one in which it is assumed that all operations have the same processing time, set equal to unity (called the non-numeric problem) and (2) the complete numerical problem, which is the sequencing problem in the usual form. For both of these, they develop algorithms which reduce the set to be searched for an optimum solution.

The nature of Giffler and Thompson's approach is as follows. First, they define an "active, feasible" schedule such that "no commodity is idle for a period during which it could be completely processed by a simultaneously idle facility and the processing of each commodity and facility starts in the same instant the commodity and facility will become idle." They then introduce a notion of *permissible* interchanges of tasks and *equivalent* schedules as follows. Suppose in a row of a Gantt chart there is an idle time of length p, beginning at time u, and that an operation begins at $u+s$, on facility j, and lasts q units of time. Then it is *permissible* to interchange (part of) the idle time and the job if, and only if, $q \leq p$ and the index j does not occur at the kth time interval where $u \leq k < u+s$. This concept of a permissible interchange of an idle time with a processing time may be extended to an exchange between two processing times. "Two schedules are said to be *equivalent* if, and only if, one can be obtained from the other by a sequence of permissible interchange of processing times and idle times or with each other." The relation of equivalence divides schedules into equivalent classes.

It then can be shown that "every optimal schedule is equivalent to an active optimal schedule," so that it is necessary to examine only the active schedules. The procedure may be viewed best by considering the next-follows matrix, Fig. 7.3. The problem is to fill in the diagonal subsets. A procedure for doing this is derived, which is straightforward, except when conflicts occur. A *conflict* occurs if "the proposed assignment sequence has the machine completing the job before it is physically possible it could complete it"; that is, two jobs are in conflict at a facility if neither job can be started without delaying the start of the other. Whenever a conflict occurs, two procedures are possible; one can either resolve all conflicts in all possible ways, that is, to generate the complete set of active numeric schedules, or one can choose resolutions at random. Giffler and Thompson's theoretical work is complete (it has not been described in detail here). They are now running simulation experiments. Their algorithm appears to be a promising approach which will lead economically to optimum schedules.

Monte Carlo. Efforts toward demonstrating specifically how rapidly a Monte Carlo approach will "converge" toward the optimum solution have been made by Heller and Smith. Heller considers a model equivalent to case IV, Table 7.1, in which it is assumed that all commodities have the same routing. He refers to this as the "assembly-line" type of situation. He also considers "active" sequences (assumption 8), which he refers to as *conservative* schedules (Heller, 1959, p. 12). Using conservative sequences, he deduces that the number of *different* "scheduling" times is much smaller than the number of different feasible schedules. Thus Heller uses the conservative characteristic to show that Monte Carlo methods can lead to near-optimum solution in not too many samples; whereas Giffler and Thompson use it to derive an algorithm for eliminating some sequences from consideration.

Three main results come from this [Heller's] study:

(i) the number of different schedule times is very, very much smaller than the number of feasible schedules,
(ii) the limit distribution of schedule times over the feasible schedules is asymptotically normal as the number of jobs becomes large, and
(iii) the sampling for a "good" schedule can be formulated as a statistical decision problem and estimates on the amount of sampling to obtain a good schedule can be obtained (J. Heller, NYU, letter, July 14, 1959).

The first of these results is obtained in terms of well-ordered sets, a logical deduction from the assumptions.

One result is:

$$N(T) \leq 2^{MJ} - \sum_{K=0}^{M+J-2} \frac{(MJ)!}{(MJ-K)!K!} \tag{7.7}$$

If all jobs have the same order over all machines:

$$N(T) \leq \frac{(MJ)!}{(MJ-M-J+1)!(M+J-1)!} \tag{7.8}$$

(Heller, p. 38). For example, in the first case, $N(T) < N(S)$ if $J > 4$ for $M = 5$. For $M = 5$, $J = 30$; the number of sequences $N(S) \sim 10^{162}$ while $N(T) \sim 10^{45}$.

Heller demonstrates (ii) by showing that a suitably defined random variable forms a finite Markov process. From this it is shown that the probability, p_i, that a schedule time is T_i is given for a sufficiently large J by

$$p_i \backsim \frac{1}{\sqrt{2\pi}\,\sigma_0} \exp\left[-\frac{1}{2}\left(\frac{T_i - \overline{T}}{\sigma_0}\right)^2\right] \tag{7.9}$$

a normal distribution (Heller, p. 59). He shows that it is often useful to sample from the population of sequences in which the jobs are processed in the same sequence on all machines, since, although permitting different $\mathfrak{M}_m$ may lead to a better sequence, the probability of finding it is significantly smaller. Heller reports on several simulation experiments (see Table 7.2).

TABLE 7.2

RESULTS OF SIMULATION TRIALS

(From Heller, p. 77)

M	J	Max t_{mj}	Min t_{mj}	Estimated Min T (1)	Sample Min	Min at Trials	Trials Total
2	30	9	0	133 *	133	62	
						981	
						1,187	2,000
5	30	997	3	15,851	16,350	8,083	11,250
.							
.							
.							
10	20	99	1	1,393	1,598	2,296	10,000
.							
.							
.							
10	100	9	0	577	577	1,154	3,000

* "...agrees with the minimum computed by Johnson's algorithm (Johnson 1954), although the order relation is different..." (there being several optimum sequences).

(1) From Heller, p. 23:

$$\min_{\mathcal{S}} T \geq \max_{m} \sum_{j'=1}^{J} t_{mj'} + \min_{j} \sum_{m'=1}^{m-1} t_{m'j} + \min_{j \neq j} \sum_{m'=m+1}^{M} t_{m'j}$$

where m in the second and third sums is that m giving the maximum in the first expression, and j in the third sum is that j giving the minimum in the second sum.

Result (iii) is based on a decision-theory approach, a "reasonable" sampling procedure. Estimates are made for the expected value of $T_{\min}$, using the normal approximation derived above, and of the cost of processing. Then it is shown that, if the number of samples which minimizes the (economic) risk is n_b,

$$n_b < \frac{KN^*}{2eC} \tag{7.10}$$

where K = cost of "running the assembly line" for one unit of time
C = cost of computing a sample
e = base natural log
N^* = number of different T found in the sampling

(It is possible that Heller's approach to determining the economic number of samples, combined with Giffler and Thompson's method of eliminating certain sets of sequences from those that must be considered, will lead to efficient computing procedures for economical sequences, that is, sequences as near optimum as one can afford with given computer costs.)

Another approach to demonstrating that a sampling procedure can lead to selecting a reasonable distribution and therefore to a solution as near optimum as can be afforded is presented by Smith. The method is based on

> the following rule of rational action (Bayes, Savage): If action is called for at any time, it is based on assumed probability distributions of the variates involved and of their populations, as appropriate; if additional information is obtained by experiments, the assumed probabilities are adjusted in accordance with the Bayes rule for *a posteriori* probabilities.
>
> We shall hypothesize that our observations are chosen from any of a set of *populations* P_i with *a priori* probability $g(P_i)$. Let A represent an observation or set of observations (or events): this probability is denoted by $P_i(A)$. Then by Bayes formula, the modified (*a posteriori*) probability attached to the population P_i is given by
>
> $$\bar{g}(P_i) = \frac{g(P_i)P_i(A)}{\sum_i g(P_i)P_i(A)} \tag{7.11}$$
>
> Having computed this *a posteriori* probability for all populations under consideration we then can obtain a complete (composite) *a posteriori* distribution. We then test our hypothesis by determining whether or not it would be probable for the event A to have come from a population governed by the *a posteriori* distribution (Smith, 1959, p. 1).

If so, then the complete distribution can be used as the basis of sampling decision rules.

The procedure as applied to sequencing is, in summary, this: create random sequences S^*. Consider a number G of distributions P_i, taken, for example, to be normal. Assume *a priori:* $g(P_i) = 1/G$. Then for each distribution, $P(A)$ may be determined. Calculate $\bar{g}(P_i)$ the *a posteriori* probabilities and

$$\sum_i \bar{g}(P_i)P_i \tag{7.12}$$

the *a posteriori* complete distribution. From this we can obtain the probability of a value T lying in any given interval.

Test the hypothesis to see if the distribution of the samples S^* is consistent with the *a posteriori* distribution, for example, by taking some extreme intervals and computing the probability of a value lying in each interval (using the usual 1 to 5 per cent confidence level). If the test is satisfied, the complete *a posteriori* distribution is used as the probability function for T as a function of sequences. "Having obtained the probability function, if we assume a value function and cost of further sampling, the computation of the expected gain in further sampling is straightforward" (Smith, 1959, p. 12).

General simulations. Finally, in the more complex cases, several researchers report the use of general simulations (approach C). Jackson has done this for one-machine cases with complex objectives (case I, Table 7.1). Rowe (1959) in particular has published results, and other groups are working along similar lines. These efforts are laboratory experiments and are not always intended to optimize but to give insight. One experimental procedure has been to simulate the sequencing procedures from a specific shop (where they can be determined) and to show that the simulator will predict the shop activity. Then, using a "better" procedure, the simulation is rerun and shown to give what would be better results in the actual shop. Dr. W. E. Barnes, of General Electric, Schenectady (letter, Aug. 4, 1959), using Rowe's approach, reports, "Some of the sequencing techniques under study here have been tried in a job shop of another General Electric Department. No results have been released, but in general they proved [the] validity of simulation and improved the scheduling of the shop."

Rowe's work actually considers a much larger segment of a manufacturing business than is normally represented by a sequencing model. See Fig. 7.4. In the figure "Scheduling" and "Dispatching" taken together are a form of sequencing. Breaking sequencing into two parts permits flexibility in actual shop control ("Factory monitor" due to "Perturbations" in Fig. 7.4) as well as the use of "sequential decision

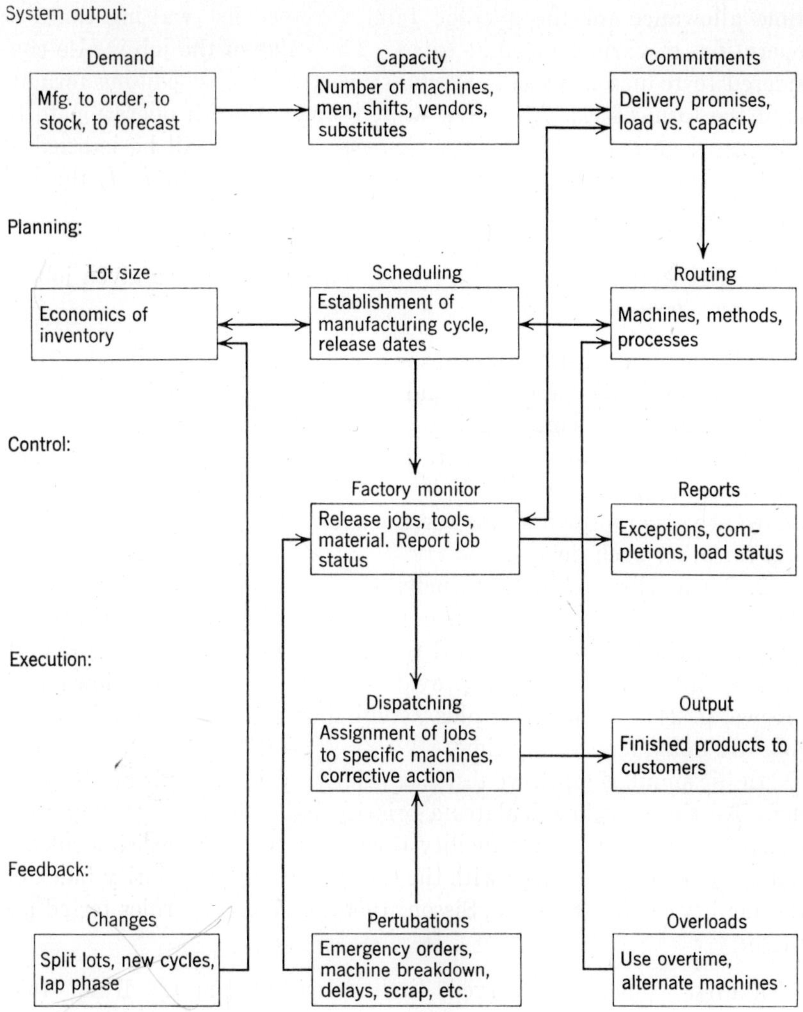

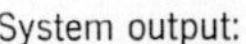

Fig. 7.4. Operating characteristics of a production system. (From Rowe, 1959, p. 3.)

rules"—the making of decisions as needed rather than in advance for an entire period. This method also permits handling situations in which new jobs and job changes periodically enter the system.

The two steps are these:

1. Jobs are first "scheduled," that is, timed, for release to the shop. This is done by taking into account due dates, processing time, and a

time allowance for the average (and variance in) waiting times of operations at various machine types. The value of the job is also considered to reduce in-process inventory costs. One scheduling formula is of the form of Eq. 7.13. (In what follows, the ith operation to be performed on a job, that is, the element m_{ij} of J_j, will be indexed as i. Let $i=n$ be the operation under consideration and $i=I$, the last operation on job j.)

$$S_i = D - \sum_{i=n}^{I}(t_i + \tau_{i-1}) - \sum_{i=n}^{I}(f_{ij} + V_i) \pm \text{constant} \qquad \text{(for a given job)} \tag{7.13}$$

S_i is the planned start-time of the operation, where D = job due time, the first sum is the processing and transportation time for operations yet to go, and the second sum is the empirically determined flow allowance (queue time) for these operations. Flow allowance f_{ij} is based on job value and machine type; V_i is a "cycle variance allowance." Flow allowance also represents time (on the average) for reprocessing rejects and for other such delays.

2. Then "dispatching is principally concerned with assigning jobs that are available in a given queue without explicitly considering other queues. Scheduling is presumed to have previously taken the overall loading into account, and provided appropriate flow allowances" (Rowe, p. 24). Scheduling plus actual shop progress determine what jobs are in a queue at any time.

In his simulation, Rowe tests six priority-rule methods of dispatching. A priority rule calculates a priority index, and a sequencing decision is made whenever a facility becomes free. The decision rule is: put the job from the queue with the smallest (largest) priority index on the facility next. (See also, Sisson, 1959, p. 17.) The rules tested are these:

i. First come, first served (index = arrival time). Rule: take smallest.

ii. First come, first served within value classes. The jobs are classified into three classes by value. High-value jobs are taken first, first come, first served within the class and so on [index = arrival time + (value class)B, where highest value-class number = 0, next highest = 1, etc., and B is some large number]. Rule: take smallest.

iii. Sequential rules of forms such as:

$$\pi_i = \frac{(t_0 - S_i) - A_i}{N^{\pm b}} \tag{7.14}$$

where π_i = index, S_i = planned start-date, t_0 = time when index is being compared, A_i = a flow allowance, N = number of operations remaining for the commodity j, b = an empirically determined constant. Rule: process job with largest algebraic π.

Another sequential rule is:

$$\pi_i = (t_0 - S_i)^c + \frac{N^b \sum_{k=i+1}^{I} t_k}{\sum_{k=i+1}^{I} t_k + \sum_{k=i}^{I} A_k - (t_0 - S_k)} \tag{7.15}$$

where c is a constant. Again the job with highest index is processed first.

The first index (Eq. 7.14) takes into account the scheduled start-date and the number of operations yet to be done; the second (Eq. 7.15) includes the effect of future processing times. Non-linear forms of the second rule can also be used.

iv. Minimum imminent processing time: process next the job in the queue with the lowest t_{mj}. This tends to minimize total expected waiting time.

v. Maximum imminent waiting time: the converse of above. This tends to reduce in-process inventory costs, if long jobs and high-value jobs are correlated.

vi. Earliest start date: take the job with the earliest planned start date (derived from a previous scheduling process) first. This is a rule in common use in industry.

Several simulation experiments were run with small samples. "A true Monte Carlo sampling . . . would require extensive runs to find the distribution of completions under many different conditions" (Rowe, p. 38). Some tentative results are these:

1. The distribution of completion times for the various rules were obtained. "Sequential" priority rules (type iii above) appeared to permit meeting due dates most closely.

2. Use of minimum imminent processing time, rule iv, does tend to minimize waiting time.

3. In using sequential rules, various flow allowances (A_i) are possible. These are derived from previous experience. A typical good allowance is the mean waiting time plus one standard deviation (assuming a Poisson distribution) for each machine group.

4. Assigning a flow allowance at each machine group according to

the value class of the commodity tends to improve sequential rules (but not first-come, first-served rules), insofar as meeting due dates and reducing costs are concerned.

5. Further improvement is possible by using the results of one simulation to develop better flow allowances in a second iteration.

The simulation was run with eighty-five machines in seventeen groups. There were some assumptions made, such as no lot-splitting, lap-phasing, or removal of job for a higher priority job.

Rowe summarizes his results thus:

> The behavior of a job lot production system is extremely complex and determination of optimal decision rules is a difficult problem. The present study was concerned with evaluating the applicability of Sequential Decision Rules to the scheduling problem. Decision rules which are based on the value of parts being processed appear to provide reduced costs while still assuring a desired completion level. . . . To insure that the planned flow rates would be carried out, a priority queue discipline was established based on correcting for deviations from the planned flow. In this way, decisions were made sequentially rather than attempting to predict the precise job assignment permutation.
>
> Monte Carlo simulation was used to evaluate the sequential rules under various shop conditions. This approach appears to provide an extremely flexible means for studying the behavior of complex systems where analytical formulations are not available. Statistical experiments can be carried out, including replication, which would otherwise be impossible directly in the factory. Computer simulation also provides a means for evaluating some of the interdependencies in a production system (Rowe, 1959, pp. 48–49).

R. W. Conway at Cornell University reports a similar study:

> With the assistance of several graduate students I am presently working on an investigation of the properties and behavior of networks of queues. We are concerned with three measures of performance: system inventory, throughput, and the distribution of unit completion times. We are investigating the effect upon these measures of different precedence (dispatching) rules; different disciplines (flexibility in routing, in specification of servor); different arrival and service distributions; and different load characteristics (intensity, balance, routing). We are interested in both steady-state and transient behavior.
>
> Most of this investigation is experimental and is being conducted by means of digital simulation (letter, June 15, 1959).

A group at UCLA (J. Jackson, Y. Kuratani, J. McKenney, R. Nelson) describe their work thus:

> We have a simulation model of a general job shop production process (general, in the sense that it is meant to include the basic common properties of such job shop production processes with no attempt made to simulate the details of any particular shop).

The model is a simulation model which takes into account the following basic factors:

1. Mean arrival rate of jobs in shop ⎫
2. Mean service time at each machine center ⎬ Load Factors
3. Shop size ⎭
4. Form of distribution of job arrivals in shop
5. Form of service time distributions
6. Job routing probability distribution
7. Lot size variation vs. operation complexity variation
8. Priority rule for job assignments (queue discipline)

The actual simulation of production deals with a continuous statistical input of jobs to the shop. The factors above will be assigned different levels with each combination of parameter values constituting one run. Output such as flow time distributions, tardiness, etc. will be recorded for each run. Experimentation will include:

1. Analyses of variance to measure effects of the factors in the model on certain output quantities.
2. Evaluation of the decision parameter (priority rules) over a range of parameter values and relative to various output quantities (letter from Nelson, June 2, 1959).

5. SUMMARY OF RESEARCH STATUS

The model described as case V in Table 7.1 might be taken as *the* sequencing model. For this model and simpler versions of it, algorithms for solution are available which lead monotonically to optimum solutions. For very simple (yet often useful) cases (I, II, III) the algorithms can be carried out in reasonable times on computers and, for small numbers of jobs, even by hand.

For cases IV and V, although the algorithms are available, computational costs are at present unreasonable for practical cases. To solve these cases one must resort to a Monte Carlo approach. Here it is of great value (1) to reduce the population from which samples are to be taken by using algorithms which isolate subsets containing an optimum solution or by statistical considerations and (2) to derive a likely form for the distribution of objective values, so that an economic sampling decision-rule can be obtained to permit minimization of total cost. These steps have all been taken, some for models more general than others. We can expect, within the next year, computational procedures for the Monte Carlo solution of models of case-V type, perhaps even with some of the assumptions (such as 3 through 7 and 9) modified or removed. These procedures should begin to find use in actual situations.

For models which are intended to represent actual situations, such as a job shop, there are no methods of finding "solutions." At the moment there are not even algorithms for reducing the size of the set of solutions to be considered. Smith provides the only method for estimating an appropriate distribution so that a cost-minimizing sampling procedure can be determined. General simulation does, however, provide a useful laboratory for the further investigation of sequencing, and as in any laboratory experimentation, practical results (better sequencing procedures) often appear, even though theoretical optimization (or even good) models are not available.

6. SUMMARY OF ENGINEERING STATUS

Operations research now covers a wide spectrum of activity: from applied mathematics, through research into operational situations, to the application of OR techniques to actual situations, i.e., industrial engineering. This chapter has dealt with a topic which is still in the research stage. It has therefore dealt with various mathematical and experimental approaches for developing general techniques for solving sequencing problems. In this section we come to the practical question: How can I improve sequencing operations in my particular situation? In spite of the fact that the research is still incomplete a number of techniques are available to the industrial engineer or his equivalent for improving a particular operation.

6.1. Possible Practical Solutions

This review of sequencing methods would indicate that, for one machine (or one bottleneck facility), the methods of Johnson (1954), Mitten (1959), and Smith (1956) will apply. An integer-linear-programming formulization (Wagner, 1959) might prove feasible, also. For small numbers of machines and not too many jobs, these methods should prove practical: Mitten (1959) (two-machine), possibly integer linear programming, and Giffler and Thompson's method with Monte Carlo resolution of conflicts in the large cases. Heller (1959) and Smith (1958) provide methods of minimizing the cost of sampling in the Monte Carlo process.

For large numbers of machines or for cases where there are many other factors such as job-parameter changes, shortages, rejects, etc. (Sisson, 1959, p. 25) experiments using simulation (as Rowe, 1959) may provide guides to good solutions.

A good engineer will, of course, adapt a method to his particular needs. Simulation is a good method of testing any sequencing procedure before its actual introduction.

6.2. Computational Requirements

Another parameter which the researcher can provide the engineer is an estimate of the number of computations required by a method as a function of M, J, range or average t_{mj}, etc. To date, researchers have been lax in providing this data. The following estimates will give some idea of the orders of magnitude involved:

Mitten's method for $M=2$ (with start- and stop-lags) requires about $5J$ computational steps (a step is one arithmetic manipulation, one comparison, etc.). Integer linear programming requires the solution of some $4J$ equations in J^2 unknowns for the three-machine case. For the M-machine case with $N(\mathcal{J}_j)=1$, the number of equations $\doteq MJ$. Manne (letter, Nov. 3, 1959) has estimated the variables in a sequencing situation with ten jobs which have to be processed on each of five machines, but not necessarily in the identical order on each machine. For Wagner's linear-programming formulation one has 600 variables and for Manne's formulation 275. Wagner's approach will be more efficient where the order of processing on each machine is constrained to be identical.

Algorithms (Wagner and Manne) for larger cases lead to apparently unmanageable numbers of variables.

Heller (1959) and Smith (1958) imply that the Monte Carlo methods require from 1,000 to 50,000 samples where each sample requires many thousands of computational steps. Giffler and Thompson's algorithm may reduce this some.

6.3. Case Histories

I have "heard" of several actual applications of sequencing theory to actual cases during the past year, but no results have been announced. General Electric is the only company name which has been mentioned, although several computing centers are concerning themselves with sequencing work for their computers. It is hoped that the use of sequencing theory in an operating situation will be described soon, even, if necessary, with disguised figures.

7. NOTE ON NOTATION

For the guidance of researchers, Table 7.3 lists the various notations which have been used. It is hoped that the compromise used in this chapter will be intelligible.

TABLE 7.3

NOTATION

(According to Various Researchers)

	Giffler and Thompson	Heller	Manne	Mitten	Sisson (earlier)	Smith	Wagner	This Chapter
Machine Index	F_j	m	—	I,II	e	i	k	m
Job Index	C_i	j	j	i	i	j	i	j
No. of Machines †	n	M	—	—	M	m	m	M
No. of Jobs †	m	J	n	n	I	n	n	J
Operation Notation	(C_i,F_j)	mjk	—	—	ij	ij	$x_{ij}^{(k)} = 0,1$	mjk
Process Time	t_i	t_{mj}	a_j	A_i,B_i	$P(i,j)$	t_{ij}	$T_{ij}^{(k)}$	t_{mj}
Sequence Completion Time	—	$t(p)$	—	C	—	C	h^*	T
Start Operation Time	—	—	x_j	—	—	S_i	$h_{ij}^{(k)}$	h_{mj}
Due Time	—	—	d_j	—	D	—	—	D
Sequence of Machines for Job (Routing)	C(matrix)	$\mathcal{J}_j$	—	—	—	—	—	J_j
Sequence of Jobs through Machine (Queue)	F(matrix)	$\mathfrak{M}_m$	—	—	—	—	—	$\mathfrak{M}_m$
Total Sequence	—	$\mathcal{S}_{JM}$	—	S	—	π	—	$\mathcal{S}$
Relationship	Next follows; Follows	Is processed before; The same job	—	—	—	—	Order position	Next follows; Order position on machine; Follows
Symbol for Relationship	$\ll$; $<$	$\prec$; $\simeq$	—	—	—	—	subscript j	$\prec\prec$; subscript k; $\prec$

† This chapter also uses $N(\;)$ to mean "number of," after Heller.

8. ACKNOWLEDGMENTS

The following were major contributors to this survey, and their assistance is certainly appreciated:

Baker, Charles T., Jr.	International Business Machines Corporation
Barnes, W. E.	General Electric Company
Conway, Richard W.	Cornell University
Fine, Gerald H.	System Development Corporation
Giffler, Bernard	International Business Machines Corporation
Heller, Jack	New York University
Jackson, James R.	University of California, Los Angeles*
Johnson, S. M.	RAND Corporation
McKenny, James	University of California, Los Angeles*
Manne, Alan S.	Cowles Foundation, Yale University
Nelson, Ross T.	University of California, Los Angeles*
Rowe, Alan J.	System Development Corporation
Sherman, Gorden R.	Purdue University
Wagner, Harvey M.	Stanford University

BIBLIOGRAPHY

Akers, S. B., and Friedman, J., "A Non-Numerical Approach to Production Scheduling Problems," *Opns. Res.,* **3,** 429–442 (1955).

Bellman, R., "Some Mathematical Aspects of Scheduling Theory," *J. Soc. Indust. and Appl. Math.,* **4,** 168–205 (1956).

Bowman, E. H., "The Schedule-Sequencing Problem," *Opns. Res.,* **7,** 621–624 (1959).

Churchman, C. W., Ackoff, R. L., and Arnoff, E. L., *Introduction to Operations Research,* John Wiley and Sons, New York, 1957, Chapter 16.

Dantzig, G. B., "Recent Advances in Linear Programming," *Mgmt. Sci.,* **2,** 131–144 (1956).

———, Fulkerson, D. R., and Johnson, S. M., "Solution of a Large-Scale Travelling Salesman Problem," *Opns. Res.,* **2,** 393–410 (1954); also see these authors' later paper on "Linear Programming, Combinatorial Approach to the Travelling Salesman Problem," *Opns. Res.,* **7,** 58–66 (1959).

Giffler, B., *Mathematical Solution of Explosion and Scheduling Problems,* IBM Research Report RC-118 (June 18, 1959), IBM Research Center, Business Systems Research, Yorktown Heights, N.Y.

———, and Thompson, G. L., *Algorithms for Solving Production Scheduling Problems,* IBM Research Report RC-118 (June 18, 1959).

* Management Sciences Research Project, supported by the Office of Naval Research.

Gomory, R. E., "Outline of an Algorithm for Integer Solutions to Linear-Programs," *Bull. Amer. Math. Soc.,* **64,** 275–278 (1958).

Gumbel, E. J., *Statistics of Extremes,* Columbia University Press, New York, 1957.

Heller, J., *Combinatorial, Probabilistic and Statistical Aspects of an* M$\times$J *Scheduling Problem,* Report NYO-2540, AEC Computing and Applied Mathematics Center, Institute of Mathematical Science, New York University, New York (Feb. 1, 1959).

Jackson, James R., "An Extension of Johnson's Results on Job Lot Scheduling," *Nav. Res. Log. Quart.,* **3,** 201–203 (1956).

———, *Some Problems in Queueing with Dynamic Priorities,* Management Sciences Research Project, UCLA, Research Report 62 (Nov. 1959).

Johnson, S. M., "Optimal Two and Three Stage Production Schedules with Setup Times Included," *Nav. Res. Log. Quart.,* **1,** 61–68 (1954).

———, "Discussion," *Mgmt. Sci.,* **5,** 299–303 (1959).

Kuratani, Yoshiro, and Nelson, R. T., *A Pre-Computational Report on Job-Shop Simulation Research,* Management Sciences Research Project, UCLA, Oct. 1959.

Manne, Alan S., *On the Job-Shop Scheduling Problem,* Cowles Foundation Discussion Paper No. 73 (May 8, 1959).

Mitten, L. G., "A Scheduling Problem," *J. of Ind. Engr.,* **10,** 131–134 (1959). This includes results of Mitten's "Sequencing in Jobs on Two Machines with Arbitrary Time Lags," *Mgmt. Sci.,* **5,** 293–298 (1959).

Nelson, R. T., *Priority Function Methods for Job-Lot Scheduling,* Management Sciences Research Project, UCLA, Discussion Paper No. 51 (Feb. 24, 1955; out of print).

Rowe, A. J., *Toward a Theory of Scheduling,* Report SP-61, System Development Corp., Santa Monica, Calif. (April 1, 1959).

Sasieni, M. W., Yaspan, A., and Friedman, L., *Operations Research: Methods and Problems,* John Wiley and Sons, New York, 1959, Chapter 9.

Sherman, G. R., "The Use of a Computer for Scheduling Students," speech before annual meeting of ORSA, Washington, D.C., May 14–15, 1959. (Purdue Statistical Computing Lab., Purdue University.)

Sisson, R. L., "Sequencing in Job Shops—A Review," *Opns. Res.,* **7,** 10–29 (1959).

Smith, W. E., "Various Optimizers for Single Stage Production," *Nav. Res. Log. Quart.,* **3,** 59–66 (1956).

———, *Applications of A Posteriori Probability,* Research Report No. 56, UCLA, Management Sciences Research Project (Sept. 19, 1958).

Wagner, H. M., "An Integer Linear-Programming Model for Machine Scheduling," *Nav. Res. Log. Quart.,* **6,** 131–140 (1959).

Wyatt, J. K., "Prediction by Computer," *Data Processing (London),* **1,** 137–141 (1959).

Recent and Related Papers

Blake, K. R., and Stopakis, W. S., *Some Theoretical Results on the Job Shop Scheduling Problem,* Report M-1533-1, United Aircraft Corp., Research Dept., East Hartford, Conn. (July 1, 1959).

Conway, R. W., Johnson, B. M., and Maxwell, W. L., "Some Problems of Digital Systems Simulation," *Mgmt. Sci.,* **6,** 92–110 (1959).

McNaughton, Robert, "Scheduling with Deadlines and Loss Functions," *Mgmt. Sci.,* **6,** 1–12 (1959) [sequencing where the objective is to meet due dates].

Chapter **8**

REPLACEMENT THEORY

Burton V. Dean

Case Institute of Technology, Cleveland, Ohio

Contents

1. INTRODUCTION

Equipment is normally replaced for two reasons. First, degradation or deterioration occurs and the equipment is subject to replacement because newer equipments offer improved, faster, or cheaper service. The problem involves (1) determining the optimum point in time or cumulative usage to replace and (2) choosing the best of available equipment to be purchased for replacement. We will refer to these as the *economic-life* and *equipment-selection* problems.

The second type of equipment replacement is required by the failure of the original unit or units. The item is no longer acceptable for its original purpose and may have negligible salvage value, such as in the case of a light bulb or an electron tube. The problem is one of determining whether to individually or group replace, and if the decision is to group replace, to determine the optimum group-replacement interval.

An item of industrial equipment may be considered as competing with alternative items for survival as it deteriorates in performance. For example, in manufacturing systems, machine tools may be transferred into lower grades of service that require less precision, reliability, or continuous service until they cannot be used economically to perform any useful function, at which point they are sold or discarded. Degradation in service for a machine tool is represented as a decline in service and in value due to better substitutes or in increased maintenance cost required to sustain a specified level of output. (See Fig. 8.1.)

1.1. The Importance of Replacement Theory

A survey conducted in 1956 by the Machinery and Allied Products Institute indicated that 54 per cent of the firms asked have staff with responsibility for conducting economic-replacement studies. A valid theory of replacement is important because it can provide the organization with a means for controlling the borrowing and expenditure of capital. In addition, operating rates and costs may be better established and controlled. For items that are subject to failure, replacement theory can offer solutions to the scheduling of equipment maintenance and the design of system-reliability problems.

Replacement theory is an important aspect of operations research

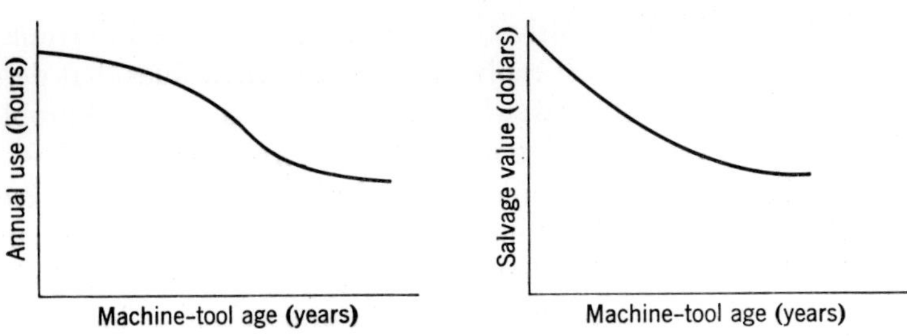

Fig. 8.1. Machine-tool degradation.

as it offers opportunities in many organizations for sizable payoffs at reasonable levels of investigative effort. As this chapter will indicate, most models of replacement problems that have been formulated can be solved by means of analytic or iterative methods. Furthermore, the information required to formulate and solve replacement models can usually be found in company records or in industrial and governmental reports. Finally, solution to replacement questions are often required by the operations researcher to solve other problems in long-range planning, product development, and capital borrowing.

Two national groups have been concerned with economic-replacement studies. One is the Machinery and Allied Products Institute and the other is the National Center of Education and Research in Equipment Policy.

1.2. Classification of Replacement Studies

This discussion will be divided into three parts:

1. *Replacement of Items That Deteriorate.* When should items be replaced (timing) and with what should the equipment be replaced (selection)?

2. *Replacement of Items That Fail.* Should all items be replaced in a group and, if so, when?

3. *Mathematics of Failure.* The mathematical theory of failure as related to the types of failures and derived functional forms, the nature of the age distribution, and methods for calculating survival probabilities.

1.3. Costs and Returns

All models presented in this chapter make assumptions concerning the nature of the relevant costs and returns. A number of studies have been performed on the sensitivity of solutions to errors in estimating parameter values. For most replacement problems, values that depend on equipment age are relevant, whereas for selection or choice problems costs that do not vary with age may be considered.

Acquisition costs are assumed to be known and may be fixed or variable with chronological time. Operating-cost rates are generally assumed to be known and to have specified functional forms. Salvage values are either considered to be negligible or specified as known functions of the equipment age. The rate of return on corporate capital investment is assumed to be either fixed or to be within a specified range of values. The rate of obsolescence of equipment is either ignored or assumed to be the same as in the past. Replacement opportunities are either discrete or continuous. Taxation and depreciation procedures are fixed. In the case of replacement timing, the allowance for depreciation will affect the direct costs and is to be considered. Failure-rate functions are generally assumed to be known and parameter values specified. As the equipment-replacement problem incorporates that of timing, the above costs and returns are expressed as functions of equipment age or cumulative service.

Typical cost and return relationships are shown in Fig. 8.2.

1.4. The Methods of Replacement Theory

The general methods of operations research have been applied to the replacement problems presented in this chapter. For an operating system requiring replacements, such as a truck fleet or a machine shop, a measure of system performance is developed that expresses the objective function of the manager in quantitative terms. This measure is generally one of the following:

1. The cost or return during a specified period of time.
2. The average cost or return per time period.
3. The present value of the discounted future costs or returns.
4. The average number of items produced or used per maintenance dollar spent.

The control variables are specified as one or more of the following:

1. The life of an item.
2. The selection of alternative items to acquire.
3. The methods or procedures for replacement or maintenance.

Consideration is seldom, if ever, given to variations from the steady-state condition of the system. Expected values are considered, and

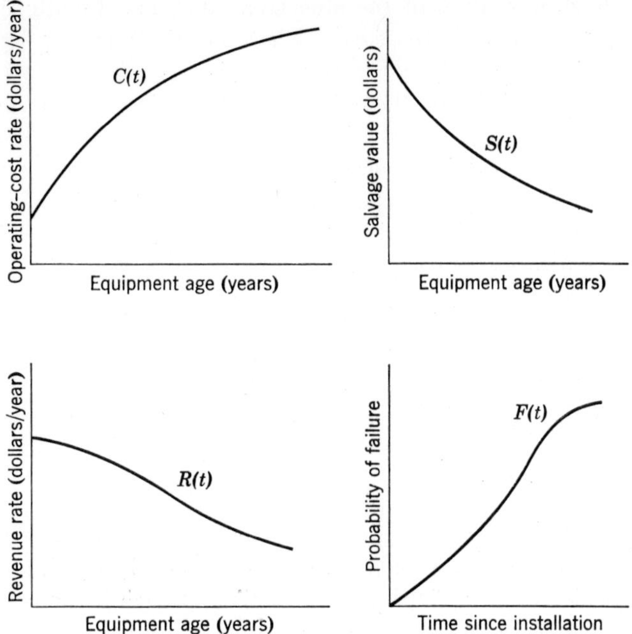

Fig. 8.2. Typical equipment-performance relationships.

the effect of deviations from the expected level of performance is not evaluated.

Deterministic models have been developed for most problems. An analytic or mathematical form is established,

$$E = E(X_i, Y_j)$$

which relates the system's performances as measured by E to the values of the control variables X_i and the uncontrollable variables Y_j. The Y_j are usually expressed in terms of the time parameter t where $Y_j(t)$ is assumed to be a known function of t.

The procedures by which the optimum value of each X_i is found depend on the nature of the E-function. In the case where E is a continuous function in each of the variables the optima are determined by the methods of the differential calculus. Wherever E is expressed as a discrete function of integral values of the time parameter, the difference calculus is applied to finding the extreme values. Dynamic programming is used in those cases where the objective function is defined as one that takes on the maximum of several values which are defined in terms of other values of the objective function. Finally, iterative methods are employed in those cases where the $Y_j(t)$ are not expressible in analytic form.

In some cases, solutions have been developed in policy form. That is, the solution is expressed as criteria for replacement or as procedures to be employed in solving a class of similar problems. In most cases the data required to solve replacement problems can be found in the history of the system's previous performance supplemented by estimates of its future performance.

2. REPLACEMENT OF ITEMS THAT DETERIORATE

2.1. *Terborgh's Model (1)*

Terborgh (1949) was the first to develop a theory for equipment replacement based on explicitly stated assumptions of a linear operating-cost function that is time-dependent with known constant parameter values. He presented procedures for comparing current equipments with challengers and descendants. The analysts before him did not include obsolescence explicitly, whereas his approach involves extrapolating the historical rate of obsolescence into the future on the principle of a uniform rate of technological discovery.

The combined cost per year E is a sum of two terms; the first increases with equipment age (operating inferiority) and the second decreases with increasing age (capital cost):

$$E=\frac{(n-1)c}{2}+\left[\frac{A-S}{n}+\frac{r}{2}(A+S)\right] \tag{8.1}$$

where c = the inferiority gradient, or the constant rate of cost accumulation due to operating inferiority

A = the acquisition cost

S = the salvage value

r = the rate of return on capital investments within the firm

n = the age of the equipment

The first term in Eq. 8.1 is the average operating-cost increase per year, since

$$\frac{0+c+2c+\cdots+(n-1)c}{n}=\frac{1}{n}\left[\frac{n(n-1)c}{2}\right]=\frac{(n-1)c}{2}$$

and the operating inferiority in the first year is zero.

The first term in the brackets of Eq. 8.1 is the average capital cost per year. The second term in the brackets is approximately the average yearly cost of money over the period calculated by taking the cost of $(A-S)$ dollars for a period of $n-1$ years, in which payments are made annually, plus the cost of borrowing S dollars for n years.

The adverse minimum, n_0, is the age that minimizes E, and thus

$$\frac{dE}{dn}=\frac{c}{2}-\frac{A-S}{2}=0$$

$$n_0=\sqrt{\frac{2(A-S)}{c}} \tag{8.2}$$

or

$$\frac{n_0 c}{2}=\frac{A-S}{n_0} \tag{8.3}$$

Thus the average increase in costs due to operating inferiority is equal to the average annual depreciation in capital at the optimum. Terborgh neglects the salvage value S and assumes that future challengers will have the same adverse minimum as the present one.

2.2. *Terborgh's Model (2)*

In a research project conducted by the Machinery and Allied Products Institute (MAPI) Terborgh extended his earlier work to cover general problems of capital investment. The reformulation and extension of the basic principles are applied to the acquisition of plant and equipment for the purposes of improving existing processes and of introducing new processes. In the published results of this work (Terborgh, 1958) Part I provides an introductory background to the subject and develops the requirements of a good approach. These include consideration of obsolescence, service values, taxes, salvage values, alternative forms of investment, and ease of application. This part states the organizational requirements for effective investment analysis and examines alternative formulas. Part II develops the theory of the MAPI system, which ranks alternative investments by the relative rate of return for the year following the decision point. Charts and forms are developed which permit the analyst to include the relevant factors. Part III applies the theory to a number of illustrative cases, giving detailed procedures for using the charts and forms. Methods for using the charts to evaluate salvage values and taxes are developed. Part IV is concerned with the problems facing top management in formulating policy affecting investment decisions in such cases as plant operating rate, tax treatment, and debt policy. The appendices present the mathematical theory for determining relative returns and for determining capital-consumption values under various depreciation rules, and the various charts. This book offers a clear-cut approach to identifying the relevant factors in investment analysis and is aimed at developing a system for ranking investment projects in order of urgency, as measured by relative return on investment. It presents the individual with the opportunity to reach replacement or acquisition decisions based on explicitly stated assumptions.

2.3. *Grant's Model*

A number of authors have simplified the cost-minimization model developed by Terborgh. Grant (1950) discusses in qualitative terms the problem of when existing equipment should be replaced on the basis of inadequacy, obsolescence, excessive maintenance, and declining efficiency. He summarizes the qualitative formulations to date and presents procedures for analyzing and reaching solutions to the economic-replacement problem where (1) more efficient equipment is introduced before replacement, (2) the value of money is constant over the life of the equipment, and (3) the annual operating costs are non-decreasing.

2.4. *Dean's Model*

Joel Dean (1951) was the first to state explicitly that capital investments for replacement purposes ought to compete with other investments the firm is capable of making. He argues that the return on investment should be used to evaluate alternative possibilities of capital investment. The combined cost for current equipment (the sum of relevant operating costs and the capital-wastage cost) is expressed as a function of equipment age. Replacement occurs when the combined costs equal the average cost per year of the new equipment plus the annual return on the capital outlay for the new equipment less the salvage value of the old equipment. The point of replacement occurs after the annual cost of the old equipment exceeds the average cost per year of the new equipment. A forecast of the latter quantity is required.

2.5. *Orenstein's Model*

An interesting result developed by Orenstein (1956) in the event of equal depreciation payments is that the economic life is independent of rate of return for an annual-cost-minimization model. Orenstein considers three costs:

1. Acquisition cost, A.
2. Annual rate of return on capital, r.
3. Linear operating cost, $F+dt$.

He defines the economic life as one that minimizes the average annual sum of the above,

$$E=\frac{A}{t}+r\frac{A}{2}+\left[Ft+\frac{t(t+1)}{2}d\right]\frac{1}{t} \tag{8.4}$$

$$\frac{dE}{dt}=-\frac{A}{t^2}+\frac{d}{2}=0$$

or

$$t_0=\sqrt{2A/d} \tag{8.5}$$

The economic life is then the value of t_0 such that

$$\frac{dt_0}{2}=\frac{A}{t_0} \tag{8.6}$$

or the average increase in operating cost is equal to the annual depreciation value of the equipment. The selection of alternative equipments would depend on the minimum values of the total average costs over the life of each. Obsolescence is considered to be introduced by increasing the interest rate, decreasing the life expectancy, or decreasing the salvage value.

2.6. Clapham's Model

A cost-minimization model that neglects opportunities for alternative investments was developed and solved by Clapham (1957). He determines the economic lives of locomotives and cars used in English coal mines by minimizing the average annual sum of capital depreciation and maintenance costs $K(t)$ where

$$K(t)=\frac{A}{t}+\frac{1}{t}\int_0^t f(x)\,dx \tag{8.7}$$

A is the acquisition cost, A/t is the annual capital depreciation, and $f(x)$ is the annual maintenance cost of equipment of age x. The solution of this model, which does not consider discounting, is found by the methods of the calculus. The minimum value of K occurs when

$$K(t_0)=f(t_0) \tag{8.8}$$

or when the average total cost to date equals the current annual maintenance cost. By verifying that the maintenance-cost function is linear in two cases,

$$f(x)=sx \tag{8.9}$$

the expression for $K(t)$ becomes the economic lot-size inventory equation. The optimum value of t is

$$t_0=\sqrt{2A/s} \tag{8.10}$$

or

$$\frac{A}{t_0}=\frac{st_0}{2} \tag{8.11}$$

and the annual depreciation payment equals the average maintenance cost for the optimum.

2.7. Smith's Model

Smith (1957) constructed an economic-equipment-replacement model that is based on maximizing the present value of all future returns V for an optimal replacement policy for truck-tractors. Consider the factors:

A = initial cost of the equipment
$S(n)$ = salvage value of the equipment after n years
r = rate of interest on capital investment
$Q(kn,t)$ = annual rate of earnings as a function of purchase time kn and age t.

The present value of net earnings is then

$$V=\sum_{k=0}^{\infty}e^{-rkn}\left\{\int_0^n Q(kn,t)e^{-rt}\,dt-A+S(n)e^{-rn}\right\} \tag{8.12}$$

where the net earnings could be written as

$$Q(kn,t)=R(kn,t)-E(kn,t)$$
$$R=\text{gross-revenue rate}$$
$$E=\text{operating-expense rate}$$

A detailed analysis was performed to determine the functional forms and parameter values of R, E, A, and S. Obsolescence was considered by forecasting future obsolescence rates from the historical values in greater payloads and engine improvements. The optimum values of n that minimized V were found to be from 5 to 6 years. The analysis indicates that, in the region of the economic life, profits are not very sensitive to the age of the equipment. Errors in estimating parameter values, as, for example, changing opportunities for investment of funds, do not seriously affect economic life. It was demonstrated that a change of the truck-tractor power unit had a significantly greater effect on profitability than did the timing of replacement.

2.8. The Model of Sandiford, Bernholtz, and Shelson

The models considered so far have assumed analytic forms for the cost functions. Sandiford, Bernholtz, and Shelson (1956) considered arbitrary values for the annual costs and developed numerical, iterative procedures for determining the economic life. They investigated replacement policies for a truck fleet which operated at a specified size and usage where only new vehicles were purchased for replacement. The measure of performance chosen was the average annual cost over the replacement interval. The optimal policy was use of that replacement interval which minimized the average annual cost, to be determined for each group of vehicles.

The total average cost C_n was considered to be the sum of capital wastage (acquisition cost less salvage value), interest, repair costs, and unserviceability costs. Values of C_n were calculated from historical data for each vehicle class by taking the cumulative averages and the minimum obtained by inspection.

The authors used historical data to obtain optimum replacement intervals. A modification was developed which assumed that the costs expected in future years for a given vehicle would be the same as the costs of current vehicles with the same age. This change increased the number of vehicle classes, as the original costs included the costs from all the years of service of each vehicle. Graphs were plotted for each truck type; the axes of these graphs were age and mileage, on which were indicated hold and sell regions. These graphs could be used to identify replacement intervals. An additional result of the reclassification of costs was that those vehicles which departed significantly from the average-cost values could be identified and repaired or removed from the system.

The method developed by V. L. Smith (1957) may be applied to this truck-fleet problem to extend this model to a dynamic one where obsolescence in capacity, fuel, and horsepower can be considered.

2.9. The Analogue of Fetter and Goodman

Fetter and Goodman (1957) have developed an electronic analogue of the equipment-replacement model and have used it to solve the cost-minimization model formulated by Terborgh as one application. In addition, a number of models are developed where the solution is that replacement interval that maximizes the present value of all future returns from the firm's use of equipment. For a single purchase of an item,

$$V_1=\int_0^T Q(t)e^{-rt}\,dt+S(T)e^{-rT}-A \tag{8.13}$$

is the present value of future returns, and for an optimal policy,

$$\frac{dV_1}{dT}=Q(T)e^{-rT}-rS(T)e^{-rT}+S(T)e^{-rT}=0$$

and the optimal solution satisfies the equation

$$Q(t_0)=rS(t_0)-S'(t_0) \tag{8.14}$$

For a single purchase, the economic life is the age at which the net annual earnings are equal to the interest on the salvage value plus the loss in salvage value.

For an assumed infinite chain of equipment replacements at equal time intervals $T, 2T, \cdots$, the present value of future earnings is given by

$$V=V_1\sum_{j=0}^{\infty}e^{-jrT}=\frac{V_1}{1-e^{-rT}} \tag{8.15}$$

Equating dV/dT to zero yields

$$Q(t_0)=rS(t_0)-S'(t_0)+\frac{r}{1-e^{-rt_0}}V_1 \tag{8.16}$$

The optimal replacement interval for an infinite chain is that interval for which the net annual earnings are equal to the interest on the salvage value plus the loss in salvage value plus the interest on the present value of all future earnings of a single machine.

For a firm which is interested in the acquisition of one machine, and wishes to minimize the present value of future costs with a specified productive capacity, the cost may be given by

$$C_1=A-S(T)e^{-rT}+\int_0^T E(t)e^{-rt}\,dt \tag{8.17}$$

and the optimum life is given by the value of t_0 such that

$$E(t_0)=S'(t_0)-rS(t_0) \tag{8.18}$$

For an infinite chain of equipment replacements at times $T, 2T, \cdots$ the present value of future costs is given by

$$C=C_1\sum_{j=0}^{\infty}e^{-jrT}=\frac{C_1}{1-e^{-rT}} \tag{8.19}$$

and the optimum life is given by the value of t_0 such that

$$E(t_0)+rS(t_0)-S'(t_0)=\frac{r}{1-e^{rt_0}}C_1 \tag{8.20}$$

A machine should be replaced when the expenses plus interest on salvage value plus the loss in salvage value equal the interest on the capitalized value of future costs. For various alternatives the minimum values of C can be compared and the one selected which yields the least value.

The model of the equation for C was selected for analogue solution and the analogue computer yielded solutions for various functional forms of the cost functions and determined sensitivity of equipment-replacement decisions to changes in parameter values. For small values of the operating costs, the economic life is not sensitive to operating-cost errors. Errors in predicting the rate of return on alternative funds for investment affect the importance of all other variables, and for $r>0.3$, replacement decisions are insensitive to the values of the other parameters. Overestimating salvage values led to earlier replacement intervals than the optimal value where the cost of error is dependent on the rate of return.

2.10. Rifas's Model

Rifas (1957) has developed a discrete-replacement theory that compares alternative policies for replacement on the basis of discounted value of all future costs associated with each policy. For periods of equal duration, $i=1,2,\cdots$, operating costs, $C_1, C_2, \cdots$, acquisition cost, A, and a replacement interval of n periods,

$$K_n=\frac{A+\sum_{i=1}^{n}[c_i/(1+r)^{i-1}]}{1-[1/(1+r)]^n} \tag{8.21}$$

where K_n is the present value of all future costs, and the cost of money is $100r$ per cent per period. Equation 8.21 assumes an infinite chain of equipment purchases, negligible salvage value at the end of n periods, and that the costs are incurred at the beginning of the period.

For monotonically increasing costs the optimal value of the replacement interval that minimizes K_n is determined, using the difference calculus, and the optimal policy is as follows:

1. Do not replace if the next period's cost is less than the weighted average of previous costs.
2. Replace if the next period's cost is greater than the weighted average of previous costs.

The weighted average of previous costs for a given period n is to be computed as

$$\frac{A+\sum_{i=1}^{n-1} C_i X^{i-1}}{1+\sum_{i=1}^{n-1} X^i} \tag{8.22}$$

where $X=\dfrac{1}{1+r}$

For each proposed new equipment with known specified $\{C_i\}$ the minimum value of K_n is to be calculated. The present equipment is replaced with the best available substitute when its operating cost per period reaches the least weighted average cost of using the new equipment.

2.11. Computational Procedure of Sasieni, Yaspan, and Friedman

Sasieni, Yaspan, and Friedman (1959) present a procedure for computing the economic life of a machine that assumes the purchase of only a single item. The present value of future costs is the numerator in the expression for K_n in the Rifas model, in Eq. 8.21, expressed as

$$P(n)=A+\sum_{i=1}^{n} C_i X^{i-1} \tag{8.23}$$

Since $P(n)$ increases as n increases, the company is considered to set up an annual amount y in the form of an annuity such that

$$P(n)=y+yX+yX^2+\cdots+yX^{n-1}=\frac{y(1-X^n)}{1-X} \tag{8.24}$$

The optimal value of the replacement interval n is that which minimizes y, or which minimizes

$$\frac{P(n)(1-X)}{1-X^n} \quad \text{or} \quad F(n)=\frac{P(n)}{1-X^n} \tag{8.25}$$

since $1-X$ is a constant. An iterative method is presented which yields the economic life based on the condition that $F(n)$ be a minimum,

$$\Delta F(n-1)<0<\Delta F(n)$$

where $\Delta F(n)$ is the difference operator, $\Delta F(n)=F(n+1)-F(n)$.

2.12. Bellman's Model

Bellman (1955) constructs a dynamic-programming model for equipment replacement that begins by considering that at each time t there are two possible courses of action. Either a machine is kept for another period or it is replaced by a purchased machine. He defines

$f(t)=$ over-all return from a machine of age t employing an optimal replacement policy

In the event that the machine is kept, $f(t)=f_K(t)$, where

$$f_K(t)=r(t)-u(t)+af(t+1) \tag{8.26}$$

for an output-return function $r(t)$, maintenance-cost function $u(t)$, and discount factor a. In the second case, $f(t)=f_P(t)$, where

$$f_P(t)=s(t)-p+r(0)-u(0)+af(1) \tag{8.27}$$

with salvage-value function $s(t)$ and acquisition cost p. Hence the expression for f is:

$$f(t)=\max_{0\leq t}[r(t)-u(t)+af(t+1),s(t)-p+r(0)-u(0)+af(1)] \tag{8.28}$$

The value t_0 that maximizes f, is found by means of successive substitution in an expression involving $r(t)$, $u(t)$, $s(t)$, p, and a. Extensions of the dynamic-programming technique to the problems of replacement of over-age machines and technological improvement are also presented. For the over-age machine, whose age (T) is greater than t_0, Eq. 8.28 is modified so that the maximization is taken for $T\leq t$.

2.13. Elmaghraby's Stochastic Conversion

Elmaghraby (1958) has indicated the need for considering obsolescence of equipment and, therefore, for converting deterministic models into ones that are stochastic. His method of converting an exact-replacement model into a stochastic one involving uncertain demand is to assign confidence weights to the demand parameter in accordance with company expectation and to compute a replacement policy that maximizes the expected return.

2.14. Barber's Probabilistic Returns

Barber (1958) has presented a method for introducing probabilistic functions for returns, as forecasted by manufacturing engineers, to determine the economic feasibility of purchasing an automatic machine. By weighting the possible payoffs with the probability of achieving the payoff, and comparing the expected return with the rate of return on other corporate investments, which machine to purchase is decided.

3. REPLACEMENT OF ITEMS THAT FAIL

The principal objective in this type of problem is to determine the amount and timing of replacement (or maintenance) of equipments that have not failed but which are subject to increasing opportunities for failure as cumulative usage or age increases. The problems are:

1. Should a group of items be replaced in entirety or should they be individually replaced upon failure?
2. If group replacement is the best policy, what is the optimum group-replacement interval?
3. How much and how often should preventive maintenance be performed?

To solve the first problem the cost of group replacement is compared with that of individual replacement upon failure. Whenever group replacement leads to reduced costs, the optimum group-replacement interval is computed using the differential calculus for continuous-cost functions and the difference calculus for discrete-cost functions. The same methods may be used to solve preventive-maintenance problems. Dynamic programming may also be used to solve group-replacement and preventive-maintenance problems.

3.1. Rifas's Model

Rifas (1957) develops and solves the group-replacement problem where the failure rates and costs of unit replacement after failure and group replacement are known. Letting

C_1 = unit cost of group replacement
C_2 = unit costs of individual replacement after failure
$f(X)$ = expected number of failures in the Xth period
N = number of units in the group

the total cost of group replacement after t periods will be given by

$$K(t) = NC_1 + C_2 \sum_{X=1}^{t-1} f(X) \tag{8.29}$$

where the first term is the cost of group replacement and the second term is the cost of replacing the individual items upon failure.

He selects as the measure of performance, the average total cost per period, $F(t) = K(t)/t$. The replacement-cost function may be represented graphically as in Fig. 8.3. At the optimum value of t, t_0, the function $F(t)$ has the property that

$$\Delta F(t_0 - 1) < 0 < \Delta F(t_0)$$

where Δ is the difference operator defined as

$$\Delta F(t) = F(t+1) - F(t)$$

Applying the above criteria to the cost equation for $F(t)$ results in the following two conditions on t_0:

$$C_2 f(t_0) > \frac{NC_1 + C_2 \sum_{X=1}^{t_0-1} f(X)}{t_0} \tag{8.30}$$

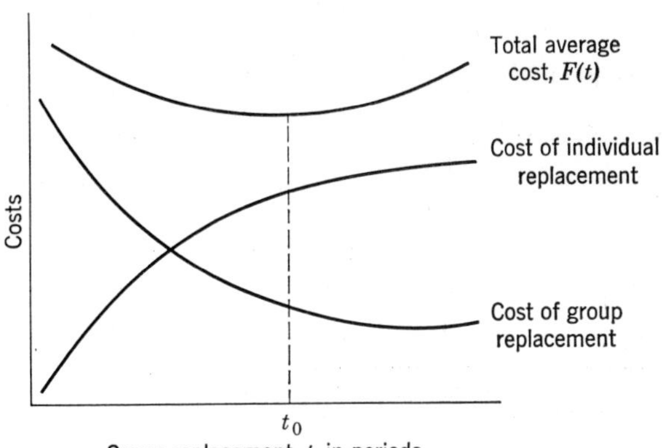

Fig. 8.3. Replacement costs.

and

$$C_2 f(t_0-1) < \frac{NC_1 + C_2 \sum_{X=1}^{t_0-2} f(X)}{t_0-1} \tag{8.31}$$

The optimum group-replacement policy is the following:

1. Group replace at the end of the tth period if the cost of individual replacement for the tth period is greater than the average cost per period through the end of t periods.
2. Do not group replace at the end of the tth period if the cost of individual replacements at the end of the tth period is less than the average cost per period through the end of t periods.

3.2. Extension by Rutenberg and Gupta

Rutenberg and Gupta (1959) have extended the results of Rifas to the case where the form of the failure-density function $f(X)$ is known but the parameters are unknown. The policy to follow in this case is not to set the group-replacement interval in advance, but to observe the cumulative number of failures at successive time intervals and to use this information to decide whether to group replace or to continue to replace individually. The policy is one of group replacing at the time of a failure if the expected cost through the next failure is higher than the average cost to date. Costs of group replacement are reduced more when this policy is followed than when the fixed-replacement rule is used, because of uncertainty in estimating the number of failures.

3.3. Rutenberg's Model

Rutenberg (1960) has constructed a dynamic-programming model for group replacement. He considers the possibility of group or individual replacement at any point, in time, when an individual failure has occurred. Suppose that failures $1,2,\cdots,n,\cdots$ have occurred at times $t_1,t_2,\cdots,t_n,\cdots$ and let

g_i = minimum average cost obtained by following an optimum policy of replacement through the ith failure $(i=1,2,\cdots,n,\cdots)$

Then

$$g_1 = \min\left\{\frac{NC_1}{t_1}, g_2\right\}$$

$$g_2 = \min\left\{\frac{NC_1 + C_2}{t_2}, g_3\right\}$$

$$\vdots$$

$$g_{n-1} = \min\left\{\frac{NC_1 + (n-2)C_2}{t_{n-1}}, g_n\right\} \tag{8.32}$$

define a set $\{g_i\}$. The solution of the set yields values $\{t_i^*\}$ which are the critical values such that individual replacement is optimal whenever $t_i \leq t_i^*$ and group replacement is optimal at the first point where $t_i > t_i^*$.

3.4. Some Illustrative Industrial Problems

Sasieni, Yaspan, and Friedman (1959) have considered a number of illustrative replacement problems in industry. They illustrate procedures for determining the hiring policies in replacing airline stewardesses, given the present age distribution and survival distribution. They determine the break-even prices for a battery manufacturer with a fixed guarantee policy and a known battery-failure distribution. They determine the optimum adjustment interval for a machine with a specified linear operating cost with no adjustment, a known cost-density function with adjustment, and a known adjustment cost.

3.5. Sasieni's "Bladder" Replacement Policy

Sasieni (1956) has investigated a replacement problem in the tire-manufacturing industry where a machine is capable of making two items at a time. The solution is a "bladder" replacement policy that minimizes the total cost of replacement divided by the number of good tires produced. Because bladder failures can result in (1) replacing the bladder, (2) scrap produced if failure occurs during the manufacturing period, (3) a machine stoppage, or (4) lost production time if the bladder is replaced during the production shift, there are four costs C_1, C_2, C_3, C_4 associated with each of the above.

Letting $h(i,j)$ represent the probability that a machine is in state (i,j), where i and j are the ages of the individual bladders in terms of numbers of good tires produced, the average cost of purchasing bladders per replacement cycle is

$$C_1[2h(0,0)+\sum_{j=1}^{t}h(0,j)] \tag{8.33}$$

the average cost of scrap produced is

$$C_2\sum_{i,j}h(i,j)(p_i+p_j) \tag{8.34}$$

the average cost of machine stoppages is

$$C_3\sum_{j=0}^{t}h(0,j) \tag{8.35}$$

and the average cost of lost production time is

$$C_4\sum_{i,j}^{t}h(i,j)(p_i+p_j-p_ip_j) \tag{8.36}$$

where t is the bladder-replacement interval and p_i is the probability that a bladder will fail at age i. The optimal (m,n) policy was found, which specified:

1. The point to replace a bladder after a specified age m (number of good tires produced) of the bladder.
2. When a machine is stopped to replace one bladder, replace the second one if its age is greater than n.

3.6. Dreyfus's Extension

Dreyfus (1957) has extended the bladder-replacement problem stated by Sasieni to one taking into account the totality of possible policies, rather than one following the two-stage (m,n) rule, by considering a dynamic-programming approach. He defines

$f_n(i,j)$ = total expected cost of producing n additional tires, where bladder 1 is of age i and bladder 2 is of age j, and where an optimal replacement policy is used (8.37)

A functional equation is derived for f_n in terms of $f_{n-1}, f_{n-2}, p_i, p_j$, and the costs C_1, C_2, C_3, and C_4. The equation for f_n is evaluated for expected costs of each admissible decision as the sum of the immediate cost plus the expected cost of optimally producing the remaining tires.

Using the parameter values of Sasieni, the dynamic programming results agree closely with Sasieni's (m,n) ploicy. But with different acquisition costs, the dynamic-programming approach yields a different policy at a reduced minimum cost. The advantage of the dynamic-programming approach is that it does not involve any assumption about the form of the optimal policy.

3.7. *Pennycuick's Replacement-Timing Model*

Pennycuick (1956) develops a replacement-timing model that does not consider costs but determines the number of replacements for a specified repair rule. The equipments analyzed are radios used by a British army division. Analysis of available data showed that in general the repair rates were increasing, suggesting wear-out as a major cause. It was not possible to determine the statistical distribution of periods between repairs for either new or current equipment. Knowing the number of sets sent to repair in each four-week period, the measure of performance was taken as the percentage increase in unserviceability between periods one year apart. The desired repair rates were specified to be those of the previous year; the problem was to determine the number and timing of units of each type of equipment to be replaced necessary to satisfy the repair-rate criteria. For a given class of equipment let

m = mean time to repair all existing sets
m_1 = mean time to repair the worst n per cent, $n = 100w$
m_2 = mean time to repair stock after replacing worst n per cent with new units

$$r_n = \frac{m_1}{m}$$

Pennycuick assumes that the life of the new sets is large compared to the life of the old sets and that the mean life of the n per cent removed is not less than n per cent of the mean life of the existing stock. The mean life of the best $100(1-w)$ per cent $= [(1-wr_n)/(1-w)]m$. Injection of the new sets decreases the number sent to repair each period by a factor $1-w$, so that

$$\frac{m_2}{m} = \frac{1-wr_n}{(1-w)^2}$$

Now $0 \leq r_n \leq 1$, and for $r_n = 1$, injection of new sets has the least effect. On the other hand the greatest effect occurs for $r_n = 0$ (all existing sets are useless). Normally r_n increases with n, and w never exceeds r_n. As a typical value $r_n = (1+w)/2$ was selected. A table of m_2/m was constructed using w and r_n as the variables ($r_n \geq w$). It was then possible to estimate the decrease in mean life over the year and hence determine the increase in mean life (by percentage) required to achieve the desired repair rate. By considering the effect of time on the decrease in mean life the number and timing of future replacements were estimated.

3.8. The Multistage Replenishment Model of Fennell and Oshiro

Fennell and Oshiro (1956) have constructed and solved a theoretical model for studying multistage-replenishment systems. An item, after installation into the system, may occupy any one of the following states:

1. A number of operational phases.
2. A number of routine or emergency overhaul phases.
3. Exit from the system.

Associated with the passage from one state i to another state j is a transition probability p_{ij}, where it is assumed that the p_{ij} are time-independent and do not depend on the states prior to the ith one. The elements p_{ij} form a square matrix P, and the elements $p_{ij}^{(n)}$ of the matrix product P^n are the probabilities that an item in the initial state i will occupy state j after n time units. The questions answered are:

1. How many items will be operational in each of n time periods?
2. How many items will be in overhaul in each of n time periods?
3. How many items must be introduced into the system, at specified intervals, to meet current and future operational requirements?

Let $\phi_n = \sum_j p_{ij}^{(n)}$, where summation is over operational states, be the probability that an item which is in state i initially will be in an operational state (one of the j's) after n time periods. Then for operating requirements $G_0, G_1, G_2, \cdots$ in periods $n = 0,1,2,\cdots$ the required inputs into the system are given as solutions of the following system of linear equations:

$$\begin{aligned} &N_0\phi_0 = G_0 \\ &N_1\phi_0 + N_0\phi_1 = G_1 \\ &N_2\phi_0 + N_1\phi_1 + N_0\phi_2 = G_2 \\ &\cdots\cdots\cdots\cdots \end{aligned} \tag{8.38}$$

The answers to questions 1 through 3 can be found by computing the various ϕ_n and using the solutions $\{N_i\}$ of the above system (Eqs. 8.38). The airline-stewardess problem solved by Sasieni, Yaspan, and Friedman (1959) can be considered as a special case of the above.

3.9. Queuing Theory Applied to Replacement: Taylor and Jackson

Taylor and Jackson (1954) have applied queuing theory to the replacement of spare parts for aircraft engines. In case of failure an engine is removed from the operational aircraft, sent to a repair facility where it may wait for service, is repaired, and then is transported to a stock area where it may wait to be installed in an aircraft. Their method uses the differential equations developed by Feller (1949) to determine expected waiting time and number of engines waiting for service, in service, and waiting for installation. It must be noted that the method of Fennell and Oshiro (1956) can also be used to solve this problem.

3.10. Senju's Preventive-Maintenance Models

Senju (1957) has constructed a number of models for solving preventive-maintenance problems in the event of uncertainty about time of machine breakdown. He considers the total cost of maintenance as the sum of cost of replacement with failure (a_1 is the unit cost) and cost of replacement without failure (a_2 is the unit cost). The total cost of maintenance, without a preventive-maintenance policy, during a specified time period T, is

$$C_1 = a_1\left(\frac{T}{m}\right) \tag{8.39}$$

where $m = \int_0^\infty x\,f(x)\,dx$, and $f(x)$ is the probability-density function of survival times. In the case of preventive maintenance performed at time t, since the previous repair, the total cost is

$$C_2 = \frac{a_1 p + a_2 q}{\int_0^t x\,f(x)\,dx + tq}\,T \tag{8.40}$$

where $p = \int_0^t f(x)\,dx$ and $q = 1 - p$. The minimum value of C_2 occurs at time t_0 where

$$t_0\,f(t_0) + \frac{1}{q}\,f(t_0)\int_0^{t_0} x\,f(x)\,dx - p = \frac{a_2}{a_1 - a_2} \tag{8.41}$$

4. MATHEMATICS OF FAILURE

The fundamental mathematics and statistics of renewal and replacement processes have been developed over a long period of time and have been intensively investigated during the last fifteen years. With the recent development of operations research these problems have also been brought to the attention of economists and engineers. The types of problems involved may be classified in three categories:

1. To characterize the survival probability distribution and to determine methods for estimating the relevant parameter values.
2. To determine the age distribution and mean replacement rate of items that are subject to individual replacement upon failure.
3. To predict the effect of system design and development upon system reliability.

This section reviews results in each of these areas as they affect replacement theory. Only a small sample of the important studies in each area is presented.

4.1. Survival Probabilities

Equipment that is subject to failure may be characterized by a survival curve defined by

$$P(t) = \text{probability that the item is operating for a time } t \text{ after its installation}$$

where $P(0)=1$, and $1 \geq P(t) \geq 0$ for $t \geq 0$

A survival curve may take the exponential form

$$P(t) = e^{-At} \qquad (A \geq 0) \tag{8.42}$$

or the more general form described in the curve shown in Fig. 8.4.

The rate of failure $f(t)$ is defined in the following way:

$$f(t)\,dt = \text{the probability that the item which has not failed up to time } t \text{ will fail between } t \text{ and } t+dt$$

Now the probability that an item will survive to a time $t+dt$ is given by

$$P(t+dt) = P(t) + P'(t)\,dt$$

and since $P(t+dt) = P(t)[1-f(t)\,dt]$, we have

$$f(t) = -\frac{P'(t)}{P(t)} \tag{8.43}$$

The probability that a new item will fail between times t and $t+dt$ is given by

$$P(t)\,f(t)\,dt = -P'(t)\,dt$$

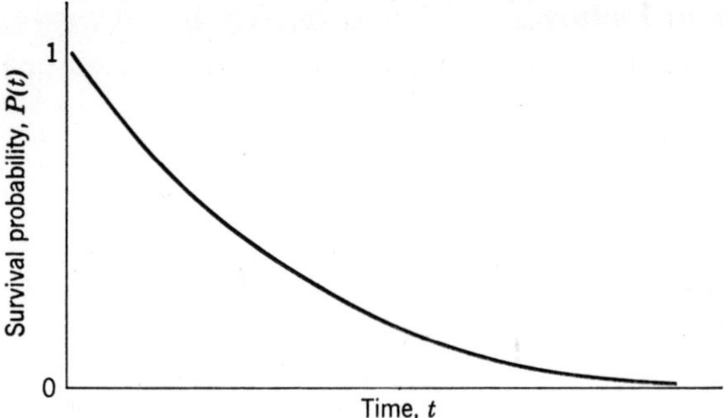

Fig. 8.4. Survival probability.

and thus the mean time to failure for a new item is given by

$$T = \int_0^\infty tP(t)\,f(t)\,dt = \int_0^\infty -tP'(t)\,dt$$

$$T = \int_0^\infty P(t)\,dt \tag{8.44}$$

From Eq. 8.44 the mean time to failure for a new item is the area under the survival curve. If an item has survived to a time t_1, the mean time to failure is given by

$$T(t_1) = \int_{t_1}^\infty \frac{P(t)\,dt}{P(t_1)} \tag{8.45}$$

In the exponential case,

$$P(t) = e^{-At}$$

$$f(t) = A$$

$$T(t_1) = \frac{1}{A}$$

whence the failure rate is constant and the life expectancy is the reciprocal of the mean failure rate regardless of the age of the item. In this case preventive maintenance and group replacement are not optimal policies.

4.2. Types of Failure

As discussed by many authors, there are three types of failures:

1. Initial failures.
2. Random failures.
3. Wear-out failures.

In some equipments all three types are present in successive periods, the first being associated with failures due to defective construction or design, the second being associated with random or chance events, and the third caused by wear and tear on the equipment.

To overcome initial failures, an item is used under test conditions for a period s, and at the end of the break-in period, the new survival curve is given by

$$P^*(t) = \frac{P(t+s)}{P(s)} \tag{8.46}$$

and the new life expectancy is given by

$$T^*(t) = T(t+s) \tag{8.47}$$

where t is measured from the end of the break-in period. Usually the break-in period results in $T^*(t) > T(t)$.

4.3. Life Tables on Industrial Equipment

The first year of published life tables on industrial equipment was 1903. In that year Alvord published life tables of forty-eight waterworks pumps and thirty-two waterworks boilers. In 1910, the New York Telephone Company presented detailed records of the life experience of aerial, underground, and submarine cables. Kurtz (1930) was the first to construct a probabilistic model for determining life tables. He fitted a Pearson Type VII curve to historical data on telegraph-pole life records.

4.4. Some Applications

Kao (1955) has demonstrated the applicability of the Weibull distribution for failure of electron tubes. Acheson (1956) has presented a general discussion of different types of failure-rate curves. Goodman (1953) developed statistical procedures for measuring and comparing items of alternative equipments without recording failures of individual items. Armstrong (1956) applied standard statistical techniques such as correlation, sampling, and hypothesis testing to determine causes of equipment failure in a chemical plant. Lotka (1939) was the first to investigate the mathematics of replacement for the Metropolitan Life Insurance Company in a series of papers beginning in 1922.

4.5. *Rifas's Computational Procedure*

Rifas (1957) has developed a procedure for calculating the number of units failing in a time interval t for an initial number of items N as

$$f(t)=N\{p(t)+\sum_{x=1}^{t-1}p(x)p(t-x)+\sum_{b=2}^{t-1}\sum_{x=1}^{b-1}p(x)p(b-x)p(t-b)+\cdots\} \quad (8.48)$$

where $p(x)$ is the probability of failure at age x and each sum is the probability for exactly one failure, two failures, three failures, etc. $f(t)$ is calculated for an illustrative case using Eq. 8.48 and is compared with a Monte Carlo calculation for a sample of three-hundred items.

Rifas (1957) also presents a matrix method for computing the rate of replacement. Let

$$V=\{v_{ij}\} \quad (8.49)$$

be the matrix component of transition probabilities where

v_{ij} = the probability that a unit at age i will be transformed into a unit at age j in the next period

Thus

$$v_{ij}=0 \quad \text{if} \quad j\neq 0 \text{ and } j\neq i+1$$

and

$$v_{i,0}+v_{i,j+1}=1$$

If A_n is the row vector which gives the age distribution of the units at the beginning of time period n,

$$A_n=A_{n-1}V=A_{n-2}V^2=\cdots=A_2V^{n-2}=A_1V^{n-1} \quad (8.50)$$

Now

$$\lim_{n\to\infty} V^n=V^* \quad (8.51)$$

and for n sufficiently large,

$$A_n=A_1V^* \quad \text{and} \quad A_{n+1}=A_1V^* \quad (8.52)$$

so that $A_n=A_{n+1}$, which states that a stable age distribution is obtained. This result has been proved by Feller (1941), who also presents a method for computing the age distribution.

4.6. Feller's Distribution of Ages

Feller (1941) has shown that for individual replacement the number of items to be replaced per unit of time will approach

$$U_t = \frac{N}{T} \tag{8.53}$$

where N is the number of items and T is the mean item life. The age distribution will approach

$$V_k(t) = \frac{N}{T} P_k \tag{8.54}$$

where $V_k(t)$ = number of items of age k at time t
P_k = probability of survival to age k

4.7. Railroad Equipment Failures: Crane and Brown

Crane and Brown (1954) have classified railroad-equipment failures as

1. Wear-out—an item fails because of usage or aging.
2. Chance—fixed probability of failure in a specified time interval characterized by exponential survival probability as a function of time.
3. Initial—failure occurs during the initial period because of a flaw in the equipment.

The first type of failure is analyzed as susceptible to preventive maintenance. An economic maintenance policy is determined as one that minimizes the sum of inspection costs, replacement costs with no failure, and replacement costs with failure.

The problem is extended to that of a system with serially connected components, where the failure of any component results in a system failure, and the probability of survival is thus the product of the component survival probabilities. Equipment reliability is a monotonically decreasing function of the number of components. If components are replaced as they fail, a steady state is ultimately reached and a uniform rate of replacement is achieved. However, an economic operation is one that combines the replacement of two or more components at the same time. An extension of the dynamic-programming approach used by Dreyfus may prove fruitful.

4.8. *Reliability of Aircraft Radar*

Boodman (1953) has analyzed the reliability of aircraft radar, considering failures as being of three types: initial, wear-out, and random. It was found that radar-equipment failure times were given by the same exponential distribution under both normal and combat conditions,

$$P(t)=e^{-At}$$

Total-system failure rate was expressible as the sum of component failure rates. Equipment reliability was found to decrease with system complexity as measured by number of components.

Increasing the reliability of a chance-failure system is an important problem. The development of maintenance procedures can only be applied to problems of wear-out failures, whereas in chance-failure systems only better equipment or varying the environment are solutions.

Stoller (1958) has developed failure models for equipment that generalize Boodman's exponential failure function. If an equipment has an exponential reliability formula

$$P(t)=e^{-At}$$

where $P(t)$ is the probability that the equipment will function in a specified way in the time interval $[0,t]$, then under k successive cycles of operation, of duration $t_1,t_2,\cdots,t_k$, the reliability of the equipment is given by

$$P\left(\sum_{i=1}^{k} t_i\right)=\exp[-A\sum_{i=1}^{k} t_i] \tag{8.55}$$

In the case of equipment subject to stress intervals, $E_1,E_2,\cdots,E_k$, where during each interval the equipment is susceptible to a particular type of failure, Stoller shows that

$$P\left(\sum_{i=1}^{k} t_i\right)=\exp[-A_0\sum_{i=1}^{k}(t_i+A_1k)] \tag{8.56}$$

where the expression within the brackets, on the right side of Eq. 8.56, depends on the number of on-off cycles and the cumulative operating time. The parameters in the above equation may be interpreted as follows. The probability that equipment does not fail during k trials is

$$(S^k)\exp[-A_0\sum_{i=1}^{k} t_i] \tag{8.57}$$

where S is the probability of stress failure not occurring during the ith trial, $\exp(-A_0 t_i)$ is the probability that the equipment does not fail during the ith trial after a time t_i, and $A_1 = -\log_e S$. A method for evaluating the parameters A_0, A_1 is presented. The model was applied to failure data of airborne electronic systems.

4.9. Weiss's Treatment of a Complex System

Weiss (1956) considers a complex system which in the course of development is to be tested n times under realistic environmental conditions. Improvements are to be made in the system between tests so that, although at each stage the hardware is similar to that used in preceding stages, all n test items will differ in some significant way. A test is to be conducted to a specified time unless the item fails. The basic survival density function is assumed to be negative exponential in the test time where the parameter of this density function is the reciprocal of the mean time to failure. It is assumed that each observation comes from such a distribution but that all n items will have different mean failure times owing to successive changes in the equipment.

There will be present in the system several causes of failure, each of which, in general, is associated with a different mean time to failure. Those causes with the smaller means will be detected first and remedial action will be taken to remove them. As the series of tests proceeds, the mean failure time of the system will be lengthened and consequently the reliability will be increased. It is assumed that the mean time to failure increases by a *constant* percentage on each trial. By means of the theory of maximum likelihood, estimates of the parameters of this assumed function are obtained. A growth curve for reliability and a method for estimating magnitudes of errors are developed.

5. CONCLUSIONS

The effect of replacement timing, selection, and method decisions is an important factor in the efficient design and operation of most systems. Replacement decisions are usually important in the operation of those processes that are undergoing rapid technological change or where the return from alternative investments is large. Yet the development of a theory of replacement is only ten years old.

The actuarial theory of renewal and replacement and the mathematical theory of failure have been developed over the past sixty years. Today, this aspect of the theory is related to the characterization of a process as one of an established class and the estimation of the values of the relevant functional parameters. However, only in a few simple situations have a number of elementary replacement models been constructed and solved and optimal replacement policies determined. Some replacement decision rules that are in use and which are *not* based on the development and solution of a mathematical model are:

1. Replace when equipment is fully depreciated.
2. Replace when the unit cost of production is a minimum.
3. Replace when equipment is worn out.

These can be compared to those derived in the studies cited in this chapter. The rules above have *not* been established as solutions to any of the elementary replacement models. One may conjecture that in spite of their popularity and wide use they would not be optimal in any situation.

Three areas of significant difference occur in the replacement models developed to date:

1. The use of different measures of system performance.
2. The use of different mathematical techniques for model representation and solution.
3. The recent development of probabilistic replacement models.

All replacement models have used as a measure of performance an expected or average value. These are described in the Introduction of this chapter and, in general, are adequate. However, deviations from the expected value have not been considered and the costs of transient behavior of the system are not included in the steady-state analysis.

No new mathematical techniques or tools have been developed in the economic theory of replacement. The principal results in the form of optimal replacement policies have been obtained through the use of standard optimization techniques involving the differential and difference calculus and dynamic programming. With the development of stochastic models, statistical methods will come to be employed.

In almost all replacement studies only exact models have been developed, for which it is assumed that all cost and return functional forms and parameters are assumed to be known when the system is placed in operation or before a replacement decision is to be made. Exact models are adequate in the event, for example, where obsolescence and failure costs are small, as in the case of truck-fleet operation. But in airline operation, for example, where obsolescence and failure costs are high, stochastic replacement models must be developed and decision rules and policies obtained.

A significant area for the development of replacement theory is in the area of system design. In the design of a complex chemical process and plant or an automated manufacturing system, replacement analysis ought to be performed prior to the installation of the system. Particularly in those cases where the demand for the system's output is only approximately known, a stochastic replacement model ought to be constructed incorporating a probabilistic-demand variable.

Four areas of significant research problems are:

1. The development and solution of mathematical models that include replacement decisions as *one* of the control variables.
2. The incorporation of *lead-time* considerations in replacement models where the physical replacement of an item occurs at a significant time after the decision to replace is made, as in cases of utility-generator replacement or airline aircraft replacement.
3. The development of replacement models that utilize the *collection* of additional information on the system's operating characteristics in making replacement decisions.
4. The further development of *stochastic* replacement models to better utilize probabilistic estimates of parameter values and to control the transient behavior of systems.

BIBLIOGRAPHY

Acheson, M. A., Electron Tube Life and Reliability, Sylvania Electric Products, Inc., 1956 (unpublished).

Alchian, A. A., *Economic Replacement Policy,* RAND Corp. Report R-224 (April 12, 1952), 129 pp. Reprinted as RM-2153 (April 9, 1958).

Armstrong, James, Jr., "Some Uses of Statistics in Plant Maintenance," *Industrial Quality Control,* **12,** 12–17 (1956).

Barber, Bruce M., "The Use of Probability-Multipliers in Replacement Analysis," *The Engineering Economist,* **4,** 17–34 (1958).

Bellman, Richard, "Notes on the Theory of Dynamic Programming III, Equipment Replacement Policy," RAND Paper 623 (1955).

———, "Equipment Replacement Policy," *J. Soc. Industrial and Applied Math.,* **3,** 133–136 (1955).

Boodman, D. M., "The Reliability of Airborne Radar Equipment," *JORSA,* **1,** 39–45 (1953). Also in McCloskey and Trefethen, *Opns. Res. for Mgmt.,* **1,** 324–351 (1954).

Chung, K. L., and Pollard, H., "An Extension of Renewal Theory," *Proc. Amer. Math. Soc.,* **3,** 303–309 (1952).

Chung, K. L., and Wolfowitz, J., "On a Limit Theorem in Renewal Theory," *Ann. Amer. Math. Soc.,* **55-56,** 1–6 (1952).

Clapham, J. C. R., "Economic Life of Equipment," *Opnal. Res. Quart.,* **8,** 181–190 (1957).

Crane, R. R., and Brown, F. B., Jr., "Theory of Maintenance of Rolling Stock," *Mechanical Engineering,* **76,** 999 et seq. (1954).

Davidson, H. O., "George Terborgh, 'Business Investment Policy,'" *Engineering Economist,* **4,** 22–36 (1959).

———, "The MAPI Formula," *J. of Ind. Eng.,* **8** (1957).

Dean, J., *Capital Expenditures—Management and Replacement of Milk Trucks* (pamphlet), Joel Dean Associates, New York.

———, "Replacement Investments," Chapter VI in *Capital Budgeting,* Columbia University Press, New York, 1951.

Dreyfus, S. E., "A Note on an Industrial Replacement Process," *Opnal. Res. Quart.,* **8,** 190–193 (1957).

Elmaghraby, S. A., "Probabilistic Considerations in Equipment Replacement Studies," *The Engineering Economist,* **4,** 1 (1958).

Epstein, Benjamin, *Tests for the Validity of the Assumption That the Underlying Distribution of Life is Exponential,* Wayne State University, Detroit, Michigan, 1959, p. 80.

Epstein, B., and Sobel, M., "Some Theorems Relevant to Life Testing from an Exponential Distribution," *Ann. Math. Stat.,* **25,** 373–381 (1954).

Feller, W., "On the Integral Equation of Renewal Theory," *Ann. Math. Stat.,* **13,** 243–267 (1941).

———, "On the Theory of Stochastic Processes, with Particular Reference to Applications," *Proc. First Berkeley Symposium on Math. Statistics and Probability,* 1949, p. 403.

———, "Fluctuation Theory of Recurrent Events," *Trans. Amer. Math. Soc.,* **67,** 98–119 (1949).

Fennell, J., and Oshiro, S., "The Dynamics of Overhaul and Replenishment Systems for Large Equipments," *Nav. Res. Log. Quart.,* **3,** 19–43 (1956).

Fetter, Robert B., and Goodman, Thomas P., "An Equipment-Investment Analog," *Opns. Res.,* **5,** 657–669 (1957).

Goodman, L., "Methods of Measuring Useful Life of Equipment under Operational Conditions," *J. Amer. Stat. Assn.,* **48** (1953).

Grant, Eugene L., *Principles of Engineering Economy,* 3rd edition, Ronald Press, New York, 1950.

Kao, J. H., "Quantifying the Life Quality of Electron Tubes with the Weibull Distribution," Technical Report No. 26, Cornell University, Ithaca, N.Y., 1955.

Karlin, S., "On the Renewal Equation," *Pacific Journal of Mathematics,* **5,** 229–258 (1955).

Kimball, G. E., "Reliability and Maintenance," Chapter 8 in *Notes on Operations Research,* Operations Research Center, M.I.T., The Technology Press, M.I.T., Cambridge, Mass., 1959.

Kurtz, E. B., *Life Expectancy of Physical Property,* Ronald Press, New York, 1930.

Lotka, Alfred J., "A Contribution to the Theory of Self Renewing Aggregates, with Special Reference to Industrial Replacement," *Ann. Math. Stat.*, **10**, 1–25 (1939).

Machinery and Allied Products Institute, *Equipment Replacement and Depreciation—Policies and Practices,* 1956.

Orenstein, R. B., "Topics on the MAPI Formula," *J. Ind. Eng.*, **7**, 283–294 (1956).

Pennycuick, K., "A Problem of Replacement," *Opnal. Res. Quart.*, **7**, 12–17 (1956).

Preinreich, G. A. D., "The Economic Life of Industrial Equipment," *Econometrica,* **8**, 12 (1940).

———, "The Present Status of Renewal Theory," Waverly Press, Baltimore, 1940.

Rifas, B. E., "Replacement Models," Chapter 17 in *Introduction to Operations Research,* edited by Churchman, C. W., Ackoff, R. L., and Arnoff, E. L., John Wiley and Sons, New York, 1957.

Rutenberg, Y. H., Sequential Decision Rules, unpublished paper, Case Institute, Cleveland, Ohio, January 1960.

Rutenberg, Y. H., and Gupta, S. K., *Sequential Decision Rules for Minimum-Cost Replacement of Equipment,* Abstract F6, Program of the Sixteenth National Meeting of ORSA, Pasadena, California, 1959.

Sandiford, P. J., Bernholz, B., and Shelson, W., "Three Applications of Operations Research in a Large Electric Utility," *Opns. Res.*, **4**, 663–673 (1956).

Sasieni, M. W., "A Markov Chain Process in Industrial Replacement," *Opnal. Res. Quart.*, **7**, 148–155 (1956).

Sasieni, M., Yaspan, A., and Friedman, L., *Operations Research Methods and Problems,* John Wiley and Sons, New York, 1959, pp. 102–124.

Senju, Shizuo, "A Probabilistic Approach to Preventive Maintenance," *J. of Opns. Res. Soc. of Japan,* **1**, 49–58 (1957).

Shellard, G. D., "Failure of Complex Equipment," *JORSA,* **1**, 130–136 (1953). Also in McCloskey and Coppinger, *Opns. Res. for Mgmt.*, **2**, 329–339 (1956).

Smith, V. L., "Economic Equipment Policies: An Evaluation," *Mgmt. Sci.*, **4**, 20–37 (1957).

Stoller, D. S., "A Failure Model for Equipments Undergoing Complex Operations," *Opns. Res.*, **6**, 723–728 (1958).

Taylor, J., and Jackson, R. R. P., "An Application of Birth and Death Process to the Provision of Spare Machines," *Opnal. Res. Quart.*, **5**, 95–108 (1954).

Terborgh, G., *Dynamic Equipment Policy,* McGraw-Hill Book Co., New York, 1949.

Weiss, H. K., "Estimation of Reliability Growth in a Complex System with a Poisson-Type Failure," *Opns. Res.*, **4**, 532–545 (1956).

Chapter 9

THE THEORY AND APPLICATION OF SIMULATION IN OPERATIONS RESEARCH

George W. Morgenthaler
University of Illinois, Chicago, Illinois
and
Caywood-Schiller, Associates

Contents

1. INTRODUCTION

Simulation, in its various forms, has established itself as an OR technique. Ten years ago it was a technical curiosity which some prophesied would be a panacea for systems-analysis studies, and others viewed as a sort of mathematician's sedative, which held no technical promise, but consumed all too large a share of available time, manpower, and money. To say that all is well today with simulation would be ostrich-like. However, in view of the applications which have already been made, to dismiss it as a second-rate tool of no promise would be equally unwarranted. Realizing that simulation is a young method, still in its developmental throes, it seems justified to believe that concentrated research on simulation methodology will ultimately result in a tool of considerably more usefulness and reliability. To this end, a definition of terms, examination of existing theory, indication of strengths and weaknesses, and study of recent applications,[1] may be a step in orderly development. Such is the general motivation for this chapter and, for that matter, of the volume of which this chapter is a part.

2. SIMULATION, MONTE CARLO, GAMING, MODEL SAMPLING: TERMINOLOGY

The scientific method is our principal tool for prediction and estimation. Among the steps usually identified in this method we find: close observation of the physical phenomenon, creation of a theory or model which explains the observations, prediction of observables from the theory by using mathematical or logical deduction, and performance of experiments to test the validity of the model.

Sometimes it is not possible to follow this procedure for a given problem or system. It may not be possible to observe the phenomenon in its desired environment. This is true of studies of the thrust of rocket motors for use in interplanetary space. The phenomenon or system may be too complex to summarize in a compressed mathematical formulation. It has not been possible thus far, for example, to

[1] The author wishes to thank many colleagues and friends at the various OR organizations who have supplied information on the recent simulation applications of their respective agencies.

reduce the operation of a large business activity to a few simple equations. Analytical techniques may not exist for solving the mathematical formulation once it has been achieved. This is often the case in solving the diffusion equation or other partial-differential equations when the boundary conditions are time-dependent or complicated by other demands of realism. Even when analysts have the confidence and ability to arrive at a theoretical prediction of the behavior of a large system, it may not be possible to perform validating experiments. You cannot, for example, test conclusions about global strategic war by trying them even once. *When any of these difficulties occur, as they do daily in the attempts of OR to tackle previously untouched, unmanageable problems, some form of simulation is the obvious tool to be tried.*

For some time, the words "simulation," "gaming," "Monte Carlo," "model sampling," and related names were used interchangeably or with special nuances dictated by the personal experiences of each particular author. While there is still some apparent disagreement, the author of this chapter is personally inclined toward the distinctions and emphases described in Thomas and Deemer (1957) and shall adopt them for this chapter. The accord given the Thomas-Deemer work [2] may be taken as a sort of Society acceptance of their terminology. While names themselves are not important, it *is* important for the development of the simulation technique and for keeping issues clear in the still-unsettled arguments on simulation that some terms be agreed upon. These definitions also serve to distinguish the content of the present chapter from that of the two which follow.

Figure 9.1 displays one interpretation of the relationship of the terms under discussion. To *"simulate"* means to duplicate the essence of the system or activity without actually attaining reality itself. In the broadest sense, any applied mathematics or analytic formulation of a problem is a simulation; however, we shall completely exclude analytic treatments from our restricted meaning of the term "simulation."

Perhaps the most traditional use of simulation has been in the engineering sciences, where analogue simulation devices have long been used for scientific prediction of system performance. REAC, GEDA, EA function generators, and other computers are used daily to obtain mathematical solution of difficult differential equations, and in performing parameter studies which describe the behavior of guidance systems, network flow, rocket motor performance, re-entry vehicle flights, etc. (Eckstrand and Rockway, 1959; Chambers and Doerfel, 1959). More recently, the whole hierarchy of space medicine and

[2] The paper shared the Lanchester Prize in OR for the year 1957.

human engineering of space craft has been viewed from the simulation viewpoint (Hardy and Clark, 1959). These types of simulation, which have been very valuable work horses of development programs, do not generally involve Monte Carlo, gaming, or training notions (Fig. 9.1).

Flight simulators are used to train civilian jet pilots in emergency procedures, and in the landing problems of the runway approaches at major airports. Driver-training devices for high-school driver courses, and the use of various simulators in bombing and gunnery training are other examples of *simulation training devices.* If the training device has random elements as an intrinsic part of the stimulus to the trainee, it might be called a Monte Carlo device by some. If the coach or trainer manipulates the device in competition with the student, we may consider it a gaming device.

Large-scale *digital simulations* of strategic systems have been performed at several agencies. At RAND, the Madam and Super Straw models were early simulation models. The Air Battle Analysis Division at Headquarters USAF has applied the RAND Air Battle Model to study the complicated interaction of total air warfare. At the Institute for Air Weapons Research (IAWR), University of Chicago, several such large strategic air warfare models were conceived and run, both manually and on an IBM 704 computer (Morgenthaler and Hesse, 1957; Strauss and Feurzeig, 1957). The machine version of the IAWR model was called SCRAMBLE. The Operations Research Office of Johns Hopkins University has also employed such strategic simulation models (Adams and Forrester, 1959). The computer models were not games (no play involving human choice or will, all decisions fixed by calculation or by codified rules). Runs were reproducible to within statistical variation. Portions of these models used random numbers to determine outcomes, and hence they might be called Monte Carlo models by some. However, it is possible to have a digital simulation which involves no Monte Carlo, no gaming, and which is not a training device. In the most general sense, a digital numerical integration of the equations of perturbed motion to give a satellite orbit is such an example. As another example, Caywood-Schiller, Associates has employed a digital simulation of an analogue antiaircraft fire-control system in order to study its error susceptibility. This is a simulation of a simulator!

"Monte Carlo" is the code name given by von Neumann and Ulam to the mathematical technique which they applied to solving a category of nuclear-shielding problems which were too expensive for experimental solution and too complicated for analytical treatment. Origi-

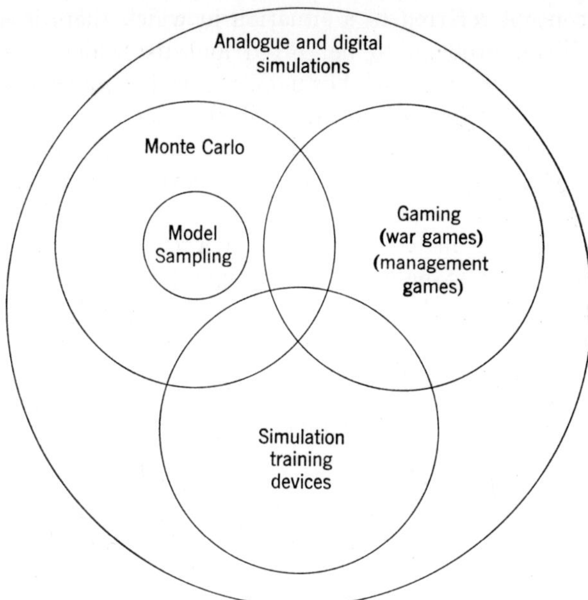

Fig. 9.1. Schematic relationship of various simulation terms.

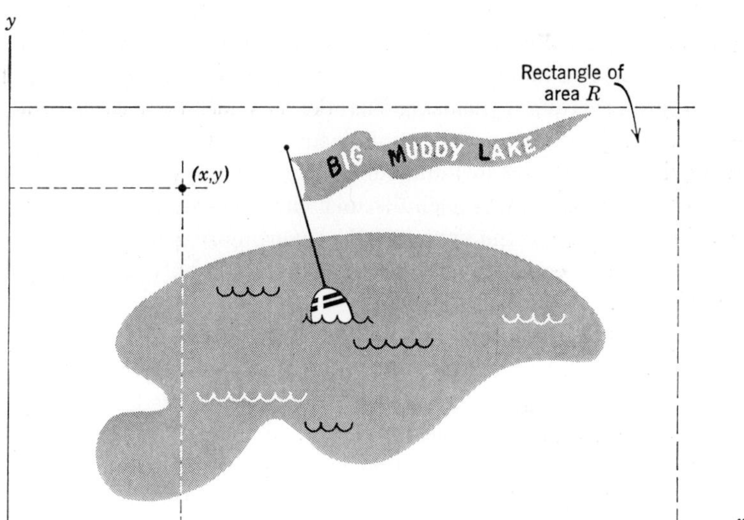

Fig. 9.2. Example of stochastic experiment to solve non-probabilistic problem.

$$\left[x \text{ and } y \text{ are uniformly distributed.} \quad \text{Area} = R\left(\frac{\text{No. of trials with } (x,y) \text{ in lake}}{\text{No. of trials}}\right). \right]$$

nally, the concept referred to a situation in which there is a difficult non-probabilistic problem to be solved and for which a stochastic process may be invented which has moments or distributions satisfying the relations of the non-probabilistic problem. As a simple example of this idea, we consider the problem of finding the water surface area of an irregularly shaped lake which contains several irregularly shaped islands (Fig. 9.2).

Enclose the lake in a rectangle of area R, and randomly select points (x,y) in the rectangle by selecting x and y from the appropriate uniform distributions along two sides of the rectangle. Then the product

$$R\left(\frac{\text{number of points } (x,y) \text{ falling in the water}}{\text{total number of trials } N}\right)$$

approximates the water area. Since this approximation is statistical in nature, its error is usually measured by the standard deviation,

$$\sigma=\sqrt{\frac{a(R-a)}{N}},$$

where R is the rectangle's area, a is the true water area, and N is the total number of trials.

The foregoing example was an inefficient Monte Carlo application, since no variance-reducing techniques were employed. We observe that by making the rectangle enclosing the lake as small as possible, that is, $(R-a)$ small, the variance is minimized for a given sample size N. This is evident from the formula for σ. Some analysts do not use the term "Monte Carlo" unless such distinct variance-reducing devices are present in the design of the process. However, more general acceptance has employed the term for any problem which is solved by use of a chance process.

Model sampling is a technique which has been used for some time in statistics. In cases where one has a complicated stochastic process, one too difficult to analyze by standard statistical procedures, it can be studied by collecting many case histories. In this way, not only the moments of the outcome distribution may be estimated, but the shape of the distribution itself. If one wishes to know the distribution of x/y, for example, x and y $(y\neq 0)$ being random variables from bizarre distributions, one may sample several hundred x- and y-values in pairs and form x/y for each pair. The histogram of the resulting x/y values will approximate the distribution of x/y.

A concrete example (due to R. Sebastian) involves finding the distribution of $\sqrt{x^2+y^2}\,|z|$, where $\sqrt{x^2+y^2}$ is the radial distance from origin to the circularly normally distributed impact point (x,y), and $|z|$ is the absolute value of the independently distributed normal deviate z. This product can easily be shown by standard methods to be exponentially distributed. However, if one did not know this, and sampled, using a table of normal random deviates, one would obtain a histogram for the product values which would approximate an exponential curve.

Thomas and Deemer have distinguished *operational gaming* by the idea of play. If human beings perform the decision or will function at some stage of the calculation, the process has an arbitrary character to it and it is an extension of the ideas of Kriegspiel, war game, and map exercise of earlier days (Thomas, 1957). Parlor games such as Monopoly and Auto-bridge are also examples of gaming simulation. A business example of this type of activity is the large game used in the American Management Association's management-decision course (Bellman, 1958; Bellman et al., 1957).

Operational gaming is not to be confused with the theory of games. The theory of games is a well-defined mathematical discipline in which each side may be assumed to know the payoff values in the payoff matrix corresponding to the various strategies (moves) it and the opposition may make. Mathematical techniques exist for obtaining optimal strategies for each opponent. In operational gaming many plays of the game must occur before any pattern can be expected to emerge regarding which strategies are rewarding and which unrewarding. Even then, the presence of humans in the opposition makes it difficult to know whether the apparently good plays were not just the result of opponent stupidity or carelessness.

The interesting possibility that business gaming may be used as a laboratory tool to study the psychological behavior of humans in competitive and pressure situations has been suggested (Kennedy). Operational gaming may, by simulation, put people into realistic situations in order to *derive what assumptions to make about human behavior,* while game theory *proceeds from simplified assumptions concerning the behavior of human beings* in conflicting situations to a guide on how to win at least a definable "game value."

No doubt other variants of simulation will be developed in time. It is felt that each of the above has a certain usefulness in OR work. Continued research, experience, and mistakes (we must not underestimate the value of mistakes for improvement) will ultimately strengthen each technique and display its proper area of application. Such optimism is justified only if continued serious efforts toward improvement and understanding are continued. H. H. Watson [3] has described the situation by saying that simulation should be viewed as a spectrum of techniques.

Moss (1958), in commenting on simulation, has offered an interesting observation on the possibility of classifying stochastic models in terms of degree of abstraction.

> On the basis of the criteria: (*a*) number of elements reproduced, (*b*) essentiality of elements, (*c*) faithfulness of reproduction, and (*d*) replicability, we can determine five degrees of abstraction:
>
> 0. The process, activity, or situation on which the model is based.
> 1. A replication of the initial process or situation; examples of this are controlled "runs" in industry, maneuvers in the area of military science, and (not to omit the arts) the drama, a model of a real or hypothetically real situation.
> 2. A controlled, laboratory-type model, capable of repetition; laboratory models of industrial processes, war games, and the cinema (as opposed to live drama) are examples of this.
> 3. A completely synthetic extraction of essential elements of the initial situation; computer models of industrial or military situations and (to maintain a labored analogy) the play-script.
> 4. A closed analytical model, usually merely nominally stochastic (p. 591).

The remainder of the chapter will deal entirely with simulations which do not involve play of humans. Operational gaming will be dealt with in the next chapter.

3. WHY PERFORM SIMULATION?

We have already mentioned the use of simulation to compensate for *difficulties: of duplication of environment, of mathematical formulation, of lack of analytical solution techniques, or of experimental impossibilities.* Some of the simulations which will be described in later sections have been motivated by still other factors, some of undoubted validity. A few of the other reasons more commonly given for simulation are:

a. The task of laying out and operating a simulation of a process is a good way to systematically gather the pertinent data about the process. It makes necessary a broad education in the process or operation being simulated, on the part of all who participate seriously in the simulation.

[3] Personal correspondence.

b. Simulation of a complex operation may provide an indication of which variables are important and how they relate. This may lead to later successful analytic formulations. Rich (1955) indicates that the use of a simple air-defense simulator which dealt with surface-to-air missiles led to the observation that each attack had a definite transient phase followed by a steady state. Analytic formulations later reflected this observation successfully.

c. A physical simulation device can sometimes play a useful training or briefing role. When answers to a management problem have been obtained the mathematician or analyst may be prone to wish to hurry on to another challenging assignment. However, operations-analysis work cannot be considered complete until the executive or customer has received the ideas and concepts and is ready to use them in his decisions. Simulations are valuable in conveying the meaning and implications of proposed policy changes.

d. Simulations are sometimes valuable in that they afford a convenient way of breaking down a complicated system into subsystems, each of which may then be modeled by an analyst or team which is expert in that area. It affords a vehicle for orderly incorporation of many skills and for pooling of expert opinion and information. A business simulation, for example, may have separate submodels which compute the effect of inventory policies, of advertising expenditures, of shipping schedules, etc.

e. Some simulations have led to the evolution of new policies and new ideas, or to the realization of simple but hidden truths concerning the nature of the operation. The author participated in a talk-through of a simulation of a supply-base operation for nuclear aircraft. In the course of the building of this simulation model interesting "free associations" were developed. It seemed possible, for example, that because of high reactor costs and the difficult reactor-handling and -refueling problems involved, one might consider the nuclear power plant to be the tail-numbered or inventoried item in base operations, and a fuselage as only a spare part, rather than using the current concept of engines as spare parts for tail-numbered fuselages.

f. Simulation is cheaper than many other forms of experiment or test facility. Product development or introduction of new equipment usually involves pilot plant runs. If a valid simulation of the operation exists, the businessman can "look before he leaps," as some authors have stated it, at less expense than that involved in layout for actual trial runs.

g. Simulation may be used to develop enthusiasm and gain acceptance for a proposed change. This is different from mere understanding. Some employees of a firm may have hostility toward change because they are unsure of its overtones as regards their jobs. Observing the simulation of the revised operation may reassure them or may indicate new tasks which will have to be performed.

h. In some problems information on the probability distribution of the outcome of a process is desired, rather than only averages or moments. If the process is complicated, standard analytic methods are helpless and Monte Carlo is the only tool which can give the full distribution.

i. Understanding gained through simulation may enable human judgment to intuit a good solution. "There is indeed a good deal of evidence that human beings have a great capacity for understanding the workings of complicated systems, and can find near optimum decision rules, operating procedures, etc., if they have enough experience with the system and it is stable enough" (Marshall, 1958, p. 4).

j. The results of simulating an operation are data (albeit fictitious) concerning the operation. These data may now be adapted to answer many types of questions. It is not necessary to know beforehand which specific questions will be asked, nor which index-factor preferences the customer has, if only proper records are kept. In fact, different executives may prefer different measures of system performance. There is no "best" measure. Data kept from runs of the IAWR strategic-penetration model have been assembled and reassembled in a variety of ways to answer questions posed much later concerning various weapons and tactics. Usual analytic OR models, on the other hand, must involve an irrevocable decision at the outset of the analysis as to which are the independent and which the dependent variables, and what the index of performance shall be.

k. Sometimes a Monte Carlo OR simulation is performed to check an analytic solution. In a recent missile study, the author arrived at a closed-form expression for the approximate expected damage to a circular target area due to an impacting circular cluster of warheads whose mass center was normally distributed about the target center. There were no tabled values against which to check the accuracy of the approximation. It seemed desirable to "check" the formula against some known cases before employing it widely in the OR study. Using cut-out paper damage circles, a circular target, and a table of random normal deviates, it was possible to obtain "experimental" data which checked out the analytic result (Morgenthaler, 1959).

At the 2nd Symposium on System Simulation (Northwestern U.,

1959) D. B. Hertz indicated an example of checking out proposed inventory rules against the historical market data for the years 1900–1958 to see that the proposed rules would have handled the emergencies of wars and depressions.

l. Simulation gives a control over time. In fact, it is a way of incorporating time into an analysis of an essentially dynamic situation. In simulation of business operations, one can compress real time and observe the results of a given policy for a ten-year period in just a few minutes' running time. Or, one can expand time. The many activities of an interceptor base during scrambling can be simulated and run slower than real time so that a single person can comprehend the complexity of *all* phases of the operation. It is like having a Fastax camera filming a system in motion.

Another time advantage is the ability to handle objects which move at different time rates. The interaction of air-defense systems with incoming attackers depends at each instant upon how many and which types of attackers are present at a defensive site. Simulation enables one to permit the variation in vehicle speeds to enter the interaction calculation in an essentially correct way. This is true also of highway-traffic simulations involving vehicles of different speeds. Any analytic approaches here would be very complicated indeed.

m. When new equipment or weapons are introduced unforeseen bottlenecks and problems in the operation may arise. Simulation can help to foresee these difficulties. It forces attention on problems which might otherwise be ignored.

n. Simulation makes generalists out of specialists. Analysts are forced into an appreciation and understanding of all facets of the system, with the result that final conclusions are less apt to be biased by particular inclinations and less apt to be unworkable within the system framework.

4. ON THE THEORY OF SIMULATION AND MONTE CARLO

When we speak of a theory of simulation, we cannot yet mean a polished, logical structure having the beauty and richness of the elegant mathematical theory of functions of a complex variable. But then, the theory of functions has been with us for more than a hundred years and many of its concepts go back twice that far. What we mean is that serious analysts have by this time recognized a certain pattern to simulations, a pattern not only in the method of performing a simulation, but also in the problems which simulation faces, and they have made progress in solving some of these problems. Here and there a concentrated effort has succeeded in developing a basic building block of the systematics of the technique itself.

In this section some of the problems of formulating a theory of simulation are mentioned and the present modest triumphs noted. A theory of functions was able to be developed by a few mathematical geniuses, working in relative isolation, but it is likely that expensive and bold experiments on digital and analogue simulations performed for the sake of simulation alone, may be required to make the substantial progress needed to put simulation on a truly satisfactory scientific basis.

4.1. On Analogue-Error Theory

The main interest of this chapter lies in simulations used in OR other than gaming. We have already mentioned the older analogue simulations which appear in design and development. It is of further interest to note in passing that this older type of simulation of dynamic systems (flight tables, network-flow simulators, guidance simulators, etc.) has already undergone a scrutiny of its logical foundations and a study of its mechanization accuracies and how best to do it. In a sense a "theory" exists for this technique.

The Air Force and its contractors have long been heavy users of analogue simulators in the development of dynamic systems and subsystems of air vehicles. In 1951, a project, The Advisory Board for Simulation (later Institute for System Research), was created at the University of Chicago under Air Force contract for the purpose of examining methods of dynamic analysis (simulation) of flight-control systems and formulating requirements for facilities to perform such analyses. (See bibliography, U. of Chicago.)

The interesting feature for us is that in addition to the usual questions of what type of equipment and how much equipment is needed, what type of personnel to hire, how to organize, and so on, for the proposed facility, the project personnel soon found it necessary to address themselves also to the basic question of the validity and error of such simulations. In order to answer questions such as "How good is this simulation device?", "How accurate is this answer?", an adequate theoretical error analysis had to be devised.

Most analogue simulations reduce to solutions of sets of ordinary differential equations. At the onset of the project, an extensive literature already existed on various facets of the problem of the effect of errors on the solution of differential equations by continuous computers.

Miller and Murray (1953) evolved a general methodology and point of view which enable one to integrate the separate error studies for components of the computer into the total effect on the analogue solution. Their theory, applicable also to non-linear systems, recognized three distinct types of error:

λ Errors: errors in the actual functional form computed by the computer due to the inability of the machine to realize a specified function and which are severe enough to change the order of the system. Higher-order derivatives are introduced.

α Errors: errors which are not severe enough to affect the order of the differential system. For example, instead of mechanizing $\dot{x} = -x$, the machine actually mechanizes $\dot{x} = -x + (0.001)(\text{sgn}\dot{x})$, because of backlash.

β Errors: errors which arise in the course of the machine computation as a result of instantaneous disturbances of the solution. These may be due to a sudden transient in the computer ("shot" effect) or to errors in setting of initial conditions, and so on.

The project attempted to apply the Miller-Murray theory to various simulation devices and to extend the theory to still other situations. The thesis of J. Winson (1954) developed the theory in a practical vein for linear differential systems with constant coefficients. Some success of the theory can be claimed, although much additional work remains to be done.

For example, output errors in a continuous computer are time-dependent and grow with time. As a result, the solutions generated by most analogue computers are meaningful only over limited time intervals. By replacing the given equations to be mechanized by a new set of equations which include corrective factors that depend on the errors, it is possible to obtain solutions having error bounds which are not time-dependent. This was done specifically for sine- and cosine-function generators and for a system which generated a set of three orthonormal vectors (Hochfeld, 1957).

Another particular approach to understanding errors in analogue simulations was that used by Caywood and Caviness (1959) in the analysis of a regenerative computing fire-control device for an anti-aircraft weapon. The computer solved a set of sixteen simultaneous differential equations to give the fire-control prediction. These equations were written down from a study of the complete circuitry. Error terms for the components (dashpots, amplifiers, multipliers, etc.) were introduced into the equations. The resulting equation set was simulated on the ORDVAC digital computer and direct numerical insight into the behavior of the fire-control device for particular target motions could be obtained.

Analogue simulation devices have already appeared in OR studies. As typical examples one might cite the papers of Dunn, Flagle, and Hicks (1956); Rich (1955); and Beer (1957); and the report of Himes (1949).

The Dunn, Flagle, Hicks paper describes the Queuiac, an electronic, tape-fed, analogue computer designed for studying queuing problems. This device is reported to be capable of using quite arbitrary input and service distributions (fed in by tape) to maintain a continuous net inventory of arrivals and departures, and to provide for direct computation of state probabilities. Many problems of queues not yet able to be handled by analytic methods may be investigated on this device.

The machine described in Beer's paper is a mechanical device using a series of synthetic data generators. Each of these has an output of ball bearings such that the time interval between balls is directly proportional to a time occurring in the distribution being simulated. Complex interacting industrial situations with feedback can be run rapidly by interconnecting these synthetic data generators. The paper emphasizes the fact that the machine has the advantage that management can watch the solution of problems and thereby support is gained for adoption of results.

The simulator described by Himes is a photoelectric coverage machine constructed by the RAND Corporation in the late 1940's. Given a target-vulnerability function, an impact-distribution function, and a weapon-lethality function, the machine used various types of transparencies and estimated the expected damage to specified target regions from photoelectric meter readings. This device has been superseded by digital simulation for damage-estimation techniques at RAND and elsewhere, but it is another interesting example of the whole class of special-purpose operations research simulators.

The importance of the fact that some error theory of analogue simulation has been evolved seems to lie chiefly in the course that it charts, and the hope it may hold for ultimate understanding of the newer digital systems simulations. The greatest progress here has been with respect to the subclass of strictly Monte Carlo simulations. These will be separately discussed later in this section.

4.2. On Digital-Simulation Theory

How does one obtain a digital simulation of a complex system, say a logistics-supply system, or a strategic-penetration interaction? A series of steps might be outlined in the evolution of the simulation. The steps are applied here to simulation of strategic aerial warfare:

a. Detailed acquaintance on the part of the analyst with the operating realities of the system is necessary. Which bombing vehicles are involved? How many? What are their flight profiles? What defensive and offensive aids may they carry? What maintenance, readiness, and operating constraints apply to the force? What are the likely defensive weapons which will be met? Where are the offensive bases and the defensive sites? Where are the defensive warning devices? How well do they perform? And so on.

b. Determination of the exact nature and scope of the simulation is an important early task. One must determine what financial, computer, and manpower support will be available for the simulation. One must determine when, where, and in what form strategic plan input data will be available, in what form, detail, and accuracy the air-battle data and bombing results must be recorded, and so on.

c. Once analysts have a thorough picture of the operation and have agreed on what level of simulation will be desirable, an effort is made to divide the real system into meaningful subcomponents linked together by a master flow diagram. The flow diagram asks a series of questions and the submodels are used to answer the questions during the simulation run. Figure 9.3 shows a typical simulation flow diagram. Examples of such subcomponents or submodels in the case of the strategic model are: a radar detection submodel which determines when a bomber has been detected by the defensive system, a submodel whose output is an assignment of defensive vehicles to the existing bomber threat, an air-battle routine which determines the outcome of interaction between interceptor vehicles and bombers under a variety of possible combat side-conditions, a submodel for estimating damage to defensive sites after a bomber has completed a delivery, and so on.

Often a submodel computes an outcome based upon the knowledge that the system is in one of several "states." Perhaps the use of electronic countermeasures has momentarily confused the defense. Or, the defense may be in a state of saturation; that is, more offensive vehicles are present than the defensive-information network can keep track of. The behavior and effectiveness of defensive vehicles will be different for the various states.

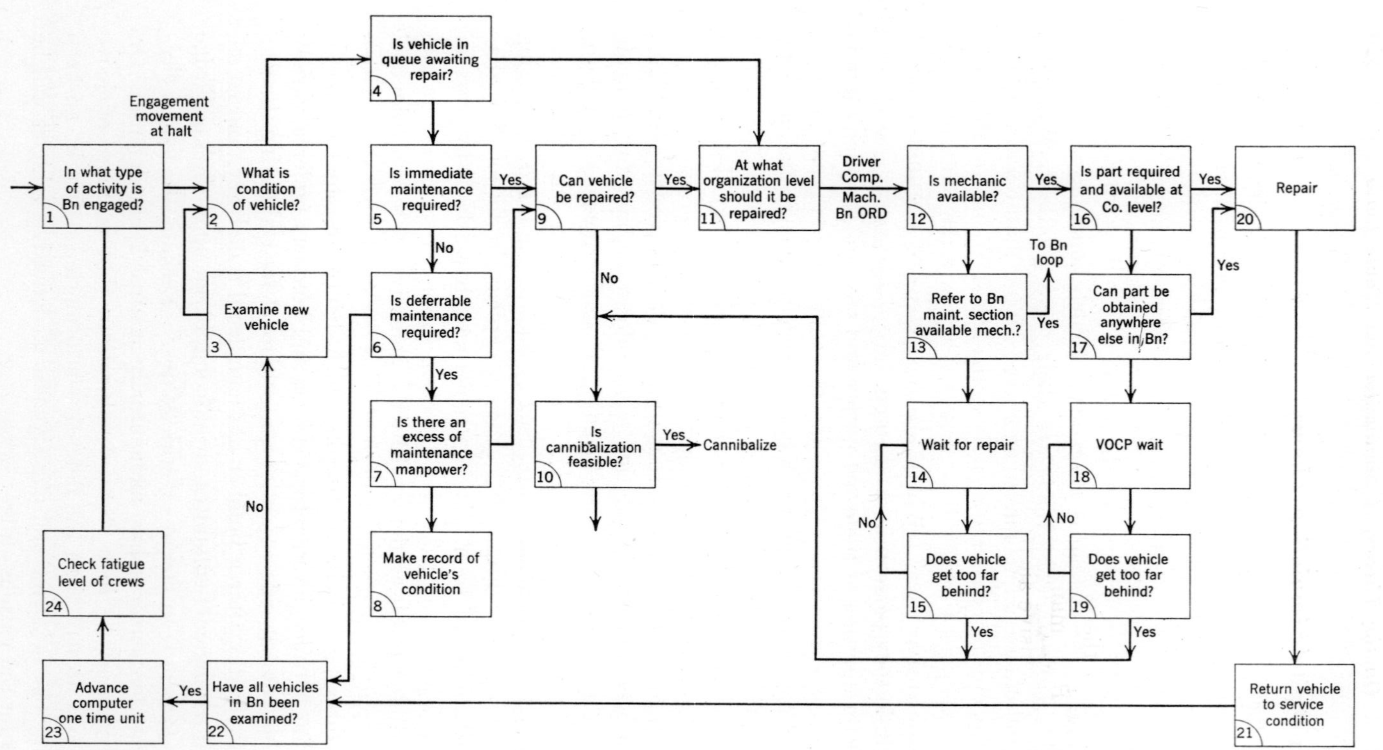

Fig. 9.3. An example of a summary flow diagram for a battalion maintenance system. [From D. G. Malcolm, "Army Battalion Maintenance Simulation," in *Report of System Simulation* (8th National Convention of the American Institute of Industrial Engineers, New York, May 16 and 17, 1957), p. 91.]

These submodels may be devised separately by analyst experts in the particular areas, the only constraint being that any particular submodel should accept those inputs and deliver those particular outputs specified in the master flow diagram. A basic strength of simulation is that unlike standard mathematical techniques, the models need not be linear or easily manipulated. Here realism may dictate the mathematics.

d. Space and time must be suitably coordinated and cut up into discrete units. In a strategic model, for example, a time pulse of appropriate magnitude may be selected, and either the actual coordinates of vehicles vs. time can be retained at each stage, or a set of cells can be used with the vehicles moving from cell to cell at appropriate times in accordance with strike plans.

e. After developing the space-time movement subroutine, the submodels, and the master flow chart, the entire simulation recipe should be thoroughly tested. This is best done by exercising the proposed simulation through a number of time pulses, carrying out by hand each subcalculation and operation, determining that each input is received from the appropriate source and that each output is acceptable to the next submodel.

f. If the simulation is to be operated by hand, the inputs may be prepared for the various runs and the simulation can now commence. If the simulation is to be done on a computer, programmers must be taught the model, and the main flow chart and all the submodels must be translated into a machine program in the appropriate computer language. After program debugging (and this will almost certainly be required) the simulation can then be run.

g. The simulation must now be replicated sufficiently often, if it contains stochastic aspects, to yield averages or distributions which have statistical stability.

The words of the Conway, Johnson, Maxwell article (1959) serve well to convey the ultimate philosophy and spirit of the technique:

> Consideration of the atomistic characteristic of simulation reveals much about its properties. First, it suggests a condition for feasibility of simulation; a system, however complex, can be simulated if it can be broken down into a set of elements for which operating rules can be given. If the smallest elements into which we can divide a system are themselves unpredictable (even in a probabilistic sense) digital simulation is not feasible. Second, it is a mathematical model that is "run," rather than one that is "solved." It is not inherently optimizing; rather it is descriptive of the performance of a given configuration of the system. Optimization must be superimposed upon this

model by varying the configuration in search of a maximum of performance. Third, the simulation does more than yield a numerical measure of the performance of the system. It provides a display of the manner in which the system operates. Finally, this discussion of the description of individual elements, the recording of individual events, and the frequent necessity of replication is rather suggestive of the reason why this form of system simulation was not widely used before the advent of the modern high speed stored-program digital computer. There is certainly nothing in the process that could not be executed manually and, in fact, there have been instances of manually-executed simulations. It is simply the tremendous volume of logical, numerical and bookkeeping operations that must be performed that makes this procedure a very natural application for digital computer (pp. 94–95).

Cohen (1959) has distinguished two basic viewpoints in simulating. When the submodels of a process are understood and known to be valid to a high degree of accuracy, but their interaction as a complete system is not known, the simulation is used as a *synthesis*. "The synthetic use of simulation is an example of pure deductive logic. The operating characteristics of the individual components are essentially the postulates of a formal deductive system, the programmed interactions of the components with each other are the rules of inference, and the over-all patterns of behavior traced out by the complete system are the derived theorems" (Cohen, 1959). If we agree with the postulates and rules of inference, we necessarily agree with the theorems (simulation results) as being empirically true.

When the over-all behavior of the system is known and observable, but the characteristics of the components and their relationships are not, simulation may be used to theorize and then test to see if the theory, when modelized and run in simulations, leads to the observed results. This is the *analytic* use of simulation. "The analytic use of simulation is an example of pure inductive logic, that is, of empirical inference. Although the underlying operating characteristics of the microunits of the system are formally treated as postulates, the fundamental interactions of the individual units as rules of inference, and the over-all system behavior as theorems of a formal deductive system, empirical testing is carried out at the level of the theorems, that is, with regard to the behavior of the complete system. If the over-all system behavior is in fact found to be in serious disagreement with the 'theorems' derived from the model, we then must infer that the micro-level model is in some way an inadequate representation of the world" (Cohen, 1959). If agreement is observed, the microlevel model is accepted in the sense of not being refuted by the facts.

It is perhaps worth emphasizing the fact that a simulator will not inherently optimize. It is essentially an "if-then" computer. "If the bombers carry such and such defensive aids, and the defense uses such and such a tactic, the results (statistically averaged) will be so and so." Wester (1959) has emphasized that the simulation itself will not make the military or business decisions. It is merely a tool for generating pertinent information and data for the decision maker.

To push the "if-then" philosophy to a currently completely unwarranted degree, we might, in the strategic-war context, view the results of replicating a particular run as determining one payoff value in a huge offense-vs.-defense game-theoretic payoff matrix.

Suppose the several offensive strategies (various choices of penetration equipment and tactics) are listed along the horizontal side of the payoff matrix and the defensive strategies (various defense forces and tactics) are listed on the vertical side. Then the simulation can conceptually provide the interaction payoff value (expected number of bombs reaching target, expected number of bombers surviving, etc.) for each offense-defense strategy pair. It would then be ideally possible to solve the resulting rectangular game for the optimum strategies of the offense and defense.

For many reasons one must very soon renounce this naive scheme. Runs of such large simulations are too lengthy and expensive for adequate replications. The defensive and offensive strategies are legion. Input values are too uncertain to warrant so grandiose an approach. Practical methods for solving such large games are lacking. The only value, if any, in articulating this type of scheme is that such technical pipe dreaming often sets a pattern for useful research.

In summary, a digital simulation may be viewed schematically as follows:

a. Collections of elements $\{x_i\}_j$ $(j=1,2,3,\cdots)$ are enumerated, whose movements in space-time through the system are to be observed.

b. Ordered submodels $\{M_k\}$ are defined which determine the interaction of the $\{x_i\}_j$ with the total system and with each other.

c. The submodels $\{M_k\}$ are connected in specific manners by input-output flow lines (feedback). At each time of application, M_k receives inputs from several sources: from without the system, from within the system, from the $\{x_i\}_j$, and/or from other M_k submodel outputs.

d. At each time pulse the sequence of submodels are applied *in a specific order, and subject to specific logical rules.*

e. At the end of the cycle, all submodel outputs are transferred to the next points of input, the $\{x_i\}_j$ are moved ahead according to their system-passage rules, the system registers are advanced or "updated," and the cycle is repeated. This continues until a prearranged stop signal is received. The final simulation output is then punched out.

This modular construction with simple linkages has the important advantage of being flexible. It is relatively easy to replace a submodel with an improved version if one is careful that the new submodel accepts exactly the same inputs, and yields exactly the same outputs, as the submodel it is replacing. Also, if the customer or analyst wishes to change the question being asked of the simulation, it is easier to identify the new observables which are to be summed and transmitted as outputs if all parts of the simulation model are identifiable wholes.

How good is the resulting digital simulation? No theory now exists for answering this question in general. But where can things go wrong?

Perhaps not all of the important variables in the real situation have been included in the simulation. To this danger an analytic solution is just as vulnerable.

Perhaps particular submodels are poor representations of their respective system interactions. This type of difficulty can generally be remedied by side experiment to check submodels. Physicists, who calculate shielding factors using Monte Carlo methods, have some confidence in their scattering submodel and in the submodel for remaining energy which they use in the Monte Carlo, because these have been cross-checked in other experiments. This particular weakness of simulation can often (but not always) be remedied.

The time required for transient decay may be long, and may introduce transient quantities into what the analyst believes is the steady state of the process. For example, suppose that a waiting-line operation is to be simulated. Suppose that the analyst desires to know the probability that the line has length n during the middle of the working day. If the simulation starts from the opening time of the service facility, it will take some unknown time for the steady state to be attained. If sampled before waiting long enough, the data will contain the transient error. Proper loading with initial conditions can reduce transient errors greatly.

Sometimes a submodel or a codified decision rule in the simulation utilizes only a few discrete states in place of a continuous reality. Interceptors are under perfect close-control, or are in a state of confused random search. In reality, many in-between combat conditions would surely exist. The author has never seen studies of the effect of such discrete states on very detailed simulations. It is something which can be studied, however, if analysts are willing to engage in some simulation for simulation's sake.

A frequent error that is made in the interest of simplicity is the use of expected values in place of random variables at intermediate stages. For example, in a problem in which a wave of bombers must fly through several waves of interceptors, the number of bombers surviving each wave is a random variable. This random variable is the bomber input to the next stage of the calculation. Sometimes the expected number of survivors is entered into the next stage. There is some evidence that this is a permissible approximation over some ranges of the variables involved. However, it is basically an incorrect procedure. The expected value of a function is not equal to the function of the expected value, in general $[E\,f(x) \neq f(E)]$.

Machine errors, round-off errors, and random-number-generation errors are inevitable in large simulations. All these problems have been, and will be, better understood with more concentrated study.

There is an inherent approximation in those cases where the digital simulation is imitating a continuous looped or feedback process. Certain events in the real process happen simultaneously, whereas in the simulation all computations proceed stepwise. For example, in an electronic circuit a certain component may receive input or load from three sources. At any time, the real output is determined by the instantaneous values of the three inputs. In the sequential calculation of a digital simulation of this system, it may be necessary that the component's output at the time t_i be computed on the basis of one or more of the inputs at time t_{i-1}. In the simulated system some components thus always lag their real counterparts.

Numerical digital integrations of systems of differential equations often attempt to get around this by using various finite difference formulas to extrapolate an input to a future time before using the input in a subroutine calculation. Such refined devices may ultimately enter digital operational simulation.

In the IAWR SCRAMBLE strategic model, Feurzeig[4] reports that a "future polynomial" is generated to predict the x-ray dosage at later times due to currently detonating warheads, thus reducing time-lag effects.

Given that these various types of errors are someday understood, how may they be coupled to indicate the over-all quality of the simula-

[4] Personal correspondence.

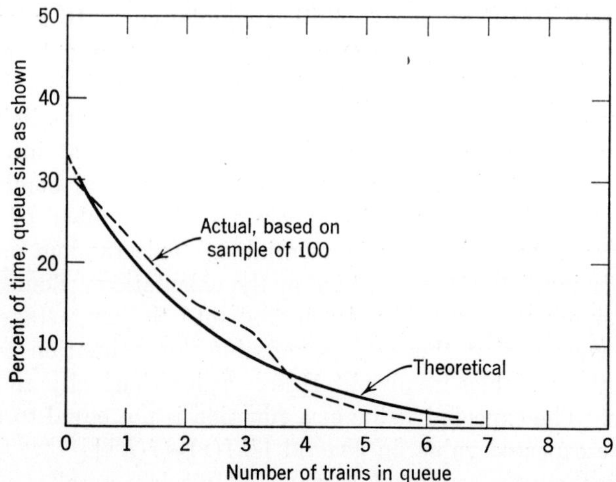

Fig. 9.4. Check on simulation probability distribution for queue lengths. [From Crane, Brown, and Blanchard, *J. Opns. Res. Soc. of Amer.*, **3**, 265 (1955).]

tion? What Miller-Murray type of theory can be evolved? What is needed is some empirical or theoretical rules which estimate the error in the total simulation as a function of the errors of the submodels and the degree and type of their interconnection. Nothing at present seems to be on the horizon. The most optimistic comment which may be made at this time is to note that in those cases of simulation application in which later check with reality was possible, very good results have been reported. Figure 9.4, taken from the railroad-classification-yard study of Crane, Brown, and Blanchard (1955) is typical of many checks on simulation accuracy. Other examples are given later in this chapter.

Various computer tricks to increase inadequate storage, improve accuracy, or increase the speed of the simulation might also be considered to belong to the theory of simulation. However, except for proven rules of thumb about organization of the program, these tricks are rather specialized for particular computers and can be viewed as belonging to the programmer's art. They must be appreciated by the analyst, however, in designing the simulation. Otherwise, he may design a model not practically computable on his available equipment, or he may unnecessarily restrict his model development by not realizing what can be done by programmers.

One important development in the attempt to make digital simulation more scientific and efficient has been the introduction of statistical tests. The philosophy of this has been to overlook the possible simulation errors alluded to above, and to view the synthetic simulation data as data gathered from the real process. As such, it is amenable to standard statistical tests.

In addition to the standard tests for normal and other common distributions, Kupferburg (1958) has developed extensive tests of hypotheses and estimators for use in those cases where the simulation data are neither normal nor exponential. These methods were developed for use with the IAWR digital simulation model of strategic aerial warfare. He also discusses the problem of determining the sample size necessary to achieve a given level of accuracy, and that needed so that a given size and power of the test meet a preset level of probability.

Granting a frame of mind which permits the synthetic data to be received as actual data, the standard techniques for design of experiments and analysis of variance may be used to minimize the number of "runs" for a specified amount of information. Such extensions of simulation philosophy have been considered by Conway, Johnson, and Maxwell (1959).

The potentiality afforded by sequential sampling methods has already been explored on a small scale by some simulation users. Randomized methods for exploring a response surface, of discovering parameter combinations which optimize system effectiveness with as few runs as possible, are currently under development (Brooks, 1959; McKown, 1958). However, such methods have not yet been successfully coupled with large simulations to the author's knowledge.

One must of course stress that questions still remain concerning the validity of the simulation data itself.

4.3. On the Theory of Monte Carlo

We have used the word "Monte Carlo" to apply to those simulations or to those portions (submodels) of larger simulations in which random sampling is used. An activity is simulated which in real life may have one of several (or a continuum) of outcomes. Repeated samples are drawn according to the probability laws which describe the activity, and, by collecting the resulting data, conclusions may be drawn concerning the activity and the parameters associated with the outcome population. This is a more embracing meaning than the original narrower view, that Monte Carlo must be a stochastic activity for solving a nonstochastic problem, or that it must involve variance-reducing devices.

Under these several meanings, however, the Monte Carlo technique has attained theoretical growth and a degree of sophistication. We shall here outline and enumerate the direction and extent of this theoretical growth and indicate sources for further study by the reader. Neutron-transport problems usually satisfy the Boltzmann equation. For these and other reactor calculations, Monte Carlo seems very well suited. In many cases the discrepancies between diffusion theory and transport theory are not known. Monte Carlo is useful in determining to what extent diffusion theory is applicable and adequate. Where diffusion theory is known to be inadequate, Monte Carlo provides a way of obtaining transport-theory results. The only other approach may be to replace the transport equation with finite difference approximations and try to solve these (see Spanier, 1959). Perhaps the following very simple description of such calculation, due to McCracken (1955), will aid our discussion.

Suppose we want to know what percentage of the neutrons in a given beam would get through a tank of water of a given size without being absorbed or losing most of their speed. No formula could describe precisely the fate of all the neutrons. The Monte Carlo approach consists in pretending to trace the "life histories" of a large sample of neutrons wandering about in the water and colliding occasionally with a hydrogen or oxygen nucleus—remember that to a neutron water looks like vast open spaces dotted here and there with tiny nuclei. We shall follow our neutrons one by one through their adventures.

We know how far a neutron travels, on the average, before it encounters a nucleus, the relative probability that this encounter will be with oxygen or with hydrogen, the relative chances that the neutron will be absorbed by the nucleus or bounce off, and certain other necessary information. Let us, then, take a specific neutron and follow its life history. It is a slow-moving neutron, and its first incident is a collision with a hydrogen nucleus. We know (from experiments) that the chances are 100 to one the neutron will bounce off from such a collision. To decide what it will do in this instance, we figuratively spin a roulette wheel with 100 equal compartments marked "bounced off" and one marked "absorbed." If the wheel says "absorbed" that is the end of the neutron's history. If it says "bounced off," we perhaps spin another appropriately marked wheel to decide what the neutron's new direction is and how much energy it lost. Then we must spin another wheel to decide how far it travels to the next collision and whether that collision is with oxygen or hydrogen. Thus we follow the neutron until it is absorbed, loses so much energy that it is no longer of interest, or gets out of the tank. We go on to accumulate a large number of such histories and obtain a more or less precise figure for the percentage of neutrons that would escape from the tank. The degree of precision depends on the number of trials.

In practice, of course, we do not use roulette wheels but random numbers, as in the previous example. I have omitted much of the detail of the calculation for the sake of simplicity and clarity. In one very simple problem on which I assisted, an electronic calculator labored for three hours to trace the life histories of 10,000 neutrons through 1.5 million collisions. I would have had to sit at a desk calculator for some years to accomplish the same results (pp. 92–93).

The areas open to theoretical consideration in Monte Carlo methods may now be enumerated. First, there is the underlying probability theory for Monte Carlo. For an elegant discussion of the basic theoretical foundation of sampling processes of this type couched in the modern language of sample space, Borel field of subsets, and probability measure, the reader should consult the exposition of Spanier (1959).

Secondly, there will certainly be problems dealing with the best methods of generating uniform deviates in a computer so that random choices can be made rapidly during the simulation. Also, the question of generating deviates from normal, exponential, and more general probability distributions during computer runs arises. Methods for accomplishing this are discussed in Appendix to Part II of Orcutt, Greenberger, and Riven (1958), and in the two classics on Monte Carlo methods, one issued by the U.S. Department of Commerce, National Bureau of Standards (1951), and the other the report of the Symposium on Monte Carlo Methods (1954) (an authoritative volume on the subject).

Thirdly, a number of elegant techniques have been devised for determining sample size to attain a given precision in Monte Carlo applications. These include importance sampling, Russian roulette, weighted sampling, systematic sampling, stratified sampling, splitting, and correlated sampling. These techniques are discussed in the works of Kahn and Marshall (1953), in the report on the Symposium on Monte Carlo Methods, and in the additional papers referenced in the bibliographies of these studies. Kahn and Marshall state:

> In general the authors believe that some design of the sampling almost always pays off. No practical problem is known to us where it is not possible with only a modest increase in the cost per sample observation to obtain a reduction, by a factor of 10 or 20, in the sampling variance of the estimate of the expected value of the outcome of the process encountered in the problem (p. 275).

As a typical example of the methods devised for random-number generation in computers, one can mention the famous midsquare method. From the middle of the square of the preceding "random" four-digit number b_i a new four-digit number b_{i+1} is extracted by the computer. It is used in the Monte Carlo trial to be decided at that instant and is then stored for the next application. For example, suppose a bomber is to "die" if a sampled uniform deviate is less than $p=0.7$, and is to "live" otherwise. If $b_i=1{,}097$, $b_i^2=1{,}203{,}409$, and thus $b_{i+1}=2{,}034$. Since $0.2034<p=0.7$, the bomber dies.

Much more sophisticated methods than the midsquare method for uniform deviates now exist. These newer multiplicative or additive congruence techniques generate random-number sequences whose periods are larger than sequences generated by the midsquare method. Clever tests (χ^2-tests, tests for "runs," "odd" and "even" tests, etc.) have been applied to the random numbers produced by these methods to determine the extent to which pseudorandomness is present.

Methods for generating non-uniform deviates include summing uniform deviates (gives approximate normal deviates by the central-limit theorem) and various rejection procedures. Bradford and Fain (1959) list the following rejection procedure:

> Suppose one wishes to generate random samples from the interval (a,b): $a<x<b$, which have the probability density function $f(x)$, where $0 \leqq f(x) \leqq c$. The procedure is to sample by random digits for an x' from the uniform distribution on (a,b) and a y' from the uniform distribution on (o,c). If $y' \leqq f(x')$, the x' sample is used, otherwise it is rejected.
>
> To see that this procedure does generate samples with the desired frequency function, notice that for a given x', the probability that a randomly drawn y' will be less than $f(x')$ is $f(x')/c$ since $f(x')$ is the length of the interval sampled from. Since the probability that x drawn at random will lie in the interval $(x',x'+\Delta x)$ is $\Delta x/b-a$, the probability that x and y will simultaneously be so drawn is
>
> $$\frac{f(x')}{c}\frac{\Delta x}{(b-a)}$$
>
> This probability is proportional to $f(x')\,\Delta x$ which is that given by the density function $f(x)$ (pp. 2–16).

As an example of the various variance-reducing methods, the picturesque Russian roulette is easily described. In many Monte Carlo operations the "random walks" or individual case histories are of two types, those which are "interesting" and enter into the determination of those parameter estimates for which the experiment is being run and "uninteresting" walks which contribute nothing to the answer. The idea is to terminate the "uninteresting" random walks because they add greatly to the variance of the process and contribute nothing. On the other hand, it is desirable to magnify the number of samples of the "interesting" random walks. Russian roulette does just this.

It involves the use of an auxiliary game of chance played with each of the "uninteresting" walks. The game is rigged to terminate most of the "uninteresting" walks as soon as their character is apparent and it attaches an excess weight or emphasis to the surviving "uninteresting" walks so that the over-all Monte Carlo estimate remains unbiased.

Space is too limited here to cover the full extent of the progress on Monte Carlo proper. Marshall (1958) has made an interesting observation, however. While the use of Monte Carlo is now widespread in large OR digital simulations, the use of various variance-reducing techniques is seldom seen in these large OR simulations. He attributes this to the availability of large computers which have permitted brute-force approaches, to the fact that analysts have not always been aware of variance-reducing methods, and to the fact that because analysts have realized that owing to the uncertainty of inputs and lack of knowledge concerning the operation itself, precision of answers has not been as meaningful in the sense that it has been to the physicist who uses Monte Carlo methods. Also, there has been a desire not to distort the outcome of the simulation because then the benefits accruing from showing the simulation or its results to customers may be jeopardized. Marshall re-emphasizes the possibility and desirability of introducing improved Monte Carlo designs into simulations used in OR, and gives several concrete suggestions for doing so.

There is, finally, the same question concerning the validity of classic Monte Carlo simulations as has arisen for the analogue and large-scale digital processes. Here, much more data exist on the success of Monte Carlo calculations in physics and engineering. The papers of Fosdick (see bibliography) and other sources cited by Fosdick attest to the ability of the method to give valid results.

Continuing activity aimed at further understanding of the method is proceeding at the National Bureau of Standards. The children's game of "Chutes and Ladders" [5] is composed of a path of one-hundred squares leading from start to goal. A player moves a given number of squares at each move as determined by a throw of the dice. In certain squares there is a "ladder" leading to free advancement to a further square, and at other squares there is a "chute" leading back to a previous square. The first player to reach the goal is the winner.

N. Bazley [6] of NBS reports that this game, which forms a Markov chain with one-hundred states, has been investigated both experimen-

[5] Manufactured by Milton Bradley Company, Springfield, Mass.

[6] Personal correspondence.

tally and theoretically. The average length of the game as computed from Markov-chain theory was compared with that computed by playing the game 10^4 times. The experimental results agreed to within the known $\sqrt{N}$ law.

Recently the Operations Research Project at MIT has been studying Monte Carlo simulation methods with emphasis on: methods for increasing the speed of simulation, statistical versatility in simulating various patterns of randomness, and synthesis of subroutines to simulate large, complex inventory systems (see H. P. Galliher's article in the *Report of the System Simulation Symposium*, New York, 1957).

5. *OR* APPLICATIONS AND ACCOMPLISHMENTS OF SIMULATION

During the preparation of this chapter, an effort was made to survey current applications of simulation and Monte Carlo in OR, and a cross section of this recent work will be discussed in this section. One cannot overestimate the importance that new and successful applications of OR techniques can have in opening wider the door to fuller utilization of OR in government and industry.

The applications have been divided into four groups for efficiency of presentation: (*a*) recent papers on the more classical Monte Carlo type of application, (*b*) descriptions of large-scale military simulations, (*c*) industrial applications which already appear in the literature of the Operations Research Society, and (*d*) other industrial applications.

The items in the last category are least well known and least available, and shall occupy our major attention.

5.1. Classical Monte Carlo Applications

The classical engineering Monte Carlo type of application is already well documented in the National Bureau of Standards study, the Monte Carlo Symposium volume (1954), and elsewhere, and little more will be said here.

The Ising lattice paper of Fosdick, mentioned earlier, describes tests of the applicability of the Monte Carlo method to a simple cooperative system (a system wherein the thermodynamic properties are the result of a strong cooperative or coherent interaction among the elementary parts). The two-dimensional Ising model of a ferromagnet was used. The Ising model assumes an arrangement of magnetic dipoles on the sites of a regular lattice. The method consists of generating a set of spin configurations with a probability distribution approaching the canonical distribution, $e^{-(E/kT)}$, where E is internal energy, k is Boltzmann's constant, and T is absolute temperature. The problem was run on the University of Illinois' ILLIAC, with satisfactory accuracy being obtained. For one pass through the 10×10 lattice, 0.033 minutes was required.

Spanier's papers, and the Spanier, Kuehn, Guilinger paper, discuss Monte Carlo computer applications to neutron-transport and capture-fraction problems. Fosdick's second paper further cites application to the calculation of order parameters in a binary alloy, which again gave satisfactory results when compared with data obtained from more conventional approaches. This program was given the imaginative pseudonym of Monte Crysto. Jones, Heit, and Livingston (1958) cite an interesting Monte Carlo simulation of claim distribution in a life insurance company.

L. Thomas (1953), in an article which compared Monte Carlo and direct methods for solution of some concrete mathematical and physical problems, gives a critical appraisal of the Monte Carlo method. He concluded that the stochastic methods were not as efficient as the more traditional methods for the particular problems considered. The problems included numerical integrations, linear partial-differential equations, and multiple scattering. He felt that Monte Carlo should be used only on those problems which really involve a stochastic element, provided other methods fail and high accuracy is not required. It is possible that some of the recent advances in computer capability would alter this appraisal if it were made at this time.

5.2. Military Simulations

These applications were among the first of the large-scale digital simulations and are probably not more widely known only because of security restrictions. In addition to the large air-battle models previously noted, at the RAND corporation, ORO, and the Institute for Air Weapons Research, almost all military study groups and weapons-system manufacturers have employed this technique in some form [see, for example, Brotman and Seid; McKown, Rudy and Poe; Dunne and Sebastian (1959); Taylor (1959); and Driggs (1956)]. Applications have ranged from vulnerability and armament-effectiveness studies for particular devices to recent large-scale studies dealing with the mechanics of recovery of the U.S. economy and estimates of civil defense capability subsequent to all-out nuclear attack. The Air Force's project OMEGA has extended the RAND Air Battle Model into what is claimed to be the largest and most detailed simulation to be realized on a digital computer. These simulations are largely probes of unknown phenomena. They provide insight and data which can be obtained in no other way.

A special OR application of simulation is that being accomplished at the System Development Corporation of Santa Monica [see Carter; Biel (1959); Ford (1959); and Brown, Freed, and Jordan (1959)]. The Air Force Air Defense Command is a large man-machine system which has the responsibility for detecting and destroying hostile penetration vehicles. There are over 150 radar stations organized into 16 divisions, each with a control center to which the sites report. A system training program (STP) has been developed to improve the performance of the air-defense system through training and/or modification of operating procedures as necessary. Simulated air situations have been developed and are presented to crews at radar sites, control centers, and higher headquarters, through several media.

At a site, combat radar data, which normally enters through the antenna, is fed to radar scopes via 70-mm. prepared film. Radar crews work the scopes, detect aircraft, and report them to plotting boards as though they were real. Friendly flights and other background data also appear as per usual. The area director might send up interceptors which, by means of radar generators, also "fly" on the radar scopes. The same type of simulation is going on in an integrated way at other sites in the division, and normal between-sites communications are thus also simulated. System performance is observed and recorded, and feedback is given to crews so that improvement is accomplished. System Development Corporation also utilizes simulation techniques in analyses and improvement of the control system of the Strategic Air Command. These are large-scale OR problems where, fortunately, the analyst has an unusual amount of control over the circumstances of the analysis, and much can be accomplished.

A less common military application is the determination of the number of missiles needed to meet missile-site operational requirements. A certain number of missiles must always be ready to fire, and yet periodic maintenance and checking are needed. Randomness of malfunctions and the variations in the time spent in missile repair make this a waiting-line type of situation. Goen (1959) uses a simple graphical model to simulate the flow of missiles through the maintenance cycle, with the position and status of each missile continuously recorded along a time scale. Data and distributions so generated were used to optimize the system.

Carlisle (1957), of the Broadview Research Corporation, has reported an interesting simulation of an army communications system of about division size. The model permits officers to test proposed communications systems in various tactical situations.

5.3. Industrial Simulation Applications from the Operations Research Society Literature

Operations Research, the journal of the Operations Research Society of America, contains a number of interesting non-military systems simulations.

Truck-dock determinations. Schiller and Lavin (1956) applied simulation to determine the extent of new truck-dock facilities at a central warehouse that would be required to handle the volume of truck traffic which was formerly accommodated at three separate warehouse facilities of the Wieboldt Department Stores in Chicago. The problem was essentially a waiting-line problem to which current waiting-line theory was not applicable. Truck arrival-time and service-time data were gathered and a program was prepared for computing the length of waiting-line and amount of service for various numbers of docks. Total machine computing time did not exceed three hours. Swensson (1958) has also applied Monte Carlo techniques to a complicated waiting-line problem.

Ground-controlled approach. With the aim of making recommendations to traffic-control authorities, Blumstein (1957) devised and ran a simulation model of the all-weather, airplane landing system (ground controlled approach, GCA). A ground controller watches the airplane on a radar scope and transmits maneuver orders to produce a proper approach path. The model stepped the aircraft through its flight path in 5-second increments, and, by random-number sampling, selected appropriate values of the landing events: initial A/C approach position, radar errors, controller estimates of A/C position, pilot errors in carrying out commands, etc. By running a large number of sample flight paths, an envelope of approach behavior is determined. The probability of a successful approach (an approach not requiring maneuvers exceeding a certain acceptable level) can be determined for specified weather conditions and equipment performance. Poor input data and lack of model refinement prevented concrete recommendations from being made, although the method was demonstrated to be a practical tool.

Barge-line scheduling. The colorful Ohio-Mississippi river system is the setting for a large-scale management problem with a happy simulation ending. The paper of O'Brien and Crane (1959) is a fascinating case history involving complicated difficulties of the proper number of tugs to operate, the proper ratio of barges to tugs, the question of when to permit return-trip hauling, and what round-trip scheduling time to impose on equipment. After several futile attempts at direct mathematical formulation of the problem, the analysts resorted to simulation of the fleet operation. At first, standard Monte Carlo sampling from distributions was employed. To save time and computer expense, this was soon replaced with a method of employing averages, which could be carried out by hand. Concrete recommendations were made to management based on the simulation results. The recommendations were adopted and gratifying simulation agreement with subsequent operational data were found. The supreme test, company revenue increase, was also reported.

Traffic analysis of communications systems. The purpose of the analysis of Coe (1959) was to assess the traffic-handling capability of small telephone switchboards having twelve or fewer subscribers, handling conversations of one to six minutes duration. The average time to place the call, and measures of other limitations on service, were desired. The study developed a mathematical model, and actual and simulation tests were carried out to check the theoretical results. The paper gives considerable detail on the equipment and methods of simulation.

Telephone-traffic problems which are not on a scale of a modest number of interconnections, such as the above, most often deal with systems so large that the switching centers in the system have fifty or more operators each. Then assumptions of independence of traffic between various component circuits may be assumed, and standard queuing techniques applied. Brotman and Minker (1957) have simulated a communications system in which the independence assumption was not warranted.

Their simulation model was very flexible, any type of arrival-time and service-time distributions could be used, many network configurations could be handled, automatic dialing and other realistic features were incorporated. The simulation output data included: percentage of time station lines were used, number of calls encountering an "all-busy" signal, operator-usage percentages, average call duration, total-system service times, etc. On a fast computer the program could handle 4,000 messages (three hours real time) in three hours, plus fifteen minutes to compile statistics. Comparison of simulation results with actual field tests have indicated the validity of the simulation.

Evaluation of multimoded-system reliability. In a multimoded system, the system components can be switched into modes which give varying degrees of task performance. If one mode fails, the system may operate in a mode of less effectiveness. For example, if the search radar fails in a weapon system, the search mode may be accomplished by optical means. Various hardware components: servos, computers, indicators, power supply, can each cause one or more mode failures. The complexity of the reliability analysis is studied by Monte Carlo sampling on a digital computer. Such analysis can indicate whether or not it will pay to include alternative modes of operation, and how much these are worth to the system (Curtin, 1959).

Numerous interesting reports on commercial OR simulation applications are found in the *Report of System Simulation Symposium* (1957), sponsored jointly by the AIIE, TIMS, and ORSA. These include inventory-control studies, profit-planning, and airline-waiting-line problems, simulation of peak-hour bus operation, a cargo-handling problem, logistic-system studies, and others. A few moments spent with this report will give the reader an excellent feel for the generality and flexibility of the simulation technique.

On the international scene, the *Proceedings of the International Conference on Operational Research* (1957) contains several papers which indicate growing use of simulation methods in other countries. The next examples come from this book.

In the article by R. Hypher, several OR problems of the Canadian mining industry are discussed. Among them is a queuing problem in which waiting times occurred at the inflowing and outflowing ends of an ore reservoir at the mine head. Ore was scraped into the reservoir in a non-steady-state manner and cars then took the ore from the reservoir. A simulation study of the effect of various rates of filling the reservoir and rates of emptying it on the length of queues formed, led to a fuller understanding of the problem by management.

Monte Carlo was part of a study of how well colliery telephone communications systems at various colleries in the United Kingdom would work during an emergency (Clapham and Dunn). Robinson and Duckworth also reported a novel application of Monte Carlo. It was necessary to speed up the procedure for quoting prices to customers of a British metal company. The OR team found that the delays were in the estimating department and they applied a queuing analysis. Monte Carlo was used to assess the merits of proposed modifications, and successful recommendations were obtained.

In the Netherlands, Monte Carlo was used to study the problem of how the number of ladles of hot metal affects bunching delay of the furnaces (Santman). The frequency of a given number of furnaces bunching was computed by assuming a Poisson distribution. Monte Carlo runs, to determine the frequencies of two or three furnaces bunching, served to check out the Poisson hypothesis and the analysis was then completed.

Japanese OR personnel at the International Conference also reported simulation applications by the industrial and defense agencies of their country.

5.4. Other Industrial Simulation Applications

Job-shop simulations. In the literature, the term "job shop" generally refers to a production or processing facility comprised of collections of machines and workers of various types. In a woodworking shop, for example, there are drills, lathes, band saws, sanders, bench saws, planers, etc., together with the corresponding craftsmen. The shop may have a variety of finishing machines: paint sprayers, waxers, polishers, etc.

Each operation requires a different amount of time and hence there may be different numbers of machines of the various types. Each worker's time to perform a given type of job is different from that of a fellow worker because of skill differences and variance in worker motivation. A given worker will even vary in his time to do a certain job depending on his fatigue level, his momentary psychological mood, personal factors, etc.

The load or input to the shop is subject to wide variation. There is usually a scheduled standard input to the shop. In addition, large special orders will be received with advance notice. At other times, last-minute rush orders, both large and small, are received. Market changes, model changes, and changes in the quality-control tolerances may from time to time change the nature of the load as far as shop scheduling is concerned.

The basic problem of shop scheduling is to schedule the operation so as to maximize production during the working day, to establish various priority and work-splitting policies which enable the total facility task to be accomplished on time and with the minimum use of overtime, subcontracting, or hiring of extra help.

Such complicated operations are almost impossible to represent with a few mathematical equations (see Sisson, 1959). Simulation, an excellent tool for studying this type of problem, has been tried with encouraging results. Priority-dispatching studies, which gave valuable data and insight, have been run on the Cornell Research Simulator (see Conway, Johnson, and Maxwell articles, 1958 and 1959). Moreover, UCLA, General Electric, and International Business Machines all have machine simulation programs dealing with various forms of a job shop, each having slightly different rules for their simulation.

At the 1959 Washington meeting of the Operations Research Society, Baker and Dzielinski reported on a simulation of a small shop having nine to thirty single process facilities. Each facility is different from any of the others and could work on one and only one job at a time. The simulation could be used to study the effect of a set of alternative policy changes on the shop output.

The Martin Company, Denver, has attempted to use a digital computer to study alternative work schedules for a large-scale job shop. As input, this program receives shop configurations, capacities, work loads, and standard production times. The parameters used include availability and skill level of manpower; amount, type, and availability of equipment; dispatching system; scheduling technique; expected performance; and time periods. The computer program determines the work load by shop area, utilization of manpower and machines, waiting times and number of orders, the cost of in-process inventory, and a summary of completion dates of orders. The work confirms that simulation has promise of widespread application in industry.

Heller (1959) has carried out an analytic investigation which tends to corroborate the validity of simulation as a tool for job-shop study. The basic problem is to find an order of processing objects through machines which will minimize the total time of processing. If we sample (simulate) and take the job order giving the minimum schedule time for the sample, is it close to the actual minimum schedule time? IBM 704 experiments with six, ten, twenty, fifty, and one-hundred jobs, and with two to ten machines, suggested that schedule times are normally distributed. Detailed stochastic analysis was carried out to prove this conjecture as a theorem. A sampling procedure is then given for the probable determination of a minimum time schedule.

Simulation of the United States economy. Economists, too, have found that their traditional tools of investigation: time series, linearized economic theories, money and banking models, etc., have been unsuccessful in analyzing those problems which deal with dynamic processes. It has been found necessary to return to the individual decision unit, the family and the single corporation, and to permit these to make time-dependent decisions if valid economic predictions are to be made, and if the results of imposed controls and stimuli are to be understood. Older models deal only in aggregates and lack this dynamic attribute. Simulation is the answer.

Orcutt, Greenberger, Rivlin, and their associates (1958) have devised a simulation routine for the IBM 704 in which individuals, households, firms, banks, governments, etc. are the decision units. Each unit has time-dependent actions: individuals are born and die, households form and dissolve, firms produce and market, banks extend credit, etc. Each activity is governed by rules and submodels, and actual choices are made by Monte Carlo sampling.

The model has a "time-space" coordinate system. Time moves forward in jumps of one month, and the spatial unit or "point" is from the population of decision units mentioned before. The simulation proceeds serially and recursively along the time axis in steps of the discrete one-month periods. Within each month it proceeds serially and recursively along the population axis, one decision at a time.

Detailed realistic input data are fed into the model for each decision unit. For example, for each household unit there will be specified the number of children of each sex, the race identification, educational level of male adult, occupation of male adult, income, mortgage debt, male-adult age, number of years married, etc. Output variables of household units are births, deaths, purchases of various durable goods, and changes in mortgage and non-mortgage debt, liquid assets, etc. Comparable detail appears for the other decision units.

The major objective of this activity is to provide an instrument for consolidating past, present, and future research efforts of many individuals in various economic and social science areas into one effective model. Such a model can be used for short-run or long-run forecasting by appropriate selection of initial conditions. It can be used for unconditional forecasting, for predictions of what would happen given specified external conditions and governmental actions. It can be used to select the more desirable of two economic-policy decisions.

Simulation of transmission-system errors. A problem now being studied by J. Graves[7] of the Stromberg Carlson Company is to determine the error rate of a particular system of wire transmission. A wire-transmission system is being developed in the laboratory which employs a method of detection other than the usual amplitude method. It is desired to compare the error rate of this system, which will be

[7] Personal correspondence.

determined experimentally, to the error rate of the amplitude detection system. Since only the method of detection is being studied, it is necessary to hold all other operating characteristics constant. For instance, the system being developed employs three voltage levels which are called "positive mark," "negative mark," and "space." The positive and negative marks are alternating. It was this feature in particular which eliminated the possibility of solving the problem analytically.

The necessary programs have been written to solve the problem on the IBM 650 computer. The first step was to determine the filtering effect of various types of telephone lines on a single square pulse. Monte Carlo techniques were then used to generate random sequences of positive marks, negative marks, and spaces which conform with the operating characteristics of the system. With the known filtering effect of the transmission medium, it was possible to determine the output of any combination of signals. The final phase of the program was to simulate the amplitude-detection scheme on the computer and to thus determine the error rate of the system.

Digital simulation in perceptual research. E. E. David (1959) of the Bell Telephone Laboratories has suggested the use of simulation in the improvement of visual-auditory communications systems. The physically measurable properties of communications systems: bandwidth, signal-to-noise ratio, power, etc., are not enough to give the true judgment as to how human perception will evaluate the system. When a breadboard model is made, prepared known distortions can be fed into the unit and the output subjectively evaluated. However, in the case when no breadboard model exists, when a system is a drawing-board model, the "canned" input method cannot be tried in reality. In such cases, a digital computer can often be programmed to simulate the proposed system and to generate data for a realistic evaluation.

Investigations using this technique for audio and visual material have been carried out. Given a signal pattern, a data translator to convert analogue picture and speech signals into digital form was used to provide an input-output link to the computer. This is done by time sampling and amplitude quantizing. This simulation technique has also been used to more closely study properties of sets for which workable models exist. One can switch from study of one communication set to another merely by changing the program in the computer. Picture-processing simulations ran on an average of less than one minute per picture. It takes from ten to one-hundred times as long to process speech signals as to speak them. The work has included artificial recognition of speech and speech-like sounds. The use of these techniques to simulate design systems, which can then be evaluated subjectively, and the possibility of special-purpose, real-time digital transmission systems for future pictorial devices make this a promising area of application.

Simulation of RAMAC computer. Operation of the IBM 305 RAMAC computer has been simulated on the IBM 704 by Licht of General Motors Research Laboratories.[8] In building up a file of addresses for part numbers, an algorithm must be developed which maps the part numbers into RAMAC addresses. Because the range of part numbers is in general much larger than the total number of parts, difficulty is encountered in developing a mapping which can be computed simply and which will not assign the same address to different part numbers. Consequently, provision is made for "chaining" and "searching" for an appropriate address when the initial computed address has already been assigned.

However, "chaining" and "searching" require machine time. Consequently, the machine time required to build up the file is a function of both the number of duplications of initial addresses and the time required for seeking if an initial address is duplicated. The amount of duplication which occurs depends upon both the distribution of part numbers and the mapping function used. For this reason, the mapping function should be tailored to the specific distribution of part numbers. Developing an analytic method of determining an optimal mapping function does not appear to be feasible.

It has been possible, however, to prepare a program for the 704 computer so that the assignment of addresses duplicates the proposed procedure for the RAMAC and computes the time that the RAMAC would require for the operation. The 704 also computes the time which the RAMAC would have required to maintain the file, once it is established. Because of its high speed of computation, the 704 can in a matter of minutes duplicate a file build-up requiring many hours of RAMAC operations. Using the simulation program, the cost of a study of alternative algorithms to select the best one is modest.

Simulation of aircraft spare-parts inventory. B. L. Schwarz[9] reports an inventory simulation in which he was engaged at Battelle. The question under study was the suitable inventory level to be main-

[8] Communicated by A. V. Butterworth.

[9] Personal communication.

tained of certain original aircraft spare parts. On aircraft in the study, parts were separated into two classes, one of which comprised the critical parts under study, and the second, all others. In each class, two types of failure were recognized: limited failure, which did not cause the aircraft to go out of commission, and complete failure, which did. The failure rates were obtained from actual field-use data, as was the distribution of resupply times.

Using a digital computer, a simulation was effected in which the effect of the inventory level of the critical parts was studied for various combinations of size of aircraft fleet and the extent of the scheduled flying program. Maintenance programs included partial scheduled maintenance on weekends and one-shift service available on week days. Aircraft and service men were followed individually through the course of the digital simulation and service queues were considered. Part failures, both critical and non-critical, and service times were determined in each run by a Monte Carlo draw. The middle-square technique was used for generating quasi-random ten-digit numbers on an IBM 650. Running time on the 650 to simulate thirty to sixty days of operation was between one and two hours. A dozen runs or so proved sufficient to provide the required information about any particular configuration. Since about ten different configurations were being investigated, the total use of computer time amounting to several hundred hours was required. The results permitted the user to determine the appropriate inventory level of the critical parts for the various ranges of operating conditions covered by the simulation, as soon as he decided on a specific performance level.

Optimizing assignment of machines to a service man. Attached to each loom in a cloth-weaving plant is a bobbin winder which runs independently of the loom. This winder takes yarn from a creel package and winds it onto an empty bobbin. The winder operates faster than the loom and a reserve of up to six wound bobbins is able to form.

A winder tender is present whose first responsibility is to "tie in" a new creel package. If a malfunction occurs, such as breaking of yarn, jamming of a bobbin, bobbin becoming cocked, etc., the loom uses up the reserve bobbins and then stops. The tender must correct these malfunctions.

The tender had been assigned a specific number of winders to service. The assignment had heretofore been based on past experience and guesswork. A simulation model was set up on an IBM 650 which mimicked the operation of tender, looms, and winders in detail. By considering the cost in labor and the cost of any losses in loom efficiency, it was possible to determine the optimum number of machines to assign to a tender (Woodall, 1959).

Simulation of operation of a developed river basin. R. Dorfman[10] of Harvard University reports a program for simulation of river-basin operation (main stream, four tributaries, four dams, two power plants, irrigation works) for a random, but realistic, hydrology with due allowance for floods, water shortages, and other natural occurrences. Every two minutes the program performs an operations study that would occupy a team of engineers equipped with slide rules for several man-years. It is used to test alternative designs for developing the basin and is apparently a useful tool in the design of optimal large-scale water-resource developments.

Logistics study by simulation. Enke (1958) and Geissler (1959) describe the large-scale simulation activities of the RAND Logistics Systems Laboratory. Here the problems confronting the Air Force's logistics system are studied and new policies formulated and tested by simulation. Broida (1958) has used simulation to study Navy supply-system procurement rules.

Central-warehousing study. Robinson (1957) describes a long-term system warehousing inventory study which was accomplished by simulation and which has resulted in savings for Imperial Oil Limited of Canada.

Simulation of manpower requirements. Simulation is used to predict the manpower requirements and the best manner of using manpower to operate and maintain a complex of equipments in a dynamic setting (Vacherot and Teeple, 1958).

Weather simulation. A semianalytical model has been generated which simulates real weather by the random determination of representative weather conditions as a function of latitude and altitude. Kurlat and Johnson (see bibliography) report that the model is currently being extended to include longitudinal effects. The model is limited to the northern hemisphere between 20 degrees north latitude and 90 degrees north latitude and consists of a winter and summer terminal weather model, and a winter and summer upper-wind model.

Inventory allocation of pineapple produce. A model for giving pineapple-produce inventory requirements at each of several warehouses for specified protection against an out-of-stock condition was developed. Feasibility of the allocation method was checked by a

[10] Personal correspondence.

simulation of inventory fluctuations over a hypothetical year of operations. The simulation demonstrated the savings potential of the proposed allocation program (Eagle, 1957).

Digital simulation of air-traffic-control systems. Bond, Gale, and Moore (1958) studied air-traffic control by programming the rules for a digital computer for keeping track of positions, altitude, and speeds of aircraft and the rules for detecting and resolving air-traffic conflicts. Particular aircraft were then allowed to enter and climb-out into air corridors. Results were compared with results obtained by older graphical methods, and good agreement was found.

At the November, 1959, Pasadena meeting of the Operations Research Society a number of interesting simulation examples were presented. R. F. Reiss discussed the possibilities of digitally simulating neuromuscular organisms to observe total motor response to an environment. D. A. Bly of Texas Instruments, Inc., used a simulation model to study the effects of given degrees of error in forecasts of inventory requirements on the average inventory and average unit failures per week. J. M. Kibbee devised a simulation (computer version) of a management information and decision system. Management decisions are implemented and results are fed back for further decisions.

Additional simulation examples from governmental, industrial, and scientific areas might readily be cited. Other interesting material is found in Chapter III of *Simulation: Management's Laboratory* (see bibliography), a thorough survey of simulation activity. However, the pattern is clear. The same digitalized techniques developed during and after the war at Los Alamos and in military-operations-analysis units have now proved to be a boon to many problem areas. The foregoing applications have great structural similarities. With a stronger theory of simulation, more efficient techniques, and more efficient methods of measuring validity, a significant advance in man's ability to solve dynamic problems will have been made.

6. COMPUTERS AND SIMULATION

Assuming that the analyst has decided to simulate the system under study, the question of how to perform the simulation becomes of importance. A basic knowledge of the capabilities of available analogue and digital machines and of the time and costs of programming and then running the program must be obtained in order to decide on the proper level of detail of the simulation model. While the latest word on computer capabilities is best obtained from the research laboratories of universities and from computer companies, it may be helpful in this section to discuss a few actual experiences of the past. Experiences of the future are apt to differ more in degree than in kind.

6.1. Manual vs. Machine Simulation

Whether simulating by analogue means, digital means, or a combination of both, there is always the possibility of manual simulation. Rich (1955) describes a mechanical air-defense simulator with which two analysts could run about thirty attacks of ten planes each in a working day. At IAWR the author used an "expected value" air-penetration model to evaluate the capability of air-to-surface missiles. In this model the penetrating vehicles (of several types) were represented by cards of different colors and were pushed across a conventionalized map in accordance with their speeds and a basic computation time pulse. At each pulse attrition calculations were carried out on slide rule or desk calculator, and were marked onto the cards. A team of six analysts employing this model manually calculated the results of about a dozen air wars in two weeks. A larger team of IAWR personnel carried out a manual simulation of a very detailed air war (see Strauss and Feurzeig) working in three shifts for six weeks. A war calculation of this type (without data collation) later took about two hours on an IBM 704 computer.

The advantages of a manual simulation are several. First, the analyst team can see, understand, and develop more intuition for the operation being simulated than they can by reading computer outputs alone. (This intuition development can be good or bad, depending on whether the simulation is valid.) The analyst can see at each stage that the program is correctly performing the simulation, that no programming blunders are occurring, and that the model is not developing a ridiculous image of life. This cannot always be appreciated from model equations alone. For this reason, it is desirable to carry out a hand-simulation run as a check case for a computer-simulation program.

The most striking disadvantage of manual simulation is due to the statistical nature of Monte Carlo. Basically, a given case or a given set of inputs must be run again and again to get a stable mean value for that case. The preparation to run each case, as well as the actual run, is time consuming when done manually. Repetition is the forte of a digital computer. Of course, one sacrifices the ability to develop the intuition generated in the hand-operated simulation. One idea which tends to combine the benefits of each approach is to use the computer, but also to have intermediate punch-out. For example, in the aerial-penetration problem, the computer can run a given case for the desired number of times to give statistical stability, and it can also punch-out a report on the position of the penetrating bombers, the number of targets bombed, and the condition of defensive stockpiles after each ten minutes of the war. By plotting these ten-minute "snapshots" on charts, a sort of motion-picture version of the war is recreated.

Midway between a manual simulation and a computer simulation is the combined form of activity. A simulation model (not gaming with human decision makers) may be played on a large chart or map and whenever interaction is to be computed, inputs may be fed to a computer and the output used to move the pieces or to make the next calculation in the process. For some large-scale simulations which are to be run a limited number of times, this may be more efficient than the large investment in programming which is required to have the fully mechanized process. Also, a limitation of computer storage could force the simulation into this variety.

6.2. Selecting the Computer

F. W. Bratten (1956) has surveyed the status of analogue computation equipment for the simulation of dynamic systems. The basic requirement for training equipment is that flight simulators develop the solution in real time so that pilot response is correctly trained. Experience has shown that equipment failure *is* a problem and that it usually occurs in electromechanical elements such as electromagnetic choppers used in operational amplifier stabilization. Also the electromechanical elements ordinarily are the limiting factors in the upper frequency limit of operation. Newer equipment tends to use all-electronic devices. Errors due to human programming are also common. This indicates a need for more automatic programming techniques such as are being evolved for digital machines. Combination digital-analogue devices are also becoming common. Bratten concludes that equipment is available, or is being developed with the accuracy, speed of response, and range of parameters required by most aircraft and missile analogue-simulation problems.

When selecting a digital computer for a simulation problem, there are questions of computer speed, storage capacity, availability, costs, and ease of programming. Arithmetic computer operations are generally quite fast. In a 1956 survey Farrell gave a comparison of the speed for various digital computers to carry out a step in each of two typical methods of numerical integration and the time to perform an interpolation formula with forward differences (memory-access time not included). (See Table 9.1.) These data are now superseded by the

TABLE 9.1

ESTIMATED COMPUTATION SPEED FOR SEVERAL DIGITAL COMPUTERS

Computer	Arithmetic Operations (in seconds)		Interpolation Time (in seconds)
	Milne	Runge-Kutta	
IBM Defense Calculator	1.023	1.296	0.368
UNIVAC	1.740	2.280	0.520
ORDVAC	0.718	0.920	0.177
AVIDAC	0.198	0.261	0.056
ORACLE	0.269	0.348	0.075
MANIAC	1.558	2.029	0.413
SEAC	2.357	2.970	0.661
Statac Scoop	0.199	0.269	0.065
OARAC	4.104	5.978	1.713
WHIRLWIND	0.067	0.088	0.024
Consolidated Engineering	5.040	6.516	1.324
Elecom 210	54.516	70.278	19.984

performance of the new generation of computers. The big need for operational simulation is not that the computer have many-digit accuracy, as in numerical work, but that it have flexibility of computer logic.

The slowest operations for digital computers are input, output, placing data into storage, and retrieving data from storage. Great progress in input-output devices has been made in the last few years, but this is still a limiting factor. Various types of storage have now been devised: tapes, magnetic drum, magnetic core, etc. Of these, most rapid access can be obtained to magnetic-core storage. The size of the magnetic-core storage unit is the predominant factor in determining whether or not a large problem may be computed efficiently on a given machine.

Early IBM 704 machines had core storage of 4,096 words, and later models made 32,000 words available. The add time of the 704 is 0.000024 sec.! The newer IBM 7090 is approximately six times as fast as the IBM 704 and has 32,000 words of magnetic-core storage. The IBM STRETCH computer has an asynchronous (parallel operating modules) memory with "look-ahead" features which permit it to attain a speed of about seventy-five times that of the 704. The memory of STRETCH is magnetic core, up to 260,000 words of storage. Ever-greater-capacity, more-rapid-access storage devices are becoming available as research continues.

The storage problem may be broken into several parts, corresponding to the basic program elements. Perhaps the following description of a consideration of computer needs on a traffic simulation, from Goode (1957), will serve to portray the problem of selection, even though larger, faster, computers now exist.

> The size of a practical problem on the computer may be estimated as follows: In the model discussed above some 25 words (registers) of information storage were required to keep account of cars, condition of light, etc. In addition there were some 150 words of instruction, but in any computer these may be handled in various ways and in connection with the problem we are interested in here, extensions of intersections, routines, etc., do not increase the required storage of instructions rapidly since the routines are repeated. Thus we need consider only storage of information. To store several lanes would probably double the number of required words to 50. To store parking and pedestrians would probably triple to 75. To allow speed changes might make this 100 as a requirement per intersection. As for time, the MIDAC required 3.2 times real time as noted above. When extending the problem we may use a faster computer either to go faster, or to handle a larger problem. Therefore interpolation on the figure must be used as required for the particular extension at hand. Some of the resulting points are marked off in the diagram (Fig. 9.5).
>
> It is noteworthy that each piece of information that is used in the computer, as for example the position of a particular car, is used in the same order each time the model is traversed. This makes it possible to consider relatively slow methods of storage, such as magnetic drums, and to store in such a fashion that as a piece of information is required it comes up on the drum in position to be read. It has been estimated that an ordinary drum machine such as the Datatron or the 650 may be made to look like four-micro-second access time if the programming is done carefully with regard to the machine itself. Therefore, the above picture is not quite a complete statement of the situation. However, as may be seen from the diagram, a fairly large model may be handled in terms of presently available computers (pp. 786–787).

Other statements on simulation computer usage may be helpful. The air-traffic-control simulation of Bond, Gale, and Moore (1958), a typical small simulation problem, required about 1,300 instructions and 500 locations out of the available 2,000 ten-digit storage on the magnetic drum of an IBM 650. Computing time required to follow from 35 to 75 aircraft for 200 minutes ranged from 20 to 55 minutes. The medium-sized program of Brotman and Seid for simulating a massed-bomber, manned-interceptor encounter utilized 10,000 storage locations of the 32,000 available in the IBM 704. About 10 per cent of the

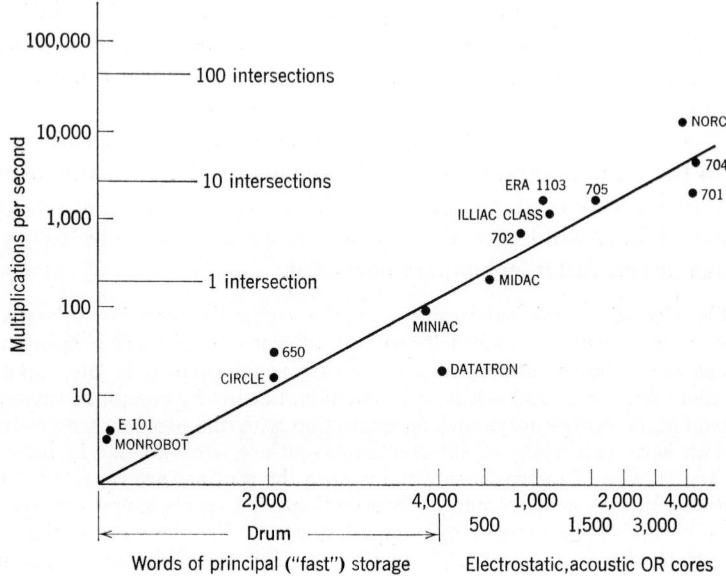

Fig. 9.5. Comparison of computers for traffic problem. [From Goode, *Opns. Res.,* **5,** 787 (1957).]

storage used was devoted to instructions. Computer running time varied from real time to twice real time. The IAWR SCRAMBLE model, some of the recent air-battle models at RAND, and those of various defense agencies are very large, requiring hours per 704 run. R. Dorfman claims that the river-basin simulation, which was mentioned earlier, will be one of the largest ever programmed for the 704.

The time involved to devise a simulation model and to program it is considerable, and it should not be underestimated. McKown, Reedy, and Poe record that their air-battle simulation on the IBM 704 took ten man months to formulate, one man month to code, and one man month to check out. This is a medium-sized simulation.

The IAWR SCRAMBLE model required about nine months to develop and about nine more months to program. The program length is about 25,000 words. Data storage (core/drum) is about 25,000 words, in addition to which about six tape-storage units are required. A single complete run requires about five hours of computer time, two hours of battle interaction and several hours of pre- and post-statistical and summarizing work. The Project OMEGA model also utilizes 25,000 words of instructions for the main part of the program. Dorfman cites eighteen months of programming on the large river-basin problem.

There are analyst, computer, and programming developments which promise improvement in the amount of time required to perform a simulation. First, as an early participant in large-scale simulations, the author believes that next time, his experience will enable him to accomplish much more model building in much less time. Analysts now have that priceless commodity, experience. Secondly, computers are becoming faster: input, output, and storage-access times are being lessened dramatically. Storage capacity is being greatly increased. Finally, all major computer manufacturers are "educating" their computers to recognize standard English commands, to recognize certain problem types, to decide how to compute, and to self-program to do so. New programming tricks and subroutines are appearing every day, and the end is not yet in sight. In the running of the SCRAMBLE program, analysts have devised pre- and post-routines to help get the run started and to cull the data when finished. OMEGA uses the Plan Converter to convert Air Force plans into input and the Output System to sort, compile, and tabulate detailed results. Simulation mechanics is becoming easier for the analyst every day.

7. FUTURE PROSPECTS FOR SIMULATION

In the author's opinion, simulation is here to stay, and a theory and practice of simulation have established themselves. In 1957 a Symposium on Simulation was held in New York City, and in 1959 a second one was held at Northwestern University. Drozda [11] of General Electric indicates plans for a College of Simulation which will develop a detailed report on the topic, and other professional activity on simulation is evident. Simulation is still evolving, and the basic question of validity of results must be further resolved theoretically. Certain challenges and dangers remain, either because of this theoretical vacuum, or because of the lack of efficiency of simulation (see Kellogg)—analysts must strive to correct these:

a. There is a tendency for analysts to construct a policy or decision rule which "beats" the simulated model instead of maximizing against reality.

b. Monte Carlo is essentially imprecise. Unlike numerical integration, iterations give a mean value and a confidence interval about the

[11] Personal correspondence.

mean, not an absolute interval of error. In some large military-simulation models whose outputs were "bombs on target," standard deviations of about 10 per cent of the mean have been informally reported.

c. Simulation is basically a very slow way to do research. If a new case is raised, new simulator runs must be made. In a sense, good simulation and good Monte Carlo should be self-annihilating. When you learn enough to make an analytic model, make it.

d. Simulation is inherently costly. To the large expenditures of analyst and programmer time must be added machine running time, sometimes at hundreds of dollars per hour. Often one underestimates the initial cost and the number of cases which will be run. The results are tragic for research budgets.

e. There is a tendency to investigate *every* problem by simulation because it is "fashionable," without carefully considering whether alternative standard methods might not be more efficient.

f. Another difficulty with large-scale simulation is that the analyst cannot foresee beforehand exactly which variables will be needed to resolve the issues. He therefore collects all manner of data from the runs, thereby encouraging numerical indigestion. The human mind just cannot absorb the reams of computer output. J. Hall [12] has noted that this uncertainty also has prevented introduction of variance-reducing techniques because: (1) one must know which random variables should have their variance reduced, and (2) there is a fear of violently warping some aspect of the process whose output may later turn out to be essential for a complete solution.

g. Those who listen to the results of large-scale simulation but who are not well read in its philosophy and limitations may read more into the results, or place complete, unquestioning faith in the numerical values themselves, without attempting to ask what phenomena in the process led to the observed values.

h. Some simulations are needlessly ponderous. In an attempt to be "realistic," unnecessary detail has been carried over into the model. The only cure for this is analyst judgment, experience, and better comprehension of the problem. It is generally better to start simply, with as little detail as possible, and to progress to greater detail only as the work indicates this to be necessary.

i. Cohen (1959) has pointed out the danger that even though the correct probability laws are known for all of the submodels in a simulation, the model flow chart may combine them as though they were stochastically independent, neglecting important correlations. In the

[12] Personal correspondence.

interest of avoiding this, at least one case of the total simulation output should be validated against reality if possible. It is not enough just to check out all of the submodels.

j. Each simulation usually turns out to be a specific tool. Perhaps the author is a cynic, but all too often he has heard the phrase, "This model may be plugged into a larger simulation model as an input." This *has* happened, but seldom. Scaling, machine differences, analyst taste, etc., all seem to demand that each new application require a new simulation model and a new program.

Some work on generalized simulation models is now being done, however. For example, it may be possible to establish a generalized inventory model and to prepare a general simulation routine. Then as particular inventory problems arise, the parameters can be specified and answers rapidly generated. This approach is similar to the gradual emergence of subroutines and simplified computer-programming methods. With such computer devices, important building-block units may now be combined easily to perform complicated calculations. Previously, detailed and time-consuming programming, different for each computer, was required to complete any computing job.

Despite the listed dangers, simulation must be considered a wonderful tool if used with discretion. It can be of real value as a check on other methods, and invaluable in those cases when all else fails.

BIBLIOGRAPHY

Only within the last few years have several publications become available which furnish extensive bibliographies on simulation and Monte Carlo. Because so much of the work in these areas has been held back owing to security or company proprietary regulations, it seems worth while for this reading audience to list the cross section of simulation work which was surveyed in compiling this review chapter, even though this may appear to duplicate existing bibliographies. The four publications which list extensive simulation bibliographies are given first, followed by the remaining entries in alphabetical order.

1. Case Institute of Technology, Operations Research Group, *A Comprehensive Bibliography on Operations Research* (and supplement), John Wiley and Sons, New York, 1957.
2. Simulation Associates, *Simulation, Management's Laboratory,* Harvard University, Graduate School of Business Administration, 1959. This publication contains a thorough survey of the present-day activity in simulation as compiled by several graduate students at the School of Business, Harvard University. It contains over 200 references to work on simulation.

3. University of Florida, *Symposium on Monte Carlo Methods,* John Wiley and Sons, New York, 1956. The extensive bibliography in this excellent volume is divided into four parts: I. Monte Carlo proper (75 entries and 4 addenda); II. Generation and testing of random digits and known sources of random-digit tables (42 entries); III. Articles and books, mostly without abstracts, in which sampling is primarily relied upon for a solution or verification (91 entries); IV. Selection of articles and books on, or making use of, stochastic processes, mostly without abstracts (170 entries). Most entries have descriptive remarks.
4. Batchelor, J. H., *Operations Research,* St. Louis University Press, 2nd ed., 1959. An annotated bibliography.

Adams, E. A., and Forrester, R. D., *Carmonette: A Computer Combat Simulation,* Operations Research Office, Johns Hopkins University, Washington, D. C., 1959.

Baker, C. T., and Dzielinski, B. P., *Simulation of a Simplified Job Shop,* IBM Research Center, Yorktown Heights, N. Y., 1959.

Beer, S., "The Mechanical Simulation of Stochastic Flow," *Proc. of the First Inter. Conf. on OR,* ORSA, Baltimore, 166–175 (1957).

Bellman, R., "Top Management Decision and Simulation Processes," *J. Indust. Eng.,* **9,** 459–464 (1958).

Bellman, R., Clark, C., Craft, C., Malcolm, D., and Ricciardi, F., "On the Construction of a Multi-Person, Multi-Stage Business Game," *Opns. Res.,* **5,** 469–503 (1957).

Biel, W. C., *Operations Research Based on Simulations for Training,* SP-16, System Development Corporation, National Conf. of Aeronautical Electronics (1958).

Blumstein, A., "A Monte Carlo Analysis of the Ground Controlled Approach System," *Opns. Res.,* **5,** 397–408 (1957).

Bond, G. W., Gale, K. S., and Moore, C. J., *Digital Simulation of Air Traffic Control Systems,* presented at Natl. Conf. on Aeronautical Electronics, Dayton, Ohio, 1958.

Bouckaert, Louis, "Les Methods de Monte Carlo," *Rev. Questions Sci.,* **5,** 344–359 (1956).

Box, G. E. P., and Muller, M. E., "A Note on the Generation of Random Normal Deviates," *Annals of Math. Stat.,* **29,** 610–611 (1958).

Bradford, J. C., and Fain, W. W., *Operations Research for Weapon System Analysis,* Chance Vought Aircraft, Inc., Dallas, Texas, 1959.

Bratten, F. W., *Dynamic System Studies: Analog Computation,* WADC Tech. Report 54-250, Part 5 (1956).

Broadview Research Corp., *Instruction Manual Intermediate (IBM 650) Computer Simulation of Army Communication Systems,* Burlingame, Calif., 1957.

Broida, T. R., *Computer Simulation of a Procurement Decision Rule for Complex Supply Systems,* Stanford Research Institute, presented at ORSA Meeting, Boston, Mass., 1958.

Brooks, S. H., "A Comparison of Maximum Seeking Methods," *Opns. Res.,* **7,** 430–457 (1959).

Brotman, L., and Minker, J., "Digital Simulation of Complex Traffic Problems in Communications Systems," *Opns. Res.,* **5,** 670–679 (1957).

Brotman, L., and Seid, B., *Digital Simulation of a Massed Bomber–Manned Interceptor Encounter,* Hughes Research and Development Labs. (no date).

Brown, P., Freed, A., and Jordan, N., *Training for Duty Directors Through STP,* TM-285, System Development Corporation, Santa Monica, Calif. (1958).

Campbell, F. M., *Monopologs: Management Decision Making Game Applied to Tool Room Management,* Oklahoma State U., Stillwater, Okla., 1959.

Carlisle, R., *Model Techniques for Communication Systems,* Broadview Research Corp., Burlingame, Calif. (1957).

Carter, L. F., *Matching the Man System and the Electronics System in Design and Operations,* System Development Corporation, Santa Monica, Calif. (no date).

Caywood, T., and Caviness, J., *Digital Simulation of Vigilante Fire-Control,* Caywood-Schiller, Assoc., Chicago, Ill., 1959.

Chambers, R. M., and Doerfel, H. V., *Closed-Loop Centrifuge Simulation of Space-Vehicle Performance,* presented at the ARS Semi-Annual Meeting, San Diego, Calif., 1959.

Clapham, J. C. R., and Dunn, H. D., "Communications in Collieries," Proc. of the First Inter. Conf. on OR, 291–305, 1957.

Coe, J. C., "Traffic Analysis of Small Telephone Switchboards," *Opns. Res.,* **7,** 347–361 (1959).

Cohen, K. J., *Computer Simulation, Some Methodological Problems,* Carnegie Institute of Technology, Graduate School of Industrial Administration, Pittsburgh, Pa., 1959.

Conway, R. W., Johnson, B. M., and Maxwell, W. L., *An Experimental Investigation of Priority Dispatching,* Dept. of Indust. and Eng. Admin., Cornell U., Ithaca, N. Y., 1959.

Conway, R. W., Johnson, B. M., and Maxwell, W. L., "Some Problems of Digital Systems Simulation," *Mgmt. Sci.,* **6,** 92–110 (1959).

Conway, R. W., Johnson, B. M., and Maxwell, L., *The Cornell Research Simulator,* Cornell U., Ithaca, N. Y., 1958.

Craft, C. J., *Integrated Materials Management Simulation Exercise,* paper presented at meeting of Assn. for Computing Machinery, MIT, Cambridge, Mass., 1959.

Craft, C. J., *Management Games Using Punched Cards and Computers,* Peat, Marwick, Mitchell & Co., New York (no date).

Crane, R. R., Brown, F. B., and Blanchard, R. O., "An Analysis of a Railroad Classification Yard," *Opns. Res.,* **3,** 262–272 (1955).

Curtin, K. M., "A 'Monte Carlo' Approach to Evaluate Multimoded System Reliability," *Opns. Res.,* **7,** 721–727 (1959).

Dahlquist, G., "The Monte Carlo Method," *Nordisk Mat. Tidskr.,* **2,** 27–43 (1954), expository paper, Swedish (English summary).

David, E. E., Jr., *Digital Simulation in Perceptual Research,* Bell Telephone Laboratories, Inc., Murray Hill, N. J. (no date).

Driggs, I., "A Monte Carlo Model of Lanchester's Square Law," *Opns. Res.,* **4,** 148–151 (1956).

Dunn, O. E., *Simulation of Traffic Loading in a Single Communication Center System,* Data Reduction Center, Applied Research Lab., U. of Arizona, Tucson, Ariz. (no date).

Dunn, P. F., Flagle, C. D., and Hicks, P. A., "The Queuiac: An Electromechanical Analog for the Simulation of Waiting-Line Problems," *Opns. Res.,* **4,** 648–662 (1956).

Dunne, J. J., and Sebastian, R. A., *Computer Played War Games,* Office of Ordnance Research, Report No. 59-3, Ordnance Corps, Durham, North Carolina (1959).

Dupac, V., "Stochastic Numerical Methods," *Casopis Pest. Mat.,* **81,** 55–68 (1956), Czech., Russian and English summaries.

Eagle, A. R., "Distribution of Seasonal Inventory of the Hawaiian Pineapple Company," *Opns. Res.,* **5,** 382–396 (1957).

Eckstrand, G., and Rockway, M. R., *Role of Simulators in a Holding Facility,* presented at the ARS Semi-Annual Meeting, San Diego, Calif., 1959.

Enke, S., *Use of a Simulation Laboratory to Study the Organization and Effectiveness of Air Force Logistics,* P-1343, The RAND Corp., Santa Monica, Calif. (1958).

Fair, W. R., "Analogue Computations of Business Decisions," *Opns. Res.,* **1,** 208–219 (1953).

Farrell, R. H., *Dynamic System Studies: Digital Computers,* WADC Tech. Report 54-250, Part 7 (1956).

Flannagan, J. C., *A Monte Carlo Computer Simulation for the Evaluation of Anti-Armor Weapon Systems,* presented at 15th Annual Meeting of ORSA, 1959.

Ford, J. D., Jr., *Test Plan for the Multiple Purpose System Training Project,* TM-348, System Development Corp., Santa Monica, Calif. (1959).

Ford, L. R., Jr., Isaacson, H. S., and Pethel, F. C., "Computer Terrain Simulation for Line-of-Sight Calculations," *Opns. Res.,* **7,** 478–482 (1959).

Forrester, J. W., "Industrial Dynamics, A Major Breakthrough for Decision Makers," *Harvard Business Review,* **36,** 37–66 (1958).

Fosdick, L. D., *Calculation of Order Parameters in a Binary Alloy by the Monte Carlo Method,* Digital Computer Laboratory, U. of Illinois, Urbana (no date).

Fosdick, L. D., *Studies of the Monte Carlo Method Applied to the Ising Lattice Problem,* Midwestern Universities Research Association (no date).

Franckx, E., "La Methode de Monte-Carlo," *Assoc. Actuair. Belges, Bull.,* **58,** 89–101 (1956).

Geissler, M. A., *The Use of Man-Machine Simulation in the Design of Control Systems,* P-1780, The RAND Corp., Santa Monica, Calif. (1959).

Goen, R. L., *Monte Carlo Simulation of Missile Maintenance Cycling,* No. Am. Aviation, Inc., Downey, Calif., 1959.

Goetz, M., "An Application of a Dynamic-Simulation Model to a Scheduling Problem," *Proc. of the First Inter. Conf. on OR,* 1957.

Goode, H. H., "The Application of a High Speed Computer to the Definition and Solution of the Vehicular Traffic Problem," *Opns. Res.,* **5,** 775–793 (1957).

Goode, H. H., and True, W. C., *Simulation and Display of Four Inter-Related Vehicular Traffic Intersections,* U. of Michigan, Ann Arbor, 1958.

Hammersley, J. M., and Morton, K. W., "A New Monte Carlo Technique: Antithetic Variates," *Proc. Cambridge Philos. Soc.,* **52,** 449–475 (1956).

Hammersley, J. M., and Nelder, J. A., "Sampling from an Isotropic Gaussian Process," *Proc. Cambridge Philos. Soc.,* **51,** 652–662 (1955).

Hardy, J. D., and Clark, C. C., "The Development of Dynamic Flight Simulation," *Aero/Space Engineering,* **18,** 48–52 (1959).

Harling, J., "*Simulation Techniques in Operations Research—A Review,*" *Opns. Res.,* **6,** 307–319 (1958).

Heller, J., *Combinatorial Probabilistic and Statistical Aspects of an* M × J *Scheduling Problem,* AEC Computing and Applied Math. Center, Inst. of Math. Sciences, N.Y.U., 1959.

Himes, B. T., *Photoelectric Coverage Machine,* RM-227, The RAND Corp., Santa Monica, Calif. (1949).

Hochfeld, E., ed., *Stabilization of Computer Circuits,* System Research, U. of Chicago, WADC Tech. Report 57-425 (1957).

Jennings, N. H., and Dickins, J. H., "Computer Simulation of Peak Operations in a Bus Terminal," *Mgmt. Sci.,* **5,** 106–120 (1958).

Jeske, J. W., Jr., *A Case Study of the Use of Simulation and Computer Application to a Production Control Problem,* Western Electric Co., Inc. (no date).

Jones, N. F., Heit, P. B., and Livingston, D. G., *Monte Carlo Simulation of Claim Distribution in a Life Insurance Company—A Case History,* presented at 5th Annual International Meeting of TIMS, Philadelphia, Pa., 1958.

Kahn, H., and Mann, I., *Techniques of Systems Analysis,* The RAND Corp., Santa Monica, Calif., 1957.

Kahn, H., and Marshall, A. W., "Methods of Reducing Sample Size in Monte Carlo Computations," *Opns. Res.,* **1,** 263–278 (1953).

Kellogg, C. M., *Difficulties of Simulation,* General Electric Co., Home Laundry Dept. (no date).

Kennedy, J. L., *Gaming Theory and Its Relation to Industrial Psychology,* Princeton U., Princeton, N. J. (no date).

King, G. W., "The Monte Carlo Method as a Natural Mode of Expression in Operations Research," *Opns. Res.,* **1,** 46–52 (1953).

Kupferberg, S., *Statistical Estimation and Test of Hypotheses as Applied to Non-Deterministic Models,* Institute for Air Weapons Research, Report 58-7, U. of Chicago (1958).

Kurlat, S., and Johnson, J., *A Method for Introducing Weather into a Simulation Model,* Technical Operations, Inc., Burlington, Mass. (no date).

Law, C. E., *War Gaming in the Canadian Army,* Department of National Defence, CAORE Memo No. 59/5, Ottawa, Canada (1959).

Malcolm, D. G., "System Simulation, A Management Wind Tunnel," *Nation's Business,* February, 1958.

Marshall, A. W., *Experimentation by Simulation and Monte Carlo,* P-1174, The RAND Corp., Santa Monica, Calif. (1958).

McCracken, D. D., "The Monte Carlo Method," *Sci. Amer.,* **192,** 90–96 (1955).

McDonald, J., and Ricciardi, F., "The Business Decision Game," *Fortune,* March, 1958.

McKown, D. C., *Survey of Methods for Finding Maximum Values Experimentally,* Chance Vought Aircraft, Inc., Dallas, Texas, 1958.

McKown, D. C., Reedy, D. M., and Poe, P. H., *Air Battle Simulation Experiences with the IBM 704,* Chance Vought Aircraft, Inc., Dallas, Texas (no date).

Meyer, G. L., *Image Simulation and Interpretation,* Astro-Electronic Products Div., Radio Corporation of America, Princeton, N. J. (no date).

Miller, K. S., and Murray, F. J., *Dynamic System Studies: Error Analysis for Differential Analyzers,* WADC Tech. Report 54-250, Part 14 (1956).

Miller, K. S., and Murray, F. J., "A Mathematical Basis for an Error Analysis of Differential Analyzers," *J. Math. Phys.,* **32,** 136–163 (1953).

Moore, C. J., and Lewis, T. S., *Digital Simulation of Discrete Flow Systems,* presented at meeting of Assn. for Computing Machinery, MIT, Cambridge, Mass., 1959.

Morgenthaler, G. W., and Hesse, H., *A Conceptual Model for Studying Strategic Aerial Penetration,* Institute for Air Weapons Research, Report 57-3, University of Chicago, Chicago, Ill. (1957).

Morgenthaler, G. W., *Some Target Coverage Problems,* The Martin Co., Denver, Colo., 1959.

Moss, J. H., "Commentary on Harling's Simulation Techniques in Operations Research," *Opns. Res.,* **6,** 591–593 (1958).

Muller, M. E., "Continuous Monte Carlo Methods for the Dirichlet Problem," *Annals of Math. Stat.,* **27,** 569–589 (1956).

O'Brien, G. G., and Crane, R. R., "The Scheduling of a Barge Line," *Opns. Res.,* **7,** 561–570 (1959).

Orcutt, G. H., "A New Type of Socio-Economic System," *Review of Econ. and Stat.,* **39,** 116–123 (1957).

Orcutt, G. H., Greenberger, M., and Rivlin, A., *Decision-Unit Models and Simulation of the United States Economy,* preliminary draft, 1958.

Rich, R. P., "Simulation As an Aid in Model Building," *Opns. Res.,* **3,** 15–19 (1955).

Robinson, P. J., *Cases in Simulation—A Research Aid as a Management "Demonstration Piece,"* Presentation at Seminar on Techniques of Industrial Operations Research, Ill. Inst. of Technology, Chicago, Ill., 1957.

Schiller, D. H., and Lavin, M. M., "The Determination of Requirements for Warehouse Dock Facilities," *Opns. Res.,* **4,** 231–242 (1956).

Sisson, R. L., "Methods of Sequencing in Job Shops—A Review," *Opns. Res.,* **7,** 10–29 (1959).

Spanier, J., Kuehn, H., and Guilinger, W., *A Two-Dimensional Monte Carlo Calculation of Capture Fractions on the IBM-704,* WAPD-TM-125, Office of Tech. Services, Dept. of Commerce, Washington, D. C. (1959).

Spanier, J., *Monte Carlo Methods and Their Application to Neutron Transport Problems,* WAPD-195, Office of Technical Services, Dept. of Commerce, Washington, D. C. (1959).

Spanier, J., *The Physics and Mathematical Analysis for the Monte Carlo Code TUT-T5,* WAPD-TM-186, Office of Technical Services, Dept. of Commerce, Washington, D. C. (1959).

Strauss, W., and Feurzeig, N., *IAWR-SAC Penetration Campaign Model as Applied in March, 1957,* Institute for Air Weapons Research, Report 57-4, University of Chicago, Chicago (1957).

Swensson, O., "An Approach to a Class of Queuing Problems," *Opns. Res.,* **6,** 276–292 (1958).

Swift, C. W., *The Significance of Management Games,* presented to Institute of Management Science, Chicago Chapter, 1958.

Taub, A. H., "A Sampling Method for Solving the Equations of Compressible Flow in a Permeable Medium," *Proceedings of the Midwestern Conf. on Fluid Dynamics, 1950,* 121–127, J. W. Edwards, Ann Arbor, Mich., 1951.

Taylor, J. L., "Development and Application of a Terminal Air Battle Model," *Opns. Res.,* **7,** 783–796 (1959).

Thomas, C. J., "The Genesis and Practice of Operational Gaming," *Proc. of the First Inter. Conf. on OR,* 64–81, ORSA, Baltimore, 1957.

Thomas, C. J., and Deemer, W. L., Jr., "The Role of Operational Gaming in Operations Research," *Opns. Res.,* **5,** 1–27 (1957).

Thomas, L. H., "A Comparison of Stochastic and Direct Methods for the Solution of Some Special Problems," *Opns. Res.,* **1,** 181–186 (1953).

Tomkins, C., "Machine Attacks on Problems Whose Variables are Permutations," *Proceedings of Symposia in Applied Mathematics, Vol. VI, Numerical Analysis,* McGraw-Hill Book Co., New York, 1956, pp. 195–211.

University of Chicago, *Dynamic-System Studies: Conclusions and Recommendations,* Advisory Board on Simulation, WADC Tech. Report 54-250, Part 1 (1956).

U.S. Dept. of Commerce, National Bureau of Standards, *Monte Carlo Method,* Applied Math. Series 12, 1951.

Vacherot, M. G., and Teeple, J. B., *Dynamic Analysis of Manpower Requirements on a Digital Computer,* Radio Corporation of America, Tucson, Ariz., 1958.

Vazsonyi, A., *Electronic Simulation of Business Operations* (*The Monte Carlo Method*), presented to 2nd Annual West Coast Engineering Management Conf., 1957.

Ware, E. B., *Job Shop Simulation on the IBM-704,* presented at meeting of Association for Computing Machinery, MIT, Cambridge, Mass., 1959.

Webb, K. W., and Moshman, J., *A Simulation for Optimal Scheduling of Maintenance of Aircraft,* C.E.I.R., Inc., Arlington, Va., 1959.

Wendel, J. G., "Groups and Conditional Monte Carlo," *Annals of Math. Stat.,* **28,** 1048–1051 (1957).

Winson, J., *The Error Analysis of Electronic Analog Computation, Linear Differential Equations with Constant Coefficients,* Ph.D. Thesis, Columbia U., New York, 1954.

Woodall, H. McG., *A Simulation Model for Determining Optimum Machine Assignment,* M.S. Thesis, North Carolina State College, Raleigh, N. C., 1959.

Chapter **10**

MILITARY GAMING

Clayton J. Thomas

Operations Analysis Office, Headquarters, U.S. Air Force, Washington, D. C.

Contents

1. INTRODUCTION [1]

Military gaming comprises a vast jumble of techniques used for the study of military problems. At a large number of military establishments, university groups, and research organizations, teams of military and scientific experts are using a great variety of techniques to tackle some of the tough questions that confront the military decision maker. Some of these methods are classic; to a reincarnated von Reisswitz, Jr., they would seem almost identical with the Kriegspiel that he introduced into the Prussian Army in 1824, a war game that itself had antecedents stretching far back to the early chess of a dimly seen antiquity. Some of the present methods, however, involve radical departures from the classic game; an enthusiastic war gamer, transported to the present from days as recent as those of World War II, would find much that is strikingly new in the modern appeal to the computing capacity of electronic calculators or to the rigorous concepts of the theory of games.

The exact scope of military gaming, though admittedly large, is itself a subject of some debate. It is a question that might be resolved by fiat, if one were devising a language like Esperanto by starting with concepts and then constructing words to represent them. In the present situation, however, where "military gaming" is given as a particularly vital phrase of a living language, one must, conversely, seek the concepts that underlie existing words. Such a search was one of the functions of a survey which sampled some of the work currently being done in the name of "military gaming."

Present usage, it turns out, definitely favors a broad interpretation of the phrase "military gaming." Some experts consciously use it to include a vast array of techniques, among which are such diverse elements as the theory of games and classic war gaming. Other experts, individually, use "military gaming" to refer to a smaller family of techniques, but the families differ from expert to expert, so that in the aggregate one is led, again, to a broad interpretation.

Efforts to find a definition to fit the broad interpretation of "mili-

[1] This chapter is based on a survey conducted in the summer of 1959 by C. J. Thomas and W. L. Deemer, Jr., and reflects the joint assessment they formed at that time.

tary gaming" tend to result in something like the following paraphrase: "Military gaming is the investigation of future military reality through its representation as a game." In this crude characterization, the term "game" must, in its turn, be interpreted rather broadly as something that may have fewer than two players, exactly two players, or more than two players, and whose rules may be in one of various stages of incompleteness. Such definitions, which are made broad enough to include most of the major activities that are frequently termed "military gaming," usually seem to be too broad, in that they threaten to encroach on all of military operations research.

Thus this chapter does not base its treatment of military gaming primarily on such a definition, but it seeks the essence of the subject through an inquiry into the development of the major modes of gaming that flourish today. Section 2 gives a brief account of the history of gaming. Section 3 lists examples of present military-gaming applications in order to set the stage for more detailed descriptions to follow. Sections 4, 5, 6, and 7 then treat in greater detail major families of applications that cluster, respectively, about the classic three-team war game, the large computer simulation model, the mathematical theory of games, and laboratory simulation. Finally, in Section 8, there is some discussion of the validity of the multifarious gaming applications.

This chapter, then, is to a large extent descriptive, and, as a further reflection of the sprawling and amorphous nature of military gaming, it does not contain the kinds of systematizing possible with better-ordered subjects. The present discussion, particularly that of Section 8, contains some implications for contemplated future applications of gaming, but nowhere does the present chapter give the kind of prescription for problem solving that could be found in texts on analytical chemistry or elementary differential equations. The chapter gives many problems to which techniques of gaming are applied with varying success, but it cannot give a simple classification into solved and unsolved problems, such as one finds in a discussion of subjects like queuing theory and mathematical programming that partake to a greater extent of the clarity and discipline of mathematics. The present chapter gives many examples of the kind of gaming applications that are being made, but it does not give either a general catalogue or a complete description of any single application, such as one might expect if the chapter were longer or the subject smaller. Many of the details of present applications, moreover, are available only in classified publications.

2. THE HISTORICAL DEVELOPMENT OF MILITARY GAMING

The aim of the present section is to present just enough of the historical development of military gaming to show the principal forces responsible for its growth. Part 2.1 outlines the development of the classic war game to the end of World War II. Parts 2.2 and 2.3 then touch, respectively, on the subsequent contributions of electronic computing machines and the mathematical theory of games. In Part 2.4, the roles of the separate contributions of war games, computing machines, and game theory are then used as a guide to an understanding of the diversity of techniques that today coexist under the name of "military gaming."

2.1. The Development of the Classic War Game

The present discussion is intended primarily to capture the spirit of the classic game. For this purpose it suffices to give only a few illustrative details of a few of the many species of gaming whose development led ultimately to the war game as it was known at the end of World War II. Those who are interested in a fuller treatment of this interesting evolution will find a good account and an extensive bibliography in Young (1959).

In Sayre (1908) it is said that "The game of chess is the oldest form of war game, and modern map maneuvers have grown out of the game of chess by a long process of evolution" (p. 5). This account says that species flourishing in the seventeenth and eighteenth centuries still "may be designated as war chess" (p. 7). Outstanding examples were introduced by Christopher Weikhmann in 1664, by Hoechenberger in 1770, by Helwig in 1780, and by Georg Venturini in 1798. Helwig, a master of pages at the court of Brunswick, wrote that his game was devised ". . . for attracting the attention of young men destined for military service . . . and lessening the difficulties of instruction" (p. 6). These games became more and more elaborate, with that of Venturini requiring 3,600 squares for the representation of troop marches and sixty pages of rules for the movement and fighting of the troops. From the point of view of later developments, an outstanding contribution of Venturini's "New Kriegspiel" was the introduction of maps to replace the older game boards.

The artificialities and complications of these early games should not be characterized simply as mistakes introduced by their inventors. Sayre (1908) quotes von der Goltz as saying that Venturini's game ". . . is a bad product of the refined military education of the period, which had piled up so many difficulties that it was incapable of taking a step in advance" (p. 7). And it should be remarked that many of the "difficulties" encountered in military education resulted from the restricted nature of war itself as it was then known. Many of these restrictions were brushed away as the grand armies of Napoleon swept over the face of Europe, and warfare became more like the "total war" that is known today. Concomitant with this modernization of warfare was the modernization of the war game.

The credit for the actual invention of the modern war game is shared by the Prussian War Counselor von Reisswitz, a civilian, and his son, Lieutenant von Reisswitz, of the Artillery of the Prussian Guard. In 1811 the father invented a game played in a sand box with blocks of wood to represent troops. The son modified details of the game to reflect actual military operations. The junior von Reisswitz and other officers devised an elaborate set of rules, which they published in 1824 under the title *Instructions for the Representation of Tactical Maneuvers Under the Guise of a War Game.* The new game has been said by Sayre (1908) to have been "a great step forward in that the exercises were to be conducted on maps, and that any military situation could be represented" (p. 8).

The game of von Reisswitz soon won approval at high levels. Sayre (1908) relates that:

> . . . In 1824, von Mueffling, then chief of the German General Staff, consented to witness an exhibition of the game. He received the players somewhat coldly, but as the operation expanded on the map, the old general's face lighted up, and at last he broke out with enthusiasm, "It's not a game at all! It's a training for war; I shall recommend it most emphatically to the whole army" (p. 8).

King Wilhelm III gave his blessing also. Sayre (1908) records that:

> The king directed that each regiment be supplied with one of these games and Lieutenant von Reisswitz was employed to superintend the preparation of the new maps. The maps which he used were on a scale of 1:8,000 and were as complete in details as they could be made, but showed only four square miles of ground. The troops were represented by blocks cut to the scale of the map and painted, red for one party and blue for the other, and showing by conventional signs the strength and arm of service of the organizations represented. Only the troops supposed to be seen by the enemy were shown by blocks.
>
> The exercises were begun by giving to the commanders general and special situations in writing, and requiring them to prepare written orders. It was carried on in "moves" of two minutes each, but when the opposing parties were not in contact the director could order several moves to be made at once (pp. 8–9).

The game of von Reisswitz incorporated many elements that are still familiar to participants in three-room war games. Moreover, its employment immediately encountered the basic dilemma that has always plagued simulation—the opposition between faithfulness of representation and ease of play or manipulation. In the efforts to evade the horns of the dilemma, or sometimes to grapple with one of them directly, many modifications of the Kriegspiel of von Reisswitz were introduced during the next century throughout many armies of the world. The varieties that emphasized faithfulness of representation were classified as forms of "rigid Kriegspiel," and the opposing varieties that emphasized ease of play were classified as forms of "free Kriegspiel."

The proponents of the more rigid war gaming sought to modify the rules of the games in such a way as to reflect accurately the changing nature of war. Elaborate tables, charts, and calculations were considered necessary in order to incorporate properly the details of troop movements, effects of fire, and so on. Dice were used to represent effects of chance.

The spirit of the freer war gaming is well described by the words of one of its chief advocates, Verdy du Vernois (1897):

> In the excursions of the General Staff, the military results that are sought are the same as in the War Game. . . . In no case do they decide upon the success of an operation by the cast of the die, but each time the umpire decides according to his own views. It is not thought necessary to decide in every case the effects of fire, shock, etc. All that is necessary is to reach the general result, to determine if a body of troops has had great losses. . . . Therefore, the means employed on the ground in these staff excursions can be easily applied in the lecture room with maps . . . in a few hours we show operations which would require several days on the open ground (pp. 8–9).

In most applications, the paramount requirement that a war game be playable led to at least some concessions in the direction of the free Kriegspiel. Thus even Livermore (1882), whose analysis of operational data contributed much to the use of rigid Kriegspiel, concedes that:

> Although the methods . . . will enable the umpire to determine . . . any doubtful point . . . of the game, it cannot be too strongly stated that all these computations not only need not, but must not, be made in every case, after the players and umpire have had a little practice, especially if they are at all familiar with military operations. They are intended to facilitate and hasten the game and should not be so perverted as to retard it (p. 26).

Although use of war games increased in many countries during the present century, Germany continued to furnish some of the more notable examples. After 1918 particularly, restrictions on the size and budget of the German Army encouraged the use of war games as a substitute for field experience. By this time, moreover, war games were being used not only for tactical training but also for the exploration and rehearsal of projected campaigns. The German spring offensive in 1918 had been so rehearsed, and Hofmann (1952, pp. 81–83) also cites, as examples from World War II, the invasion of France in 1940 and the invasion of the Ukraine in 1941. The memoirs of Erich v. Manstein (1958, pp. 131–133) mention the inclusion of relevant political considerations in the German gaming, and the Tokyo Trials (1946) of "war criminals" give evidence of similar interests in the extensive Japanese gaming of World War II.

In his summary of the German use of war games, General Hofmann (1952) has given a very useful evaluation of the classic war game as it was at the time of World War II:

> Whether they were the simplest sandbox exercises . . . or whether they were the war games . . . of the intermediate command levels, or finally whether they were the big operational games . . . of the Commander in Chief of the Army, all these exercises completely fulfilled their purpose as a training device, as a means for testing new ideas of command and as a preparation for future operations. . . . However, in spite of all this esteem in which they were held, the value of war games should not be overestimated. . . . They can no more simulate real warfare than can maneuvers. For what is missing are the impressions of combat, the live ammunition, the genuine tensions and the far-reaching responsibilities. . . . They likewise give only a limited impression of the character of the participant . . . there are officers who feel constrained and nervous when under the spotlight of a war game, but who later prove to be clear-thinking and decisive commanders in war. In the same way an intelligent participant in a war game who has perhaps known the director for a fairly long time can sometimes guess the latter's intention exactly; this same man, who is so brilliant in a game, may be unsure of himself and fail when actually under fire (pp. 64–65).

2.2. The Growth of Computing Aids

The discussion of the present part seeks to portray a little of the breathless awe inspired by the meteoric advent of the electronic computing machine. The interaction of the computing machine with the classic war game and mathematical game theory in the bubbling pot of military gaming will be considered in Part 2.4 of the present section.

Whereas the classic war game was born in the direct consideration of military problems, the modern computing machine arose to meet the data-processing needs of business and government and the computational needs of science and engineering. Whereas the classic war game had essentially achieved its modern form by World War I, and from many points of view considerably earlier, an electronic computer presently becomes "obsolete" in a very few years, and improved methods of programming are also developing very rapidly.

Of the various incentives for the development of better computing methods, the one most important for the present historical sketch is that provided by the subject of nuclear physics. An illuminating account of early applications is outlined by Ulam (1958) in his memorial article on the late John von Neumann. Ulam writes of the basic need and how it was met:

> I remember quite well how, very early in the Los Alamos Project, it became obvious that analytical work alone was often not sufficient to provide even qualitative answers. The numerical work by hand and even the use of desk computing machines would require a prohibitively long time for these problems. This situation seemed to provide the final spur for von Neumann. . . .
>
> . . . to examine, *from its foundations,* the problem of computing on electronic machines and, during 1944 and 1945, he formulated the now fundamental methods of translating a set of mathematical procedures into a language of instructions for a computing machine. The electronic machines of that time (e.g., the Eniac) lacked the flexibility and generality which they now possess in the handling of mathematical problems. Speaking broadly, each problem required a special and different system of wiring, in order to enable the machine to perform the prescribed operations in a given sequence. Von Neumann's great contribution was the idea of a fixed and rather universal set of connections or circuits in the machine, a flow diagram, and a code so as to enable a fixed set of connections in the machine to have the means of solving a very great variety of problems. . . .
>
> It is easy to underestimate, even now, ten years after the inception of such methods, the great possibilities opened through such theoretical experimentation in problems of mathematical physics. . . . the already accumulated mass of theoretical experiments . . . allow one to hope that good syntheses may arise from these computations (p. 31).

A particular form taken by the "theoretical experiments," that associated with the name "Monte Carlo method," has been of predominant importance, not just in military gaming, but throughout current operations research. Ulam (1958) describes its origin in mathematical physics:

> The simplicity of mathematical formulation of the principles of mathematical physics hoped for in the nineteenth century seems to be conspicuously absent in modern theories. A perplexing variety and wealth of structure found in what one considered as elementary particles, seem to postpone the hopes for an early mathematical synthesis. In applied physics and in technology one is

forced to deal with situations which, mathematically, present mixtures of different systems. . . .

From the point of view of combinatorics alone, not to mention the difficulties of analysis in the handling of several partial differential and integral equations, it is clear that at the present time, there is very little hope of finding solutions in a closed form. In order to find, *even only qualitatively,* the properties of such systems, one is forced to look for pragmatic methods.

We decided to look for ways to find, as it were, homomorphic images of the given physical problem in a mathematical schema which could be represented by a system of fictitious "particles" treated by an electronic computer. It is especially in problems involving functions of a considerable number of independent variables that such procedures would be applied. To give a very simple concrete example of such a Monte Carlo approach, let us consider the question of evaluating the volume of a subregion of a given n-dimensional "cube" described by a set of inequalities. Instead of the usual method of approximating the volume required by a systematic subdivision of the space into its lattice points one could select, *at random,* with uniform probability, a number of points in space and determine (on the machine) how many of these points belong to the given region. This proportion will give us . . . an approximate value of the relative volumes, *with the probability as close to one* as we wish, by employing a sufficient number of sample points. . . .

Another instance of such methodology is, given a set of functional equations, to attempt to transform it into an equivalent one which would admit of a probabilistic or game theory interpretation. This latter would allow one to play, on a machine, the games illustrating the random processes and the distribution obtained would give a fair idea of the solution of the original equations. Better still, the hope would be to obtain directly a "homomorphic image" of the behavior of the physical system in question. It has to be stated that in many physical problems presently considered, the differential equations originally obtained by certain idealizations, are not, so to say, very sacrosanct any more. A direct study of models of the system on computing machines may possess a heuristic value, at least (pp. 33–34).

A different line of development, important in its own right for the role it has played in the shaping of military gaming, is that of the electronic analogue computer. The applications of its principles in control systems and training devices have been particularly suggestive for gaming. For use in "pure computing," or any application where special-purpose design may be a handicap, however, the analogue computer has been largely overtaken by the digital computer.

The spectacular increase in computational speed and capacity brought about in the last fifteen years has not come without the confusion, the false hopes, and the excesses that seem, inevitably, to accompany a brilliant new development. Koopman (1956), as he exposes fallacies in operations research, points an accusing finger:

Mechanitis is the occupational disease of one who is so impressed with modern computing machinery that he believes that a mathematical problem, which he can neither solve nor even formulate, can readily be answered, once he has access to a sufficiently expensive machine. "Monte-Carloism" is a special case; and so is the dangerous notion that a war game can serve as a means of computing probabilities of the results of various tactics (p. 424).

Kahn and Marshall (1953), emphasizing a careful use of Monte Carlo techniques, give a similar warning:

Monte Carlo, in its most primitive form at least, is in danger of being oversold . . . too much emphasis has been laid on the brute-force multiplication of sample observations. This emphasis, usually associated with the "Monte Carlo will do anything view," is, we believe, misplaced. . . . The general rule should be (*a*) never use random sampling in lieu of any easy exact method for any part of a problem, and (*b*) never act as if the problem determines the sampling design to be used . . . (p. 278).

2.3. The Introduction of a Mathematical Theory of Games

Mathematical game theory, a third major force important in the shaping of modern military gaming, derives neither from classic war gaming nor from physical science but rather from application of mathematics to economics. Although von Neumann (1928) gave some of the principal results quite early, it was the publication of the classic by von Neumann and Morgenstern (1943) during World War II that marked the beginning of popularity for the theory.

Although designed with economic problems in mind, the theory of games was soon applied to military problems. The basic part of the theory, that which has been best worked out and is most free from objection, pertains to zero-sum, two-person games, conflict situations involving two diametrically opposed interests. Certain military situations afford some of the examples where such a theory seems to be most applicable, and many of the early applications, as reported in Dresher (1951) and Caywood and Thomas (1955), were made in connection with research on military problems.

Some of the early successes of the theory in the years immediately after World War II aroused exaggerated hopes. The gradual recognition of many formidable problems still remaining has brought about, in reaction, an equally exaggerated despair. From some of the popular literature, one might well conclude that game theory deals exclusively with two-by-two matrices. To see that the scope of the theory is considerably greater than that, and still broadening, one may consult Berkovitz and Dresher (1959) and Isaacs (1955 and 1958) for example.

Now that much of its early glamor has fled, the general role of the theory of games is often considered to be suggestive and inspirational. The theory has provided precise notions of such terms as "game," "game value," and "optimum strategy," notions now seen to be conspicuously absent from the ardent play of games during several preceding millennia. Moreover, in its provision of unexpected solutions for some relatively simple games the theory of games suggests some limits to the validity of intuition that may well apply to more complicated games. Some of the suggestive definitions and examples may be found in Luce and Raiffa (1957), or in sources to which one is there referred by an excellent bibliography.

2.4. The Confluence of the Streams of Military Gaming

The three preceding parts of this section have described three forceful streams that began to commingle about the end of World War II. The resulting river of military gaming may be pictured as still consisting of the three streams, which, far from having merged or blended together into a homogeneous whole, are flowing along side by side with a modest amount of mixing. The large central current from classic war gaming has neither absorbed nor been absorbed in the flow of the two younger tributaries representing computing machines and game theory, but there have been various interactions and suggestive eddies. The present discussion is directed toward an examination of such interactions as a basis for the description of some examples in the next section.

It may be appropriate in the beginning, while the picture of the newly formed river is still vivid, to inquire into its name. How did it come about that "military gaming," a term very similar to "war gaming," connotes such a broad stream that includes currents of such diverse degrees of abstraction? Whereas any answer must be somewhat speculative, the name in this case may well have resulted from historical forces not unlike those responsible for the naming of some of our geographical rivers. As historical background, one may recall that, prior to the introduction of computing machines or game theory, war gaming represented one of the more abstract techniques utilized in the study of military problems. A common attitude is recorded in a comment of Feldmarschall List (Hofmann, 1952), "One occasionally hears that there is too much theory in a war game and that too little practical training value is derived from it" (pp. 135–136). It was not unnatural then, as techniques of a still more theoretical nature were used for military problems, that they also were often termed "gaming" techniques.

One of the striking features of the newly formed stream was the speed with which it moved. Speaking of the remarkable interest that developed in game theory when "much of the material had lain dormant in the literature for two decades," Luce and Raiffa (1957) give an explanation that applies generally to the techniques introduced during that period:

> Presumably the recent war was an important contributing factor to the later rapid development of the theory. During that period considerable activity developed in scientific, or at least systematic, approaches to problems that had been previously considered the exclusive province of men of "experience." These include such topics as logistics, submarine search, air defense, etc. (p. 3).

The prevailing air was one of hopefulness as connoted by the phrase "operations research."

Among the first hopes was the natural expectation that the new computing machines would help to extend the classic war game. Thus Mood (1954) says, "Modern high-speed computers will enable the number of factors which can be included in a game to be increased tremendously, if necessary, without adding to the complexity of the game from the player's standpoint" (pp. 9–10). Starting as a tool, the computing machine shows signs of asserting a dominance that makes the man seem more like a tool. Thus Mood and Specht (1954, p. 1) speak of the human in gaming as playing the role of an analogue computer, and a little of this point of view is reflected in the comment of Rich (1955), "From the present point of view, then, a war game is just a special type of simulator . . ." (p. 15).

Another hope of the early postwar years was that the theory of games would help to extend the classic war game. The novelty of this hope is seen with especial clarity when it is contrasted with an older view as expressed by Sayre (1908) a half century ago:

> Although map maneuvers owe their origin to a game, the game feature is no longer an important element of them. A predominance of the game idea has always been an obstacle to the proper development of these exercises as a means of military instruction and training. . . . The questions which we should keep uppermost in maneuvers are—What principles of the art of war are illustrated? Have the troops been handled to the best advantage? . . . The question as to which side has the advantage at the close of the maneuver is relatively unimportant. . . . In order to give a needful variety of instructions, too great a proportion of the available time should not be devoted to the consideration of the closing stages of battles (pp. 28–29).

The new thought, that the "game idea" might be something other than an "obstacle," is expressed in extreme form by Young (1959), "The growth of the rigid type of game, from the prototype of von Reisswitz, and from those more sophisticated games of Livermore and Totten, with the added mathematical power given to it by von Neumann's theories, has been rapid during recent years" (p. 105). Again, referring to these theories, Young (1959) says that "The rigorous treatment applied to games . . . has been transferred to war gaming techniques, providing for a scientific analysis of decision making in warfare with a considerable future potential" (p. 96). It is difficult to reconcile such claims for added "power" with the more common view expressed in Mood (1954) that, while the theory of games "has developed a considerable body of clarifying ideas and a technique which can analyze quite simple economic and tactical problems, . . . these techniques are not even remotely capable, however, of dealing with complex military problems" (pp. 3–4).

Finally, there has been a mingling of the hopes inspired by computing machines and game theory. Smith (1956) expresses a common aspiration when he makes the definition "gaming is a Monte Carlo method for solving games" (p. 1). For many common simulation problems or "one-person games," there are, indeed, Monte Carlo methods for insuring a statistical adequacy of plays. In order to solve games with more players, however, it is necessary for the collection of plays to be stategically adequate as well. This problem is discussed in Thomas and Deemer (1957), where it is concluded that "In gaming, generally, there is no way of knowing with certainty when a sample of plays is both strategically and statistically adequate for a required decision" (p. 19).

These early interminglings of the different streams in gaming give abundant evidence that hopes ever spring up profusely, whereas the means of accomplishment may lag far behind. There is no easy, direct means for immediately incorporating into a new magical form of gaming all of the separate virtues—the resourcefulness of the players in the classic game, the speed of computing machines, the rigor of game theory. It is still necessary to pick and choose, and almost every new application of gaming represents some new compromise, some new mixture of men, machines, and mathematics. Some such mixtures are briefly described in the next section.

3. ILLUSTRATIVE APPLICATIONS OF MILITARY GAMING

In order to illustrate some of the diverse activities in current military gaming, a dozen typical applications will be sketched:

1. The use at a military war college of a standard war game with the conventional red team, blue team, and control team for teaching doctrine.
2. The employment of such a three-team (or three-room) game at a military headquarters for elaborating and testing a war plan.
3. The maintenance of a three-room game at a research organization for the provision of context and the suggestion of problems related to future military operations.
4. The use of a game for practicing or testing field maneuvers.
5. The design and use of an elaborate game by a war college to give officers simulated experience in commanding operational units.
6. The use of a game whose players simulate decision makers of a logistics organization in order to investigate the effects of their interacting decisions.
7. The simulation of a computer-based military command or control system with players chosen from actual operators of the system in order to increase operating efficiency.
8. The design and use by research organizations of large-scale models, programmed for electronic computers and intended to simulate combat interactions of opposing offensive and defensive units, with no intervention of actual human decisions between the formulation of inputs and the interpretation of outputs.
9. The study of cold-war or limited-war problems at a research organization by assembling political and military experts around a table for a joint, stepwise arguing out of proposals for move and countermove.
10. The effort by a research organization to formulate a partial or complete set of rules for a game involving a complicated military system as a device for learning how the system operates, without necessarily intending to play the game thus formulated.
11. The formulation of a game and the derivation of its game-theoretic solution for the determination of optimal strategies and game value.
12. The effort to find optimal strategies and game value by use of a three-room war game.

Each of these phrases refers not just to one application but to a whole class of somewhat similar applications, which may, however, differ among themselves in scope and spirit. To say, for example, that a research organization is paying engineers, scientists, and retired military officers to play a three-room war game with the hope of developing a combat context for future weapon systems, is not to identify a specific application or even a specific organization. This statement does, however, involve examples of four basic elements that interact in a gaming application—the kind of organization involved, the types of people participating, the objectives or purposes of the gaming, and the kind of techniques employed.

Although the actual character of a particular gaming application depends on the interaction of its elements, on the way in which the resources of men and machines are structured, the skill with which they are managed, and the clarity with which objectives are seen, it is useful in a preliminary discussion to consider the elements separately. That will be done in the remainder of this section. Then, in the following four sections, major families of applications will be treated in greater detail.

There are many organizations, of several different kinds, where current applications of gaming are being made. The war colleges, service schools, military academies, and military headquarters are both continuing a long tradition and also experimenting with new methods. There are non-profit research organizations directly sponsored by the military services and a host of consulting organizations and university research groups largely dependent on military support. Finally, somewhat further removed, but still closely tied to military support, are many operations research or systems evaluation departments of corporations that produce aircraft, missiles, or electronic equipment.

As would be expected, the people actively involved in gaming include many military personnel at the military establishments and many scientists and engineers at the research establishments. It is remarkable, however, as an extreme example of the mixed-team approach in operations research, that there has been a large influx of military officers, active or retired, into research organizations and a large influx of scientists, civilian and military, into military establishments. In all this activity a great many different kinds of expertness are represented. On the military side there are experts on the major arms or branches of all services. On the scientific side there are representatives of mathematics, various physical sciences, branches of engineering, machine programmers, and the behavioral sciences.

The fundamental purpose or objective of military gaming is learning. The learning usually involves military systems that will be subjected to a rigorous test as they confront a formidable enemy or a formidable nature. The learning, moreover, may take one of a variety of forms. Efforts to learn something about the universe that has never been known before may be termed *research*. The process by which a learner acquires what is new to him from a teacher to whom it is well known constitutes *education*. When one entrenches his learning through practice so as to acquire facility or endurance in its application, he is *training*. The examples given earlier illustrate all of these aspects of learning. Research efforts may concern such varied topics as the concept of deterrence, bomber-penetration problems, and the determination of optimal strategies. Educational applications of gaming are illustrated by the teaching of doctrine at war colleges. A good example of training is the exercise of the operators of a command and control system through their participation in a faithful simulation of a typical situation.

A great variety of techniques is represented in the gaming examples given earlier, and almost every new application brings forth some new modification or combination of methods previously employed. Out of this diversity, however, some order can be made by noting that each technique, basically, represents one of the ways of combining and structuring three basic resources. These resources may be denoted mnemonically as the "three M's"—men, machines, and mathematics—and they correspond roughly to the three currents of development described, respectively, in Parts 2.1, 2.2, and 2.3. Moreover, for each of the principal resources, there is a family of techniques in which its use is dominant. Section 4, for example, describes techniques that cluster about the classic, three-room war game, techniques that depend strongly on resourceful men but make relatively little use of large computing machines or the mathematical theory of games. Section 5 deals with techniques patterned after the modern, large simulation model, in the application of which both men and mathematics are often dominated by a computing machine whose memory, word length, speed, and input-output requirements constitute the basic mold. Section 6 is concerned with the use of mathematical techniques, like the theory of games, which are dominated by ideals of generality, rigor, and depth of understanding, and an insistence that conjectures be validated and computations be pertinent. Various ways of organizing the topics of the next four sections are illustrated by Kahn and Mann (1957), Paxson (1957), and Weiner (1959).

4. APPLICATIONS BASED ON THE CLASSIC THREE-ROOM GAME

This section discusses a family of applications based on elements that were already familiar in the time of von Reisswitz. These applications, compared with those to be described in later sections, make relatively little use of either computing machines or mathematical theories of conflict. Much emphasis is placed, however, on human knowledge and ingenuity. Men with command experience, military or political expertness, resourcefulness as role players—such men are sought for team members.

The proliferation, which began when von Reisswitz introduced what is essentially the modern game, still continues, and it prohibits a detailed discussion of applications. Part 4.1 of this section will present a discussion of an idealized version of the classic war game that applies also to minor variations. Part 4.2 will then present some more major deviations from the classic pattern.

4.1. The Classic Three-Room War Game

The idealized version of the classic game may be pictured as the kind that is played largely for "research" purposes, at several military and research organizations which maintain gaming facilities on a more or less continuing basis. Typically, there may be from ten to fifty players organized into three teams, a room for each team, maps, counters, slide rules or desk computers, clocks keeping "game time," and appropriate communication channels between rooms. The red team and the blue team represent opposing forces or nations or blocs of nations, with their players assuming pertinent military or political roles. Other nations, and the laws of nature generally, both deterministic and stochastic, are represented by the control team in accordance with a set of rules which it enforces. Play starts from the initial condition of a scenario, goes through a succession of red moves and blue countermoves, and finally is terminated at the discretion of the control team, usually after several days or weeks have elapsed. There may then be one or more replays starting from the same basic situation. After the play has concluded, there may issue from it a succession of analyses, reports, and summaries.

The description given above applies to a great many different applications that vary considerably among themselves. The actual problem to be solved and the actual resources of experts available for its solution determine to a large extent the scale of simulation, the placing of the emphasis, and the structure of the gaming. Essentially the same facilities and resources might be applied at different times to such varied questions as the suitability of certain weapon systems for European ground war five years hence, the possibility of limiting war should it break out in one of the world's trouble spots, the logistic problems of a future war several thousand miles away, or the feasibility of a proposed future organization for one of the military services. Each such application, however, would demand its own rules and planning factors, its own body of expert knowledge, and its own structuring.

In a large gaming activity there are several stages that, to a certain extent, occur sequentially. At the beginning it is quite important, particularly when a period of several months or even a year or two of gaming is involved, to decide on the purposes of the gaming. Although this initial decision helps to limit the task remaining to be completed before play can commence, this task of developing planning factors and rules is often quite arduous. At this stage one may also be concerned with the question of how to record and document the play of the game. At last there is the play itself, and finally there is analysis of the play. There is often feedback from one of the later stages of early play to an earlier stage in later play. It may develop that purposes must be narrowed or rules modified, for example.

The administration of a war-gaming group often demands a rather delicate balance of firmness and imagination. There may be one series of plays in a late stage at the same time that another series is beginning. There may be times when activity lags and dullness threatens. On still other occasions, enthusiasm for collateral investigations suggested by the gaming, ordinarily valuable, may get out of hand. It is necessary to place some constraints on the gaming activity without stifling the creativity that is its ultimate end.

Some of the administrative difficulties of the research war game are seen to be associated with the general uncertainty of the results of research. Because of its great cost, the three-room war game, even more than most research techniques, is properly restricted in its employment to those problems where it seems that "nothing else will work." In a typical application, therefore, prior efforts to simplify the problem further have failed, and the residual formulation is full of complexities.

In research involving the classic game, as in research generally, it is often found that some avenues turn out to be unexpectedly fruitful while others that had been thought promising seem not to be very valuable. One particular evidence of this phenomenon in three-room gaming is the frequency with which there issues out of the elaborate, but seemingly necessary, cycle of preparation, play, and analysis some striking, transcendent conclusion that it now appears could have been reached independently. It may happen, for example, that, after a series of plays lasting several months or more, the most valuable result by far is a set of planning factors prepared prior to play, such as more accurate numerical estimates of kill probabilities or of unit logistic capabilities. Or it could be, as in some applications, that the players see in their preparation of the rules a principal source of learning, beyond which play is largely unnecessary. In still other applications, the outstanding conclusion may be a result of play that seems rather insensitive to the precise set of rules and planning factors used, as, for example, the recognition that some particular politicomilitary situation is unexpectedly unstable. Such examples illustrate the general recognition, often somewhat sheepish, that the principal results of applications of a three-room game do not depend essentially on the game for their derivation.

It is very important to recognize not only that such results of the three-room game do not depend essentially on the game for their derivation but also that such results cannot depend on the game for their substantiation. Kahn and Mann (1957) make this point forcefully, that conjectures based on play of the game must be verifiable by other means. For the classic game constitutes the kind of test that gives primarily negative results—a plan is unworkable, a logistics scheme unfeasible, a weapon system unsuitable, a proposed organizational structure unsound. A proposal that is not shown by the game to be unsound is not, thereby, proved sound. It has merely passed one of the tests to which it can be subjected.

An important key, then, to the proper employment of the classic game is the recognition that it is a test, complicated, expensive, and often severe. It is a mechanism for eliciting "buried" knowledge from experts, files, latent sources of all kinds, and then assembling it into a coherent totality that provides a test context. Since it is expensive in time and men, its use is properly restricted to be a "last resort." Since its success depends crucially on the expertness of the players, their selection is most important. When a very specific situation is to be gamed, it may be possible to have some of those destined to play a role in that situation chosen to play the representative role in the game. In any event, the experts should be selected with the objective of providing, for the questions to be examined, the most pertinent tests possible.

Finally, it must be recognized that the most realistic war game is still far from reality itself. The references cited at the end of Section 3 all emphasize that a war game is not oracular. To mistake a game for reality or to think that enough complication in a game converts it into an oracle is to miss the true role of the game as a test. Its function is not to predict the future but rather to help preserve the future from the consequences of bad present decisions.

4.2. Variants of the Classic War Game

The classic game as discussed above is primarily an exploratory research tool to be employed in those difficult situations where there is as yet little true understanding and every detail is suspected to have potential importance. When it is thought that some particular aspects of a problem situation deserve special attention, it may be considered more efficient to depart from the classic game. This part of the present section lists some of the standard variants.

In some situations it is possible to compress the "move structure" of the classic game, and so to obtain greater speed in the play as well as greater use of some of the experts. The prime motivation for the use of separate secret-move preparation by Red and Blue with adjudication by the control team in the classic game is the desire to simulate "intelligence interplay," the ignorance and doubts that each opponent may have about the actions of the other. When this is not considered to be a major effect, or when its incorporation is thought possible without the elaborate move structure, it is possible to "streamline" the play of the game. In one such form, sometimes termed "joint adjudication," moves are still prepared in private by individual teams, but their discussion and implementation now occurs in joint session of all three teams. In a second, more extreme departure, often termed "seminar war gaming," the formulation of moves, argumentation, and arbitration all are conducted publicly around a table. Such forms of collective adjudication permit the expertness of players of the Red and Blue teams to be brought to bear on questions that are resolved solely by members of the control team in the classic version. Some experienced gamers believe that these modified methods may be used safely only by groups that have first developed knowledge and insight pertinent to the questions at hand through long use of the classic game. Other experienced gamers, however, believe that something like the seminar method not only can be, but should be, employed in first attacking a problem area.

Some variants arise through the desire to emphasize certain stages of a conflict situation. Political maneuvering, already seen to be important in the war gaming of small, local wars, may be singled out for special attention in what is termed "political gaming," a subject discussed by Goldhamer and Speier (1959). Or, recognizing the importance of research and development decisions that precede the acquisition of weapon systems, one may produce a "force posture" game like that described by Helmer and Shapley (1957), in which such decisions play a more central role than combat interaction.

For educational purposes, where what is to be learned by the student has already been discovered or decided by the instructor, it is possible to produce extremely simplified games. A common form for military education is a one-sided game, in which students constitute the Blue team and an instructor plays the part of both the Red team and the control team. Or, when the rules can be sufficiently simplified without doing violence to the subject matter, it may be possible to revert to a board game for which no control team is needed. Such games may be used, for example, to introduce the complexities of modern military decision making to the players.

Finally, there are variants like command-post exercises and field exercises that constitute what the press terms a "war game." Such exercises involve hundreds or thousands of men and thus include many effects that are often only imperfectly simulated in the classic game. Outcomes may depend, for example, on the speed with which low-level decisions are made and communicated as well as on the quality of the decisions made by the high-level personnel who are represented in the classic game. Since large-scale exercises have as one defect tremendous expense, it is efficient to make as much use as possible of "laboratory simulation," a subject to be discussed later.

5. APPLICATIONS ESSENTIALLY BASED ON COMPUTING MACHINES

This section emphasizes, primarily, applications based on large-scale simulation models programmed for large digital computers. These applications, though numerous and spectacular, do not comprise all the applications based on computing machines, nor even the most obvious. As evidenced in Part 2.4, those familiar with the classic war game early entertained hopes that the computational capacity of the promising new machines could be harnessed to the game. To some extent this hope has been realized. Large analogue devices incorporated in the framework of a war game now help to provide command experience for military officers. Analogue representation of sets of differential equations with human decision making performed by men sitting at the console constitutes one approach to certain allocation games. Digital computers also lend themselves to easing the computational burden of players, as some of the management games attest.

There is a twofold reason, however, for giving such applications little attention in the present section. First, the use of a machine chiefly to give somewhat greater speed or scope to a game merely aids the kind of application that has already been discussed. Second, the more important, the use of machines in gaming, as in other fields, has led, not just to changes in speed or scope, but to new applications structured in new ways. These new applications to large-scale simulation models have caught the fancy of gamers to such an extent that they seem most characteristic of machine applications. A classified description of one large model that is something of a prototype is given by Dalkey and Wegner (1958), and an unclassified summary is available in OMEGA (1958).

A large simulation model is not, of course, entirely dissimilar to a classic game in spirit. In each type of simulation one is often motivated by the desire to see events unfold before one's eyes and seeks to produce what Ulam (1958) terms "homomorphic images" (or at least what might be termed "piece-wise homomorphic images" when some parts of the problem get more emphasis than others). A computing-machine program for a simulation model, however, has a rigidity that goes far beyond that of "rigid Kriegspiel," and this is true in two senses. First, it often turns out that rules, which are rigid by ordinary standards and quite satisfactory for a game, require the elimination of loopholes and the addition of further specifications when programmed for a computing machine. Second, because one often desires a machine program to run with almost no human intervention between the entering of inputs and the recording of outputs, the program is made to contain rigid decision rules that replace the human decisions made by players in a war game.

The steps involved in the construction and use of a machine simulation model parallel to some extent those involved in the design and use of a game. One should decide the objectives of the simulation. Such objectives, together with the availability of computing machines and programmers, play a large part in determining the size and scale of the simulation. It is necessary then, at least in principle, to prepare a flow chart. A complete flow chart corresponds closely to a combination of rules, as known in the classic game, and decision rules, to replace players. Given a flow chart, programmers and coders exercise one of the more popular postwar arts in preparing a translation pleasing to the computing machine. In order to apply the resulting program, it is necessary to obtain pertinent numerical inputs, sometimes well over a hundred thousand, and to convert them into a form acceptable to the machine. An actual machine "run," then, in which the given operation is simulated in terms of the program and inputs, may require from a few minutes to a few hours of computer time. It is in this step that the speed of the electronic computer has compressed the time that would be required for play in the classic war game. For a particular application, runs may be made for several sets of inputs, and several runs may be made for one set of physical inputs when the machine calculates pseudorandom numbers for the generation of a probability distribution. On the basis of the runs, there may be voluminous output, a printed record of the simulated events. Although the output may already reflect some "preanalysis," or prior efforts in writing an output program to select pertinent results of the run, to arrange them conveniently, and to make rather obvious calculations, it is usually necessary to devote considerable time to an analysis of the results of machine calculation.

The step of choosing the size and scope of a machine simulation model may be taken in one of a great many directions. To say merely that this important choice depends upon the problem and upon the capacity of the available computing machines is only to begin the story. For the dependence has such complication that one may have great difficulty allowing for it in beginning the construction of a model. As in the design of a game, it is difficult to decide just how much detail the underlying problem dictates. Moreover, there is the added uncertainty in machine simulation of not knowing in advance just how successful the machine programmers will be as they ply their art. The final outcome may be almost as unexpected to the programmers as it is to analysts ignorant of programming. Because the outcome of model construction can not be foreseen with great accuracy from the beginning, when one has had no experience, it is common to proceed along a spiral path by acquiring experience with relatively simple models that may in turn be used as a basis for the design of larger models. It may be remarked, as well, that experience with a large model has occasionally led to the introduction of a simpler version, which may be essentially a fragment or component of the larger model that has proved particularly useful.

Whatever the choice of size and scale for a simulation model, one has several options as to basic structure. There are two extreme possibilities often termed the "time-step" and the "event-store" methods, both of which permit the simulation of randomness in the course of events. They may be illustrated in terms of a model that simulates the interaction of two opposing forces, such as strategic penetrators versus air-defense units or a group of tanks versus anti-tank weapons. In the time-step method, one divides the duration of the simulated combat into a number of successive time intervals displaced by "time steps." The status of the opposing forces in one interval, movement, detection, destruction, etc. is then calculated from the status in the previous interval and preplanned intentions. Thus a time-step program keeps asking, "What will the situation be one time unit from now?" In the event-store method, on the other hand, after a given event has occurred, one determines and "stores" a set of "imminent" significant events and times at which they will occur, and selects the earliest. The occurrence of this next significant event may alter the possibility or timing of other events that had been listed, so that a new set of events and times may then be calculated. Thus, an event-store program keeps asking, "What will happen next?" In practice, of course, the time-step and event-store methods may be implemented in many ways and partially combined, in order to produce a program that is artfully suited to the problem.

One of the most striking problems encountered in the preparation of a machine simulation model is the difficulty of producing a machine program that does exactly what it is intended to do. In effect, this difficulty adds another level of uncertainty: whereas there is already uncertainty as to the faithfulness with which a model represents reality, there is now uncertainty as to the faithfulness with which a program represents a model. Since programming mistakes shatter human self-esteem, it is probably fitting that they are termed "bugs" and their removal, "debugging." One approach to debugging, which grapples directly with the compound uncertainty of a programmed model, compares the output of an over-all program with the "real" situation being simulated. Despite an occasional success, this "over-all" approach is not considered to be as efficient as that of first separately debugging smaller segments of a program by comparing their results with those of desk calculators, and secondly removing errors introduced in the combination of the separate segments. For the future, there is hope that the increasing development and use of automatic programming methods will decrease the number of errors introduced in the programming of a simulation model. More automatic methods should also decrease the time required for programming, which, exclusive of debugging, may presently require many man-months or man-years for a large model.

The preparation of inputs is also often very time consuming. The numerical values of many parameters, sometimes well over a hundred thousand, must be determined and put in such form that they can be utilized by the computing machine. Since such inputs are to be used by a specific program, they must be compatible with the program and with one another. This requirement prohibits the uncritical use in a new program of a parameter value that was acceptable in a former program. Similarly, there must be a check of compatibility when separate blocks of inputs are prepared by separate organizations, such as military commands. Since many of the inputs to a machine program themselves depend upon calculations that may be performed by a machine, there is hope that some of the tedious labor now associated with the preparation of inputs can be eliminated. If the subprograms for such calculations are written by those familiar with the major model, it may help also in the achievement of compatibility of inputs.

The choice of inputs, in the more fundamental sense of the selection of situations to be simulated in a study, is a subject that may be discussed together with that of output analysis in terms of the question "How does one use a computer simulation model?" Various applications suggest quite different answers to this basic question. Reminiscent of the classic war game is the thesis that a large-scale simulation, undertaken in desperation when other methods seem to offer little promise, almost inevitably adds something to the understanding of the problem merely by requiring the preparation of a flow chart or program. At the other extreme is the thesis that it is possible to devise a simulation model of such realism as to encourage use of standard statistical techniques for the design of experiments. Most applications seem to be based on the intermediate thesis, which does not claim that one obtains extreme realism from machine runs but does suggest that their results may be considerably more valuable than just the preparation of a program in itself.

Each of these attitudes toward the use of simulation models has a domain of validity that depends on the size of the model and the difficulty of the problem. In some relatively simple problems where the number of variables is small, one may have a well-defined mathematical problem whose solution is sought by simulation, as, for example, when one determines a probability distribution through use of the Monte Carlo method. In dealing with exceedingly complicated problems, on the other hand, the process of arriving at a machine program may often bring a more orderly view of the problem than was previously available, without, however, yielding a formulation that will serve as a firm basis for calculations of great validity.

The variety of approaches to the use of computer simulation models reflects the absence of any standard technique that insures good results from a merely mechanical application. The large simulation models that have been most successfully applied owe their successes to the extremely thoughtful and imaginative care lavished upon them, the constant attention that has been bestowed upon them by their creators and users. New auxiliary programs have been written for them to provide ever more useful print-outs of results. In any given application, their results have been carefully scrutinized to see if simpler analytic models are suggested. Such tentative models have been useful as a means of choosing the situations to be simulated in later runs. When such models have been validated, they have been used as a means of interpolation to yield results for situations not directly simulated by machine runs.

The frequent failure to give to individual simulation models the personal attention they demand arises from a false attribution to machine models of such "machine virtues" as automaticity, transferability, and speed. When one hears of the flexibility of computing machines that "can do anything," one sometimes forgets that a machine solves no problem entirely by itself, in some magical, automatic way of its own. Similarly, one sometimes falsely believes that a large simulation model, like a precisely machined automobile engine, may be produced in one city and transferred to another for use, forgetting the intimate care presently required for successful employment of even a debugged model. Finally, it is perhaps most difficult to remember that the lightning speed of a computer run, like the flash of human insight, must be preceded by long and careful preparation and, if it is to be fully exploited, followed by long and careful analysis of results, so that the over-all process is far from speedy.

Recognizing that the full attainment of "machine automaticity" still lies in the future, the designer of a simulation model can do much to exploit human skills. There are, for example, such human abilities as decision making and perception, which are as yet duplicated by machines only with great difficulty, and complication. Thus it may be more efficient in some simulations to employ a man in those roles. Rather, for example, than to simulate several days of military operations, involving many contingencies and decisions, entirely with one large machine model, one may produce a variety of machine simulation models, each of which represents a smaller operational segment, and let human judgment link the smaller models together serially. In similar spirit, the powers of human perception can be utilized, sometimes by the relatively simple device of arranging an output for presentation on a cathode-ray tube.

6. APPLICATIONS OF MATHEMATICAL TECHNIQUES

This section deals principally with what are commonly considered to be over-all mathematical approaches to conflict situations. Besides these outstanding examples, there are many other instances where it is well recognized that mathematics makes valuable contributions to military gaming, though of smaller scope. In addition to these commonly recognized areas of mathematical interest, however, there are many others to which, in a proper sense, mathematics also applies. The totality of these domains, in fact, makes up a very large fraction of military gaming, almost all of it that goes beyond intuition.

Since the mathematics in military gaming is very often considered to be more restricted, it is important to explain the sense (or *a* sense) in which it can be said to apply to a much larger region. An extreme interpretation is given by Stone (1957), who makes a good case for the syllogism: "science is reasoning; reasoning is mathematics; and therefore, science is mathematics" (p. 61). It is not necessary to go so far, however, in order to justify the assertion that a precise set of rules for a war game or a computer program for a simulation model may well be considered mathematically. One need merely note and reflect upon the current use of rules in mathematics under the name of the "postulational method." Referring to this latter instrument, Stone (1957) writes:

> Rather it is what this instrument has made possible—the dissection of mathematical concepts into their elemental components, the recombination of these components into new constructs of intrinsic interest, the critical evaluation of alternative approaches to the important mathematical theories, the unification of hitherto unconnected branches of mathematics—that best expresses the spirit of modern pure mathematics (pp. 68–69).

In this statement, one discerns as elements of the mathematical spirit a generality, a precision, and an inventiveness which very few would want to bar, permanently, from any branch of military gaming.

If one grants that there is a proper sense in which mathematics is seen to be quite generally applicable to military gaming, or even to include a large fraction of it, then one is left with the problem of explaining the more restricted meaning of "mathematical gaming techniques." If a machine program is seen to characterize a "mathematical model," how does its use differ from that of what is commonly termed a "mathematical technique"? Recognizing that any simulation is only a representation of reality, and not reality itself, how does what is called a "simulation model" differ from what is often called a more "mathematical approach"?

A survey of common usage suggests that the restricted sense of "mathematical" in gaming or simulation derives from the concept of an ideal investigation that is particularly successful, successful in going beyond an unimaginative "homomorphic" representation to obtain results of striking generality or simplicity. In this sense, "mathematics" tends to be narrowed to "techniques for finding 'closed forms' " or to "techniques for solving overly simplified problems." One may illustrate the process of identification by considering the problem of summing a large number of terms, as in a direct computation for a problem involving compound interest. The determination, for example, of the sum to which one hundred dollars grows in 17.5 years with an interest rate of 4 per cent per year, compounded semiannually, may be made by straightforward simulation (involving remarkable "time compression") of the calculations that would actually be performed by bank tellers over the 17.5 years, but this approach is ordinarily considered to be still too tedious for use except by school children and computing machines. The strikingly quick solution to such a problem, based on a use of tables justified by "mathematics," obscures the fact that the longer simulation is also "mathematics." For this reason, one tends to forget that the summation of any finite series or convergent infinite series, even when there is no "closed form" for partial sums or simple expression for the total sum, is a subject of mathematics where general theories have often been put to "practical" use. And one could multiply such examples endlessly.

The recognition that the more remarkable simplifications achieved in certain special problems do not constitute all of the mathematics in gaming should not lead us to underestimate their very substantial and inspirational contribution. Very few analysts who have once seen the cluttering details of a problem subsumed under a beautifully elegant simplification will ever again be fully satisfied with any of the other expedients to which they may sometimes resort. The appeal of the "understanding" that a simple model permits is reflected in the following statement of Weiss (1959) on the choice of a model:

> The present paper employs these concepts as a stepping stone to a simple mathematical model. . . . The model is still too great an oversimplification of real tactical problems for conclusions to be taken seriously with regard to real weapon systems; however, in model building we must choose between a model that is sufficiently complex to represent a real tactical situation accurately, and a model simple enough to allow the basic interrelations to be clearly seen. We choose the latter here on the ground that general results obtained with it can always be employed as guides to computer manipulation of more complex models, while the simple model may yield understanding of important relations that would be difficult to perceive in a more complex model (pp. 180–181).

The remainder of this section describes very briefly a few of the applications that come to mind when "mathematical techniques" are mentioned in connection with military gaming. These applications represent two main streams. One, based on the theory of games, reflects a preoccupation with strategic choice reminiscent of the war game. The other stream, illustrated by Lanchester's differential equations, is predominantly concerned with the nature of the interaction and attrition of opposing forces, a subject also of central interest in many applications of large simulation models. In some of the recent work on multimove games emphasizing allocation decisions these two streams have come together.

Some of the early applications of mathematics to the study of conflict were made by Lanchester (1916) during World War I, when he wrote farsightedly on the use of aircraft in warfare. In this connection he investigated "mathematics in warfare," particularly mathematics concerned with the effects of concentration. Thus Lanchester (1916) introduced the consideration from which he deduced the famous "square law" according to which the fighting strength of a force is proportional to the square of its numerical strength multiplied by the fighting strength of one of its units:

> There is an important difference between the methods of defense of primitive times and those of the present day. . . . In olden times, when weapon directly answered weapon, the act of defense was positive and direct. . . . But the defense of modern arms is indirect: tersely, the enemy is prevented from killing you by your killing him first, and the fighting is essentially collective. As a consequence of this difference, the importance of concentration in history has been by no means a constant quantity. . . .
>
> Now let us take the modern conditions. If, again, we assume equal indi-

vidual fighting value, and the combatants otherwise (as to "cover," etc.) on terms of equality, each man will in a given time score, on an average, a certain number of hits that are effective; consequently, the number of men knocked out per unit time will be directly proportional to the numerical strength of the opposing force. Putting this in mathematical language, and employing symbol b to represent the numerical strength of the "Blue" force, and r for the "Red," we have:—

$$\frac{db}{dt} = -r \times c$$

and

$$\frac{dr}{dt} = -b \times k$$

in which t is time and c and k are constants ($c = k$ if the fighting values of the individual units of the force are equal) (pp. 40–42).

The time of World War I was too early for such contributions to be appreciated, a result also not unforeseen by Lanchester:

> There are many who will be inclined to cavil at any mathematical or semi-mathematical treatment of the present subject, on the ground that with so many unknown factors, such as the morale or leadership of the men, the unaccounted merits or demerits of the weapons, and the still more unknown "chances of war," it is ridiculous to pretend to calculate anything. The answer to this is simple: the direct numerical comparison of the forces engaging in conflict or available in the event of war is almost universal. It is a factor always carefully reckoned with by the various military authorities; it is discussed *ad nauseam* in the Press. Yet such direct counting of forces is in itself a tacit acceptance of the applicability of mathematical principles, but confined to a special case. To accept without reserve the mere "counting of the pieces" as of value, and to deny the more extended application of mathematical theory, is as illogical and unintelligent as to accept broadly and indiscriminately the balance and the weighing-machine as instruments of precision, but to decline to permit in the latter case any allowance for the known inequality of leverage (pp. 46–47).

By the time of World War II, the differential-equation approach, like other applications of mathematics, was more generally accepted, and its use has continued in the postwar period. The recent work has proceeded in several directions. Historical records have been investigated to obtain statistical validation for the use of equations like Lanchester's. Considerably more complicated systems of differential equations have been introduced to represent other factors affecting the strength of forces and other measures of a nation's strength. Lanchester's equations have been modified to represent probability distributions rather than "averages." Finally, the strategic element, recognized in some of Lanchester's own work, has been brought to the fore again with recent interest in differential games. Weiss (1957, 1959) exemplifies current activity in some of these areas and gives references to work in others.

The theory of games also, despite some earlier work, has only been generally accepted since the time of World War II. In this instance an important cause was the publication of the first edition of a provocative and remarkably complete book (von Neumann and Morgenstern, 1943). The preface mentions the early work and its primary aim:

> This book contains an exposition of various applications of a mathematical theory of games. The theory has been developed by one of us since 1928 and is now published for the first time in its entirety. The applications are of two kinds: On the one hand to games in the proper sense, on the other hand to economic and sociological problems which, as we hope to show, are best approached from this direction.
>
> . . . our aim is primarily to show that there is a rigorous approach to these subjects, involving, as they do, questions of parallel or opposite interest, perfect or imperfect information, free rational decision or chance influences.

One of the first sociological phenomena to be studied with the aid of the new theory was military struggle, involving questions of "opposite interest," very often "imperfect information," "rational decision," and "chance influences." Many of the examples given in Dresher (1951) and Caywood and Thomas (1955) depend upon games with an infinite number of strategies. The application of such games involves the same basic aims as that of finite games, but different mathematical techniques. Typical of such early applications is that to a duel involving two armed opponents separated by a distance that constantly decreases, where the role of game theory is, essentially, to resolve the dilemma between shooting early with a high chance of missing and shooting late with a high chance of dying.

A very fertile field of applications, largely developed by Isaacs (1955), has arisen from an interesting modification of the duel problem. Instead of assuming, as in the original problem, that the two opponents are fated to come ever closer, one may single out the element of the "chase" for special attention. One thus arrives at what Isaacs termed a pursuit game, in which the two players may be designated as "pursuer" and "evader." "At each instant," each of the two players exercises his volition through choice of the values of certain "navigation variables." These values, together with the present values of other "descriptive variables," determine the time rate of change of the "descriptive variables," variables that characterize the position or present state of the two players. The solution of such a game is based on what Isaacs termed the "tenet of transition," a two-sided version of the "principle of optimality" of dynamic programming; essentially, this is a recognition that each set of values of the state variables may be regarded as an initial condition with an assigned payoff value, so that in his choice of values for the navigation variables each player seeks to change the descriptive variables in the direction of higher payoff for himself. Having established this general approach and having solved several interesting pursuit games, Isaacs then found a broader field of applications for his theory, which he renamed "differential game theory." In an application to a game involving sets of Lanchester equations, for example, the sizes of various forces would be represented by descriptive variables, and the fractions of various forces allotted at any instant to the various possible tasks would be represented by the navigation variables.

Games of the latter type have been cast in discrete form where the allocation decisions of the players are made on each of a succession of "strikes." An early version was formulated and solved by Fulkerson and Johnson (1957), following which various games of a more elaborate nature have been formulated and solved by Berkovitz and Dresher. A useful summary of the results presently available is given in Berkovitz and Dresher (1959), together with an indication of the method of proof. Their results dash hopes that even relatively simple allocation games can be solved by play.

7. APPLICATIONS INVOLVING LABORATORY SIMULATION

This section deals with the application of laboratory simulation, often large-scale, to the investigation of military systems. Such systems may involve many men and many machines in complicated interaction. Some of these systems are only now being designed, and the problems with which they must cope are so novel that past experience offers only vague guidance. The techniques described in the preceding sections bear on such problems, of course, and their applications have often been considered very valuable. After their application, however, there may remain some troublesome residuals whose resolution demands other methods. In the past it has largely been possible, or even necessary, to ignore such effects or, at best, to sum them up in a highly aggregated treatment. Increasingly, however, such effects are becoming amenable to more extensive study, and they often intrude into the forefront of analysis. Unclassified discussions of an example are available in Enke (1958) and Geisler (1959).

These effects that are being newly studied are human effects, and it is the behavior of people in military systems that is the object of study in these new laboratory simulations. Individual applications, of course, emphasize quite different aspects of behavior. In one study the basic question may concern the interaction of people and machines, and in another the basic problem may hinge on the interaction of people with other people. The source of the original problem in a particular military command or research organization also adds its own flavor to any given application. But human behavior is the common subject of study, and psychologists, as students of human behavior, are the specialists common to the applications.

The applications of laboratory simulation in military gaming may be viewed as outgrowths of training applications. In some instances the same equipment and largely the same personnel may be used at one time for training purposes and at another time for evaluation or research purposes. Moreover, it is often difficult in one activity to separate training from evaluation although their ends may be quite distinct. In large-scale military exercises, for example, whether in the field, at sea, or in the air, one very often finds the somewhat conflicting objectives of giving valuable experience to personnel at the same time that their over-all effectiveness in a system is being tested.

The old-style, large-scale military exercise is a useful example, for its defects suggest the need for, and the desirable characteristics of, laboratory simulation. A rather obvious defect is the difficulty of determining and recording what happens in an exercise. Thus the feedback of such information may be impossible, or so slow as to make it of little value either for improving or for evaluating the system. Another defect of the exercise is a lack of uniform realism. There may be a superficial appearance of great realism in an exercise, as large numbers of uniformed men and military vehicles are shuffled about, but this often serves only to conceal unrealities that are variously introduced by the desire to exercise as many men as possible, conflicting aims of different participating commands, conflicts between training and evaluation, friction with neighboring organizations (military or civilian) where "life goes on as usual," and failure to implement either a plausible threat or realistic doctrine. Some of these defects can be reduced or eliminated. A direct effort to improve the field exercise, however, because of its expense and possible interference with military readiness, does not appear as immediately promising as the use of laboratory simulation.

In order to remedy the defects listed above, a laboratory simulation of a military system must meet basic requirements identical with those governing the effective use of many pilot and gunnery training devices in World War II. The simulation must be appropriately realistic. There must be adequate instrumentation to record what happens. Finally, there must be provision for utilizing this record for training or evaluation. What is new in the present applications is the central interest in the collective behavior of groups of people involved in military systems.

An interest in such collective human behavior can arise as an extension of an application from any one of the three families already discussed, the traditional war game, the computer simulation, or the mathematical approach. Any one of these applications may reach the point where it is necessary to know something more, and often something rather specific, about the way people actually behave in a system. How do they share responsibility? What is the effect of personal jealousies? How do the aims of top management conflict with the interests of lower management? How rapidly can people assimilate information? Will people trust a central computer to keep records and make routine decisions? How much will learning improve behavior as a new system or a new policy is implemented? How do people actually make decisions involving risk? How do people actually play games with three or more players? What do people actually learn from playing games? All of these are questions to which laboratory simulation can contribute.

Since such questions arise in the context of specific systems, a simulation laboratory is typically based on a specific system or type of system. The general size of laboratory, the kind of equipment, and the scale of representation all reflect the kind of problems to be solved. For an air-defense laboratory simulation, one may utilize a room of the same size, arrangement, and equipment as an actual defense control room, or several such rooms connected with appropriate communications. For a logistics laboratory simulation, of lower scale, about the same amount of space may house appropriate representatives of both a logistics command and a using command. Some simulations find their laboratories in the great out-of-doors, where proving grounds may be elaborately instrumented for the study of combat problems that cannot be confined to a control room. Some simulation techniques, such as those used for air-defense training and evaluation, are being taken from the laboratory back to the command for standard use, thus closing the cycle that started with the military exercise.

Examples like those above show a considerable variation in scale of representation and suggest the question of how to determine when a simulation is "appropriately realistic." Since simulation in a large laboratory or proving ground is still very expensive, despite savings over the exercise of an entire military service or command, there is strong incentive to adopt the lowest scale that is at all adequate. In the general design of a laboratory, where one has in mind a whole set of possible problems, one must be prepared to meet the maximum of several minimum sets of requirements. Given a laboratory and a relatively fixed staff, however, the expense may also be relatively fixed. Then, the appropriate question may be: What portion of the proposed system should be simulated with the available resources?

Though the structuring of a simulation clearly depends to a great extent on individual circumstances, there are some generally useful principles of simplification such as those enunciated in Koopman (1957). Noting the difficulty of analyzing operations whose elements permit an "astronomical" number of possible combinations or states, Koopman observed that solutions of such problems generally depend on the possibility of using at least one of three simplifying principles—homogeneity, localization of effects, and minimization or maximization of some function of the system. In most laboratory simulations, as in many other applications of military gaming, one uses a minimization or maximization principle, often unconsciously, to eliminate vast categories of logically possible systems as unworthy of study. Simulations of air-defense systems and logistics systems both illustrate, also, the advantages of homogeneity, as they apply similar treatment to each of a set of equivalent bases or units and concern policies for general implementation throughout a command. Air-defense and logistics systems exhibit illuminating differences, however, with respect to the localization of effects. Whereas the operation of an air-defense control center may be largely isolated from the system as a whole, except for "crosstelling" from other centers that are geographically proximate, a supply depot may have nationwide responsibilities. When, as in some logistics simulation, less localization is permitted, then a reduction in scale is required for the representation of a larger fraction of the system within the limitations of fixed resources.

8. EVALUATION OF MILITARY GAMING

This section offers a tentative evaluation of the current intense activity in military gaming, in which there are a great many applications that involve a considerable variety of different techniques. Part 8.1 rejoices in some encouraging trends, Part 8.2 condemns some discouraging practices, and Part 8.3 offers a partial explanation of some present attitudes toward gaming. This section offers no handbook of prescriptions of the form "for problem number 3 use technique D_2," for it maintains, as in Part 8.2, that there is already too great a tendency to apply techniques mechanically without adequate reflection, or even to profess to see in some one technique a panacea for all problems.

There is another sense of evaluation of military gaming, in which one asks how well it achieves its ends, that is considerably more modest than a handbook but still difficult of attainment at present. For the terms in which one asks and answers the basic questions of gaming achievement are often ill-defined or poorly stated. Sometimes no purposes are stated for an application of gaming. The accomplishments are very often difficult to measure, and the assignment of credit for them to some one technique may be very uncertain. Thus it is impossible in an evaluation to maintain a high level of precision, and it is necessary to glean what one can from practices, trends, and such rationale as can be discerned.

8.1. Encouraging Trends

One of the most encouraging general developments is a growing awareness of what different techniques of military gaming can do and what they cannot do. There is increasing recognition of the inability of any one technique to do everything, and, thus, of the necessity for matching techniques to problems. There has been a corresponding decrease in exaggerated claims. It is more clearly seen that in most applications a concept or a proposal is subjected to a test but not rigorously proved.

Each of the families of applications discussed in the preceding sections has been seen to have encouraging trends of its own. The three-room war game has given birth to new varieties that facilitate an increasing appropriateness and efficiency of application. Computer simulation promises to become less cumbersome with the introduction of improved programs for preparation of inputs and interpretation of outputs, and new, more nearly automatic methods of programming;

it is also encouraging to see the continued use of human skills for tasks that cannot yet be efficiently performed by machines. In the mathematical area it is encouraging to see that the patient work of talented individuals is extending the domain of reason, and is gaining increasing recognition. The increasing use of laboratory simulation promises new insights into human behavior in military systems that should bring greater accuracy and relevance into all areas of military gaming.

8.2. Unfortunate Practices

One of the most unfortunate present tendencies is to confuse distinct techniques under some such broad terms as "military gaming" or "simulation." Although such inclusive terms are sometimes useful, they are often misused. A characteristic of one technique may be falsely assigned to a different technique, for example, because both come under "military gaming." And some prospective gamers have even been misled to the extent of thinking that there is a unified technique of military gaming, universally applicable, with all the separate virtues of the three-room war game, computer simulation, game theory, and laboratory simulation.

Partly as a result of such terminological confusion, and partly as the result of hope for a panacea, there is an unfortunately common tendency to think of "military gaming" as being not only universally applicable but also mechanically applicable. The failure to match technique with problem is often expensive and almost invariably produces disappointment. This is evident in the learning experience of those who know now that the instrumentation of three rooms for war gaming does not solve all problems, and that a large computer simulation model originated at one organization is not painlessly transferred to another organization. Unfortunately, many have not learned from the experiences of their predecessors. Some still establish war-gaming facilities without having problems amenable to war gaming. Some still think that in the two or three months allotted to them for a short study, they can "borrow" a gigantic computer simulation model developed elsewhere, understand it, input to it, and make sense of the outputs.

Not anticipating the kind of difficulty mentioned above, some tend to be overly ambitious in undertaking study projects. Now that more and more problems are being subjected to a scientific, or at least systematic, treatment, there is a tendency to think that for every problem there must be some appropriate technique. In extreme form, one feels that if $n-1$ of n techniques have been excluded as inapplicable, then the nth must necessarily be chosen. Errors of this kind would not be as serious as they are, if there were better means of measuring success in gaming, or even if there were closer control of gaming activities. Once started, however, a study is hard to stop, for without clear aims and frequent review, its failure may not be easily discernible.

8.3. Vogues in Gaming

The diversity of attitudes and opinions engendered by the techniques of military gaming exceeds the diversity of the techniques themselves. The different viewpoints of different scientists, even in the same organization, seem very striking to one who first encounters gaming. This part of the present section offers a partial explanation of these differences and of the vogues that exist in gaming.

Part of the diversity in attitudes, of course, goes back to the diversity of historical sources described in Section 2. The different techniques of military gaming arose from quite different academic backgrounds. The war game suggests graduates of a military academy, a computer simulation suggests physicists or engineers, particularly electronic engineers, game theory was introduced by mathematicians and economists, and laboratory simulation heavily involves psychologists. Corresponding to such different academic backgrounds are quite different viewpoints.

The effect of academic background on the formation of attitudes towards techniques of gaming is often reinforced by an effect of quite a different character. This other effect is the human tendency to become enamoured of a path of thought one has taken in reaching a conclusion, to regard it as the unique route, to consider it as having proved or established the conclusion beyond any further doubt. Often one who has used a given technique of gaming to reach a satisfying conclusion, or to fail, is so impressed with his experience, happy or sad, that he finds it difficult not to generalize from a sample of one. Yet the fallacy is evident. The conclusion may be good and the path bad, as in Dalton's atomic hypothesis, which he reached by combining three false steps, or as in the numerous true theorems which are falsely "proved" in the journals each year. But a bad path may lead to an equally bad conclusion, as mathematical experience again shows.

In dealing with most of military gaming, however, there is nothing to fill the fundamental role assumed by the concept of proof in mathematics, with the result that an appearance of reality becomes a dominant criterion. To an extent the dependence on an appearance of reality is well motivated. No one wants to see poor, "sophomoric" theorizing. Everyone dreads an inappropriate suboptimization that wastes an elegant investigation on what turns out to be an entirely inapplicable region. There is a common fear that a mathematical discipline cut off from its empirical source tends to become, as von Neumann (1947) put it, "more and more purely aestheticizing, more and more purely *l'art pour l'art*" (pp. 195–196). There is general uplifting of spirits with the hope that laboratory simulation will give a good factual grounding to all manner of theory of human behavior in military systems. All of these emotional responses evidence a striving for reality.

What happens, unfortunately, is that the search for reality is shunted into a search for the appearance of reality. One is fascinated by the appearance of real events unfolding before one's eyes, and may forget that the appearance does not in itself prove or disprove the reality or faithfulness of the representation. It is interesting to inquire into this appearance of reality and to see why certain types of simulation do, or do not, tend to produce it.

Very often it is not recognized, or remembered, that the full blazing glory of reality itself is rarely experienced, even when one has extremely vivid impressions of reality. Consider, then, the additional filtering that comes between reality and its common representations during military combat. The enemy bomber, no longer even a dot in the sky, becomes a blip on a radar scope, a counter on a plotting board, or even a number on a vertical screen. The "fog of battle" becomes a blur of numbers on a tote board or a battery of blinking lights at the computer console. Thus much of our relatively direct "experiencing" of reality is flooded with abstraction. And what is needed, then, to produce an appearance of reality is just to produce similar abstractions.

Much of the simulation in war gaming and computer simulation is admirably suited to the production of the standard abstractions. The colored pins in the maps of the game room are hardly distinguishable from those of the command post. The intelligence reports of the game may use a standard form. The computer output of the simulation can certainly emulate the clickety-clack of the teletype or even the cathode-ray tube of the radar. These results surely look real.

Contrast such simulation with what often happens when mathematics is applied. Mathematics, too, may start with fundamental, individual elements, with the separate terms of a series (as in the example of Section 6), with the numerous slender rectangles whose combined area approximates the area under a curve. But the well-known examples of elementary mathematics concern problems where it is possible and desirable to pass quickly from the individual elements to an elegant summation. The student is drilled in the manipulation that finds such "closed forms" and often forgets the "duller" theorems where one finds the detailed roots of brilliant florescence. Add to this the occasional perversions of mathematical applications where a closed form is unduly sought at the expense of vital realism, and it is easy to understand the too-common picture of mathematics as a technique for producing closed forms that are usually inapplicable. This is particularly ironic in that the spirit of mathematics, as going beyond simulation to become almost "metasimulation," could contribute much to many of the more straightforward simulations.

There are, of course, still deeper veins in the opposition of "experiential reality" to "mathematical reality." In a sympathetic recollection, Polya (1954) is especially illuminating:

> I remember a conversation on invention and plausible reasoning. It happened long ago. I talked with a friend who was much older than myself and could look back on a distinguished record of discoveries, inventions, and successful professional work. As he talked on plausible reasoning and invention, he doubtless knew what he was talking about. He maintained with unusual warmth and force of conviction that invention and plausible reasoning have no rules. Hunches and guesses, he said, depend on experience and intuition, but not on rules: there are no rules, there can be no rules, there should be no rules, and if there were some rules, they were useless anyway. I maintained the contrary—a conversation is uninteresting if there is no difference of opinion—yet I felt the strength of his position. My friend was a surgeon. A wrong decision of a surgeon may cost a life and sometimes, when a patient suddenly starts bleeding or suffocating, the right decision must come in a second. I understand that people who have to make such responsible quick decisions have no use for rules. The time is too short to apply a rule properly, and any set pattern could misguide you; what you need is intense concentration upon the situation before you. And so people come to distrust "rules" and to rely on their "intuition" or "experience" or "intuition-and-experience."
>
> In the case of my friend, there was still something else, perhaps. He was a little on the domineering side. He hated to relinquish power. He felt, perhaps, that acknowledging a rule is like delegating a part of his authority to a machine, and so he was against it (pp. 109–110).

Cannot this basic conflict, so well brought out in Polya's conversation, be expected to persevere in military gaming so long as it includes the frontier between an expanding realm of reasoned rules and the enduring realm of intuition?

BIBLIOGRAPHY

Berkovitz, L. D., and Dresher, M., "A Game-Theory Analysis of Tactical Air War," *Opns. Res.*, **7**, 599–620 (1959).

Caywood, T. E., and Thomas, C. J., "Applications of Game Theory in Fighter versus Bomber Combat," *Opns. Res.*, **3**, 402–411 (1955).

Dalkey, N. C., and Wegner, L. H., "The Strategic Operations Model" (confidential), RM-2250, The RAND Corporation, September 2, 1958.

Dresher, Melvin, "Theory and Applications of Games of Strategy," R-216, The RAND Corporation, December 1, 1951.

Enke, Stephen, "On the Economic Management of Large Organizations: A Case Study in Military Logistics Involving Laboratory Simulation," P-1368, The RAND Corporation, May 8, 1958.

Fulkerson, D. R., and Johnson, S. M., "A Tactical Air Game," *Opns. Res.*, **5**, 704–712 (1957).

Geisler, M. A., "The Use of Monte Carlo Models, Man-Machine Simulation, and Analytical Methods for Studying Large Human Organizations," P-1634, The RAND Corporation, March 11, 1959.

Goldhamer, H., and Speier, H., "Some Observations on Political Gaming," P-1679-RC, The RAND Corporation, April 30, 1959.

Helmer, O., and Shapley, L. S., "Brief Description of the SWAP Game" (confidential), RM-2058, The RAND Corporation, December 12, 1957.

Hofmann, Rudolf, List, Wilhelm, et al., "War Games" (trans. by P. Luetzkendorf), F. B. Robinson (ed.), MS. No. P-094, Department of the Army, Office of Military History, Washington, D. C., 1952.

Isaacs, Rufus, "Differential Games—I. Introduction, II. The Definition and Formulation, III. The Basic Principles of the Solution Process, IV. Mainly Examples," RM-1391, RM-1399, RM-1411, RM-1486, The RAND Corporation, March 25, 1955.

———, "The Theory of Collisions Between Moving Craft," SRSM1-189, Hughes Aircraft Company, April 1, 1958.

Kahn, Herman, and Mann, Irwin, "War Gaming," P-1167, The RAND Corp., July 30, 1957.

Kahn, H., and Marshall, A. W., "Methods of Reducing Sample Size in Monte Carlo Computations," *Opns. Res.*, **1**, 263–278 (1953).

Koopman, B. O., "Fallacies in Operations Research," *Opns. Res.*, **4**, 422–426 (1956).

———, "Combinatorial Analysis of Operations," *Proc. of the First Inter. Conf. on OR*, Oxford, September 1957.

Lanchester, F. W., *Aircraft in Warfare; "The Dawn of the Fourth Arm,"* Constable and Co., London, 1916.

Livermore, W. R., *The American Kriegspiel*, The Riverside Press, Cambridge, 1882.

Luce, R. Duncan, and Raiffa, Howard, *Games and Decisions*, John Wiley and Sons, New York, 1957.

Manstein, Erich v., *Aus Einem Soldatenleben*, Athenaeum-Verlag, Bonn, 1958.

Mood, A. M., "War Gaming as a Technique of Analysis," P-899, The RAND Corporation, September 3, 1954.

———, and Specht, R. D., "Gaming as a Technique of Analysis," P-579, The RAND Corporation, October 19, 1954.

OMEGA, "A Guide to the Air Battle Model" (Vol. I on Flow Charts, Vol. II on Notations), SM58-5, Technical Operations, Inc., Washington, D. C., April 10, 1958.

Paxson, E. W., "Joint War Games" (confidential), Danish Academy of Defense, Copenhagen, December 6, 1957.

Polya, George, *Patterns of Plausible Inference,* Volume II of *Mathematics and Plausible Reasoning,* Princeton University Press, Princeton, N. J., 1954.

Rich, R. P., "Simulation as an Aid in Model Building," *Opns. Res.,* **3,** 15–19 (1955).

Sayre, Farrand, *Map Maneuvers and Tactical Rides,* Springfield Printing and Binding Company, Springfield, Massachusetts, 1908.

Smith, N. M., Jr., "A Rationale for Operational Gaming," paper presented to 8th National Meeting of ORSA, Ottawa, Canada, January 10, 1956.

Stone, Marshall H., "Mathematics and the Future of Science," *Bull. of the Amer. Math. Soc.,* **63,** 61–76 (1957).

Thomas, C. J., and Deemer, W. L., Jr., "The Role of Operational Gaming in Operations Research," *Opns. Res.,* **5,** 1–27 (1957).

Tokyo Trials, *Proceedings of the International Military Tribunal for the Far East,* Tokyo, 1946–1947 (mimeographed transcript of charges, testimony, and exhibits, numbering approximately 50,000 pages, record held by the Library of Congress).

Ulam, S., "John von Neumann, 1903–1957," *Bull. of the Amer. Math. Soc.,* **64,** No. 3, Part 2, 1–49 (1958).

Vernois, Verdy du (trans. by Eben Swift), *A Simplified War Game,* Hudson-Kimberly Publishing Company, Kansas City, Missouri, 1897.

von Neumann, John, "Zur Theorie der Gesellschaftsspiele," *Math. Ann.,* **100,** 295–320 (1928).

———, "The Mathematician," *The Works of the Mind,* University of Chicago Press, Chicago, 1947.

———, and Morgenstern, Oskar, *Theory of Games and Economic Behavior,* Princeton University Press, Princeton, N. J., 1943.

Weiner, M. G., "An Introduction to War Games," P-1773, The RAND Corporation, August 17, 1959.

Weiss, Herbert K., "Lanchester-Type Models of Warfare," *Proc. of the First Inter. Conf. on OR,* Oxford, September 1957.

———, "Some Differential Games of Tactical Interest and the Value of a Supporting Weapon System," *Opns. Res.,* **7,** 180–196 (1959).

Young, John P., "A Survey of Historical Developments in War Games," ORO-SP-98, Operations Research Office, The Johns Hopkins University, Bethesda, Maryland, March 1959.

Chapter **11**

PROGRESS IN OPERATIONS RESEARCH: The Challenge of the Future

JOHN F. MAGEE AND MARTIN L. ERNST
Arthur D. Little, Inc., Cambridge, Massachusetts

Contents

1. INTRODUCTION

Ten years ago, a small group of hopeful, enthusiastic scientists met at Arden House to found the Operations Research Society of America. That ten years later operations research has a firm place in American business, professional, and military life, is hardly in doubt. One needs only to look to the hundreds attending Society meetings, the number of strong, well-established military groups, and the steady increase and spread of industrial groups.

Operations research has been a tradition in the military services since the beginnings of World War II. Though one cannot yet call operations research a "traditional" business service, there is some evidence that it is receiving growing acceptance: some business publications have even consented to write operations research in lower-case type. A few "what is it" meetings still are held, but increasing numbers of businessmen are growing familiar with the more common concepts and jargon. Professionals themselves are devoting minimal time to defining operations research, more to practicing it. Operations research is slowly fading into the landscape, acquiring more opportunity to work, and presenting less of a target to the sniping of the suspicious and unfriendly.[1]

Progress in operations research to date has been modest but steady. But what of the future? Into what areas will operations research grow? Will operations research survive as a distinct field? Will it outgrow the stigma of a "technique" and hold the status of a professional field of learning? Will opportunities for work of greater significance be presented; will professional competence in the field grow adequately to meet the opportunities? To answer these questions, to forecast the future significance of operations research, is impossible; but a review of past developments and their causes will help indicate the lines of growth that exist, and clarify some of the conditions and problems which we must face.

[1] A happy future forecast by Philip M. Morse (1953) in his address as retiring president of ORSA.

2. TEN YEARS OF GROWTH

Basic acceptance of operations research already existed in military circles ten years ago, and techniques for handling many tactical problems were in hand. Based on the simple fact that operations research had been useful during the war, groups had been established in the three services—often at several command levels—and in the Department of Defense. Further support was provided by outside organizations such as the RAND Corporation, and by sections of several military-equipment suppliers. Almost without exception these groups were expanding, and were being provided with increased opportunities to participate in military planning and operations.

Operations research had started ten years previously with heavy emphasis on the collection of statistical data, and application of the simple variational techniques used so effectively by P. M. S. Blackett and other early British workers. By 1950, methodology had made notable advances leading to the development of considerable theoretical background, such as that presented in *Search and Screening* by B. O. Koopman, portions of which have since been published in *Operations Research* (1956 and 1957).[2] The concept of mathematical models of operations was widespread, and many of these models had developed a high level of sophistication. However, with the exception of some of the work done by RAND, and a few broad studies of air defense and antisubmarine warfare, almost all work was still being done at the tactical level. Most operations research problems dealt with the requirements and use of individual weapons, with only limited attention devoted to the larger problems of allocation and integration of effort (see Brothers, 1954).

Ten years of growth has led to even greater acceptance of operations research techniques, and to a continual broadening of the problems presented to the service operations research groups. The increased acceptance has largely meant more participation by workers at higher staff levels, with more confidence being placed in the results achieved. Almost without exception the major operations research groups have devoted large portions of their recent efforts to important strategic problems. Notable areas of work include the analysis of air defense integrated into the entirety of our national military effort, the choice of strategic alternatives between widely different types of weapons systems, analysis of the implications of different military postures, reviews of military-aid programs, analyses of research and development efforts

[2] See also Chapter 2, *Notes on Operations Research 1959.*

in major areas of warfare, and participation in very large-scale war games.

So far so good; but at least some warning signs are available to the critical observer that this rosy picture has flaws which may impose obstacles to future growth. Two elements in particular present severe threats. First, the acceptance of operations research has all too often been based on standards far different from those which scientists would desire. In recent years the competition and rivalry between military services over the allocation of the national defense budget has reached a degree of severity which probably far exceeds any equivalent in industry. One result has been a steady increase in emphasis on the "packaging" of weapons systems proposals, and a great incentive to "dress it up with science."

This remark is not necessarily derogatory to either the scientists or to the officers of military services. The scientists have often taken stands opposed to the policies of their own services or companies, when data and analyses so warranted. Military leaders have carefully examined and respectfully treated reports which were in strong opposition to their traditions and immediate viewpoints. However, the role of security tends to distort efforts at objective analysis. It is almost inevitable that one finds a study supporting a given service position widely distributed by that service, while a critical evaluation—even though it may receive careful attention and action—will normally never see the light of day outside the organization for which it was prepared. Although members of one military operations research group may have high regard and respect for members of another group, it is quite typical for one service to regard another's group as the latter's creature, devoted to finding (or making) evidence which will support a one-sided point of view. This situation—which is by no means unknown in industry—is compounded by the limited information and data available to an operations research worker when dealing with operations outside his immediate command. Survival in this atmosphere will take its toll of objectivity, and the military groups, regardless of their internal merit, face an uphill battle to maintain a reputation for integrity.

While the above problem is largely one of environment, the second critical element is purely technical, and deals with the methodology available for working on strategic problems. In blunt terms, very little exists. Most of the colorful techniques we have at our disposal—such as game theory, value theory, linear and dynamic programming, Monte Carlo and war gaming—are completely out of their depth when applied to the practical problems facing military operations research workers today. Even when unquestionably useful for some purposes, these techniques may be quite dangerous if employed as a basis for decisions; the limitations of some of them are covered in the literature (see Haywood, 1954, and Thomas and Deemer, 1957).

In time, these techniques may develop to help fill the gap, but at present the content of most strategic operations research work is primarily the elaborate manipulation of uncertain and controversial assumptions. Some of this work has been excellent in its analysis of the implications of various assumptions, but almost without exception, any major strategic study by a military operations research group can be torn to shreds by an opposing group using different—but equally supportable—assumptions. Unless improvement in the use, handling, and interpretation of these vital assumptions is forthcoming, it is difficult to see how real confidence in the results of analyses can continue to grow. And unless increasing confidence is developed, the environment may take over, and military operations research workers may find their main function the supplying of window dressing to combat the equivalent window dressing of groups in other services.

The growth of industrial operations research has in many ways shown striking parallels to the development of operations research activities in the military field. The greatest effective contributions and the most numerous illustrations of work exist in specific tactical problems of rather limited scope. Edie's paper (1954), awarded the first Lanchester Prize, is an outstanding example of this type of work. *Operations Research, Management Science,* and the business literature are filled with technical discussions and case histories in the field of inventory control. Much of this work has been devoted to what is probably the lowest level of management decision in the business structure, namely, how much of an individual item to put on a shelf in a warehouse.

The interest in and productivity of work in tactical issues has strongly influenced the subject matter of professional journals, as well as the texts in operations research and related fields which have been published. The Ackoff, Arnoff, and Churchman book (1957), for example, which is probably the first professionally recognized text on operations research produced outside the military services, is devoted largely to methods applicable to tactical issues, and to case histories drawn from such subject matter. Of the series published by ORSA, perhaps only McKean's book (1958) gives more than passing attention to other than immediate short-term problems.

The basis for attention to detailed questions such as inventory control is sound. It can be argued with some force that only when the smaller-scale problems are understood, in the sense that useful concepts and valid quantitative bases exist to analyze them, can operations research workers extend their efforts into broader problems of business strategy and planning. Furthermore, in industry as in the military, constructive work on the smaller problems is needed to provide the basic confidence of business management in operations research efforts which can in time lead to a hearing on the broader issues.

There is evidence that beginnings are being made in problems of broader scope. The Allais paper (1957) on exploration of the Sahara is an example. The Hetrick-Kimball effort to understand the role of basic research is another.[3] Progress is being made to exploit the work in inventory control and production planning to study broader questions:

1. The design of distribution systems incorporating field inventory control, the interaction of manufacturing facilities, and the distribution system, transportation methods, and information processing.[4]
2. The use of business models, again in many cases heavily dependent on the contributions of inventory theory and the transportation problem, for the analysis of facility requirements to meet forecast demand, as a basis for long-term planning.[5]

Through these steps, industrial operations research is following the lead of the military field in building on tactical studies toward eventually making significant contributions in broader strategic applications.

There are, however, some vital differences between the introduction and growth of operations research in the industrial and military spheres. Industrial operations have been far more stable, until recently, than were military activities in World War II and after. Stability has given business management the opportunity to arrive at effective policies and procedures, through a slow process of experimentation and buildup of experience.

Over the course of the last forty years, business management has acquired a number of supporting service activities—industrial engi-

[3] *Basic Research in the Navy,* a report to the Secretary of the Navy by the Naval Research Advisory Committee, Volume II, Appendix B, June 1, 1959.

[4] See Hanssmann (1959) and Simpson (1958 and 1959).

[5] This work is essentially unpublished. Scattered references may be found in the literature to the problems of balancing demand, transport, and production cost, but as static problems.

neering, marketing research, and accounting, for example—all of which have had the objective of providing management with analytical support, or at least with data for business-management purposes. In most organizations these services had arrived at a modus vivendi, and business management was not apparently left without sources of analytical assistance on the problems that it recognized. The operations research worker could not very well defend his right to a livelihood on the ground that his sphere of interest was new, and his demands for support have represented simultaneously a challenge to existing business services and a challenge to the business decision practices themselves. The development of operations research in industry, therefore, has been an attempt to impose a new discipline rather than a recognition of existing fact and accomplishment. In the face of business stability and entrenched services, when one takes account of natural human instincts, it is hardly surprising that the growth of operations research in industry has been halting and that to date the claims of its adherents are largely undemonstrated.[6]

In assessing the strength of operations research in industry, it is not fair to include the many large and powerful groups serving companies that are principally military suppliers, e.g., the aircraft and computer manufacturers. To a substantial extent, the work of these groups parallels the efforts of military groups. The greatest true industrial growth appears to exist in technologically based industries such as petroleum or chemicals—perhaps because of the close coupling between physical processes and operating practices, perhaps because of the greater familiarity with quantitative method and engineering practice existing in the middle and upper management of these companies. Even in these industries, the efforts have been heavily confined to the extension of studies where quantitative method was well established, e.g., plant utilization. There are signs of growth in other spheres, as demonstrated by recent surveys.[7] In some industries where operations research would appear to have an important natural role, such as in transportation companies and other public utilities, growth has been hampered by the degree to which management freedom is hemmed in by regulation or labor restrictions. In almost all industries, however, the slowness in growth may be attributed to the inability of the operations research field to contribute to truly significant industrial prob-

[6] "Operations Research: What It Is, How It Is Conducted, What It Offers Business," National Industrial Conference Board, Studies in Business Policy No. 82, 1957.

[7] See Churchman (1955) and Hertz (1957).

lems, to management's inability to integrate and use staff services such as operations research, and to the limitations on the number and quality of personnel.

3. BASIS FOR GROWTH

This restrained view of the position of operations research to date provides us at least with some measure of the requirements for the further active and healthy spread of operations research as a new discipline. Fundamentally:

1. There must be a requirement for work. There must be significant problems to be solved which are not adequately handled by existing doctrine and managerial experience.
2. There must be a recognition of the requirement. Business or military management must recognize the problems, if indeed they do exist, and must recognize the nature of the contribution that operations research can make. Edison's work for the Navy in World War I is an outstanding example of solid technical effort which came to nought because existing doctrine appeared to be adequate, and because Naval management was neither forced nor able to see the value of Edison's effort.[8] Members of the Operations Research Society scattered throughout industry find themselves in much the same position. Inspired by the technical literature, they see opportunities for contribution, but often get nowhere because of lack of management recognition.
3. We must be able to achieve effective solutions. We must have method and theory which make some valid contribution to the solution of problems if we are to presume to ask for support. To date, operations research has had little to contribute to many significant military and business issues such as questions of broad allocation of resources, risk taking, organization, and competition. Truly effective methods in these areas do not exist, so the decision makers are left to their own devices.

As the limitations implied by these requirements are overcome, the operations research field will maintain healthy growth only if it can meet two significant internal challenges.

Operations research must amount to more than a concept. It must identify a body of people of growing professional stature, professional in the sense of having an ability to blend solid technical competence

[8] See Whitmore (1953).

with an understanding of practical affairs, and an ability to guide the implementation of results.

Operations research must maintain vision; as a profession it must continue to be dissatisfied with the adequacy and breadth of its work and must push for understanding of increasing scope; it must avoid turning inward to a concentration on sharpening techniques for increasingly better solutions to ever-narrower problems. The inventory problem alone provides an almost inexhaustible subject for technical investigation.[9] Concentration on knowing more and more about how to control a stock-keeping unit represents, however, abdication of our responsibility. The opportunity for contribution can be realized only by the efforts to explore and understand increasingly significant business and military activity.

As a corollary, operations research must hold to the role of building organized knowledge of operating processes and management, rather than of serving as a storehouse for technique. Concentration on technique rather than discovery will reduce the members of the profession to the role of technicians, albeit highly "sophisticated."

The growth of future application and opportunity of operations research can be put into perspective by examining in greater detail the three basic requirements for growth, in order to identify present trends and suggest how these requirements will influence the future scope of work.

4. DO REQUIREMENTS EXIST?

One needs but little acquaintance with modern military or industrial activities to answer this question—not only do requirements in the sense of significant problems exist, but they are increasing daily. Some of these problems have been with us a long time, but are now being re-examined in a new light. Others are arising for the first time, or in such a radically new and more vital form that they effectively constitute new problems. Industrial and military staffs are endeavoring to formulate solutions to these problems, but the doctrine, techniques, and experience available to assist them provide far less support than in the past.

If any single factor is primarily responsible for the size and urgency of these requirements, it is unquestionably the rapid and competitive

[9] As a cursory review of professional literature such as *Operations Research, Management Science,* and *Naval Research Logistics Quarterly* will show.

growth of technology. In the military field, it is unnecessary to describe the radical changes in the last decade in the use of nuclear weapons and propulsion, in aircraft and missile design, in detection and communications equipment, and in the beginnings of the use of high-speed data-processing equipment to assist the formation of command decisions; these advances are common knowledge. More to the point are the problems which our technology poses. Perhaps the most critical are the greatly increased requirements for procurement lead time and the spiraling costs of modern equipment. For the first time in history during a period of peace—and much against well-supported tradition and experience—it has become necessary to make major procurement decisions long before weapons systems have been thoroughly developed, debugged, and evaluated. The expense of these systems precludes the previously possible development of and selection among a family of similar systems. The cost and lead times imply a degree of complexity and interrelationships which forecast changes in the operation of customary command structures; even more, they suggest that major procurement decisions can come close to freezing the national military and political posture in a mold determined by the anticipated technical capabilities of our weapons.

This situation is so strikingly different from all past developments that previous experience has only limited value. Military organizations have attempted to respond by great increases in staff sizes, and by expansion of the analytical capabilities of these staffs. This has all too often resulted in a pyramiding of subcommittees, panels, and committees, with the obvious danger of near strangulation of individual initiative when faced with the inertia provided by massive organizational structure. The question of how effectively operations research can contribute to the solution of these problems will be considered later, but it is clear that analysis increases in importance as experience proves less applicable in reaching valid decisions. The requirements exist and all current indications forecast their increase.

Meanwhile, similar events are taking place in industry.[10] As the rate of change in industrial technology accelerates, business management finds itself faced with increased lead times—because of the larger size and greater scope of projects—whether for procedural change or new plant or equipment. The threat, for example, of obsolete systems has haunted banking and other industries with heavy clerical content which have been installing data-processing equipment. The rate of

[10] See Drucker (1959).

equipment development threatens to outstrip the capability to plan and install.

Opportunities for increasingly radical change are presenting themselves to business management: higher speeds, lower costs, greater flexibility and interchangeability in transport; mechanization and automatic process control systems; and revolutionary changes in marketing due to, for example, increased or novel emphasis on style, shifts in selling methods and consumer incentives, and radical changes in advertising media. The changes in marketing in the 1950's are exemplified by the growth of style-consciousness in formerly prosaic fields such as office furniture, the dominance of advertising and heavily merchandised industries by television, and the growth of interest in specialty/convenience shopping. These changes have hardly come to an end.

The changes forcing themselves on business are increasingly costly. Notwithstanding the social consequences, the replacement of, first, human muscle and, latterly, human mental effort by mechanical devices takes capital in huge quantities, capital permanently committed. An automated factory presents a vastly different problem in investment than does a skilled worker.

Business, in the face of the rate of change in industrial processes, increasing lead times, and higher investment requirements, is losing its capability for incremental improvement, its ability to experiment with alternatives. Systems analysis, common in military weapons design for the past ten years, is finding use in industry: selection of equipment in transportation, analysis of control systems and unit investments in chemical processing, material and information flow or facilities planning in manufacturing industry. Lessened opportunity for incremental change, and accumulation of experience, forces analysis as a last resort.

Industry also faces other changes, some of which were encountered in the military field many decades ago. Business management is becoming less personal; and the pattern of functional specialization is increasing. Thus there is an increasing need for conscious—quantitative—planning and control to balance functional interests and to resolve the internal conflicts these generate, conflicts which often in the past centered in and were resolved by one man, the "boss."

The inventory problem—perhaps the "classic" problem in industrial operations research—illustrates the resolution of functional conflict, the competing pressures of production efficiency, sales service, and financial investment.[11] Distribution system design introduces further matters of information-processing efficiency, locational economics, facility design, and traffic. Information-system design forces a resolution of clerical data-processing efficiency, organization, and managerial needs. Marketing programs must reconcile long- and short-run positions and profits.

As a result of the trend to depersonalization and functional specialization, greater need exists for explicit demonstration of conflict and tradeoffs. Opportunity for study of functional interdependencies, broad questions cutting across functional areas, exists. The abilities to meet these needs are two key strengths claimed by the operations research profession from inception. The growing need challenges the growing capability for intrafunction detailed study.

In addition to the large issues, the opportunities for technical growth in operations research are still tremendous in tactical operations. In the military field, for example, we lack a basic understanding and measure of the operational performance of most of our primary detection systems. The process of search, perhaps the best studied of all true operations, still has unexplored aspects. Some work has been done in the study of special search techniques when high-quality "noise" is present (Engel, 1957), but we have much to learn with regard to search in the presence of countermeasures by an opponent—and, on the other side, with respect to the employment of countermeasures against a searching enemy.

No analytical models exist of individual unit interactions, with ships, aircraft, land vehicles, or men, which are adequate both to describe past history and to predict future trends. At the mass-action level, where equations of the Lanchester type apply, the situation is better, and some progress has been made in broadening the scope of earlier work (Weiss, 1957 and 1959). The influence of communications on operational effectiveness is not understood in any general quantitative fashion, in spite of some worthwhile and interesting initial studies (Page, 1957). The effects of the level of logistic support on two sides engaged in combat cannot be evaluated in other than gross fashion. The proper role of costs in military procurement decisions has been examined with limited success, but the relations of such costs to inven-

[11] The breadth of validity of the inventory concept is probably generally unrecognized. The concept of lot size, fundamental to the inventory problem, applies with equal force to such diverse questions as facilities planning and some personnel-manning problems.

tory sizes, transportation methods, and service standards have received only little analytical investigation. Our current position represents a mass of doctrine based on experience and judgment, supplemented with a leavening of quantitative knowledge based on analysis. Current procedures will usually work fairly well, provided the situations encountered are not too radically different from those in the past, but the process of adjusting to new environments is slow.

Industries also have their tactical problems: we have yet to solve the inventory problem. For example, an inadequate standard or measure of effectiveness exists for unifying the presently incommensurable goals of service, cost, and investment. Even investment, which appears deceptively straightforward, is clouded by inadequate explicit knowledge of the cost of money, its relation to risk, and the risk that inventory represents. We have made substantial progress in recognizing inventory control as a servo system; we have just begun to concern ourselves with monitoring of the system itself. In other tactical areas, the shop-scheduling problem remains a practical puzzle; we can observe, simulate, and make wise comment on the job shop, but we cannot yet practically control it. Some progress has been made in marketing studies and in the measurement of payoff for effort expended; exceedingly little has been accomplished, or at least published, in the development of an operational theory of price. The effort in these areas has been far short, in relation to importance.

The operations research field has the beginnings of methods to investigate and characterize integrated systems. Distribution problems have been mentioned; the analyses of broad-scale physical distribution systems have probably been the first "strategic" problems to be studied extensively from the foundations of inventory theory and its extension to stock allocation, cascaded-stock, and control-system problems. Integrated information handling and retrieval systems are receiving some attention; here, military efforts offer a tremendous technical stimulus to industrial work. However, we must yet develop meaningful measures of information content and significance, and an adequate explicit understanding of the retrieval process. Transportation offers an exciting opportunity for integrated systems study. As industrial requirements for transport services become better understood, gross volume and cost per ton-mile fall in significance, relative to, e.g., reliability. In the face of a revolution in facilities, the transport systems are faced with major problems in reconciling equipment investment, unit operating costs, speed, flexibility and reliability of service, and facilities or switching costs in the face of the mix of market requirements. Fundamentally similar problems exist in rail, air, trucking services, road design, and communications such as the postal service.

Product design promises to be a fruitful field for operations research work, because of the business system implications and the need to find and quantify adequate measures of design efficiency. Though product design will never be a rational process until, God forbid, esthetics is reduced to a true experimental science, at least a rational engineering base should be possible. We find once more a conflict among functional interests: product diversity to satisfy market requirements, whether use or esthetic needs; functional efficiency of the individual product; and production efficiency. Some interesting progress has been made. Exploitation of the concept of product families, diversity achieved by capitalizing on the combinatorial possibilities of limited component lines as in automotive manufacture, has begun in other industries in the face of increased process mechanization and the pressure to cut scheduling, stock-keeping, and distribution costs.

Product redesign to postpone specialization is another attractive possibility. Changed design concepts in typewriter manufacture to minimize the burden of a wide product line resulting from sudden emphasis on color and style is a striking example. Economic substitution of materials of higher-than-necessary specification to cut down the total number of items or components carried is yet a third possibility, as in packaging materials or equipment components. These and other devices are at work here and there in industry. Operations research has the opportunity to build these devices into a set of generally useful concepts and theory for product-design analysis over a broad industrial field.

At least three fundamental areas exist in industrial operations—with counterparts in the military area—where operations research should offer significant help, and where advances in concepts and technique are needed. These are: the handling of risk, competition, and analysis of organization.

Risk and decision making in the face of uncertainty are at the core of our economic and military systems. Surprisingly, while risk-taking decisions are faced every day, our conceptual understanding of the problem is weak. This is not so much a matter of technique; certainly the technical possibilities of, e.g., statistical decision theory are not exhausted. The difficulties in the analysis of risk are illustrated by the problems of pricing capital or computing capital costs. It is generally recognized, for example, that an enterprise cannot survive if its expected earnings merely match the time-cost of capital. There is no point in borrowing money at 5 per cent to invest in an activity which will yield only a 5 per cent gross return. But what standard of return should be required and how is this related to the risk of the activity, to the distribution of earnings vs. expectation? Today, we are forced to deal with relatively arbitrary rules of thumb. With a proper operational understanding of the concept of risk, the operations research profession will have the basis for really significant contributions in the area of long-range planning and allocation of resources.

The theory of games received significant publicity in the business and military worlds essentially coincidentally with operations research (McDonald, 1949). It was heralded as the basis for rational investigation and formulation of competitive policies and tactics. Though a monumental effort, both its industrial significance and its military significance have been trivial as a method for analysis. The difficulties are simple: the conventional criteria for strategy choice are objectionable and intuitively dissatisfactory, and the technical apparatus is hopelessly complex except in a few special cases. Just as important, we characteristically cannot evaluate competitive strategies. These are characteristically implemented in the market, or on the political scene, probably our weakest areas as regards ability to define and measure functional dependence. Difficult as the problem is, the operations research profession must continue efforts to understand and measure competitive forces.

Existing organization theory is largely dogma. Organization studies are today characteristically clearly separated from operations research efforts. The lack of real industrial organization theory is evident in the fads of change, staff/line realignment, centralization/decentralization. While the desirability of continuous change in organization can be argued with some force, especially under the stimulation of spirits, the tremendous direct cost of organizational change is rarely borne for the sake of change itself. Some significant and interesting progress is being made to understand organization, witness the work of March and Simon (1958) and others, and the efforts in group dynamics.[12] Organization study is probably one of the more valid of the reasons for the current interest in gaming. Operations research has a potential contribution to make to organization theory. The analysis of decisions, business control mechanisms, and information requirements to support these may, we hope, open an attack on organization issues through effort to minimize information-transmittal effort and

[12] See also Clark and Ackoff (1959).

noise generation and to match decision-making activity with relevant information channels.

In the discussions so far we have made no mention of operations research in the field of civil government, where our past history has been distressingly weak. Certainly requirements exist for more effective use of resources in this area. Some outstanding examples of work exist, such as those reported by Edie, McKean, and others, and a great deal of scattered work closely akin to operations research has been done for many years. In any event, widespread opportunities exist in the fields of slum clearance, city planning, highway routing and design, medical care and hospital management, mail handling, and a host of other governmental activities at the local, state, and national level. While some efforts are under way in the Federal Government—notably, for example, in the FAA—the field is at yet relatively untouched, while the needs are great.

There is, then, no shortage of problems or of new fields for exercise of operations research talent. The critical question is, simply, Will we meet the challenge?

Operations research has been defined semifacetiously as "the application of big minds to small problems." For reasons noted above, the concentration on tactical problems has been a necessary and healthy aspect of growth of the field. Nevertheless, the profession must continue to look outward to problems of greater scope, to development of concepts of greater power and depth, to deepened understanding of operating processes and the management of them. If we turn inward in our interests, if we concentrate on ever-finer techniques for solution of defined problems, we will deserve the jibe.

5. RECOGNITION OF NEED OR VALUE

Before we can make use of our talents on the multitude of problems recounted above, management must be aware of the existence of these problems, and must have faith in the potential contributions which analytical techniques can provide. This is not always a simple process; the origin and rapid growth of military operations research would have been most unlikely if the military situation had not been desperate at the time this work started. Even then, the growth process was very uneven, and it required a considerable length of time before military operations research groups had established a relatively secure position. In industry the parallel situation has never arisen; there has been little demand for operations research within industries in difficulty.

In foreign countries, notably in England, there have been opportunities provided through industry research institutes, and in nationalized industries. The significant progress in the United States, however, has been made principally within successful companies, with management personnel sufficiently sophisticated and self-confident to recognize realistically the values and limits of quantitative study, to know how to use staff services, and to gamble on an unproven concept in staff work.

As modest demonstrated success has been achieved, there has been a significant growth in companies with a serious interest in operations research, accompanied by a drop in lunatic-fringe activities, within companies, the press, and consulting services. There is hope, therefore, that the contributions being made will be recognized and the growing body of accomplishment will serve as a stimulus.

Still another stimulus to growth is the radical change in attitude of business schools toward training in quantitative methods. Ten years ago, the spokesmen for operations research on the faculties of leading business schools were few indeed, and operations research was viewed as a transplant from military services, its existence more a measure of the lack of conventional business staff work in the military than a concept with any enduring vitality. Only in the last few years, have businessmen and students begun to realize that the military services had developed effective techniques of training, organization, and staff work to cope with planning, logistics, and operational problems which are immense compared with even the largest business operations. We can expect to find in business a growing number of men in managerial positions who are familiar with the elements of operations research method and who have some acquaintance with the work and products of an operations research group, much as managers today have a basic understanding of accounting. Such men will be able not only to recognize opportunities for operations research assistance but also to talk with and understand professionals in the operations research field.

A similar process has taken place within the military organizations. Perhaps the most advanced efforts in this respect have been the two-year course in operations research offered by the United States Navy Postgraduate School, and the special systems analysis courses that are given periodically at the USAF Institute of Technology, and by the RAND Corporation and elsewhere. Graduates from such classes have carried on active operations research, and even more have assisted civilian operations research workers by finding appropriate problems, by supplying needed practical advice, and by interpreting and assisting in the implementation of the results of their work. As these graduates advance in rank, operations research should gain great benefits through their knowledge of both its capabilities and its limitations.

Meanwhile communications have been a serious problem and a retardant. Meaningful terminology to the operations research worker has been viewed as unnecessary jargon introduced to obscure, and there has been some truth in this. One hopes that the apparent trend is a real one: the drop in the activities of the charlatan fringe, the growth in self-confidence of industrial operations research workers and in their acquaintance with business practices and language, and the growing knowledge business has of operations research concepts and the words used to describe them, all of these should contribute to understanding. Eliminating the charges of "jargon" will remove one of the principal sources of business irritation now retarding growth in operations research activity.

Finally, we have the environment itself. As discussed earlier, a host of technologically based decisions are being forced on management, and traditional techniques are hard pressed to provide adequate solutions. As this process continues, management will seek new methods, and in doing so will steadily improve its acquaintance with the possibilities of analytical applications to the solution of its problems. If the contributions prove valuable there need be little worry over future recognition; the requirements are present, the opportunities exist, and the most vital question is whether we will live up to them.

6. WILL WE BE UP TO THE OPPORTUNITY?

The existence of a need for operations research on a growing scale and recognition of this need in business is no guarantee that operations research will meet the challenge. We only have to look to other business services to see how easily a field like operations research can stagnate. Many claim, for example, that a good deal done in the name of operations research lies within the scope of industrial engineering, and at least potentially is a part of industrial engineering. Certainly the early industrial engineers like Taylor or Gantt had vigorous inventive minds. The pity is that industrial engineers concentrated on exploiting, refining, and economizing on the work of these pioneers, rather than on maintenance of equivalent vitality and inquisitiveness. Though unfair as a generalization, it is not unreasonable to characterize industrial engineering by its concentration on details of manual work, methods, time and motion, and newer systems for these same purposes.

Market research has suffered from a somewhat similar affliction. The goals and charter of market research are broad indeed. The principal technical challenge has, since the early thirties, been the acquisition of valid data. In meeting this challenge, tremendous technical effort has been devoted to improvement of survey and sampling methods, with enormous contributions. Yet this creature of the field has shown signs of choking its creator; the concentration on improved survey precision has threatened to turn market research into a body of technique rather than a field of inquiry. The analogue of the potential threat to operations research is obvious.

Statistical quality control has shown a somewhat similar history. From its initial development by men such as Dodge and Shewhart, with fruitful concepts having potentially very broad implications, this activity to a large extent has degenerated into a body of statistical technique and practical lore applied to problems far narrower than those to which the concepts of statistical stability or quality of system performance potentially apply.

If these characterizations seem unfair, let us say in defense that they are not aimed as criticisms of the examples cited, but as warnings to workers in operations research: the conditions necessary for operations research to fill its potential role include maintenance of vision and pressure to expand our scope of work, insistence on improvement of professional skills, better basic training as research men—not as efficient technicians, more understanding of military and business activity, and increased concentration on the phenomena of the real world.

It is still too early to tell how well we will meet the problem of training men for the operations research profession. The evidence shows a substantial growth in the number of institutions giving some attention.[13] We are, however, caught with a lack of professional standards *and* of trained people in the face of a growing demand for workers. Business organizations that do have an interest are being driven to compromise on people, too often settling for a man or two with a smattering of technique. It is surprising how many people in this circumstance know a little linear programming, how few know an equivalent amount about statistical methods. The doom of operations research

[13] "Formal Educational Offerings in Operations Research 1959," a report of the Education Committee of the Operations Research Society of America, June 1959, *Operations Research* (Bulletin), Vol. 7, Supplement 2, 1959.

will be sealed if its educational programs follow a shallow, technique-oriented pattern. If the operations research field is to grow to meet its challenge, we must find people—presumably from our universities—trained in the standards, the ethics, and the basic methods of science, and in the concepts, objectives, and organization of business.

Just as importantly, we must devote increasing time to observation or experiment. It is shocking for a field, most of whose professional members claim to live by the standards of the experimental sciences, to find so little in the way of experimental or observational results in its professional journals. Both military and commercial security present problems, but hardly so severe as the journals would suggest. Much data of fundamental value is of no commercial or military significance, for example, the statistical characteristics of demand. We are able to publish volumes of refinements in inventory control technique, but practically nothing on, e.g., the observed influence of lead time on forecast error. It is much easier to assume!

Operations research, in fact, has had a shock effect on other business services and business training. The reaction in many cases, notably within industrial engineering, is evident in the greater emphasis on broader training in method. The effect is evident in business training, where new emphasis is being placed on statistics, systems analysis, and mathematics. It is still too early to tell what the effect will be. It may conceivably lead to other business functional services or professions reclaiming their role of analysis within their functions, and much of the field of tactical studies in operations research may be subsumed under reinvigorated functional services.

What will be the effect on operations research as a profession? If other services respond to the challenge, operations research might well disappear. After all, much of the growth of operations research to date in industry has resulted from the void left by existing services in their concentration on technique, and their failure as a result to meet new managerial needs created by the changing post-World War II business environment. Operations research, on the other hand, might increasingly assume the role of a general management service; however strong functional services may be, there still remain problems of integration and balance, and the problems of the whole business as a system.

Another most likely effect, we feel, would be that operations research will develop less as a unified profession than as a rallying point, a point of common interest among functional professional groups. To some extent the Operations Research Society of America performs in this manner now. If the functional services such as industrial engineering or marketing develop strong experimental and theoretical capabilities, the opportunity may exist for a true multidisciplinary attack on business system problems.

In matters concerning future training and the general scope of operations research, the military portion of our profession will eventually follow the lead of the academic and industrial components. In applications, the military groups have generally been the leaders, but these groups must be fed from our civilian universities. As long as the military establishments are the largest organizations in our country, workers there will normally be the first to encounter new problems arising from the tremendous management structure, the huge procurement requirements, and the difficulties of long-term operational planning. However, as long as the country is dominantly civilian in thinking, the universities and industry are apt to establish the ethics, the standards, and the professional environment.

In short, operations research may develop in many ways, and probably will, to some extent dependent on the nature of development of other functional research fields. It can continue to grow as a profession devoted to problems of the whole business system. It will grow only if it meets the challenge of professional standards, an interest in expanding our understanding of the real world rather than technique, and professional education.

7. METHODS OF SOLUTION

Much emphasis has been given in this chapter to the significance of tactical problems, the problems of finite scope, essentially procedural, which do not directly challenge management strategy or policy. The present volume in the subjects treated demonstrates the debt owed by operations research in the development of its own background of method to the analysis of tactical questions, queues, inventory questions, chance processes of specific form. Some areas of growth—actual or potential—into strategic, policy, and organizational issues have been suggested: integrated logistics and processing-distribution systems, risk, competition and conflict, and organization. The theory, concepts, or technical apparatus to handle these problems will not be borrowed from other fields. It must be developed within the context of business/military operations, management, and environment.

Before considering the various technical elements at our disposal, it is worth emphasizing that our greatest needs in the strategic areas are conceptual. It is difficult to believe that an extension of our mathematical methods will solve problems of risk, or provide a quantitative measure of effectiveness of national military posture. Gross assumptions, some of which will never be fully comprehended, will always have to appear in long-term analyses. While sensitivity tests can and should be conducted, these will often simply shift the assumptions—to cloud the issue in one area while clarifying it in another. The problem here is one of learning to view the strategic situations in an effective manner, one which produces more invariance and results which are less sensitive to the exact nature of the minor assumptions. The main assumptions must remain as assumptions, but it is often possible to clear away immense masses of underbrush. A few notable examples of such work exist, but they are far too few, and for security reasons are necessarily too little known.

On the more technical side of affairs, there are many subjects worth continual attention. Optimization methods will form an important area of growth. Techniques such as simulation—viewed by many as a far from satisfactory, or even a potentially dangerous approach—offer possibilities for providing analogues to complex operating systems for analysis purposes. As contrasted with analytic methods, we lack today adequate procedures, whether practical or not, for choosing optimum conditions in simulated processes. True, we have the opportunity to attempt point-by-point evaluation, but often over impossibly large sets of possible conditions. True also, the unit cost of simulation trials may be expected to drop. Great opportunity still exists, however, for development of optimum-locating procedures of greater efficiency for complex systems.

The algorithms of linear programming illustrate one type of possible method, the iterative procedure which yields an exact solution. While less neat, a more promising approach appears to be development of statistical surface exploration procedures. Box's methods are an important contribution, although they probably still require an excessively large number of experiments, observations, or simulation trials.[14]

Optimization of processes under way is another field for development of method. The assumption that the optimum position can be found with any time lag—that is, that it can be predicted—is contingent on the process being stationary to some "reasonable" degree. If, however, true quantitative control systems are to be built, monitoring, "learning," and control techniques must be utilized which recognize the internal correlations within such systems.

[14] See Davies (1954) for references to Box's work.

Equally important will be techniques for observation and analysis of on-going processes, since in many sizable problems our ability to experiment is seriously limited. Under such conditions, observation and inference of input-output of effort-effect-functional dependences is complicated by internal and, at times, only partially identified interactions. In military work, the reduction of intelligence data is an obvious example. Analysis of market structure, marketing effort, and strategy illustrates this problem well on the industrial side. In most cases, classical experimentation is extremely costly or impossible. Elimination of the confounding of experimental results with other time-dependent elements—economic conditions, competitive reactions, etc.—may not be possible. Where experiments are possible, the costs and risks to management of adequate experiments to make meaningful measurements may be excessive. On the other hand, inferences from observations suffer from the conditions imposed on the data by continuing attempts under normal operations to adjust effort to approach an optimum. Attempts to ferret out sense from such data may lead to entirely spurious correlations or no apparent effects whatsoever.

Statistical techniques such as evolutionary operation offer some hope. These still suffer in many business applications from the presence of unavoidably large dynamic or chance influences, relative to the effects of controllable actions. In such problems, greater attention to observation of detailed operations and behavior is needed, first, to give us the basis for more complete hypotheses concerning joint effects of variables; thereafter we will need and be in a position to use methods for analysis of complex systems with feedback and internal correlation.

Quantitative models of human behavior will be another important field of growth in operations research. These are needed in numerous fields: in marketing, we are faced with a requirement to understand buyers' activity in a statistical sense. The interaction of men with men, and men with machines, has received much military attention, and will require more. In organizational and information problems—both military and industrial—much is to be gained by understanding human activity in using information to formulate alternatives, predict outcome, evaluate, and choose or decide. We have made some progress in the tactical problems—e.g., inventory control—in separating the elements of the control/decision process and thereby improving information flow, providing mechanical assistance to prediction or calculation, and clarifying the nature and levels of responsibility of decisions required. Extension of this capability to achieve an understanding of the role of information, analysis, and value judgment in business operating decisions will give operations research a lever it can exploit in organizational and business information system problems.

Before we can expect to break through into truly constructive work on major issues, our grasp of the problems of risk and competition must be strengthened. In both of these areas, questions of value are central. We are faced with very hazy statements of objectives, of measures of effectiveness. We have, however, an opportunity to develop technical methods to describe risk-taking and competitive processes. The work stemming from the concepts of Wald (1951), of von Neumann and Morgenstern (1944), and from the dynamic programming methods offers some promising initial suggestions. However, we must not confuse the elegance of this work with solution of the technical, observational, and value problems existing in questions of risk and competitive action in the real world.

These illustrations will support, we hope, the contention that the operations research field is far from mature, that challenging technical and professional opportunities exist if the field is to meet the needs of management in a world of dynamic change, where effective use of economic and human resources and efficient planning in the face of competition and uncertainty will determine industrial and national survival. We can no longer play on naïveté; if operations research is to exist as a professional field, the "fresh viewpoint" must be replaced by the fruitful concept and method, built on observation and experimentation within the field of management.

The growth of operations research during the past decade has demonstrated that the field has promise. The realization of this promise in the decade to come rests with the profession, on its ability to avoid the cult of technique, its recognition of a twofold mission—to assist management in practical affairs while drawing on problem-solving activities to achieve growing organized understanding of the real world of management affairs.

The field of operations research now has the capital represented by the progress described in earlier chapters. We could choose to live on this capital for some time to come, the probable outcome being the progressive degeneration of operations research into a field of handbook technique. As a professional field, our real responsibility is to use these assets, developed so extensively in the fifties, to support professional growth and to formulate the experiments, concepts, and method needed to meet the challenge of the sixties.

BIBLIOGRAPHY

Allias, M., "Method of Appraising Economic Prospects of Mining Exploration over Large Territories: Algerian Sahara Case Study," *Mgmt. Sci.,* **3,** 285–348 (1957).

Brothers, L. A., "Operations Analysis in the United States Air Force," *Opns. Res.,* **2,** 1–16 (1954).

Churchman, C. W., "A Survey of Operations Research Accomplishment in Industry," *Proceedings of the Conference on What Is Operations Research Accomplishing in Industry,* Case Institute of Technology, Cleveland, 1955.

Churchman, C. W., Ackoff, R. L., and Arnoff, E. L., *Introduction to Operations Research,* John Wiley and Sons, New York, 1957.

Clark, D. F., and Ackoff, R. L., "A Report on Some Organizational Experiments," *Opns. Res.,* **7,** 279–293 (1959).

Davies, O. L. (ed.), *Design and Analysis of Industrial Experiments,* Oliver and Boyd, Edinburgh, 1954.

Drucker, P. F., "Long-Range Planning, Challenge to Management Science," *Mgmt. Sci.,* **5,** 238–249 (1959).

Edie, L. C., "Traffic Delays at Toll Booths," *Opns. Res.,* **2,** 107–138 (1954).

Engel, J. H., "Use of Clustering in Mineralogical and other Surveys," *Proc. of the First Inter. Conf. on OR,* ORSA, Baltimore, 1957, pp. 176–192.

Hanssmann, Fred, "Optimal Inventory Location and Control in Production and Distribution Networks," *Opns. Res.,* **7,** 483–498 (1959).

Haywood, O. G., Jr., "Military Decision and Game Theory," *Opns. Res.,* **2,** 107–138 (1954).

Hertz, D. B., "Progress of Industrial Operations Research in the United States," *Proc. of the First Inter. Conf. on OR,* ORSA, Baltimore, 1957, pp. 455–468.

Koopman, B. O., "Search and Screening," *Opns. Res.,* **4,** 324–346 (1956); **4,** 503–531 (1956); and **5,** 613–626 (1957).

March, J. G., and Simon, H. A., *Organization,* John Wiley and Sons, New York, 1958.

McDonald, John, "A Theory of Strategy," *Fortune,* June 1949, pp. 100–110.

McKean, R. N., *Efficiency in Government through Systems Analysis,* John Wiley and Sons, New York, 1958.

Morse, P. M., "Trends in Operations Research," *Opns. Res.,* **1,** 159–165 (1953).

Notes on Operations Research 1959, The Operations Research Center, Massachusetts Institute of Technology, The Technology Press, Cambridge, 1959.

"Operations Research: What It Is, How It Is Conducted, What It Offers Business," National Industrial Conference Board, Studies in Business Policy, No. 82, 1957.

Page, Thornton, "The Value of Information in Decision Making," *Proc. of the First Inter. Conf. on OR,* ORSA, Baltimore, 1957, pp. 306–316.

Simpson, K. F., Jr., "In Process Inventories," *Opns. Res.,* **6,** 863–873 (1958).

Simpson, K. F., Jr., "A Theory of Allocation of Stocks to Warehouses," *Opns. Res.,* **7,** 797–805 (1959).

Thomas, C. J., and Deemer, W. L., Jr., "The Role of Operational Gaming in Operations Research," *Opns. Res.,* **5,** 1–27 (1957).

von Neumann, John, and Morgenstern, Oskar, *Theory of Games and Economic Behavior,* Princeton University Press, Princeton, N. J., 1944.

Wald, Abraham, *Statistical Decision Functions,* John Wiley and Sons, New York, 1951.

Weiss, H. K., "Lanchester-Type Models of Warfare," *Proc. of the First Inter. Conf. on OR,* ORSA, Baltimore, 1957.

Weiss, H. K., "Some Differential Games of Tactical Interest and the Value of a Supporting Weapon System," *Opns. Res.,* **7,** 180–196 (1959).

Whitmore, W. F., "Edison and Operations Research," *Opns. Res.,* **1,** 83–85 (1953).

AUTHOR INDEX

SUBJECT INDEX